THE LOGIC OF AMERICAN POLITICS

THE LOGIC OF AMERICAN POLITICS

SAMUEL KERNELL and **GARY C. JACOBSON**
University of California, San Diego

CQ PRESS
Washington, D.C.

CQ Press

A Division of Congressional Quarterly Inc.

1414 22nd Street, N.W.

Washington, D.C. 20037

202-822-1475

800-638-1710

http://books.cq.com

The Logic of American Politics was designed and typeset by Kachergis Book Design,
Pittsboro, North Carolina.

Printed and bound in the United States of America

03 02 01 00   5 4 3 2

Library of Congress Cataloging-in-Publication Data

Kernell, Samuel

The logic of American politics / Samuel Kernell and Gary C. Jacobson

    p.   cm.

Includes bibliographical references and index.

ISBN 1-56802-395-2

1. United States—Politics and government.   I. Jacobson, Gary C.

II. Title.

JK274.K43   1999

320.473'01—dc21   99-38744

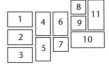

Acknowledgments, cover images

1. Douglas Graham / Congressional Quarterly

2. PhotoDisc

3. Reuters / Sam Mircovich

4. Ken Heinen for the Supreme Court

5. Bettmann-UPI

6. AP / Wide World Photos

7. PhotoDisc

8. Reuters / Mark Wilson

9. File photo

10. Scott J. Ferrell / Congressional Quarterly

11. Scott J. Ferrell / Congressional Quarterly

To our favorite students—our daughters, Georgia and Karen

The following dedication to James Madison is from the oldest American government textbook we have found: William Alexander Duer's *Outlines of the Constitutional Jurisprudence of the United States,* published in 1833.

To you, Sir, as the surviving member of the august assembly that framed the Constitution, and of that illustrious triumvirate who, in vindicating it from the objections of its first assailants, succeeded in recommending it to the adoption of their country; to you, who, in discharging the highest duties of its administration, proved the stability and excellence of the Constitution, in war as well as in peace, and determined the experiment in favour of republican institutions and the right of self-government; to you, who in your retirement, raised a warning voice against those heresies in the construction of that Constitution which for a moment threatened to impair it; to you, Sir, as alone amongst the earliest and the latest of its defenders,—this brief exposition of the organization and principles of the National Government, intended especially for the instruction of our American youth, is most respectfully, and, in reference to your public services, most properly inscribed.

Columbia College, N. Y.
August 1st, 1833.

BRIEF CONTENTS

CONTENTS

BOXED FEATURES

FIGURES AND TABLES

Figures

Tables

PREFACE

This book is the product of our nearly thirty years of trying to teach American politics in a way that goes beyond the basics. In addition to introducing students to the fundamental principles, we have sought to help them develop an ability to analyze and understand American politics for themselves. Neither of us would be considered an authentic member of the rational choice school. Yet we think many of its insights, especially those exploited by the new institutionalism, are broadly applicable and, even if used only informally, are often helpful in making sense of American politics in a way that students intuitively can grasp. We have absorbed these ideas into our own scholarly thinking, as have many of you. Here, we put them to work to help students understand not only *what* the American political system looks like but also *why* it has assumed its present shape.

Our goal in this book is to help students discern the logic—the rationale—embedded in the extraordinary and complex array of American political institutions and practices that we observe today. To accomplish this goal, we analyze political institutions and practices as (imperfect) solutions to problems facing people who need to act collectively. We highlight the typical obstacles to collective action—conflicts over values and interests, the need for coordination, the threat of free riding—as they recur in a great variety of contexts in order to illuminate the diverse institutional means that American politicians have created to overcome them. Because the means adopted to deal with the problems of collective action at one historical moment can continue to shape politics long after those problems have receded, we pay a good deal of attention to the historical development of political institutions as well.

We also delve into the unavoidable difficulties associated with delegating authority in a large-scale democracy—of citizens to elected officials, of Congress to the president, of elected officials to civil servants, and the like—and explore how these affect the design of institutions. And throughout the book we emphasize the strategic dimension of political action, from the Framers' tradeoffs in crafting the Constitution to contemporary officeholders' efforts to shape policy, for we want students to understand current institutions as the products of, as well as venues for, resolving political conflicts. Finally, we encourage students to consider how they can themselves participate effectively in politics and urge them to think analytically about proposed reforms of political institutions.

Organization of the Book

Our emphasis on the logic of institutions, including their historical development, has led us to adopt a somewhat unorthodox structure for the book. We cover the rules of the game and the formal institutions of government before discussing the "input" side of the political process—public opinion, elections, parties, and interest groups—because our emphasis is on how rules and institutions structure the actions and choices of citizens and politicians alike.

The introductory chapter presents the concepts and ideas that form the framework for the substantive chapters, which are arranged in four parts. Part I covers the foundational elements of American politics: the Constitution, federalism, civil rights, and civil liberties. The chapters that cover these topics give students an understanding of political origins and development of the basic structure and rules of the national polity.

Part II examines the major formal institutions of national government: Congress, the presidency, the bureaucracy, and the judiciary. These chapters reveal how the politics and logic of their development have shaped their current organizational features, practices, and relations with one another.

Part III analyzes the institutions that link citizens with government officials, again in terms of their historical development, political logic, and present-day operations. Chapters in this section are devoted to public opinion; voting, campaigns, and elections; political parties; interest groups; and the news media.

The concluding chapter, found in Part IV, assesses the biases inherent in the system of formal and informal political institutions that have developed over the course of American history and discusses how to think about proposals for changing them. Rather than devote separate chapters to public policy, we weave it throughout the book; policies and policy making are integral elements of our analysis of institutions.

Instructional Features

The Logic of American Politics includes special features designed to engage students' attention and to help them think analytically about the subject. Thematic questions at the beginning of each chapter preview important themes and set the tone for critical thinking about the subject matter. Each chapter then begins with a story that sets the scene, often dramatically, for the topic at hand. The federalism chapter, for example, begins with a vignette contrasting federal disaster relief following the San Francisco earthquakes of 1906 and 1989, which highlights the expanded reach of the national government in the intervening years.

Within the text itself, important terms and concepts appear in boldface the first time they are used. These key terms are summarized at the end of each chapter and are defined in a glossary at the back of the book. To encourage students to continue their studies of American politics beyond the pages of this volume, we have included annotated reading lists at the end of each chapter.

Instructional features also appear on *The Logic of American Politics* Web site (http://logic.cqpress.com), which is rich in exercises and materials that go far beyond the text. Among them is a study guide that includes chapter summaries, learning objectives, and review questions. Students also will find electronically graded practice quizzes to test their mastery of the material. Exercises drawing on a wealth of information (such as CQ's *Politics in America*) allow students to analyze how interest groups rate specific members of Congress, compare President Eisenhower's daily schedule with that of President Clinton, or check out who's giving money to whom for campaign contributions. A section called "Explore" offers links and images so that students can observe Congress in action, listen in on White House conversations during the Cuban missile crisis, or compare today's tabloid journalism with the yellow journalism of another era.

The Web site is just one item in a valuable instructional package that accompanies the text. Our *Instructor's Resource Manual* includes a test bank, transparencies, and study materials that professors can give to students who do not have easy access to the Web. The test bank contains 1,000 questions, combining multiple choice, true-false, short-answer, and essay formats.

Two outstanding references are offered to professors who adopt the text (subject to restrictions by the publisher). First, what we find to be the best single-source reference, *Vital Statistics on American Politics* by Harold W. Stanley and Richard G. Niemi, is available on CD-ROM. Whether you need to look up a statistic before a lecture or wish to prepare slides of tables and figures for overhead presentation, Stanley and Niemi's treasure trove of statistics will be a wonderful resource. Second, subscriptions to the *CQ Weekly*, the same source on which political Washington relies for nonpartisan coverage and insightful analysis, are available. For more information about any of these supplements, contact CQ Press, 800 638-1710, ext. 363.

Acknowledgments

Without the help and encouragement of department colleagues, friends, students, and the editorial staff at CQ Press this book would never have been completed. The book also has benefited from the insightful and astute comments of colleagues at other institutions who took time from their busy schedules to review chapters. We are deeply obliged to everyone who has helped the project along.

Our colleagues and students at the University of California at San Diego have contributed to every aspect of the book, often in ways they might not realize, for the way we think about politics is permeated with the intellectual atmosphere they have created and continue to sustain. Among department colleagues, we are indebted particularly to the sound advice, leads, and careful reading of earlier drafts offered by Neal Beck, Amy Bridges, Gary Cox, Steve Erie, Liz Gerber, Harry Hirsch, Sanford Lakoff, Skip Lupia, Mat McCubbins, and Samuel Popkin. Among our graduate students, Scott Basinger, Greg Bovitz, Jamie Druckman, and Michael Molloy served as teaching assistants in courses that used manuscript versions of the book and provided us with invaluable feedback on what worked and what did not. Erik Engstrom and Jeff Lazarus did yeoman work on ancillary material.

Tim Groeling applied his special talents to developing the book's Web site and supplied essential research assistance. Numerous other colleagues came to our assistance from time to time in our search for information, advice, and ideas. We would be remiss not to mention the special efforts of Keith Bybee, Charles Cameron, Larry Jacobs, Elliott King, and Robert Shapiro.

We also are grateful to Dianne Kernell for editorial help, to Georgia Kernell for comments and help in preparation of the test questions, and to both for help with proofreading.

We are indebted to the director of the college publishing group of CQ Press, Brenda Carter, for her enthusiasm in taking up this project and bringing it to fruition. Ann Davies, as the managing editor, oversaw all of the editing and production. Sabra Bissette Ledent and Carolyn Goldinger were the assiduous, talented copy editors, and, although they let us have our own way with words once in a while, the book is much clearer and tighter for their efforts. Sandy Adams, James Headley, Carrie Hutchison, Gwenda Larsen, Jerry Orvedahl, Jon Preimesberger, and Julie Rovesti all contributed their talents and energy to various essential parts of the project. Nadine Steffan ably handled final production and photo research under a very constricted time schedule. We thank them all.

Colleagues around the country who read parts of the manuscript gave us an abundance of good advice, much of which we took, and, equally essential, kept us from many embarrassing mistakes. A list follows, but we would be remiss if we did not give special recognition to Andrew J. Polsky of Hunter College for his extraordinarily thorough and helpful comments on the manuscript. Whatever CQ paid him, it was not enough.

Scott H. Ainsworth, *University of Georgia*
Stephen Amberg, *University of Texas at San Antonio*
Lydia Andrade, *University of North Texas*
Ross K. Baker, *Rutgers University*
Thomas J. Baldino, *Wilkes University*

William T. Bianco, *Pennsylvania State University*

Sarah Binder, *Brookings Institution and George Washington University*

John C. Domino, *Sam Houston State University*

Kenneth Entin, *California State University, Stanislaus*

Lee Epstein, *Washington University*

Larry Evans, *The College of William and Mary*

Pauline M. Harrington, *Bridgewater State College*

Carol E. Hays, *University of Illinois at Urbana—Champaign*

Scott P. Hays, *University of Illinois at Urbana—Champaign*

Valerie Heitshusen, *University of Missouri—Columbia*

Brian D. Humes, *University of Nebraska—Lincoln*

Elkin Terry Jack, *Gulf Coast Community College*

D. Roderick Kiewiet, *California Institute of Technology*

John S. Klemanski, *Oakland University*

Joseph R. Marbach, *Seton Hall University*

Mark C. Miller, *Clark University*

Jeff Mondak, *Florida State University*

Glenn R. Parker, *Florida State University*

Andrew J. Polsky, *Hunter College*

Stephen C. Roberds, *Southern Utah University*

Peregrine Schwartz-Shea, *University of Utah*

Bartholomew Sparrow, *University of Texas at Austin*

John E. Stanga, *Wichita State University*

Charles E. Walcott, *Virginia Polytechnic Institute and State University*

Hanes Walton Jr., *University of Michigan*

John R. Wright, *Ohio State University*

Garry Young, *University of Missouri—Columbia*

Finally, our families. Dianne and Georgia Kernell already have been thanked for editorial services, but they and Marty and Karen Jacobson also deserve our gratitude for putting up with what at times seemed an interminable drain on our time and attention. We are sure that they are as delighted to have the book finished as we are.

A NOTE TO STUDENTS

The two of us—the authors of this text—have spent our entire adult lives examining, teaching, and writing about American politics because we find the subject endlessly fascinating, intellectually challenging, and vitally important. We hope that you, our readers, will come to share our excitement while developing your own coherent understanding of the complex institutions and practices that populate the world of politics.

Understanding politics is no trivial endeavor. To the casual observer, American politics seems alternately chaotic, mundane, infuriating, hilarious, tedious, dramatic, sinister—and sometimes even noble and inspiring. Indeed, it can be all these things and more, as politics in the year of scandal and impeachment that ended with President Bill Clinton's acquittal by the Senate in February 1999 certainly confirmed. The institutions of American politics, probably the most complex of any in the world, also seem to defy comprehension, not to mention common sense. Yet an intelligible logic underlies America's political institutions and practices, and our goal is to provide you with the concepts, histories, examples, illustrations, and plain old facts that will enable you to grasp it. If we succeed, you will come away with a sophisticated appreciation of the possibilities and limits of American politics and the knowledge with which to play your own effective part in the political system—as voter, activist, observer, taxpayer,

gadfly, or whatever other role you choose. A few may even decide to join us as political scientists.

Plan of the Book

Our analysis of the logic of American politics begins in Chapter 1 with an introduction to the analytical concepts we will draw on throughout the text. Although these concepts are straightforward and intuitive, we do not expect you to understand them fully until they have been applied in later chapters. The rest of the text is arranged in four main parts. Part I looks at the foundational elements of the political system that are especially relevant to understanding modern American politics. It begins with the constitutional system (Chapter 2, The Constitution) and then moves on to the relations between the national government and the states (Chapter 3, Federalism), the evolution of civil rights and the definition of citizenship (Chapter 4, Civil Rights), and the establishment of civil liberties, such as freedom of speech and religion (Chapter 5, Civil Liberties). A recurring theme of Part I is *nationalization,* the gradual shift of authority from state and local governments to the national government.

Part II examines the four basic institutions of America's national government: Congress (Chapter 6), the presidency (Chapter 7), the bureaucracy (Chapter 8), and the federal judiciary (Chapter 9). The development of effective, resourceful institutions at the national level has made it possible for modern-day politicians to tackle problems that in an earlier time they would have been helpless to solve. We explain how all four institutions have evolved along the paths initiated and confined by the Constitution in response to the forces of nationalization and other social and economic changes.

Part III surveys the institutions that keep citizens informed about what their representatives are doing and enable them to influence their elected officials through voting and other forms of participation. Chapter 10, Public Opinion, explores the nature of modern political communication by focusing on the ins and outs of mass public opinion. Chapter 11, Voting, Campaigns, and Elections, examines the ways in which candidates' strategies and voters' preferences interact at the polls to produce national leaders and, on occasion, create mandates for policies. The Constitution mentions neither political parties nor interest groups, and the Framers were deeply suspicious of both. But they are vital to helping citizens make sense of politics and pursue political goals effectively. In Chapter 12, Political Parties, and Chapter 13, Interest Groups, we explain how and why parties and interest groups have flourished as intermediaries between citizens and government officials. President Woodrow Wilson once aptly observed that "news is the atmosphere of politics." Chapter 14 looks at the news media both as channels of communication from elected leaders to their constituents and as independent sources of information about their performance.

Part IV, which consists of Chapter 15, concludes our inquiry by reviewing the biases inherent in the institutions we have examined and considering how to evaluate proposals to reform current political arrangements.

Special Features

This book contains several special features designed to help students grasp the logic of American politics. At the outset of each chapter are questions that preview important themes and, we hope, will pique your curiosity. Each chapter then opens with a story from the real world of politics that introduces one or more of the central issues to be explored. Within each chapter, thematic boxes labeled "The Logic of Politics" provide concrete examples of the political logic underlying different aspects of political life. Another set of thematic boxes, "Politics to Policy," scattered throughout the chapters, treat some of the public policy issues that have sprung forth from the political process. Additional boxes, tables, figures, photographs, and other visuals clarify and enliven the text. Since these features, including the substantive captions, play an integral role in the presentation and discussion, you should read them with as much care as the text. Key terms, another feature, appear in boldface when first introduced and are summarized at the end of chapters. Definitions of these terms are listed in the glossary at the back of the book. Finally, to encourage you to pursue more information on topics you find particularly interesting, we have included annotated lists of suggested readings at the end of each chapter.

But more lies beyond the covers of this book. Be sure to check out *The Logic of American Politics* Web site (http://logic.cqpress.com), where you will find study materials and electronically graded practice quizzes that will give you a chance to test your knowledge of the material. The site offers a wide variety of exercises, games, images, and links to some of the best political and government sites on the Internet.

Politics, like every significant human endeavor, becomes more intriguing the more deeply it is explored and understood. Our book aims to give you not only a strong basic foundation for understanding political life in the present-day United States but also a glimpse of how intellectually enjoyable it can be to grapple with its puzzles and paradoxes.

THE LOGIC OF AMERICAN POLITICS

Chapter 1

THE LOGIC OF AMERICAN POLITICS

⭐ *Why do people need politics to help them solve their common problems?*

⭐ *Do institutions matter? When, say in a democracy, a majority agrees on a course of action, do the particular institutional arrangements really affect the majority's ability to do what it wants?*

⭐ *Are politicians necessary evils, or do they have any redeeming qualities?*

⭐ *Since everyone dislikes auto pollution and we know what causes it, why don't we just agree to end it?*

The objects of the decade-long rancorous political and legal wrangling between loggers and environmental activists stood majestic and serene along the Northern California coast, indifferent to the negotiations under way to determine their future. But on Friday, February 26, 1999, the talks between federal and state officials, trying to save the ten thousand acres of California redwoods, and Pacific Lumber, trying to protect its lumberjacks and profits, collapsed. The breakdown in negotiations was a major blow—not only to the Clinton administration and California state officials, but also to the debt-ridden lumber company. Failure would guarantee another round of expensive, vicious lawsuits. Another victim might be the Endangered Species Act if the lumber company one day succeeded in convincing the Supreme Court that the government had unfairly denied its right to harvest timber.

On Friday evening the threats began. Pacific Lumber suggested it might begin cutting down the old trees. The government vowed to overrun the lumber company with regulators. But hopes rose over the weekend as federal and state officials approached the lumber company again. Then, through complicated maneuvers by the government, the impasse was broken on Monday, March 1. The government agreed to purchase the redwood forests from Pacific Lumber for $480 million; the lumber company agreed to restrictions on its adjacent logging operations to prevent destruction of habitats and endangered species such as the coho salmon and spotted owl.[1]

In the end, then, choices were made—among scarce species, jobs, profits, and taxpayer dollars. Such choices are at the heart of American politics. Politics arises from the need to choose among alternatives when scarcity makes it impossible for people to get what they want. These choices frequently involve material things such as redwoods, salmon, and profits, or may concern moral and aesthetic values. For example, a society cannot have both a "freedom to choose" policy for abortion and "right to life" for the unborn. Likewise, it cannot preserve the towering, irreplaceable redwoods, yet allow lumber companies unlimited access to the redwood domains so loggers can feed their families.

Inevitably, choices breed conflict: conflicting interests, conflicting values, conflicting ideas about how best to allocate limited resources and whose values will be served. Politics is how people try to manage such conflicts. But try as they may, successful politics does not always lead to a happy ending. The problems of scarce resources and conflict bred by competing values may persist; so may disagreement over the appropriate course of action. After the redwood deal, environmentalists remained wary and complained that the lumber company was paid too much for too little protection of the environment. Yet, despite conflicts, politics allows us to live together, enjoying the fruits of social exchange. In fact, politics, like the air we breathe, is essential to our existence. Only when the air becomes dark and dirty—when politics fails and societies collapse into anarchy and civil war—do we grasp the significance of politics in sustaining our everyday lives as well as our plans for the future.

In more formal terms, **politics** is *the process through which individuals and groups reach agreement on a course of common, or collective, action—even as they continue to disagree on the goals that action is intended to achieve.* This definition of politics covers a great variety of social relations from negotiations between parents and teenagers over use of the family car, to talks between bosses and employees over working conditions and pay, to disputes among smugglers over territorial jurisdictions for their illicit activities. Each of these situations is ripe for politics because solutions must be found in conflicting choices. One party wants the other party to pursue a course of action that requires its cooperation even when that cooperation is costly.[2]

Successful politics almost invariably requires bargaining and compromise. Where the issues are simple and the participants know and trust one another, bargaining, such as that between teenagers and their parents, may be all that is needed for the group to reach a collective decision.

But as participants multiply and as issues become more complex and divisive, unstructured negotiation rarely yields a collective decision all parties can accept. It may simply require too much time and effort. More crucially, it may expose each side to too great a risk that the other side will not live up to its agreements. Fear of reneging may foster mutual suspicions and lead each side to conclude that "politics" will not work. When this occurs, war may become the preferred alternative.[3] The recent conflict in Bosnia among the Serbs, Croats, and Muslims followed such a dynamic. The collapse of Yugoslavia's communist government in 1990 resurrected ancient enmities among people who had lived peacefully as neighbors for decades. In the absence of effective political institutions they could count on to manage potential conflicts, ethnic rivals became trapped in a spiral of mutual suspicion, fear, and hostility. Within a year they were joining militias and killing one another.

Whether at war or simply at odds over a matter as mundane as scheduling employee coffee breaks, the parties to a conflict will benefit from prior agreement on a set of rules and procedures for negotiations. Indeed, this theme reappears throughout this book: a stable community, whether a social club or a nation-state, persists by establishing rules and procedures for reaching and enforcing agreements necessary for successful collective action. In January 1999, when the U.S. Senate turned to the impeachment trial of President Bill Clinton, the stage was set for an escalation of the partisan rancor that had so marred the impeachment proceedings in the House of Representatives. Yet the Senate managed to perform its constitutional responsibility expeditiously and with a surprising degree of decorum thanks to an early, closed-door meeting in which all hundred senators endorsed a resolution that laid out the trial's ground rules. More important, in their desire for partisan and institutional comity senators gave Majority Leader Trent Lott and Minority Leader Thomas Daschle de facto vetoes over any changes in these rules. Thus members on both sides of the partisan

THE POLITICS OF ANTIPOLITICS

It happens all too often. Candidates take a firm stand on an issue in the election, only to have to compromise their positions once elected. The voters shake their heads, frustrated with their representatives who appear to be saying one thing and doing another. Sensing this frustration, third-party presidential candidate Ross Perot campaigned in 1992 and again in 1996 on the single issue of taking politics out of government. His appeal struck a responsive chord with professional wrestler Jesse Ventura, who also was mayor of a medium-sized town in Minnesota. In 1998, taking up Perot's mantle and his Reform Party label, Ventura defeated both the Democratic and Republican candidates for Minnesota's governorship. During his first months in office, Ventura's perceived contempt for negotiation and compromise won him few allies in the legislature, and politicos predicted his style eventually would "wear thin" with voters. "He's fond of saying he's not going to play the games politicians play," noted departing Democratic Party chairman Dick Senese, "but it's not only the game of politics, it's the game of life. You and your friends can't decide what restaurant to go to without discussion and compromise."[1]

1. Dirk Johnson, "Ventura Is Leading, But Is Offering No Examples," *New York Times*, April 17, 1999.

divide could proceed toward a decision without fear that the other side would resort to trickery to get the decision it favored. That the Senate would find a way to manage its disagreements is not so surprising. Its leaders take pride in finding collegial ways of containing the potential conflicts that daily threaten to disrupt its business.

Reliance on rules and procedures is nothing new, of course. Even in an era of arbitrary kings and aristocrats, republican political theorists understood their value. In a 1656 treatise exploring how republican institutions might be constructed to allow conflicting interests to find solutions, the English political theorist James Harrington told the story of two young girls who were arguing about how to share a single slice of cake. Suddenly one of the

girls proposed a rule: "'Divide,' says one to the other, 'and I will choose; or let me divide, and you shall choose.'" With that ingenious rule, both girls were able to pursue their self-interest (the largest possible slice of cake) and yet have the collective decision result in a division both could happily live with.[4]

Over a hundred years after Harrington's treatise, the Framers of the Constitution spent the entire summer of 1787 in Philadelphia debating what new rules and offices to create for the new government. They were guided by their best guesses about how the alternatives they were contemplating would affect the interests of their states and constituencies (see Chapter 2). The result of their efforts, the Constitution, is a collection of rules fundamentally similar to the one discovered by the girls in Harrington's story, and intended to reassure diverse interests that they would be better off under the proposed system than under the institutions already in place under the Articles of Confederation. The politics of drafting the Constitution also reminds us that the design of governmental institutions may confer advantages on some parties over others. Thus agreements about which rules to adopt typically follow the requirements of competing political interests.

Constitutions and Governments

All organizations are governed by rules and procedures for making and enforcing decisions. Within colleges and universities, the student government, the faculty senate, staff associations, academic departments, and, of course, the university itself have their own rules and procedures to follow when they transact regular business. Although rules and procedures go by different names (constitution, bylaws, charter), their purpose is the same: to guide an organization's members in making essentially political decisions—that is, decisions in which the participants disagree about what they would like the organization to do.

And what happens when the organization is a nation? Consider the problems: the number of participants is great, the many issues to be settled are complex, and each participant's performance in living up to agreements cannot be easily monitored. Yet, even with their conflicts, entire populations engage in politics every day. Their degree of success depends largely on whether or not they have developed constitutions and governments that work.

The **constitution** of a nation creates its governing institutions and *the set of rules prescribing the political process these institutions must follow to reach and enforce collective agreements.* A constitution may be a highly formal legal document, such as that of the United States, or it may resemble Britain's unwritten constitution, an informal "understanding" based on centuries of precedents and laws. A **government,** in turn, consists of *those institutions creat-*

ed by the constitution and charged with making and enforcing collective agreements. It may assume various forms, including a monarchy, a representative democracy, a theocracy (a government composed of religious leaders), or a dictatorship.

The simple observation that governments are comprised of institutions actually says a great deal and implies much more. Institutions consist of *roles* that are designed and linked together with *rules* to perform some intended purpose. In government the roles often are formalized as *offices,* positions that confer on their occupants specific authority and responsibilities. *Authority* is the acknowledged right of the office to make a particular decision for all participants. For example, the chief justice of the United States exercises the office's authority when selecting a colleague to write the Supreme Court's opinion on a case.

Rules prescribe what the authority relations among institutions will be. The Constitution assigns Congress the legislative tasks and the president the executive duties of government such as appointing officers to the various administrative departments. Authority is assigned to the office, not to the individual holding the office. Thus institutions exist—and endure—independently of those who occupy them. A university remains the same institution even though all of its students, professors, and administrators are eventually replaced. Institutions, therefore, contribute a fundamental continuity and orderliness to collective action, enabling people to plan for the future.

Institutions are by no means immutable, but they are difficult to change for two basic reasons. First, the people whose lives are affected by them usually are content with the current arrangements. Imagine how senior art majors would react if, during their last semester, their college or university closed the art department because of budget deficits. Or consider the anxiety that the millions of workers approaching retirement must feel whenever politicians in Washington talk about the need to pare Medicare benefits or change eligibility requirements for Social Security. Second, even those who want change typically find it hard to agree on a proposed alternative. While most members of Congress have expressed support for campaign finance reform, they disagree sharply over the direction of reforms. Some advocate government subsidies; others want mandated free television time; and still others favor caps on expenditures. As a result, the current rules, though preferred by only a few members, appear unlikely to change anytime soon.

When institutional reform does occur, it rarely involves wholesale restructuring. Rather, change is gradual, usually consisting of periodic tinkering with the rules or the duties and authority assigned to offices. Like rings within a tree, the history of long-standing institutions rests in the layers of rules and offices that have accumulated in response to successive demands and challenges. Before the modern White House Office was created, presidents relied informally on a handful of assistants loaned to them from the executive departments. In the late 1930s Congress, acceding to President Franklin Roosevelt's request, created a separate staff and designated six assistants to the president. Gradually, as presidents took on more responsibilities, the White House Office grew in number and complexity. Today its staff is composed of over five hundred policy and political specialists, occupying two office buildings.

Sometimes reform is undertaken to make institutions perform more efficiently. During the opening session of the First Congress in 1789, James Madison, member of the House of Representatives from Virginia, observed that "in every step the difficulties arising from novelty are severely experienced. . . . Scarcely a day passes without some striking evidence of the delays and perplexities springing merely from the want of precedents." Then, more sanguinely, he predicted that "time will be a full remedy for this evil." And time has proven Madison right. By setting rules and following precedents, the House of Representatives has become a well-regulated machine, allowing members to concentrate on lawmaking.

On other occasions, reforms enable institutions to accomplish new collective goals. In 1970 the Environmental Protection Agency was created through an executive reorganization plan that consolidated components of five executive departments and agencies into a single independent agency with strong regulatory authority to protect the environment. By coordinating their actions and centralizing authority, these formerly dispersed agencies could more effectively monitor and regulate polluting industries.

The quality of democracy in modern America reflects the quality of its governing institutions. Embedded in these institutions—initially by the Framers in the Constitution and later by amendment and two centuries of political evolution—is a logic based on principles about how members of a community engage one another politically. When we understand this logic, we will understand why America's political institutions, the politicians who occupy them, and the citizens who monitor and respond to their actions behave as they do. To that end, the concepts presented in the remainder of this chapter are the keys we can use to "open up" America's political institutions to reveal their underlying logic.

Organizing Collective Action

By virtue of their size and complexity, nations encounter special difficulties in conducting political business. In those nations where citizens participate in decisions through voting and other activities, still more complex issues arise. Every aspect of a political choice presents a challenge: combining and ranking preferences, agreeing on a course of action, and implementing the collective choice, especially when it involves enforcing commitments. This section looks at these challenges, specifically at three barriers to successful **collective action**—coordination, free riding, and the prisoner's dilemma—which reappear in virtually every chapter of this book.[5]

Coordination is in some sense the simplest barrier to overcome: each member of the collectivity agrees on what it wants, is prepared to contribute to the collective effort, but must figure out how to coordinate his or her effort with those of others. Free riding is a special instance of the broader prisoner's dilemma. In these cases the members of the group agree to a joint action but fail to deliver on their commitments.

Although the Framers did not use the vocabulary of modern political science, they well understood these problems and that the young nation must solve them if what skeptical Europeans called the "American Experiment" was to succeed. For five months they pondered, argued, voted, and occasionally changed their minds, struggling to design a set of national institutions that could overcome the formidable barriers to successful collective action the new nation faced. The American political system's extraordinary durability stands as a testament to the Framers' success.[6]

Coordination

A string quartet offers an education in the costs of coordinating collective action. During a concert the performers coordinate their individual performances by spending nearly as much time looking at each other as they do at their music. Volume, tempo, and ornamentation must all be executed precisely and in tandem. By the end of a successful concert, the effort required is evident on the triumphant musicians' perspiring faces. A symphony orchestra, by contrast, achieves comparable coordination, despite its greater numbers, by retaining one of its members to put aside the musical instrument and take up the baton. Keying on the conductor, orchestra members are able to coordinate their contributions to making beautiful music. Not surprising, at the end of the concert the conductor is the first one to reach for a handkerchief to mop a perspiring brow.

Coordination problems increase with the size of a group. Large groups trying to reach a shared goal might follow the symphony's solution in designating and following a leader. But there are other solutions. Members of the House of Representatives and the Senate all strive to configure procedures to enable Congress to decide policy

for hundreds of issues presented to it each session. But to achieve the same objective the 435-member House and the 100-member Senate proceed quite differently, following a logic reflecting the size of their organizations. The House delegates to a Rules Committee responsibility for scheduling the flow of legislation onto the floor and setting limits on deliberations and amendments. Thus this important committee becomes the "leader" in setting the body's agenda. The entire House cedes this authority to a committee not because it is unimportant and they do not want to be bothered, but because coordination is vital to the chamber and can best be done this way. By contrast, the smaller Senate has found that it can achieve comparable levels of coordination through informal discussions among members and party leaders. Members need not surrender formal responsibility and authority to a specialized committee to manage their business successfully.

Free Riding

Coordination is not the only collective action problem that increases with the size of a group. Suppose, for example, a violinist is tempted to skip practice and party with friends the evening before a performance. If the violinist plays in the quartet, he will face powerful incentives to fulfill his obligation. If he performs poorly, his three colleagues will quickly notice and the audience will soon detect problems with the performance. After all, they are cueing their actions in part to his. Since his contribution is manifestly vital to the group's collective product, he is likely to stay home and practice.

But if the would-be party-goer is a member of the symphony, he might make a different decision. As one of twenty violinists in the orchestra, his contribution to the collective product is much smaller than that of a member of the string quartet. Since almost any performance problem could be easily concealed from his colleagues and the audience, he might be tempted to spend the night on the town. After all, practice or no practice, he and his professional reputation will still bask in the orchestra's beautiful music. His colleagues, however, might accuse him of taking a "free ride." Citizens confront the **free-rider problem** daily. While within their families and workplaces they may be no less conscientious than the member of the string quartet, in their collective civic behavior they have every incentive to become free riders. They know their small contribution to the collective enterprise will not affect its success or failure.

Even those citizens who enthusiastically support an enterprise realize that they (and others) can escape fulfilling their obligations. If many people think this way—and many do—and suspect their neighbors of doing so as well, too few people will contribute to collective endeavors and some may fail. A good example of free riding is membership support of public television. Less than 10 percent of its regular viewers ever donate to their local PBS affiliate, which explains why the public television system requires an annual government subsidy to stay in business. Another astonishing example can be drawn from World War I. Because of the risk associated with exposing their heads to enemy gunfire while aiming, less than half of the American soldiers stationed in the trenches reportedly ever fired their rifles.

Given the logic of nonparticipation, why does anyone ever contribute to a collective enterprise? Clearly some people find some activities intrinsically rewarding, however minor their contribution to the collective effort. Or the adventure and excitement of participating may be the real goal. Whatever the case, had free riding prevailed there would have been no civil rights marches in the 1960s to propel the civil rights movement into the national limelight (Chapter 4) or anti-Vietnam protests in the 1970s when the police deployed levels of force and tear gas to encourage protesters to consider free riding.

This being said, most of the people, most of the time are inclined to free ride. A reliable way to elicit contributions to a collective effort lies in providing potential participants with a private inducement to take action or dig into their pockets. A few PBS viewers become members of their local station because they want to express their fondness for public television (or perhaps their dis-

gust with commercial television). But many others are lured into membership by the monthly program guide subscription, license plate holders, discount coupon books, and other "rewards of membership." See Chapter 13 for more on the variety of services that another class of private associations, interest groups, provide their members. Government has an important advantage when it comes to inducing contributions to collective efforts: force. Imagine how few people would pay income taxes if there were no Internal Revenue Service waiting in the wings.

The Prisoner's Dilemma

The free-rider problem is part of a more general collective action problem called the **prisoner's dilemma.** (This term originates in the longtime police tactic of separating crime suspects and inducing them to confess by suggesting that their partner is "singing like a canary" in another room in exchange for a reduced sentence.) Every successful political exchange must tacitly solve this dilemma of whether to trust the other side to abide by its commitments. This problem arises because each side, to get something, must typically give up something of value in return.

In 1997, despite repeated overtures, neither Democratic president Bill Clinton nor Republican House Speaker Newt Gingrich would publicly advocate changing how cost of living adjustments, or COLAs, were calculated for Social Security payments. Each side conceded that the current formula for calculating COLAs overstated inflation and that correcting it would improve the long-term financial soundness of the Social Security system. But each side also feared the other would renege on a call for change, leaving it at election time to bear the wrath of the nation's senior citizens who enjoyed their generous annual COLA increases to their retirement checks.

A simple graph illustrates the prisoner's dilemma Clinton and Gingrich confronted. (The numbers represent each politician's hypothetical cost in public approval from each possible outcome. The first number in each pair

Democratic president Bill Clinton and Republican House Speaker Newt Gingrich shake hands amicably at the president's 1995 State of the Union appearance on Capitol Hill. Behind the scenes, however, neither trusted the other to tackle politically risky Social Security reform.

refers to Clinton's loss in percent approval, the second to Gingrich's.) If the two politicians continue to criticize one another for being unwilling to make tough choices without offering a solution, each loses public support (–5,–5). If they work together to solve the Social Security problem by, for example, reformulating COLAs, they will see the comparative benefits of cooperation (–1,–1) versus continuing to do nothing (–5,–5). The problem is they cannot move easily to that position. If one of them proposes cooperation, the other will be tempted to accuse the reform advocate of "selling out the nation's senior citizens." By doing so, the accuser (that is, the defector) imposes the maximum penalty on the reformer (–10) while wholly escaping the wrath of senior citizens (0). Each side, then, appreciates the value of defecting from reform and so prudently distrusts the other. The result: Clinton and Gingrich remain stuck in mutual criticism and suffer the public's displeasure (–5,–5).

A key ingredient of the prisoner's dilemma is that each side is better off defecting no matter what the other side chooses to do. In the case of Clinton and Gingrich, if the other side cooperates, 0 is better than –1; if the other side defects, –5 is better than –10. For each person, criticizing is the rational choice, but acting rationally leaves them both worse off than if they cooperated (with –5 rather than –1), making them collectively irrational.

How, then, do people solve dilemmas in which individual rationality produces irrational outcomes? One solution: make defection very expensive. In some settings this can be achieved informally. For example, politicians who repeatedly renege on agreements will find that others will refuse to deal with them in the future. Thus for them, defection imposes costs down the road and makes politicians think twice before doing so.

Another common solution is to create institutions that guarantee agreements are honored. Here the government's coercive authority is useful. An anthropologist once reported that two tribes in a remote region of New Guinea lived in a state of continual warfare, to the point that many more men from both tribes had died in battle than from natural causes. The anthropologist summed up

		Gingrich's Choice	
		Cooperate	Criticize
Clinton's Choice	Cooperate	–1, –1	–10, 0
	Criticize	0, –10	–5, –5

LOGIC OF POLITICS

Hobbes on Monarchs

In 1651 Thomas Hobbes used his work *Leviathan* to defend the English monarch as a necessary guarantor of collective agreements.[1] He proposed that since the king and his offspring derived their wealth directly from the population in taxes and labor, they would pursue the nation's welfare because it would enrich them as well. Even if the monarch were wicked and expropriated too much of the nation's wealth for himself, the citizenry was still better off with him wielding power arbitrarily than if no one had enforcement authority.

1. Thomas Hobbes, *Leviathan, or The matter, forme, & power of a common-wealth ecclesiasticall and civill* (1651; reprint, Oxford: Clarendon Press, 1958).

their dilemma: "In the absence of any central authority, they are condemned to fight forever . . . since for any group to cease defending itself would be suicidal." He added that these tribes might "welcome pacification." One day the distant government in Papua sent a ranger armed with a handgun to establish territorial boundaries between the tribes and rules governing their chance encounters. Suddenly, the decades-long warfare ended. Each side believed the ranger with his single sidearm presented sufficient force to punish any breach of peace agree-

ments, and the now-peaceful neighbors began to use politics—not war—to solve any conflicts.[7] Members of a society must be able to engage one another politically. Without confidence that agreements will be enforced, the political process quickly unravels as participants balk at undertaking obligations they suspect their bargaining partners will not honor.

The seventeenth-century political philosopher Thomas Hobbes, in his 1651 treatise on the origin and purposes of government, *Leviathan,* examined the straits to which society is reduced when its government is unable to enforce obligations. In a famous passage he warned that life would return to "a state of nature . . . solitary, poor, nasty, brutish and short."[8] The mortality rate of New Guinea tribesmen confirmed Hobbes's insight. They were not naturally bellicose; rather each side simply could not trust the other side not to strike first. Thus enforcement succeeded in inducing a cooperative outcome, not by flaunting overwhelming force and imposing a solution on the different parties, but simply by rendering any party's defection more costly than its compliance.

The Costs of Collective Action

Collective action offers its participants benefits they cannot achieve on their own. The potential benefits, however, must be weighed against the risk that the other side might free ride or renege in some other fashion. Moreover, collective action is costly in various ways. This section examines these costs and their implications for the design of governmental institutions.

Some of the costs associated with participation in collective enterprises are not hard to spot. An obvious one is each person's contribution to the enterprise—for example, the tax payments funding road construction or staffing a police department. Less obvious are the overhead costs of enforcing agreements such as the ranger's salary in New Guinea or the costs associated with the judicial system and the lawyers needed to ensure that those

In January 1798 Matthew Lyon, a member of Congress from Vermont known for his fiery temper, brawled with Roger Griswold from Connecticut in the chamber of the House of Representatives. The lesson here: transaction costs are real—and sometimes painful.

who enter into business agreements live up to their contracts. "Overhead" costs also include the government's effort to combat free riding—for example, the cost of conducting smog tests on vehicles up for state license renewal.[9]

Two additional costs that are a little less obvious but have special significance for designing constitutions are **transaction costs** and **conformity costs**. In the prisoner's dilemma just described, both Clinton and Gingrich already knew the contours of the agreement that would allow them to move from mutual defection to cooperation. The problem they never solved was how to move *together.* Sometimes, however, the parties seeking to cooperate may not know whether a mutually attractive outcome exists or what it would look like. They compare preferences, explore alternative courses of action, and enter into agreements. The time and effort required to compare preferences and make joint decisions are the transaction costs of collective action. These costs can pose a formidable barrier to political agreements.

Transaction costs rise sharply as the number of participants whose preferences must be taken into account increases. In the absence of institutions for negotiating and implementing collective agreements, these costs might overwhelm the ability of the parties to identify and to commit themselves to implementing solutions. With the presence of well-designed institutions, however, agreements become easier. For example, shortly after ratification of the Sixteenth Amendment in 1913 allowed the national government to levy an income tax, the resources available for national programs soared (Figure 1–1). But would tax revenues have grown so rapidly had Congress had to amend the Constitution each time it wanted to change the tax code? Certainly not. The key to successful federal actions lay in reducing the transaction cost of raising federal revenue.

Sometimes, though, high transaction costs are intentionally put in place to make some decisions and agreements more, not less, difficult. Having spent a long, hot summer fashioning a delicately balanced plan of govern-

Figure 1–1 Government Revenue 1910–1970

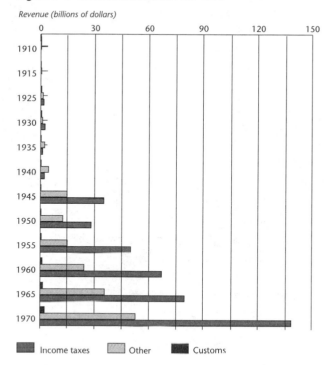

Revenue (billions of dollars)

■ Income taxes ▨ Other ■ Customs

Source: U.S. Department of Commerce, Bureau of the Census, *Historical Statistics of the United States, Colonial Times to 1970* (White Plains, N.Y.: Kraus International Publications, 1989), Tables Y343–351, Y358–373. (No data provided for 1920.)

cost.[11] That person is, after all, contributing to a policy that does not best serve his or her interest. In countries characterized as dictatorships, the dictators themselves may incur few conformity costs, but the rest of the citizenry will be saddled with the extraordinary conformity costs required to maintain the dictator's opulent lifestyle. Not only do the citizens receive few benefits from their collective efforts, but their contribution taxes their ability to look after their own welfare. At the opposite end of the conformity cost continuum is government by consensus. Each citizen retains a veto over the collective decision, and thus any conformity costs are voluntarily agreed to.

Transaction and conformity costs tend to be inversely related: those forms of government that minimize transaction costs, such as dictatorships, tend to impose excessive conformity costs. In the 1930s Italian dictator Benito Mussolini famously "made the trains run on time," but he also dragged his nation into a disastrous world war. Con-

ment, the Framers of the Constitution were understandably not interested in allowing some group down the road to rewrite it easily. One solution was to ratchet up the transaction costs, making change difficult. And that is exactly what the Framers did. A proposed amendment to the Constitution must be endorsed by two-thirds of the membership of both houses of Congress and ratified by three-fourths of the states.[10] The total transaction cost: forty legislatures (the House, Senate, and the governing bodies of thirty-eight of the fifty states) must sign on to any change in the Constitution.

In negotiating a common course of action, competing interests rarely discover they want precisely the same thing. Politics thus invariably involves compromise. The difference between what any one person prefers and what the collectivity actually agrees to represents a *conformity*

"It's either this or a country run by lawyers."

Not just another lawyer joke. . . . Clearly the guards prefer the limited conformity costs imposed by this hapless leviathan to the transaction costs of more democratic institutions. © *The New Yorker Collection 1997 Frank Cotham from cartoonbank.com. All Rights Reserved.*

sensus governments, conversely, shield individual members from imposed collective undertakings but quite possibly at exorbitant transaction costs. Chapter 2 examines America's unhappy experience in its earliest days with government by consensus. The Articles of Confederation, the nation's first constitution, allowed any state to block national action on important policies such as taxes. Moreover, free riding was rampant because the national government lacked the authority to make the states "conform" to agreed-upon policies. Thus even in a country with only thirteen participating states—each state had one vote in the Confederation Congress—the transaction costs imposed by consensus government proved impossibly difficult and prompted all but one state, Rhode Island, to send delegates to the reform convention to redesign the national constitution.

Designing Constitutions for Collective Action

What constitutional arrangements best solve the problems and costs associated with collective action? It depends on what is being decided. If citizens are worried the government might intrude too far into their private lives, they might want to build in high transaction costs and require something close to a consensus to make collective decisions. Perhaps with this in mind, some of the early nation's best political minds drafted the Constitution's Bill of Rights, which limits the ability of majorities in control of government to impose certain kinds of conformity costs on individuals and minorities (see Chapter 5, Civil Liberties). If, by contrast, citizens greatly value a quick, firm collective response, such as defense against foreign threats, they may create institutions that minimize transaction costs. Article II of the Constitution declares that the president is the commander in chief of the nation's military—that is, a single government officer has the authority to send fellow citizens into the field of battle. Clearly, delegates to the Constitutional Convention harbored both kinds of concerns and many shadings in be-

tween. Consequently, the Constitution contains a rich variety of institutional rules and offices.

Among the design principles that reappear explicitly or implicitly throughout the Constitution, two of the most important are **majority rule** and **delegation.** The Framers ingeniously found all kinds of ways to modify and combine these principles to achieve the desired mix of transaction and conformity costs.

Majority Rule

Majority rule, a very special principle in democratic theory, normally refers to *simple majorities,* or one-half plus one. But other kinds of majorities are possible as well. For example, the Constitution prescribes that removal of an impeached president by the Senate requires "the Concurrence of two thirds of the Members present." In this text, however, "majority" refers to a simple majority unless otherwise designated.

Majority rule embodies another hallowed democratic principle, political equality. Equality means that each citizen's vote carries the same weight and all citizens have the same opportunity to participate in the nation's civic life. When all votes count the same, majority rule becomes an obvious principle—that is, when disagreements arise, the more widely shared preference will prevail. Yet majority rule offers no magic formula for balancing transaction and conformity costs. It is just one possible constitutional rule midway on a scale between dictatorship and consensus. Governments controlled by popular majorities are less likely to engage in tyranny—that is, impose very high conformity costs—than are dictators, but this knowledge did not fully assuage the Constitution's Framers. Worried about tyranny by the majority, they devoted a large part of their deliberations to constructing institutions that would temper the power of majorities in the new government.

While majority rule figures prominently in the Constitution, it is explicitly required in only a couple of instances: a majority of the electoral college elects the president and a majority of the membership of the House of

Representatives must be present (quorum) before the institution can conduct business. Most of what the government is authorized to do requires the backing of Congress, which, the Framers seemed to assume, would conduct its business by majority vote. Yet a variety of other rules also appear, or are tacitly permitted, in the Constitution. Rather than prescribing majority-based rules for electing members of Congress, the Constitution leaves it to the states to specify such rules, and they almost always have preferred the **plurality** rule in deciding winners. Under this rule, whoever receives the most popular votes in the election wins whether or not the plurality reaches a majority. When more than two serious candidates run for an office, the winners often receive less than majority support. In the 1992 presidential election, for example, Bill Clinton, the winner, received only 43 percent of the popular vote, thanks largely to third-party candidate Ross Perot who won 19 percent of the vote. Elsewhere in the Constitution *supermajorities* are required. If the president vetoes a bill passed by both houses of Congress, two-thirds of the House and of the Senate must vote to override the veto or the bill is defeated. The Framers raised the bar even higher for constitutional amendments: the approval of three-fourths of the states is required.

The trade-off between transaction and conformity costs thus depends entirely on the kind of decisions the rule—whether majority or otherwise—governs. For some important decisions majority rule, hand in hand with high transaction costs, could lead to undesirable policy. For example, the government allocates space on the frequency band to prevent radio or television stations from interfering with each other's signals. In 1933 Congress removed these decisions from the legislative arena and gave them instead to the five members (and the expert staff) of the Federal Communications Commission. In this instance, assigning frequencies portended high transaction costs for Congress and comparatively modest conformity costs for interested constituencies. Congress therefore *delegated* this class of decisions to an organization of experts while retaining the authority to override their decisions by passing a new law. Thus, though delegated, the authority to set the nation's technical broadcasting policies remains ultimately subject to majority control.

Delegation

Delegation is by far the favored solution to controlling transaction costs. Frequently, this involves assigning authority to make and implement decisions to some smaller number of persons who are expected to act in behalf of the larger group's interest. Social clubs, for example, elect officers each year because members do not enjoy making political decisions. They want to pay their dues and let others worry about providing the services that attracted them to join the club.

Delegation is ubiquitous within government. Every time Americans go to the polls, they delegate to some representative the responsibility for making collective decisions for them. Similarly, members of the House of Representatives elect party and institutional leaders to orchestrate their chamber's business, thereby reducing coordination and other costs of collective action. These politicians also delegate the tasks of writing legislation to more manageable subsets of their members organized into standing committees. Presidents appoint hundreds of staff members to monitor and promote the administration's interests within the bureaucracy. And citizens have agreed to delegate to the Internal Revenue Service the authority to deter any of them from free riding on April 15. Delegation is indispensable whenever the number of people and the number of choices are large and the quality of the choice will improve with expertise.

Social scientists who analyze delegation designate as **principals** those individuals who possess the **authority**—the right—to make certain decisions. Principals then delegate to **agents** the authority to make and implement these decisions for them. For example, every spring millions of Americans hire an agent—say, H&R Block—to fill out their tax forms for them and, they hope, to save them some money. The terms *principal, authority,* and *agent* are used throughout this text to identify and understand a variety of important political relationships that involve some form of delegation.

Delegating authority solves some problems for the collectivity, but it introduces others. Principals run the risk that the agents to whom they have delegated power might use it to improve their own welfare to the neglect of the principal's interest. The discrepancy between what principals would ideally like their agents to do and how these agents actually behave is called **agency loss.** Losses might take the modest form of shirking in which the agent simply does not work as diligently as the principal would like. For example, the agent might attend to personal business rather than "public" business, nod off in committee meetings, or accept tickets to the Super Bowl from someone who wants a special favor. Then there is the more virulent form of agency loss called tyranny. When agents exercise sufficient authority to guarantee that everyone complies with collective decisions (thereby solving the prisoner's dilemma), what is to prevent them from exploiting their advantage to enrich and entrench themselves and to prevent challenges to their authority? Certainly many have. History is rife with stories of government officials who imprisoned their opponents or drained their nation's treasury into Swiss bank accounts.

This risk raises another fundamental question: how much authority must the citizenry surrender to allow it to achieve its collective goals? In the next chapter we find the Constitution's Framers struggling mightily with this conundrum. For James Madison, who played a dominant role in drafting the Constitution, this question was critical. "In framing a government," he wrote, "the great difficulty lies in this: you must first enable the government to control the governed; and in the next place oblige it to control itself."[12] How to design government to manage this "great difficulty" preoccupied the Framers of the Constitution and the political philosophers who influenced them.

But how can principals determine whether their agents are being faithful when they cannot see what their agents do or know why their agents did it? It is the kind of

problem car owners face when an auto mechanic says the strange engine noise will require replacement of some obscure part at the cost of a month's pay. How do owners know whether to trust the mechanic, especially since they know the mechanic's financial interest in the matter clashes with theirs? They could get a second opinion, ask around about the mechanic's reputation, or learn more about cars and check for themselves, but all these solutions take time and energy. Keeping tabs on agents is costly—particularly when the principals may need information from someone who might have a stake in keeping them in the dark. Principals try in various ways to minimize agency loss, but none works perfectly. Delegation always entails a trade-off between the benefits of having the agent attend to decisions in the principal's behalf and the costs of agency loss and the effort required to monitor the agent's behavior.

Representative Government

Modern democracies blend delegation with majority rule into what is known as **representative government.** Citizens limit their decisions to the selection of government officials who, acting as their agents, deliberate and commit the citizenry to collective enterprises. This form of democracy eliminates the massive confusion that would ensue if large communities tried to craft policies directly and frees most citizens from having to attend constantly to civic business. For a large group or society, representative government, through delegation, makes large-scale democracy possible. **Direct democracy,** where citizens participate directly in collective decision making, is reserved for small communities and organizations.

Majority Rule versus Republics

In the era in which the U.S. Constitution was adopted, the idea of majority rule was controversial. Of the few experiments in democracy until that time, the most famous, the ancient city-state of Athens, had ended ignominiously in mob rule and ultimately dictatorship. The eighteenth-century political theorists[13] who influenced the Constitution's Framers endorsed a form of government called a **republic**, designed to allow some degree of popular control and avoid tyranny (see Chapter 2). In a republic voters elect their representatives, but these representatives are constrained in following the majority's dictates by constitutional guarantees for minorities and by institutions and rules requiring exceptionally large majorities for some kinds of decisions.

The notion of an independent, unelected judiciary also may run seriously afoul of the paramount democratic principle of majority rule, but it presents no problem for the republican creed. By ratifying the Constitution and retaining the power to amend it, the people may, if they wish, set up an institution independent of the others and unconcerned with short-term swings in public opinion to serve as a kind of referee for the political process and to preserve the values on which the government is founded. In short, republican theorists, who had the allegiance of virtually everyone who attended the Constitutional Convention in 1787, *really* believed in the role of institutions in reaching and preserving agreements. And by making some collective decisions more difficult than others, the Framers consciously built in higher transaction costs, even if they did not call them that.

Since the American experiment was launched over two hundred years ago, majority rule has proved to be a viable approach to self-governance. As a result, although constitutions written in the twentieth century—for example, in France and modern Germany—may still divide authority in ways that allow their countries to be referred to as republics, they do not contain the elaborate rules and institutions designed to constrain majority rule that are characteristic of the U.S. Constitution. Rather than separating the executive from the legislature, most of the world's modern democracies have fused them in **parliamentary government.** Many varieties of parliamentary government exist, but they all lodge great authority in a popularly elected legislature. It in turn elects a team of executives called a **cabinet,** one of whose members serves as the premier or prime minister (see Figure 1–2). This system

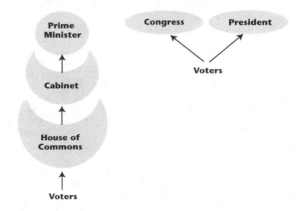

Figure 1–2 Comparison of the American and British Constitutional Systems

British Parliamentary System   *U.S. Presidential System*

promotes majority rule in the sense that the political party or coalition of parties that controls the legislature also controls the executive. In effect, by worrying less about conformity costs, parliamentary systems are able to forgo the higher transaction costs embedded in the U.S. Constitution's **separation of powers.**

Politicians

Another innovation of representative government is elected politicians. Politicians are a class of professionals who specialize in providing compelling reasons for people with different values and interests to join in a common action. These elected agents are sometimes called "public servants"—a euphemism they prefer because such a self-effacing image tends to allay fears of agency loss.

A much more apt term for a politician, however, is *entrepreneur.* Like entrepreneurs, politicians are deal makers, but instead of putting together financial partnerships and other ventures, they assemble coalitions. A **coalition** is a combination of *unlike*-minded interests who nonetheless agree, for their own distinct reasons, to a common course of action. Even to win elections, politicians must succeed at coalition building. The successful candidates persuade a plurality of voters to vote for them (a common action) by offering different constituencies their own reasons for doing so. For many Americans, the "ideal" politician is a

During the Great Depression, when millions of Americans were suddenly impoverished, billboards like this one sprouted up across the country to counter calls for radical reform of the economic and political systems.

dutiful, selfless public servant who is pursuing a principled vision of the public good. But they probably would not be satisfied with his or her performance. A polity in which numerous competing interests are well represented and governing power is widely shared is better off with politicians whose ambitions lead them to become deal-making entrepreneurs.

Upwardly mobile politicians have reason to look beyond the local concerns of those who elected them to identify new issues that will attract a larger and more diverse constituency. In 1957 Senate Majority Leader Lyndon Johnson, a Texan from the segregationist South, pushed the first civil rights law since Reconstruction through the Senate. He did so to prepare the way for his candidacy for the 1960 Democratic presidential nomination. His support for civil rights for African Americans may not have been popular among white voters in Texas, but it gave him sufficient "national" credentials for John Kennedy, who won the nomination, to find LBJ an attractive running mate in the 1960 presidential election.

Ambitious political leaders, however, are a mixed blessing. Citizens want their politicians to act as faithful agents—diligent custodians of their interests—and yet they fear that, once elected to office, politicians will pursue their own interests and neglect the concerns of the people who put them there. Such fears recently spawned a movement to limit the number of terms representatives can serve in Congress and in state legislatures. But politicians' responsiveness is linked to their desire to get reelected or to create a firm base for advancing to higher elective office. Thus the term-limit "solution" eliminates the one real device that democracy provides citizens for keeping these agents responsive.

The Work of Government

Given the variety of costs and risks associated with collective action, Americans tend to weigh such undertakings carefully. Among other things, they calculate whether the prospective gains from a collective public effort are sufficiently greater than what they could achieve privately. The vast majority of these calculations favor private action, perhaps explaining why most of what Americans do and consume as individuals has little or nothing to do with government. Their homes, cars, clothes, food, and sources of entertainment fall into a realm called **private goods**—that is, things people buy and consume themselves in a marketplace that supplies these goods according to the demand for them.[14]

An altogether different kind of good is collectively produced and freely available for anyone's consumption. An example of these **public goods** is a freeway which, as its name implies, may be used by anyone. The distinguishing feature of a "public good" is that its consumption has been disconnected from its production. A toll road, then, is a private good since its costs are met by the motorists who pay a fee (toll) for its use. A quintessential public good is national defense. Although in the early 1950s, at the beginning of the cold war, some homeowners tried to provide their own private defense against nuclear attack by installing backyard bomb shelters, the shelters eventually were replaced by swimming pools as just about everyone accepted the superiority of the nation's nuclear deterrence strategy.

Sometimes public goods are generated as a byproduct of people's private activities. Many such byproducts are undesirable and are more accurately called "public bads." Economists and political scientists prefer to call these byproducts **externalities**.[15] Automobile pollution is a classic example of an externality. It is produced by motorists who act as free riders in serving their own interests over those of society at large. Even the motorists who profess to hate pollution and despise "polluters" rationalize that their own contribution to pollution (the externality) is minuscule and so will not appreciably affect air quality. Collectively, then, drivers gripe about this public bad even as they contribute to it.

Citizens frequently look to government to provide positive public goods: national defense, public order, a legal system, civil liberties, and public parks. They also count on government to prevent negative externalities by passing laws that control pollution, protect endangered species, and establish residential, commercial, and indus-

In 1776 the Scottish economist Adam Smith laid the intellectual foundation for capitalism by declaring in his treatise The Wealth of Nations *that the exchange of goods and services among private parties in an open marketplace generates a public good in the form of prosperity.*

trial zones. Using government has two important advantages: the government has sufficient resources to undertake expensive projects, and it has the coercive authority to prevent or compensate for free riding. Some public goods simply cannot be produced any other way. Other goods offer better value when converted from a private to a public good. The history of fire protection in America is one example (see box).

Because public goods are free, consumers might be tempted to overuse or waste them. When Medi-Cal, California's health care program for the poor, treated eye-

LOGIC OF POLITICS

FIRE PROTECTION
From a Private to a Public Good

The history of fire protection in America offers a classic example of the evolution of private goods to a government responsibility. During the nation's colonial era, fire protection assumed the form of an insurance policy. Homeowners subscribed to a local protection service, mounted its identifying shield on the front of the house, and hoped that if they had a fire it would show up. Aside from the serious coordination problem of identifying the service provider during an emergency, this approach to fire protection was susceptible to a serious externality: when a neighbor's house burned to the ground because he failed to pay his premiums, the fire-protected house stood an excellent chance of catching on fire as well.

In many small communities voluntary fire departments formed to turn fire protection into a public good. The coordination problems were resolved, and the service's responsiveness limited the spread of fires across structures. This arrangement worked reasonably well in towns and villages where everyone knew everyone else. Any "volunteer" who chronically slept through the fire bell might well have found his neighbors doing the same when the bell sounded for his house.

As communities grew and social controls on free riding weakened, voluntary fire protection gave way to government-run, professional fire protection. Typically, governments created a special fire district with taxing authority and hired professional firefighters to supply this public good.

glasses as a public good, it soon discovered that its patients consumed almost twice as many pairs of glasses on average as the people who bought them in the private market. The solution: introduce a modest co-payment, partially privatizing consumption. It promptly brought consumption rates in line with the national averages.

In another variation, governments may regulate aspects of the consumption of private goods in order to achieve a public good. Most kinds of pollution, for example, are created as byproducts of private activities, which means that the government, to protect the public from these byproducts, must intrude on private behavior. For example, the government requires auto manufacturers to produce cleaner-burning engines, forces power plants to install scrubbers on their smokestacks, mandates periodic auto emission inspections, and controls the disposal of toxic waste (see box "Evolution of Smoking from a Private to a Public Issue").

Another large class of goods and services are those that are consumed privately but, because they are undersupplied in the private marketplace, are provided by the government for the public good. In offering federal deposit insurance the government was responding to the widespread bank failures that accompanied the depression in the 1930s. Its solution was to create an insurance program for the benefit of the banks and their depositors. Similar steps have been taken over the years to provide tax deductions for home mortgage payments, federally subsidized college loans, price support subsidies and controls on agriculture, safety regulations in the workplace, and food stamps.

In reality, most of the goods and services that governments are asked to provide cannot be easily sorted into either the private or the public bin. Public education is a classic example. A well-educated citizenry undeniably strengthens the civic and economic life of a society, but public education also bestows substantial *private* benefits on students and educators. Because the work of modern governments typically belongs in this class of mixed

POLITICS ➞ POLICY

Evolution of Smoking from a Private to a Public Issue

An example of the government's intrusion into private behavior is the evolution of the nation's policy toward smoking (see chart). Before the 1980s lighting up a cigarette was regarded as a strictly private activity. There were externalities, to be sure, but as long as the smoke was believed to be no more than a nuisance, nonsmokers endured the fumes with resignation and no one seriously proposed a ban on smoking in public places. In the 1960s, as the externalities of smoking came to be regarded as serious—that is, costly to public health and budgets—the government undertook collective action by requiring health warning labels on cigarette packages. Today, the array of "public bads" associated with smoking—public health care costs, the carcinogenic properties of secondhand smoke, and teenage smoking—has transformed smoking into a prominent public policy issue.

	Discerned Externalities	Nature of Collective Action
1950s and earlier	Nuisance smoke	Voluntary "no smoking"
1960s	Carcinogenic	Package labeling
1970s	Greater scientific evidence and rising public health care costs	Advertising restrictions
1980s–1990s	Secondhand smoke	Smoke-free zones in public facilities
1990s	Rising public health costs and teenage addiction	Settlement of lawsuit between tobacco industry and states' attorneys general to compensate states for public health costs of smoking and agreement

goods, public policy is frequently referred to as **collective goods,** a less-restrictive term.

Mitigating "Popular Passions"

Americans live in a republic whose framework is defined by its Constitution. As we will see in the next chapter, the Framers succeeded in installing in that document the institutions, rules, and procedures intended to mitigate the "popular passions" so feared by James Madison. Separation of powers, staggered legislative terms, an unelected judiciary, limited national authority, and the other features explored in the chapters that follow effectively constrain majority rule. The implication of the Framers'

success for this book is apparent. Any inquiry into understanding how we, as citizens, govern ourselves as a nation must begin by taking a close look at how America's institutions work—how they structure choices and how they blend citizens' preferences into a course of action. Only then can we begin to appreciate the opportunities we have to influence the political process.

The American political system is arguably the most complex of any in the world and the product, in so many ways, of the nation's rich history and its evolving culture. But American politics, in all of its complexity, represents much more than, as one political scientist once put it, "the accretion of so much coral rock."[16] A logic, a rationale, is embedded in American institutions and political

For most of its history the National Park Service was financed by tax revenue and operated as a public good. With the introduction of significant user fees in the 1980s, national parks became partially privatized.

processes. The challenge is to understand this logic. Thus this book not only describes America's political system but also seeks to explain why it takes the form it does.

Key Terms

Suggested Readings

Safire, William. *Safire's New Political Dictionary*. New York: Ballantine Books, 1993. Arguably, Safire understands the American version of English better than any modern popular writer. Fortunately, the former presidential speechwriter also has an especially keen eye for politics.

Shepsle, Kenneth A., and Mark S. Bonchek. *Analyzing Politics: Rationality, Behavior, and Institutions*. New York: Norton, 1997. This book, aimed at the undergraduate audience, elaborates on many of the rational choice concepts presented in this chapter.

Smith, Hedrick. *The Power Game: How Washington Works*. New York: Ballantine Books, 1988. This longtime *New York Times* journalist offers a trove of revealing anecdotes.

Stanley, Harold W., and Richard G. Niemi. *Vital Statistics on American Politics, 1997–1998*. 6th ed. Washington, D.C.: Congressional Quarterly, 1998. If the text does not satisfy your appetite for tables and figures, this book, filled with well-organized data about American politics, will.

Tocqueville, Alexis de. *Democracy in America*. Many good paperback translations of Tocqueville are available, but beware of abridged versions where, invariably, the lively asides and incidental observations are lost.

Chapter 2

THE CONSTITUTION

★ *Why is America's Constitution so complicated, and are the elaborate rules promoting "checks and balances" really necessary?*

★ *How can we call ourselves a democracy when so many features of our national political system are designed to frustrate majority rule?*

★ *The present-day United States is a very different country than the one for which the Framers drafted the Constitution, and yet the Constitution has not changed much over the past two hundred years. Were the Framers really geniuses, or are we simply very lucky?*

Militarily, 1780 was a disastrous year for the American Revolution. Three years into the war the army teeters on total collapse. In May an entire garrison of 5,000 men surrenders to the British at Charleston, South Carolina. In late summer, across the state in Camden, nearly 900 Continental soldiers are killed and 1,000 are taken prisoner in a single engagement. When the army regroups, only 700 of the original 4,000 men show up. The fall brings no respite from the army's woes. Indeed, the young nation learns that one of its few illustrious military commanders, Gen. Benedict Arnold, has switched sides.

By the end of 1780, the American forces, under Gen. George Washington, have shrunk from 26,000 to 15,000. New Year's Day 1781 sees even further deterioration in the army's situation; 1,300 mutinous Pennsylvania troops, camped in Princeton, New Jersey, demand from Congress a year's back pay and immediate discharge. A congressional committee meets the soldiers outside Philadelphia and agrees to some of their demands.

Although all these problems may appear to stem from unfit commanders or unwilling troops, the real problem was the fledgling national government. It simply did not have the capacity to take decisive action since all decisions of consequence such as taxes required approval by all state governments. And it had virtually no administrative apparatus for implementing even those policies that enjoyed unanimous support. As a result, long into the war the army remained underfed, ill-clothed, poorly armed, unpaid (at least in currency of value), and despised by civilians uncompensated for its requisition of supplies. The troops struggled just to survive as a unit. During the winter of 1780, General Washington desperately exhorted Congress, "Where are the Men? Where are the provi-

COUNTDOWN TO THE CONSTITUTION

EVENT	DATE	COLONIAL ACTION
	1750	
French and Indian War (1754–1763) drains the British treasury		Albany Congress calls for colonial unity (1754)
	1760	
Stamp Act enacted by British Parliament (1765)		Stamp Act Congress attended by delegates from nine of the thirteen colonies (1765)
	1770	
Tea Act (1773)		Boston Tea Party (1773)
British adopt Coercive Acts to punish colonies (1774)		First Continental Congress rejects plan of union but adopts Declaration of American Rights denying Parliament's authority over internal colonial affairs (1774)
Battles of Lexington and Concord (1775)		Second Continental Congress assumes role of revolutionary government (1775); adopts Declaration of Independence (1776)
Thomas Paine's *Common Sense* (1776) published		
		Congress adopts Articles of Confederation as constitution for new government (1777)
	1780	
British defeat Americans at Camden and Charleston (1780)		
British surrender at Yorktown (1781)		Articles of Confederation ratified (1781)
Hartford Convention (1781)		
Shays's Rebellion (1786)		Annapolis Convention calls for consideration of a stronger central government (1786)
		Constitutional Convention drafts blueprint for new government (1787)
Federalist Papers (1788)		

sions? Where are the Cloaths?" And ultimately, of course, this emaciated army had to confront the well-equipped British on the battlefield.

The bitter irony was that many of the desperately needed provisions existed in ample supply. The war was causing shortages, but they were not severe enough to account for the deprivations hampering the army. Nor was the problem strictly one of logistics—that is, keeping a traveling army supplied. Despite the difficulty of that task, British troops and their German mercenaries were reasonably well provisioned. Undermining the Revolution's cause was an epidemic of free riding by Americans—from political leaders to ordinary soldiers. States agreed to contribute money and supplies but failed to do so in a timely fashion, if at all. Contractors, paid with a currency that was losing about 10 percent of its value every month, sold the American army spoiled food, shoddy clothing, and poorly manufactured arms, and then shortchanged it even on these inferior provisions when they thought they could get away with it. Many recruits enlisted, received their requisitions, and then deserted with their new booty.

Although the politicians, merchants, and soldiers involved in the war effort were likely all patriots, they were not prepared to shoulder the costs of serving the public good while their neighbors and colleagues conspicuously shirked the same duties. After all, enforcement of contracts and agreements is a fundamental responsibility of government. Was it their fault that lack of government enforcement encouraged free riding, thereby sapping the community's will to achieve its collective goals? General Washington understood the problem and warned darkly that if the government did not soon take charge, "our Independence fails, [our government] will be annihilated, and we must once more return to the Government of Great Britain, and be made to kiss the rod preparing for our correction."[1] Over the next year Washington endured the government's ineptitude and avoided a catastrophic military defeat. Then, with time, the Revolution gained

credibility abroad, which persuaded England's arch rival, France, to loan Congress money to continue the war effort and, finally, to commit its naval and land forces to the battlefield. On October 17, 1781, the collaboration paid off with a decisive victory at Yorktown, Virginia, which ended the war.

The year 1783 brought a formal end to the hostilities and independence for the American colonies. But the young nation, still saddled with a government that could not act, was forced to contend with many of the same problems it had labored under during the war. Indeed, many observers feared that independence, won in war, would soon be lost in peace as the nation threatened to unravel into thirteen disputatious nations.

In the summer of 1787 fifty-five delegates from all the states except Rhode Island assembled in Philadelphia to consider ways of revising the nation's constitution, known as the **Articles of Confederation.** General Washington, presiding over this convention, and the twenty other delegates who had served under him in the field knew firsthand the failings of the current government. The rest of the delegates similarly drew on their varied governing experiences, some stretching back into the colonial era, as they worked together first to revise the Articles and then to formulate an entirely new constitution. How did these delegates use their experience and their familiarity with the new nation's struggle to solve the problems inherent to collective action? A closer look at the events leading up to the Constitutional Convention and the creative process it spawned will reveal the thinking that gave birth to and buttresses today's institutions of government.

The Road to Independence

Geographically, America was well situated to be the first nation to break with monarchy and embrace republicanism; distance limited Britain's capacity to govern the colonies—a problem that gained painful significance during the Revolutionary War. Beginning early in the colonial era, Britain had ceded to Americans responsibility for managing their own domestic affairs, including taxation. The colonists enjoyed this **home rule,** and the British found it agreeable as well. After all, Britain's first concern was to control America's foreign commerce, thereby guaranteeing itself a market for British manufactured goods and a steady supply of cheap raw materials. Thus for more than a century before independence the colonists had routinely elected their own leaders and held them accountable for local policies and taxes. Breaking with Great Britain may have been emotionally wrenching for many Americans, but unfamiliarity with self-governance was not a factor in their hesitancy to seek independence.

A Legacy of Self-Governance

The first colonial representative assembly convened in Virginia in August 1619. By about 1650 all of the colonies had established elective assemblies, which eventually gained the authority to initiate laws and levy taxes. The British appointed governors, colonial councils, and judges in most colonies, and some of these officials vigorously resisted the expansion of local prerogatives. But because the elective assemblies paid their salaries and funded their offices, these officers of the Crown found that they too had to accommodate popular opinion. The colonial experience thus taught Americans that a popularly elected legislature in control of the purse strings could dominate other governmental institutions. With this in mind, the Constitution's Framers turned first to designing a new Congress, but not before encountering the most serious and hard-fought disagreements to surface among convention delegates during the summer of 1787 in Philadelphia.

In addition to experience in self-governance, the state assemblies supplied the nation with another vital resource: elective politicians experienced in negotiating collective agreements. As the vanguard of the independence movement, these politicians provided the nation with an era of exceptional leadership.

Americans also entered independence well versed in constitution writing. A royal charter or contract between the Crown and a British company or business entrepreneur had provided the foundation for most colonies. Later, the colonists themselves wrote constitutions, which they periodically revised. When in 1776 and again in 1787 the nation's leaders confronted the task of designing new government institutions, a constitution was, not surprisingly, the instrument of choice.

Home rule may have had its benefits for the American colonies, but in important respects it also shortchanged the nation's civic education in the requirements of self-governance. In ruling its far-flung empire, which included the American colonies, Britain regulated all of its colonies' commerce, as well as provided them with military security by means of its navy, the world's largest. Thus the colonies prospered and managed their own domestic affairs while Britain dictated their foreign relations and bore the substantial costs of providing their security. Britain found it easier to maintain control by dealing with the thirteen colonies individually rather than through some national assembly that represented their collective interests. As a result, instead of gradually assuming greater responsibility for their common destiny, America's colonial governments found few occasions to work together. Later, after the nation declared its independence, politicians who had stridently resisted the Crown's incursions into their local authority found themselves unwilling to bear the costs of addressing their collective problems. With nationhood, the free ride was over.

Home rule experienced its first strains during Britain's war with France in the 1750s. Known in America as the French and Indian War and in Europe as the Seven Years' War, this lengthy, far-flung conflict drained Britain's treasury and its military resources. Searching for assistance, Britain in 1754 summoned delegates from each of the colonies to a conference in Albany, New York, to invite their collective assistance in defending the western frontier against the French military and its Indian allies. Since six of the thirteen colonies failed to send delegates, this

In what is recognized as America's first political cartoon, Benjamin Franklin depicts the colonies as caught in a classic collective action dilemma. If united, the colonies represent a formidable force for England to reckon with. But the snake will not exist if any of its parts—the individual colonies—are missing.

would-be first national assembly failed even before it convened.

Yet the Albany Congress produced the first serious proposal for a national government. One of Pennsylvania's delegates, Benjamin Franklin, already renowned throughout the country as the man who had tamed lightning, proposed a "Plan of the Union" which would have created a national government. It called for an American army to provide for the colonies' defense, a popularly elected national legislature with the power to levy taxes, and an executive appointed by the British king.[2] But none of the colonial assemblies could muster much enthusiasm for Franklin's ideas. Why should they share their tax base with some new governmental entity with a dubious mandate? And why should they undertake Britain's burden of providing for the colonies' security and overseeing trade? For them, free riding made eminent sense as long as they could get away with it. And they did get away with it; another decade would pass before Britain tried to force Americans to contribute to their defense. Only then did Franklin's proposal begin to make sense and attract interest.

Dismantling Home Rule

France's defeat in 1763 ended its aspirations for extensive colonization of America. The British, relishing their victory, had little idea, however, that the war would trigger a chain of events that would, over the next decade, severely compromise Britain's claims in America as well.

By the end of the war Britain was broke. With its citizenry already among the most heavily taxed in the world, the British government looked to the colonies to share in the empire's upkeep.[3] To get the tax revenues it needed, Britain had to assert its power to impose taxes. Moreover, to consolidate its power it had to violate home rule. This it proceeded to do. Every revenue law the British government enacted during the decade after the French and Indian War contained provisions tightening its control over the internal affairs of the colonies.

The most aggressive challenge to home rule came in 1765 with passage of the Stamp Act.[4] This law imposed a tax on all printed materials, including legal documents, licenses, insurance papers, and land titles, as well as a variety of consumer goods, including newspapers and playing cards (proof of payment of the tax was the stamp affixed to the taxed document). The tax had been long familiar to the British public, but Americans greeted it as a personal affront. It inflamed American public opinion, not so much because of the money but because of the instruments employed to extract the money. Americans had paid taxes before, but they had been self-imposed, levied by the colonial assemblies to provide local services. Thus the American response, "no taxation without representation," was not simply the rallying cry of a tax revolt. In fact, Americans were not genuinely interested in representation in the British Parliament. Rather, it was an assertion of home rule.

The colonial assemblies passed resolutions demanding repeal of the tax, and most sent delegates to a national conference, the Stamp Act Congress, to craft a unified response. For the first time they united against Britain by agreeing unanimously on a resolution condemning the

On March 5, 1770, British troops fired into a crowd of men and boys in Boston, killing five men and wounding others. The massacre gave the word tyranny *new meaning. This and other events were instrumental in rousing colonial resistance to British rule on the eve of the American Revolution.*

tax. They could not agree, however, on a course of action.

The organized resistance of ordinary citizens was more successful.[5] Throughout the colonies local groups confronted tax collectors and prevented them from performing their duties. Over the next decade these scenes were repeated as Britain imposed a half dozen new tax and administrative laws designed to weaken the colonial assemblies. Americans countered by boycotting British products and forming protest organizations, such as the Sons of Liberty, the Daughters of Liberty, and the more militant Committees of Correspondence. Vigilantism and public demonstrations overshadowed assembly resolutions.

Justly, the most famous of these demonstrations was the Boston Tea Party. No colony had chafed under Britain's new rules and taxes more than Massachusetts. On a winter night in 1773 a group of patriots donned Indi-

an dress and dumped 342 chests of tea owned by the East India Company into Boston harbor to protest a new tax on Americans' favorite "soft drink." Britain responded with the Restraining Acts and Coercive Acts, which closed the port of Boston to all commerce, dissolved the Massachusetts assembly, decreed that British troops in Boston must be quartered in American homes, and ordered that Americans charged with protest crimes and British soldiers charged with crimes against the colonists be sent to England for trial. Colonists viewed these last provisions as assuring serious punishment for the first group and lax punishment for the second.

The Continental Congresses

When colonists elsewhere witnessed Britain's heavy-handed policies in Massachusetts, they recognized their own vulnerability. Without hesitation, then, they an-

In this eighteenth-century satirical drawing by a British artist, Bostonians gleefully pour tea down the throat of a customs official, who has just been tarred and feathered. In the distance colonists dump tea into Boston Harbor, just as they did in 1773 at the Boston Tea Party. And, lest one British misdeed go unnoticed, a symbol of the hated Stamp Act, passed in 1765, appears on the tree at right.

crees. When the idea of creating a national government was raised, Franklin's plan of union, the only extant proposal for unification, was introduced and briefly but inconclusively debated. The most significant actions taken by the First Continental Congress were adoption of a Declaration of American Rights, which essentially reasserted home rule, and endorsement of an agreement to ban all trade with Britain until it rescinded despised taxes and regulations. To enforce the boycott against the prospect of massive free riding, the Congress called for the formation of local elective "committees of observation" in every county, town, and hamlet in the country. Soon, many of these newly formed organizations began imposing a kind of patriot morality. "Treasonable" conversations were investigated; more ordinary vices were publicly rebuked. Earlier import boycotts had been modestly successful—successful enough to alter British policy—but the new boycott was almost totally effective.

The eight thousand or so members of these local committees provided a base for the statewide conventions that sprang up throughout the colonies when the British prevented the colonial assemblies from meeting. Unhampered by local British authorities, these conventions quickly became de facto governments.[6] They collected taxes, raised militias, passed "laws" forbidding the judiciary from enforcing British decrees, and selected delegates to the Second Continental Congress which met in Philadelphia in May 1775.

By the time the Second Continental Congress met, war had broken out. Spontaneous bloody uprisings in the spring of 1775 at Lexington and Concord in Massachusetts had provoked the state conventions to begin mobilizing local volunteer militias and disarming suspected British loyalists. Events demanded concerted action, and the Second Continental Congress responded by acting like a national government. Congress had no legal authority to conduct a war effort, but throughout the colonies patriots desperately required coordination, and it was the only national institution available.

The first action by Congress was to instruct the con-

swered the call of Boston resistance leader Samuel Adams to assemble in the fall of 1774 at Philadelphia for what became the First Continental Congress. Each colony sent its leading professionals, merchants, and planters. These men had mostly known one another only by reputation, but at this meeting they would form a nucleus of national leadership for the next decade. Among them were the nation's first presidents: George Washington, Thomas Jefferson, and John Adams.

The Continental Congress promptly passed resolutions condemning British taxes and administrative de-

ventions to reconstitute themselves as state governments based on republican principles, which all promptly did. Using their former colonial governments as a model, most states adopted **bicameral** (two-chamber) **legislatures,** and all created a governorship. Accustomed to difficult relations with the royal governors, the states imposed severe limits on the terms and authority of these newly minted American executives. This anti-executive bias would persist and influence deliberations at the Constitutional Convention a decade later.

Then, acting even more like a government, the Second Continental Congress issued the nation's first bonds and established a national currency. It also authorized delegate George Washington to expand the shrinking Massachusetts militia into a full-fledged national army. (As if his colleagues had needed a hint, Washington attended the convention in full military dress of his own design.)

The Declaration of Independence

During its first year's work of creating states and raising and financing an army, Congress did not consider the fundamental issue of separation from England. But it was being discussed on street corners and in taverns throughout the nation. In January 1776 the writer Thomas Paine published a pamphlet entitled *Common Sense.* It moved the independence issue to center stage. Within three months 120,000 copies had been sold, and Americans were talking about Paine's plainly stated, irresistible argument that only in the creation of an independent republic would the people find contentment.

The restless citizenry's anticipation that Congress would consider a resolution of separation was realized in June when Virginia delegate Richard Henry Lee called for creation of a new nation separate from Britain. Congress referred his proposal to a committee of delegates from every region with instructions to draft the proper resolution. One member of this committee was a thirty-three-year-old lawyer from Virginia, Thomas Jefferson. Asked to draft a statement because of "his peculiar felicity of ex-

pression," Jefferson modestly demurred. This prompted the always direct John Adams of Massachusetts to protest, "You can write ten times better than I can."[7]

Jefferson's qualifications to articulate the rationale for independence extended well beyond his writing skills. A man of aristocratic tastes but democratic values, he never wavered from an abiding confidence in the innate goodness and wisdom of common people. "State a moral case to a ploughman and a professor," he once challenged a friend. "The former will decide it as well, and often better than the latter, because he has not been led astray by artificial rules."[8] In the end, Jefferson agreed to draft the resolution of separation.

Jefferson concurred with the other delegates in many of the specific grievances itemized in the resolution he drafted, but for him the real rationale for throwing off British rule rested on the fundamental right of self-government. Such conviction produced this well-known passage:

We hold these truths to be self-evident, that all men are created equal, that they are endowed by their creator with certain unalienable Rights, that among these are Life, Liberty and the pursuit of Happiness. That to secure these rights, Governments are instituted among Men, deriving their just powers from the consent of the governed. That whenever any form of government becomes destructive of these ends, it is the Right of the People to alter or abolish it, and to institute new Government. . . .

Jefferson's colleagues did not tamper with this crown jewel of the **Declaration of Independence,** but they did amend his list of grievances. Foreshadowing the future conflict over race, Jefferson's indictment of Britain for introducing slavery into the colonies offended the sensibilities of slave-owning southern delegates. Thus at their insistence this grievance was stricken from the final resolution.[9] (The full text of the Declaration of Independence appears in the Appendix.)

In a solemn ceremony on July 4, 1776, each member of the Second Continental Congress signed the document. Rebelling against a colonial power with a huge occupation army was a dangerous enterprise. The conclusion of the Declaration—"we mutually pledge to each other our lives, our Fortunes, and our sacred Honor"—was no mere rhetoric.

America's First Constitution: The Articles of Confederation

With the Declaration of Independence in hand, the delegates to the Second Continental Congress proceeded to "institute new Government" as called for in the Declaration. Over the next several weeks they drafted and sent to the new states for ratification the nation's first constitution known as the Articles of Confederation. Though not ratified until 1781, the Articles served as the nation's de facto constitution during the intervening war years.

As its name states, the first American constitution created a **confederation,** a highly decentralized governmental system in which the national government derives limited authority from the states rather than directly from the citizenry. Not only do the states select officials of the national government, but they also retain authority to override the government's decisions.

The Articles transferred the form and functions of the Continental Congress to the new, permanent Congress in which each state received one vote. Major laws—such as those dealing with taxes and constitutional change—required unanimous agreement. National authority was so circumscribed that the delegates saw little purpose for an executive branch or a judiciary.[10] From time to time administrators might be required, but they could be hired as needed and directly supervised by the new Congress.

In adopting a confederation, the delegates sought to restore a semblance of the home rule they had lost in the 1760s. Clearly, after years of free riding under British rule, they were not yet willing to absorb the collective action costs associated with nationhood. Yet they also recognized that in declaring their independence they thrust upon themselves responsibility for supplying essential public goods—most important, defense and commercial markets—that Britain had provided under home rule. The same delegates who had pressed hardest for independence, knowing that it was likely to lead to war, were among those who most vigorously favored a confederation over more powerful alternatives. Clearly, the new nation's leaders still had a great deal to learn about the logic of collective action. But they would learn in time—the hard way. Their suspicion of national authority very nearly cost the fledgling nation its independence.

The Confederation at War

Faced with a war raging for over a year, the states, unwilling to give the national government sufficient authority to conduct the war, became chiefly responsible for recruiting troops and outfitting them for battle. The national military command, which would be answerable to Congress, assumed responsibility for organizing the various state regiments into a single fighting force. In principle, Congress was assigned the role of coordinator. It would identify military requirements, assess the states, and channel their (voluntary) contributions to the army.[11] Congress also was empowered to borrow money through bonds, but its lack of taxation authority made bonds a risky and expensive venture for the government, which had to offer high interest rates to attract investors.

The public's deep suspicion of government also prevented national officeholders from creating the administrative structures suitable for the new government's wartime responsibilities. John Adams even wanted to prevent Washington from appointing his own staff officers for fear that "there be too much Connection between them." Instead, he argued, Congress should select all officers so that these "officers are checks upon the General." Adams's appeal to the "proper Rule and Principle" stimulated serious debate, but he did not prevail in this instance. He was, however, more successful in most other attempts to dilute executive powers.

The administrative vacuum sucked congressional committees into the daily affairs of requisitioning an army. These legislators struggled mightily, even heroically, to do their duty, but most were unskilled in administration and frequently unable to make timely decisions. In fact, the members of one committee expressed such a variety of views on the number of uniforms to be ordered they found themselves unable to come to a decision. The desperate plight of General Washington's army as the war continued attests to the naiveté and ineffectiveness of the structure of the confederation. Thus the collective action problems described in Chapter 1 were evident in America's war effort: contagious levels of free riding and the reluctance of some states to contribute their fair share for fear that the other states would hold back (prisoner's dilemma). Moreover, the undeveloped national administration provided fertile soil for equally debilitating free riding in the form of corruption.

Prevented by the Articles of Confederation from playing a more central role in administering the war, Congress responded to the quickly deteriorating military situation by decentralizing authority even further. Among other things, it passed resolutions instructing the states to supply their troops directly. Perhaps, some members reasoned, the states would be more forthcoming with support for their own sons in uniform. This scheme had the merit of converting a public good—military supplies that all state regiments could consume regardless of their state's contribution—into a more or less private good that linked the welfare of each state's own sons to its legislature's effort. But the notion of thirteen states locating and supplying intermingled regiments scattered up and down the Atlantic seaboard presented a logistical nightmare. On hearing of it, General Washington caustically remarked that members of Congress "think it is but to say 'Presto begone,' and everything is done."

At the same time pressure was mounting on various fronts, including within Congress itself, for Congress to assume greater authority to conduct the war.[12] Understandably, the military commanders were the most outspoken in lobbying Congress and state governors for a "new plan of civil constitution."[13] General Washington ad-

vised Congress that an "entire new plan" providing it with the authority "adequate to all of the purposes of the war" must be instituted immediately. Washington's aide Alexander Hamilton, later one of the architects of the Constitution, showered members of Congress with correspondence urging them to grasp the emergency authority he claimed was inherent in the Articles. Without the "complete sovereignty" that could only come with an independent source of revenue, he argued, Congress would have neither the resources nor the credibility necessary to conduct the war. And, as the states' dismal performance had proved, if Congress did not take control, no one else could.[14]

The addition of the second major group—state officials—to the chorus for reform reveals the pervasiveness of frustration with the confederation. Although the confederation had sought to empower these officials above all others, many found themselves trapped in a classic prisoner's dilemma. Each was prepared to sacrifice for the war, but only if they could be confident that the others would. Moreover, many of their colleagues who had been outspoken champions of volunteerism were defeated in the 1780 elections by challengers calling for a strengthened national authority that could enforce agreements.

By the summer of 1780 some states had decided to take direct action. In August representatives of several New England states met and passed a resolution calling for investing Congress with "powers competent for the government." Several months later five northern states met at what is now known as the Hartford Convention to urge Congress to grant itself the power to tax. In a remarkable resolution the convention called for Congress to delegate to General Washington the authority "to induce . . . punctual compliance" from states that ignored their obligations to supply the army. As delegates saw it, only under threat of coercion would the states cooperate (and end their prisoner's dilemma).

Congress responded as best it could, but it labored under a constitution designed to frustrate national action. In 1781 Rhode Island, with less than 2 percent of the nation's population, vetoed a bill giving Congress the authority to levy taxes. Various administrative reforms were enacted, but they had to be watered down to win unanimous endorsement. Although Congress did create executive offices, it was unable to agree on what kinds of independent authority to delegate to them. As a result, the offices had no authority, and their occupants were reduced to serving at the beck and call of the legislature's committees.

Perhaps the only change of consequence was the appointment of the able commercial leader Robert Morris as the government's finance secretary. Convinced that the British would quit the battlefield only when the states demonstrated a capacity to continue the fight indefinitely, Morris worked mightily to restore the nation's credit, even guaranteeing government debts with his own fortune. Encouraged by Morris, France lent the government hard currency. By 1782 General Washington could write for the first time since the beginning of the war that his army was well fed, clothed, and armed.

A recuperating American army and France's continued participation in the war presented Britain with the prospect of a far longer conflict. (France formally recognized American independence and agreed to support the United States unilaterally in 1778.) In October 1781 British troops, under Gen. Charles Cornwallis, suffered defeat at Yorktown, Virginia, and Britain sued for peace. Thus the United States had somehow survived a war with an occupying army. In the jubilation of victory, however, momentum for political reform was lost.

The Confederation's Troubled Peace

Shortly after signing the peace treaty with Britain, the nation lunged toward new perils—indeed, to the point that many Americans and even more Europeans began to question whether the hard-won independence might still be lost in national disintegration. By 1787 American leaders were openly speculating about the prospect of Britain reasserting its authority over the barely united and internally divided states.

The War-Torn Economy. After six years of war, the nation's debt was staggering. Congress owed Americans about $25 million and foreign governments another $10 million. The most urgent concern was the back pay owed the army. In the spring of 1783 General Washington learned of a conspiracy forming among disgruntled officers to march on Congress. Greatly alarmed, he wrote his former aide Alexander Hamilton, now a member of Congress, that the army should be paid and "disbanded without delay." The army is "a dangerous instrument to play with," he warned ominously. Prudently, Congress followed Washington's advice.

Creditors who had supplied the troops formed another long line. But Congress was more successful in ignoring these unarmed claimants, some of whom eventually received partial payment from the states. Abroad, debts to Britain negotiated in the peace settlement and loans from European governments and private interests all had to be repaid before normal commercial relations with these countries could be resumed. In the face of so much debt, the national currency plummeted to approximately one-tenth of its prewar value.

The complexities of governing by confederation compounded the problem. Congress held the debt, but the states controlled the purse strings. As it had during the war, Congress prescribed annual state contributions to reduce the debt over twenty-five years. But no one expressed confidence that the states, having proven so unreliable in war, would step forward in peace to accept fiscal responsibility for the nation. Thus in the same bill Congress proposed that it be given a source of direct revenue in the form of import duties. Once again, however, the Articles' unanimous consent rule frustrated action. Unwilling to share the revenue from its already active port city of New York, the delegates from New York state killed this proposal.

Trade Barriers at Home and Abroad. The nation's shaky finances were not helped by its trade problems, which also stemmed from the terms of the confederation. (The Articles of Confederation explicitly reserved all matters of commerce to the states.) For example, Congress lacked the authority to negotiate credible trade agreements with other nations. European governments found this arrangement, in which trade agreements required the endorsement of each state's legislature, unwieldy. The national government also proved incapable of responding to discriminatory trade sanctions and other actions abroad. When the British and later the French closed their West Indies possessions to U.S. exports, the effects played havoc with the fragile, war-torn economy that depended heavily on exports.

Economic relations among the states were nearly as unsatisfactory. States with international ports charged exporters from other states stiff user fees. New York victimized New Jersey; Virginia and South Carolina both extracted a toll from North Carolina. And each state minted its own currency. Some states, responding to political pressures from indebted farmers, inflated their currencies. Exchange rates fluctuated widely across states, which made interstate commerce a speculative financial exercise.

To no one's surprise, many sectors of the economy clamored loudly for reform. The nation's creditors wanted a government able to pay its debts. Importers and the mercantile class desperately needed a sound currency and an end to capricious state policies toward one another's goods. The profits of southern growers of tobacco and indigo depended wholly on open export markets, which only a national government could negotiate effectively. The need for a central authority that could create and manage a common market at home and implement a unified commercial policy abroad stirred diverse economic interests to call for a revision of the Articles of Confederation.

In the summer of 1786 Virginia made the first move, inviting delegates of other states to convene that fall at Annapolis, Maryland, to consider ways of strengthening the national government's role in commerce. Eight states named delegates, but when those from only five states showed up, the Annapolis convention adjourned after passing a resolution calling for another convention in Philadelphia nine months later. Thus the Annapolis convention earned a place in history by setting the stage for the Constitutional Convention in May 1787. Although the delegates had no reason to believe the next meeting would generate any better turnout, something happened during the intervening months to galvanize interest in constitutional reform. That event was Shays's Rebellion.

Popular Discontent. In the economic depression that followed the Revolution, many small farmers lost their land and other assets. Markets were disrupted, credit became scarce, and personal debt mounted. The financial straits of small farmers spawned occasional demonstrations, but none so threatening as the one that erupted in the fall of 1786 in western Massachusetts where taxes were especially onerous and the local courts unforgiving. Not only were farmers losing their possessions at the auction block, but some were even being hauled off to prison for their debts. The protest movement began with town meetings and petitions to the state legislature to suspend taxes and foreclosures. When their appeals failed to win much sympathy, these disaffected citizens found more aggressive ways to remonstrate their grievances. Under the leadership of Daniel Shays, a former captain in the Continental army and a bankrupt farmer, an armed group composed mostly of farmers marched on the Massachusetts supreme court session in Springfield to demand that state judges stop prosecuting debtors. Shays's band was met by the state militia, but the confrontation ended peacefully after the magistrates adjourned the court.

In late January 1787 Massachusetts erupted once more, this time with enough violence to convince the states to convene in Philadelphia. Having learned that Shays planned an assault on a government arsenal in Springfield, delegates from Massachusetts appealed to the national government to send troops, but, once again unable to muster unanimous support in the states, Congress could offer neither troops nor money. A similar appeal to neighboring states proved no more productive. Finally, a local militia organized with private donations intercepted and repulsed Shays's "army" of about a thousand farmers outside the arsenal. Over the next several weeks some of Shays's men were captured, others dispersed, and the rebellion ended.

Had it been an isolated incident even this event might not have persuaded state leaders of the need for a stronger national government. But Shays's rebellion incited a wave of popular uprisings that swept across the country. The same winter, two hundred armed farmers in Pennsylvania had tried to reclaim neighbors' possessions that had been seized by tax collectors. On the same day as Shays's defeat, these farmers rescued a neighbor's cattle from a tax sale. Virginia protesters, following the example of the insurgents in Massachusetts, burned down public buildings. Their favorite targets were jails and courthouses where tax and debt records were kept.

State legislatures, either intimidated by threats of force or genuinely sympathetic with farmers' demands, caved in to the slightest pressure from these constituencies. At times, these bodies' knee-jerk responses caused them to behave in ways more in keeping with revolutionary tribunals than with deliberative republican legislatures. Throughout the country they summarily overturned unpopular court decisions, altered property assessments, and issued quickly devalued paper money which they then forced creditors to accept as full payment of farmers' debts.[15] Observing all this, the troubled James Madison of Virginia wrote his friend Thomas Jefferson in Paris, where Jefferson was serving as the states' ambassador: "In our Governments the real power lies in the majority, and the invasion of private rights . . . chiefly [arises] . . . not from acts of Government contrary to the sense of its constituents, but from acts in which the Government is the mere instrument of the major number of the constituents."[16] Madison's discomfort with arbitrary majority action was to guide his efforts and those of like-minded delegates throughout the Constitutional Convention.

To many observers, Shays's rebellion represented a wildfire threatening to sweep the country to anarchy.[17] No matter how persuasive Hamilton, the beloved Washing-

Despite their defeat, the protesting farmers led by Daniel Shays won a number of reforms from the Massachusetts state legislature, which lowered court costs and exempted household necessities and workmen's tools from the debt collection process. The unintended impact of Shays's Rebellion on national reform was far more dramatic. It demonstrated that the confederation could not perform the most basic function of government—keeping the peace.

ton, or any of the other nationalists were in promoting the cause of constitutional reform, it was Daniel Shays who offered the most compelling reason to the state legislatures to send delegates to the upcoming convention in Philadelphia. When they assembled the next May in Philadelphia, delegates from all states except Rhode Island were present.

Drafting a New Constitution

In their deliberations the fifty-five youngish, well-educated white males who gathered in Philadelphia in 1787 drew on their shared experience of war and its aftermath, but they did not do so reflexively or out of narrowly construed self-interest. They also were highly conversant in the ideas and theories swirling "in the air" in the Age of

Reason, as the eighteenth century was known. Influenced by recent advances in science, scholars, and even America's politicians, sought through careful reasoning to discern the "natural laws" that governed economics, politics, and morality. The impact of these ideas was not merely a matter of their novelty and intellectual appeal, but also in how they illuminated Americans' experiences.

Thus the Constitution that eventually arose out of the convention was grounded in theories of politics, economy, and even science that were attracting attention at the time throughout Europe. The delegates cited dozens of contemporary and ancient philosophers during floor deliberations, often quoting them in their original language of Latin or French. Of these thinkers, several deserve to be singled out because their ideas are clearly discernible in the Constitution.

Heading any list is the English philosopher John Locke (1632–1704), whose brilliant writings on political theory and design of government read in some places as if the Framers were his sole audience. In 1690 Locke vigorously defended the still-novel idea of *popular sovereignty*—that is, citizens delegate authority to their agents in government knowing they can rescind it.[18] This argument clearly influenced Jefferson's pen in the Declaration of Independence. Moreover, Locke stressed individual rights and the limited scope of government authority. If Locke's ideas strike the modern student as unexceptional, it is because they are so thoroughly embedded in the Constitution and governmental system that they are taken for granted.

During the same era another Englishman, Sir Isaac Newton (1642–1727), was laying the foundations for the study of modern mechanics and physics. His discovery of the laws of physical relations (such as gravity) inspired the Framers to search for comparable laws governing social relations. Evidence of Newton's influence can be seen in the Framers' imagery as they described their design proposals to each other and later to the nation. Concepts such as "force," "balance," and "fulcrum," and phrases such as "laws of politics" and "check power with power" were bandied about with great familiarity.

When the youthful James Madison was introduced with the accolade "Father of the Constitution," he frequently demurred, probably less from modesty than from disagreement with many of its provisions.

Perhaps more than anyone else, the French philosopher Baron de Montesquieu (1689–1755) supplied the Framers with the nuts and bolts of a design of government, particularly his classification of governmental functions and forms as legislative, executive, and judicial. Like Locke, Montesquieu championed limited government—limited not only in the nature of its authority but also in the size of the political community it encompassed. Thus during and after the convention opponents of reform invoked Montesquieu as a powerful counterargument to those who advocated empowering the national government.

Finally, the Scottish philosopher David Hume (1711–1776) treated politics as a competition among contending interests, in much the same way that his fellow countryman Adam Smith described competition in the marketplace of an emerging capitalist economy. An ocean away, James Madison adapted Hume's arguments to his own purposes, much as Jefferson did Locke's.

From May until September 1787 the delegates to the Constitutional Convention drafted the rules and procedures that would govern the new nation. Unlike in this engraving, the shutters remained closed—in one of the hottest summers in Philadelphia history—to guarantee the privacy of their deliberations.

America's leaders, though politicians, often behaved as if they were philosophers, carefully studying and even writing treatises on government. The most important is James Madison's three-thousand-word essay "Vices of the Political System of the U. States," which he drafted in the spring of 1787 after extensive research on ancient and modern confederations. (Madison had Jefferson scour Paris bookstores for source materials.) Madison circulated copies of his manuscript among fellow Virginians who would be attending the Philadelphia convention to prepare them for the reform proposal he was writing. Madison's sophisticated understanding of politics is apparent in a passage attributing the confederation's failure not to a moral breakdown of the citizenry but to the prisoner's dilemma embedded in faulty institutions: "A distrust of the voluntary compliance of each other may prevent the compliance of any, although . . . [cooperation is] the latent disposition of all."

Getting Down to Business

Most of the delegates chosen to represent their states in Philadelphia probably were unaware of the grand scope of the enterprise on which they were about to embark. Some undoubtedly assumed that the convention would simply return to the Annapolis agenda which sought to resolve commercial disputes at home and coordinate the states' commercial policies abroad. Others anticipated minor reforms of the Articles and were prepared to take the positions dictated by their state legislatures. But at least a few, most notably James Madison, were planning—indeed, plotting with others of like mind—to scrap the Articles of Confederation altogether and start over.

Sensing his fellow Virginian's hidden agenda, war hero Patrick Henry announced he "smelt a rat" and refused to join the delegation to Philadelphia. The Delaware legislature was similarly suspicious and instructed its delegates to oppose any scheme that undermined the equality of the states. Another small state, the ever-independent Rhode Island, boycotted the convention.

The convention opened on a rainy Friday, May 25, 1787. By acclamation, the delegates elected General Washington to preside over the deliberations, and the convention began on a harmonious note. Madison sat at the front where he could easily participate in floor debates and record the arguments of his colleagues.[19] The convention agreed to keep the proceedings secret in order to allow a frank exchange of views and to facilitate compromise. This decision meant keeping the window shutters closed during one of the hottest summers in Philadelphia's history.

The Virginia and New Jersey Plans

On the first day of substantive business Madison and his nationalist colleagues sprang their surprise. Edmund Randolph, also from Virginia, introduced Madison's blueprint for a new constitution. Known today as the Virginia Plan, it dominated floor debate well into July. While few of its provisions survived intact in the final draft of the Constitution, the Virginia Plan succeeded in shifting the focus of deliberations from patching up the confederation to considering anew the requirements of a national union.[20]

The centerpiece of the Virginia Plan was a bicameral national legislature. Members of the lower chamber would be apportioned among the states by population and directly elected by the citizenry. The lower chamber would, in turn, elect the members of the upper chamber from lists of nominees supplied by the state legislatures. It also would elect the officers of the proposed executive and judicial branches (see Figure 2–1). Madison's intent was clear: by controlling the selection of the other officers of government, representatives of the people could claim the special legitimacy that comes with democratic election.

The Virginia Plan also stipulated that the national government could make whatever laws it deemed appropri-

Figure 2–1 The Virginia Plan

Organization of the National Government

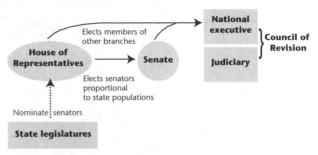

How a Bill Becomes a Law

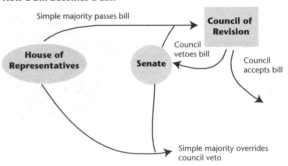

ate and veto any state laws it regarded as unfit. If a state failed to fulfill its legal obligations, the national government could summon military force against it. This provision proved to be a tactical mistake because it inflamed opposition. In the meantime, the nationalists realized belatedly that military force would never be needed since the national government could directly implement its own policies and would no longer depend on the cooperation of the states.

With the states reduced to the status of junior partners, the national legislature would assume a standing comparable to that of the British Parliament. Madison did provide one check on this legislative dynamo: a Council of Revision, composed of the executive and certain judges, which could veto legislation. Its members, however, would be elected by the legislature. Thus skeptical delegates reasonably questioned how effective such a check could be. In any event, Madison proposed allowing a simple majority of Congress to override a council veto.

After Madison achieved early success in some preliminary floor votes, opposition to his radical reforms stiffened. It came from two directions. Delegates representing the less populous states were understandably upset. They could easily calculate that they (and their citizens) would have far less representation under the Virginia Plan than they presently enjoyed with equal state representation and the one-state veto rule. Another bloc (mostly from small states as well) wanted stronger safeguards of state sovereignty. For these states' rights delegates, continued state participation in the selection of national officeholders was as important an issue as how legislative seats were to be apportioned.

Both groups coalesced around an alternative proposed by New Jersey delegate William Paterson, known as the New Jersey Plan. This late, hastily drafted response to the Virginia Plan was not as thoroughly thought through as Madison's proposal. For example, it failed to propose the organization of the executive and judiciary. It satisfied the requirements of its states' rights supporters, however, by perpetuating the composition and selection of Congress as it functioned under the Articles of Confederation and continuing to give each state one vote. But the New Jersey Plan broke with the Articles by giving Congress the authority to levy taxes and to enforce compliance by the states with their obligations. This plan also allowed a simple majority vote to enact national policy rather than the unanimous agreement required in the Articles. The New Jersey Plan thus eliminated the most objectionable features of the confederation. But its retention of a Congress representative of the states rather than the citizenry, and thus seriously malapportioned, did not come close to satisfying the demands of the nationalists.

Debate on the composition of Congress raged for weeks, each side steadfastly and heatedly refusing to budge.[21] Stalemate loomed. As the meetings neared a Fourth of July recess, the delegates agreed to send the question of Congress—its selection and composition—to a committee with instructions to report out a recommendation after the break. Madison was not named to the committee.

The Great Compromise

The committee's solution was a Solomon-like compromise in which each side got one of the two legislative chambers fashioned to its liking. The upper chamber, or Senate, would retain many of the features of Congress under the Articles of Confederation: each state legislature would send two senators to serve six-year terms. Madison's population-based, elective legislature became the House of Representatives. To sweeten the deal for the nationalists, who had rejected a similar compromise earlier in floor deliberations, the committee reserved to the House alone the authority to originate revenue legislation (see Figure 2–2).

The unanimous agreement rule of the states that had hobbled the confederation Congress was gone, replaced by a rule allowing a majority of the membership to pass legislation. Moreover, the severe limitations on the legislature's sphere of action disappeared. In addition to specifying a broad list of enumerated or expressed powers (see Article I, Section 8, of the Constitution), the committee proposed a clause that authorized Congress to "make all Laws which shall be necessary and proper for carrying into Execution the foregoing Powers, and all other Powers vested by this Constitution in the Government of the United States. . . ." This critical provision, called the **necessary and proper clause,** left the door open for a major expansion of Congress's legislative power and with it the nationalization of public policy during the twentieth century.[22]

The committee's proposal was adopted by a vote of 5–4, with the other states abstaining or absent. Opposition came uniformly from the nationalists who viewed the compromise as one-sided. Through the Senate a majority of the states could still prevail over national policy. But the nationalists also recognized that this was the best deal they could get. Because the preferences of the states'

Figure 2–2 Virginia Plan, New Jersey Plan, and Great Compromise

Virginia Plan

☆ Two-chamber legislature, representation based on state population

☆ Lower chamber of legislature elected by the citizenry; upper chamber, executive, and courts elected by the lower house

☆ Legislature can make any law and veto any state legislation

☆ Council of Revision (composed of executive and court) can veto legislation, but legislature can override by majority vote

New Jersey Plan

☆ Single-house chamber; equal representation for each state regardless of population

☆ Legislature has same power as under Articles, with added authority to levy taxes and regulate commerce; can exercise supremacy clause over state legislation

☆ Plural executive can be removed by legislature (on petition of a majority of states); courts appointed by executive

☆ Supreme Court hears appeals in limited number of cases

Great Compromise

☆ Two-chamber legislature, with lower chamber (House of Representatives) representation based on population, and upper chamber (Senate) representation equal for every state

☆ Authority to levy taxes reserved to the lower chamber

rights delegates were more closely aligned with those of the status quo, they could more credibly present the nationalist side with a take-it-or-leave-it proposition.

Two centuries later, the political logic of dividing representation in Congress between the citizens and the states no longer matches reality. The supremacy of the national government over the states was decided by the Civil War. Senators have been elected directly by the voters since adoption of the Seventeenth Amendment in 1913. Yet the Senate, the institution that embodied the initial logic, persists. Indeed, as noted in Chapter 1, once in place an institution tends to survive long after the circumstances that fashioned it in a particular form have changed beyond all recognition. Although it is difficult today to justify a system in which, for example, citizens of Wyoming count for sixty-five times as much as citizens of California in one chamber of the national legislature, Americans are stuck with it. Yet, while still badly malapportioned, the modern Senate has become as attuned as the House of Representatives to changes in popular sentiments (see Chapter 6, Congress).

Because the compromise plan substantially strengthened the national government's capacity for action, most nationalists reconciled themselves to it—except Madison, at least initially. The man who during his lifetime was called "the father of the Constitution" maintained that ultimately the nationalists would prevail by letting the country stew a while longer under the Articles. Eventually he was talked out of that idea, but he remained profoundly disillusioned. Then, perhaps literally overnight, Madison scrapped the rest of the Virginia Plan and made what amounted to a 180-degree turn in his views on the proper relations among government institutions. His hurried reassessment might have gone something like this: if the state legislatures could corrupt the new Congress through their hold on the Senate, they also could corrupt the entire national government through Congress's power to select the officers of the other branches of government. The solution: insulate the executive and judicial branches and enlist them in containing any efforts by the states through the Senate to subvert national policy. Suddenly, Madison became interested in a genuine separation of powers between the branches with each side exercising **checks and balances** over the others. Thus in early July, with the summer half over and the proceedings gathering momentum, Madison turned his attention to fashioning an independent executive and judiciary.

Checks and Balances in the Constitution

The Framers feared that a concentration of power in any one group or branch of government would lead to tyranny—that is, one group would gain enough power to dominate the government and strip other groups of their basic rights. Thus they devised in the Constitution something of a political game in which each of the three branches of government has some capacity to limit, or trump, the power of the other two.

This system of "checks and balances" largely originated with the French philosopher Charles de Montesquieu (1689–1755), who argued that the power to govern could be effectively limited by dividing it among multiple branches of government and making the power of the branches interdependent.

**President
Executive Branch**

Congress passes legislation, controls the federal budget, can override a presidential veto, and can impeach the president. The Senate confirms top executive branch appointments and ratifies treaties.

**Congress
Legislative Branch**

The president can veto legislation.

The president nominates judges to the federal courts, including the Supreme Court.

Courts can declare executive acts unconstitutional.

Courts can declare laws unconstitutional

Congress can impeach federal judges, set size of Supreme Court and jurisdiction of lower courts, and determine judicial salaries and budget. The Senate confirms all federal judges.

**Supreme Court (and federal courts)
Judicial Branch**

Designing the Executive Branch

Of all the delegates, Alexander Hamilton had shown the most consistent interest in the office of the executive. His fixation on an executive elected for life, however, left him so far on the fringe that he enjoyed little influence on the rest of the delegates as they turned their attention to this institution. His eloquent speeches were "praised by everybody . . . [but] supported by none," reported one candid delegate.

The delegates' difficulty in envisioning such an office was rooted in the young nation's experience with executives. During the colonial era they had endured an arbitrary king and his agents, the vilified colonial governors, who chronically were at loggerheads with the colonial legislature over who had what authority. With this memory in mind, the new states had created governors with little administrative discretion. Jefferson, who had served briefly as Virginia's wartime governor, described the office as a "cipher," a nonentity. In the end the only acceptable model was, in the words of one historian, "sitting there in front of them . . . dignified, silent, universally admired and respected . . . impartial, honored for his selfless devotion to the common good, not intervening in, but presiding over, their councils—a presider, a *president*. The executive was to be—George Washington."[23]

But the presence of a real-life model for the executive did not stifle the debate. Only through arduous committee deliberations and floor wrangling was a compromise reached. Earlier at the convention the delegates had found that the only workable formula for agreement between the nationalists and states' rights advocates was to give both sides pretty much what they wanted. This approach had yielded the Great Compromise, and later in the convention it would generate multiple routes for amending the Constitution. But when the drafters sought to specify the procedure for election of the president, this pragmatic strategy produced the most convoluted concept found in the Constitution: the **electoral college.**

As a device, the electoral college tries to mix state, congressional, and popular participation in the election process and in doing so has managed to confuse the citizenry for nearly two hundred years. Each state is awarded as many electors as it has members of the House and Senate. The Constitution left it to the states to decide how electors are selected, but the Framers generally and correctly expected that the states would rely on statewide elections. If any candidate fails to receive an absolute majority (270) of the 538 votes in the electoral college, the election is thrown into the House of Representatives, which chooses from among the three candidates who received the largest number of electoral votes. In making its selection, the House votes by state delegation; each state gets one vote, and a majority is required to elect a president (see Chapter 11, Voting, Campaigns, and Elections, for more on the electoral college). Until the Twelfth Amendment corrected its most egregious flaws, votes for the president and the vice president were tallied side by side, resulting in a vice-presidential candidate almost winning the presidency in the 1800 election.

In the end, Madison and Hamilton largely succeeded in fashioning an independent executive branch capable of checking any excesses of an overreaching legislature. The president's device of choice in checking the power of Congress is the **veto.** By requiring a supermajority vote of two-thirds of the members of each house to override a presidential veto, the Framers carved out a major role for the president in domestic legislation. But in enumerating presidential powers in Sections 2 and 3 of Article II, the Framers deliberately included congressional checks on those powers. For example, the president is designated commander in chief of the army and navy, but only Congress has the authority to declare war. In receiving and appointing ambassadors, the president conducts the nation's foreign policy and negotiates treaties, but, again, the Framers tempered presidential prerogatives by requiring Senate approval of ambassadorial appointments and treaties. Domestically, the president's chief administrative duty is the appointment of officers to fill vacancies in the executive departments. Yet the Senate, which must confirm all appointments, has the final say.

Just as the necessary and proper clause has enabled the modern Congress to enlarge on its enumerated powers, Article II has opened an avenue for greater presidential authority in its provision that the president "shall take Care that the Laws be faithfully executed." Twentieth-century presidents have asserted that the take care clause allows them to undertake whatever actions national policy may require that are not expressly forbidden by the Constitution or public law (see Chapter 7, The Presidency).

Designing the Judiciary

The convention spent comparatively little time designing the new federal judiciary, a somewhat surprising development given that the Constitution gives the Supreme Court exclusive jurisdiction in resolving differences between the state and national levels of government. Armed with that jurisdiction and with the **supremacy clause** (Article VI), which declares that national laws take precedence over state laws when both properly discharge their governments' respective responsibilities, the Supreme Court emerged from the convention as a major, probably underappreciated, lever for expanding the scope of national policy making.

States' rights advocates and nationalists did, however, have a tug-of-war over two lesser questions: Who would appoint Supreme Court justices—the president or the Senate? And should a network of lower federal courts be created or should state courts handle all cases until they reach the Supreme Court? The convention split the difference over appointments by giving the president appointment powers and the Senate confirmation powers, and they left it to some future Congress to decide whether the national government needed its own lower-level judiciary. Congress exercised this option almost immediately.[24]

An important issue never quite resolved by the convention was the extent of the Court's authority to overturn federal laws and executive actions as unconstitutional—a concept known as **judicial review.** While the supremacy clause appears to establish the Court's authority to review state laws, there is no formal language extending this review authority to federal laws. Yet many of the Framers, including Hamilton, claimed that the Constitution implicitly provides for judicial review. Later in life Madison protested that he never would have agreed to a provision that allowed an unelected branch of government to have the final say in lawmaking. But in one of the great ironies of American history, Madison was a litigant in an early Supreme Court decision, *Marbury v. Madison* (1803), in which the Court laid claim to this authority.[25] In Chapter 9 we will return to this historic case and its profound effects on the development of the federal judiciary.

Solving the States' Collective Action Problems

The remapping of federal–state responsibilities was largely intended to eliminate the collective action dilemmas that had discouraged voluntary compliance by the states under the Articles of Confederation. The Framers recognized that the states, to undertake joint activities successfully, had to surrender some of their autonomy to a central agency—the national government—and give it the authority to prevent any state from free riding or otherwise violating their collective agreements.

Trade and foreign policy probably were at the top of the list of federal–state issues the Framers wanted the Constitution to solve. Shortly after the Revolutionary War, the states had found themselves engaged in cutthroat competition for foreign commerce. The Framers solved this dilemma by placing foreign policy under the administration of the president and giving Congress the explicit legislative authority to regulate commerce. As for the common defense and security, the Framers placed those responsibilities squarely on the shoulders of the national government. The Constitution (Article I, Section 10) forbids any state from entering into a foreign alliance or treaty, maintaining a military during peacetime, or engaging in war unless invaded.

WHY WOMEN WERE LEFT OUT OF THE CONSTITUTION

Why is it that nowhere in the original Constitution or in the floor debates at Philadelphia are women mentioned? One reason is that the delegates to the Constitutional Convention, faced with the glaring deficiencies of the national government under the Articles of Confederation, were less concerned with individual rights than with making government more effective and establishing proper relations among the institutions they were creating. Early on, delegates agreed to allow the individual states to continue to decide which citizens should have the right to vote. Thus no one gained the right to vote in the Constitution.

Second, although it tacitly accepts franchise restrictions imposed by the states, the Constitution reads as though it was drafted to be as free of gender bias as eighteenth-century usage allowed. Throughout, the words *persons* and *citizens,* not *men,* appear. Eligibility to serve as a member of Congress, for example, begins with the statement "No *Person* shall be a Representative. . . ." Elsewhere: "The *Citizens* of each State shall be entitled to all Privileges and Immunities of Citizens in the several States." A few passages of the Constitution use the pronoun "he" (in each instance, however, the masculine pronoun refers back to a gender-free noun), but until the twentieth century this referent was commonly employed and legally interpreted to include women. In this respect, then, women were not left out of the Constitution.

The third reason is that women's political rights simply had not yet become an issue. Absence of the issue, howev-

er, did not mean that women remained apolitical during the Revolution and the subsequent crisis in governance, or that they failed to protest other aspects of their inferior legal standing. The ample evidence in private correspondence indicates that many women followed politics carefully. A few even published monographs that received wide circulation. One of the most famous correspondents of either sex during this era was Abigail Adams, the wife of John Adams and the mother of John Quincy Adams. Her numerous letters to her husband and leaders, such as Thomas Jefferson, exhibit a candor and insight that make them compelling to modern readers as well. To her husband, who was away attending the Continental Congress, she wrote, "In the new code of laws which I suppose it will be necessary for you to make, I desire you would remember the ladies, and be more generous to them than your ancestors. Do not put such unlimited power in the hands of husbands. Remember, all men would be tyrants if they could." This passage often has been celebrated as one of the first expressions of women's political rights in America. But, in fact, Adams was addressing various civil laws that allowed husbands to confiscate their wife's property and made divorce all but impossible. Lack of a woman's rights in marriage—not suffrage—was the grievance of these early feminists.

Not until publication of Sarah Grimké's *Letters on the Condition of Women and Equality of the Sexes* in 1838 and the Seneca Falls Convention declaration—"All men and women are created equal"—a decade later would women's suffrage be placed on the national political agenda. In 1869 Wyoming became the first state to add women to the voter rolls. Later in the nineteenth century, Susan B. Anthony of Massachusetts led a suffragist movement that claimed the right to vote under the Fourteenth Amendment and sought a constitutional suffrage amendment. In 1887 Congress defeated the proposal of the amendment, but the suffrage movement continued. President Woodrow Wilson (1913–1921) initially opposed the amendment, arguing that state action was more appropriate (see photo, taken in 1916). But when protests grew into hunger strikes in 1918, he announced his support. The Nineteenth Amendment to the Constitution, guaranteeing women the right to vote, was ratified in 1920.

Source: Adapted from James Q. Wilson and John J. DiIulio Jr., *American Government: Institutions and Policies,* 7th ed. (Boston: Houghton Mifflin, 1998), 43.

Relations among the states, a longtime source of friction, also figured prominently in the Framers' deliberations. As a result, Article I, Section 10, prohibits states from discriminating against each other in various ways. They may not, for example, enter into agreements without the consent of Congress, tax imports or exports entering local ports, print money not backed by gold or silver, or make laws prejudicial to citizens of other states.

The Framers balanced these concessions with important benefits for the states. The new national government would assume outstanding debts the states had incurred during the war, protect the states from invasion and insurrection, and guarantee that all states would be governed by republican institutions.[26]

All these provisions of the Constitution are less well known than those creating and conferring powers on the several branches of government or the amendments known as the Bill of Rights. But the fact that Americans take them for granted reflects their success, not their irrelevance. Because by means of these provisions the Framers solved the most serious collective action dilemmas confronting the young nation, including trade. Taken together, the provisions that prevented states from interfering with commerce that crossed their borders established the essentials of a common market.[27] As a result, the Constitution contributed vitally to the nation's economic development during the next century.

The Issue of Slavery

Throughout America's history the issue of race has never been far removed from politics. It certainly was present in Philadelphia, despite some delegates' best efforts to prevent a regional disagreement on slavery from thwarting the purpose of the convention. But how could delegates construct a government based on popular sovereignty and inalienable rights without addressing the fact that one-sixth of Americans were in bondage? They could not. Slavery figured importantly in many delegates' private calculations, especially those of the southern delegates. At several junctures, it broke to the surface.

The first effort to grapple with slavery was the most acrimonious and threatening. How should slaves be counted in allocating congressional representatives to the states? Madison had persuaded delegates to postpone this issue until they had finalized the design of the new Congress, but the issue soon loomed again. Trying to maximize their representation in the population-based House of Representatives, southern delegates insisted that slaves were undeniably people and should be included fully in any population count to determine representation. Northerners resisted this attempted power grab by arguing that since slaves did not enjoy the freedom to act as autonomous citizens, they should not be counted at all. In the end each side accepted a formula worked out under the Articles of Confederation that assigned states their financial obligations to the national government. Accordingly, the Constitution apportioned each state seats in the House of Representatives based on population totals in which each slave would count as three-fifths of a citizen.[28]

Later in the convention some southern delegates insisted on two guarantees for their "peculiar institution" as conditions for remaining at the convention and endorsing the Constitution in the ratification debates. One was the unrestricted right to continue importing slaves. The delegates from northern states, most of which had outlawed slavery, preferred to leave the issue to some future government. But in the end they conceded by writing into the Constitution a ban on regulation of the slave trade until 1808.[29] (A total ban on slave imports went into effect on January 1, 1808.) Late in the convention southerners introduced the Constitution's second slavery protection clause. It required northern states to return runaway slaves to their masters. After some delegates first resisted and then softened the language of the clause, the proposal passed.

Southern intransigence paid off handsomely: slavery was sanctioned by the U.S. Constitution. Why did the delegations from the more numerous northern states cave in to the southerners? Two explanations are possible—and both are probably true. First, the handling of the slavery issue was likely another instance of intense private interests prevailing over more diffuse notions of the public good. Reporting to Jefferson in Paris, Madison wrote that "South Carolina and Georgia were inflexible on the point of slaves," implying that without the slave trade and fugitive provisions they would not have endorsed the Constitution.

The second explanation stems from the economic interests driving some northern delegations. New England delegates came to Philadelphia largely out of their desire to strengthen the nation's commercial policies at home and abroad. Fearful that its agricultural exports to Europe might be taxed and regulated, the South had opposed giving the national government such authority except with the consent of two-thirds majorities of both houses of Congress. Such majorities, however, would presumably have given the South a veto over any objectionable policy. But if the national government insisted, as in time it did, that a substantial share of exports must travel on U.S. ships, the Northeast with its ports and shipping companies would gain financially at the expense of the southern producers.[30] So in the end, in a classic logroll, New England and the South accommodated each other's dominant economic interests: Article I, Section 9, protects the importation of slaves and Article IV, Section 2, requires the return of fugitive slaves; Article I, Section 8, allows the national government to regulate commerce and tax imports. In his detailed minutes of the proceedings, Madison recorded the circumlocutions of delegates from both regions who took the floor to seal their deal. His footnotes further clarify the political arguments behind these formal agreements.

Amending the Constitution

In their efforts to provide a suitable means for amending the Constitution, the Framers broke new ground. (Amendment of the Articles of Confederation required the unanimous consent of the states, and the constitution creating the French republic in 1789 contained no amendment procedure whatsoever.) Perhaps the futility of trying to win unanimous consent for changing the Articles

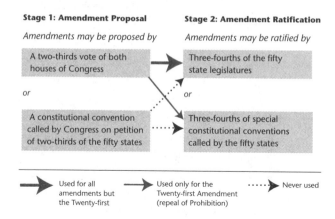

Figure 2–3   Process for Amending the Constitution

persuaded the Framers to find a more flexible method for amending the Constitution.

The concept of providing for future amendment of the Constitution proved less controversial than the amendment procedure itself. Intent on preserving their hard-won gains in the face of future amendment proposals, both the nationalists and states' rights advocates approached this matter warily. Delegates from small states insisted on endorsement of amendments by a large number of states, while the nationalists argued that the Constitution derived its legitimacy directly from the citizenry and that the citizenry alone should approve any change. Unable to muster a majority for either position, the delegates again employed the formula of accepting parts of both proposals. As a result, the Constitution allows an amendment to be proposed either by a two-thirds vote of both houses of Congress or by an "application" from two-thirds of the states. Enactment occurs when three-fourths of the states, acting either through their state legislatures or in special conventions, accepts the amendment (see Figure 2–3). Since its ratification the Constitution has been amended twenty-seven times. In every instance Congress initiated the process, and in all but one case the state legislatures did the ratifying. (The Constitution and its amendments appear in the Appendix.)

Even though the New York ratification convention narrowly approved the Constitution, its final adoption by the states occasioned celebration. The parade was graced by a "ship of state," an already well-developed metaphor. At the time, New Yorker Alexander Hamilton was widely regarded as one of the Constitution's most effective sponsors.

The Fight for Ratification

The last sentence of the Constitution spells out an important procedure endorsed by delegates in the final days of the convention: "The Ratification of the Conventions of nine States, shall be sufficient for the Establishment of this Constitution between the States so ratifying the Same." Everyone knew that this deceptively straightforward provision was critical for the success of their enterprise. It replaced the unanimous assent rule of the Articles of Confederation which had thwarted any attempt at reform. And it withdrew ratification authority from the state legislatures, which might have misgivings about surrendering autonomy, and gave it instead to elective special conventions. In the end, the only way to escape the confederation's bind was to ignore it.

The Federalist and Antifederalist Debate

Only three of the delegates still in Philadelphia in September 1787 at the close of the convention refused to sign the Constitution. This consensus, however, is misleading; others who probably would have objected left early, and many prominent political leaders such as Patrick Henry and Richard Henry Lee of Virginia had refused even to participate.

Over the next year every state but Rhode Island (it held out until 1790) elected delegates to state conventions which proceeded to dissect the Constitution and ponder its individual provisions. This was truly a time of national debate over the future of the country. As one observer noted, "Almost every American pen . . . [and] peasants and their wives in every part of the land" had begun "to dispute on politics and positively to determine upon our liberties."[31] On a lighter note, the *Boston Daily Advertiser*, responding to General Washington's call for public debate, admonished its readers: "Come on brother scribblers, 'tis idle to lag! The Convention has let the cat out of the bag."[32]

Delegates to the state conventions concentrated, predictably, on the concerns of their states and communities. Southern states carefully inspected each article for a northern avenue of attack on their "peculiar institution." Finding none, all of the southern states except South Carolina lined up behind the Constitution. Constituencies and their delegates similarly aligned themselves for or against the Constitution according to its perceived impact on their pocketbooks. Small farmers, struck hard by declining markets and high property taxes after the war, had succeeded in gaining sympathetic majorities in many of the state legislatures. Thus they looked suspiciously on this attempt to shift fiscal policy to the national government.[33]

In the public campaign for ratification these issues tended to be reduced to the rhetoric of nationalism, voiced by the Federalists, versus the rhetoric of states' rights, voiced by the Antifederalists. The divisiveness characterizing the Philadelphia convention thus continued. But the labels given the two sides were confusing. While they consistently distinguished the Constitution's

Table 2–1 The First Ten Amendments to the Constitution: Bill of Rights

Amendment	Purpose
I	Guarantees freedom of religion, speech, assembly, and press, and the right of people to petition the government for redress of grievances
II	Protects the right of states to maintain a militia
III	Restricts quartering of troops in private homes
IV	Protects against "unreasonable searches and seizures"
V	Assures the right not to be deprived of "life, liberty, or property, without due process of law," including protections against double jeopardy, self-incrimination, and government seizure of property without just compensation
VI	Guarantees the right to a speedy and public trial by an impartial jury
VII	Assures the right to a jury trial in cases involving the common law (judge-made law originating in England)
VIII	Protects against excessive bail or cruel and unusual punishment
IX	Provides that people's rights are not restricted to those specified in Amendments I–VIII
X	Reiterates the Constitution's principle of federalism by providing that powers not granted to the national government are reserved to the states, or to the people

supporters and opponents, the labels confused the positions of these camps on the issue of federalism. Many of those who opposed ratification were more protective of state prerogatives, as the term *federalist* implies, than were many of the prominent "Federalists." Appreciating the depth of state loyalties, Madison and his colleagues early on tactically maneuvered to neutralize this issue by claiming that the Constitution provided a true federal system, making them Federalists. Their success in expropriating this label put their opponents at a disadvantage in the public relations campaign. One disgruntled Antifederalist proposed that the labels be changed so that Madison and his crowd would be called the "Rats" (for pro-ratification) and his side the "Antirats."

Although in the end the Federalists prevailed and are today revered as the nation's "Founders," the Antifederalists included a comparable number and quality of proven patriots. Foremost among them was Patrick Henry, who led his side's counterattack. With him were fellow Virginians Richard Henry Lee, George Mason, and a young James Monroe, who would become the nation's fifth pres-

ident under the Constitution he opposed. Other famous outspoken opponents included Boston's Revolutionary War hero Samuel Adams and New York governor George Clinton.

In their opposition to the Constitution, the Antifederalists raised serious theoretical objections—objections that can still be heard two hundred years later. They argued that only local democracy, the kind found in small homogeneous communities, could approach true democracy. The United States, they asserted, already was too large and too diverse to be well ruled by a single set of laws. Turning their sights to the Constitution itself, the Antifederalists argued that a stronger national government must be accompanied by explicit safeguards against tyranny. Specifically, the Constitution needed a bill of rights—a familiar feature of most state constitutions.[34] Some delegates to the convention proposed a bill of rights, but Madison and others had argued that it was unnecessary because the Constitution did not give the national government any powers that could be construed as invading the citizenry's rights. This argument, however, worked better at the convention than it did in the public campaign. The Antifederalists quickly realized they had identified a chink in the Constitution's armor and began pounding the issue hard. Even Madison's ally Jefferson wrote him from France insisting that individual rights were too important to be "left to inference." Suddenly on the defensive, Madison made a strategic capitulation and announced that at the convening of the First Congress under the new Constitution, he would introduce constitutional amendments providing a bill of rights. His strategy worked; the issue receded. In a sense, though, the Antifederalist strategy had worked as well. Madison kept his promise, and by 1791 the Constitution contained the Bill of Rights (Table 2–1).

In June 1788 New Hampshire became the ninth and technically decisive state to ratify the Constitution. But Virginia and New York had still not voted, and until these two large, centrally located states became a part of the Union, no one gave the new government much chance of getting off the ground. But by the end of July both states had narrowly ratified the Constitution, and the new Union was a reality.

The Federalist Argument

Aside from eventually yielding a new constitution, the ratification debates fostered another national resource: eighty-five essays that were collected under the title *The Federalist*. Published under the shared pseudonym Publius in 1787–1788, the essays were written by Alexander Hamilton (who wrote the majority), James Madison (who wrote the best ones), and John Jay (who wrote five). It was only years later, after Madison's death in 1836, that the original manuscripts were found and the authors identified.

Because their immediate purpose was to influence the delegates to the New York convention, where ratification was in trouble, the *Federalist* essays first appeared in New York City newspapers. At one point Hamilton and Madison were cranking out four essays a week, prompting the Antifederalists to complain that by the time they rebutted

THE

FEDERALIST:

ADDRESSED TO THE

PEOPLE OF THE STATE OF NEW-YORK.

NUMBER I.

Introduction.

AFTER an unequivocal experience of the inefficacy of the subsisting federal government, you are called upon to deliberate on a new constitution for the United States of America. The subject speaks its own importance; comprehending in its consequences, nothing less than the existence of the UNION, the safety and welfare of the parts of which it is composed, the fate of an empire, in many respects, the most interesting in the world. It has been frequently remarked, that it seems to have been reserved to the people of this country, by their conduct and example, to decide the important question, whether societies of men are really capable or not, of establishing good government from reflection and choice, or whether they are forever destined to depend, for their political constitutions, on accident and force. If there be any truth in the remark, the crisis, at which we are arrived, may with propriety be regarded as the æra in which
A   that

one argument in print, several others had appeared. Reprinted widely, the essays provided rhetorical ammunition to those supporting ratification.[35]

Whatever their role in the Constitution's ratification, *The Federalist Papers,* as they also are called, have had a profound effect on the way Americans then and now have understood their government. A few years after their publication, Thomas Jefferson, describing the curriculum of

Today the Federalist Papers *continue to find popularity, most recently and most publicly in the 1999 impeachment trial of President Bill Clinton. From the well of the Senate chamber, the House impeachment managers (shown here entering the chamber) and the president's counsel frequently summoned the words of Alexander Hamilton and James Madison to support their interpretations of the Constitution and their respective arguments for and against removing the president from office.*

the University of Virginia to its board of overseers, declared *The Federalist Papers* to be indispensable reading for all undergraduates. It is "agreed by all," he explained, that these essays convey "the genuine meaning" of the Constitution.

The Theory Underlying the Constitution

Two of Madison's essays, *Federalist* No. 10 and *Federalist* No. 51, offer special insights into the theory underlying the Constitution. (For the full text of both essays, see the Appendix.) In different ways, each essay tackles the fundamental problem of self-governance, which Madison poses in a famous passage from *Federalist* No. 51:

If men were angels, no government would be necessary. If an-

gels were to govern men, neither external nor internal controls on government would be necessary. In framing a government which is to be administered by men over men, the great difficulty lies in this: you must first enable the government to control the governed; and in the next place oblige it to control itself.

The last goal is tricky. *Federalist* No. 10 tackles the problem by both exploring the likelihood that tyranny by the majority would arise within a democracy and identifying a solution. It is a powerful, cogent argument grounded in logic. *Federalist* No. 51 deals with the delegation problem of keeping agents honest. The solution lies in pitting politicians against one another through the Constitution's principles of separation of powers and checks and balances. This way, politicians are able to counteract each other's temptation to engage in mischief. Whatever their differences, these two essays can be read as following parallel paths—one at the societal level, the other at the governmental level—toward the same destination of a polity free from tyranny.

Federalist *No. 10*

Madison's first and most celebrated essay appeared in the November 24, 1787, issue of the *New York Daily Advertiser. Federalist* No. 10 responds to the strongest argument the Antifederalists could muster—that a "large Republic" cannot long survive. This essay borrows from the writings of David Hume, but over the course of a decade of legislative debate and correspondence Madison had honed his argument to fit the American case.[36] Indeed, Madison had made the argument before—at the Constitutional Convention when defending the Virginia Plan in a floor debate.

The major task Madison sets out for himself in *Federalist* No. 10 is to devise a republic in which a majority of citizens will be unable to tyrannize the minority. Madison wastes no time identifying the rotten apple. It is factions, which he describes as "mortal diseases under which popular governments have everywhere perished." He defines a **faction** as "a number of citizens, whether amounting to a majority or minority of the whole, who are united and actuated by some common impulse of passion, or of *interest,* adverse to the rights of other citizens, or to the permanent and aggregate interests of the community" (emphasis added). Madison's factions have many of the attributes of modern-day interest groups and even political parties.

Madison then identifies two ways to eliminate factions, authoritarianism or conformism, neither of which he finds acceptable. Authoritarianism, a form of government that actively suppresses factions, is a remedy that would be worse than the disease. In a famous passage of *Federalist* No. 10 Madison offers an analogy: "Liberty is to faction what air is to fire, an aliment without which it instantly expires."

Conformism, the second solution, is, as Madison notes, "as impracticable as the first would be unwise." People cannot somehow be made to have the same goals, for "the latent causes of faction are . . . sown in the nature of man." Thus two persons who are precisely alike in wealth, education, and other characteristics will nonetheless have different views on many issues. Even the "most frivolous and fanciful distinction" can "kindle their unfriendly passions," Madison observes, but most of the important political cleavages that divide a citizenry are predictably rooted in their life circumstances. In another famous passage the author anticipates the German political philosopher Karl Marx and his analysis of class in capitalism by nearly a century:

But the most common and durable source of factions has been the various and unequal distribution of property. Those who hold and those who are without property have ever formed distinct interests in society. . . . A landed interest, a manufacturing interest, a mercantile interest, a moneyed interest, with many lesser interests, grow up of necessity in civilized nations, and divide them into different classes, actuated by different sentiments and views.[37]

If the causes of faction cannot be removed without snuffing out liberty, then one must control their effects. Madison identifies two kinds of factions—minority factions and majority factions—that have to be controlled in different ways. During the late eighteenth century, the ubiquitous problem of factional tyranny occurred at the hands of the monarchy and aristocracy, a "minority" faction. Democracy remedies this: a minority faction "may clog the administration, it may convulse the society; but it will be unable to execute and mask its violence under the forms of the Constitution." Democracy, however, introduces its own special brand of factional tyranny—that emanating from a majority. In Madison's era many people equated majority rule with mob rule. Thus supporters of the new constitutional plan had to explain how a society could give government authority to a majority without fear it would trample on minority rights. Madison explained: "To secure the public good and private rights against the danger of . . . a [majority] faction, and at the same time to preserve the spirit and the form of popular government, is then the great object to which our inquiries are directed."

Parting ways with some of the leading political philosophers of his era, Madison dismisses direct democracy as the solution:

[T]here is nothing to check the inducements to sacrifice the weaker party or an obnoxious individual. Hence it is that such democracies have ever been spectacles of turbulence and contention; have ever been found incompatible with personal security or the rights of property; and have in general been as short in their lives as they have been violent in their deaths.

So much for town meetings.

Madison contends that the republican form of government, in which elected representatives are delegated responsibility for making governmental decisions, addresses the majority tyranny problem in two ways. First, representation dilutes the factious spirit. Madison does not trust politicians to be more virtuous than their constituents, but he recognizes that, to get elected, they will tend to moderate their views to appeal to a diverse constituency. Here, Madison subtly introduces his *size principle* on which the rest of the argument hinges: up to a point, the larger and more diverse the constituency, the more diluted is the influence of any particular faction on the preferences of the representative.

A legislature composed of representatives elected from districts containing diverse factional interests is unlikely to allow a faction or a small coalition of them to so dominate the institution that it can deny rights to factions in the minority. This line of reasoning allows Madison to introduce a second distinct virtue of a republic. Unlike a direct democracy, it can advantageously encompass a large population and a large territory. As Madison argues,

Extend the sphere, and you take in a greater variety of parties and interests; you make it less probable that a majority of the whole will have a common motive to invade the rights of other citizens; or if such a common motive exists, it will be more difficult for all who feel it to discover their own strength and to act in unison with each other.[38]

In other words, their differences will pose a collective action problem, which tends to prevent them from colluding to do mischief.

What has Madison accomplished here? He has turned the Antifederalists' "small is beautiful" mantra on its head by pointing out that an encompassing national government would be less susceptible to the influence of factions than state governments: "A rage for paper money, for an abolition of debts, for an equal division of property, or for any other improper or wicked project, would be less apt to pervade the whole body of the Union than a particular member of it. . . ." A geographically large republic would encompass diverse interests, thereby minimizing the prospect of majority tyranny. Madison concludes: "In the extent and proper structure of the Union, therefore, we behold a republican remedy for the disease most incident to republican government."

Until the twentieth century, *Federalist* No. 10 attracted less attention than did some of its companion essays. Yet as the nation has grown in size and diversity, the essay has won new prominence for the prescience with which Madison explained how such growth strengthens the re-

public. This Madisonian view of democracy often is referred to as **pluralism.** It welcomes society's numerous diverse interests and generally endorses the idea that those competing interests most affected by a public policy will have the greatest say in what the policy will be.

Federalist No. 51

By giving free expression to all of society's diversity, *Federalist* No. 10 offers an essentially organic solution to the danger of majority tyranny. *Federalist* No. 51, by contrast, takes a more mechanistic approach of separating government officers into different branches and giving them the authority to interfere with each other's actions. The authority of each branch must "be made commensurate to the danger of attack," Madison asserts. As for incentive: "Ambition must be made to counteract ambition. The interest of the man must be connected with the constitutional rights of the place." In other words, the Framers' efforts will have failed if future generations of politicians do not jealously defend the integrity of their offices. Here, then, is the rationale for separating governmental authority among several branches with each having the authority to check the other.

Since popular election is the supreme basis for legitimacy and independence in a democracy, no constitutional contrivances can place appointive offices on an equal footing with elective offices. Madison explains:

In republican government, the legislative authority necessarily predominates. The remedy for this inconvenience is to divide the legislature into different branches; and to render them, by different modes of election and different principles of action, as little connected with each other as the nature of their common functions and their common dependence on the society will admit.

Bicameralism is intended to weaken the legislature's capacity to act too quickly and impulsively, but even so it may not prevent the legislature from encroaching on the other branches. Madison offers the president's veto as a strong countervailing force and speculates that, by refusing to override the president's veto, the Senate might team up with the executive to keep the popularly elected House of Representatives in check. Madison even finds virtue in the considerable prerogatives reserved to the states: "In a compound republic of America, the power surrendered by the people is first divided between two distinct governments. . . . Hence a double security arises to the rights of the people. The different governments will control each other, at the same time that each will be controlled by itself."

Could this be the same James Madison who wanted to abandon the convention rather than agree to a Senate elected by the state legislatures, the same man who had wanted Congress to have an absolute veto over state actions? Madison's Virginia Plan had vested ultimate authority in a popularly elected, national legislature, and this model of a legislature became the House of Representatives. So why is he commending a Constitution that severely constrains this institution's influence over policy?

Madison probably was playing to his audience. *Federalist* No. 51 seeks to reassure those fence sitters who were listening to Antifederalist propaganda that the Constitution would take a giant step down the short path to tyranny. After all, the Antifederalists were presenting the specter of a powerful and remote national government and, within it, the possible emergence of a junta comprised of unelected senators and an indirectly elected president bent on usurping the authority of the states, undermining the one popularly elected branch of government (the House of Representatives), and ultimately subjugating the citizenry. Madison is countering with a portrait of a weak, fragmented system that appears virtually incapable of purposive action, much less of hatching plots.[39] He must have grimaced as he (anonymously) drafted the passage extolling the Constitution's checks on his House of Representatives.

In summary, *Federalist* No. 10 conveys the theory that guided the Constitution's chief architect; *Federalist* No. 51 explores how the governmental system that emerged from the political process in Philadelphia might actually work. Since these essays were written, Madison's insight into the operation of the Constitution has been largely borne out. As we shall see in Chapter 4, Civil Rights, government policy sometimes fails to implement the preferences of national majorities for reasons he identifies in this famous essay.

Both the pluralism of competing interests and separated institutions have been judged less favorably by many modern students of American politics. With authority so fragmented, they argue, government cannot function effectively. And by adding a layer of institutional fragmentation on top of pluralism, the Framers simply overdid it. The result is an inherently conservative political process in which legitimate majorities are frequently frustrated by some minority faction that happens to control a critical lever of government. Furthermore, if the logic of *Federalist* No. 10 is correct, Americans do not need all of this constitutional architecture of checks and balances to get the job done.[40] Critics also point to the many other stable democracies throughout the world that function well with institutions designed to allow majorities to govern effectively. Would Madison have privately agreed with this critique? Probably so—after all, his Virginia Plan incorporated those checks and balances necessary to foster the healthy competition of factions and no more.

The Constitution: Borne of Sweet Reason or Politics?

"America is a nation without a national government," one critic observed during the last days of the confederation, "and it is not a pretty sight." The Constitution was adopted to correct the problems inherent to localism. But rather than making a break with the past, as the nationalists had sought, the new Constitution simply veered in a somewhat more national direction. In the end, a century and a half of home rule, as well as the loyalty to state governments felt by those who had served successfully at that level, could not be denied. The new national government had to accommodate the states by allowing their participation in the selection of senators and reserving to them certain prerogatives and responsibilities.

It is deeply ironic that the kind of national pluralism Madison and his allies were trying to install already was at work at the convention, frustrating their success. Present were the contending interests that closely resembled the factions of *Federalist* No. 10. Large states competed with small over representation; the South pushed for constitutional protection for slaveholding, and the Northeast worked for favorable commercial regulations. The absence of a dominant majority faction meant intense bargaining resulting in shifting alliances that led to a novel, hybrid governmental system that is neither national nor confederative in nature. Many of the Constitution's provisions have no theoretical rationale; they are simply the hammered out products of compromise. How does one justify the three-fifths rule, the malapportioned Senate, or the byzantine procedures for electing a president, if not by explaining that each was borne of political necessity? The Constitution is, in other words, a fine document arising not from the application of sweet reason but from politics. The document produced by the Constitutional Convention was a plan no delegate favored or could even have imagined on the opening day of the convention. It was, however, a plan that a substantial majority favored over the status quo and all could live with.

Despite their efforts, Madison and the nationalists won only a partial victory with the launching of the Constitution; the nation still added up to little more than a collection of states. Nevertheless, America's political development since 1787 has seen the realization of many of the goals that eluded the nationalists at the Philadelphia convention. For example, by building the Constitution on the consent of the governed rather than endorsement by the states, the nationalists successfully denied state governments any claim that they could ignore national policy. Over the next several decades, however, state politicians unhappy with national policy routinely threatened to secede or to "nullify" objectionable federal laws. But none of these threats became a full-fledged constitutional crisis until the eleven southern states seceded from the Union shortly after Abraham Lincoln was elected to the presidency in 1860. With the Union victory in 1865, this threat to nationhood ended conclusively. A central government capable of forcing compliance was finally achieved by war. Yet as we shall see in Chapter 3, Federalism, the nationalization of government authority remained limited by modern standards. Nowhere is this more evident than in the domain of civil liberties, the subject of Chapter 5.

But what about Madison's other goal of building a national society that could prevent majority factions from tyrannizing local minorities? The two-hundred-year history of governance under the Constitution has been one of gradual nationalization—so gradual, in fact, that the nation only recently realized Madison's aspiration. In slavery, segregation, and the disenfranchisement of southern black citizens, Madison's worst dreams were realized, and nearly two hundred years would pass before these citizens were able to achieve equality in civic life. Chapter 4 surveys this inglorious history to illuminate the weaknesses and limitations of the constitutional system. In the process, we shall see that Madison correctly identified the U.S. Senate as an institutional barrier to establishing a national community and quelling the threat of state-level tyranny of the majority.

Key Terms

Articles of
    Confederation / 27
bicameral legislature / 32
checks and balances / 42
confederation / 33
Declaration of
    Independence / 32
electoral college / 44

faction / 52
home rule / 28
judicial review / 45
necessary and proper
    clause / 41
pluralism / 54
supremacy clause / 45
veto / 44

Suggested Readings

Draper, Theodore. *A Struggle for Power: The American Revolution.* New York: Times Books, 1996. According to Draper, the Revolution represented the politics of self-interest rather than ideology. His account also examines the greater political context of the Revolution, in particular the long-standing conflict between the French and British.

Ketcham, Ralph. *James Madison: A Biography.* Charlottesville: University Press of Virginia, 1990. An authoritative and highly readable biography of America's first political scientist.

Miller, William Lee. *The Business of May Next: James Madison and the Founding.* Charlottesville: University Press of Virginia, 1992. A lively and absorbing account of the politics leading up to and at the Convention. This history served as the chief source of the account reported in this chapter.

Norton, Mary Beth. *Liberty's Daughters.* Boston: Little, Brown, 1980. A systematic and persuasive assessment of the considerable behind-the-scenes contribution of women during the Revolution and the impact of the war on the transformation of family relationships.

Rossiter, Clinton. *1787: The Grand Convention.* New York: Macmillan, 1966. This classic portrayal of the Constitutional Convention remains the most readable and lively treatment of the Framers at work in Philadelphia.

Wills, Garry. *Explaining America.* New York: Doubleday, 1981. An analysis of the logic and ideas of *The Federalist Papers.* Few authors can match Wills's talent for rendering abstract concepts and ideas intelligible to the general audience.

Wood, Gordon S. *The Creation of the American Republic, 1776–1787.* New York: Norton, 1972. An indispensable intellectual history of the transformation of America from the Revolution through the adoption of the Constitution.

Chapter 3

FEDERALISM

☆ *Is there a logic or rationale for having some government services supplied locally, others by the states, and still others by the national government?*

☆ *Given the Framers' efforts to keep the national government out of the states' business, why are so many policies once left to the states now handled by the national government?*

☆ *To what extent are the political relations among the fifty states subject to the same collective action problems that plagued the colonies?*

☆ *Is federalism dead?*

In the early morning of April 18, 1906, an earthquake registering 8.3 on the Richter scale struck San Francisco. After initial reports from the scene came an ominous twenty-four-hour silence. The telegraph lines had snapped, and San Francisco was cut off from the rest of California and the nation. The fire that swept through the city far eclipsed the quake's direct damage; the broken natural gas and water mains had created a highly flammable combination. In the end, the fire and the aftershocks produced by a shifting fault line cut a swath of destruction roughly 450 miles long and 50 miles wide. Seven hundred people died. Two hundred and fifty thousand were homeless. By some estimates, property damage reached $500 million. The 1906 San Francisco earthquake easily qualifies as one of the worst natural disasters in American history.[1]

After hearing a brief report of the quake, President Theodore Roosevelt sent a telegram to California governor George Pardee in Sacramento: "I feel the greatest concern and sympathy for you and the people—not only of San Francisco, but of California, in this terrible disaster. You will let me know if there is anything that the *national government* can do" (emphasis added). Late that night Governor Pardee replied from Oakland, across the bay and as close as he could get to the stricken city: "Owing to the interruption of telegraphic communication, the extent of the disaster in San Francisco is not well known here. People of California appreciate your prompt inquiry and offer of assistance. State troops are doing patrol duty and if *Federal* assistance is needed, will call on you" (emphasis added).

The breakdown in communication delayed the immediate mobilization of outside support because government and private relief officials in San Francisco were un-

The buildings of San Francisco loom starkly against the skyline after the earthquake and fire of 1906. Public charity was short-lived and federal assistance proved chaotic and ineffective, paving the way for the nationalization of disaster relief.

able to file requests for emergency assistance or obtain authority to take exceptional measures to deal with the crisis. This said, Gen. Frederick Funston, commander in chief of the Pacific Division stationed just outside the city, did not wait for instructions. He promptly ordered federal troops into the city to assist state troops and local police. His first communication to Secretary of War William Howard Taft confirmed the extent of the disaster: "We need thousands of tents and all the rations that can be sent. Fire still raging . . . troops all on duty assisting police . . . 100,000 homeless."

On April 19, the day after the quake, President Roosevelt called on Americans to lend a hand. The American Red Cross, he added, would coordinate the relief effort and receive any donations. The Red Cross named Dr. Edward Devine to head relief work in San Francisco; he started west that day. Because Secretary of War Taft also served as president of the Red Cross, Roosevelt assigned the army a major, if unofficial, role in distributing aid to residents who had suffered severe losses. Over the next month Americans contributed millions in cash and tons of clothing and food to the relief effort. Millionaire philanthropists John D. Rockefeller, Andrew Carnegie, and William Astor each publicly pledged $100,000; Wall Street firms collected over $500,000, as did residents of Philadelphia. Chicago contributed almost $400,000. Even Tammany Hall, New York's notoriously corrupt Democratic Party machine, responded with a $10,000 contribution.

Also on April 19, Roosevelt requested and Congress promptly appropriated $1 million in emergency relief. Two days later the president returned to Congress requesting another $1.5 million. Most of the money was earmarked to reimburse the military for direct costs such as that of setting up a large tent city in Golden Gate Park.

San Francisco mayor Eugene Schmitz, acting under a dispatch from President Roosevelt, placed the city under martial law and proclaimed: "The Federal troops, the members of the regular police force, and all special police officers have been authorized to kill any and all persons engaged in looting or in the commission of any other crime." The presence of these patrols, independently policing the city and issuing curfews, soon kindled massive confusion and resentment. In some locales overly vigilant militias prevented fire-fighting and relief teams from entering disaster zones. Until April 28, when the governor formally asked the president to bring in U.S. Army troops to assume full command, the relief operation was in chaos.

The Red Cross's role in relief efforts became controversial as well because the organization insisted on coordinating those efforts from its headquarters in Washington. Meanwhile, the mayor and other local authorities—the only ones in a position to know what to do—had few resources at their disposal. Recognizing this, Roosevelt urged that further donations go directly to a local relief committee; the Red Cross complied as well and turned over much of the relief money to local leaders. Back on the disaster front, the limitations of patchwork assistance based mostly on volunteerism had become painfully evident to the earthquake victims. Then, shortly after the fire was extinguished, so too was public charity. The citizens of San Francisco were left to their own devices in clearing away the rubble and rebuilding their lives.

Eighty-three years later, San Francisco was again the scene of an earthquake, the largest since the one in 1906. This quake occurred only moments before the first game of the 1989 World Series between the Giants and their Bay area rivals, the Oakland A's, at San Francisco's sold-out Candlestick Park. Millions of viewers around the world were just tuning into the broadcast when they saw the stadium suddenly tremble and fans and players scurry for cover. Clearly it was not one of those routine tremors that Californians take in stride. Within moments the

quake, scoring 7.1 on the Richter scale, had pulled down portions of four freeways and snapped sections of the San Francisco–Oakland Bay Bridge. Thousands were injured; sixty would die. Bay area residents would suffer over $7 billion in property losses.

Unlike in 1906, however, long-distance telephone service was the sole communication system interrupted by the quake, and this happened only because hundreds of thousands of TV viewers rushed to call friends and family in the quake area. Within the hour, officials in Sacramento and in Washington had assessed the magnitude of the disaster and gone to work. The next morning President George Bush formally declared the region a disaster area, thereby triggering massive federal assistance.

Two days after the quake, high-level administration officials arrived in the Bay area to evaluate the damage. The Federal Emergency Management Agency (FEMA) already was in place, coordinating the rescue and relief activities of state and local officials as well as representatives of other federal agencies. Unlike the confusion

The 1989 San Francisco earthquake snapped sections of the San Francisco–Oakland Bay Bridge. The disaster triggered massive federal assistance and efficient disaster relief efforts, in stark contrast to the failures of volunteerism and state relief efforts so evident in 1906.

that reigned after the 1906 disaster, public and private agencies were prepared to work as a team. Indeed, the federal Earthquake Hazards Reduction Act of 1977 requires FEMA to play a lead role in preparing contingency plans for just such a disaster; only two months earlier it had led state and other federal agencies in a major earthquake training exercise.

When President Bush arrived on the scene several days later, he was greeted at the airport by San Francisco's mayor who publicly demanded that federal checks be "written on the spot." The president demurred but shortly announced an initial $273 million relief allocation. Almost everyone in Washington agreed with local officials that far more money would be needed to fulfill the federal government's responsibilities. In fact, a bidding war soon erupted between the Republican White House and congressional Democrats. The administration proposed between $2 and $2.5 billion. Congress countered with a bid of $3.45 billion. Bowing to the cross pressures of fiscal and political prudence, Bush temporized but then accepted the Democratic figure. Private donations poured in from all over the United States, but this time they played a secondary role to that of the government, particularly the national government. Overall, charitable contributions represented less than 5 percent of the total expenditure.

Over the next five months FEMA opened seventeen centers in the region, processed more than 77,000 applications for assistance, and distributed $31 million to individuals. Moreover, FEMA and eight other federal departments and agencies spent, under FEMA's direction, $2 billion on emergency relief, insurance, and repair of roads, highways and buildings.[2]

A look back reveals that although the devastation of the 1906 quake and fire far exceeded that of the 1989 quake, substantially less aid was provided in 1906 than in 1989. The legacy of the 1906 disaster is the lesson it offers on the limits of volunteerism and state resources—a lesson not lost on present-day national policy makers. In the 1906 quake the absence of a central authority doomed coordination, ranging from the collection of funds at the national level to cordoning off neighborhoods from potential looting. As for volunteerism, Americans initially donated—some anonymously, some ostentatiously—impressive amounts of supplies. Ultimately, however, their contributions were inadequate. Then, characteristic of volunteerism, as the earthquake receded to the inside pages of the newspapers both the self-interested and true charity dried up.

The virtues of a national policy for disaster relief are revealed in the deficiencies of volunteerism and exclusive reliance on state resources. A national "insurance policy" gives individuals, businesses, and local governments the resources they need when they need it. Financed out of general revenues, such a policy spreads "exposure" to these chance events across the entire population, freeing up resources that states and local communities would otherwise have to hold unproductively in reserve to deal with catastrophes.

More broadly, the San Francisco earthquakes tell a story of subtly evolving federal-state relations—a story that has been repeated many times for other policies that once belonged exclusively to the states. Over time, the national government has entered virtually every sector of public policy, typically not to wrest authority away from the states but to produce collective goods that the states are unwilling or unable to undertake on their own. The national government's assumption of responsibility has not always been so congenial, however. As we shall see in Chapter 4, in the 1860s the national government went to war to end slavery and prove to the states that they could not unilaterally withdraw from the Union. Some hundred years later another struggle between southern states and the national government ensued as the latter outlawed segregation and black disenfranchisement against the official resistance of state governments throughout the South.

American-Style Federalism

In a federal system, authority is divided between two or more distinct levels of government. In the United States the division is between the national (*federal*) government and the states.[3] **Federalism** is a hybrid arrangement that mixes elements of a *confederation,* in which lower-level governments possess all real authority, and **unitary government,** in which the national government monopolizes constitutional authority.

Before adopting a federal system in the Constitution the nation had experienced both of these alternatives. The decision by the distant British government to exercise its option as the central, unitary authority to tax and administer the subordinate colonies had precipitated the American War of Independence. After the war the citizens of the newly independent states had reacted to the colonial experience by rejecting unitary authority in favor of confederation. But because the Articles of Confederation allowed state delegations to veto any major legislation in Congress, the states rarely achieved a consensus and the national government accomplished little.

Worldwide, unitary governments are far more common than federations and confederations combined. Under unitary systems, shown in Figure 3–1, the lower-level governmental entities—such as counties and metropolitan districts in Britain and departments in France—are created by and ultimately dependent on the national government for authority and resources. Typically, the central government establishes national policies and raises and distributes funds to the local units to carry them out. However deliberative and authoritative these subnational units may appear, they function largely as part of the administrative apparatus of the national government.

To qualify as a federal system, a government must have constitutional relations across levels that satisfy three general conditions:

• The same people and territory are included in both levels of government.

Figure 3–1 Three Systems of Government: Unitary, Federation, and Confederation

Unitary System

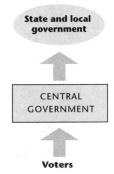

Authority is centralized with state and local governments administering authority delegated from central government. Examples: United Kingdom, France, and Japan

Federation

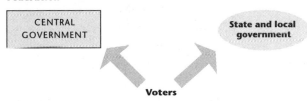

Authority is divided between central and state or local governments. Examples: Canada, United States under the Constitution.

Confederation

Authority held by independent states and delegated to central government by consensus agreements. Example: United States under the Articles of Confederation

• The nation's constitution protects units at each level of government from encroachment by the other units.

• Each unit is in a position to exert some leverage over the other.[4]

The second condition, independence, is critical because it sets the stage for the third condition, mutual influence. Independence was the missing ingredient that rendered the national government impotent under the Articles of Confederation. With every state commanding a veto over major national policies, the national government lacked the resources and authority to act independently of the states.

Occasionally, observers of American federalism refer to local governments as if they were a separate level in a three-tiered federal system. This characterization is inaccurate. Local governments, which include thousands of counties, cities, and specialized divisions such as school districts and port authorities, are established by the states (Table 3–1). In providing a limited range of government services, local governing bodies may pass laws, worry each year about balancing their budgets, generate revenue through taxes and fees, and spend public money through their own agencies, but these bodies do not exercise independent, constitutional authority. Their responsibilities and the extent of their discretion are established by state law.

Even when metropolitan areas are ceded great discretion to decide local policies through state home rule provisions, they remain the legal creations of states, which retain the authority to rescind local ordinances or otherwise preempt their policies. In 1999, for example, the gun industry fought a gun safety civil suit brought against it by the city of Atlanta by persuading the Georgia legislature to pass the first bill in the nation designed to block such suits. With other cities considering similar legal action, the gun industry and its user support groups launched legislative campaigns to ward off those plaintiffs as well. And they are likely to succeed; forty states already have laws on the books preventing their cities and counties

Table 3–1	U.S. Governments, 1997	
National		1
State		50
Local	County	3,043
	Municipal	19,372
	Township and town	16,629
	School district	13,726
	Special district	34,683
Total		**87,504**

Source: Bureau of the Census, *Statistical Abstract of the United States: 1998* (Washington, D.C.: Government Printing Office, 1998), 305.

from enacting local gun control ordinances.[5] This example demonstrates that whereas the relations between the state and national governments are premised on separate constitutional authority and qualify as "federal," those between state and local governments are not and therefore can best be classified as "unitary."[6]

Dual Federalism

Two distinct relations between the national and state governments satisfy the specific conditions of federalism. American federalism contains elements of both. The first, a simple arrangement called **dual federalism,** leaves the states and the national government presiding over mutually exclusive "spheres of sovereignty." James Madison described this arrangement (and the intent of the Framers of the Constitution) in *Federalist* No. 45: "The powers delegated by the proposed Constitution to the Federal Government are few and defined. Those which are to remain to the State Governments are numerous and indefinite." For example, foreign policy and national defense are purely national concerns; matters that "in the ordinary course of affairs, concern the lives" of the citizens are the responsibility of the individual states.

The nation, however, has never divided authority so neatly. Nineteenth-century governments at both levels assumed what by modern standards were quite limited responsibilities and thus found it easier to divide domains. Yet from the outset, states exercised national authority on

Figure 3–2 The Constitutional Basis for "Dual" and "Shared" Federalism

National Government

Exclusive Powers
- Coin money
- Regulate interstate and foreign commerce
- Tax imports and exports
- Make treaties
- Make all laws "necessary and proper" to fulfill responsibilities
- Make war
- Regulate postal system

Powers Denied
- Tax state exports
- Change state boundaries
- Impose religious tests
- Pass laws in conflict with the Bill of Rights

State Governments

Exclusive Powers
- Run elections
- Regulate intrastate commerce
- Establish republican forms of state and local governments
- Protect public health, safety, and morals
- All powers not delegated to the national government or denied to the states by the Constitution

Powers Denied
- Tax imports and exports
- Coin money
- Enter into treaties
- Impair obligation of contracts
- Enter compacts with other states without congressional consent

Shared Authority
- Tax
- Borrow money
- Charter banks and corporations
- Take property (eminent domain)
- Enforce laws and administer a judiciary

Source: Adapted from Lee Epstein and Thomas G. Walker, *Constitutional Law for a Changing America: Short Course* (Washington, D.C.: CQ Press, 1996), Table III–1.

some important matters. In the Civil War the Union forces assembled to put down the Confederacy were recruited and initially provisioned by the states. Only after the men joined the ranks of other states' enlistees did the federal government assume control.

Since those days, nationalization has shifted the "indefinite" authority Madison assigned to state governments to the national side. Today, in fact, the national government has a hand in almost all policies that "concern the lives" of the citizenry. While the image of dual federalism remains popular among those who oppose federal action, it no longer accurately describes federal–state relations (see Figure 3–2).

Shared Federalism

The second and more accurate conception of federalism, called **shared** (or "cooperative") **federalism,** recognizes that the national and state governments jointly supply services to the citizenry. Over the years progressive nationalization has transformed American federalism from mostly dual to mostly shared. As citizens have come to expect "the government" to provide services and solve problems, they have not worried much about maintaining clear federal–state boundaries. Moreover, the scope and complexity of modern problems mandate a joint, cooperative strategy across states and levels of governments. Pollution does not honor state boundaries; neither do unemployment, inflation, crime, drugs, or homelessness. Then there is the Internet which knows no boundaries whatsoever.

Modern federal–state relations defy easy description, much less assessment. Certainly the idea of dual federalism with its carefully observed "spheres of sovereignty" that guided many of the Framers belongs to history. And the concept of shared federalism can mean almost anything other than dual federalism. Another difficulty in assessing federal–state relations is that they vary greatly from one policy to the next. For example, the Social Security system closely conforms to national policy, but major parts of the program are administered by the states. Here, federal–state relations satisfy the conditions of a unitary governmental system. Federal participation in local police services, by contrast, remains marginal.

Critics of nationalization argue that the federal government has so intruded into the traditional responsibilities of states and local communities that even "shared" federalism is a misnomer. As they see it, the federal government now calls the shots; the states merely implement federally mandated programs. Indeed, the modern ascendancy of the national government surely would have amazed all (and horrified most) of the delegates to the Constitutional Convention. After all, protecting the states from encroachment by a stronger national government was, in the words of one nationalist delegate, "the favorite object of the Convention." All but a handful of the states' rights delegates were satisfied with the final product, and most of them later spoke in favor of the Constitution's ratification. So why have their efforts to partition federal and state responsibilities into separate, self-contained spheres been so thoroughly eclipsed?

The answer is straightforward. As national politicians sought over the years to expand their authority and responsibilities, they discovered that the wall between the federal government and the states was not so impregnable as most of the Framers had apparently supposed. The Constitution's provisions and language leave ample room for a variety of federal–state relations. Thus nationalization of public policy proceeded to reshape federalism largely unfettered by constitutional constraints and without triggering a constitutional crisis. The nationalization of policy did not just happen, however. Granted, as many problems outgrew state borders pressure usually built for the states to surrender control to the national government. But whether the federal government actually assumed responsibility for a specific policy remained—and still is—a political decision.

The Logic of Nationalization

As we shall see in this chapter, and indeed throughout this book, the forces favoring nationalization are many and varied. They can be simply classified, however, according to whether they follow a logic based on the realities of collective action or whether purely political considerations are at work. Perhaps a simple hypothetical situation best illustrates how both types of forces can push policy to the national level. Consider the decisions of a small farming community that is trying to upgrade its local roads (see box "Nationalization as a Road-Building Game"). After a bitter winter, the farmers' driveways and neighborhood roads are in disrepair. Moreover, new markets for their crops are opening up nearby, but access to the markets will require construction of a new road.

How will these sixteen farmers approach their road improvement and construction decisions? For the driveways, we can assume the farmers have always maintained their own and that this policy will not change. Each driveway represents a quintessential private good: one person benefits and no one else suffers from its consumption.

The neighborhood roads (A–D) qualify as public goods, at least for the local residents. As such, the issue is whether those who use them will contribute to their maintenance. Because the number of users is small, informal negotiations will likely reveal who favors and who opposes the resurfacing project. This said, there is no guarantee that each neighborhood will maintain its road. That decision will depend on the cost of the project in relation to each farmer's perceived benefit. In fact, in this hypothetical community some farmers (shaded) have weighed the benefits against their one-fourth share of the regrading cost and decided against it. Each of the other farmers, however, is willing to pay up to a third of the total road improvement cost. Thus roads A and B will be improved even though farmers 2 and 8 do not contribute and get their roads graded for nothing.[7] Meanwhile, farmer 9 is not prepared to bear the full cost of regrading road C, nor are farmers 13 and 14 willing to split the cost for road D. These roads, then, will not be improved.

For these small-scale collective activities, informal negotiations and voluntary compliance yield a fairly successful final outcome. The roads were regraded in those neighborhoods where most of the farmers wanted to do so and unchanged where demand fell short. Overall, thirteen of the sixteen farmers benefited in some fashion (five by not having to pay for something they did not want). Only farmers 9, 13, and 14 found their preferences frustrated by their neighbors' choices.

If one thinks of the four neighborhoods as four states, the implications of these separate road-building projects for federalism are evident. The organization of collective action at the "state" level where the project represents a public good introduces a commendable level of efficiency and responsiveness in public policy to the preferences of the citizenry. With each farmer weighing the value of the good against the individual cost of providing it, neighborhoods avoid the inefficiencies of supplying goods for which there is little demand. By keeping road improvement decisions local, the farmers also avoid the substantial transaction costs entailed in community-wide decisions. Finally, this decentralized approach minimizes the conformity costs imposed on individual members; neighborhoods where most of the farmers want a newly paved road undertake the project while those in which the project attracts too little support do not. The lesson of this ex-

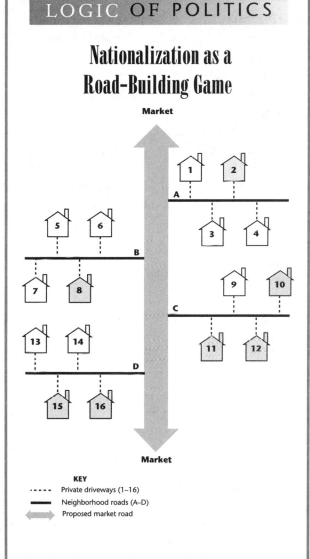

LOGIC OF POLITICS

Nationalization as a Road-Building Game

KEY
- - - - Private driveways (1–16)
――― Neighborhood roads (A–D)
⬍ Proposed market road

Building hypothetical roads and lighthouses is a favorite pastime of political scientists and economists. Such "games" allow the players to isolate the essential features of a problem and inspect how they relate to one another. Here the problem (described fully in the text) is one of replicating the forces of nationalization as they influence the road improvement choices of a hypothetical farming community.

ercise for federalism is clear: state jurisdiction over public goods that fall within its borders offers real advantages.

But once the public good encompasses the larger community, the logic for local control (that is, states' rights) disappears. Consider the third road-building decision facing this hypothetical farming community: whether to build a road to the new markets for its crops. Each farmer figures that the profits gained by access to these markets would well exceed his or her one-sixteenth share of the cost of road construction. But now comes the hard part. To transform their sixteen private preferences into actual construction of the market road, the farmers must clear several of the formidable hurdles to successful collective action introduced in Chapter 1. First, they must identify their mutual interest in such a project. For this limited task, community leaders, the functional equivalent here of politicians, will prove invaluable. Second, the farmers must agree on the specifics of the project such as the kind of road to be built, where it will run, and how it will be financed. Again, a low-key political process such as a series of meetings might be enough to allow the farmers to make these decisions and build their new road. But not all farmers will contribute voluntarily; even in this small community some will be tempted to free ride. Thus the third hurdle facing farmers is finding a way to enforce their collective agreements against the temptation to free ride. They might create a construction committee and delegate to certain members responsibility for negotiating with contractors and assessing each farmer. Better yet, they might create a *special district* that would piggyback onto the state government's taxation authority. The farmers would then be obliged to pay for the road as part of their property taxes.

But why stop there? Now that a special district is in place, the farmers can reconsider their other road improvement decisions. Recall that a clear majority (nine of the sixteen farmers) initially favored regrading their neighborhood roads. In the end, two neighborhoods (A and B) regraded, but two (C and D) did not. Moreover,

every member of the majority had reason to feel exploited by the local decisions. Three had to forgo road improvements, and the rest had to contribute extra money to cover the neighbors who refused to participate. With the new special district, however, the majority finds itself in a stronger position. If the new district assumes responsibility for the neighborhoods, all the roads could be resurfaced with no farmer having to pay more than one-quarter of the cost. For the majority, still resentful that some farmers got something for nothing when these decisions remained in the neighborhoods, this outcome would seem altogether equitable. The shaded farmers, however, would object; they did not want to pay for road improvements in the first place.

Whether the special district takes up the regrading project depends on the rules governing its decisions. If majority rule holds sway, the farmers might well vote 9 (unshaded farms) to 7 (shaded farms) to have the district take on neighborhood road maintenance.[8] Democracy, then, has prevailed. But has it produced a more desirable outcome than when these decisions were strictly local matters? Probably not. When the decision was left at the local level, only three of the sixteen farmers failed to achieve at least part of their desired outcome. With the decision now at the community level, the number of unsatisfied farmers has grown to seven. And what is the significance of this finding? The special district makes good *economic* sense in solving the free-riding problem and allowing the community to construct a market road, but the decision to shift road grading to this higher level of government lacks the same compelling rationale. Only the farmers who wanted their roads regraded would be happy with the latter decision. For them, it makes good *political* sense.

As we will see in the next section, the history of American federalism has followed a course that resembles that of the hypothetical farmers. Both the logic of collective action and the opportunities for political advantage have worked at times to shift policy from the states to Wash-

At the outset of World War I the states ratified the Sixteenth Amendment, allowing Congress to levy a national income tax to pay for the war. Later this tax provided a revenue stream that Congress used to finance thousands of other projects, few of which had anything to do with the nation's security. Once the states open the door to nationalization of policy, it often is hard to shut.

ington. If there is any lesson to be learned from the road-building farmers it is that by giving the national government the authority and resources to nationalize policy when it is essential, the states may open the door to national action even when it is not.

The Paths to Nationalization

Throughout the first half of the nineteenth century, America remained a nation of segmented communities whose commercial intercourse required minimal coordination across states. But just as the arrival of distant markets caused our hypothetical farmers to expand their concerns from local potholes to a new market road, so too did America shift its attention from strictly state and local

matters to national problems and solutions. With growth, industrialization, urbanization, and the development of national transportation and communication systems, the nation's appetite grew for the kinds of public goods that outstripped the scope and resources of local communities and states.[9] In the early 1870s, for example, the farm states tried in vain to prohibit the railroads from engaging in rate discrimination and exorbitant charges. They finally turned to Washington for regulation, and in 1887 Congress obliged by passing the Interstate Commerce Act. A similar process spurred the federal government to enforce national food safety standards, enact antimonopoly laws, and undertake numerous other services.

This nationalization of public policy, which altered America's federal–state relations, was propelled by a rationale, or logic, that grew out of the requirements of collective action. Played out historically, the logic of collective action has assumed several forms. First, it has produced historic movements of large blocks of domestic policy from the state capitals to Washington as problems have become national in scope.

Second, states have solicited federal intervention when they cannot solve their problems by working together individually. The Constitution prohibits formal interstate agreements (Article I, Section 10), and voluntary cooperation holds the potential for reneging, particularly when serious, costly commitments are required. For that reason, in the years following the 1906 San Francisco earthquake the states welcomed a national insurance policy against such disasters even though it meant surrendering control of disaster relief to federal agencies.

Finally, the political considerations that inspired the farmers to assign road grading to the special district has been at work at the national level where national majorities have insisted on federal involvement in what were formerly state and local matters. Sometimes mere expediency is at work as a national majority finds it easier to succeed in Washington than in each of the states. On other occasions, the cause has been just and noble. The history

Officials of the Union Pacific and Central Pacific companies shake hands at Promontory Point, Utah, on May 10, 1869, after the last spike has been driven to join the two lines and complete the nation's first transcontinental railroad. Several years later the farm states would turn to Washington to regulate the railroads and halt rate discrimination and exorbitant charges.

of civil rights policy in America is but one of many examples. In the course of asserting its authority to protect the rights of African Americans—from the Civil War in the 1860s to the civil rights laws a century later—the national government breached the wall separating national from state spheres of control. While the impact of civil rights for federalism has been profound, it is a subject with broad implications for all Americans and warrants separate consideration in the next chapter.

Historic Transfers of Policy to Washington

Two equally historic moments of nationalization were contained in President Franklin Roosevelt's New Deal, enacted in the 1930s, and President Lyndon Johnson's Great Society program, realized in the mid-1960s. In addition to broadening the scope of federal responsibilities, these watershed programs were accompanied by the election of large national majorities to Congress from the

president's party, with an apparent mandate to create a broad new array of collective goods.

Roosevelt's New Deal was a comprehensive set of economic regulations and relief programs intended to fight the Great Depression (1929–1940). The innovation of the New Deal stemmed less from the form of its policies than from their size and scope. During Roosevelt's first two terms (1933–1941), he and the huge Democratic majorities in Congress established economic management as one of the national government's primary responsibilities. Federal policy took two basic forms: regulating and financing (and with it, prescribing) state action. Despite the continuing debate between present-day Republicans and Democrats over the proper federal role, no one has seriously proposed dismantling the framework of economic management constructed by the New Deal.

At the outset of the depression, 40 percent unemployment rates were not uncommon in many communities.

The states, which were responsible for welfare programs, had to reduce services to fend off insolvency. In the process, they also had to abandon those in need of help.[10] When the Roosevelt administration's offer to fund 90 percent of the costs for relief and new make-work programs finally came, the principle of federalism did not prevent state leaders from cheerfully accepting the help. All forty-eight states rapidly signed up for the Works Progress Administration, Old Age Assistance, Civilian Conservation Corps, Social Security, and other federally sponsored public assistance programs. The states that complied with federal guidelines for these programs retained a large measure of administrative control over them. Those that balked at having to contribute 10 percent of the costs of services saw the national government reduce their funding. During these depression years the dramatic growth in federal spending, coupled with corresponding reductions at the state and local levels, provided evidence of the sharp shift in government responsibility for social programs to Washington (Figure 3–3).

To justify its unprecedented intervention in the economy, the Roosevelt administration invoked Article I, Section 8, of the Constitution, known as the **commerce clause.**[11] Although demands for national regulation of the

economy had begun modestly in the late nineteenth century, they reached a new level of intensity with the onset of the Great Depression. FDR's New Deal introduced regulations that touched virtually every aspect of the nation's economic life, from how securities were sold on Wall Street to the amount of feed corn a Kansas farmer could grow for his livestock. At first, a conservative Supreme Court resisted. Narrowly interpreting the commerce clause to include only direct trade among the states, the Court ruled that federal workplace policies such as child labor restrictions were unconstitutional because they acted as regulation of intrastate commerce, an area left to the states. Under great political pressure, however, the Court eventually relented by extending its interpretation of the commerce clause to include intrastate commerce that indirectly affected commerce across state lines.

Another great wave of nationalization of domestic policy occurred in the mid-1960s. Elected in 1964 in an even larger landslide than FDR's in 1932, Lyndon Johnson and the overwhelmingly Democratic Congress launched a War on Poverty as part of its Great Society agenda. In 1964–1965 Congress passed more than a hundred new categorical grant programs, spending over $5 billion. As with

The depression of the 1930s bankrupted the states and forced the federal government to take over national relief. Breadlines such as this one were widespread.

Figure 3–3 Nonmilitary Expenditure Shares by Level of Government, 1927–1942

(percent)

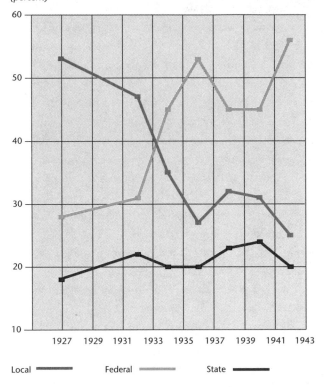

Local ▬▬▬   Federal ▬▬▬   State ▬▬▬

Source: John Joseph Wallis, "The Political Economy of New Deal Fiscal Federalism," *Economic Inquiry,* 29 (July 1991), 511.
    Note: About half of the increase in federal spending in this figure took the form of direct financial support to indigent citizens.

the New Deal, these grants subsidized state programs that implemented national goals. Traditional state and local responsibilities such as school construction, teacher training, urban renewal, and public housing became important federal responsibilities.

But all these grants came with strings attached. To qualify for funding, state and local authorities had to follow detailed programmatic guidelines prescribing how funds were to be spent. The War on Poverty also undermined traditional federalism by cutting the states out of the partnership. Local officials, and in many instances private community groups, applied directly to Washington for funds and the authority to set up local Headstart schools and many other programs designed to lift the urban poor from poverty. States found themselves reduced to bystanders. During the 1960s the Council of State Governments plaintively implored Washington to notify state officials when programs were introduced in their communities.[12]

State Responses to Collective Action Problems

When modern state governments have encountered the same dilemmas of collective action that plagued their eighteenth-century counterparts, they have solved the dilemmas the same way—by shifting responsibility from the state to federal authorities. The kinds of collective action problems that prompt states to ask Washington for help often fall into one of three categories: coordination problems, free riding, and cutthroat competition.

Coordination Problems. A nation composed of fifty states is bound to face coordination problems—some dramatic, some rather mundane. Until 1986, the principle that each state administers its own driver's license laws appeared unassailable. But after heavy lobbying by state officials, Congress passed the Commercial Motor Vehicle Safety Act which standardized state driver's licenses for interstate truckers and created a bureau within the Department of Transportation to centralize records of traffic violations. Prompting federal intervention was the practice common among truckers of obtaining licenses in several states in order to maintain a valid license regardless of the number of traffic tickets accumulated. Centralized record keeping offered a far simpler solution to state coordination than requiring each state to update its records with those from every other state. Disgruntled truckers charged that the new law was another example of interference by "heavy-handed Washington bureaucrats," but in fact the law precisely fulfilled the states' request.

Free Riding. In the nation's early years, the new national government solved many of the most serious free-riding problems arising from the Revolutionary War and later the Articles of Confederation. New problems continually arise, however, with changing conditions and policies. One realm in which classic free riding remains commonplace is protection of a region's natural resources. During the 1950s and 1960s, for example, no state on the eastern seaboard desired the loss of the cod fishery, but in the absence of a collective mechanism to assure each state's compliance, none controlled its harvest and the fishery collapsed. Today a half dozen midwestern farm states face the same dilemma as farms steadily draw down the regional water aquifer by irrigation. After all, why should Kansas impose water usage quotas on its farmers in order to conserve the public good if it suspects that none of the other states will require their farmers to curtail irrigation?

Such crises arise not because the states are irresponsible but because they confront a dilemma that one state, acting alone, cannot solve. The solution lies in agreeing to cede authority to an outside party—the national government—to make and *enforce* allocation decisions. For example, the federal Fishery Conservation Management Act of 1976 established regional councils composed of state representatives to set fishing quotas for threatened species. Their decisions carry the force of federal authority.[13]

Cutthroat Competition. Under the Articles of Confederation each state was free to conduct its own international trade policy. This arrangement allowed foreign governments and merchants to play states against one another when negotiating trade agreements. The losers were American producers and the states, which found themselves in a classic prisoner's dilemma. Searching for a solution, both nationalists and advocates of states' rights readily agreed at the Constitutional Convention that the states' interests were best served by the national government assuming control in foreign affairs, including trade.

At various times the dilemma of cutthroat competition has prompted state officials to lobby Washington to prevent bidding wars. When the national government defended a 1937 minimum wage law before the Supreme

Some states like California test their coastal waters for bacterial pollution and, when necessary, close beaches. The states that do not test derive a competitive edge in tourism by keeping their beaches open. In 1999 several House lawmakers from California introduced the Beaches Environmental Assessment, Cleanup and Health Act to encourage all state and local governments to test their coastal waters. In addition to directing the U.S. Environmental Protection Agency to establish minimal quality standards, the legislation offers states $150 million in subsidies for testing. Pictured (left to right) are lobbyist Darryl Hatheway of the Surfrider Foundation and California's surfing House members: Republican Brian Bilbray, Democrat Sam Farr, and Republican Dana Rohrabacher.

Court, it reminded the justices that rather than usurping state prerogatives, Washington was actually serving the states: "State legislators, . . . over a period of time have realized that no state, acting alone, could require labor standards substantially higher than those obtained in other states whose producers and manufacturers competed in the interstate market."[14]

Environmental regulation is another area in which the national government has taken action. To lure new business, states sometimes are tempted to relax their environmental standards to give them a competitive edge over their neighbors. Thus one state's strong environmental policies may expose it to other states' gamesmanship. As much as state officials like to complain about the policies of the Environmental Protection Agency, the presence of national standards tends to insulate environmental protection from cutthroat competition.

Competition among states can take other forms as well. Companies considering relocating facilities will strategically select two or three "finalist" sites in different states and then sit back and let them bid against one another by offering tax breaks or special services. While the states generally would be better off if they could avoid this competition, they cannot afford to do so.

The Political Logic of Nationalization

Sometimes those who are promoting a policy will try to shift it from the states to the national government because either they expect more sympathetic treatment in Washington or they find it easier than lobbying fifty state governments. National campaigns for legislation banning automatic weapons and handguns, regulating hazardous waste disposal, and mandating special education programs in public schools are instances in which "state" issues have been strategically shifted to Washington.

If a cause enjoys widespread national support, lobbying Congress is far more efficient than lobbying fifty state legislatures. After all, a single federal law can change a policy in all fifty states. In 1980 a mother whose teenage daughter was killed by a drunk driver formed Mothers Against Drunk Driving (MADD) which quickly mushroomed into a national organization with thousands of members. Initially, MADD pressed state legislatures for stiffer laws and higher drinking ages. But states with lower drinking ages benefited via free riding from the additional business of underage customers from neighboring states. As a result, variations in the states' drinking ages perversely forced some young people to take to the highways in search of alcohol.

MADD may have eventually prevailed in state legislatures, nevertheless in 1984 it took its case to Congress.[15] Few politicians proved willing to defend drunks or federalism. In 1985 Congress passed legislation that instituted a simple, effective way to regulate drinking age laws. If a state failed to raise its drinking age to twenty-one in 1986, it would lose 5 percent of its federal highway funds. Failure to do so in 1987 would trigger a 10 percent deduction. All the states got the message and promptly raised the drinking age. They also cried "Foul!" to the Supreme Court, claiming extortion and federal intrusion into strictly state jurisdictions. The Court sided with the national government.[16]

Even those who do not desire national action sometimes invite it as a way of avoiding burdensome and varied regulations from each of the states. In recent years the attorneys general of many states have charged the airlines with practicing illegal "bait and switch" advertising when they run local newspaper promotions for steeply discounted fares that few customers find available. The airlines, however, have successfully evaded state prosecution by persuading the Department of Transportation to assert its preemptive federal authority over airline rates. Thus even businesses wanting to remain free of any government regulation may prefer to deal with one federal agency than have to fend off attempts at regulation from fifty states.

Perhaps the most compelling strategic reason for a group to prefer national policy over state policy is that the national arena may be the only place in which it can hope to prevail, especially when policy preferences are concentrated geographically. This situation characterized civil rights in the South during the 1960s, and today it often is found in efforts to enact environmental policy. Protection of environmental resources can be costly—directly or indirectly. Either way, local residents pay the bulk of the costs. Idaho ranchers worry that the reintroduction of wolves in the nearby national parks will endanger their sheep. And, as we saw in Chapter 1, the lumber industry believes jobs will be imperiled if it must curtail the harvest of old-growth forest to protect the endangered spotted owl. The Navajos' coal-burning, electric-generating plant in Arizona may cast a London fog over the Grand

Despite his outspoken opposition to the intrusion of the federal government into longtime state domains, President Ronald Reagan did not hesitate to sign the popular legislation requiring states to change the drinking age to twenty-one to qualify for federal highway funds.

Canyon, but they prefer the profits gained from selling electricity to a national market.

The rest of the country, by comparison, bears little of these costs. It can "afford" the appropriate environmental measures far better than can those whose livelihoods are adversely affected by them. Restoring the original ecology of Yellowstone National Park, protecting an endangered owl, and maintaining a smoke-free Grand Canyon are desirable and essentially free collective goods. Thus conflicts arising over the environment frequently pit local resource users (such as ranchers and developers) against a nationally organized environmental constituency.

Sometimes, political strategy forces groups that lose at the national level to seek smaller victories in those states where they enjoy majority support. For example, social conservatives, frustrated in their efforts to rescind abortion rights and validate school prayer at the national level, have sponsored drives to put these issues on state ballots. Similarly, gun-control groups, unable to persuade Con-

gress to adopt tougher handgun laws, have taken their campaign to the legislatures of sympathetic states. By the end of 1997 at least fifteen states had passed laws mandating safety devices for firearms to prevent accidents.[17]

As James Madison emphasized in *Federalist* No. 10, states and the national government aggregate the citizenry's preferences into different groupings, with the result that the two levels of government may adopt different, even opposite, policies to address the same problem. Thus federalism presents opportunities for two kinds of majorities—state and national—to pursue their interests. For better or worse, national majorities have the institutional resources to nationalize many policy questions that once were the exclusive domain of state majorities.

The Constitution and Federalism

The greatest victory gained by states' righters at the Constitutional Convention was the creation of a Senate whose members would be selected by the state legislatures. This victory nearly drove the nationalist James Madison from the convention. He and everyone else assumed that in making decisions, senators would, like delegates to today's United Nations, follow the instructions of the government officials who elected them. States' rights advocates also won other skirmishes at the Convention; the evidence of their victories is found throughout the Constitution (see Chapter 2).

Transformation of the Senate

In countering Antifederalist alarms about an overly powerful national government, Madison cited the "structure of the Federal Government" as the foremost bulwark of federalism.[18] He was referring to the separation of powers among the branches of government generally and to the Senate in particular. In the nineteenth century the equal representation of states regardless of population, combined with the selection of senators by state legislatures, gave the Senate both the motive and the means to defend state prerogatives against national encroachment. The history of slavery reveals just how effective the institution was in this task. At first, some state legislatures took such a possessive view of the Senate and its members that they would pass resolutions instructing their senators how to vote on particular issues. Senators who failed to comply were asked to resign, and some did.[19] Even after this practice died out in the 1840s, most senators continued to regard themselves as agents of the state party organizations who controlled the state legislatures and elected them.

In 1913, amid persistent, widespread, and well-founded charges that senators were buying seats by bribing legislators, public pressure forced Congress and the state legislatures to ratify the Seventeenth Amendment mandating popular election of senators. The amendment, however, while targeting corrupt political practices, also incidentally knocked out an important prop of federalism. Today the Senate is a central pillar of the national government. Major innovations in domestic and foreign policy originate on the floor of the Senate, as more than a few of its members cultivate a national constituency with an eye toward future presidential campaigns.[20]

Constitutional Provisions Governing Federalism

In his first inaugural address in 1981 President Ronald Reagan decorated his attack on federal regulations by reminding his audience that "the federal government did not create the states; the states created the federal government." Reagan, however, was wrong. Twelve independent states did send representatives to the Philadelphia convention, but neither they nor their state governments *created* the new national government. Foreseeing such a claim, Madison had persuaded fellow delegates to require ratification by state conventions that directly represented the people, not the state governments.

In fact, the Constitution gives the national government at least as much responsibility for overseeing the integrity of the states as it gives the states for overseeing the integrity of the national government. All but the original thirteen states entered the Union by an act of Congress; the national government defined the boundaries of territories, oversaw their administration, and eventually ushered them into the Union. Moreover, Article IV of the Constitution obliges the national government to ensure that all states adhere to republican principles. But while Congress may create new states, it cannot destroy an old one—say, by dividing it in half—without that state's consent. For their part, two-thirds of the states may petition Congress to convene a special constitutional convention to propose amendments which that body is obliged to do. The Constitution enlists each level of government to keep the other in check.

Language distinguishing the authority and responsibilities of the states from those of the national government runs throughout the Constitution. In partitioning responsibilities, the Framers worked within a framework of dual federalism. Thus in three major sections of the Constitution they took a stab at specifying boundaries between the two levels of government. By understanding what these provisions sought but largely failed to do, we can better appreciate how America's governmental system has yielded to nationalizing forces.

The Supremacy Clause. The provision of the Constitution with the most profound implication for modern American federalism is the so-called supremacy clause in Article VI: "This Constitution, and the Laws of the United States which shall be made in Pursuance thereof [that is, in keeping with the principles of the Constitution] . . . shall be the supreme Law of the Land." Although this clause appears to give the national government license to do whatever it wants, the text actually contains an important qualifier: the national government enjoys supremacy, but only insofar as its policies conform to a Constitution that prohibits certain kinds of federal activities.[21] This qualifier restricted national authority throughout most of the nineteenth century. The original intent was simply to have the national government prevail when both governments were acting in a constitutionally correct manner. Thus the supremacy clause was framed to avoid impasses

THE CONSTITUTION'S PROVISION FOR FEDERALISM

Article I, Section 8 Commerce Clause

The Congress shall have Power ... To regulate Commerce with foreign Nations, and among the several States, and with the Indian Tribes; ...

Article I, Section 8 Elastic Clause

The Congress shall have Power ... To make all Laws which shall be necessary and proper for carrying into Execution the foregoing Powers, and all other Powers vested by this Constitution in the Government of the United States, or in any Department or Officer thereof.

Article IV, Section 3 Admission of New States

New States may be admitted by the Congress into this Union; but no new State shall be formed or erected within the Jurisdiction of any other State; nor any State be formed by the Junction of two or more States, or Parts of States, without the Consent of the Legislatures of the States concerned as well as of the Congress.

Article IV, Section 4 Enforcement of Republican Form of Government

The United States shall guarantee to every State in this Union a Republican Form of Government, and shall protect each of them against Invasion; and on Application of the Legislature, or of the Executive (when the Legislature cannot be convened) against domestic Violence.

Article VI Supremacy Clause

This Constitution, and the Laws of the United States which shall be made in Pursuance thereof; and all Treaties made, or which shall be made, under the Authority of the United States, shall be the supreme Law of the Land; and the Judges in every State shall be bound thereby, any Thing in the Constitution or Laws of any State to the Contrary notwithstanding.

Tenth Amendment

The powers not delegated to the United States by the Constitution, nor prohibited by it to the States, are reserved to the States respectively, or to the people.

over jurisdiction rather than to cede to the national government broad, preemptive authority over the states. Over the next two hundred years, however, the sphere of legitimate national action expanded, allowing national policy to enter domains once only occupied by the states. Wherever the national government carved out new authority, it automatically became supreme.

The Powers of Congress. Article I, Section 8, lists the powers reserved to Congress. But these provisions have as much to do with federalism—that is, creating jurisdictional boundaries between the states and the national government—as they do with parceling out authority among Congress, the president, and the Supreme Court. After protracted deliberations in which many possibilities were considered, the Framers finally agreed to list in the Constitution a dozen or so **enumerated powers** that should be in the domain of the national government—powers that would enable the government to address the problems the states had not grappled with effectively under the Articles of Confederation. One example: even Antifederalists conceded that a national postal system made better sense than trying to stitch together thirteen individual state postal systems.

Some of the powers enumerated in Section 8 are broadly stated. For example, as we learned earlier in this chapter, the commerce clause has opened vast areas of traditional state policy to national intervention. As a result, the twentieth century has seen the nation's economy become quite integrated. The variety of economic transactions that directly involve interstate commerce has grown sharply, and the sphere of policy in which the federal government can claim some jurisdiction has expanded. Moreover, laws governing a broad variety of social relations that are only incidentally economic—such as racial discrimination in access to public accommodations and possession of handguns near public schools—have invoked the commerce clause to justify federal involvement in these longtime state responsibilities.

Recognizing that contingencies requiring a national response might arise in the future, the Framers added to Section 8 what is now known as the **elastic clause.** It allows Congress to "make all Laws which shall be necessary and proper for carrying into Execution the foregoing Powers."[22] This open-ended provision, whose interpretation later would undermine the restrictive purpose of the carefully worded list of enumerated powers, apparently escaped the attention of many of the delegates since the convention accepted it with little debate. Later, the Antifederalists detected in it an opening for broad national authority, as did the generations of national officeholders who followed them.

The Tenth Amendment. In the ratification debates Madison answered Antifederalist charges of impending tyranny by promising that once the new government was in place, he would immediately introduce a Bill of Rights (see Chapter 2). In view of the controversy surrounding federal power in the ratification debates, it is not surprising that many members of the First Congress insisted that the first ten constitutional amendments include protections for the states as well as for individual citizens.[23]

The Tenth Amendment offers the most explicit endorsement of federalism to be found in the Constitution: "The powers not delegated to the United States by the Constitution, nor prohibited by it to the States, are reserved to the States respectively, or to the people." Yet, despite its plain language, the Tenth Amendment has failed to play a major role in fending off federal authority. The powerful combination of the supremacy and the elastic clauses reduces the Tenth Amendment to little more than a truism: those powers not taken by the national government *do* belong to the states. About all that it offers critics of nationalization is lip service to the principle of states' rights.

Interpreting the Constitution's Provisions

The sweeping language with which the Constitution variously endorses national power and states' rights has given politicians easy openings to interpret the Constitu-

tion according to their own political objectives. Just before the Civil War, as the crisis over slavery escalated, southern leaders could be heard invoking the Tenth Amendment to support their pet belief, **nullification**—the doctrine that the states are no less sovereign than the national government and retain the prerogative to ignore federal law. If their interpretation had prevailed, the nation would have returned to a confederation. A century later, their segregationist descendants, in the name of "states' rights," resisted national intervention against racial segregation and by association tainted federalism with an unsavory reputation as a reactionary doctrine (see Chapter 4).

The Framers envisioned that the Supreme Court would referee jurisdictional disputes among the states and between states and the national government. Among the thousands of judicial decisions that have grappled with the appropriate roles of the national and state governments, one early Supreme Court ruling stands out for protecting the national government from incursions by the states. In 1816 Congress created a national bank that proved unpopular with many state-level politicians who preferred the state-chartered banks over which they exercised control. To nip this federal meddling into what it viewed as a state matter, Maryland levied a heavy tax on all non-state-chartered banks. James McCulloch, an agent for the national bank in Baltimore, refused to pay the tax and the two sides went to court. The historic decision, *McCulloch v. Maryland* (1819), brought together the supremacy and elastic clauses and moved them to the forefront of constitutional interpretation.[24] Writing for the Court, Chief Justice John Marshall declared that since the national bank assisted Congress in performing several of its responsibilities enumerated in Article 8—namely, borrowing money, levying taxes, and issuing a national currency—the elastic clause gave the national government the implicit authority to create the bank. In one of the most famous passages in Supreme Court opinion, Marshall enunciated this definitive constitutional doctrine:

Let the end be legitimate, let it be within the scope of the Con-

POLITICS ➤ POLICY

George Wallace and States' Rights

In the 1960s Alabama governor George Wallace correctly claimed that the federal government's actions against segregation were compromising federalism, or "states' rights." But however vociferously he denounced Washington in the name of federalism, few people mistook the real reason for his wrath. Wallace blockaded the entrance of the University of Alabama in 1963 and prevented the admission of black students to preserve a different value: "segregation, now and forever." Facing him in this photo is U.S. Deputy Attorney General Nicholas Katzenbach.

stitution, and all means which are appropriate, which are plainly adapted to that end, which are not prohibited, but consistent with the letter and spirit of the Constitution, are constitutional.

Marshall iced the cake by removing the young national government from the purview of the states. Since "the power to tax involves the power to destroy," the suprema-

cy clause implicitly exempts the federal government from state taxes.

Five years later, in 1824, the Marshall Court handed down another decision that must have appeared far less significant to contemporaries than it came to be regarded in the twentieth century. In settling a dispute between New Jersey and New York over each state's effort to give a favored steam company a monopoly over shipping on the Hudson River, the Court held in *Gibbons v. Ogden* that neither state could control such a concession.[25] Only Congress possessed the authority to regulate commerce.

In combination, these two cases created powerful precedents that would allow future national policy to develop free of the constraints of state prerogatives. Once the Court in *Gibbons* had sanctioned federal authority to regulate commerce, the supremacy clause kicked in to give the national government the authority to preempt the states in virtually all policies involving interstate commerce. Many traditional tasks of states such as providing for public safety, enforcing fair advertising laws, and overseeing waste disposal easily slipped into federal control via the commerce clause. At first, these decisions merely staved off predatory state policies. Not until a national political coalition took control of Washington during the Great Depression in the 1930s with the intent to regulate the economy did *McCulloch* and *Gibbons* fully blossom to legitimize an activist national government.

Indicative of how far nationalization has shifted the balance of power, today's constitutional litigation over federalism typically concerns direct efforts by the federal government to regulate the activities of state and local governments and their employees. In *Garcia v. San Antonio Metropolitan Transit Authority* (1985) the Supreme Court approved the application of federal wage-and-hour laws to state and local employees. Writing for the majority, Justice Harry Blackmun dismissed the Tenth Amendment as too ambiguous to guide federal–state relations. But this was no great matter, he added, because the proper relations between the states and the national government were protected in other ways. The states' "sovereign interests," wrote Blackmun, "are more properly protected by procedural safeguards inherent in the structure of the federal system than by judicially created limitation on federal power." Because members of Congress come from the states, the majority opinion concluded, "the political process ensures that laws that unduly burden the States will not be promulgated."[26] Such an argument may have befitted federalism during the days when senators really were agents of their state legislatures, but, as we shall see, the Court had little basis for expecting the states' interests to win a sympathetic audience in Washington. Indeed, this decision illustrates just how much over the years the Supreme Court favored the national government in refereeing federal–state relations.

In recent years the Supreme Court has begun to take a more circumspect view of federal authority and has sought to preserve some semblance of state independence in federal–state relations. For example, in *United States v. Lopez* (1995) the Court narrowly decided in favor of a student who had been caught carrying a handgun onto campus in violation of the federal Gun-Free School Zones Act of 1990.[27] For the first time in many years the Court held that some "empirical connection" needed to be established between a law's provisions and its actual effect on *commerce* before the national government could enter a traditional domain of the states.[28] However heartening this and other recent small victories may be for defenders of states' rights, they do not seriously undermine the extensive authority nationalization has thrust upon the federal government.

Modern Federalism

Today the clearest and most unequivocal expression of the impact of nationalization on public policy can be found in the growth of **preemption legislation**—federal laws that assert the national government's prerogative to control public policy in a particular field. Preemption owes its existence to the supremacy clause and its frequent

use to the nationalizing forces just described. Over the 150 years prior to the New Deal, Congress enacted eighty-three laws that in some way substituted federal policy for that of the states. From 1933 to 1969, 123 such statutes were adopted, and since 1969 twice that number.[29] If preemption were all that had changed federal–state relations, modern American federalism might still be described as dual. The national government's "sphere of sovereignty" would merely have grown at the expense of the states'. But preemption describes only a small part of the impact of nationalization on federal–state relations. Generally, the jurisdictions of the states have been not so much curtailed as the national government has joined with the states in formulating policy. The result is the kind of shared federalism described earlier in this chapter.

A cursory examination of trends in government growth during the twentieth century might raise the question of whether the impact of nationalization on reshaping modern federalism has been overstated here. Today the states employ more workers than ever before, their largest increases occurring since the nationalizing thrust of the New Deal (Figure 3–4). Paradoxically, state governments have grown because of, rather than despite, nationalization. Just as the New Deal grafted national policy onto state administrations, much of federal domestic policy continues to be implemented through the states instead of directly through the federal bureaucracy.

The national government has developed two ways to induce cooperation from the constitutionally independent states: the carrot and the stick. The carrot consists of financial inducements, usually in the form of grants to states. The stick is regulation and mandates. Over the last two decades, chronic federal budget deficits have led national politicians to rely more heavily on the stick to achieve their policy objectives; in this way they can pass the costs on to the states.

The Carrot: Federal Grants to the States

Although federal aid dates back to the Articles of Confederation when the national government doled out pub-

Figure 3–4 Federal, State, and Local Government Employees, 1946–1995

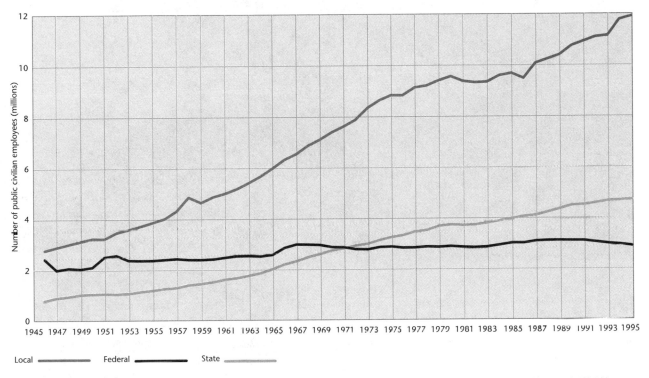

Local ━━━━━   Federal ━━━━━   State ━━━━━

Sources: 1949, 1952, 1954, 1959, 1964, 1969–1988: U.S. Advisory Commission on Intergovernmental Relations, *Significant Features of Fiscal Federalism, 1990,* vol. 2 (Washington, D.C.: U.S. Advisory Commission on Intergovernmental Relations, 1990), 177; 1989–1992: *1994,* 151; other years: U.S. Bureau of the Census, *Historical Statistics of the United States,* Series Y189–198 (Washington, D.C.: U.S. Government Printing Office, 1975), 1100; Bureau of the Census, Statistical Abstract of the United States: 1998 (Washington, D.C.: Government Printing Office, 1998), Table 530.

lic lands to the states, only during the last half-century have federal **grants-in-aid** become an important feature of intergovernmental relations. By one count, only a handful of such programs existed before the New Deal; today they number in the hundreds. All of these programs enlist **categorical grants,** in which federal dollars are tied to particular programs, or categories, of spending.

Although after World War II the depression was well behind the nation, federal grant programs were not dismantled. Reacting to this dramatic expansion of federal responsibilities, two Republican presidents, Richard Nixon (1969–1974) and Ronald Reagan (1981–1989), sought to restructure intergovernmental relations by relying on different kinds of grants. In 1973 President Nixon intro-

duced **revenue sharing** as a way of returning policy making to the states. Unlike grants-in-aid, revenue sharing was based on a state's size and wealth and came with few obligations. Because these grants did not replace categorical commitments, the Democratic Congress accepted the concept—at least until the steep federal budget deficits of the 1980s sharply curtailed and then ended the program.

Another alternative favored by Republican administrations is the **block grant.** Like categorical grants, funds are appropriated to achieve a particular policy goal with specific administrative procedures. But in contrast to categorical grants, the policy targets are only generally stated—such as improving maternal and child health services and responding to high unemployment—and fewer strings are

In 1862 Congress, though preoccupied with turmoil of the Civil War, established federal support for land-grant colleges. Today these institutions, built with the proceeds from the sale of early federal land grants to the states, are among the nation's finest universities. Here students plow the campus of Pennsylvania State University, one of the first land-grant colleges.

attached. Neither Nixon nor Reagan embraced block grants simply to restore the traditional equilibrium in federal–state relations. Rather, they sought to decouple federal dollars from the liberal social policies enacted during past Democratic administrations. (This strategy for reducing social policies was dramatically evident in the welfare reforms passed by the Republican 104th Congress in 1995–1997.[30]) Although in the end both presidents achieved modest success in loosening federal supervision of state policy, block grants have never endangered categorical aid as the way the federal government does business with the states. In 1978 nearly 25 percent of all federal aid was delivered in block grants. By the 1990s this figure had fallen to about 10 percent. So why is the federal government so fond of categorical grants? The answer is easy. Those appropriating the money want to have a say in how it is spent. Having prevailed in the legislative struggle to create and finance a new federal program, the victors and their supporters have no incentive to allow state politicians to design it.[31]

In the early 1990s the federal government, seeking to promote a more comprehensive approach to homeless-

ness in America's cities, consolidated six categorical grants into a single block grant program. Under this program, the Department of Health and Human Services evaluates proposals submitted by the cities and funds those that qualify. The guidelines for evaluation prescribe that the local government work closely with local social service providers and interested groups. In practice, however, this prescription gives these special constituencies a veto over proposals. In Washington, D.C., for example, officials had their proposal held up for two years because a local, militant homeless rights organization demanded greater financial commitment by the city before endorsing it. Perhaps the lesson learned from this story is that the decisions surrounding apportionment of federal funds within a community best rest with its local elected officials who are uniquely able to survey citizen demands for services and apportion limited resources to provide them. Any move to shift such decisions to federal agencies undermines the abilities of mayors and other key officials to act as brokers among the constituencies that make up a community.

The Stick: Unfunded Mandates

Until the 1960s the only federal regulations applied to the states were those governing the routine reporting and accounting for grants.[32] Since then, Washington has relied increasingly on rules to pursue policy objectives. Not only are states required to administer policies they might object to, but, adding insult to injury, the federal government may not even compensate the states for the costs of administration.

The national government uses four basic methods to prescribe state policy and supervise its administration: cross-cutting requirements, crossover sanctions, direct orders, and partial preemption. The states have challenged each before the Supreme Court and lost. Taken together, these methods allow the national government to create new state responsibilities, stipulate eligibility requirements, and monitor the implementation and enforcement of these requirements. In many areas of social policy, such as welfare and medical care for the indigent, the states have, until recently, acted as little more than extensions of the federal bureaucracy.

Cross-cutting requirements are statutes that apply certain rules and guidelines to a broad array of federally subsidized state programs. Since the 1960s this device has been used widely to enforce civil rights laws. For example, the failure of any state to follow federal guidelines that prohibit discriminatory employment practices can result in prosecution of state officials as well as loss of grants. Another prominent area of cross-cutting requirements is the environment. All state programs that include major construction and changes in land use must file environmental impact statements with the federal government.

Crossover sanctions are stipulations that a state, to remain eligible for full federal funding for one program, must adhere to the guidelines of an unrelated program. One example, mentioned earlier, is Congress's stipulation that federal highway funds be tied to state adoption of a minimum drinking age of twenty-one. Similarly, the Education for All Handicapped Children Act requires that

The welfare reform law of 1996 returned the primary administrative controls for welfare to the states by transforming some welfare programs such as Aid to Families with Dependent Children (AFDC) from categorical to block grants. The federal government is still in the picture, however. Among other things, it created a Welfare to Work program that includes training and day care grants for the states and tax breaks to the companies that hire welfare recipients. This former welfare recipient is now a supervisor at United Parcel Service.

states and their school districts offer prescribed levels of special education in order to maintain their eligibility for a variety of subsidies ranging from school construction to teacher training.

National politicians frequently find crossover sanctions irresistible in trying to influence state policies beyond their jurisdiction. In 1994 Senator Patrick Leahy, Democrat of Vermont, proposed legislation banning the sale of soft drinks on public school campuses, and California Democratic Senator Dianne Feinstein introduced a bill requiring that all students caught entering school with a handgun be suspended for a minimum of one year. Both bills provided for a cutoff in school aid funds if the districts failed to comply.

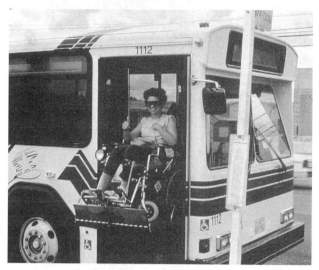

The only controversial feature of the 1990 Americans with Disabilities Act was the way in which Congress implemented it. Imposing a classic unfunded mandate, it required businesses and state and local governments to follow strict national standards and bear the full expense of redesigning curbs, access to buildings, public transportation services, restrooms, and the like.

Direct orders are requirements that can be enforced by legal and civil penalties. The Clean Water Act, for example, bans ocean dumping of sewage sludge. In 1996, when the city of San Diego resisted a multibillion-dollar investment in a sophisticated sewage treatment facility that would alleviate the problem, the Environmental Protection Agency brought suit in federal court to impose punitive financial penalties on the city.

Certain federal laws allow the states to administer joint federal–state programs so long as they conform to federal guidelines—a practice known as *partial preemption*. If a state agency fails to follow the instructions of federal agencies, the state might lose control of the program altogether; alternatively, federal grants might be suspended via crossover regulations. A good example of this form of federal regulation is state air pollution policies. Public law and the Environmental Protection Agency set minimally acceptable standards, but enforcement of these standards rests mostly with state agencies.

Hardly any area of state policy is unaffected by federal regulations of one kind or another. A close look at the major federal laws listed in Table 3–2 reveals several interesting trends and characteristics. First, although federal grants were plentiful prior to the 1970s, few regulatory policies were in place. Second, since the 1970s the more coercive forms of regulation—direct orders and partial preemption—have been favored. Finally, the content of the policies reveals the political process that produced them. Federal regulation of the states is concentrated in the domains of civil rights and the environment—the two sectors in which national majorities are likely to be at odds with state majorities. The same policy disagreements also may explain why coercion is such a favored policy instrument today. Regulatory statutes compel states to administer policies they would spurn if federal regulations did not legally require their compliance.

When members of Congress pass a law that obligates the states to provide particular services, they are yielding to a temptation all politicians share: the desire to respond to some citizens' demands without imposing costs on others. In forcing the states to pay for a program, members are imposing costs for which they will not be held accountable. Like the grants process, mandates deprive state political representatives of their rightful decision-making authority. Of greater concern to fiscal conservatives, unfunded mandates increase government spending. In 1995 President Bill Clinton and the Republican Congress agreed to rein in future temptations to "spend" the states' revenues; the result was the Unfunded Mandates Reform Act. A 1998 study, however, found that the new law was exerting minimal constraint on mandates.[33] Perhaps the temptation to respond to demands for services while avoiding costs overwhelms the ideologies of even conservative politicians. In any event, Table 3–3 shows that the Republican Congress has continued to enact preemptive and mandate legislation.

Table 3–2 Examples of Major Unfunded Mandates

Public Law	Kind of Mandate
Davis-Bacon Act (1931) — Assured that locally prevailing wages were paid to construction workers employed under federal contracts and assistance programs.	Cross-cutting
Hatch Act (1940) — Prohibited public employees from engaging in certain political activities.	Cross-cutting
Civil Rights Act of 1964 (Title VI) — Prevented discrimination on the basis of race, color, or national origin in federally assisted programs.	Cross-cutting
Age Discrimination in Employment Act (1967) — Prevented discrimination on the basis of age in federally assisted programs.	Cross-cutting
Clean Air Act Amendments of 1970 — Established national air quality and emissions standards.	Cross-cutting, crossover sanctions, partial preemption
Occupational Safety and Health Act (1970) — Set standards for safe and healthful working conditions.	Partial preemption
Endangered Species Act of 1973 — Protected and conserved endangered and threatened animal and plant species.	Cross-cutting, partial preemption
Fair Labor Standards Act Amendments of 1974 — Extended federal minimum wage and overtime pay protections to state and local government employees.	Direct order
Education for All Handicapped Children Act (1975) — Provided a free appropriate public education to all handicapped children.	Crossover sanctions
Hazardous and Solid Waste Amendments of 1984 — Reauthorized and strengthened scope and enforcement of the Resource Conservation and Recovery Act of 1976; established program to regulate underground storage tanks for petroleum and hazardous substances; required annual EPA inspections of state and locally operated hazardous waste sites.	Partial preemption
Asbestos Hazard Emergency Response Act of 1986 — Directed school districts to inspect for asbestos hazards and take the necessary actions to protect health and the environment; required state review and approval of local management response plans.	Direct order
Americans with Disabilities Act (1990) — Established comprehensive national standards to prohibit discrimination in public services and accommodations and to promote handicapped access to public buildings and transportation.	Cross-cutting, direct order
Clean Air Act Amendments of 1990 — Imposed strict new deadlines and requirements dealing with urban smog, municipal incinerators, and toxic emissions; enacted program for controlling acid rain.	Partial preemption
National Voter Registration Act of 1993 — Required states to provide all eligible citizens the chance to register to vote when they apply for renewal of their driver's license.	Direct order

Sources: Advisory Commission on Intergovernmental Relations and various issues of *Congressional Quarterly Weekly Report.*

Table 3–3 Federal Statutes Enacted in 1997 Imposing Mandate or Preemption

Name or Topic	Preemption or Mandate
Airport and Airway Trust Fund Tax Reinstatement Act	Requires state and local governments to pay tax on airline travel
Bank branches	Preempts state bank laws related to out-of-state branches
Charitable Donation Antitrust Immunity Act	Preempts state antitrust laws related to certain charities
Balanced Budget Act	Includes multiple mandates related to Medicare, tax preemptions, legal aliens and Supplemental Security Income, requirements on District of Columbia government
Labor and Health and Human Services Appropriations Bill for Fiscal Year 1997	Prohibits states from requiring standardized testing of private school students
National Defense Authorization Act for Fiscal Year 1998	Exempts Department of Defense workers from certain state medical licensing requirements
Adoption Promotion Act	Requires states to make changes to foster care programs
Veterans benefits	Preempts state taxing authority for private facilities on Department of Veterans Affairs property
Food and drug regulation	Preempts state cosmetic and drug laws
Amtrak reform and accountability	Preempts state and local taxes on Amtrak tickets

Source: L. Nye Stevens, "Unfunded Mandates—Reform Act Has Had Little Effect on Agencies' Rulemaking Actions, Report to the Committee on Governmental Affairs, U.S. Senate," General Accounting Office, Washington, D.C., 1998.

Federalism: A Byproduct of National Policy

No feature of American government has undergone a more dramatic transformation during the twentieth century than federal–state relations. In some instances, special interests have pressed for national action when they have failed to win in the states. In other instances, the states have invited federal participation so that they can either seek federal funding to bankroll their programs or to solve their own collective action problems. By shifting regulations and programs to Washington, states can avoid cutthroat competition and free riding by their neighbors.

The nationalization of public policy that proceeded from these causes did not arise from some grand design. Rather, it proceeded incrementally as politicians sought to solve problems and serve constituencies. No one had an interest in trying to rationalize intergovernmental relations or wrest authority away from the states. In this sense, then, modern federalism is not so much a product of constitutional revision as it is a byproduct of national policy. And if the behavior of recent presidents and Congresses is any indication, it will continue to evolve in this direction, despite their sincere declarations that they will stop issuing mandates to the states. Finally, some of the most important contributions to the development of federalism in America came not through largely transparent, incremental change but through brief bursts of national policy in which the federal government assumed jurisdiction and responsibility for large sectors of public policy once reserved to the states. President Roosevelt's New Deal response to the depression and President Johnson's Great Society initiatives against poverty in America are two notable examples. It is instructive that both occurred when the same party (Democratic) controlled the White House and enjoyed the largest majorities in Congress ever seen in the twentieth century.

In Chapter 4 we turn to a series of national decisions that even more dramatically refashioned federalism in America. The issue is civil rights for African Americans. The Civil War, Reconstruction, and the civil rights movement of the 1960s all required the vigorous national action against entrenched state policies instituting slavery and, later, segregation. The result was a decisive victory for civil rights—initially for African Americans and more recently for numerous other groups—and defeat for assertions of states' rights.

Key Terms

block grant / 81

categorical grant / 81

commerce clause / 71

dual federalism / 64

elastic clause / 78

enumerated powers / 77

federalism / 63

grants-in-aid / 81

nullification / 78

preemption legislation / 80

revenue sharing / 81

shared federalism / 65

unitary government / 63

Suggested Readings

Beer, Samuel H. *To Make a Nation: The Rediscovery of American Federalism*. Cambridge, Mass.: Belknap Press of Harvard University Press, 1993. Beer reviews the history of American federalism, its roots in traditional republican theory, and its modern evolution.

Campbell, Ballard C. *The Growth of American Government: Governance from the Cleveland Era to the Present*. Bloomington: Indiana University Press, 1995. Another historical survey of nationalization during the late nineteenth and twentieth centuries, which focuses almost exclusively on the national government.

Lowry, William R. *The Dimensions of Federalism: State Governments and Pollution Control Policies*. Durham, N.C.: Duke University Press, 1992. A careful study of shared federalism in national water pollution policy. Lowry finds a stronger state presence in providing this public good than is commonly assumed.

Peterson, Paul E., Barry G. Rabe, and Kenneth K. Wong. *When Federalism Works*. Washington, D.C.: Brookings, 1986. A thorough and authoritative study of modern federalism in America.

Skowronek, Stephen. *Building a New American State: The Expansion of National Administrative Capacities, 1877–1920*. New York: Cambridge University Press, 1982. A modern classic on the institutional conflicts involved in shifting the center of public policy from the states to Washington.

Wiebe, Robert H. *The Search for Order, 1877–1920*. New York: Hill and Wang, 1967. An authoritative, well-written historical survey of the nationalization of American life.

Chapter 4

CIVIL RIGHTS

★ *How could a nation that embraced the Declaration of Independence's creed that "all men are created equal" condone slavery?*

★ *Why would a majority in society ever seek to extend and protect the rights of its minorities in the face of huge costs—even those imposed by a tragic civil war?*

★ *Has America's constitutional system impeded or promoted the cause of civil rights?*

★ *Why, after nearly a century of segregation and disenfranchisement, did the civil rights revolution burst onto the national scene in the 1960s and in short order succeed in dismantling segregation throughout the South?*

On November 21, 1997, the Piscataway, New Jersey, school board announced it had settled an eight-year-long lawsuit with one of its teachers. Although the Supreme Court had agreed to hear the case within two months, the teacher decided to drop her suit in return for a $433,500 settlement. On its face, the case seemed to be no more than a typical employment discrimination lawsuit—one of many court cases stemming from claims of racial or sex discrimination or **reverse discrimination,** the unfair loss of a job because of **affirmative action** (preferential hiring practices). The Piscataway case, arising from familiar circumstances, belonged in the reverse discrimination category. Its abrupt conclusion with a settlement, however, is highly peculiar and reveals the strategies employed by both sides in the present-day politics over civil rights.

The case dated back to 1989 when the Piscataway school board, facing a budget shortfall, decided to lay off one of its business administration teachers. The lowest-seniority positions were occupied by two women—one white, one black—who had been hired on the same day in 1980. After reviewing their files and finding the women equally qualified for the position, the school board laid off the white teacher. It cited the need for diversity within its teaching staff; at the time 30 percent of the students enrolled in the business program—but only one of the ten business teachers—were African American. The white teacher went to court charging illegal reverse discrimination. Although she was rehired in 1992, she continued to press her lawsuit to gain back pay and legal fees.

The lawsuit charged that racial preference had been inappropriately applied in this instance. A coin toss to determine which teacher to retain would have been fairer, lawyers for the white teacher argued. The Piscataway school board, however, seemed to be on solid ground. Although it had never been accused of practicing discrimination for which racial preference might serve as an appropriate remedy, some federal courts had shown a willingness to condone hiring preferences in the name of diversity. Universities were employing affirmative action to provide "educational enrichment." Some urban police departments, seeking to improve community relations, also were using affirmative action when hiring and promoting officers. Ostensibly, then, the school board, in enlisting diversity, was following a widely established practice. So why did it settle?

This is where the case took an unusual and instructive turn. The school board's attorneys appeared eager to test their case before the Supreme Court, but they were importuned by various national civil rights organizations to quit the case. These organizations feared the school board would lose and that, with its decision, the Supreme Court might take the opportunity to strike a sweeping blow against diversity as an appropriate justification for affirmative action. They noted that in recent decisions the mostly Republican-appointed Court had been shifting to more conservative ground on civil rights issues. During 1997 it had let stand, and thereby tacitly endorsed, blows to affirmative action from lower courts. Some civil rights leaders believed the only way to preserve some semblance of legitimacy for the diversity standard was to settle, in effect taking the case out of the Court's hands. Indeed, the Piscataway case was the only affirmative action case on the Supreme Court's 1997–1998 docket. Settling the case would at least buy those supporting affirmative action another year, with the possibility that one of the conservative justices might retire and a more compelling case might appear on the docket.

Civil rights organizations backed up their request with an offer to pay 70 percent of the settlement. Throughout the fall the civil rights leader Jesse Jackson had discreetly appealed to sympathetic donors who anonymously con-

tributed from $1,000 to $5,000 each to the settlement fund. In the end, then, the white teacher "won" her case and settlement—not from the school board but from those civil rights organizations who had opposed her suit. Conservative groups, who similarly sensed that an important victory was at hand, were upset. "I'd like to think that if I were embroiled in a major constitutional case, I'd have the fortitude to see it through," complained the spokesperson of the Independent Women's Forum which previously had filed a "friend of the court" brief against affirmative action.[1] Having already set the docket for their session, the Supreme Court justices must have looked on ruefully as well. Their only opportunity for the year to review affirmative action had just slipped away.

This nondecision is noteworthy because of the way its potential impact was nipped by a carefully calculated, strategic *political* maneuver. Americans may not associate civil rights with politics, yet politics is the chief mechanism available to them for collectively defining and pursuing civil rights. Indeed, these rights represent society's most basic and controversial collective choices about the rules that govern how classes of citizens relate to one another. James Madison, who understood these choices only too well, prescribed factional competition for keeping a majority of the citizens in a democracy from tyrannizing a minority. This chapter, then, follows Madison closely in locating the course of civil rights in America as a product of its political process.

What Are Civil Rights?

Throughout the nation's history, Americans have applied the term **civil rights** to a variety of rights and privileges. In colonial times civil rights took the form of "civic" rights—protections against arbitrary action by the distant British crown. Although the term *civil rights* did not enter common usage until the late 1860s, colonial Americans were clearly thinking about these rights when they rallied to the slogan "No taxation without representation." Thomas Jefferson's eloquent statement in the Declaration of Independence that all governments must defer to mankind's "unalienable Rights" of "Life, Liberty and the pursuit of Happiness" gave the Revolutionary War its moral certitude.

Once they had gained their independence and established republican institutions, Americans turned from seeking protection from an arbitrary and distant government to looking for protection from one another. In *Federalist* No. 10 Madison entertained the possibility that a majority of citizens could use government authority to gain a permanent advantage by stripping adversaries of their rights. This prospect bothered leaders on both sides of the Constitution's ratification issue. For Madison and the other nationalists, the pluralism offered by a large republic provided the best insurance against such factionally inspired tyranny. But Patrick Henry and others opposing ratification insisted on a Bill of Rights to further deter the new national government from usurping power. Along with voting (an issue the Constitution already had resolved by allowing the states to set voting requirements), freedom of speech, free assembly, and a free press appeared on virtually everyone's list of freedoms being proposed in Congress for the new Bill of Rights.

Modern-day "civil rights" encompass much more than these "civic" rights of political expression and participation. They also include safeguards against any effort by government and dominant groups in a community to subjugate another group and take unfair, mostly economic, advantage of it. In the slavery era, southern governments teamed up with white slave owners to configure state laws and institutions to legalize and preserve this tyranny. In most southern states, for example, it was illegal for slave masters to free their slaves. Many decades later, segregation in the South, also regulated by the states, was applied to virtually all interpersonal contact between the races. Civil rights, then, also include the rights of individuals in their relations with one another: to live free from bondage and intimidation, to enter into contracts and own property, and to have access to businesses that serve the public and equal educational opportunities, among many other things.

A closely related set of principles and issues, known as **civil liberties,** defines the fundamental personal freedoms that lie beyond government interference. Freedom of speech, freedom of religion, and the right to privacy are examples of civil liberties. Typically, violations of these liberties occur when some government agency, at any level, oversteps its authority. For example, for years the courts have consistently ruled that a school district's practice of opening each school day with recitation of the Lord's Prayer infringes on the religious freedom of those students and their families who worship a different god or none at all. Likewise, when a majority of citizens or some governmental entity decides that a particular behavior—such as flag burning, assisted suicides, or nude dancing—is objectionable and seeks to suppress it, the court battles begin.

Definitions and lists help to distinguish between civil rights and civil liberties, but when the private behavior of a class of people is the object of judicial scrutiny, the boundary between these concepts can become ambiguous and arbitrary. The controversial abortion rights issue falls in this category. On the one hand, the Supreme Court has ruled that a woman's decision to have an abortion is protected by an implicit constitutional right to privacy—that is, the right to an abortion is a civil liberty. On the other hand, abortion policy affects women as a class and so is debated and reported as a civil rights issue. Chapter 5 examines the state of civil liberties in America.

The Civil Rights of African Americans

In December 1997 Bill Lann Lee, a second-generation Chinese American, opened his acceptance statement as President Bill Clinton's acting assistant attorney general for civil rights by characterizing his post as one "haunted by the ghosts of slavery, the Civil War, Jim Crow." He then proceeded to cite modern instances of racial, ethnic,

Do not look at the Negro.

His earthly problems are ended.

Instead, look at the seven WHITE children who gaze at this gruesome spectacle.

Is it horror or gloating on the face of the neatly dressed seven-year-old girl on the right?

Is the tiny four-year-old on the left old enough, one wonders, to comprehend the barbarism her elders have perpetrated?

Rubin Stacy, the Negro, who was lynched at Fort Lauderdale, Florida, on July 19, 1935, for "threatening and frightening a white woman," suffered PHYSICAL torture for a few short hours. But what psychological havoc is being wrought in the minds of the white children? Into what kinds of citizens

Between 1882 and 1950, 4,729 lynchings were reported in the United States. African Americans were the victims in about three-quarters of cases. In the 1930s the NAACP graphically featured this tyrannical practice designed to intimidate the entire black population.

and religious discrimination.[2] Indeed, as Lee knew and the history books describe, African Americans have been engaged in a two-hundred-year struggle for civil rights—a struggle that has spanned slavery to full citizenship. As we shall see in this chapter and the next, the results have redefined the rights and liberties of *all* Americans.

A more theoretical reason for concentrating on the history of black civil rights is that it contains all of the essen-tial ingredients for testing James Madison's ideas on democracy in America, laid out in his *Federalist* essays. The treatment of African Americans in the South before the civil rights victories of the 1960s corresponded closely to the factional tyranny Madison warned against in *Federalist* No. 10. Dominant white majorities throughout the South instituted slavery—and later segregation—to gain a permanent advantage over the black minority. And what is the solution to such tyranny? As Madison argued, a diverse national community will be less inclined than state-level majorities to engage in tyranny and more inclined to halt it.

The history of African American civil rights may follow the broad contours of Madison's script, but one fact is unsettling to his theory: slavery and then segregation with their myriad abuses endured almost two centuries before the national majority struck out against local tyranny. Several factors related to institutions and their effects on democracy shed light on this fact. For one thing, the Framers, instead of providing for a national veto over all state laws, as Madison had proposed, ceded in the Constitution a broad, exclusive jurisdiction to the states. In the South, slavery and later segregation flourished within that jurisdiction. The Constitution also originally called for members of the Senate to represent the interests of the majority in the state legislature that elected them. Had some oracle told Madison that the Constitution would occasionally fail to protect citizens' civil rights, he surely would have pointed an accusing finger first at the states and then at the Senate.[3]

African Americans, then, faced two obstacles in securing rights. The first was the Constitution itself. It reserves important authority for the states, such as determining voting eligibility, and separates powers among the three branches of government, making it difficult for national majorities to control the national government to the extent required to strike against tyranny in the states.

Madison's observation that "Men are not angels" sums up the second obstacle facing efforts to secure civil rights for African Americans. People do not engage in costly behavior without some expected return. Madison, recognizing that citizens and politicians alike act most forcefully when they have a personal stake in the outcome, believed that tyranny could best be avoided by empowering every faction to look out for its own interests. But what becomes of the faction that does not possess the capacity to defend itself? This predicament is at the heart of the nation's long ordeal over civil rights for African Americans. Indeed, the politics of self-interest in a fragmented constitutional system largely answers the question of why it took so long to eradicate slavery, segregation, and other forms of discrimination. Instead, the real question is why they were ever addressed at all.

The Politics of Black Civil Rights

Over the decades, efforts to seek civil rights for African Americans have taken different forms at different times. From well before the 1787 Constitutional Convention until the emancipation of black slaves during the Civil War, a small but persistent abolitionist movement forced the nation to face the discrepancy between its creed "Life, Liberty and the pursuit of Happiness" and the enslavement of 10 percent of its population.[4] Emancipation shifted the issue from fundamental "life and liberty" rights to those of full citizenship.[5] Several years later former slaves gained the right to vote through the Fifteenth Amendment,[6] but another century would pass before most could safely exercise this right. With civic rights secured, the dominant issue again shifted, this time to equal opportunity in the marketplace—particularly in education, employment, and housing.

By and large, national majorities have over the decades consistently favored the cause of civil rights for blacks, but only twice did they strike out forcefully against the sources of discrimination. The first was Reconstruction after the Civil War; the second was the national attack on segregation in the 1960s. Why were rights advanced at these particular moments in American history and not at

others? A look at the occasions of success and of failure will reveal the answer to this question and shed light on the conditions that must be satisfied for national majorities to dictate national policy.

The Height of Slavery: 1808–1865

Late in 1807, with the Constitution's prohibition against regulation of the slave trade about to expire, Congress passed a law ending the importation of slaves. Southern representatives in Congress, not yet aware that the rise of "King Cotton" would soon place a premium on a slave-centered, plantation economy, did not vigorously contest the new law. In fact, some of their slave-owning constituents probably anticipated that the restricted supply might drive up the market value of their human property. Thus the nation took its first step toward civil rights for African Americans with deceptive ease. It would never be easy again.

Over the next decade slavery remained off center stage, but only because the northern and southern states carefully maintained regional balance in the Senate, thereby preserving the South's veto over national policy. Balance was achieved by matching states' entry—one slave state with one free state—into the Union. Although many northerners found slavery objectionable, they were not prepared to press for its eradication. Indeed, the conventional wisdom in the North seemed to be that slavery would eventually wither away.

Then in 1819 the citizens of Missouri, most of whom had emigrated from the slave states of Kentucky and Tennessee, petitioned Congress for admission as a slave state. Instead of shriveling up, slavery was threatening to expand beyond its southern borders and become a national cancer. "Like a fire bell in the night," wrote Thomas Jefferson from retirement, this prospect "awakened and filled me with terror."[7]

After months of debate in Washington and throughout the country, Congress enacted the Missouri Compromise in 1820. The plan matched Missouri's entry as a slave state with Maine's entry as a free state, thereby maintain-

Figure 4–1 The Missouri Compromise and the State of the Union, 1820

Closed to slavery by Missouri Compromise

Open to slavery by Missouri Compromise

Free states and territories

Slave states and territories

Source: Mary B. Norton et al., *People and a Nation: A History of the United States,* 2 vols., 5th ed. (Boston: Houghton Mifflin, 1987), 1: 250.

ing a balance in the Senate between free and slave states. Moreover, the South agreed to accept Missouri's southern border as the northern boundary beyond which slavery could not extend in the future (Figure 4–1). The boundary, known as the Mason–Dixon line (after the English surveyors Charles Mason and Jeremiah Dixon who had established these early colonial borders), stretched to the end of the Louisiana Territory, where Spain's territories began. Once again, slavery appeared to be fenced in. The compromise itself was a classic "political" solution—one that was not entirely satisfactory to either side but that allowed the competing sides to agree to a national policy applicable to the foreseeable future.

For the next decade or so this compromise worked. As each side became dissatisfied with the results, however, it began to unravel. Territories applying for statehood did not conveniently pair off as slave states and free states, and each statehood petition threatened the agreement. Gradually, southern senators realized that, under the current formula, their ability to block national policy was doomed: continued westward expansion would result in more free states than slave states joining the Union. Thus they began searching for an effective alternative to their Senate veto—an alternative that would allow them to ensure continuation of the institution of slavery.

Meanwhile, the containment strategy also was losing favor in the North, where a small but highly vocal group of abolitionists had never accepted the compromise. More broadly, the abolitionist movement, under the banner of the Liberty Party, reminded the nation of its hypocrisy in condoning slavery. Although few voters would endorse the outright eradication of slavery, they were angry about slavery's territorial expansion. After its recent war with Mexico, the nation had annexed territory in the southwest, almost all of it falling into the slavery zone. Moreover, California was petitioning for statehood and southerners were proposing that the Mason–Dixon line be projected to the Pacific Ocean and California be split into two states—one slave, one free.

In 1846 David Wilmot, a Democratic representative from Pennsylvania, introduced a bill that would have gutted the compromise by banning slavery in the recently acquired territories. Asked to explain his position on the slavery issue, Wilmot denied any "squeamish sensitivities" or "morbid sympathy for the slave." Rather, he professed devotion to "the rights of white freemen . . . [and] white free labor."[8] The issue was simply this: the presence of slaves depressed wages. The Wilmot Proviso was introduced twice and passed the House of Representatives both times, but it made no headway in the still evenly divided Senate. All was not lost, however. The political considerations surrounding the failure of Wilmot's proposal eventually led significant numbers of northern whites to recognize they had a stake in containing slavery.

By 1848 Wilmot's allies had joined the abolitionists in the new antislavery Free Soil Party. Its election slate that year was headed by presidential candidate Martin Van Buren who already had served one term as president, elected on the Democratic ticket in 1836. His 1848 campaign re-

volved around a single issue: opposition to the extension of slavery in behalf of "free labor." The Free Soil Party managed to scare the two major political parties, the Democrats and the Whigs, by winning 10 percent of the national popular vote and finishing second in several states. Six years later the Free Soil Party joined a broader coalition against slavery's extension that called itself the Republican Party.

The year 1850 saw the Missouri Compromise collapse under the weight of southern and northern grievances. Southerners complained that runaway slaves who reached the North via the underground railroad—a network of abolitionists who hid slaves and provided them with transportation northward—were not being returned to their owners. At the same time, northerners were repulsed by the presence of slave auctions in Washington, D.C., "within the shadow of the Capitol." But the final straw was California's 1849 application for admission to the Union as a free state. If the South agreed to admit California, it would lose its ability to block legislation in the Senate. Ultimately the South did agree, but only in return for passage of the Fugitive Slave Law compelling northerners to honor southerners' property claims to slaves. Moreover, the new Compromise of 1850, introduced by the aging Whig senator Henry Clay of Kentucky, allowed the residents of the territories to decide for themselves whether to apply for statehood as a slave state or a free state.

The South may have lost its Senate veto, but a few years later it would unexpectedly acquire a new one. In 1857 the Supreme Court delivered one of its most unfortunate decisions in *Dred Scott v. Sandford*.[9] With every justice writing a separate opinion, a narrow 5–4 majority of the Court concurred that the federal government could not prevent slavery in the territories. The herculean effort to legislate mutually acceptable policy over the previous half-century was undone in a single decision by the nine unelected justices. The mostly southern majority argued that the Constitution's Framers had never intended blacks to be citizens. Consequently, blacks enjoyed "no rights

The Fugitive Slave Law of 1850 forced law enforcement authorities in both the North and South to act as slaveholders' agents in seizing and returning their "property." As this broadside warned, even free blacks were in danger of being seized and sent into slavery as unscrupulous law enforcement officials colluded with slaveholders in making bogus claims that these free citizens were actually runaway slaves.

which a white man was bound to respect," and any federal law that interfered with the right of an individual to his property, including slaves, was unconstitutional. Sympathetic lower-court judges appeared ready to extend the logic of this argument and rule that *state* laws banning slavery also were unconstitutional. The specter of the whole nation being opened to slave holding by judicial fiat galvanized the North. Campaigning vigorously on the is-

sue "Free Soil, Free Labor, Free Men" in the 1860 presidential election, the Republican candidate, Abraham Lincoln, was swept into office. So too were other Republican candidates—so many, in fact, that they enjoyed a commanding majority in the House of Representatives and, in alliance with splinter parties, formed a narrow antislavery majority in the Senate. For the first time in American history, the president and a majority of both houses of Congress were aligned against slavery's extension. The Supreme Court, by a single vote, remained the only roadblock to national action.

Recognizing the inevitable, the South did not linger long once Lincoln announced that the national government would no longer tolerate "the minority [the South] over the majority." South Carolina bolted before Lincoln's inauguration and proclaimed its independence on December 20, 1860. By June 1861 ten more states had left the Union and established a new, confederation-styled government. On April 12, 1861, the "Confederates" fired on Fort Sumter, a federal garrison in Charleston harbor. The Civil War had begun. It would leave more than 600,000 American soldiers dead and many thousands more maimed for life.

Thus the first half-century of racial politics in the United States closely followed Madison's prediction of tyranny in the states unconstrained by national majorities. In the South white majorities enlisted state authority to preserve slavery. They were aided and abetted by their agents in the Senate who, as Madison had warned, succeeded in frustrating national action. Only a decisive Republican victory in 1860 and the exit of the slave states from the Union gave the national majority sufficient control over government to enforce its preferences. Along the way, strategic politicians—men like Wilmot and Lincoln—transformed a losing issue into a winning issue by remaining narrowly focused on the territories and the interests of their constituencies. Because they knew they had the support of abolitionists by default, they ignored this "captive" constituency and appealed to those northern whites more

THE EMANCIPATION PROCLAMATION

Emancipation of the slaves was borne of war rather than politics, but its planning and implementation were nonetheless highly strategic. When read carefully, President Abraham Lincoln's Emancipation Proclamation, issued in the fall of 1862, appears to have been composed more with an eye to encouraging southern defections from the Confederacy than to emancipating slaves. Lincoln announced that slaves would be freed in those states that persisted with the rebellion. Slavery was to remain intact in the border states that had stayed in the Union, and even in those sections of the Confederacy that had fallen under Union control.

This policy exposed the president to the criticism that he had failed to free the slaves where he could and freed them where he could not. But by mapping emancipation this way, he prevented it from becoming politically divisive among the Union states (a few still allowed slave ownership), while simultaneously trying to drive a wedge into the Confederacy. Moreover, the rebel states might have to deal with slaves asserting their freedom. Not until the 1864 presidential campaign did Lincoln openly endorse the universal abolition of slavery.

In 1863 David Gilmour Blythe depicted a homespun Lincoln (his rail-splitter's maul is in the foreground) at work in his study writing the Emancipation Proclamation. Pushed to one side, unheeded, are the states' rights theories of John C. Calhoun and John Randolph. Instead, Lincoln rests his hand on the Holy Bible and heeds Andrew Jackson's call: "The Union Must & Shall Be Preserved."

concerned about their own welfare than that of slaves. In the end, this appeal enabled these politicians to win control of government and eventually eradicate slavery.[10]

Reconstruction: 1865–1877

In the short span of five years, from 1865 to 1870, slaves were formally emancipated (Thirteenth Amendment), granted citizenship (Fourteenth Amendment), and guaranteed the right to vote (Fifteenth Amendment). At the close of the Civil War, however, only a handful of Union states gave black citizens equal access to the ballot box.

Some subjected African Americans to special criteria—such as proof of property ownership and literacy—that effectively disenfranchised most of them. Other northern states simply barred African Americans from voting.[11] For most states, then, freeing slaves and granting them full-fledged citizenship were two different things, and the latter was regarded as radical even by abolitionists.[12] So how did the Fifteenth Amendment manage to clear the formidable hurdles of the amendment process, and do so with remarkable alacrity?

The ability to count is an invaluable asset for a politician. Shortly after the war ended in 1865, House Republican leader Thaddeus Stevens of Pennsylvania began calculating the probable partisan makeup of Congress after the South returned to the Union. Taking into account that blacks now counted as full rather than three-fifths citizens for the purpose of apportioning congressional seats across the states, Stevens estimated that the South would gain thirteen seats over its prewar level.[13] Moreover, with southern legislatures busily enacting laws, called black codes, that would effectively prevent former slaves from voting (and thus from supporting the party of Lincoln), Stevens rightly suspected that all thirteen seats would be added to the Democratic column.[14] Southerners, he noted, "with their kindred Copperheads [Democrats] of the North, would always elect the President [as well as] control Congress."[15]

The outlook, then, was bleak. Even as Andrew Johnson of Tennessee, Lincoln's Democratic successor in the White House, was readying plans for the South's rapid readmission to the Union, congressional Republicans were staring at possible defeat in the next national election.[16] Something had to be done in a hurry. That "something" was Reconstruction; under the watchful eye of federal troops, the South would be transformed from a slave society into a free society where African Americans would fully enjoy the privileges of citizenship. At least that was the plan.

The Fourteenth and Fifteenth Amendments. The Republicans' foray into the unfamiliar business of political and social reconstruction began with the Fourteenth Amendment. It opens with a straightforward definition of citizenship that encompasses former slaves: "All persons born or naturalized in the United States and subject to the jurisdiction thereof, are citizens of the United States and of the State wherein they reside." It then declares that no state shall "deprive any person of life, liberty, or property, without the *due process* of law; nor deny to any person within its jurisdiction the *equal protection* of the laws" (emphasis added). (The full impact of the due process and equal protection clauses on the liberties of all Americans is examined in Chapter 5.)

Section 2 of the Fourteenth Amendment turns to the immediate business of reconstruction. It reaffirms the constitutional prescription of apportioning seats in the House of Representatives according to a state's population, but it then makes an exception: if a state fails to allow black males to vote in federal and state elections, the number of seats allocated to it will be reduced proportionately. The political principle was that the additional seats would be provided only where the Republican Party stood a fighting chance of winning. The amendment was intended to protect two constituencies: African Americans in the South and the Republican majority in Washington. After the war, as before, civil rights rode on the shoulders of partisan, self-interested politics.

But would this adroitly crafted amendment ever find the support it needed? By the time it was sent to the states for ratification, several of the rebel states had, at the urging of President Johnson, already convened new legislatures and applied for readmission to the Union. The new legislatures also had rejected the Fourteenth Amendment, in each instance by nearly unanimous majorities. If their votes counted in the drive for ratification, the Fourteenth Amendment—the legal cornerstone of Reconstruction—would be doomed. Once again, it seemed, the South had found, in a sympathetic president and the Constitution's difficult amendment rules, a couple of veto levers for defeating the national majority.

The Republican majority in Congress, however, held its own formidable assets. First, it attacked President Johnson's sympathy for the enemy and was rewarded with a landslide victory in the 1866 midterm elections. Then, enjoying veto-proof majorities, congressional Republicans devised an ingenious plan to foil southern opposition to the Fourteenth Amendment. The First Reconstruction Act of 1867 disbanded the governments of the southern states (with the exception of Tennessee which already had been readmitted to the Union), thereby voiding their votes against the amendment. It then replaced the state governments with five military districts headed by generals and administered by more than twenty thou-

When a procession of former slaves and Republican politicians were met by a white mob in New Orleans in 1866, one of the bloodiest riots of Reconstruction ensued. The local police joined white rioters, killing thirty-four blacks and two white Republicans.

sand northern troops. To assure ratification once the state governments were reinstituted, the law bluntly extended the vote to all freedmen and withheld it from the white, rebel ex-soldiers. In Louisiana, where the racial composition of the adult male population was roughly equal, black voter registration was soon double that of whites.[17] Then, putting one last nail in the Confederacy's coffin, Congress made readmission to the Union contingent on a state's ratification of the Fourteenth Amendment.

The narrow partisan purpose of Reconstruction also can be found in what the Republican policy omitted. Abolitionists and black leaders had pressed Congress for land reform, and with it a degree of economic independence for slaves from their former masters. Instead, all that the freed slaves got from Congress was the ballot. This prompted Republican cabinet secretary Gideon Welles to conclude cynically, "It is evident that intense partisanship rather than philanthropy is the root of the movement."[18]

Two years later congressional Republicans sought to make the black franchise inviolable by passing and send-

ing to the states the Fifteenth Amendment. Quickly ratified, it simply states, "The right of citizens of the United States to vote shall not be denied or abridged by the United States or by any State on account of race, color, or previous condition of servitude."

Rights Lost: The Failure of Reconstruction. Despite these efforts, Reconstruction's advancement of black civil rights proved temporary. Relying heavily on black support, Republicans maintained control of southern state legislatures for a few years, but white Democrats seized control of Tennessee and Virginia as early as 1869, and by 1877 all of the former Confederate states had reverted to white Democratic control. Once this happened, Reconstruction was doomed and African Americans saw their newly acquired status as freed men and women slide back to one of near servitude.

Power slipped away from African Americans during these years for several reasons. The late 1860s saw the rise of vigilante violence as a political resource. Murderous white riots in New Orleans, Memphis, and other southern cities targeted politically active African Americans and their white allies. In the countryside, the Ku Klux Klan, a secret society of white men seeking to maintain white supremacy, perfected intimidation through selective brutality.

Meanwhile, northern politicians' commitment to Reconstruction was waning. After many Republicans went down to defeat in the 1874 midterm congressional elections, apparently because of an economic recession, the new Democratic majority in the House of Representatives refused to appropriate funds to support the military forces that remained in the South. Constituents wanted their sons returned home. Congress passed additional laws to protect the freed slaves, but because none contained serious enforcement provisions, they offered blacks in the distant South little substantive support. With the rise of the Ku Klux Klan accompanied by the rapid demobilization of the occupying Union Army, the trajectory of southern politics became clear.

Killed by the same short-term partisan considerations that gave birth to it, Reconstruction met its end with the 1876 presidential election. The Democratic candidate, Samuel Tilden, came within one vote of a majority in the electoral college, but in the disputed states of Florida and Louisiana both parties managed to come up with their own favorable vote counts. As a result, the election was thrown into the House of Representatives, where a Republican pledge to end Reconstruction induced southerners to break ranks and support the Republican candidate, Rutherford B. Hayes. In 1877 federal troops pulled out of the South, leaving African Americans at the mercy of their former masters.[19]

During the early post–Civil War years, then, the Constitution presented fewer barriers to majority rule than in any other period in American history. The Republican majority in Congress and the White House—or the "radical Republicans," as their opponents and historians later misnamed them—were able to dictate the terms of the South's readmission to the Union. Yet they opted for a middle course of political reform. Rather than undertake a massive social and economic reconstruction of the South, they limited Reconstruction to making the South Republican, thereby realizing the party's national goals and satisfying the interests of the citizens they represented. Even so, local interests soon rose against the limited reconstruction under way. Twenty thousand war-weary northern sons remained in the South, and the government continued to assess high wartime taxes to achieve in the South what few white citizens anywhere would have tolerated in their own communities—the creation of a sizable black electorate. In the North, voters no longer wanted to sacrifice to solve someone else's problem. Reacting to these sentiments, the Republican majority soon lost the will to act. Full citizenship for African Americans would have to await the emergence of a group of northern politicians whose constituencies favored intervention in race relations in the South. Such a mandate would come, but not for nearly a hundred years.

The Jim Crow Era and Segregation: 1877–1933

In the 1890s **Jim Crow laws** were adopted throughout the South to disenfranchise black citizens and segregate—physically divide—blacks and whites. The result was **segregation** of blacks and whites in their access to schools, hospitals, prisons, public parks, restrooms, housing, and public conveyances. Indeed, hardly any government service or social interaction between the races was unaffected.

But to secure segregation the southern states had to prevent black citizens from voting, and so they did. By the end of the century all southern states had constructed a maze of electoral laws that systematically excluded African Americans from civic life. One commonly employed device was the **white primary,** which excluded African Americans from voting in primary elections. Since winning the Democratic primary in the solidly Democratic South was tantamount to winning the general election, this law effectively disenfranchised southern black voters. Another effective barrier was the **poll tax** levied on all registered voters which typically had to be paid months before the election.

Perhaps the most notorious and effective legal barrier was the **literacy test.** Local white registrars would require prospective voters to read and interpret arcane passages of the state's constitution. Few could satisfy the registrars' rigorous demands, and by 1910 less than 10 percent of black males were voting in the South. These restrictive laws also netted many poor and illiterate whites. Most states, however, provided **grandfather clauses** which exempted from these registration requirements those whose grandfathers had voted before the Civil War.

Without the backing of the Supreme Court, the southern state legislatures would have found it harder to strip away black civil rights. When segregation and disenfranchisement laws were challenged, the Court generally sustained them. Conversely, when federal laws extending rights were challenged, the Court summarily overturned them. The Court based these decisions on a tortuously narrow reading of the Fourteenth and Fifteenth Amendments. Consider this passage from the Fourteenth Amendment: "No State shall make or enforce any law which shall abridge the privileges or immunities of citizens of the United States." The Supreme Court interpreted this clause to mean only that states could not abridge privileges conferred explicitly by the Constitution to the national government such as unrestricted interstate travel and open navigation of rivers. The justices excluded the Bill of Rights from the federal guarantees that applied to the states. Decades later, the Supreme Court would reject this interpretation of the Fourteenth Amendment and rediscover the broad national guarantees this clause provides.[20]

The *coup de grâce* came in 1896 when the Supreme Court, ruling in *Plessy v. Ferguson,* blessed the Jim Crow laws and declared the South's segregation laws constitutional.[21] The case arose when Homer Plessy, who was seven-eighths white, appealed his conviction for having violated Louisiana's segregation law by sitting in a "whites only" railroad car. The Court argued that the Fourteenth Amendment's guarantee of equal protection of the law referred only to "political" equality. If African Americans

Until federal laws in the 1960s banned segregation in public accommodations, the doctrine "separate but equal" pervaded every aspect of social contact between the races throughout the South. The policy differed little from South Africa's recently dismantled apartheid.

were socially inferior to whites, the Court reasoned, laws such as Louisiana's could reflect that inferiority so long as political equality was not compromised. The Court then ruled that government-enforced segregation of the races was constitutional as long as the facilities for blacks and whites were equal. With that ruling, the Court established nationally the **separate but equal doctrine** which officially sanctioned segregation throughout the South.

Why would a mostly Republican-appointed Supreme Court strain to interpret the Fourteenth and Fifteenth Amendments in ways that negated Reconstruction? The answer is a complicated story beyond the bounds of this chapter,[22] but it is clear that, given the broad sweep of the Court's decisions, Republican presidents and members of Congress would have had to change the Constitution or change the Court in order to fulfill the intent of the Fourteenth and Fifteenth Amendments. With the South restored to the Union, neither of these changes was possible.

Eleanor Roosevelt's civil rights activism worked to the advantage of the president. FDR was able to woo African American voters, many of whom had voted Republican (the party of Lincoln) in the 1932 election, without alienating southern Democrats in Congress whose support was essential to sustain his New Deal programs. In serving as her husband's de facto envoy to the black community, the first lady often conveyed her messages through public speeches, here to a black college in Florida. Seated is Mary McLeod Bethune, president of the college and director of Negro affairs for the National Youth Administration, a New Deal federal agency.

Democratic Party Sponsorship of Civil Rights: 1933–1940s

From 1929 until 1933 the Republican Party presided over the worst depression in American history. Among the many victims of these economic hard times was the party itself. The Great Depression ended the party's dominance in national politics for the next half-century. Ironically, while the rest of the nation was abandoning the Republican incumbent, Herbert Hoover, in favor of Democrat Franklin Roosevelt, most black voters were sticking with their party's ticket in the presidential election of 1932, despite being hit harder by the Great Depression than any group of Americans. (By 1936, however, three-

quarters of blacks had been won over to Roosevelt's reelection.) Today, the appeal of mostly liberal Democratic politicians to black voters appears quite natural, requiring no special explanation. It is a partnership, however, that took nearly three decades to establish.

Both sides first had to break enduring ties that pulled in opposing directions. For black voters, Emancipation and Reconstruction had attracted them to the Republican Party, and Democratic politicians had done nothing in the intervening years to prompt them to question their partisanship. But it was a loyalty rooted more in habit than reward and thus susceptible to a Democratic appeal. For Democratic politicians, any effort to take up the cause of African Americans was fraught with risk. Ever since its return to the Union, the South had provided the Democratic Party with the electoral base it needed to compete nationally. Northern Democratic members of Congress had long depended on the automatic victories of their southern colleagues to win majority control of Congress. Democratic presidential candidates could count on the South's large bloc of electoral votes. All they had to do was ignore segregation, just as their counterparts before the war had sought to ignore slavery.

The New Deal. Neither Franklin Roosevelt's winning electoral campaign in 1932 nor his "New Deal" to pull the nation out of the depression overtly championed the cause of African Americans. Both did, however, alter political circumstances in a way that prompted black Americans and Democratic politicians to contemplate their mutual interests. When pressed, Roosevelt refused to battle southern Democratic senators for passage of popular antilynching legislation, privately citing his need to maintain friendly relations with southern Democrats in order to enact his emergency economic policies.[23] Yet the New Deal's even-handed treatment of the black community appealed to African American voters. Many of its programs offered blacks government assistance for the first time since Reconstruction. (Other programs, however, such as Social Security, excluded many low-income occupations that were disproportionately black.) Federal authorities investigated racial discrimination in the distribution of relief aid, especially prevalent in the South, and largely rooted it out. Roosevelt also appointed over a hundred black administrators, some of them to prominent posts. Finally, the Justice Department rejuvenated its long-dormant civil liberties division.

Following the White House initiative, congressional Democrats added nondiscrimination language to a score of public laws creating federal programs. In 1941 Roosevelt issued an executive order banning employment discrimination in federal agencies, and he established the Committee on Fair Employment Practices to enforce nondiscrimination in defense-related industries. These measures, requiring that African Americans be treated as ordinary citizens, represented a major policy breakthrough for America's civil rights policy.

African Americans and the New Deal Coalition. During the Roosevelt years, Democratic politicians continued to woo black voters, but from a sufficient distance to allow the Democratic Party to maintain its southern alliance. Nonetheless, hindsight reveals that subtle changes were under way in the political landscape, creating the foundation for later advances in civil rights. First, the twenty years of nearly uninterrupted Democratic control of both the presidency and Congress that began with the Roosevelt administration guaranteed that the Supreme Court and lower federal judiciary would be replenished with judges more sympathetic to civil rights claims. This new look to the courts eliminated a major stumbling block to federal intervention against segregation.[24]

Second, African Americans, who were gradually shifting their party loyalties from the "party of Lincoln" to the "party of Roosevelt," also were migrating from the South, where they could not vote, to northern and midwestern cities, where Democratic political organizations

Table 4–1 Percentage of African Americans in Central Cities of the Twelve Largest Standard Metropolitan Statistical Areas (SMSAs), 1930–1970

	1930	1940	1950	1960	1970
All 12 SMSAs	7.6	9.0	13.7	21.4	30.8
New York	4.9	6.9	9.8	14.7	23.4
Los Angeles–Long Beach	5.0	6.0	9.8	15.3	21.2
Chicago	7.1	8.3	14.1	23.6	34.4
Philadelphia	11.4	13.1	18.3	26.7	34.4
Detroit	7.8	9.3	16.4	29.2	44.0
San Francisco–Oakland	4.9	4.9	11.8	21.1	32.7
Boston	2.9	3.3	12.3	9.8	18.2
Pittsburgh	8.3	9.3	18.0	16.8	27.0
St. Louis	11.5	13.4	5.3	28.8	41.3
Washington, D.C.	27.3	28.5	35.4	54.8	72.3
Cleveland	8.1	9.7	16.3	28.9	39.0
Baltimore	17.7	19.4	23.8	35.0	47.0

Source: Adapted from Leo F. Schnore, Carolyn D. Andre, and Harry Sharp, "Black Suburbanization, 1930–1970," *The Changing Face of the Suburbs*, ed. Barry Schwartz (Chicago: University of Chicago Press, 1976), 80. The figures were transposed to yield data on black percentages.

welcomed them and their votes (Table 4–1).[25] For a century black sharecroppers and tenant farmers had been one of the least mobile population groups in the nation. But World War II (1939–1945) sent many young black males from the segregated Deep South into the armed services where they were stationed in less-racist communities. Other rural black men and women were lured north by high-paying jobs in wartime industry. After the war, farm mechanization continued displacing rural African Americans by rendering labor-intensive farming obsolete. Migration transformed these black citizens from political nonentities into pivotal voters.

The first sign of the changing political fortunes of African Americans came in 1948 when a Democratic president, Harry Truman, openly courted the black vote even at the risk of alienating the South. A faltering, strike-plagued economy appeared to doom the unpopular president to electoral defeat. Desperately searching for a campaign plan that might lead him to victory, Truman's advisers proposed a novel strategy for the Democratic Party: "Unless there are real and new efforts . . . to help the Negro," stated one strategy memo, "the Negro bloc, which,

Figure 4–2   Presidential Election, 1948

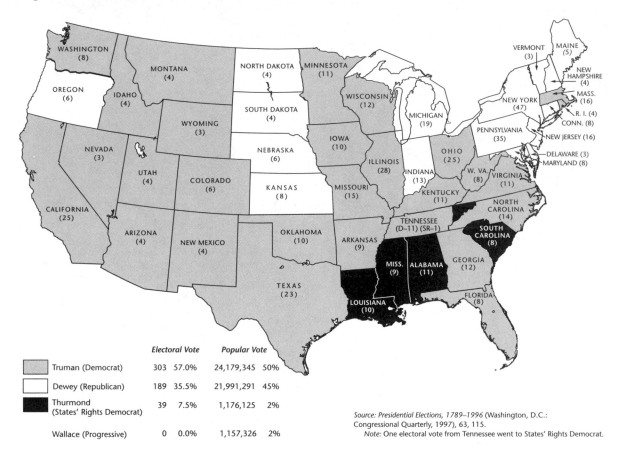

	Electoral Vote		Popular Vote	
Truman (Democrat)	303	57.0%	24,179,345	50%
Dewey (Republican)	189	35.5%	21,991,291	45%
Thurmond (States' Rights Democrat)	39	7.5%	1,176,125	2%
Wallace (Progressive)	0	0.0%	1,157,326	2%

Source: Presidential Elections, 1789–1996 (Washington, D.C.: Congressional Quarterly, 1997), 63, 115.

Note: One electoral vote from Tennessee went to States' Rights Democrat.

certainly in Illinois and probably in New York and Ohio, *does* hold the balance of power, will go Republican."[26] This strategy prompted President Truman in the 1948 election year to issue an executive order integrating the armed services, introduce legislation making the Fair Employment Practices Committee a permanent agency, and, most important, follow it with a comprehensive civil rights bill, the first since the end of Reconstruction. Among its numerous provisions, it made racial lynching a federal crime, provided federal guarantees for voting rights, and prohibited employment and housing discrimination. Although supported by most Republicans and

non-southern Democrats, the legislation, predictably, died in the Senate where southern members succeeded in preventing it from coming to a vote.

At the Democratic Party's national convention in the summer of 1948, liberal northern Democrats pressed fellow delegates to adopt a strong civil rights platform. Southern delegates became outraged and bolted from the meeting. In the fall these "Dixiecrats," as they were called, ran their own candidate under the States' Rights Party banner and pulled several southern states' electoral votes away from the Democratic ticket (Figure 4–2). The defection also served to remind national Democrats that the South could be taken for granted only so long as the party left segregation alone. Despite losing this traditional stronghold, Truman won the election.

As for the Truman administration's 1948 attempts to enact a civil rights law, the defeat of the legislation, like that of the Wilmot Proviso a century earlier, presaged a victory down the road, by identifying a political rationale for northern politicians to attack southern tyranny. With the New Deal, the Democratic Party had begun to attract activist liberals and union leaders who were ideologically committed to civil rights. Like Republican abolitionists a hundred years earlier, these activists were an important constituency of their party, more important than their numbers alone would attest.[27] But not until Democratic presidential candidates realized that the black vote might offset the potential southern losses did the party's politicians have a collective stake in advancing civil rights. Similarly, not until northern congressional Democrats discovered that speaking out against segregation in the South won them a receptive audience among recent arrivals from that region did a congressional majority committed to breaking up segregation begin to coalesce.

Emergence of a Civil Rights Coalition: The 1950s

The 1950s saw only modest advances in civil rights, but a new coalition was setting the stage for action. Success required both renewed support for civil rights from the Republican Party and profound shifts within the Democratic Party, whose elected leaders historically had been hostile to the cause of African Americans. Two landmark events of the 1950s stand out: the historic *Brown v. Board of Education of Topeka* decision and the Civil Rights Act of 1957, the first such law in eighty-two years.[28] Although important, both events proved more influential in identifying the issues and cleavages for the next decade than in yielding real gains in civil rights.

The NAACP's Litigation Strategy. In 1909 the National Association for the Advancement of Colored People (NAACP) began to defend African Americans throughout the South and to challenge the legal structure of segrega-tion. Of its landmark victories during these early years, one of its most important came in 1944, when it persuaded the Supreme Court in *Smith v. Allwright* to throw out white primary laws.[29] The Court ruled that because race was the explicit criterion for discrimination, such laws violated the Fifteenth Amendment.

Throughout the Deep South, however, many barriers to black registration had been put in place, and the removal of one did not appreciably improve conditions. In fact, nowhere in the South was the electoral potential of the black vote close to being realized. Long-standing Supreme Court doctrine requiring that plaintiffs prove a law's discriminatory *intent* rather than simply demonstrate a bias in its *effect* frustrated the NAACP's efforts to dismantle other racial barriers. For example, in trying to eradicate mechanisms like the poll tax which also disenfranchised poor whites, the NAACP could not satisfy the Court's tough requirements.

In the 1940s the NAACP launched a second line of attack against Jim Crow laws, this time targeting segregated public education. Since *Plessy v. Ferguson* in 1896, the federal judiciary had upheld segregation in the South, but the "separate but equal" doctrine contained in the *Plessy* ruling proved to be an easy target for challenges. The soft underbelly of segregation was the word "equal." Nowhere in the South did the separate facilities for African Americans equal those for whites.

The NAACP began with challenges to the most blatant disparities and gradually brought to the Supreme Court the more subtle forms of inequality inherent in segregated education. Since many states did not provide black graduate and professional schools and black residents were shut out of both public and private white facilities, the NAACP had a relatively easy time convincing the Court of the inequality of separating the races in this instance. Then, the NAACP successfully attacked segregated schools where separate facilities existed but were patently unequal in the education offered students. Less conspicuous forms of inequality were taken on next. In a 1950 decision the Court accepted the argument that intan-

Southern opponents usually were able to avoid integration of public schools through the use of legal subterfuges. Occasionally, however, confrontations occurred. In 1957 President Dwight Eisenhower had to enlist his commander-in-chief authority and deploy federal troops to usher black students into all-white Little Rock Central High School in Arkansas.

gible factors such as faculty reputation and alumni prestige contributed to educational inequality.

Having established that "separate but equal" *could* be unconstitutional, the NAACP launched a frontal assault on *Plessy.* The opportunity came in 1950 when Oliver Brown of Topeka, Kansas, violated local segregation laws by trying to enroll his daughter, Linda, in a white neighborhood public school. Representing the NAACP, future Supreme Court justice Thurgood Marshall took up Brown's case. Four years later the Supreme Court ruled in *Brown v. Board of Education of Topeka.* Writing for a unanimous Court, Chief Justice Earl Warren argued that education is the foundation of good citizenship and thus constitutes "a right which must be made available to all on equal terms." Stipulating that racial segregation "generates a feeling of inferiority as to [black children's] status in

the community that may affect their hearts and minds in a way unlikely ever to be undone," Chief Justice Warren concluded, "separate educational facilities are inherently unequal." With this 1954 ruling, *Plessy,* the principal legal prop of Jim Crow, crumbled.

The *Brown* decision had broad legal ramifications. It had been argued as a class-action suit on behalf of all citizens similarly denied access to white public schools. The next year the Court empowered lower federal courts to hear segregation cases and oversee the desegregation of public schools with "all deliberate speed."[30] Over the decade after *Brown,* hundreds of school desegregation cases were filed in the federal courts.

Yet even this flurry of litigation did not end segregation. Efforts to implement *Brown* encountered all of the problems associated with enforcing judicial rulings. The decision was met by massive resistance across the South. Acting as if the nation were still governed by the Articles of Confederation, some state legislatures boldly asserted that public education lay beyond the national government's jurisdiction and that they would ignore the Court's "illegal" decision. When this bluff failed, state politicians devised more imaginative blocking tactics. In Virginia, public schools were closed and "private" ones, created with state financing, opened in the vain hope that the new schools would be exempt from the *Brown* ruling. When these and other legal tricks were exhausted, state officials simply defied black parents and federal marshals sent to implement a desegregation ruling. The Supreme Court itself intervened in 1957, ordering the city of Little Rock, Arkansas, to enroll black students in all-white Central High School. When Arkansas governor Orval Faubus and school officials failed to comply, President Dwight Eisenhower sent in U.S. Army troops to escort black students to their new school.

The last bulwark of segregation's defense was tokenism—perhaps the most successful dilatory tactic of all. A school district would admit a handful of black students and then rush to federal court claiming compliance. Civil rights lawyers may have won many cases during this era, but their clients had little success in gaining access to "whites only" schools. In 1962, eight years after *Brown,* less than one-half of 1 percent of black students in the South were attending desegregated schools.

The 1957 Civil Rights Act: Rehearsal for the 1960s. The year 1957 was ripe with political opportunity for the Democrats. With Republican two-term president Dwight Eisenhower ineligible for reelection in 1960, the Senate was full of ambitious Democrats grooming themselves for a presidential bid. John Kennedy of Massachusetts, Stuart Symington of Missouri, and Hubert Humphrey of Minnesota would later declare their candidacies and campaign actively in the 1960 presidential primaries. Other, less-daring Senate colleagues could barely contain their aspirations for the top spot. Among them was Democratic majority leader Lyndon Johnson from Texas.

Daring or not, all would-be Democratic candidates had to demonstrate their abilities to appeal to a national constituency that now included substantial numbers of black voters in the large, vote rich industrial states. For Johnson, a southerner, this requirement posed a serious problem. How could this Texan establish his credentials with African Americans and therefore be taken seriously by the northern Democratic Party leaders who controlled the nomination?

Johnson's vehicle into the national arena was the 1957 Civil Rights Act, which he introduced.[31] This strategy was not lost on his southern colleagues who wanted to boost his presidential bid over those of the northern liberals Humphrey and Kennedy. And so they blessed the legislation the only way these agents of segregation reasonably could—by refraining from vigorous opposition and, in a few cases, by abstaining in the final floor vote. This message was reinforced by the passage of another, slightly less anemic voting rights bill in the spring of 1960, only weeks before many of these senators would head for the Democratic presidential nominating convention. Although Johnson lost the Democratic presidential nomination to Kennedy, he did succeed in winning the consolation prize—the vice-presidential nomination. And ever mindful of the black vote, Johnson and his colleagues oversaw enactment of yet another minority voting rights law during the summer before the 1960 presidential election.

With passage of the Civil Rights Act of 1957, the first civil rights law since Reconstruction, men and women who felt their right to vote had been denied for reasons of race could now file suit in federal court. But the prospect of expensive litigation and the provision that defendants—say, a local voter registrar—would be entitled to a jury trial proved such a formidable barrier that the NAACP and similar civil rights organizations filed suits designed only to establish widespread voting discrimination. To no one's surprise, few, if indeed any, black citizens gained the vote by virtue of this limited law. The significance of the 1957 Civil Rights Act, then, lay in what it represented politically than in any real gains it produced for black Americans. For the first time, Democratic congressional leaders committed themselves to passing a civil rights bill. These early civil rights laws represented a transition, not so much for African Americans seeking full citizenship but rather for the Democratic Party.

John Kennedy's narrow victory in 1960 reminded Democrats once again that winning the presidency without the South was virtually impossible. Even majority control of Congress would be jeopardized if more southern politicians decided—as a few in fact had—to disassociate themselves with northern Democrats and change parties. But even if the party accepted these risks and took up the cause of civil rights, it still lacked sufficient votes to enact the kinds of policies necessary to dismantle segregation. To jettison the party's southern wing by embracing civil rights and then fail to deliver would constitute political suicide.

Yet during the 1960s Democratic presidents Kennedy and Johnson and their congressional colleagues took this precarious course. The party leadership broke with the South and committed the nation to an activist civil rights policy before it was politically safe to do so. Why? Because doing nothing suddenly became the riskier strategy. A civil rights movement based on demonstrations and protest was generating a groundswell of support throughout the nation that the Democratic Party, which controlled Congress and the presidency, could not ignore. Failure to deal with this issue would have jeopardized the political relations of many Democrats with their core supporters. Then, in the 1964 election, an event rarer than Halley's comet occurred: the emergence of a dominant governing coalition in Washington. The Democrats won both the presidency and a large majority of seats in both chambers of Congress. Like a comet, it did not last long, but while present it burned bright. The result was half a decade of legislation followed by vigorous enforcement to dismantle segregation and voting discrimination. Finally, the national government had decided to finish Reconstruction and assume responsibility for every citizen's civil rights.

The Civil Rights Movement: 1960s

In the years leading up to the early 1960s, the civil rights movement, led by the NAACP, followed a strategy designed more to influence judges than politicians. This strategy had garnered some impressive court victories, but success at the bar had not translated into real gains in civil rights. Entering the 1960s, the civil rights movement took a new course—public protests directed against segregation and the authorities who administered it and, ultimately, toward influencing public opinion and, in turn, Congress and the president.

In December 1955 a black seamstress, Rosa Parks, refused to surrender her seat on a city bus in Montgomery, Alabama, to a white patron and move to the back of the vehicle. In doing so, she launched the historic Montgomery bus boycott, which became the model for later boycotts. In 1960 the first "sit-in" was held when several black college students in Greensboro, North Carolina, occupied seats in a local restaurant reserved for whites and refused to move until they were served or arrested.

Realizing that they needed protection if injured or arrested, demonstration participants began to look for stronger organization and leadership.[32] As the arena shifted from litigation to protest, a new class of leaders

Rosa Parks, whose refusal to move to the back of a city bus in December 1955 touched off the historic Montgomery, Alabama, bus boycott, is fingerprinted by Montgomery deputy sheriff D. H. Lackey. Her courageous act and subsequent arrest triggered massive demonstrations in the city and a boycott of local public transportation and white businesses. These events led eventually to the dismantling of local segregation policies and stimulated other acts of civil disobedience elsewhere.

emerged—men and women who were attuned more to popular persuasion than to judicial appeals. The most important of these leaders was the Reverend Martin Luther King Jr. He had gained national recognition helping to coordinate the Montgomery bus boycott and would serve as leader of the civil rights movement for most of the 1960s. During those years, King and his organization, the Southern Christian Leadership Conference (SCLC), spearheaded demonstrations throughout the South.

King's strategy of nonviolent resistance may have been inspired by the Indian leader Mahatma Gandhi (1869–1948), but his political pragmatism was a page out of James Madison's playbook. Ultimately, King reasoned,

The scene is Jackson, Mississippi, where the local lunch crowd is drenching lunch counter demonstrators with mustard and ketchup. Such demonstrations occurred throughout the South in the 1960s. Most of the participants were local black and northern white college students.

rights would be won not in the courts through reasoned argument but in legislatures through direct engagement with opponents whose interests were at stake. "Needless fighting in lower courts," King argued, is "exactly what the white man wants the Negro to do. Then he can draw out the fight."[33] If African Americans were to realize their rights, he knew they would have to claim them.

Civil rights demonstrations began in earnest in 1960, and over the next six years almost 2,500 were held, with many receiving national news coverage.[34] One of the most important, held in the spring of 1963 in Birmingham, Alabama, provided the stimulus for passage of a landmark in American history, the Civil Rights Act of 1964. It forced a reluctant Democratic Party to commit itself to an aggressive civil rights policy.

The Birmingham Demonstration. In early 1963 President Kennedy proposed a new civil rights bill that perpetuated the Democrats' historical straddle of its warring factions. But, pleading for patience from King and other leaders, Kennedy argued that Congress should enact his less-controversial social programs before tackling segregation. Civil rights leaders suspected that his real motivation was to keep the South in the Democratic column in the upcoming 1964 election. And they had their own strategic reasons for impatience. Demonstrations were turning violent, and events were only partially under their control. If King and the other leaders were to keep the movement directed toward civil disobedience and peaceful protest, they needed to start producing results.

The selection of Birmingham as a venue for protest reflected the broad strategic purpose of the demonstrations. Segregation was no worse there than in many other cities throughout the Deep South. But Birmingham did have a local police chief, Eugene "Bull" Connor, who was notorious for his intolerance and rough treatment of civil rights demonstrators. He would provide the nation with a graphic display of the institutional violence that could be marshaled to enforce segregation. As the nation watched on network television, Connor filled his jails with two thousand marchers, who were arrested for not having a parade permit. The local law enforcement officers then resorted to police dogs and fire hoses to disperse peaceful demonstrators, including children barely old enough to go to school.

The Birmingham demonstrations succeeded when the city's business community agreed to sit down with the protesters and negotiate. But, more important, protesters had created a national crisis that President Kennedy could not ignore. For years the monthly Gallup Poll had asked its national sample of respondents to name the most important problem facing the country. Until the Montgomery bus boycott in 1956, civil rights had never figured prominently in responses to this query. From April to July 1963, however, the percentage of respondents mentioning civil rights shot up from 10 to nearly 50 percent.

Suddenly, continued accommodation of southern

Protestors parading down the streets of Birmingham, Alabama, in 1963 were bent on focusing national attention on their cause. The local police were quite accommodating. To the horror of television viewers, police dogs and water hoses were used forcefully on protestors, demonstrating the brutality with which segregation was enforced.

Democrats imposed significant political costs on Kennedy. To fail to act might irreparably damage his reputation among black voters who had provided the margin of victory in critical states in 1960 and might well again in any bid for reelection. These events, orchestrated by the civil rights movement, turned the president into a reluctant champion of its cause. But the Democratic Party's predicament remained. Shortly after a televised address to the nation unveiling the new civil rights legislation, Kennedy invited movement leaders to the White House to plan legislative strategy. The president explained to the group the bind they had put him in:

This is a very serious fight. The Vice-President [Lyndon Johnson] and I know what it will mean if we fail. I have just seen a new poll—national approval of the administration has fallen from 60 to 47 per cent. We're in this up to the neck. The worst trouble of all would be to lose the fight in the Congress. We'll have enough trouble if we win; but, if we win, we can deal with those. A good many programs I care about may go down the drain as a result of this—we may go down the drain as a result of this—so we are putting a lot on the line.

Democrats were about to commit to a strong civil rights program without having the means to succeed.[35]

The Democratic Party's Commitment to Civil Rights. On June 11, 1963, President Kennedy addressed the nation, proclaiming his full support for the aspirations of African Americans and announcing a major revision of the civil rights bill then before Congress. The courts would no longer determine violations; for the first time federal agencies could independently identify discrimination and impose remedies. Although this new proposal was far weaker than what King and his colleagues had asked for, they accepted it as a solid step in the right direction.

Five months later Kennedy was assassinated, and Vice President Lyndon Johnson succeeded to the presidency. At the time, a strengthened version of the legislation, which had passed the House of Representatives on a bipartisan vote, was predictably stalled in the Senate.[36] Southern senators did not have enough votes to defeat the legislation outright, but they appeared able to filibuster it indefinitely (see Chapter 6, Congress).

Within a few days of assuming the presidency, Johnson addressed a joint session of Congress and a nationwide television audience to announce that a strong civil rights law would be the nation's memorial to the fallen president. This proclamation set the stage for a struggle in Washington. The outcome would make 1964 a year of historic successes for both civil rights and the Democratic Party.

The 1964 Civil Rights Act. Once Johnson persuaded Senate Republicans to join northern Democrats in breaking the southern filibuster, the Senate promptly passed the

For years Georgia senator Richard Russell and other southerners had blocked civil rights legislation with the threat of a filibuster. New president Lyndon Johnson, however, was not deterred in his push for civil rights legislation. Here, two weeks after President John Kennedy's assassination, Johnson warns his Senate mentor to stand aside or be run down.

POLITICS ⟶ POLICY

The 1964 Civil Rights Act and Integration of Public Schools

One of the most effective provisions of the 1964 Civil Rights Act authorized the Department of Health, Education and Welfare to withhold federal grants from school districts that failed to integrate their schools. No longer could southern school boards hide behind token desegregation and endless visits to the federal courts. The effects were quick and dramatic: within a year more black children were admitted to formerly all-white schools than in the entire decade after the 1954 *Brown v. Board of Education of Topeka* decision. Within ten years over 90 percent of black children in the South were attending integrated schools.

Percentage of All Southern Black Schoolchildren Attending School with Whites, 1955–1973

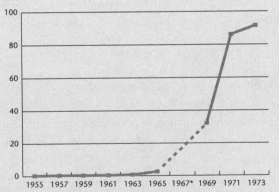

Source: Gerald N. Rosenberg, *Hollow Hope: Can Courts Bring about Social Change?* (Chicago: University of Chicago Press, 1991), 50–51.

*Dashed line indicates missing data for 1967.

Figure 4–3 Presidential Election, 1964.

Source: Presidential Elections, 1789–1996 (Washington, D.C.: Congressional Quarterly, 1997), 67.

Civil Rights Act of 1964. This law, which was substantially stronger than the legislation President Kennedy had introduced, authorized the national government to end segregation in public education and public accommodations.

The Democratic administration's high-profile sponsorship of the civil rights law set the stage for civil rights to emerge as a decisive campaign issue in the 1964 presidential election. The Republican Party in Congress traditionally had been more supportive of civil rights than the Democrats, but in 1964 it began to veer sharply away from its long-standing support. At their national convention in the summer of that year, Republicans chose Barry Goldwater of Arizona as their presidential candidate. Goldwater was one of the few senators outside the South to oppose the 1964 civil rights bill. When the Democrats convened to nominate the incumbent president Johnson, they underlined the party differences on this issue by seating delegates who challenged segregationist Democrats and by selecting Sen. Hubert Humphrey, a long-standing, vocal proponent of civil rights, as Johnson's running mate.

Rarely have the major parties staked out such divergent positions on so important an issue. As a result, public awareness of the parties' positions on the race issue was uncharacteristically high. Earlier surveys had found respondents equally divided on their views about which political party most favored school integration, but during the 1964 election campaign respondents had no difficulty identifying the Democrats, by a nine-to-one margin.[37]

The outcome of the election was the largest presidential landslide in history. The Democrats also racked up huge majorities in the congressional elections. Goldwater won five states in the Deep South and his home state of Arizona (Figure 4–3). With over 95 percent of black voters preferring Johnson, the Democratic and Republican Parties swapped constituencies in the South.[38] When the new Congress convened in 1965, northern Democrats domi-

MAJOR EVENTS IN THE CIVIL RIGHTS MOVEMENT, 1955–1968

December 1955	Blacks in Montgomery, Alabama, begin boycott of city buses in protest of segregated seating.
September 1, 1957	Central High School in Little Rock, Arkansas, engulfed in turmoil as the governor calls out Arkansas National Guard to prevent enrollment of nine black students. President Dwight Eisenhower forced to send in federal troops to restore order.
February 1, 1960	Wave of "sit-ins" touched off across the South by four students in Greensboro, North Carolina, who are refused service at a segregated lunch counter.
May 4, 1961	"Freedom rides" begin as blacks try to occupy "whites only" sections of interstate buses. U.S. marshals ultimately are called in to settle violent reaction to black efforts.
September 30, 1962	Federal troops are used to quell a fifteen-hour uprising by University of Mississippi students protesting the enrollment of a single black student, James Meredith. Two students are killed. (Televised live across the nation.)
April 1963	Demonstrations begin in Birmingham, Alabama. Local authorities use fire hoses and police dogs to disperse demonstrators.
August 28, 1963	March on Washington by over 200,000 blacks and whites. The Reverend Martin Luther King Jr. delivers his "I Have A Dream" speech, and "We Shall Overcome" becomes the anthem of the civil rights movement.
September 1963	Demonstrations begin in St. Augustine, Florida, to protest the arrest and detention of seven students. Blacks boycott several northern schools in protest of de facto segregation. Four black children are killed in bombing of Birmingham, Alabama, church.
June 1964	Three civil rights workers, two white and one black, working to register black voters are killed in Mississippi. Murderers include sheriff's deputies.
July 1964	First in a wave of ghetto riots breaks out in New York City's Harlem.
January 1965	King organizes protest marches in Selma, Alabama. Marches end in violent attacks by police.
August 11, 1965	Black riots erupt in Watts section of Los Angeles. Four thousand rioters are arrested; thirty-four are killed.
June 6, 1966	James Meredith suffers gunshot wound in march across Mississippi. March continues under "Black Power" slogan.
Summers 1966 and 1967	Riots and violent demonstrations occur in cities across the nation.
April 4, 1968	Martin Luther King Jr. assassinated in Memphis, Tennessee.

Figure 4–4 African-American Voting Rights, 1960–1971

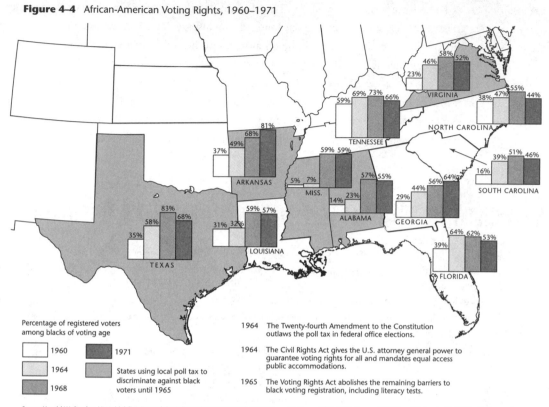

Source: Harold W. Stanley, *Voter Mobilization and the Politics of Race: The South and Universal Suffrage, 1952–1984* (Praeger Publishers, Westport, CT, 1987), 97. Copyright © 1987 by Harold W. Stanley. Used with permission.

nated both chambers. Even some border states elected Democrats who were moderate supporters of civil rights and who were prepared to support national policies that would dismantle segregation.

The Voting Rights Act of 1965. Every civil rights law enacted since 1957 had addressed voting rights, but throughout much of the South black registration remained the exception rather than the rule. Only 7 percent of eligible black citizens in Mississippi were registered in 1964; in Alabama the figure was 20 percent. Each of these civil rights laws had the same fatal flaw: they required individuals to prove discrimination in court. Black leaders thus pressed the White House to authorize federal agencies to guarantee the right to vote by taking over voter registration or directly supervising local officials, just as the 1964 Civil

Rights Act had authorized government action against segregation in education and public accommodations.

Responding to their pleas, Johnson, who was preparing a huge package of social legislation known as his Great Society program, asked King and other leaders to "give the nation a chance to catch its breath" on civil rights. After all, African Americans would be well served, Johnson argued, by his new social programs in employment, education, and health care. But for movement leaders, this was asking too much. Never before had there been such large, sympathetic majorities in the House of Representatives and the Senate. For the first time since the early days of Reconstruction, opponents of civil rights lacked a veto. In Johnson and the Democratic members of Congress, the movement leaders had politicians who had been elected largely on their commitment to civil rights. From recent experience, they knew precisely what was needed to motivate this legislative juggernaut into action.

The demonstrations in Selma, Alabama, in the spring of 1965 closely paralleled those in Birmingham in 1963. Brutal local law enforcement—club-wielding police on horseback, attack dogs, and liberal use of powerful fire hoses—yielded vivid television images of the official violence that enforced segregation. Another echo of Birmingham was that civil rights leaders knew they had succeeded when President Johnson went on prime-time television to introduce new civil rights legislation.

Table 4–2 Black Federal, State, and Local Officeholders, 1970–1997

Office	1970	1980	1990	1997
Members of Congress and state legislatures	179	365	465	646
City and county officials	715	2,807	4,481	5,052
Judges, sheriffs, and other law enforcement officers	213	528	769	996
Boards of education	362	1,214	1,655	1,962
Total	**1,469**[a]	**4,914**[b]	**7,370**	**8,656**[c]

Source: Information supplied by the Joint Center for Political and Economic Studies, Washington, D.C.

a. Nine states had no black elected officials: Idaho, Maine, Montana, New Hampshire, North Dakota, Oregon, South Dakota, Utah, and Vermont.

b. No black elected officials were identified in six states: Idaho, Montana, North Dakota, Utah, Vermont, and Wyoming.

c. Total includes one statehood senator and one statehood representative from the District of Columbia.

Ignoring the howls of southern senators, Congress passed and the president promptly signed the Voting Rights Act of 1965. The law was aggressive—the legislators who drafted it knew that virtually everyone it added to the registration rolls would soon be voting Democratic. Its main provision authorized the Department of Justice to suspend restrictive electoral tests in southern states that had a history of low black turnout. In these states the Justice Department could (and did) send federal officers into uncooperative communities to register voters directly. The states also had to obtain clearance from the Justice Department before changing their election laws. While the Antifederalist Patrick Henry might have turned over in his grave at his first sight of the Voting Rights Act and federal registrars entering his home state of Virginia, the policy was perfectly consistent with Madison's proposed national veto over objectionable state laws.

Few laws have ever achieved their goals more dramatically or quickly (Figure 4-4). Registration soared, yielding some dramatic effects. For the first time politicians from these states began paying attention to the views of their black constituents. In 1970, when several southern senators polled their colleagues about opposing an extension of the voting rights law, they found little enthusiasm. Democratic conservative Herman Talmadge of Georgia, who at one time could have been counted on, begged off: "Look, fellows, I was the principal speaker at the NAACP conference in my state last year." And South Carolina Democrat Ernest Hollings was direct: "I'm not going home to my state and explain a filibuster to black voters."[39] Moreover, Table 4–2 traces the new class of politicians emerging to represent this large, rapidly growing, and residentially concentrated constituency. From 1970 to 1997, the number of black elected officials at all levels of government grew from 1,469 to 8,656.

The 1965 Voting Rights Act was, then, a culminating achievement of the civil rights movement of the 1960s. But during the second half of the decade events began to change the way African Americans and whites looked at civil rights. In the summer of 1965 a two-week riot, in which thirty-four people were killed, exploded in the black neighborhood of Watts in Los Angeles. Over the next few summers similar riots would erupt in other cities including Oakland and Detroit. Late in 1965 the Vietnam War began to replace civil rights demonstrations on tele-

Key Provisions of Federal Civil Rights Legislation

Civil Rights Act, 1957

Established U.S. Commission on Civil Rights to investigate the status of civil rights in the country. Made it a federal crime to attempt to prevent a person from voting.

Civil Rights Act, 1960

Increased sanctions against abridging or denying the right to vote. Permitted federal government to appoint "referees," under the jurisdiction of the courts, to register voters denied the right to vote by a pattern or practice of discrimination.

Civil Rights Act, 1964

Voting: By equating a sixth-grade education with literacy, the act made it more difficult to disenfranchise blacks through literacy tests.

Public accommodations: Barred discrimination on basis of race, color, religion, or nationality in restaurants, service stations, theaters, transportation, and hotels with five rooms or more. Empowered attorney general to initiate suits.

Schools: Authorized attorney general to bring suit against segregated schools. Also permitted federal government to withhold funds from segregated schools.

Employment: Barred discrimination on the basis of race, color, religion, nationality, or sex in a range of employment practices. Established Equal Employment Opportunity Commission to enforce this provision.

Voting Rights Act, 1965

Permitted appointment, under Civil Service Commission, of voting examiners in place of local registrars in all areas where less than 50 percent of those eligible to vote actually voted in the 1964 presidential election. Use of literacy tests and similar mechanisms suspended.

Age Discrimination Act, 1967

Prevented employment discrimination based on age for workers 40–65 years old. Later amended to prevent mandatory retirement.

Fair Housing Act, 1968

Outlawed refusal to rent or sell housing on grounds of race or religion, but exempted citizens who rented or sold their homes without using a real estate agent.

Rehabilitation Act of 1973

Instituted affirmative action programs for employers to hire "qualified handicapped individuals" and barred discrimination solely on the basis of a handicap.

Civil Rights Restoration Act, 1988

Applied anti-sex discrimination standards to all institutions' programs if the institution received federal funding.

Civil Rights Act of 1991

Gave victims of intentional discrimination based on sex, religion, or disability the right to sue for monetary damages. (Victims of racial discrimination had had this right since a Reconstruction-era law.)

---

vision news, and the vocal opposition of some civil rights leaders to the war sapped support in Washington. Reflecting its waning enthusiasm for civil rights, Congress defeated a fair housing bill in 1966. (A somewhat weaker law was passed two years later, however.) Then, in 1968, Martin Luther King Jr. was assassinated in Memphis, Tennessee, after leading a march in behalf of striking sanitation workers. Riots erupted in cities throughout the nation. Shortly thereafter, "law and order" replaced civil rights as the mantra of political campaigns throughout the United States.

The Era of Remedial Action: The 1970s to the Millennium

The civil rights movement may have lost momentum, but the advances continued. Over the next thirty years,

POLITICS ➞ POLICY

THE BUSING CONTROVERSY

In the 1970s the enforcement of fair housing laws was at best only a partial remedy for preventing future discrimination. Even with aggressive federal action, segregated neighborhoods would persist for years and with them the continued racial segregation of schools. Then, in an effort to rectify the legacy of residential segregation for public education, the federal bureaucracy and courts adopted a policy of achieving racial integration by busing students to schools outside their neighborhoods. Americans, however, were not happy with this solution. Throughout the 1970s and 1980s busing scored at or near the top in public opinion surveys as the national policy most upsetting Americans.

In recent years school busing has declined in both the numbers of students affected and its importance as a political issue. Replacing it as a controversy is affirmative action—another emphasis on "equal outcomes" over "equal opportunity." To implement affirmative action, government and the private sector try to compensate individuals for the effects of past discrimination.

legislation (including the Fair Housing Act of 1968) shifted the responsibility for identifying and eradicating abuses from the injured individuals and the courts to the federal bureaucracy. Once the Department of Health, Education and Welfare (HEW) assumed control, the pace of desegregation increased sharply. In redelegating principal enforcement authority from the courts to the bureaucracy, Congress and the presidency "redefined" discrimination in a way that made it much easier for the federal agencies to administer civil rights policy. Rather than having to investigate and prove a specific discriminatory act that prevented African Americans from enjoying their rights, the government could focus instead on the "outcome" of local practices. The underrepresentation of African Americans on voter registration rolls, in apartment rentals, in schools, in employment, and the like were enough to establish a reasonable suspicion of discrimination for which the government could apply a remedial solution.

In the 1980s and 1990s civil rights enforcement moved beyond the South to include all government and private actions that yielded indicators of discrimination. A favorite target of federal investigators was schools. In fact, when these officials searched for evidence of discrimination in black versus white enrollment figures, they netted many schools outside the South where segregation arose not from school policies, but as a byproduct of discriminatory housing laws that kept neighborhoods, and consequently the neighborhood schools, segregated.[40] (This **de facto segregation** is distinguished from **de jure segregation,** which is that mandated by law as it was in the South.) When the courts, the Department of Justice, and HEW decided jointly to force school districts to bus stu-

Table 4–3 Public Attitudes toward Affirmative Action (percent)

Question		Blacks	Whites	Total
Do you favor government financing for job training for minorities to help them get ahead in industries where they are underrepresented?	Yes	95	64	69
	No	3	29	24
Is it necessary to have laws to protect minorities against discrimination in hiring and promotion?	Yes	88	65	69
	No	9	31	27
Do you favor special education programs to assist minorities in competing for college admissions?	Yes	82	59	63
	No	11	31	28
Should affirmative action programs be ended now, phased out over the next few years, or continued for the foreseeable future?	Ended now	1	13	12
	Phased out	17	45	40
	Continued	80	35	41
Should preference in hiring and promotion be given to blacks to make up for past discrimination?	Yes	62	31	35
	No	23	57	52
As a result of affirmative action, do you think less-qualified people are hired and promoted and admitted to college at least some of the time, or hardly ever or never?	At least some	67	81	79
	Hardly ever/never	28	13	15

Source: New York Times/CBS Poll, December 6–9, 1997. Cited in Sam Howe Verhovek, "In Poll, Americans Reject Means but Not Ends of Racial Diversity," New York Times, December 14, 1997.

dents to sometimes distant schools for the sake of integration, the measure produced waves of public protests. Indeed, busing proved to be one of the most controversial civil rights policies of the modern era (see box "The Busing Controversy").

The government, then, had found straightforward solutions for redressing discrimination in voting rights and schools: it enrolled black voters and redirected students to new schools. But what about past discrimination in employment? The government could not simply tell its own agencies or private businesses to hire an equal number of minorities. Instead, it resorted to a policy of *affirmative action*. This policy requires any employers or government agencies that have practiced discrimination to compensate minorities by giving them special consideration in

their selection for employment and education. Affirmative action is most controversial when applied to government contracting, university admission rules to increase minority enrollments, and employment policies to promote minority presence and advancement in business and the professions. Early efforts at affirmative action, quickly rejected by both the federal courts and the American public, involved the use of **quotas**—that is, setting aside a certain share of admissions, government contracts, and jobs for those population groups that presumably had suffered from past discrimination.

Although the Supreme Court has consistently rejected the use of quotas, apparently it is prepared to allow some consideration of an applicant's membership in a disadvantaged group. In 1987, for example, the Court ruled that sex could be considered along with other criteria in promotion decisions. This decision appeared to permit affirmative action even in realms where evidence of past discrimination was absent.[41] But even without quotas, affirmative action remains highly controversial. The results of the national survey reported in Table 4–3 indicate that a healthy majority of both white and black respondents favor special assistance for minorities subjected to past discrimination, but a majority of whites draw the line at affirmative action.

Indeed, that controversy is playing out in the Supreme Court as well. Over the past few years the Court has looked askance at any form of preferential treatment. In 1995 a narrow majority employed decisive language in *Adarand Constructors, Inc. v. Pena* to rule that affirmative action policies tailored to produce broad, equal outcomes across groups violated the Constitution's equal protection provisions. Instead, only those affirmative action policies "narrowly tailored" to achieve a "compelling government interest" would be countenanced.[42] Since *Adarand,* the Court has displayed unusual consistency in voiding affirmative action policies. (This finding accounts for efforts of civil rights groups to settle the Piscataway discrimination case and head off another Court verdict against affirmative action.) In 1996 the Court refused to review a case in which a federal court of appeals had voided race as a criterion for admission to the University of Texas Law School and in doing so rejected the state's claim that it had a "compelling interest" to produce minority lawyers.[43] More generally, this ruling undermined frequent claims by colleges and universities that they could enlist race and other criteria to achieve "diversity" on campus. In 1997 the Court continued this policy course by refusing to review an appeals court decision that upheld the constitutionality of a 1996 California proposition to end affirmative action. By a vote of 54–46 percent, Californians had added Proposition 209 to the state's constitution. It banned the use of "race, sex, color, ethnicity or national origin as a criterion for either discriminating against, or granting preferential treatment to, any individual or group in the operation of the State's system of public employment, public education or public contracting." Among civil rights groups and their opponents, debate over the value and constitutionality of affirmative action continues.

The Legacy of the Civil Rights Movement for Women, Gays, and Other Groups

Although race remained a prominent civil rights issue in the 1970s, the civil rights movement began to branch out to include women, the elderly, the disabled, homosexuals, and virtually every ethnic minority. The new directions civil rights have taken over the past several decades have deep roots, however, in the two-hundred-year struggle of African Americans for civil rights. It paved the way politically for these new efforts, both in honing the techniques of demonstrations and protest and in creating a receptive audience in the news media and American public opinion. But, most important, the black civil rights movement built a foundation of federal laws, judicial precedents, and administrative regulations that could be easily extended to other groups.

In the American constitutional system several hurdles must be cleared to establish a particular right for a particular group. First, a right must be recognized as such by those who make and enforce the law. Universal suffrage, for example, would appear to be an essential feature of any republic aspiring to be a democracy. Yet until ratification of the Fifteenth Amendment in 1870, the Constitution left the decision of who voted up to the states. Over the nineteenth century the states added and subtracted all kinds of qualifications—property, literacy, advance registration, and even whether one's grandfather had voted. Each unenfranchised group had to establish its right to vote: white males without property did so in state electoral reforms (1820s and 1830s), African Americans in the Fifteenth Amendment (1870), women in the Nineteenth

Amendment (1920), American Indians in a 1924 federal law, and young adults from eighteen to twenty-one in the Twenty-sixth Amendment (1971).

The second hurdle to establishing rights is enforcement. The sordid history of black civil rights demonstrates that unless the political will exists to implement constitutional amendments extending civil rights, the amendments may amount to little more than hollow declarations. African Americans may have won the "right" to vote in 1870, but for those in the South, winning the vote itself would take another century.

In recent years, then, activists seeking to establish and implement rights for women and other minorities have found their way paved by the slow, painstaking efforts of African Americans. The black civil rights movement established valuable precedents and administrative structures that could be easily transferred to other rights claimants.

Equal Rights for Women

Women established their right to vote nearly a century after they organized and began promoting their cause. Long before abolitionists were advancing the vote for African Americans, the early feminists, later calling themselves **suffragettes,** were campaigning for the vote. (Many also were active in the abolition movement.) Yet despite their efforts, "sex" was excluded from the Fifteenth Amendment, and none had the vote until 1869 when the territory of Wyoming passed the first women's suffrage law. Gradually, fourteen other states added women to the electorate. In 1919 Congress sent the Nineteenth Amendment to the states, and the next year it was ratified. Despite the half-century gulf between these constitutional amendments, the association between black and women's civil rights is evident in the wording of the two texts:

AMENDMENT XV (Ratified February 3, 1870)
Section 1. The right of citizens of the United States to vote shall not be denied or abridged by the United States or by any State on account of race, color, or previous condition of servitude.

Section 2. The Congress shall have power to enforce this article by appropriate legislation.

AMENDMENT XIX (Ratified August 18, 1920)
The right of citizens of the United States to vote shall not be denied or abridged by the United States or by any State on account of sex.
Congress shall have power to enforce this article by appropriate legislation.

Unlike African Americans, however, women experienced little delay between principle and reality. Although voting registration varied across states, women's registration rates approached three-quarters of men's less than a decade after ratification of the Nineteenth Amendment. Within a few years women were voting regularly at a rate slightly below that of men.

The extension of other civil rights guarantees to women clearly rode the coattails of the civil rights movement. In fact, discrimination based on sex was included in the 1964 Civil Rights Act. Its presence in the act, however, stemmed from a political miscalculation. Initially the legislation included language covering discrimination based only on religion, national origin, and race. Southern opponents proposed and voted to add sex to this list, certain that it would decrease overall support for and ultimately defeat the civil rights bill. This strategy of weighing the legislation down with controversial provisions backfired, however, when Congress accepted their amendment and proceeded to pass the legislation.

The surprising legislative victory did not lead to immediate enforcement, however, even though the 1964 law created an enforcement mechanism—the new Equal Employment Opportunity Commission (EEOC)—authorized to investigate and file suits against racial discrimination in the workplace. With one early EEOC commissioner calling the sex discrimination policy "a fluke," the commission initially balked at enforcing the employment discrimination protections for women. But the agency revised its orientation after a successful political campaign focused national attention on employment discrimination against women. Today, claims of sexual discrimination and harassment in the workplace outnumber all others filed with and investigated by this commission.

The National Organization for Women (NOW) was formed in 1966 in direct reaction to the EEOC's refusal to take up their cause. Organized along the same lines as the NAACP, NOW initially pursued a litigation strategy, which met with mixed success. So, to establish a stronger legal foundation, NOW and other feminist organizations dusted off the Equal Rights Amendment (ERA) which had been introduced in Congress in 1923 and every year thereafter with tepid enthusiasm. The amendment gave Congress the authority to implement the following statement: "Equality of rights under the law shall not be denied or abridged by the United States or by any State on account of sex."

Using many of the same tactics honed by the civil rights movement—demonstrations, televised appeals, Washington rallies, and intensive lobbying—NOW and other feminist organizations won over a sympathetic public. The mostly male members of Congress were not far behind. After languishing for years, ERA was sent to the states in 1972 by a vote of 354–24 in the House of Representatives and 84–8 in the Senate. The early response in the states was equally favorable. Within the first year twenty-two of thirty-eight states needed for ratification had indicated their approval. By 1978 thirty-five of the required thirty-eight states had ratified the amendment, but no more would. ERA hit a brick wall called the abortion issue (discussed more fully in Chapter 5).[44] Thus instead of pitting men against women, as the Nineteenth Amendment had done earlier in the century, ERA was fought between feminist and antiabortion women's groups. As the amendment became contentious, public support waned. By 1981 less than half of voters still endorsed the amendment in the states that had not yet ratified it.[45] The time available for ratifying the ERA expired on June 30, 1982.

The feminist forces may have lost the battle over ERA, but they appear to have won the war. In 1972 Congress en-

In November 1977 former First Lady Betty Ford (center right) and First Lady Rosalynn Carter (center left) took to the hustings to promote the Equal Rights Amendment. Despite their efforts, the amendment failed, largely a victim of the growing debate over abortion rights.

acted Title IX of the Higher Education Act, which prohibits funding for schools and universities that discriminate against women, including in the size of their intercollegiate sports programs. Years later, in the Civil Rights Act of 1991, Congress strengthened employment discrimination claims by requiring employers to demonstrate that unequal hiring and compensation practices do not reflect gender discrimination.

In recent years sex has eclipsed race in setting the civil rights agenda. The courts, Congress, and the state legislatures devote significant shares of their sessions to policies governing relations between the sexes in the workplace. Sexual harassment is the most prominent example of unsettled civil rights law. Other issues are comparable pay for comparable work and hiring and promotions policy.

Gay Rights

The favorable "rights" climate has encouraged other groups to come forward, particularly the LGBT (lesbian, gay, bisexual, and transgender) community. But civil rights claims remain murky for homosexuals. There is no "gay rights" policy as such—no federal statutes or Supreme

The Americans with Disabilities Act may have been signed by President George Bush in 1990, but its scope—who should be considered "disabled"—was far from settled. In 1999 the Supreme Court heard three cases initiated by workers denied jobs based on their medical conditions. The Court ruled in all three that people with physcial impairments who can function normally when they wear glasses or take medication cannot in general be considered disabled and therefore are not covered by the act's protection against job discrimination.

Court decisions have incorporated homosexuals into the inclusive 1964 Civil Rights Act or any other law. In fact, in 1995 Congress voted down legislation that would have incorporated sexual preference into existing employment rights laws. Some states have extended job protection and "hate crime" protections to homosexual men and women. Other states, however, have sought explicitly to exclude sexual orientation as a category subject to discrimination protection. After many cities in Colorado, for example, passed broadly worded ordinances banning discrimination against homosexuals, Colorado voters passed a state constitutional amendment in 1992 striking down these antidiscrimination laws. Ironically, in 1996, when the Supreme Court in turn struck down the Colorado amendment, it

established the only federal statement on gay rights. The Court ruled by 6–3 that the Colorado law violated the equal protection clause of the Constitution by singling out gays as unworthy of protections.[46]

Emerging Rights: The Disabled, the Elderly, Parents

The advances in civil rights over the past half-century have been extraordinary in both the kinds of privileges that have come under this rubric and the variety of groups in American society that have sought its protections. For example, in addition to women and gays the disabled have won significant victories. Perhaps the largest was the 1990 passage of the Americans with Disabilities Act, which bars discrimination in employment, transportation, public accommodation, and telecommunication against persons with physical and mental disabilities.

Not to be outdone, the elderly, led in part by one of America's largest interest groups, the American Association of Retired Persons (AARP), have successfully sought national legislation ending the once-prevalent practice of mandatory retirement age. And other groups are waiting on the sidelines, mustering support for their forays into the civil rights arena. Even parents—especially divorced ones who do not have custody of their children and parents of children with disabilities—have begun to draft their own bills of rights. And so the politics of civil rights will continue, building on its painful legacy.

Challenging Tyranny

This historical survey of civil rights in America has revealed selfless men and women pressing the case for their fellow citizens who were suffering injustice. But this history also has revealed that these efforts did not suffice. Just as James Madison argued in *Federalist* No. 10, civil rights advanced only when a large national majority fully took control of the national government and challenged tyranny in the states. The politicians who assembled these broad national coalitions were keen political strategists. Abraham Lincoln and the Republican Party rode into office advocating "Free Soil, Free Labor, Free Men," not eradication of slavery. Nonetheless, their political success allowed them to conduct a costly and bloody war to preserve the Union and abolish slavery.

From the 1880s through the 1950s neither party could muster a majority even within their party, much less the government, in behalf of civil rights for African Americans. Consequently, the cause languished, and generations of African Americans were doomed to lifetimes ruled by segregation's strict regimen. Then, in the 1960s, the Democratic Party rode the crest of public opinion generated by the civil rights movement. The 1964 election gave Democrats the presidency and huge majorities in both chambers of Congress. They enacted strong new civil rights policy and enforced it. Advances in civil rights since those years have rested on a firm foundation of laws and institutions spawned by these historic events.

What does the difficult history of the civil rights movement say about the operation of America's political system? The struggle for civil rights has seriously tested the politics of self-interest. Yet all of the strategic politicians who worked to advance the cause of black civil rights offer a more sanguine depiction of political ambition than the one James Madison presented in *Federalist* No. 51. Whereas Madison viewed competing ambitions as performing a limited, but vital, service of neutralizing politicians who might be inclined to serve themselves more than their constituencies, the history of civil rights portrays these same ambitious politicians as transforming moral justice into public policy. David Wilmot, Abraham Lincoln, Lyndon Johnson, and others assembled coalitions of self-interested constituencies behind policies that have rapidly evolved to secure the civil rights of all Americans.

Key Terms

affirmative action / 89
civil liberties / 91
civil rights / 90
de facto segregation / 117
de jure segregation / 117
grandfather clause / 101
Jim Crow laws / 100
literacy test / 101
poll tax / 100
quotas / 118
reverse discrimination / 89
segregation / 100
separate but equal doctrine / 101
suffragettes / 120
white primary / 100

Suggested Readings

Anderson, Kristi. *After Suffrage.* Chicago: University of Chicago Press, 1996. Anderson assembles all of the available voting and registration data in providing a detailed and varied history of the entry of women into American politics.

Black, Earl, and Merle Black. *Politics and Society in the South.* Cambridge: Harvard University Press, 1987. Weaving history and political analysis, the authors track the transformation of southern politics in reaction to the civil rights movement.

Branch, Taylor. *Parting the Waters: America in the King Years, 1954–1963.* New York: Simon and Schuster, 1988; and *Pillar of Fire: America in the King Years, 1963–65.* New York: Simon and Schuster, 1998. These two installments of Branch's detailed political history of civil rights offer a wealth of instruction to students of politics and history alike.

Carmines, Edward G., and James A. Stimson. *Issue Evolution: Race and the Transformation of American Politics.* Princeton: Princeton University Press, 1989. Although these scholars use sophisticated statistical techniques, they offer an accessible and convincing accounting of the evolution of the Democratic Party among politicians and citizens as the party of civil rights.

Garrow, David J. *Bearing the Cross: Martin Luther King Jr. and the Southern Christian Leadership Conference.* New York: Morrow, 1986. An absorbing account of the rise of King from the Montgomery bus boycott to his assassination in 1968.

Oates, Stephen B. *With Malice toward None: The Life of Abraham Lincoln.* New York: New American Library–Dutton, 1978. Our favorite Lincoln biography has two great virtues: Lincoln is shown to be a masterful politician, and the gradual emergence of emancipation as a wartime issue is described clearly.

Orfield, Gary. *The Reconstruction of Southern Education.* New York: Wiley-Interscience, 1969. A thorough case study of the enactment and implementation of the 1964 Civil Rights Act.

Chapter 5

CIVIL LIBERTIES

☆ *Has the existence of a formal Bill of Rights, which at first was omitted from the Constitution, really affected the freedoms of Americans?*

☆ *Does the Supreme Court's peculiarly large role in this area of public policy imply that democracy requires an institution of Solomon-like judges to protect it from itself?*

☆ *What roles, if any, do Congress, the president, and the states play in defining civil liberties?*

☆ *Since the Bill of Rights does not mention "right of privacy," how can the Supreme Court deem it to be a fundamental constitutional right?*

☆ *Why did the Supreme Court rule the use of the cross in a Ku Klux Klan demonstration is constitutional, but its use in a public Easter service is not?*

"Parents to Censor Children's Internet Use in Orange County Libraries"

In Orange County, California, public librarians and concerned parents meet to formulate rules requiring children to have parental permission before using the Internet in public libraries. Although the First Amendment virtually forbids the government's involvement in these matters when adults are the users, children's access—especially to pornography—remains open to regulation.

"Law to Curb Political Lies Runs Afoul of Higher Truth: The First Amendment"

The Washington State Supreme Court rules that lying in a political campaign is not a crime. Thus freedom of speech takes precedence over what some call "calculated [political] lies."

"Wisconsin OKs Civil Detention for Fetal Abuse"

The Wisconsin legislature passes a law allowing authorities to detain pregnant women who abuse drugs or alcohol. A woman's freedom of movement during the third trimester of pregnancy may compete with the state's interest in protecting fetal life.

"Not All See Eye to Eye on Biometrics"

Fingerprints, facial thermography, and iris scans may soon replace keystrokes and credit cards at America's ATM machines and checkout counters. The American Civil Liberties Union claims these procedures would violate constitutional rights to privacy and protection from unreasonable search and seizure.

"Sex Offender Notification Laws Raise Complex Issues"

"Megan's Law," which authorizes city offcials to notify parents when a convicted sex offender is living in the neighborhood where their children live or go to school, upholds a parent's "right to know," but at what cost to the sex offender's right to privacy? Publication or broadcast of the sex offender's identity by the news media is not allowed, but leaks continue to occur.

Civil liberties claims—of all kinds—dominate the headlines of today's daily newspapers and lead the television evening news programs. Some claims assert a basic freedom has been denied. Others apply established principles in new areas. Civil liberties, though, have not always occupied such a prominent spot in the nation's news. At the end of the last century readers might have had to scour newspapers for a month or more to discover such a claim. If and when gay marriages, physician-assisted suicides, and abortion occurred in nineteenth-century America, they were clandestine, and ultimately criminal, enterprises. What then has elevated individual liberty from an essentially private and local administrative matter to a prominent national policy issue?

New technologies and modern lifestyles are partly to answer for the entry of individual liberties into the public arena. Technological advances in every field from communications to medicine challenge the scope of established principles. The *principle* of free expression was not an issue in 1996 when Congress passed the Communications Decency Act allowing censorship of the Internet, or in 1997 when the Supreme Court struck it down as unconstitutional.[1] The *real* issue was how existing standards of free expression applied to this new medium in which juveniles could easily access sexually explicit language and images. Other civil liberties issues arise in response to cultural changes that give way to freer expression in lifestyle, art, and politics. Another important factor elevating civil

liberties to national prominence during the twentieth century has been the gradual recognition that personal rights belong at the national level of public policy and not under the nearly exclusive jurisdiction of states and communities. For the first hundred years of the Republic, defendants' rights amounted to little more than what the local police and sheriff would allow. And in many states local judges, prosecutors, and legal associations agreed that exclusively white (and mostly older) male jurors satisfied the standards of impartiality and that an attorney represented an unneeded luxury for indigent defendants. Local ministers tendered prayers to school principals who passed them on to teachers and students for morning recitations. Eventually, though, the national government assumed jurisdiction over defendants' rights and school prayer. With a new, expansive interpretation of the Constitution, the courts extended application of the Bill of Rights down to state and local policy as well.

The histories of civil rights and civil liberties have much in common. Chapter 4 describes how the greatest advances in civil rights occurred when a national majority took up a minority's cause; so long as the national government remained silent, slavery and segregation were secure. The federal judiciary struck the first blows against segregation, but the rights of African Americans did not substantially improve until congressional majorities joined presidents prepared to stake their party's electoral fortunes on intervening directly against segregation and black disenfranchisement. In the end, civil rights required the sustained efforts of a national majority exerting the full force of the federal government. The history of civil liberties has wound down the same path toward nationalization in that only after national institutions have assumed jurisdiction over civil liberties have claims won a sympathetic and responsive audience. But the parallels between civil rights and civil liberties are limited. Indeed, in many instances the nationalization of civil liberties policy in America has arisen from efforts to frustrate majority rule. One need look no further than the First Amendment's admonition that "Congress shall make no law . . ."

to suspect that, unlike civil rights, civil liberties are one domain in which national majorities will be constrained in fixing national policy. This language also has opened the door for the Supreme Court's involvement in defining civil liberties. Recognizing this, James Madison predicted that the courts "will consider themselves in a peculiar manner the guardians of [civil liberties]: they will be an impenetrable bulwark against every assumption of power in the legislative or executive; they will be naturally led to resist every encroachment upon rights."[2]

The first ten amendments to the Constitution were designed to limit the capacity of national majorities to impose their preferences on the press and the private behavior of the citizenry. This limitation is altogether consistent with the principle of institutional design described in Chapter 1—that is, an effective way to prevent government from imposing high conformity costs on individuals and minorities is to require broad agreement and let the resulting high transaction costs frustrate collective action. Thus in giving the Supreme Court, an institution purposely well insulated from the "popular passions of the majority," an opportunity to veto Congress in this class of decisions, the Constitution renders civil liberties one of the most difficult kinds of policies for majorities to control.

The clear and absolute language of the Bill of Rights also offers little latitude to politicians who might want to alter its constitutionally protected liberties. Some of the amendments, however, are not quite as clear-cut as they appear. For example, what does the First Amendment clause "Congress shall make no law respecting an establishment of religion . . ." really mean? It unambiguously prevents Congress from declaring one religion the "official" religion of the country, but, beyond that, the clause offers little guidance and has even fostered opposing interpretations of the relationship between church and state. For example, does it prohibit prayer in public schools? Does it deny government subsidies for transportation and textbooks for children attending private, church-sponsored schools?

Another familiar example of ambiguous language is the Second Amendment's provision that "[a] well regulated Militia, being necessary to the security of a free State, the right of the people to keep and bear Arms, shall not be infringed." When this amendment was debated in Congress, the Revolutionary War was still very much on the minds of representatives. The Supreme Court has long read the amendment as guaranteeing this right of citizens only in their capacity as soldiers in their state militias. Yet today many citizens—especially members of the National Rifle Association and callers to talk radio—persist in maintaining that the right to bear arms is an inviolable personal freedom.

Sometimes ambiguity arises when clearly worded provisions conflict with other equally clear provisions. When this happens, constitutional confusion ensues. For example, the First Amendment ensuring freedom of the press conflicts with the Sixth Amendment which guarantees the criminally accused the right to an impartial jury. Which amendment prevails when a defendant correctly complains that press coverage may make an impartial trial impossible?

Elsewhere in the Constitution the government's responsibility to pursue the country's collective interest may bring its actions into conflict with an individual's rights. For example, the preamble to the Constitution charges the national government to "provide for the common defence" and Article II assigns the president the role of "Commander in Chief." Does this presidential responsibility allow the government to restrict freedom of the press, as President Abraham Lincoln claimed, during times of war? Whether liberties are competing with one another or with other parts of the Constitution, the Bill of Rights represents a Pandora's box of unanswered policy questions.

At times all three branches of government, in grappling with an issue, disagree over what the Bill of Rights actually means. What became a protracted disagreement arose in 1990 when, in a series of rulings, the Supreme Court appeared to adopt a new standard in weighing whether state and local laws impinged on protected religious practices. In *Employment Division v. Smith* (1990) the Court ruled that laws applicable to all citizens did not violate constitutional protections just because they unintentionally burdened particular religious practices.[3] To exempt religious organizations from reasonable regulation would be tantamount to "establishing" religion, the majority of justices concluded. Suddenly religious organizations of every persuasion that had been exempt from a wide variety of laws ranging from antidrug to zoning lobbied Congress to enact a blanket law that would, in effect, exempt them from local regulations.

In 1993 Congress obliged by passing the Religious Freedom Restoration Act, which voided any law or regulation that "substantially burdened" religious practices if it could not be shown to serve a "compelling government interest . . . by the least restrictive means." In signing the new law, President Bill Clinton noted that it effectively reversed the Court's 1990 decision and was "far more consistent with the intent of the Founders than [was] the Supreme Court." Four years later the Court responded by ruling that the new law was itself unconstitutional. The Court majority reminded Congress and the president that "[t]he power to interpret a case or controversy remains in the Judiciary."[4] In response, Congress reopened hearings to consider new legislation to achieve its goals.[5] In this protracted, tit-for-tat exchange, the Supreme Court stressed the Constitution's prohibition of religious establishment; Congress and President Clinton emphasized religious freedom. The result was a rare demonstration of these institutions squaring off against each other's policy in contrast to their usual practice of jointly defining current liberties and rights. The conflict also reconfirms how the Constitution's language has permitted the modern Supreme Court to carve out a large role for itself in formulating civil liberties policy. How the judiciary moved to the forefront of civil liberties policy, and in doing so created a revolution in rights and liberties, is an important theme of this chapter.

Writing Rights and Liberties into the Constitution

The Constitution, as it emerged from the Philadelphia convention in 1787, did not seriously address civil liberties. Late in the convention George Mason of Virginia had proposed prefacing the document with a bill of rights (many state constitutions had one), but most delegates were skeptical about the need for such an addition.[6] They reasoned that the solution to tyranny lay in correctly designed institutions. Some delegates also feared that a list of rights in the Constitution might imply that the federal government had the authority to restrict the freedoms not expressly protected. Alexander Hamilton posed the question famously in *Federalist* No. 84: "Why declare that things shall not be done which there is no power to do? Why, for instance, should it be said that the liberty of the press shall not be restrained, when no power is given by which restrictions may be imposed?"

Mason was not alone in his insistence on a federal bill of rights. Throughout the ratifying process Antifederalists rallied opposition by arguing vigorously that the new constitutional plan flirted with tyranny by omitting explicit protections for the citizenry. Recognizing a chink in their armor, Madison and fellow supporters of the Constitution conceded the point and agreed that after its ratification they would introduce at the first session of the new Congress the amendments required for a bill of rights.

The Constitution actually acquired civil liberties protections in several steps. The first step was inclusion of the Bill of Rights, which insulated citizens from interference by the federal government in a variety of areas. The second step, taken over seventy-five years later, after the Civil War, was ratification of the Fourteenth Amendment, which gave the national government the authority to protect the rights of former slaves. And in the third step, which has occurred over the twentieth century, the Supreme Court has used its own various interpretations of the Fourteenth Amendment to extend the guarantees of the Bill of Rights to state and local governments. Thus the nationalization of civil liberties has not only altered the balance of power between Washington and the states, but it has also dramatically expanded the range of protections offered by the Bill of Rights. The end result is the increasingly large role the federal judiciary now plays in this area of public policy.

The First Ten Amendments

In June 1789 James Madison, elected to the First Congress as a representative from Virginia, followed through on his earlier commitment to a bill of rights by introducing seventeen constitutional amendments. His letters indicate that he may even have been persuaded of their merit. Writing to his friend Thomas Jefferson, Madison conjectured that constitutionally guaranteed rights "acquire by degrees the character of fundamental maxims of free Governments, and as they become incorporated with the national sentiment, counteract the impulses of interest and passion."[7]

Madison may have been won over to the Bill of Rights, but he remained steadfast in his belief that the states and not the national government provided the most fertile soil for tyranny. Acting on that belief, he targeted one of the amendments he submitted to the First Congress to limit state authority. It read: "No state shall infringe the right of trial by jury in criminal cases, nor the right of conscience, nor the freedom of speech or of the press." States' righters, however, were suspicious; Madison's effort to restrain the states smacked of another "nationalist" ruse, and they succeeded in striking it from the list of amendments sent to the states for ratification. Two years then passed before the required three-quarters of the states ratified the Bill of Rights. As for the Antifederalists, they may have lost the ratification fight, but they salvaged a major political concession: the Bill of Rights is their chief legacy to future generations of Americans.

In 1833 the Supreme Court secured the states' rights victory in a landmark decision that was to govern its posture and remove civil liberties from the national agenda for nearly a century. The case was *Barron v. Baltimore*.[8] Offering a glimpse at the character of civil liberties in the nineteenth century, it revolved around road repairs made by the city of Baltimore that caused a buildup of gravel and sand in the area of John Barron's wharf that impeded access of deep-bottomed vessels. Barron sued the city of Baltimore for violating his constitutionally guaranteed rights. Pointing out that the Fifth Amendment forbade the public use of private property without "just compensation," Barron argued that this provision applied to the states as well as the federal government and that Baltimore therefore owed him money.

The Supreme Court ruled unanimously against Barron, holding that the Bill of Rights restrained only the actions of the national government. The whole thrust of the Bill of Rights, the justices reasoned, was directed exclusively at federal power. In short, the federal courts could not offer relief against the excesses of state and local governments. Handed down in an era of limited federal responsibilities, the ruling rendered the Bill of Rights virtually meaningless, for most citizens' quarrels were with their state governments. If a state's residents wanted the rights that Barron claimed, they should amend their state constitution, suggested the Court. The other option—to amend the U.S. Constitution—was left unsaid. Yet achievements on the civil liberties front continued, and, instead of serving as the last word on the subject, *Barron* today is a historical relic, illustrating how Americans once regarded their rights and federal–state relations. Reflecting the low salience of civil liberties in the nation's civic discourse, an introductory American government textbook written ten years after *Barron* devoted less than 5 of its 332 pages to the Bill of Rights (see Preface).[9]

Incorporation via the Fourteenth Amendment

Among the several constitutional amendments proposed during Reconstruction, one was the Fourteenth—a

THE BILL OF RIGHTS

Amendment I

Congress shall make no law respecting an establishment of religion, or prohibiting the free exercise thereof; or abridging the freedom of speech, or of the press; or the right of the people peacefully to assemble, and to petition the Government for a redress of grievances.

Amendment II

A well regulated Militia, being necessary to the security of a free State, the right of the people to keep and bear Arms, shall not be infringed.

Amendment III

No Soldier shall, in time of peace be quartered in any house, without the consent of the Owner, nor in time of war, but in a manner to be prescribed by law.

Amendment IV

The right of the people to be secure in their persons, houses, papers, and effects, against unreasonable searches and seizures, shall not be violated, and no Warrants shall issue, but upon probable cause, supported by Oath or affirmation, and particularly describing the place to be searched, and the persons or things to be seized.

Amendment V

No person shall be held to answer for a capital, or otherwise infamous crime, unless on a presentment or indictment of a Grand Jury, except in cases arising in the land or naval forces, or in the Militia, when in actual service in time of War or public danger; nor shall any person be subject for the same offence to be twice put in jeopardy or life or limb; nor shall be compelled in any criminal case to be a witness against himself, nor be deprived of life, liberty, or property, without due process of law; nor shall private property be taken for public use, without just compensation.

Amendment VI

In all criminal prosecutions, the accused shall enjoy the right to a speedy and public trial, by an impartial jury of the State and district wherein the crime shall have been committed, which district shall have been previously ascertained by law, and to be informed of the nature and cause of the accusation; to be confronted with the witnesses against him; to have compulsory process for obtaining witnesses in his favor, and to have the Assistance of Counsel for his defence.

Amendment VII

In Suits at common law, where the value in controversy shall exceed twenty dollars, the right of trial by jury shall be preserved, and no fact tried by a jury, shall be otherwise re-examined in any Court of the United States, than according to the rules of the common law.

Amendment VIII

Excessive bail shall not be required, nor excessive fines imposed, nor cruel and unusual punishments inflicted.

Amendment IX

The enumeration in the Constitution, of certain rights, shall not be construed to deny or disparage others retained by the people.

Amendment X

The powers not delegated to the United States by the Constitution, nor prohibited by it to the States, are reserved to the States respectively, or to the people.

text crammed with now-familiar phrases (see box). Although the amendment was intended initially to protect former slaves by explicitly declaring that rights of citizenship were not subject to state controls, over time its sweeping language led other groups to seek its umbrella protections. Yet nearly a half-century of jurisprudence would pass before the Supreme Court would begin to interpret the Fourteenth Amendment language as requiring the states to adhere to the national government's Bill of Rights protections.[10] One of the great ironies of American history is that while this amendment failed to achieve its immediate objective, a century later it extended the rights and liberties of all citizens in directions unimaginable to its authors.

The first sentence of the amendment provides for a unified national citizenship and thereby directly contradicts the Court's assertion in *Barron v. Baltimore* that citizenship in a state and citizenship in the nation are separate affiliations. The second sentence states flatly that *all* citizens enjoy the same civil liberties and rights (the **due process clause** and the **equal protection clause**). To the modern reader this language is not confining in any way, but in 1868 its nationalizing thrust eluded most readers.

In 1873 the Supreme Court rejected its first opportunity to incorporate the Bill of Rights into the Fourteenth Amendment. In the *Slaughterhouse Cases,* a group of disgruntled butchers sued to invalidate a New Orleans ordinance that gave a single company a monopoly over all slaughterhouse business.[11] They based their appeal on the Fourteenth Amendment, arguing that the monopoly denied them the "privileges and immunities" of citizens. The Court did not agree. By a 5–4 decision it ruled that the monopoly did not violate the Fourteenth Amendment because the amendment was intended to protect black citizens. Moreover, application of the amendment broadly to state policy would "fetter and degrade the State governments by subjecting them to the control of Congress." With that decision, the Court effectively short-circuited any future development of the privileges

FOURTEENTH AMENDMENT
Section 1

All persons born or naturalized in the United States and subject to the jurisdiction thereof, are citizens of the United States and of the State wherein they reside. No State shall make or enforce any law which shall abridge the *privileges or immunities* of citizens of the United States; nor shall any State deprive any person of life, liberty, or property, without *due process of law;* nor deny to any person within its jurisdiction the *equal protection of the laws* (emphasis added).

and immunities clause; lawyers had to turn to the due process clause when seeking incorporation of the Bill of Rights into the Fourteenth Amendment. Although these plaintiffs consistently lost their cases as well, most justices agreed that the due process provision might be construed to protect certain unspecified "fundamental rights."[12]

Some twenty-five years into the twentieth century the Court began to incorporate into the Fourteenth Amendment those provisions of the Bill of Rights dealing with personal freedoms.[13] The justices approached this task gingerly (note the paucity of civil liberties cases in the first half of the twentieth century in Figure 5–1). Only gradually, about the same time it was relinquishing its custodial duties in behalf of laissez-faire capitalism, did the Supreme Court assume guardianship of civil liberties by applying piecemeal the various provisions of the Bill of Rights to state laws and practices. Through this process, called **selective incorporation,** civil liberties have been gradually "nationalized" (Table 5–1).

In the 1930s and 1940s the First Amendment freedoms (speech, press, and religion) were taken up by the Court, and they remain the rights most carefully protected. At first, criminal rights were viewed as a special class of rights for which incorporation did not apply.[14] But then, in the 1960s, most of the provisions of the Fourth, Fifth,

Figure 5–1 The Growth of Civil Liberties in the Supreme Court Caseload, 1923–1991

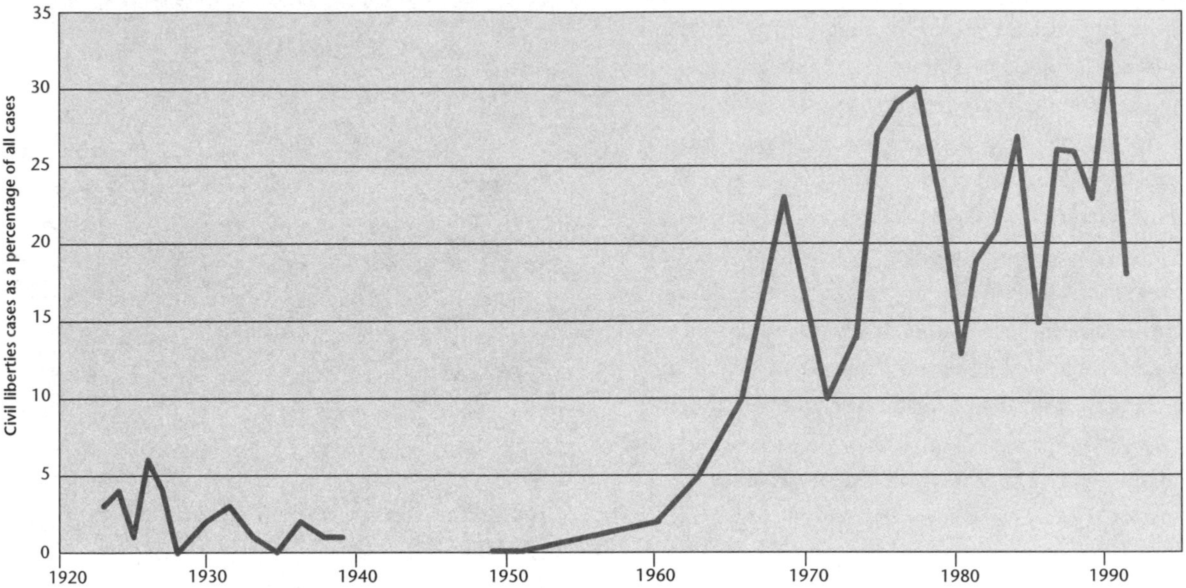

Source: Compiled from annual (1923–1938) and biannual (1948–1995) updates of the Harvard Law Review.
Note: Data unavailable for 1932, 1933, 1939–1947.

and Sixth Amendments also were covered through the due process and equal protection clauses (Table 5–1). Today, a third wave of advances in civil liberties may be forming as judges and politicians explore the right to privacy.

The incorporation decisions handed down by the Supreme Court since 1925 have served as precedents in guiding lower federal and state courts and, by offering new opportunities for litigation, have generated the dramatic growth in the civil liberties docket of the Court (Figure 5–1). Yet the case-by-case approach to incorporation has never taken the form of a sweeping ideological shifting of ground. Indeed, some provisions of the Bill of Rights are still not applied to the states: the Second Amendment right to keep and bear arms, the Third Amendment's prohibition against quartering soldiers, the Fifth and Sixth Amendment provisions concerning grand jury hearing, the Seventh Amendment right to a jury trial

in civil cases, and the Eighth Amendment right against excessive bail and fines. Nonetheless, the accumulated precedents mean that Madison's vision of the national government as the ultimate guarantor of individual rights has largely been realized.

Judicial Interpretation

The incorporation of provisions of the Bill of Rights into the Fourteenth Amendment was a historic development in civil liberties, comparable to adoption of the Bill of Rights itself. As we have seen, incorporation occurred not through legislative mandate or the amendment process but through judicial interpretation. Once this was done, the Supreme Court could turn to the more substantive issue of whether particular state policies violated constitutional protections and, if so, what the remedies should be.

Supreme Court justices agree that as jurists they are

Table 5-1 Cases Incorporating Provisions of the Bill of Rights into the Due Process Clause of the Fourteenth Amendment

Constitutional Provision	Case	Year
First Amendment		
Freedom of speech and press	Gitlow v. New York	1925
Freedom of assembly	DeJonge v. Oregon	1937
Freedom of petition	Hague v. CIO	1939
Free exercise of religion	Cantwell v. Connecticut	1940
No establishment of religion	Everson v. Board of Education	1947
Fourth Amendment		
No unreasonable search and seizure	Wolf v. Colorado	1949
Exclusionary rule	Mapp v. Ohio	1961
Fifth Amendment		
Payment of compensation for taking private property	Chicago, Burlington and Quincy R. Co. v. Chicago	1897
Protection from self-incrimination	Malloy v. Hogan	1964
Protection from double jeopardy	Benton v. Maryland	1969
When jeopardy attaches	Crist v. Bretz	1978
Sixth Amendment		
Right to public trial	In re Oliver	1948
Right to due notice of accusation	Cole v. Arkansas	1948
Right to counsel (felonies)	Gideon v. Wainwright	1963
Right to confront and cross-examine adverse witnesses	Pointer v. Texas	1965
Right to speedy trial	Klopfer v. North Carolina	1967
Right to compulsory process to obtain witnesses	Washington v. Texas	1967
Right to jury trial (felonies)	Duncan v. Louisiana	1968
Right to counsel in all cases involving jail terms	Argersinger v. Hamlin	1972
Eighth Amendment		
Protection from cruel and unusual punishment	Louisiana ex rel. Francis v. Resweber	1947
Ninth Amendment		
Right to privacy[a]	Griswold v. Connecticut	1965

Source: Adapted from Lee Epstein and Thomas G. Walker, *Constitutional Law for a Changing America: Rights, Liberties, and Justice,* 3d ed. (Washington, D.C.: CQ Press, 1998), Table 1-4.

a. The word *privacy* does not appear in the Ninth Amendment nor anywhere in the text of the Constitution. In *Griswold* several members of the Court viewed the Ninth Amendment as guaranteeing (and incorporating) that right.

obligated to interpret the Constitution as objectively as possible. Yet on any particular ruling they frequently disagree—sometimes sharply—over what an "objective" interpretation prescribes. A literalist, finding no language in the Constitution that protects burning of the U.S. flag, might conclude that this act is not protected in the Bill of Rights. Another justice might view flag burning as a kind of political expression sufficiently close to speech to deserve First Amendment protection.

All self-respecting jurists subscribe to the view that when they don their robes and take the bench they must shed all of their personal preferences, ideologies, and partisanship. But evidence reveals that their efforts are not as successful as they might think; the personal and political ideologies of the nine justices on the Supreme Court are evident in almost every decision. Consequently, as justices come and go from the Court, judicial doctrine may change. Nativity scenes deemed objectionable and removed one Christmas pass constitutional scrutiny and are reinstalled the next. Students of jurisprudence have long accepted the fact that justices, like members of Congress and presidents, can be accurately classified as liberals and conservatives. As a result, trends in civil liberties tend to reflect the shifting ideological composition of the Court (Figure 5–2).

The reality that justices do follow their ideological beliefs has its advantages, particularly for the presidents who nominate them and the senators who vote on their confirmation. By selecting nominees whose political values agree with their own, the White House and the Senate can seek to influence the course of judicial policy. Far from undermining democratic responsibility, judicial ideology allows elected officeholders to keep the judiciary from straying too far from the majority opinion in the nation. The Supreme Court shifted in a conservative direction shortly after Republican Richard Nixon, elected president in 1968, started filling vacancies to the Court, and the trend continued even after he left office (Figure 5–2). Until Democratic president Bill Clinton made his first appointment in 1993, every justice was a Republican nomi-

Figure 5–2 Supreme Court Decisions on Civil Liberties Cases, 1953–1995 Terms

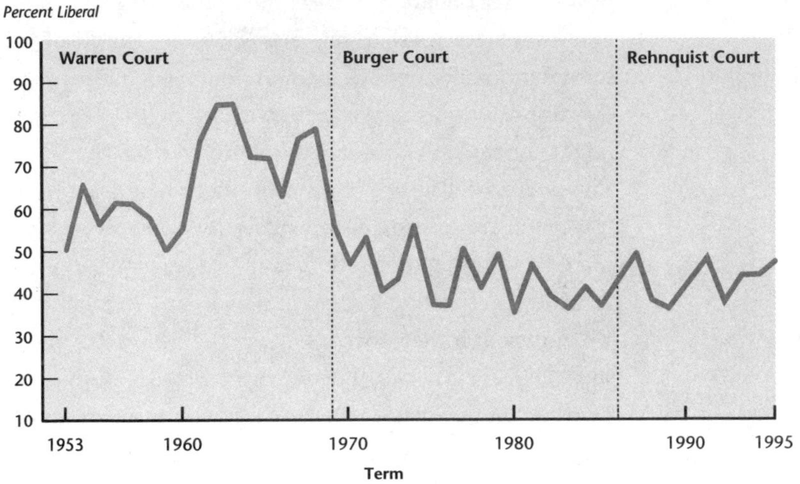

Percent Liberal

Source: Adapted from Lee Epstein and Thomas G. Walker, *Constitutional Law for a Changing America: Rights, Liberties, and Justice,* 3d ed. (Washington, D.C.: CQ Press, 1998), Figure 1–6.

nee. Chapter 9 examines this and other control mechanisms available to the elected branches to keep judicial policy from diverging sharply and potentially creating a constitutional crisis. Nowhere is this danger greater than in the delicate area of civil liberties, with its often polarizing effects on public opinion and its reliance on the Supreme Court to set national policy.

Freedom of Speech

Freedom of speech is essential to representative government and the exercise of individual autonomy. But what exactly constitutes legitimate expression? And how does one go about balancing free speech against other rights and claims?

When the issue is free speech, Americans do not always practice what they preach. Almost all survey respondents endorse the Constitution's Bill of Rights, but when they are pinned down with specific, hypothetical examples, their tolerance for freedom of speech depends on who is doing the speaking and where. In a 1996 survey, 83 percent of national respondents believed homosexuals should be allowed to speak in their communities, but only 62 percent were willing to extend this right to "an avowed

racist" (Table 5–2). Less than half were prepared to allow a racist to teach in a college. The good news, however, is that Americans have become much more tolerant across both groups and forms of expression.[15]

Free Expression and National Security

Throughout the early years of the twentieth century, the Supreme Court rejected arguments for nationalizing free speech guarantees through the Fourteenth Amendment and continued to leave protection of free expression up to the state governments. Typical of the Court's posture during this era was a 1922 judgment in which it declared, as baldly as possible, that the "Constitution of the United States imposes upon the states no obligation to confer upon those within their jurisdiction either the right of free speech or the right of silence."[16] By the end of World War I in 1918, over thirty states had enacted sedition laws aimed at pacifists, socialists, and communists.

The Court did, however, seek to define the degree to which *federal* legislation must protect free speech. That opportunity arose in the 1919 case of *Schenck v. United States.*[17] In mailings to men eligible for the military draft, Charles Schenck had argued that World War I was immoral; he urged draftees to resist. Schenck was convicted under the Espionage Act of 1917 for attempting to foment disloyalty and mutiny in the armed forces during time of war. Writing for a unanimous Court, Justice Oliver Wendell Holmes declared,

The most stringent protection of free speech would not protect a man in falsely shouting fire in a theater and causing panic. . . . The question in every case is whether the words used are in such circumstances and are of such a nature as to create a *clear and present danger* that they will bring about the substantive evils that Congress has a right to prevent (emphasis added).

Table 5–2 Attitudes of Americans on Freedom of Speech

	Should be allowed to speak (percent)	Should be allowed to teach in a college (percent)	His or her book should be allowed in your library (percent)
An admitted communist			
1954	28	6	29
1976	56	44	58
1985	59	46	59
1996	66	60	67
A person who believes blacks are genetically inferior			
1976	62	42	62
1985	57	44	62
1996	62	48	66
Someone against all churches and religion			
1954	38	12	37
1976	65	42	61
1985	66	47	62
1996	74	58	71
Homosexual			
1976	64	54	57
1985	69	60	57
1996	83	77	71

Source: General Social Survey, National Opinion Research Center, University of Chicago, various years.

When the government is unable to show that particular words demonstrate a "clear and present danger," the words are protected. Holmes's **clear and present danger test** became widely adopted throughout the federal judiciary as a criterion for distinguishing protected from unprotected expression. But the test did not ensure decisions that favored individual freedom. In Schenck's case, the Court ruled that his circulars did in fact constitute a legitimate danger, and it sent him to jail.

In 1925 the Court finally applied the First Amendment protections to the states.[18] The case was brought to the Court by Benjamin Gitlow, the leader of a radical faction of the Socialist Party who was arrested in New York City at the height of the Red Scare. Charged with advocating "criminal anarchy" through organized labor strikes, Gitlow was found guilty in a New York State court. In its review of his case, the Supreme Court ruled that states could not interfere with the "fundamental personal rights and 'liberties'" contained in the First Amendment. The Court thus established the Fourteenth Amendment's jurisdiction over the states. But, moving cautiously, the Court continued: "the State cannot reasonably be required to measure the danger from every such utterance in the nice balance of a jeweler's scale. A single revolutionary spark may kindle a fire that, smoldering for a time, may burst into a sweeping and destructive conflagration." So, Gitlow went to prison.

Even during World War II and the conflicts that followed, the Court persisted in giving the government the benefit of the doubt during times of crisis. During the Korean War (1951–1953), the Court upheld the Alien Registration Act of 1940 by affirming the conviction of eleven top members of the American Communist Party for having advocated the violent overthrow of the government.[19] The government, the Court argued, could not idly watch traitors hatch a rebellion. Indeed, Chief Justice Frederick Vinson proposed a new "clear and probable danger" test for the courts to enlist in free expression cases: "In each case [the courts] must ask whether the gravity of the 'evil,' discounted by its probability, justifies such invasion of free speech as is necessary to avoid the danger."

The evolution of the Supreme Court's thinking on the relationship of national security to free speech is important in two respects. First, it strikes at the heart of the ability of government officials to block opposition. This finding is confirmed by recent instances in which the leaders of weak or pseudo democracies have invoked national security to suppress opposition political parties. Second, this jurisprudence provides a rationale for relaxing freedom of speech in nonsecurity cases. If speech does not constitute a danger to public safety, why inhibit it?

Cracking Down on Dissent in Wartime

"Woe be to the man that seeks to stand in our way in this day of high resolution," warned President Woodrow Wilson in his April 2, 1917, speech to Congress asking for a declaration of war against Germany. Those words took on new meaning shortly after America's entry into World War I, when Congress passed the Espionage Act (1917) and then outlawed open opposition to the war. The cartoon, showing Uncle Sam towering above enemies of the state, appeared in 1918.

America's entry into World War II some twenty-three years later brought new legislation, the

Alien Registration Act (Smith Act, 1940). But none of these measures was as harsh as the martial law Abraham Lincoln declared some eighty years earlier in the Civil War. It allowed him to jail without trial thousands of newspaper editors and other southern sympathizers in the North.

Why do democratic governments limit their citizens' freedoms during war? Critics of wartime patriotism suggest that leaders who have little respect for the Bill of Rights find in war an opportunity to curb citizens' liberties. The historical record contains many examples of antilibertarian zealotry.

Nonetheless, a rational basis exists for heightened demands for conformity during wartime. Wars can demand great sacrifice in the form of higher taxes, rationing of basic consumer goods, dislocation of families, and hundreds of thousands of war casualties. Even a fully patriotic population might respond to such demands with rampant free riding if citizens feel they can successfully shirk their responsibilities. Therefore, even the most popular wars, such as World War II, trigger compulsory military service. Any dissent is countered by demands for conformity.

Dissent at home has ramifications outside the country as well. A government riddled by disagreement will be hard-pressed to convince the enemy that it will persevere to victory. If dissent strengthens the enemy's resolve, then it will prolong the war and, by extension, the deaths and deprivations that accompany war. Thus a nation at war has powerful incentives to demand greater conformity from its citizens. Presumably, such demands arise in democracies because a majority of the citizenry want them. Weakened political liberties and increased conformity do entail risks, however. Among other things, they loosen the citizens' control over leaders, who then are freer to pursue imprudent policies that the nation would not otherwise agree to.

Shortly after the attack on Pearl Harbor, President Franklin Roosevelt began issuing executive orders that placed restrictions on Japanese Americans living on the West Coast. Eventually, more than 110,000 Japanese Americans—including native-born U.S. citizens—were removed to internment camps throughout the nation. The internees were given little time to dispose of their homes, businesses, or other property, which for many, caused financial ruin.

Nonthreatening Speech and Expression

In 1969 the Court overturned the conviction of a Ku Klux Klan leader under an Ohio law that prohibited the advocacy of violence as a means to political reform.[20] The Klan leader had maintained that "the nigger should be returned to Africa, the Jew returned to Israel" and, at a cross-burning rally, had called for "vengeance" against African Americans and Jews. Yet the Court let him off, holding that speech that endorses "lawless action" cannot be punished unless such action is "imminent." In 1977 the Court also supported the right of the National Socialist Party, modeled on Adolf Hitler's Nazi Party, to parade through a predominantly Jewish community in Skokie, Illinois, while wearing full Nazi regalia.[21] Some observers found the federal government's defense of the free speech rights of the Ku Klux Klan and the American Nazi Party to be a perversion since their purpose was to intimidate fellow citizens. But others saw in the controversial decisions a commitment to civil liberties, even for marginal and offensive groups that offend the majority's values or interests.

Speech and parades are not the only kinds of expression protected by modern case law. In 1969 the Supreme Court ruled that freedom of speech allowed high school students in Des Moines, Iowa, to wear black armbands to school to express their opposition to the Vietnam War.[22] War protesters also began burning and otherwise desecrating the American flag. Court decisions protecting these highly unpopular acts soon followed. The defendant in *Texas v. Johnson* (1989) was a protester who burned an American flag outside of the 1984 Republican National Convention in Dallas, Texas.[23] Justice William Brennan, writing for the Court in a 5–4 decision, held that "if there is a bedrock principle underlying the First Amendment, it is that the Government may not prohibit the expression of an idea simply because society finds the idea itself offensive or disagreeable." The burning of the flag, in this case, was held to be an expression of a political idea and thus was constitutionally sanctioned.

Shortly after the *Texas v. Johnson* decision, public opinion polls found that two-thirds of the American public favored a constitutional amendment protecting the flag. In response, Congress promptly enacted the Flag Protection Act of 1989, which, in less than a year, the Supreme Court struck down as unconstitutional.[24] The issue did not die, however. In a national survey conducted in July 1998, 79 percent of respondents said flag burning should be illegal; only 17 percent said it should not be.[25] Such figures inspire

In the summer of 1984 Texas authorities arrested Gregory Lee Johnson for violating the Texas flag desecration law. As the flag burned, other demonstrators at the Republican National Convention chanted, "America, the red, white, and blue, we spit on you." Johnson was convicted, fined, and sentenced to one year in jail. In 1989 the Supreme Court ruled that Johnson's conviction violated his First Amendment expression rights.

elected officials, and by May 1999 the House of Representatives had passed a resolution calling for a constitutional amendment. The Senate appeared poised to do so as well.

Sexually Explicit Expression

Obscenity, whether expressed verbally, graphically, cybernetically, or via the conventional written page, is not protected by the First Amendment. The problem for the Supreme Court and law enforcement, however, has been defining obscenity and drafting objective standards that enable judges and police to distinguish the merely pornographic (sexually explicit) from the truly obscene. Until the 1950s obscenity was pretty much what local city officials, public librarians, postmasters, and movie censors

said it was. In the meantime, the Supreme Court was adhering to an 1870s doctrine that designated any material inappropriate for children as obscene. Such a doctrine, however, required a variety of officials—from librarians to the cop on the beat—to make judgment calls about what constituted obscenity.

By 1920 Hollywood was practicing self-censorship. Its film review mandated, among other things, that actors keep at least one foot on the floor during all bedroom scenes. (This proved to be an effective rule.) In the 1930s censorship found its way into a U.S. Post Office where a diligent postal official charged with enforcing the Comstock Act, which banned obscene material from the U.S. mail, presumably read and seized copies of James Joyce's novel *Ulysses,* claiming it contained "obscene" passages.[26]

Despite these restrictive rules and practices, pornography was flourishing by the 1950s. Those charged with enforcing communities' moral codes were losing the war. Yet civil libertarians, including lawyers in the American Civil Liberties Union (ACLU), were not happy either; obscenity policy allowed local officials to catch and prosecute the producers and consumers of pornography. Against this contentious backdrop, the Supreme Court reviewed obscenity policy in 1957 and issued new doctrine in *Roth v. United States.*[27] The majority ruled that a work was obscene if it was "utterly without redeeming social importance" and, "to the average person, applying contemporary community standards, the dominant theme of the material, taken as a whole, appeals to prurient interests." With this language, the Court tried to thread its way between the conservative forces calling for tight local regulation of loose morals and the libertarians who sought to banish the concept of "obscenity" from jurisprudence. But every key word in the passage is ambiguous and subject to lenient or restrictive interpretation. Who decides the tastes of the "average person?" (This standard would seem to call for elections!) Which community's "standards"—a town's, a state's, or the nation's—should be applied? How much obscene material may a work contain before it "dominates" the work's theme? And how does one begin to define "prurient" in a way that would offer clear guidelines to those charged with enforcing obscenity laws?

Only as the Court answered these questions in later rulings did the full extent of the libertarian victory become clear. One of the most important of these follow-up decisions defined "community standards" as national standards, which is itself so vague almost nothing could be deemed obscene.[28] Answers or not, these rulings propelled all federal, state, and local efforts to define and regulate pornography into federal court.

The late 1960s, however, saw the libertarian victory thwarted by the views of an increasingly conservative Court. Within five months of his inauguration in 1969, Republican Richard Nixon had made the first of the four Supreme Court appointments he would make over the next two years. These new justices quickly shifted the nine-member Court in a more conservative direction. By 1973 the Court was ready to formulate clearer and more stringent doctrine (and perhaps lighten its caseload). In the case of *Miller v. California* the Court shifted primary authority for obscenity policy back to the state—and, implicitly, local— governments.[29] Under this standard, the governments could deem as obscene those materials which "taken as a whole, appeal to the prurient interest in sex, which portray sexual conduct in a patently offensive way, and which, taken as a whole, do not have serious literary, artistic, political or scientific value." Obscene materials could then be banned from sale or exhibition. In the years since *Miller,* many commentators, including members of the Court, have argued that this test still fails to offer adequate guidelines. Indeed, it appears to offer little improvement over Justice Potter Stewart's 1964 "I know it when I see it" criterion for obscenity.[30] Yet the return of the issue to the state level has greatly strengthened local regulatory control. Moreover, since adoption of *Miller* as its prevailing doctrine, the Court has decided less than a quarter of its obscenity cases in favor of First Amendment claims.[31]

Overall, then, the Court has struggled for decades to

New York City's 1998 crackdown on X-rated enterprises put shops like this one, near Times Square, out of business. The new regulations banned sex shops, strip clubs, and adult book and video stores within five hundred feet of residences, schools, day care centers, churches, and each other.

define obscenity in a way that protects both individual liberty and public decency and leads to doctrine that can be consistently administered. But the task might be impossible, especially in view of the onslaught of new media, such as the Internet. How can local standards apply when anyone can go to the local library and instantaneously call up pornographic video from Copenhagen? As one sign of the Court's struggle to adapt doctrine to new circumstances, in 1997 it struck down the Communications Decency Act (1996), a law criminalizing the "indecent" and "patently offensive" online transmission of sexual materials accessible by children.[32] In trying to protect children from obscenity, the "vaguely worded" law would, the Court ruled, stifle adult access to protected speech. Congress and the president responded in 1998 with the Child Online Protection Act which requires Websites to require some form of adult identification such as a credit card before offering their obscene or merely pornographic products. (The law resembles city ordinances that allow barkers—but not dancers—outside topless "clubs" to entice passersby to enter.) Nonetheless, a federal judge blocked

enforcement of the law in early 1999, and a long court battle appears to be ahead for the law and its enforcers.

Freedom of the Press

An independent press plays an indispensable role in maintaining a representative democracy. Without reliable information about the performance of officeholders, citizens would find themselves hard-pressed to monitor their elected agents. Without the news media, politicians would find it difficult to communicate with their constituents and to keep an eye on each other.

As for the news media itself, freedom of the press allows reporters and editors to find and report their own news in addition to simply reporting what politicians say and do. The Framers viewed a free press as yet another "check" against political abuse and backed their view by writing sweeping provisions for press freedom into the First Amendment. In self-recognition of their special status, publishers and other news professionals sometimes refer to themselves as members of the "fourth branch" of government (see Chapter 14).

But just what freedom and license does the First Amendment offer the modern news media? Two factors define the freedom of the modern news media in American politics. The first is the extent to which the media are free from government regulation; the second is the media's prerogative to encroach on the rights and privileges of politicians, businesses, and private citizens.

Prior Restraint

When a government (or a school administration, for that matter) attempts to prevent the publication and dissemination of written and recorded speech, it is exercising **prior restraint.** Over the years the Supreme Court has taken a very dim view of this form of censorship.

The Court began to distinguish prior restraint from other kinds of censorship in 1931. Jay Near was using the small Minnesota newspaper he edited as a platform for vilifying Jews and politicians.[33] When a state judge ordered him to stop publication, Near challenged the Minnesota law that allowed local courts and law enforcement to shut down a "malicious, scandalous, and defamatory newspaper, magazine, or other periodical." Finding the state-ordered injunction especially objectionable, the Supreme Court in *Near v. Minnesota* (1931) overturned the state court and effectively incorporated state policy into the First Amendment of the Bill of Rights. In enunciating new doctrine, the Court did acknowledge that national security might sometimes require government censorship.

In 1971, however, the Court demonstrated its extreme reluctance to allow prior restraint even when security concerns were raised. The Nixon administration had won a restraining order from a lower court preventing the *New York Times* and other newspapers from publishing the Pentagon Papers, an immense top-secret compilation of U.S. decisions and information about the Vietnam War.[34] In striking down the lower court's decision, the Supreme Court once again followed its four-decades-old precedent: "Any system of prior restraints of expression comes to this Court bearing a heavy presumption against its constitutional validity." In other words, the government had to demonstrate—and in this case had failed to do so—that publication of the documents would damage national security.

Today, this presumption lives on, and prior restraint is rarely permitted, except in "troopship" circumstances, when a news report threatens to endanger the lives of American soldiers by publicly disclosing their position.

Press versus Individual Rights

While tension between the individual and the government lies at the core of freedom of speech cases, freedom of the press cases are as likely to pit the press against individual rights as against the government. For example, the Sixth Amendment guarantees that "[i]n all criminal prosecutions, the accused shall enjoy the right to a speedy and public trial, by an impartial jury of the State. . . ." The importance of an impartial jury is obvious. As for a public trial, the history of its concept has less to do with prosecuting criminals than with preventing law enforcement officials from meting out arbitrary justice. Exposing the judicial process to public scrutiny, and by implication the press, was intended to help keep police, judges, and prosecutors in check.

In one famous trial, however, public scrutiny led to public chaos that threatened the defendant's right to a fair hearing. In 1954 Ohio osteopath Samuel Sheppard (whose case inspired the long-running television series and movie *The Fugitive*) was convicted of murdering his wife. His trial attracted almost as much news coverage as the O. J. Simpson trial some forty years later. Yet the Simpson trial, however tumultuous, was a model of judicial and press decorum compared with the Sheppard proceedings. The testimony of witnesses could not be heard at times because of the din from a courtroom packed with reporters. Moreover, the jurors, who were not sequestered, were exposed to the media circus throughout the trial. Order was eventually restored, but only years after Sheppard's imprisonment: in 1966 the Supreme Court found that the "carnival atmosphere" surrounding the trial had undermined Sheppard's right to a fair day in court, and it reversed his conviction.[35]

Signaling a victory for the Washington Post *and New York Times, a pleased pressman at the* Post *holds the first edition of the paper announcing the Supreme Court's decision in* New York Times v. United States, *handed down June 30, 1971. The papers had contended that the government's attempt to enjoin publication of the so called Pentagon Papers amounted to nothing less than prior restraint.*

Does the *Sheppard* case indicate that the press should be uniformly banned from trials involving sensitive issues or famous defendants? Apparently not. In 1982 the Supreme Court overturned a Massachusetts law that excluded the public from trials of sex crimes involving victims under the age of eighteen.[36] Although it conceded the value of protecting an underage victim, the majority argued that the victim's welfare did not justify the mandatory exclusion of the public. Rather, the question of public access should be decided on a case-by-case basis.

A similar strain of judicial reasoning crops up in libel doctrine (**libel** is the issuance in written form of false and malicious information that damages another person's reputation). Well-established standards defining libel and monetary damages guide civil litigation involving private citizens, but when one party is a newspaper and the other a public figure—such as a politician, televangelist, or movie star—an altogether different doctrine kicks in. Simply stated, public figures largely forfeit their right to privacy. The injured party must prove not only that a newspaper knowingly published a false story that damaged the individual's reputation, but also that "malice" was intended—a test that raises the bar of proof so high that politicians stand little chance of winning in court.[37] Presumably, because the press is free from any real threat of being sued for knowingly spreading falsehoods about a public figure, it will feel less constrained in seeking the truth, even when public officials might find the truth embarrassing.

Freedom of Religion

Although the First Amendment is best known for its free speech guarantees, it actually begins with religion. Many of the early colonies had designated official churches, which believers and nonbelievers alike were forced to attend and support with their taxes (this practice continued in some states even after independence). And yet by the Revolution, America already was home to a great variety of religious denominations. In *Federalist* No. 10, Madison identified religious conflict as one of the issues bound to generate factional struggle.[38] In fact, Virginia's religious fights had given Madison the insight that factional conflict could provide a solid foundation for democracy.[39]

The religious freedom provision of the First Amendment prohibits Congress from passing any legislation "respecting an *establishment* of religion, or prohibiting the *free exercise* thereof" (emphasis added). But like the rest of the amendment, the **establishment of religion clause** and the **free exercise clause** at first applied only to actions of the federal government. In fact, some states retained laws discriminating against particular religions for years after the Bill of Rights was added to the Constitution.

Madison and his friend Thomas Jefferson both sub-

scribed to the frequently stated view that the First Amendment erects "a wall of separation" between church and state.[40] But theirs was merely one interpretation. Separation is not mentioned in the Constitution itself, and it has not been followed consistently by Congress or the Court. Nor can it be in many instances. Indeed, the Court has argued that tensions between the free exercise and establishment clauses may allow government to support religious institutions in various ways.

Establishment

Because the national government rarely had occasion to subsidize religious institutions or their ancillary activities during the nineteenth century, the first real establishment of religion decision did not come until 1899 when the Supreme Court allowed the federal government to subsidize a Catholic hospital that was open to all patients.[41] In 1947 the Supreme Court attached the due process clause to the establishment provision and applied it to the states.[42] As the Court entered the field of state policy, it found some states subsidizing parochial schools and others offering religious training in the public schools. A 1960 survey of school districts revealed that 77 percent of schools in the South and 68 percent in the East were conducting Bible readings.[43] And throughout the nation most students accompanied the Pledge of Allegiance to the American flag with a prayer.

Over the years, most of the controversial policies triggering establishment arguments have concerned the various ways states have sought to subsidize private schools. Tuition grants, textbooks, and school buses have all had their day in court. The most precedent-setting of these cases was *Lemon v. Kurtzman* (1971), in which the Court specified three conditions every state law must satisfy to avoid running afoul of the establishment prohibition:[44]

1. The statute in question "must have a secular legislative purpose," such as remedial education.

2. The statute's "primary effect must be one that neither advances nor inhibits religion."

3. The statute must not foster "an excessive government entanglement with religion."

If any of these conditions are violated, the policy transgresses the establishment ban. The Court was trying mightily to construct clear doctrine, but with highly subjective criteria such as "primary" and "excessive," it succeeded better perhaps in describing how justices thought through these issues than in prescribing how particular cases should be decided.

The flaws of the *Lemon* test were evident in the highly inconsistent decisions that followed its adoption. For example, sometimes the federal courts applied the test to require that nativity scenes on public property be dismantled; at other times judges enlisted the same guidelines to approve official displays of nativity scenes as a celebration of the historic origins of Christmas.[45] In the Court's view, prayers in schools and convocation exercises clearly violated the Constitution, but it had no problem with the prayers that began each day's business in Congress. In the judgment of one constitutional scholar, the vague, three-pronged *Lemon* test inspired judges to engage in reasoning "that would glaze the minds of medieval scholastics."[46]

By the 1990s the *Lemon* test was fading from establishment decisions as justices increasingly relied on the test of a policy's "neutrality." Tax credits for religious school tuition were permissible if they also were available for secular, private instruction. Religious organizations could meet on public school property, but their access could be no greater than that provided any other school club.

In 1994 the Supreme Court applied the emerging neutrality doctrine in *Board of Education v. Grumet.*[47] A sect of Orthodox Jews in upstate New York persuaded the state legislature to carve out a new, publicly financed school district that would include only their village. Since students who had no special needs attended a private religious school, the new district would offer only special education classes for the community's disabled children. The Court ruled, however, that creation of this school district breached the rule of neutrality and was thus uncon-

As part of its holiday decorations, Allegheny County, Pennsylvania, erected on public property a nativity scene and a combined Christmas tree and menorah display. In County of Allegheny v. ACLU *(1989) the Supreme Court ruled that the crèche violated the separation of church and state principle, but that the combined exhibit did not.*

What's wrong with this picture? Chief Justice William Rehnquist stands alongside Senate chaplain Lloyd Ogilvie, who is about to read the opening prayer in the January 14, 1999, session of the Clinton impeachment trial. This poignant image reveals the inconsistency that has justices praying with lawmakers while local pastors are prevented from offering a benediction at high school graduation ceremonies.

stitutional: "The district's creation ran uniquely counter to state practice, following the lines of a religious community where the customary and neutral principles would not have dictated the same result."

Of all of the establishment issues, none has aroused more enduring enmity among religious conservatives than the Supreme Court doctrine banning prayer and Bible readings in public schools. This issue is, arguably, the only real wall separating church and state not yet breached by the Supreme Court. In *Engel v. Vitale* (1962) the Court ruled the following New York State–composed prayer unconstitutional: "Almighty God, we acknowledge our dependence on Thee, and we beg thy blessings upon us, our parents, our teachers, and our country."[48] The next year it invalidated Bible readings in public schools.[49]

Over the years these decisions and the later ones that

bolstered them have angered many Americans. Indeed, neither a majority of the public nor those politicians who periodically ask for their votes have ever been won over to the Supreme Court's point of view (Figure 5–3). Congress has periodically considered a constitutional amendment allowing school prayer, most recently in 1998. Each time, however, proponents attracted majority support in Congress but failed to win the two-thirds support necessary to send an amendment to the states.

In the absence of a national policy alternative, states have continued to pass laws either trying to circumvent or accommodate the federal courts but with no success. In 1985, for example, the Court ruled unconstitutional an Alabama state law that mandated a moment of silence at the beginning of the school day.[50] Seven years later it found invocation and benediction prayers at graduation equally objectionable.[51] Moreover, in a throwback to the days of school desegregation in the 1950s and early 1960s, many local school districts throughout the South have simply ignored the federal courts' instructions on school prayer. Several years after the 1963 unequivocal banning of Bible reading, one study revealed that only one Tennessee school official of the 121 interviewed even bothered to claim compliance with the Court decision.[52] In 1997 a federal district judge found school prayers to be a pervasive feature of school life in Alabama despite the federal courts' efforts to forbid these practices. When the judge appointed a "monitor" to ferret out classroom violations of his order to end prayers, the Alabama governor denounced his action as tantamount to employing "secret police." Nearly 500 of the 636 students in the affected district protested the judge's ban by walking out of class.[53]

School prayer policy appears to be an exception to the political process that tends to ensure that the Court's decisions do not stray far beyond the bounds of citizen opinion. It is safe to assume, then, that these issues will remain contentious and be revisited frequently by both judges and elected representatives.

Figure 5–3 Public Opinion on the 1962 Supreme Court Decision Banning School Prayer, 1963–1994

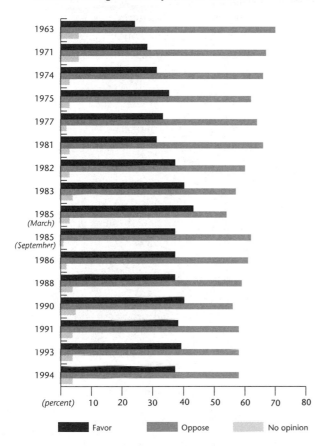

(percent) 10 20 30 40 50 60 70 80

■ Favor ■ Oppose ■ No opinion

Source: Harold W. Stanley and Richard G. Niemi, *Vital Statistics on American Politics, 1997–1998* (Washington, D.C.: CQ Press, 1998), Table 3–13.

Note: Question on school prayer: "The U.S. Supreme Court has ruled that no state or local government may require the reading of the Lord's Prayer or Bible verses in public schools. What are your views on this—do you approve or disapprove of the Court ruling?" Sources of data: 1963, 1971—Gallup Poll (1972), 1837; 1981, 1985 (September)—ABC News/*Washington Post* survey; 1974–1977, 1982–1985 (March), 1986–1994—General Social Survey, National Opinion Research Center, University of Chicago.

Free Exercise

The free exercise doctrine is relatively clear and simple when compared with the tortured history of religious establishment cases. Its incorporation into the Fourteenth Amendment began on a spring day in 1938, when the Cantwells, a family of Jehovah's Witnesses, drove into New Haven, Connecticut, to spend the afternoon proselytizing for their faith and soliciting donations. They were acting on the belief of their denomination that each member of the church, as one of its ministers, is obligated to spread the gospel of salvation. Some local residents, however, objected to the Witnesses' intrusion on their privacy and called the police, who arrested the Cantwells for soliciting money door to door without a permit.

Ruling on this case in 1940, the Supreme Court decided for the first time that First Amendment protections of free exercise of religion were *incorporated* in the "fundamental concept of liberty embodied" in the Fourteenth Amendment. Connecticut's regulation of financial solicitation by religious groups, the Court ruled, represented an unconstitutional "censoring" of religion.[54]

In recognizing that the free exercise clause "embraces" the freedom to act as well as the freedom to believe, the Court opened the door to a host of free exercise cases that sought to define the boundaries of action and answer questions such as: when may the state reject free exercise claims in favor of a "compelling government interest?" When the dust settled, the Court, in pitting the individual

About fifty students gathered outside Sardis (Mississippi) High School in November 1997 to pray and chant, "We want prayer!" They walked out of class to protest a ruling by a federal court in Alabama that restricted moments of silent prayer in public schools.

against the community, found itself relying on a case-by-case balancing of interests reminiscent of the obscenity criteria.

The present Court, which continues to distinguish beliefs from actions, claims that the state may regulate religious practice when it becomes "abhorrent to most members of society."[55] In *Employment Division v. Smith* (1990) two members of the Native American Church were dismissed from their drug counseling jobs for ingesting peyote (a hallucinogenic derived from cactus) as part of a religious ceremony.[56] When the state of Oregon denied their request for unemployment benefits, the church members sued the state for infringing on their free exercise of religion. But the Court disagreed; the use of illegal drugs, even though for a religious purpose, had crossed the boundary into illegal action. Their claim was denied.

In a 1993 animal sacrifice case, however, the Court executed a 180-degree turn—and precisely (and perhaps not coincidentally) at the time Congress was enacting the Religious Freedom Restoration Act, aimed at limiting state and judicial regulations on religious organizations and practice. The suit was brought by a Santeria church in Hialeah, Florida, that engaged in animal sacrifice as a religious rite. After the city passed ordinances effectively outlawing the practice, the church took the city to court.[57] When the case reached the Supreme Court, it held that the challenged laws were unconstitutional since the local law was directed at conduct that *only* arose as part of religious practices and thus inadvertently regulated religious practices.

Both the free exercise and establishment issues tend to spark competing rights claims that require careful balancing on the scales of justice. The problems are rooted in the language of the First Amendment. Does "free exercise" extend to behavior that imposes costs on the larger community—whether it be drug use, proselytizing, or disregard of local zoning ordinances? Does the prohibition against establishing a state religion cover moments of silence, church-sponsored school clubs, or Christmas displays that call up the holiday's religious origins? As the Supreme Court's wavering decisions reveal so clearly, there is no single "correct" answer to the questions raised by the First Amendment's guarantee of religious freedom. The courts, politicians, and public, then, have ample room to decide for themselves and thus disagree.

Criminal Rights

"The history of liberty," remarked Supreme Court Justice Felix Frankfurter, "has largely been the observance of procedural safeguards."[58] Nowhere is this insight more applicable than in the realm of criminal rights. In fact, the chance that an article on world affairs in today's newspaper will confirm Frankfurter's comment is quite good. Leaders in nondemocratic societies often throw their adversaries in prison on trumped-up criminal charges as an easy way of quelling the opposition.

But when procedural safeguards are in place, they serve to remove the criminal process from politics and protect the individual citizen from the raw power of the state. The Framers had had first-hand experience in this area: Britain had employed criminal statutes and prosecutions in its attempts to tighten its political control over the colonies. The drafters of the Bill of Rights, all the wiser then, carefully and systematically constructed barriers to arbitrary law enforcement. And how successful were they? Very successful. Defendants rarely claim they are being persecuted by law enforcement because of their politics. Indeed, the cases examined in this section, while altering criminal rights in some important way, were brought against men and women accused of committing real crimes.

Public safety and law enforcement are quintessentially state and local responsibilities. This fact probably explains why the Bill of Rights provisions in Table 5–3 were among the last to be incorporated into the Fourteenth Amendment and applied to all levels of government. Until the 1960s the Supreme Court had applied the Fourteenth Amendment's due process clause to defendants only in egregious instances of state misconduct such as a 1936

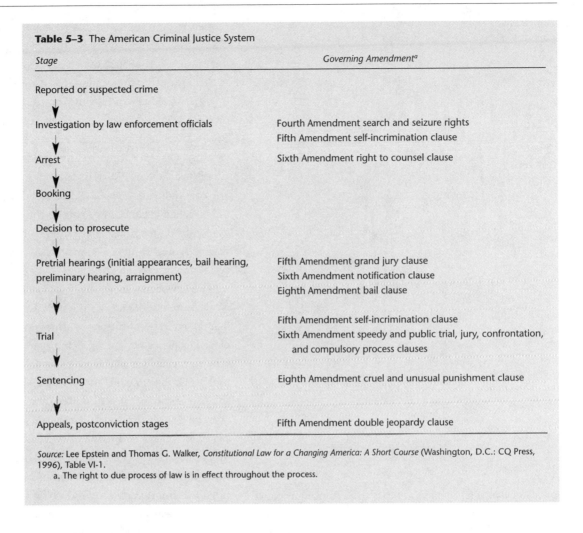

Table 5–3 The American Criminal Justice System

Stage	Governing Amendment[a]
Reported or suspected crime	
↓	
Investigation by law enforcement officials	Fourth Amendment search and seizure rights
	Fifth Amendment self-incrimination clause
↓	
Arrest	Sixth Amendment right to counsel clause
↓	
Booking	
↓	
Decision to prosecute	
↓	
Pretrial hearings (initial appearances, bail hearing, preliminary hearing, arraignment)	Fifth Amendment grand jury clause
	Sixth Amendment notification clause
	Eighth Amendment bail clause
↓	
	Fifth Amendment self-incrimination clause
Trial	Sixth Amendment speedy and public trial, jury, confrontation, and compulsory process clauses
↓	
Sentencing	Eighth Amendment cruel and unusual punishment clause
↓	
Appeals, postconviction stages	Fifth Amendment double jeopardy clause

Source: Lee Epstein and Thomas G. Walker, *Constitutional Law for a Changing America: A Short Course* (Washington, D.C.: CQ Press, 1996), Table VI-1.

　　a. The right to due process of law is in effect throughout the process.

case in which a defendant was tortured to near death before he confessed.[59] Clearly, for a long time a majority of the Court wanted to stay out of the business of overseeing the state criminal justice system. Even when it did accept the argument that a particular constitutional provision applied to the states, the Court hesitated to impose the rules and standards used in federal criminal cases.

The incorporation of criminal rights into the Fourteenth Amendment has not met with the public's approbation; law-abiding citizens and those who represent them tend to sympathize more with the victims of crime than with the accused. When a national survey asked

Americans in 1972 whether the courts treat criminals "too harshly" or "not harshly enough," two-thirds said the latter. By 1994 this figure had risen to 85 percent, but perhaps reflecting the effects of more restrictive decisions in recent years and longer sentences, it dropped to 78 percent in 1996.[60] Today criminal rights remain one of the most controversial aspects of modern civil liberties policy.

Elected officeholders have responded to these opinions and controversies by paying closer attention to the legal opinions of the men and women they are appointing and confirming to the federal judiciary. Although criminal rights have not been "unincorporated" or sharply cur-

Figure 5–4 Percentage of Supreme Court Criminal Rights Cases Decided in Favor of the Accused, 1953–1991

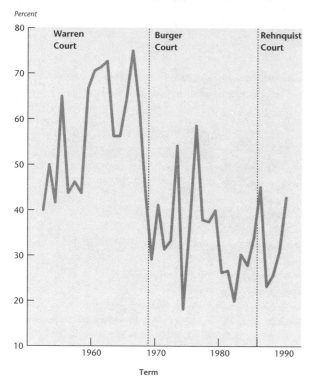

Source: Lee Epstein, et al., *The Supreme Court Compendium: Data, Decisions, and Developments* (Washington, D.C.: Congressional Quarterly, 1994), Table 3–8.

tailed, vigilant recruitment appears to have brought court rulings on them into closer alignment with the preferences of the American public. In recent years the Supreme Court has pulled back in this area of civil liberties, amendment by amendment (Figure 5–4).

Fourth Amendment: Illegal Searches and Seizures

The Fourth Amendment addresses the "right of the people to be secure in their persons, houses, papers, and effects, against unreasonable searches and seizures." Furthermore, it assures them that "no Warrants shall issue, but upon probable cause, supported by Oath or affirmation, and particularly describing the place to be searched, and the persons or things to be seized." The full historical

sequence of criminal rights is evident in the Court's efforts to determine what constitutes illegal searches and seizures. As late as 1949 the Court rejected incorporation in this area of law, reasoning that if police acted improperly, an individual could complain to the police superiors or file a private lawsuit (the main recourse provided by British law). Beginning in the early 1960s, however, an increasingly liberal Supreme Court, under the leadership of Chief Justice Earl Warren, turned to incorporation of criminal rights. In *Mapp v. Ohio* (1961) the Court extended the so-called **exclusionary rule** to the states.[61] Unlike for obscenity or religious establishment cases, the doctrine was clear and simple: no improperly obtained evidence could be admitted at a trial.

The Court majority must have believed it had created an absolute standard. Over the next few years it and lower federal courts unflinchingly threw out improperly acquired evidence no matter how incriminating. The public was outraged. But as membership on the Court became more Republican and conservative, the seemingly absolute standard set down in *Mapp* became more ambiguous and flexible. In two 1984 cases the Court ruled that if law enforcement had made a "good faith" effort to abide by established procedures, the evidence retrieved could still be introduced.[62] In yet another 1984 case the Court ruled that improperly acquired evidence was admissible if one could reasonably assume it would have been discovered anyway. (In the case on which this ruling was based, the evidence was the body of the murder victim, lying exposed in a field.[63]) More recent rulings have limited the protections against searches of automobiles or of guests in homes.[64] Court doctrine continues to change as the makeup of the Court changes.

Fifth Amendment: Self-incrimination and Double Jeopardy

The Fifth Amendment states that no person shall "be compelled in any criminal case to be a witness against himself"—a protection that applies not only to testimony in a trial but also to any statement made by a defendant awaiting trial. The principle against self-incrimination has been a bedrock of American jurisprudence. Only if granted immunity from prosecution, based on requested testimony, can an individual be legally compelled to testify. But what happens when defendants claim they were coerced or tricked into confessing?

Law enforcement officials have always preferred confessions. The alternative, gathering evidence and building a case, can be time consuming and risky. As late as the 1960s, many police departments throughout the nation routinely induced confessions by beatings, threats, and severe deprivations. Moreover, "tricks of the trade," including placing codefendants in a prisoner's dilemma, induced some of the accused—even some of those who were innocent—to confess.

In 1964 the Supreme Court took the first step toward eradicating these abuses by applying the Fifth Amendment to the states.[65] It followed that decision with a controversial ruling two years later in *Miranda v. Arizona* (1966) aimed at protecting suspects from self-incrimination during the critical time between arrest and arraignment.[66] In the *Miranda* case the Warren Court held that police custody is inherently threatening and that confessions obtained during that period can be admitted as evidence only if suspects have been advised of their constitutional right to remain silent, moreover, defendants must be warned that what they say can be used against them in a trial, informed that they have a right to have a lawyer present for any statements (and that the state will provide an attorney if they cannot afford one), and told of the right to end the interrogation at any time.

In 1968, as part of a more encompassing crime law, Congress enacted language that sought to overturn *Miranda* by permitting all demonstrably voluntary confessions. The provision was intended to return the judiciary's focus to the nature of the confession rather than strict adherence to the *Miranda* rule. In the meantime, attorneys general and local prosecutors—perhaps believing the law to be unconstitutional—did not seek to enforce it for

three decades. Then in 1999 an appeals court cited the 1968 law to overturn *Miranda* requirements. This reversal guarantees the Supreme Court an opportunity to reconsider this pillar of defendants' rights.[67] In fact, even the Court has acknowledged over the years that the *Miranda* warnings are merely a device protecting against coerced confessions and "not themselves rights protected by the Constitution."

The Fifth Amendment also protects citizens against double jeopardy (trying a person twice for the same crime). This provision was nationalized in *Benton v. Maryland* (1969), but the Court continues to reject arguments that federal and state charges for the same crime amount to double jeopardy.[68] Nowhere is this point better illustrated than in a 1991 incident in Los Angeles. When the LA police officers charged with beating motorist Rodney King were acquitted of various state felony charges of misconduct, the federal district attorney indicted them for violating the civil rights of King, an African American. Two officers were acquitted, and two eventually were convicted and sent to prison.

Sixth Amendment: Right to Counsel and Impartial Jury of Peers

Defendants in any American courtroom can take comfort in the Sixth Amendment assurances that they are entitled to "a speedy and public trial, by an impartial jury of the State and district wherein the crime shall have been committed," a "compulsory process for obtaining witnesses in [their] favor," as well as "the Assistance of Counsel." The protections offered in this amendment have been subject to little controversy.

In 1932 the Supreme Court partially applied the Sixth Amendment to the states when it required them to provide all indigent defendants in capital cases (that is, those potentially involving the death penalty) with a lawyer. Full incorporation, however, had to wait until 1963 when Clarence Earl Gideon won one of the most famous decisions in Court history.[69] Gideon was accused of breaking

PD 47
Rev. 8/73

METROPOLITAN POLICE DEPARTMENT
WARNING AS TO YOUR RIGHTS

You are under arrest. Before we ask you any questions, you must understand what your rights are.

You have the right to remain silent. You are not required to say anything to us at any time or to answer any questions. Anything you say can be used against you in court.

You have the right to talk to a lawyer for advice before we question you and to have him with you during questioning.

If you cannot afford a lawyer and want one, a lawyer will be provided for you.

If you want to answer questions now without a lawyer present you will still have the right to stop answering at any time. You also have the right to stop answering at any time until you talk to a lawyer.

WAIVER

1. Have you read or had read to you the warning as to your rights?_____

2. Do you understand these rights?_____

3. Do you wish to answer any questions?_____

4. Are you willing to answer questions without having an attorney present?_____

5. Signature of defendant on line below.

_____

6. Time_____   Date_____

7. Signature of Officer_____

8. Signature of Witness _____

---

into a pool hall. Unable to afford a lawyer, he asked the Florida trial judge for representation, but he was turned down, convicted, and sent promptly to prison. There he became an inspiration for "prison lawyers" everywhere.

With classic David versus Goliath determination, Gideon researched the law and sent a handwritten petition to the Supreme Court claiming that his five-year prison sentence was unconstitutional because he had been too poor to hire an attorney and, consequently, had been required to defend himself.

Upon taking up his case, the Court assigned Gideon a first-class attorney (and future justice), Abe Fortas, who successfully argued that Gideon's constitutional right to counsel had been denied. Indeed, the decision in *Gideon v. Wainwright* decreed that anyone charged with a felony must be offered legal representation. Later the Court expanded eligibility to include any defendant whose conviction might result in incarceration.[70]

As for the Sixth Amendment's reference to juries and their procedures, the federal courts have largely allowed the states to determine the size of juries and whether unanimous agreement is required for conviction. The courts have concentrated instead on whether juries are adequately composed of a defendant's peers. Unrepresentative juries can arise in two ways: the pool of potential jurors is itself unrepresentative or the selection process is biased. Until the 1960s African Americans in the South were effectively excluded from juries because jury pools were drawn from voter registration lists (see Chapter 4). When federal registrars signed up black voters, however, this discrimination was automatically dismantled. Not until 1975 did the Court rule the exclusion of women from the jury pool unconstitutional.

Potential jurors may be rejected from service either for "cause" (arising from suspected prejudice), or as the target of a peremptory challenge. The latter is a pervasive practice in state and local courts where it allows attorneys on both sides to reject a certain number of individuals without having to establish cause. Lawyers, seeking the most sympathetic jury possible, routinely exempt certain types of people depending on the nature of the case and the personal characteristics of the defendant. They may not, however, use their challenges to eliminate jurors on the basis of race or sex.

Eighth Amendment: "Cruel and Unusual" Punishment

The death penalty is far and away the most important and contentious policy issue falling under the Eighth Amendment, which states quite succinctly: "Excessive bail shall not be required, nor excessive fines imposed, nor cruel and unusual punishments inflicted." Does "cruel

DIVISION OF CORRECTIONS
CORRESPONDENCE REGULATIONS

MAIL WILL NOT BE DELIVERED WHICH DOES NOT CONFORM WITH THESE RULES

No. 1 -- Only 2 letters each week, not to exceed 2 sheets letter-size 8 1/2 x 11" and written *on one side only*, and if ruled paper, do not write between lines. *Your complete name* must be signed at the close of your letter. *Clippings, stamps, letters from other people, stationery or cash must not be enclosed in your letters.*

No. 2 -- All letters must be addressed in the *complete prison name* of the inmate. Cell number, where applicable, and *prison number* must be placed in lower left corner of envelope, with your complete name and address in the upper left corner.

No. 3 -- *Do not send any packages without a Package Permit.* Unauthorized *packages* will be destroyed.

No. 4 -- *Letters* must be written in English only.

No. 5 -- *Books, magazines, pamphlets,* and *newspapers* of reputable character will be delivered *only if* mailed direct from the publisher.

No. 6 -- *Money* must be sent in the form of *Postal Money Orders* only, in the inmate's complete prison name and prison number.

INSTITUTION _____ CELL NUMBER _____

NAME _____ NUMBER _____

In The Supreme Court of The United States
Washington D.C.
Clarence Earl Gideon
Petitioner | *Petition for a writ*
vs. | *of Certiorari Directed*
H.G. Cochran, Jr., as | *To The Supreme Court*
Director, Divisions, | *State of Florida.*
of corrections state | No. 890 Misc.
of Florida | OCT. TERM 1961
| U.S. Supreme Court

To. The Honorable Earl Warren, Chief
Justice of the United States
Comes now The petitioner, Clarence
Earl Gideon, a citizen of The United States
of America, in proper person, and appearing
as his own counsel. Who petitions this
Honorable Court for a Writ of Certiorari
directed to The Supreme Court of The State
of Florida. To review the order and Judge-
ment of the court below denying The
petitioner a writ of Habeus Corpus.
Petitioner submits That The Supreme
Court of The United States has The authority
and jurisdiction to review The final Judge-
ment of The Supreme Court of The State
of Florida The highest court of The State
Under sec. 344 (B) Title 28 U.S.C.A. and
Because The "Due process clause" of the

When Clarence Gideon wrote his petition in 1961 asking the Supreme Court to hear his case, he did not know that Chief Justice Earl Warren had instructed his law clerks to be on the lookout for a habeas corpus petition (one that argues that the person in jail is there in violation of some statutory or constitutional right). Apparently the chief justice was seeking to guarantee the assistance of counsel for defendants in criminal cases.

and unusual" punishment preclude the death penalty? Until the 1970s the federal judiciary rarely entertained cases raising this Eighth Amendment question.

Then, in 1972, the Supreme Court issued a stunning 5–4 decision in *Furman v. Georgia*.[71] The formula for success was the argument by the legal arm of the National Association for the Advancement of Colored People that the Georgia law allowing juries to determine whether to mete out the death penalty to a convicted murderer had led to large disparities in sentencing; African Americans convicted of murdering whites were far more likely to receive the death penalty than whites convicted of the same

crime. A close inspection of the 243-page decision, the longest in Court history, reveals that the majority declaration of the death penalty as "cruel and unusual" was not nearly so secure as it first appeared. Only three justices maintained that the death penalty inherently violated the Bill of Rights. The others who joined the majority took a narrow approach, citing discriminatory practices rather than questioning the death penalty as inherently "cruel and unusual."

Immediately the federal government and thirty-five states began to redraft laws to satisfy the justices' requirements. Some states tried to eliminate discrimination by

Figure 5–5 Trends in Executions and Public Opinion on the Death Penalty, 1972–1998

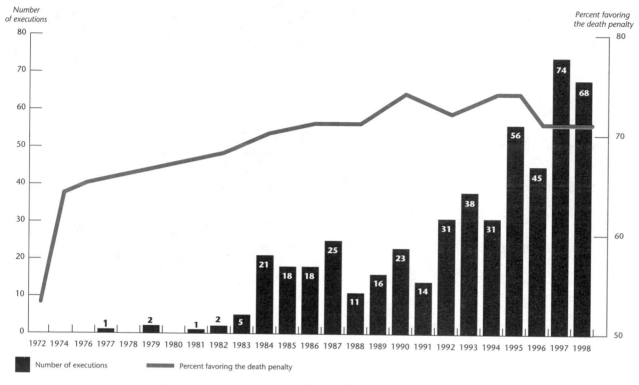

Sources: Executions—Death Penalty Information Center <http://www.essential.org/dpic/dpicexec.html>; public opinion—General Social Survey, National Opinion Research Center, University of Chicago, various years.

mandating that certain heinous crimes carry an automatic death penalty. But these laws were later rejected under the Eighth Amendment as inherently arbitrary and because they did not allow consideration of mitigating circumstances in sentencing. The solution was found in the new Georgia statute: separate the conviction from the sentencing stage of the trial, allowing juries to weigh the particular crime and the defendant and any mitigating and aggravating circumstances. In 1976 the 7–2 majority in *Gregg v. Georgia* proclaimed the new Georgia statute to be a "model" law, and the death penalty ceased to constitute "cruel and unusual" punishment.[72]

Indeed, the Georgia solution appears to have become an acceptable option for the state governments that rewrote sentencing procedures shortly after the *Gregg* de-

cision and for the prosecutors and juries that implemented them. As of October 1998, 3,517 inmates were sitting on death row. More than 500 others have been executed since reinstatement of the death penalty in 1976 (Figure 5–5). About four-fifths of all executions have been carried out in the South, with Texas, at 166 executions as of late 1998, far surpassing its neighbors.[73] The escalation of executions has been accompanied by mounting public opinion in favor of capital punishment for murderers (Figure 5–5). A consensus appears to be emerging on the bench as well. When asked his views on the death penalty at his Senate confirmation hearing in 1994, Supreme Court nominee Stephen Breyer replied that he viewed its constitutionality to be "settled law."

Time has shown that the rights of the accused are not

Table 5–4 The Meandering Path of Criminal Rights

	Early	1960s and 1970s	Recent Developments
Search and seizure (Fourth Amendment)	*Wolf v. Colorado* (1949): Fourth Amendment applies to states but exclusionary rule not mandated.	**Mapp v. Ohio** (1961): Improperly obtained evidence cannot be introduced at trial.	**United States v. Leon** (1984): Exclusionary rule not constitutionally protected but a means to deter police illegality. Allows good faith and inevitable discovery exceptions.
Non-self-incrimination (Fifth Amendment)	*Brown v. Mississippi* (1936): Outlaws confessions extracted by torture.	**Miranda v. Arizona** (1966): Officers must inform suspects of their rights before interrogation.	*Illinois v. Perkins* (1990): For confessions heard by undercover police, the Court rules: "*Miranda* forbids coercion, not strategic deception."
Right to lawyer (Sixth Amendment)	*Betts v. Brady* (1942): Denies right to lawyer in state prosecutions where special circumstances do not apply.	**Gideon v. Wainwright** (1963): Reverses *Betts*, guaranteeing all defendants charged with a felony a lawyer at trial.	*Ross v. Moffitt* (1974): Right to counsel is not required for discretionary appeals after conviction.
Double jeopardy (Fifth Amendment)		**Benton v. Maryland** (1969): Forbids state reindictment of acquitted defendant.	*Heath v. Alabama* (1985): Double jeopardy does not apply across levels of government.
Capital punishment (Eighth Amendment)	*Louisiana ex rel. Francis v. Resweber* (1947): Death penalty not inherently "cruel and unusual" punishment.	**Furman v. Georgia** (1972): "Arbitrary" sentencing process disallows death penalty.	**Gregg v. Georgia** (1976): Accepts separate sentencing trials to assign death penalty.

Note: Cases in **bold** discussed in text.

always easy to appreciate or enforce. Criminal rights almost always trigger a precarious balancing act between the defendant's interest in fair treatment and the community's interest in punishing the guilty and maintaining social order. When a court frees a guilty individual because of some technical glitch in the criminal justice system—such as from an improperly filled-out search warrant or an untimely prosecution—controversy erupts. Perhaps this and the other thorny issues described in this section account for the delayed incorporation in the criminal rights domain (see Table 5–4). By the early 1940s the Supreme Court had applied the entire First Amendment to the states, but it hesitated until the 1960s to nationalize the remainder of the Bill of Rights.

Privacy

A right to privacy, unlike other civil liberties, is not explicitly stated in the Bill of Rights or elsewhere in the Constitution. Indeed, although an implicit "right of privacy" was postulated by legal jurists as early as the 1890s, the Supreme Court did not explicitly recognize its existence until 1965.

But how could the Court "recognize" a right as constitutional that is nowhere mentioned in the Constitution? In 1965 the Court reasoned in *Griswold v. Connecticut* that Americans' guaranteed rights are not limited to those specifically identified in the Constitution.[74] Indeed, the Ninth Amendment says as much: "The enumeration in the Constitution, of certain rights, shall not be construed to deny or disparage others retained by the people." This amendment opened the door to unstated rights. Moreover, a reasonable reading of other amendments invites privacy into the Constitution's protected liberties. After all, what does the Constitution's guarantee of "liberty" mean if not privacy from state surveillance? Other explicit rights such as freedom of speech and assembly and the prohibitions against self-incrimination and unreasonable search and seizure require some measure of privacy if they are to be secure. These explicitly guaranteed rights form **penumbras,** or implicit zones of protected privacy rights on which the explicit rights depend to exist. For example, freedom of speech and a free press must include not only one person's right to engage in these activities but also the right to distribute, receive, and read others' views. Without these other rights, the specific rights would be insecure.

Once identified, the right to privacy became subject to all the complexities of interpretation and enforcement associated with other civil liberties. But the overriding question was: in the absence of constitutional standards, what actions and practices are so personal or private that they should be shielded from interference by the government and other third parties? The massive online databases maintained by employers, credit agencies, health providers, insurance companies, credit card companies, and banks are highly intrusive of privacy. So why are the courts not flooded with suits charging the people who control these databases with invasion of privacy? Perhaps the long-standing judicial doctrine that information loses its privacy privilege once conveyed to third parties has discouraged claims. Or perhaps this area of civil liberties has simply failed to attract the kinds of group sponsorship typically needed to make strong cases and sustain them

through the judicial system. Whatever the reason, when federal independent prosecutor Kenneth Starr sought in 1998 to subpoena the records of bookstore purchases made by former White House intern Monica Lewinsky, no privacy policy prevented him from doing so. Similarly, during hearings on Judge Robert Bork's nomination to the Supreme Court in 1987, journalists obtained and published the nominee's video rental records. Bork had no recourse.

Most efforts to protect privacy have emerged from the state legislatures and Congress. In 1988, perhaps to the comfort of Bork and others, Congress passed the Video Privacy Protection Act, which placed video rental records out of bounds. And lawmakers continue to deliberate more sweeping privacy legislation in the domain of medical records and the Internet.

Child-bearing Choices

The Supreme Court's attentiveness to privacy claims has largely been confined to an important but narrow domain of public policy: reproductive rights. In extending privacy in child-bearing choices, the courts began not with abortion but with a married couple's access to contraceptives.[75] In 1961 Estelle Griswold, executive director of the Planned Parenthood League of Connecticut, opened a Planned Parenthood clinic, which began to dispense contraceptives. Three days after the clinic opened, Griswold was arrested for violating an 1879 Connecticut law prohibiting the use of contraceptives. After losing her case in the state courts, the defendant appealed her test case in federal court. Not only did she win, but the decision, *Griswold v. Connecticut,* laid precedents that emboldened feminist and reproductive freedom groups to pursue abortion rights.

In 1972 Justice William Brennan's argument in *Eisenstadt v. Baird* bolstered the efforts of such groups: "If the right of privacy means anything, it is the right of the individual, married or single, to be free from unwanted governmental intrusion into matters so fundamentally affecting a person as the decision to bear or beget a child."[76]

Abortion is one of the most politicized civil liberties issues in American history. Demonstrations by right to life and pro-choice groups are scheduled regularly, complete with signs intended by demonstrators to communicate their slogans to television audiences over the evening news.

One year later, in the landmark abortion rights decision *Roe v. Wade,* a Court majority ruled: "The right of privacy, whether it be founded in the Fourteenth Amendment's concept of liberty . . . or . . . in the Ninth Amendment's reservation of rights to the people, is broad enough to encompass a woman's decision whether or not to terminate her pregnancy."[77]

Abortion rights in America did not begin with this historic and controversial decision; many states had permitted abortion until the late nineteenth century. Moreover, in the ten years leading up to the *Roe* decision, eighteen states had either relaxed or repealed their statutes prohibiting abortion. Thus the Court's nationalization in 1973 of a woman's right to terminate her pregnancy ended abortion's varying legality across the states.

This said, *Roe v. Wade* did not completely remove the states from abortion rights policy. This decision established that a woman's decision to end her pregnancy belongs within the protected sphere of privacy, but it did not wholly exempt abortion from government regulation. Rather, the Court ruled that in the interest of the mother's health and the "potential" life of the fetus, state governments could regulate abortions from the end of the first trimester of pregnancy to fetus viability (months four through six). Within the final trimester the states could forbid all abortions except those required "for the preservation of the life or health of the mother."

In 1992 the Court backed away from the first trimester standard and substituted a more ambiguous "undue burden" criterion: states may impose certain regulations on both the women who seek abortions and the doctors who perform them.[78] Waiting periods, counseling sessions, and parental consent were deemed constitutional so long as they did not place an undue burden on the abortion right.

Abortion politics remains the subject of intense political debate that takes many forms—confrontational demonstrations by the right to life movement, platform fights at the presidential nominating conventions, legislation both extending and voiding the *Roe* decision, and new state laws testing the boundaries of this privacy right. Although *Roe v. Wade* has yet to be overturned, the controversy over abortion will continue to cast a pall over politics at all levels whether reproduction rights remain a federal concern or are returned to the states.

POLITICS → POLICY

The Twists and Turns of the Right to Die

Since the issue emerged as a public and legal issue some thirty years ago, two-thirds or more of survey respondents have supported a patient's right to die. Nearly half nationally favor physician-assisted suicide in cases of intense and unremediable pain. In view of the aging of the population and advances in life-sustaining technology, it is unlikely this issue will soon recede from Americans' concerns or the policy agenda at the state level. Here are highlights of attempts by some states to deal with this sensitive subject.

1976

• New Jersey Supreme Court allows the parents of auto accident victim Karen Ann Quinlan to disconnect her life support system.

• California passes the Natural Death Act, the nation's first aid-in-dying statute.

1990

• Dr. Jack Kevorkian (see photo), a retired pathologist, assists in the death of a middle-aged woman with Alzheimer's disease. He later defies attempts by the Michigan legislature to stop him from assisting in other suicides.

• In *Cruzan v. Director, Missouri Department of Health* the Supreme Court rejects the right to die as a fundamental privacy right.

1991

• Washington State voters, by 54–46 percent, reject Ballot Initiative 119, which would have legalized physician-aided suicide.

1992

• California voters, by 54–46 percent, defeat Proposition 161, which would have allowed physicians to administer or to prescribe medications for self-administration by terminally ill patients.

Other Life Choices

In *Griswold, Roe,* and related cases, the Supreme Court enlisted the Ninth Amendment and various penumbra to broadly protect citizens against government intrusion into their private lives. Yet the Court has thus far failed to apply these rights to other kinds of private behavior brought before it. In 1986, for example, the Court turned away a suit challenging a Georgia law prohibiting homosexual acts between consenting adults.[79] The justices, in narrowly upholding the law, argued that, given America's history, traditions, and "the concept of ordered liberty," citizens simply had no "fundamental right" to engage in sodomy. Confronted with competing claims about the range of personal autonomy and lifestyle choices the community can tolerate, the Court affirmed the interests of the majority over those of a minority. Yet, just as for

1993

• Compassion in Dying is founded in Washington State to counsel the terminally ill. The group also sponsors suits challenging state laws against assisted suicide.

1994

• A district court overturns Washington State's anti-suicide law by finding in *Compassion v. Washington* that a law banning assisted suicide violates the Fourteenth Amendment.

• *Quill et al. v. Koppell* challenges the New York law prohibiting assisted suicide. Quill loses and appeals.

• Oregon voters, by 51–49 percent, approve the Death with Dignity Act ballot initiative. It would permit terminally ill patients, under proper safeguards, to obtain a physician's prescription to end life.

1995

• Ninth Circuit Court of Appeals overturns Washington State's *Compassion* ruling, reinstating anti-suicide law.

• U.S. district judge rules Oregon's Death with Dignity Act unconstitutional; it violates the equal protection clause. Ruling is appealed.

1996

• Ninth Circuit Court of Appeals reconsiders its own *Compassion* finding in Washington State and reverses itself, maintaining that a "liberty interest exists in the choice of how and when one dies."

• A Michigan jury acquits Kevorkian of violating a state law banning assisted suicides.

• Second Circuit Court of Appeals reverses the *Quill* decision, ruling that New York statutes that criminalize assisted suicide violate the equal protection clause.

1997

• The Oregon legislature votes to return Death with Dignity Act (Measure 16) to voters for repeal.

• On June 26 the Supreme Court reverses decisions in both Compassion cases—now known as *Washington v. Glucksberg* and *Vacco v. Quill*—upholding as constitutional state statutes that bar assisted suicide.

• On November 4 Oregon voters, by 60–40 percent, refuse to repeal the Death with Dignity Act.

1998

• On November 3 Michigan voters, by 71–29 percent, defeat a ballot initiative to make physician-assisted suicide legal.

• On November 22, CBS's *60 Minutes* airs a segment showing Kevorkian giving a lethal injection to Thomas Youk, who is terminally ill.

1999

• On March 26 Kevorkian is convicted of second-degree murder in the Youk death.

Sources: Lee Epstein et al., *The Supreme Court Compendium*, 2d ed. (Washington, D.C.: CQ Press, 1997), 695; "Doctor-assisted Suicide—Chronology of the Issue," *Longwood College Library*, March 29, 1999, <http://www.web.lcw.edu/administrative/library/death.htm> (May 3, 1999).

---

other civil liberties, the balance between interests struck by the Court remains incomplete and open to change.

Recently, another privacy claim emerged: the right to die. The issue arose in the 1970s over the removal of life-sustaining technology for patients in a vegetative state. In 1990 the Supreme Court rejected the right to die—even the removal of life support equipment—as a fundamental privacy right.[80] The states, the Court declared, could largely determine the level of commitment and kinds of evidence required before family members are given authority to halt medical treatment. In 1997 the Court ruled with rare unanimity that the Constitution provides no privacy guarantees for assisted suicide.[81] Policy in this area also was left to the states (see box "The Twists and Turns of the Right to Die").

Assessing Civil Liberties as Public Policy

At first, the nationalization of civil liberties in the Bill of Rights was not a popular idea. Madison's proposal to amend the Constitution to apply them directly to the states was handily defeated in Congress as those members sympathetic with the Antifederalists, who had insisted that civic freedoms be written into the Constitution, explicitly rejected the idea.

Only during the twentieth century, and gradually via incorporation, has the Bill of Rights come to be accepted as *national* policy that applies to every level of government. Yet states still have a role in formulating the rules that implement many of the rights guaranteed. For example, the Supreme Court allows states to determine the size of juries and level of agreement required to convict in state courts. Similarly, the states are free to decide the legality of physician-assisted suicide and have plenty of room to regulate the availability of abortions.

Civil liberties policy has developed on another front as well, equally unimagined by its eighteenth-century sponsors. The members of Congress who drafted and deliberated these liberties and the state legislators who ratified them probably had in mind essentially "civic" rights: the right to dissent, to organize opposition, and, in extreme instances, to resist—essential bulwarks against the impulses of any intemperate majorities and tyrannical government officials. As we have seen, these rights have been broadened, in some instances dramatically, to create personal spheres of expression and privacy. This evolution is evident in modern case law on search and seizure, unconventional religious practices, nude dancing, the right to die, abortion, and many other issues reviewed in this chapter.

Americans, however, do not see eye to eye on these matters. In fact, modern civil liberties number among the most divisive and unsettled issues facing the nation. None is more contentious than abortion rights. In the years since the 1973 *Roe v. Wade* decision, the issue has surfaced at every level of government from neighborhood rallies and demonstrations to restrictive amendments in annual appropriations legislation in Congress. At times, the intensity of disagreement even spills over into violence directed at the physicians who perform abortions and their clinics. Abortion, together with the other conflictual civil liberties issues on the modern scene—flag burning, school prayer, and assisted suicide, to mention a few—reminds us of the inherent divisiveness of public policy when it enters the realm of personal behavior.

The modern Supreme Court's preeminent role in deciding these policies contributes in part to their controversy. Once, these issues resided exclusively in the political arena—that is, with state and local governments and with Congress. But as the Supreme Court carved out a large role in these policies, its insulation from public opinion exposed its decisions to criticism and second-guessing. And, of course, its insulation has allowed it at times to issue highly unpopular decisions, such as its stance on flag burning and, during the 1960s, its restrictions on established law enforcement practices.

How does the image of a small number of unelected, life-tenured justices deciding public policy comport with the principles of democracy? Those who insist that majority rule must prevail in a democracy cannot justify the Court having any role at all other than duties delegated to it by the democratic (that is, elected) branches of government.

Others, however, may accept the authority of a national community to impose limits on itself and future majorities in making certain decisions. The elaborate rules to amend the Constitution are a prime example. Another can be found in the Bill of Rights. It removes various personal prerogatives and private behavior from casual government intrusion. The first amendment opens with "Congress shall make no law . . . ," and the list of proscriptions continues throughout the ten amendments. Madison recognized at the outset that the Supreme Court was well designed to enforce these antimajoritarian rules. The Court's unelected, life-tenured members are well insulated from the "popular passions" that can run roughshod over personal freedoms. Moreover, the explicit prohibitions to congressional action create space for the Court to enter as the Constitution's guardian.

If a national majority wants to ban flag burning, it can wait for new justices to be appointed and hope they are sympathetic with its position, or it can try to pass a constitutional amendment. Both avenues promise a lengthy delay and high transaction costs for the majority with little guarantee of success.

Finally, still others may point out that the majority is not so frustrated in exerting its preferences as it might appear. Supreme Court justices may not be elected, but voters' preferences do not go unheard. As we saw in this chapter, Court policy rarely deviates far from public opinion. Only in one small area of judicial policy—the religious establishment clause—has the Court persistently been at odds with majority sentiment. When it overturned the Religious Freedom Restoration Act of 1993, the Court found itself at loggerheads with Congress and the presidency. And in those communities, particularly throughout the South, where school prayer commands broad public support, school districts routinely ignore the Court's rulings on this controversial issue.

Supreme Court justices are not simply robed politicians who test the political waters before sending down a ruling. Far from it, they are insulated from "constituency" concerns in their decision making. Yet the Constitution provides many safeguards to ensure this institution stays on track with national majorities and the political branches of government that serve them and to limit the Court's influence when it fails to do so. Civil liberties policy may consume much of the caseload of today's Supreme Court, but the nine-member Court acts knowing that its final say rarely is.

Key Terms

clear and present danger test /135
due process clause /131
equal protection clause /131
establishment of religion clause /142
exclusionary rule /148

free exercise clause /142
libel /141
obscenity /138
penumbras /154
prior restraint /140
selective incorporation /131

Suggested Reading

Carter, Stephen L. *The Culture of Disbelief: How American Law and Politics Trivialize Religious Devotion.* New York: Basic Books, 1993. A thoughtful argument against prevailing court doctrine on the separation of church and state issue.

Epstein, Lee, and Thomas G. Walker, *Constitutional Law for a Changing America, Rights, Liberties, and Justice,* 3d ed. Washington, D.C.: CQ Press, 1998. A massive, comprehensive examination of the issues and Supreme Court opinions that define modern civil liberties policy. The authors retain a lively, pedagogic style.

Garrow, David J. *Liberty and Sexuality: The Right to Privacy and the Making of* Roe v. Wade. New York: Macmillan, 1994. A thorough, well-written survey of the circumstances and legal proceedings that culminated in this famous decision.

Hentoff, Nat. *Free Speech for Me . . . But Not for Thee: How the American Left and Right Relentlessly Censor Each Other.* New York: Harper Perennial, 1992. A highly original account of how political groups gain a political advantage through censorship.

Irons, Peter. *The Courage of Their Convictions.* New York: Free Press, 1988. Six case studies, including interviews, of defendants who took their cases to the Supreme Court.

Marshall, Thomas. *Public Opinion and the Supreme Court.* New York: Unwin/Hyman, 1989. An authoritative assessment of the extent to which judicial liberties and rights policies correspond to those of the American public.

Chapter 6

CONGRESS

⭐ *In 1995 Republicans in the House of Representatives made Newt Gingrich the most powerful Speaker in more than eighty years. Less than four years later they forced his resignation. What accounts for changes in the share of authority members are willing to delegate to party leaders?*

⭐ *Why do members of the House and Senate follow complex, arcane rules and precedents in processing legislation even when such devices keep majorities from getting their way?*

⭐ *Why, during its 1998 impeachment of President Bill Clinton, did the House never vote on censuring the president, the option most popular with the public and probably with the House membership as well?*

⭐ *Congressional incumbents rarely lose elections. Why then are they obsessed with the electoral implications of nearly everything they do?*

⭐ *Why do members of Congress show such a strong inclination to be individually responsive but collectively irresponsible?*

In 1994 the Republican Party won a majority of seats in the House of Representatives for the first time in more than forty years. The election elevated Newt Gingrich of Georgia, one-time history professor, from minority whip to Speaker of the House, next to president the most powerful position in Washington. The House Republicans intended to use their newly won power to change dramatically the direction of national policy, dismantling programs that had accumulated under decades of Democratic rule. Campaigning on their "Contract with America," Gingrich and most Republican House members had promised to cut income taxes, reduce spending on welfare programs for poor families, and in-troduce constitutional amendments requiring a balanced federal budget and term limits for members of Congress. Robert Livingston of Louisiana, elevated by Gingrich to chairman of the powerful Appropriations Committee, described Republican plans: "We are going to be re-evaluating every program, every rice bowl that the Democrats have built up over 50, 60, years. There are a lot of them that are going to be kicked over."[1] Claiming that the Democrats had used the rules governing how the House is organized and conducts its business to stifle debate on the Republicans' favorite hot-button issues, Livingston vowed that the new regime would put those issues "four-square right in their face. We are going to be revolution-

More than three hundred Republicans stepped up to sign the Contract with America during the 1994 midterm election campaign. Although it is history and its architect, Newt Gingrich, has left Congress, the contract, together with the Republican class of 1994 it helped to elect, demonstrated that a minority opposition party in Congress can present a coherent alternative to the president's policies. The fact that this opposition effort was the first to succeed is a reminder of how hard it is for political parties in America to commit their members to a course of action.

ary. . . . We are going at their throats."[2] The first order of business, then, was to change many of the rules. Only then did Republicans turn to the substance of national policy.

Voters also gave Republicans majority control of the Senate. The Senate Republicans, led by Majority Leader Bob Dole of Kansas, left the chamber's rules intact when they took over and displayed rather less revolutionary fervor than their colleagues in the House. Observers speculated as much about how the House and Senate leaders would get along as they did about how they would deal with the Democrat in the White House, Bill Clinton. The House Republicans kept their promise to act on all items in the Contract with America within the first hun-

dred days of the 104th Congress (1995–1996), but only half the items actually became law. The others fell victim to failure in the House or Senate or to President Clinton's veto.

What do the dramatic events of 1994 and 1995 say about Congress?

• Congress occupies the center stage in national policy making. Republicans were confident they could shape national policy more to their liking through control of both houses of Congress, but not the presidency, than they had been able to do during the twenty years (1967–1976, 1981–1993) a Republican had occupied the White House while Democrats held a majority of House (and usually Senate) seats.

• Electoral politics influences almost everything Congress does.

• Parties, through party leaders, direct and sometimes dominate the action in Congress.

• The rules and organizational structures the House and Senate adopt have a deliberate and crucial effect on both the distribution of power and policy making in Congress.

• The House and Senate differ in many ways; shared party labels do not guarantee cooperation and agreement between them.

• It is always far easier to stop things from happening in Congress than to make things happen.

This chapter explores each of these themes while explaining how and why the House and Senate operate as they do. It also looks at how these institutions have evolved in response to the changing motives and opportunities, personal and political, of the politicians elected to them. Any such discussion must be prefaced, however, by a review of the constitutional design of Congress and the extensive powers granted it by the Framers.

Congress in the Constitution

The basic structure of Congress is the product of the Great Compromise at the Constitutional Convention, described in Chapter 2. Balancing the demands of the large states for national representation against the demands of the small states for protection of states' rights, the Framers established in the Constitution a House of Representatives, with seats allocated by population and members elected by the citizenry, and a Senate composed of two members from each state chosen by the state legislature. Bicameralism (two houses) also helped to resolve another dispute. Delegates to the convention disagreed about the appropriate degree of popular influence on government. But, using the bicameral structure, they were able to devise a mixed solution. Representatives would be "popularly" chosen in biennial elections held in even-

Washington's city planner, the young Frenchman Pierre L'Enfant, consulted the Constitution before placing the Capitol on the highest hill in the city. From 1825 to 1856 the Capitol lacked a large dome—the original low wooden dome is depicted here—causing L'Enfant to describe it as "a pedestal waiting for a monument."

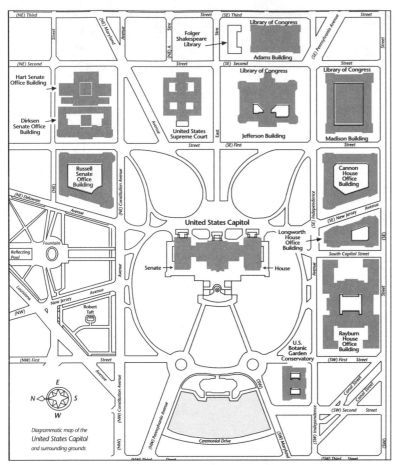

Diagrammatic map of the
United States Capitol
and surrounding grounds

The modern Congress occupies many buildings around the periphery of Capitol Hill. Although the office buildings have dramatically altered the local landscape, the map confirms preservation of L'Enfant's central concept that avenues should radiate from the Capitol to give citizens easy access to the representative branch of government.

numbered years. The two-year term was a compromise between the annual elections advocated by many delegates and the three-year term proposed by James Madison. Broad suffrage—the qualification for voting was to be the same as for the "most numerous Branch of the State Legislature" (Article I, Section 2)—and short tenure were intended to keep one chamber, the House, as close as possible to the people.

The Senate, by contrast, would be much more insulated from momentary shifts in the public mood. Senators would be chosen by state legislatures, not directly by the voters. The term of office was set at six years, another compromise; terms ranging from three to nine years had been proposed. Continuity was assured by the requirement that one-third of the Senate's membership stand for election every two years. The Senate could thus act as a stable, dispassionate counterweight to the more popular and radical House, protecting the new government from the dangerous volatility thought to be characteristic of democracies. As James Madison put it in *Federalist* No. 62, "The necessity of the Senate is . . . indicated by the propensity of all single and numerous assemblies to yield to the impulse of sudden and violent passions, and to be seduced by factious leaders into intemperate and pernicious resolutions." The Senate also incorporated remnants of state sovereignty into the new national government.

Qualifications for office also reflected the Framers' concept of the Senate as the more "mature" of the two chambers (*senate* is derived from the Latin *senatus,* old man). The minimum age for representatives was set at twenty-five years, for senators thirty years. Representatives had to be citizens for at least seven years, senators for nine years. Both were required to reside in the state they represented. Representatives do not have to reside in the district they serve, but in practice they almost always do. These are the only qualifications for office specified in the Constitution. The property-holding and religious qualifications included in many state constitutions were explicitly rejected, as was a proposal to forbid a member's reelection to office after serving a term. The Articles of Confederation had included a reelection restriction, but the Framers thought it had weakened Congress by depriving it of some of its most effective members.

Powers of Congress

As we saw in Chapter 2, the Constitution established a truly national government by giving Congress broad power over crucial economic matters. Article I, Section 8, authorizes Congress to impose taxes, coin and borrow money, regulate interstate and foreign commerce, and spend money for the "common defense" and "general welfare." Tacked on at the end of this list of specific powers is a residual clause authorizing Congress "to make all Laws which shall be necessary and proper for carrying into Execution the foregoing Powers, and all other Powers vested by this Constitution in the Government of the United States, or in any Department or Officer thereof." Accepted by many delegates as an afterthought, the necessary and proper clause—often known as the elastic clause—has proved to be the single most extensive grant of power in the Constitution, giving Congress authority over many different spheres of public policy (see Chapter 3). Indeed, it was under this authority that Congress banned discrimination in public accommodations and housing in the 1960s (see Chapter 4).

Congress was given significant authority in foreign affairs as well. Although the president is designated commander in chief of the armed forces, only Congress may declare war, raise and finance an army and navy, and call out the state militias "to execute the Laws of the Union, suppress Insurrections and repel Invasions" (Article I, Section 8). The Senate was granted some special powers over foreign relations. In its "advice and consent" capacity, the Senate ratifies treaties and confirms presidential appointments of ambassadors.

The Senate also approves presidentially appointed Supreme Court justices and top executive branch officials. These powers reveal that, in part, the Framers viewed the Senate as an advisory council to the executive, modeled on the upper chambers of some state legislatures. But they also reflect the Framers' belief that the more "aristocratic" and insulated of the two houses would keep a steadier eye on the nation's long-term interests.

In distributing power between the House and the Senate, the delegates sought a proper balance of authority. One bone of contention was the authority to raise and spend money. Some delegates wanted to give the House, as the chamber closer to the people, the exclusive authority to enact legislation to raise or spend money; the Senate would be allowed to vote on House bills but not amend them. The final compromise required merely that bills raising revenue originate in the House, with the Senate having an unrestricted right to amend them. The House was given no special authority to initiate spending bills, but it has assumed that right by custom as an extension of its special authority over revenue bills.

Despite its many legislative powers, Congress does not have exclusive authority over legislation. The president may recommend new laws and, in emergencies, call Congress into special session. Most important, the president has the power to veto laws passed by Congress, killing them unless two-thirds of each chamber votes to override the veto.

The Electoral System

Two other choices made by the Framers of the Constitution have profoundly affected the electoral politics of Congress. First, members of Congress and presidents are elected separately. In parliamentary systems like those found in most European countries, government authority rests with the legislature, and it chooses the chief executive (called the prime minister or premier). Thus voters' choices for legislators depend mainly on their preferences for leader of the executive branch. In the United States, voters are presented separate choices for senator, representative, and president.

Second, members of Congress are elected from states and congressional districts by plurality vote—that is, whoever gets the most votes wins.[3] Some parliamentary systems employ **proportional representation,** which gives a party a share of seats in the legislature matching the share of the votes it wins on election day. For example, if a party's share of votes entitles it to eighty-five seats, the first eighty-five candidates on the party's slate go to parliament. The voters, then, choose among parties, not individual candidates, and candidates need not have a local connection. Party leaders under this system are very powerful because they control parliamentary careers by deciding who goes on the list and in what order.

American legislators are elected from territorial units, not party lists. Parties do matter in congressional elections, and, with rare exceptions, only major party nominees have any chance of winning (see Chapter 12, Political Parties). In the 1990s only a single member of Congress—Rep. Bernard Sanders of Vermont—was not a Republican or Democrat. But the parties do not control nominations. Almost all congressional nominees are now chosen by voters in primary elections—preliminary contests in which voters select the parties' nominees. Candidates thus get their party's nomination directly from voters, not from party activists or leaders.

Congressional Districts

After the first census in 1790, each state was allotted one House seat for every 33,000 inhabitants, for a total of 105 seats. Until the twentieth century the House grew as population increased and new states joined the Union. Total membership was finally fixed at its current ceiling of 435 in 1911 when House leaders concluded that further growth would impede the House's work. Since 1911, states have both lost as well as gained seats to reflect population shifts between the decennial (ten-year) censuses. Changes in the size of state delegations to the House since World War II illustrate vividly the major population movements in the United States (Figure 6–1). States in the West and South, with flourishing economies based on aerospace and other defense industries, have gained at the expense of the large industrial states in the Northeast and Midwest.

Federal law may apportion House seats among states after each census, but each state draws the lines that divide its territory into the requisite number of districts. In 1964 the Supreme Court ruled in *Wesberry v. Sanders*[4] that

THE ORIGINAL GERRYMANDER

The practice of "gerrymandering"—the extensive manipulation of the shape of a legislative district to benefit a certain incumbent or party—is probably as old as the Republic, but the name originated in 1812. That year, the Massachusetts legislature carved out of Essex County a district that historian John Fiske said had a "dragonlike contour." When the painter Gilbert Stuart saw the misshapen district, he penciled in a head, wings, and claws and exclaimed, "That will do for a salamander!" Editor Benjamin Russell replied, "Better say a Gerrymander"—after Elbridge Gerry, then governor of Massachusetts.

districts must have equal populations. In *Thornburg v. Gingles* (1986) the Court ruled that district lines may not dilute minority representation, but neither may they be drawn with race as the predominant consideration.[5] Within these limits states can draw districts pretty much as they please. If one party controls both the legislature and governorship, it may attempt to draw district lines that favor its own candidates. The idea is to concentrate

Figure 6–1 Apportionment of House Seats, 1950 and 1990

WASHINGTON
1950: 7
1990: 9
change: +2

OREGON
1950: 4
1990: 5
change: +1

IDAHO
1950: 2
1990: 2
change: 0

MONTANA
1950: 2
1990: 1
change: −1

WYOMING
1950: 1
1990: 1
change: 0

NORTH DAKOTA
1950: 2
1990: 1
change: −1

MINNESOTA
1950: 9
1990: 8
change: −1

SOUTH DAKOTA
1950: 2
1990: 1
change: −1

WISCONSIN
1950: 10
1990: 9
change: −1

MICHIGAN
1950: 18
1990: 16
change: −2

NEW HAMPSHIRE
1950: 2
1990: 2
change: 0

VERMONT
1950: 1
1990: 1
change: 0

MAINE
1950: 3
1990: 2
change: −1

NEW YORK
1950: 43
1990: 31
change: −12

MASS. 1950: 14 1990: 10
change: −4

R. I. 1950: 2 1990: 2
change: 0

CONN.
1950: 6 1990: 6
change: 0

NEVADA
1950: 1
1990: 2
change: +1

UTAH
1950: 2
1990: 3
change: +1

COLORADO
1950: 4
1990: 6
change: +2

NEBRASKA
1950: 4
1990: 3
change: −1

IOWA
1950: 8
1990: 5
change: −3

ILLINOIS
1950: 25
1990: 20
change: −5

INDIANA
1950: 11
1990: 10
change: −4

OHIO
1950: 23
1990: 19
change: −4

PENNSYLVANIA
1950: 30
1990: 21
change: −9

NEW JERSEY
1950: 14 1990: 13
change: −1

DELAWARE 1950: 1 1990: 1
change: 0

MARYLAND
1950: 7 1990: 8
change: +1

CALIFORNIA
1950: 30
1990: 52
change: +22

ARIZONA
1950: 2
1990: 6
change: +4

NEW MEXICO
1950: 2
1990: 3
change: +1

KANSAS
1950: 6
1990: 4
change: −2

MISSOURI
1950: 11
1990: 9
change: −2

KENTUCKY
1950: 8
1990: 6
change: −2

W. VA.
1950: 6
1990: 3
change: −3

VIRGINIA
1950: 10
1990: 11
change: +1

NORTH CAROLINA
1950: 12
1990: 12
change: 0

TENNESSEE
1950: 9
1990: 9
change: 0

OKLAHOMA
1950: 6
1990: 6
change: 0

ARKANSAS
1950: 6
1990: 4
change: −2

MISS.
1950: 9
1990: 9
change: 0

ALABAMA
1950: 9
1990: 7
change: −2

GEORGIA
1950: 10
1990: 11
change: +1

SOUTH CAROLINA
1950: 6
1990: 6
change: 0

TEXAS
1950: 22
1990: 30
change: +8

LOUISIANA
1950: 8
1990: 7
change: −1

FLORIDA
1950: 8
1990: 23
change: +15

ALASKA*
1950: 0
1990: 1
change: +1

HAWAII*
1950: 0
1990: 2
change: +2

*Note: Alaska and Hawaii were not yet states in 1950.

Added House Seats

Lost House Seats

No Change

the opposition party's voters in a small number of districts that the party wins by large margins, thus "wasting" many of its votes, while creating as many districts as possible where one's own party has a secure, though not overwhelming, majority. Called **gerrymandering,** these tactics sometimes produce bizarrely shaped districts (see box, "The Original Gerrymander").

The constitutionality of partisan gerrymanders has been challenged in court, but so far without success. In *Davis v. Bandemer* (1986), the Court held that a gerrymander would be unconstitutional if it were too unfair to one of the parties, but as yet no districting scheme has run afoul of this vague standard.[6]

The Court's 1986 *Thornburg* decision, requiring that legislative district lines not discriminate, even unintentionally, against racial minorities, was widely interpreted as directing mapmakers to design districts in which racial and ethnic minorities constituted a majority of voters

Figure 6–2   North Carolina's First and Twelfth Districts, 1991 and 1998

1991 version (rejected by the Supreme Court)

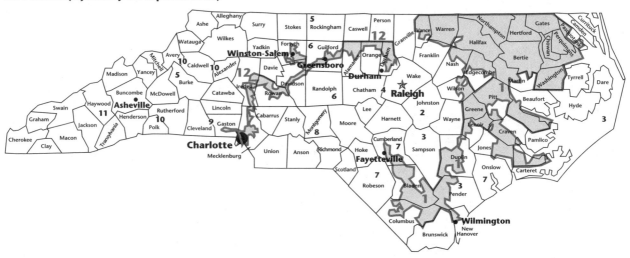

1998 version (accepted by the Supreme Court)

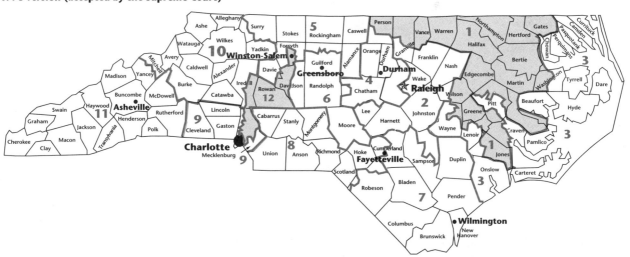

wherever residence patterns made this feasible.[7] Attempts to conform to this decision after the 1990 census inspired some artistry that would have made Massachusetts governor Elbridge Gerry, from whom the gerrymander got its name, proud (see box). For example, North Carolina legislators carved out two majority African American dis-

tricts (First and Twelfth) which eventually came before the Court (Figure 6–2). In 1993 the Court decided that such irregular districts went too far[8] and in 1995 that districts could not be drawn solely to benefit one race.[9] Thus the North Carolina districts (along with thirty-four districts in four other states) had to be redrawn. Modified twice before receiving final court approval, the districts had some of their rough edges smoothed off but retained all the earmarks of a painstaking gerrymander.

The fifty Senate constituencies—entire states—may not change boundaries with each census, but they vary greatly in size of population. Sen. Dianne Feinstein of California represents more than 32 million people, while Sen. Michael Enzi of Wyoming has fewer constituents (481,000) than the average U.S. representative (610,000). The nine largest states are home to 52 percent of the total U.S. population, while the smallest twenty-six states, with 52 percent of Senate seats, hold only 17 percent of the population. Unequal representation in the Senate sometimes matters politically. For example, Republicans held a Senate majority between 1981 and 1987 even though their candidates had received overall a smaller percentage of the popular vote than Democrats because Republican candidates won so many of the smaller states.

Until 1913 senators were chosen by state legislatures. Most Americans had long since concluded that this method of selection was undemocratic and corrupting (between 1890 and 1905 charges of bribery shadowed Senate elections in seven different states).[10] But it took the reforming spirit of Progressivism at its peak to convince senators to agree to a constitutional amendment (the Seventeenth) providing for popular election.[11] As it turned out, they had little to fear from the change; senators have been about as successful in winning reelection as they had been in persuading state legislatures to return them to office.

Congress and Electoral Politics

The modern Congress is organized to serve the goals of its members. A primary goal for most of them is to keep their jobs. And since voters have the final say in the hiring and firing, a career in Congress depends on members winning the voters' endorsement at regular intervals. Winning regular reelection is not the only goal of most congressional careers, but it is essential to whatever else members may want to achieve in office. Electoral imperatives thus shape all important aspects of congressional life.

Candidate-Centered versus Party-Centered Electoral Politics

The post–World War II era of Democratic majorities in Congress coincided with the emergence of a candidate-centered pattern of electoral politics. Similarly, the Republican takeover of Congress in the 1994 midterm elections coincided with a modest resurgence of party-centered electoral politics. Neither connection was accidental. Congressional Democrats thrived on, and thus sought to encourage, a kind of electoral politics in which candidates operated largely as independent political entrepreneurs. Republican leaders, unable to win House majorities by playing the game this way (Republicans did manage to control the Senate from 1981 through 1986), sought in 1994 to have their candidates run more as a party team, emphasizing national issues and a common program of action. The strategy succeeded beyond their expectations. Thus in triumph the Republican majority, owing their new-found control to party-centered electoral politics, immediately moved to alter the House and the Senate, long shaped by the Democrats' candidate-centered electoral politics, to suit their own electoral and policy goals.

During the long period of Democratic dominance, members of both parties had won election to Congress, and stayed there, largely because of their own efforts. Most "recruited" themselves, organized their own campaigns, and raised their own campaign money. Party organizations and **political action committees** (PACs—organizations that raise and distribute money for campaigns) were ready to help, but not until campaigns had shown promise. "Promise" usually meant the candidate had won the primary election, gained some favorable media attention, and raised a substantial amount of start-up money. Often most of the start-up money came from candidates' own pockets.

Although congressional candidates ran under party labels for national office, most congressional campaigns were personal and centered on local interests and values. National issues that did enter the campaign were given a local spin. Likewise, candidates solicited support more as individuals than as party representatives. After the election, successful candidates continued to cultivate local ties and personal relationships with constituents, and campaigns for reelection dwelled on the services, projects, and locally popular programs the incumbent had delivered to constituents. This strategy made it possible for members to separate their electoral fates from those of their party's other candidates.[12] For example, between 1972 and 1992 House Democrats won victories in 45 percent of the districts that delivered majorities to the Republican candidate in presidential elections (Republicans won in 12 percent of the much smaller number of districts that delivered majorities to Democratic presidential candidates).[13]

The local component of congressional elections had not always been so dominant. During much of the nineteenth century, party-line voting was far more common than it is now. Voters based their choices on the top of the ticket—the presidential candidates in presidential election years—and on the parties' platforms. Congressional candidates' fates were decided by national trends they could do little personally to shape or control. Changes in the laws regulating elections and parties around the turn of the century weakened parties and encouraged **ticket-splitting**—that is, voting for candidates of different parties for different offices.[14]

The most important of these changes were the introduction of primary elections for choosing the parties' nominees and the secret ballot (see Chapter 12, Political Parties). Still, party conflicts over national policy, most notably the political battles over President Franklin Roosevelt's New Deal, continued to inject a strong national component into congressional elections until the 1950s. As the New Deal controversies faded, however, the party coalitions built around them fractured under the stress of divisive new issues, most prominently civil rights, the Vietnam War, and social issues such as abortion and the environment. Party lines became blurred and party loyalty among voters declined.

The Advantages of Incumbency

Congressional incumbents both exploited and abetted the loosening of party ties. The decline in party loyalty among voters offered incumbents a chance to win votes that once would have gone routinely to the other party's candidate. Members could expand their electoral base by emphasizing their personal ties and services to constituents while downplaying partisanship. At the same time, reelection campaigns stressing individual character, legislative performance, and constituency services encouraged voters to use such criteria in deciding how to vote.[15]

Realizing that the growth of candidate-centered electoral politics worked to the advantage of incumbents willing to build a personal following, members of Congress voted themselves greater resources for servicing their states and districts—that is, higher allowances for staff, travel, local offices, and communication. In 1997 these allowances ranged from $814,090 to $1,233,780 in the House and from $1,598,472 to $2,645,845 in the Senate.[16]

Electoral data demonstrate the success of these efforts. The average share of votes won by House incumbents increased from 61 percent in the 1940s and 1950s to 67 percent in the 1980s before retreating a bit to 65 percent in the 1990s (Figure 6–3). The proportion of incumbents winning more than 60 percent of the vote grew even more steeply, from as low as 41 percent in 1948 to as high as 84 percent in 1988. Incumbent reelection rates also have generally been higher since the mid-1960s, although some years, notably in the early 1990s, have been exceptions. Even before the 1960s House incumbents were winning reelection very consistently; their overall success rate since World War II exceeds 92 percent. Even in a year like 1994, with a strong electoral tide running against one of

Figure 6–3 Success of House Incumbents , 1946–1998

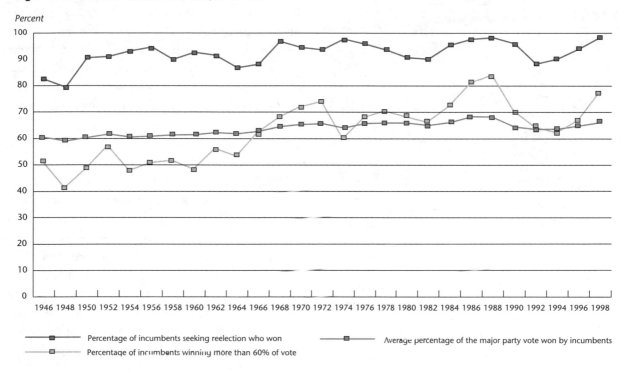

Percent

Legend:
Percentage of incumbents seeking reelection who won
Average percentage of the major party vote won by incumbents
Percentage of incumbents winning more than 60% of vote

Source: Compiled by the authors.

the parties, incumbency remained a potent advantage. Republican candidates won 71 percent (22 of 31) of the contests for open House seats (those without an incumbent running) that had been held by Democrats but only 15 percent (34 of 225) of the seats defended by Democratic incumbents. They won all six of the open Senate seats where the Democrat retired but only 13 percent (2 of 16) of the contests against Democratic incumbents.

The remarkable won–lost record of incumbents raises an important question: if incumbency is so advantageous and if members of Congress win reelection so consistently, usually by comfortable margins, why do electoral worries do so much to shape congressional life? The answer is that the incumbency advantage does not accrue automatically to officeholders; it stems from diligent use of the many resources that come with holding office. Incum-

bents win reelection consistently because they work so hard at it, and they work hard because so much of their electoral fate is in their own hands.[17]

One purpose of hard work is to discourage potential opponents. In a candidate-centered system of electoral politics, ambitious, talented people rarely challenge incumbents if they see no chance of winning; and contributors decline to waste money on hopeless causes. Obscure, underfinanced challengers simply cannot compete. The most successful incumbents win easy reelection by making themselves appear so invincible that no qualified opponent is willing to take them on.[18] But an image of invincibility is not invincible; it is vulnerable to unexpected events, such as the House bank scandal in 1992, and, for Democrats, the strong Republican tide in 1994. These events demonstrate why members of Congress—even

Members of Congress pursue job security by trying to show constituents they are responsive, accessible, and effective—in other words, that they are good agents. Thus when Republicans took over the House in 1995, they cut congressional committee staffs by one-third but rejected a proposal to reduce members' personal staff assistants— the people who answer the mail, perform casework, and otherwise help members keep in touch with constituents. Copyright, cartoon by The Birmingham News, 1998. All rights reserved. Reprinted with permission.

those with long records of past electoral success—are right to worry about reelection.

The revelation in April 1992 that 350 past and current members of the House had written some twenty thousand overdrafts on their House bank checking accounts between July 1988 and October 1991 provoked a storm of outrage from the press and public that contributed to the largest turnover of membership in fifty years. Even members who wrote no bad checks suffered in the fallout.[19] The strength of the Republican tide in 1994 also surprised nearly everyone on Capitol Hill, as Republicans succeeded in turning long-simmering public anger over stagnant incomes, declining public services, high crime rates, continuing budget deficits, high taxes, and congressional malfeasance against Democratic candidates for both national and local offices. Thirty-four Democratic House incumbents, including Speaker Thomas Foley of Washington, were defeated.

Members of Congress, then, inhabit a world fraught with far more electoral uncertainty than their won–lost record would lead one to believe. As electorates have become less partisan, they also have become more volatile. Without the anchor of party, voters are easier to attract, but they also are easier to lose. An easy victory against feeble opposition in one election carries no guarantee of success against a talented and well-financed challenger in the next.

Recognizing that they hold their jobs at the sufferance of fickle electorates, members of Congress are highly responsive to their constituencies. Decisions on legislative issues are shaped by the potential need to explain and defend them in future campaigns.[20] Most members also spend a great deal of time back home, keeping in touch and staying visible. They solicit and process **casework,** requests from constituents for information and help in dealing with government agencies. A lost Social Security check? A bureaucratic mix-up over veterans' benefits? A representative or senator is ready to help. Some requests—and services—go well beyond the expected. One constituent tried to get his senator to intercede with the head of the state university's board of regents to have the C grade his son received in a political science course raised.[21] The senator did not comply, but electoral logic makes it hard to resist almost any opportunity to please people back home.

Although senators engage in many of the same constituency-building activities as representatives, they have not been as successful in keeping their jobs. Since 1946 their overall rate of reelection, 78 percent, has left them three times more likely to lose their seats than House incumbents. But because senators face reelection only one-third as often, tenure in office tends to even out between the chambers. Overall, though, Senate election outcomes are more variable than House outcomes; in recent years incumbent reelection rates have been as low as 55 percent (1980) and as high as 97 percent (1990). Even when Senate incumbents do win, their margins of victory tend to be narrower than those of representatives. Why do Senate incumbents win less consistently and typically by narrower margins? First, because states are generally more populous and diverse than congressional districts,[22] most senators are unable to develop the kinds of personal ties to constituents that many representatives cultivate. Second, states are more likely than congressional districts to have balanced party competition; few states are securely in either party's pocket. Third, Senate races attract a larger proportion of experienced, politically talented, well-financed challengers. Fourth, states usually fit media markets—formed by cities and their suburbs reached by local TV and radio stations and newspapers—better than House districts, making it easier for challengers to get out their message. Senators receive far more attention from the news media than representatives, but so do their opponents. Representatives may be largely ignored by journalists, but this vacuum leaves them freer to shape the information that does reach constituents. And, finally, senators are more readily associated with controversial and divisive issues, and they do not have the pressure of a two-year election cycle to keep them attuned to the folks back home. All these things contribute to making senators more vulnerable to defeat by challengers.

National Politics in Congressional Elections

The modest resurgence of party-centered campaigning in 1994 strengthened the national component of congressional election politics, but even during the heyday of locally focused, candidate-centered elections, national forces continued to have a palpable effect on electoral fates. Although the fortunes of a party's House and Senate candidates are no longer as closely tied to those of their presidential candidate as they were in the nineteenth century, congressional candidates are still better off if their party's presidential candidate wins. Presidents may have shorter *coattails*—the common metaphor for the capacity of a successful presidential candidate to pull the party's other candidates into office—than they once did, but coattail effects remain significant.[23]

In midterm elections the president's party almost always loses congressional seats, but the size of its losses depends in part on the performances of the national economy and the president. Losses tend to be fewer when the economy is booming and the president is popular, greater when the economy or the administration's popularity sags. Thus, for example, congressional Democrats suffered in 1994 from, among other things, Bill Clinton's low job approval ratings and voters' doubts about the economy. In 1998, by contrast, Clinton's approval rating stood nearly twenty points higher than it had in 1994 and the economy was in its best shape since the 1960s. As a result, the Democrats broke precedent by actually gaining House seats.[24]

As the 1994 elections showed so dramatically, members of Congress cannot always dissociate themselves from their party's fate, so they retain a personal stake in their party's public image as well as the public standing of the president. Nor can they dissociate themselves from Congress itself, though incumbents frequently try to do so. Individual members remain far more popular than Congress collectively (see Figure 6–9 later in this chapter), but they still suffer at the ballot box when the public's normally mild hostility toward Congress becomes intense, as it did in 1992 in response to the House bank scandal. In 1994, when Republicans managed to transform hostility to Congress into hostility to the party controlling it, Democrats lost their majority. But individual members cannot do much about such situations by themselves, so they concentrate on activities such as casework where their individual efforts can make a difference.

Representation versus Responsibility

Different electoral processes produce different forms of representation. In a party-centered electoral process, for example, legislators represent citizens by carrying out the policies promised by the party (or parties in multiparty systems) winning a majority of seats. Legislators know they will be held responsible by voters for their party's performance in governing, so ensuring the success of their party and the government takes top priority.

The kind of candidate-centered electoral process that

POLITICS ⟶ POLICY

THE TAX REFORM ACT OF 1986

Although its instinct is to do the opposite, Congress sometimes can find a way to enact policies that impose costs on specific groups to produce benefits shared by many people. For example, the Tax Reform Act of 1986 eliminated a host of special tax favors in order to reduce tax rates for everyone. Although the law was a popular idea pushed by Republican president Ronald Reagan and embraced by Democrats who did not want their party left defending "special interests," its success nonetheless depended heavily on the procedural strategies of congressional leaders. The package was assembled behind closed doors without recorded votes so no member could be blamed personally for eliminating any particular tax break. It then came to the floor of the House under a modified closed rule that allowed only three specific amendments to be offered (see section "The Committee System" for an explanation of closed rules). Some powerful members whose support was deemed essential received special concessions in the form of breaks for specific taxpayers in their states or districts—with support for the bill set as the minimum price for any concession. Among other taxpayers, sports facilities in New Jersey (the Meadowlands complex), Miami (Joe Robbie Stadium), and New Orleans (the Superdome) received special treatment.

In the Senate, which does not use closed rules, the bill's principal sponsor, Sen. Bob Packwood, a Republican from Oregon, won agreement that amendments on the floor had to be revenue neutral—that is, any change producing a tax benefit to some group had to be offset by increased taxes on another group. This agreement prevented the kind of logrolling among proponents of special tax breaks that would have unraveled the package.

Members of both houses had to go on record as for or against a substantial cut in taxes for a large majority of taxpayers. Because members were given no opportunity to do any behind-the-scenes favors for the myriad special interest groups that traditionally have feasted at tax-writing time, they could not be blamed for not doing the favors. By agreeing to tie their own hands, then, members were able to solve the acute collective action problem that tax bills always present. In the end, the bill's success took most seasoned observers of Congress by surprise, illustrating how uncommon such an outcome is.

Sources: R. Douglas Arnold, *The Logic of Congressional Action* (New Haven: Yale University Press, 1990), chap. 8; Jeffrey H. Birnbaum and Alan S. Murray, *Showdown at Gucci Gulch: Lawmakers, Lobbyists, and the Unlikely Triumph of Tax Reform* (New York: Vintage Books, 1988).

flourished during the long period of Democratic control and has ebbed only slightly since then gives members of Congress far more incentive to be individually *responsive* than collectively *responsible*. This shift is a primary source of Congress's collective action problems. For example, electoral logic induces members to promote narrowly targeted programs, projects, or tax breaks for constituents without worrying about the impacts of such measures on spending or revenues. Recipients notice and appreciate such specific and identifiable benefits and show their gratitude to the legislator responsible at election time. Because the benefits come at the expense of general revenues (money supplied by the taxes that everyone pays), no one's share of the cost of any specific project or tax break is large enough to notice. Thus it makes political sense for members of Congress to pursue local or group benefits that are paid for nationally even if the costs clearly outweigh the benefits. Conversely, no obvious payoff arises from opposing any particular local or group benefit because the savings are spread so thinly among taxpayers that no one notices. The pursuit of reelection therefore makes **logrolling**—a legislative practice in which members of Congress agree to reciprocally support each other's vote-gaining projects or tax breaks—an attractive strategy. But this situation creates a classic prisoner's dilemma. When everyone follows such an individually productive strategy, all may end up in worse shape politically when shackled with collective blame for the overall consequences. Spending rises, revenues fall, the deficit grows, government programs proliferate, and the opposition attacks the logrolling coalition—in practice, the majority party—for wastefulness and incompetence. Individual responsiveness leads to collective irresponsibility.

Democratic candidates suffered across the board in 1994 as voters turned against the aggregate consequences of collective irresponsibility: a government they perceived as too big, too expensive, and too inept. To demonstrate that they were different, the newly elected Republican majority invited voters to hold them collectively accountable for delivering on the Republican Contract with America, with its basic promise to shrink government, cut taxes, and change how the government operates. They stuck together on the contract, but, after losing a standoff over the budget in late 1995 to President Clinton, they broke ranks on issues such as repealing the ban on assault weapons, weakening protection of endangered species, and raising the minimum wage. In 1996 it was their Democratic opponents, bolstered by independent campaigns mounted by labor unions and other activists, who sought to inject national issues into the campaign, while endangered Republicans strove to show their independence from House Speaker Newt Gingrich.[25] Thus a noticeable shift away from the candidate-centered toward a more party-centered electoral politics was evident in 1994 (for the Republicans) and 1996 (for the Democrats). By 1997 congressional Republicans were showing renewed interest in the particularistic politics of **pork barrel legislation**—earmarking construction projects for individual members' districts—that had served the Democrats so well for so long.

The same logic that encourages logrolling makes members of Congress hesitate to impose direct costs on identifiable groups in order to produce greater, but more diffuse, benefits for all citizens. For example, laws designed to clean up the environment for everyone impose direct costs on industrial firms such as those incurred in installing antipollution equipment. The cost of compliance is clear to every firm affected, but the benefit of any firm's investment is diffused across so many people that few are likely to know of it. Members of Congress, then, fear retaliation from the losers without a compensating increase in support from the winners. Congressional majorities have found ways to get around this problem. One tactic is to delegate authority to bureaucratic agencies or state governments, letting them take the heat (see Chapter 8, The Bureaucracy). Another tactic is for legislative leaders to frame the lawmaker's choice in a way that highlights credit for the general benefits while minimizing individual responsibility for the specific costs.

More broadly, the trick is to make the electoral payoffs from disregarding special interests to benefit a broader public outweigh the costs. One essential ingredient is that the issue be important (or potentially important if an opponent raises it in a future election campaign) to many voters. A challenge for legislative leaders is to frame the decision on an issue in a way that forces members to put themselves on the record for or against the issue's general benefits without having an opportunity to amend or modify the policy to serve narrower interests. Meeting this challenge requires skillful manipulation of congressional procedures. In addition, leaders may have to buy off the most powerful potential opponents with special concessions or side deals (see box, "The Tax Reform Act of 1986," which describes a classic example of successful execution of the strategy described here).

Table 6–1 Profile of Members of the 106th Congress, 1999–2000

Occupation[a]	Senate	House of Representatives
Law	55	163
Business or banking	24	159
Education	13	84
Journalism	8	9
Agriculture	6	22
Public service	18	106
Real estate	4	20
Medicine	2	15
Other	4	40
Religion		
Roman Catholic	25	126
Jewish	11	23
Protestant		
Baptist	8	62
Episcopalian	13	30
Methodist	12	50
Presbyterian	7	41
Other	23	95
Unspecified	1	7
Ethnicity		
White	97	372
African American	0	39
Hispanic	0	19
Asian and Pacific Islander	2	5
Native American	1	0
Sex		
Male	91	377
Female	9	58

Source: CQ Weekly, January 9, 1999, 63.

　a. *Because some members have more than one occupation, totals are higher than total memberships.*

Who Serves in Congress?

The people who win seats in the Senate and House are by no means "representative" of the American people in any demographic sense (see Table 6–1). Almost all members have graduated from college; 41 percent have law degrees. Next to law, business is the most common prior occupation. A large majority are professionals of one kind or another; only a handful have blue-collar backgrounds.

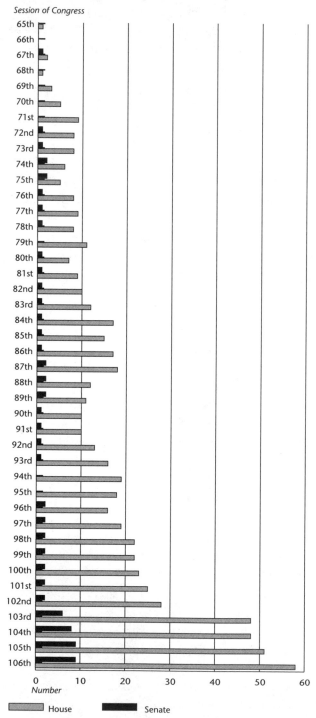

Figure 6–4 Women in Congress, 1917–1999

Sources: Norman J. Ornstein, Thomas E. Mann, and Michael J. Malbin, *Vital Statistics on Congress, 1997–1998* (Washington, D.C.: Congressional Quarterly, 1998), 40; data on 106th Congress compiled by authors.

Figure 6–5 African Americans and Hispanics in Congress, 1869–1999

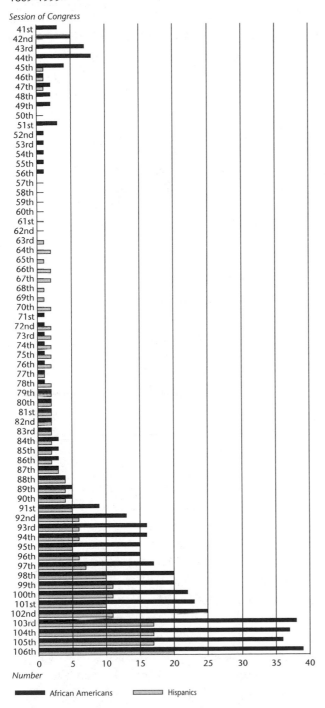

Session of Congress

Number

■ African Americans   ▢ Hispanics

Sources: Norman J. Ornstein, Thomas E. Mann, and Michael J. Malbin, *Vital Statistics on Congress, 1997–1998* (Washington, D.C.: Congressional Quarterly, 1998), 38–39; data on 106th Congress compiled by authors.

Republican representative Jennifer Dunn made history in 1998 as the first woman of either party to run for House majority leader. She lost her bid to the incumbent majority leader, Dick Armey of Texas.

Most have served in lower elected offices. The true vocation of the average member is, in fact, politics.

Women and racial minorities continue to be underrepresented in Congress, though their numbers have been increasing (see Figures 6–4 and 6–5). In 1961 only three African Americans and twenty women held House or Senate seats; by 1981 the number of African American members had grown to seventeen, while only one more woman had been added. Growth continued to be slow until 1992, when the number of blacks and Hispanics in the House increased sharply after the 1982 Voting Rights Act amendments had been interpreted to require states to maximize the number of "majority-minority" districts when drawing new district lines. The 1992 election also saw women candidates and campaign donors mobilized in unprecedented numbers in response to an event widely publicized in 1991: the insensitive handling by an all-male Senate committee of sexual harassment charges made by college professor Anita Hill against Supreme Court nominee Clarence Thomas. Women also represented a change from politics as usual in a year when most voters wanted change.

After the 1998 elections the Senate included nine women and one Native American, the House fifty-eight women, thirty-nine African Americans, and nineteen Hispanics. Despite a sharp increase in diversity in the 1990s, Congress remains overwhelmingly white and male because white males still predominate in the lower-level public offices and private careers that are the most common steppingstones to Congress. As women and minorities continue, albeit slowly, to assume a larger share of state and local offices and professional careers in law and business, their representation in Congress will continue to rise as well.

The gender and racial makeup of Congress makes a difference. For example, African American members led the fight for sanctions punishing South Africa for its apartheid system in the 1980s. The influx of women has made Congress far more attentive to issues of sex discrimination and sexual harassment.[26]

The Basic Problems of Legislative Organization

The Constitution established a basic framework for a national legislature, but Congress of today also is the product of more than two centuries of institutional development in which the House and Senate have evolved into highly complex institutions with remarkably elaborate and arcane rules, procedures, and customs. Yet a logic underlies this sometimes bewildering complexity. The way Congress operates reflects the diverse and conflicting needs and intentions of its members both now and in the past. To understand the House and Senate, one must understand what representatives and senators want to accomplish and what obstacles they have to overcome to achieve their goals.

The delegates in Philadelphia created and empowered a national legislature—on paper at least; it was up to members of Congress to make the words on paper into an institutional reality. To exercise the powers conferred on them by the Constitution, the House and Senate had to solve some basic problems: how to acquire information, how to resolve conflicts, how to coordinate action, and how to get members to work for common as well as personal goals. As these problems have become more acute over the years, members of Congress have scrambled to adapt the institution to cope with them more effectively while recognizing that every solution raises problems of its own. The challenges that spurred members to develop the modern Congress fall into two classes: problems besetting the House and Senate as organizations and problems arising from the competing individual and collective needs of members.

The Need for Information

Legislation is only as effective as the quality of knowledge underlying its inception. For example, a legislator cannot regulate the stock market sensibly without knowing how the market works or attack environmental pollution effectively without knowing how pollution is produced. As the United States has become more and more complex—socially, economically, and technologically—and the activities of the federal government have expanded, the informational demands on Congress have grown enormously.

Congress has responded with a solution common to the problem of performing complex social tasks efficiently: division of labor and specialization. The division of labor has given rise to the committee and subcommittee systems, large personal and committee staffs, and specialized research agencies that characterize the modern Congress. Specialists are able to develop a deeper understanding of their domains. By becoming specialists themselves or by drawing on the knowledge of other specialists, members of Congress can make better-informed decisions, and Congress, in turn, becomes a more effective institution. To provide the chamber with expertise, members must invest a lot of time and effort in mastering an area of specialization (as we learned earlier, public goods are more attractive in their consumption than in their production). Congress compensates members who master an area of specialization and supply specialized information with enhanced influence in their area of expertise. For example, California representative Henry Waxman's unparalleled mastery of health care issues has made him the most influential House Democrat by far in this important policy area. One problem, however, is that specialists may dominate policy making in their domains, shutting out the broader viewpoints of other members. Thus the efficiencies gained by a division of labor are paid for by diminished participation in policy making outside one's specialty.

Coordination Problems

As noted in Chapter 1, any group of people trying to act in concert faces coordination problems. Coordination becomes more difficult—and necessary—the greater the group's workload and the more elaborate its division of labor. As the volume and complexity of Congress's work have grown, so has its need for traffic management: dividing up the work, directing the flow of bills through the legislative process, scheduling debates and votes on the floor. Coordination problems of this kind usually are solved by a group giving one or several of its members the authority to do the coordinating—that is, take on the role of traffic cop. In Congress, party leaders serve as the "traffic cops." But procedures also shape policy. Control over the agenda—deciding what gets voted on when—is a powerful legislative weapon. For example, a majority of House members probably would have preferred to censure rather than to impeach Bill Clinton, but the Republican House leaders refused to allow a vote on censure, leaving a vote for impeachment as the only alternative to letting the president off completely. (Had they allowed a vote on censure, Clinton probably would have avoided impeachment and trial in the Senate.) Members thus sac-

rifice a measure of their autonomy in return for the gains in efficiency that come from delegating agenda control to party leaders.

Resolving Conflicts

Legislation is not passed until the majorities in both houses agree to its passage. The rich pluralism of American society guarantees that resolving conflicts is a fundamental task of any institution that reflects America's diversity. Agreement requires successful politicking: getting people who are pursuing divergent, even conflicting, ends to take a common course of action. Even when there is a consensus on ends, Congress often must resolve disagreements about means. During the 104th Congress (1995–1996), for example, almost all members agreed that welfare programs should be revised to discourage people from becoming permanently dependent on public assistance, but national leaders had to reconcile competing ideas about the best way to accomplish this goal in order to enact welfare reform.

Many of Congress's rules, customs, and procedures are aimed at resolving or deflecting conflicts so it can get on with the business of legislating. For example, when representatives speak on the floor of the House, all remarks are officially addressed to the Speaker, making it less likely that debates will degenerate into personal confrontations. More substantively, members delegate the task of building legislative coalitions to party leaders, who hold such positions by virtue of their demonstrated skills at negotiating legislative deals. The political parties in Congress themselves serve as ready-made coalitions. Party members agree on matters often enough to adopt a common label and to cooperate routinely on many—but by no means all—of the matters that come before the House and Senate. The presence of ready-made coalitions resolves many conflicts in advance, reducing the transaction costs of negotiating agreements on legislation. The price, however, is loss of autonomy to the party and of authority to leaders: individual members incur greater conformity costs because they cannot always do what is politically best for themselves rather than their party.

Collective Action

Everyone who wins a seat in the House or Senate wants to belong to a well-informed, effective legislature capable of fulfilling its constitutional mandate. Moreover, senators and representatives run under party labels and so have a stake in their party's reputation. But all of them have personal interests as well: winning reelection or advancing to higher office by pleasing constituents, enacting pet policies, attaining influence and respect in Washington. The problem is that what members do to pursue individual goals—tax breaks for local firms, special projects for their constituents—may undermine the reputation of their party or of Congress as a whole. In 1990, for example, Sen. Quentin Burdick, a Democrat from North Dakota, sought to appropriate $500,000 to restore bandleader Lawrence Welk's birthplace in Strasburg, North Dakota. Critics in the news media used the project to ridicule Congress for wasting taxpayers' money on "pork."

The tension between individual and collective political welfare—the standard prisoners' dilemma—pervades congressional life. The electoral process is the fundamental source of this dilemma. Congress has responded to the problem by developing devices such as the committee system that give members individual incentives to work for collectively beneficial ends. As noted, members who contribute to Congress's performance by becoming well informed about issues in their subcommittee's jurisdiction are rewarded with preeminent influence over policy in that area. Others listen to them, and they are given a chance to take personal credit for particular pieces of legislation.[27]

In trying to meet its many challenges, Congress must cope with another pressing problem: high transaction costs. These costs, as noted in Chapter 1, are the costs of doing politics—the time, effort, and bargaining resources (favors to be exchanged) that go into negotiating agree-ments on action in the absence of agreement on the purposes of the action. Because many of the transaction costs involved in building legislative coalitions are unavoidable—such as the conflicts to be ironed out, compromises to be arranged, favors to be traded—Congress has organized itself to reduce other transaction costs. One way is the use of fixed rules to automate decisions. For example, the **seniority rule,** by routinely allocating first choice in committee chairs, offices, and committee assignments to majority party members who have served longest, reduces the time and energy members would otherwise put into competing for these valued things. Another way is to follow precedent; battles over legislative turf, for example, are minimized by strict adherence to precedent in assigning bills to House committees. The pressing need to reduce transaction costs explains, then, why Congress does its work within an elaborate structure of rules and precedents. Absent these devices, transaction costs can be high. A recent example was the Senate's struggle to reach agreement on procedures for Bill Clinton's impeachment trial. Presidential impeachment trials (fortunately) occur so rarely that few usable rules or precedents were available.

The pressure to avoid unnecessary transaction costs is intensified by the ticking clock—both within the one-year session of Congress and over the two-year tenure of each Congress. The chief source of Congress's authority is its power of the purse over government spending and revenue raising. But if it fails to enact a federal budget in some form each year (or session), large portions of the federal government have to shut down, as happened in late 1995 when the Republican Congress and Democratic president played a high-stakes game of chicken over the budget. As budgets have grown larger, broader in scope, and, in recent years, more hotly contested, Congress often has found it difficult to enact them on schedule. Thus it has continued to tinker with the budgetary process. Other legislation has to pass through all the hurdles (outlined later in this chapter) within the two-year life of a

Congress. Bills in the pipeline but not enacted by the end of the second session of one Congress must be reintroduced in the next Congress.

The organization and rules of the House and Senate have evolved over two centuries through the accumulation of solutions deliberately chosen to overcome the pressing challenges just described. Because its membership substantially exceeds that of the Senate, the House experiences organizational problems more acutely than the Senate. Senators can get away with looser organization and retain more individual autonomy and equality simply because there are fewer of them. Their counterparts in the House, to solve their coordination problems, have to follow stricter rules of procedure and tolerate greater control by leaders.

Organizing Congress

To preserve the House and Senate as the powerful legislative bodies envisioned in the Constitution, members of Congress have had to devise means to overcome the formidable barriers to effective collective action discussed in the previous section. The crucial institutional structures they have created to exercise, and therefore preserve, Congress's power in the federal system are the party and committee systems.

The Parties

Decisions in the House and Senate are made (with a few important exceptions) by majority vote. Majorities not only enact bills, but also set rules, establish procedures, choose leaders, and decide how to organize their respective houses. This reality creates powerful incentives for members of Congress to both join and maintain durable coalitions—that is, political parties (for a broader analysis of the logic of party formation, see Chapter 12). What individual members give up in freedom to go their own way is more than made up by what they can gain by cooperating with one another.

Parties do not arise through spontaneous, voluntary cooperation, however. Like other coalitions, political parties arise when people recognize it is in their best interests to cooperate despite their disagreements. Party coalitions are assembled and maintained by party leaders. But leaders cannot lead without effective means to resolve conflicts, coordinate action, and induce members to cooperate when they are tempted to do otherwise. Members, in turn, must sacrifice independence by conceding some authority to party leaders. Yet as we noted in Chapter 1, when a group delegates authority to a leader to achieve coordination and reduce transaction costs, it risks incurring conformity costs and agency losses.

Members of Congress, aware of the risks, relinquish autonomy only so far as necessary, which accounts for the notable differences in the evolution of party leadership between the House and Senate as well as the changes over time in the power of House and Senate leaders.[28]

Development of Congressional Parties. Parties began to form in the very first session of the First Congress. A majority of members in the House favored the program for national economic development proposed by Alexander Hamilton, President George Washington's secretary of the Treasury, and worked together under his leadership to enact it. James Madison, a member of the House, and Thomas Jefferson, secretary of state, led the opposition to what they saw as an unwarranted expansion of federal activity. Recognizing the obvious—that, to prevail, they needed more votes in Congress—Madison's followers sought to increase their numbers by recruiting and electing like-minded men to the House.

These "factions" soon had names—the Federalists, led by Hamilton, and the Republicans (later called Democratic-Republicans and then Democrats), led by Jefferson—and party competition was under way. (See Chapter 12 for a fuller account of these developments.)

When the House and Senate divided into parties, congressional and party leadership merged. Formal leadership was established more quickly and more powerfully

Joseph Cannon was the last of a generation of powerful Speakers of the House of Representatives. During his tenure as Speaker of the House, "Uncle Joe" swatted many an opponent. Too many of his victims were fellow Republicans, however, and in 1910 thirty-six of them joined with Democrats in the historic revolt that dismantled the strong Speaker system and decentralized House administration.

in the House because, as the larger and busier body (the Senate's legislative role was decidedly secondary in the early Congresses), its collective action problems were more acute. Elected by the reigning majority, the Speaker of the House became the majority's leader and agent. Speakers were given the authority to appoint committees, make rules, and manage the legislative process on the majority party's behalf.

Centralized authority reached its peak under Thomas Brackett "Czar" Reed, a Republican from Maine, who served as Speaker in the Fifty-first (1889–1890), Fifty-fourth (1895–1896), and Fifty-fifth (1897–1898) Congresses. Reed appointed all committees and committee chairs, exercised unlimited power of recognition (that is, decided who would speak on the floor of the House), and imposed a new set of rules that made it much more difficult for a minority to prevent action through endless procedural delays. He also chaired the Rules Committee, which controlled the flow of legislation from the other committees to the floor of the House.

Although denounced by his opponents as a tyrant, Reed could not have amassed so much power without the full support of the Republican House majority. They were willing to delegate so much authority for two reasons. First, disagreements within the Republican Party were, at the time, muted; no important faction thought its interests could be threatened by a powerful leader allied with a competing faction. Second, service in the House had not yet become a career. The average member served only two terms. Indeed, in many places the local party organizations that controlled nominations enforced a two-term limit so that more of the party's stalwarts could enjoy the honor of serving in Congress. Without long-term career prospects and accustomed to party discipline, most members had little reason to object to strong leadership.

But once these conditions no longer held, the House revolted. Republican Speaker Joseph Cannon of Illinois (served 1903–1911) made the mistake of offending the progressive faction of the Republican Party that had emerged since Reed's day; he denied its members committee chairs and opposed the policies of the progressive Republican president, Theodore Roosevelt. In response, the Republican insurgents, with their Democratic allies, voted in 1910 to strip the Speaker of his power to appoint committees and chairs, forced him off the powerful Rules Committee, and limited his power of recognition. The increasingly career-oriented membership filled the power vacuum with a more decentralized and impersonal leadership structure, making seniority the criterion for selecting committee chairs. By weakening the Speaker, House members in

Figure 6–6 Congressional Party Unity, 1954–1998

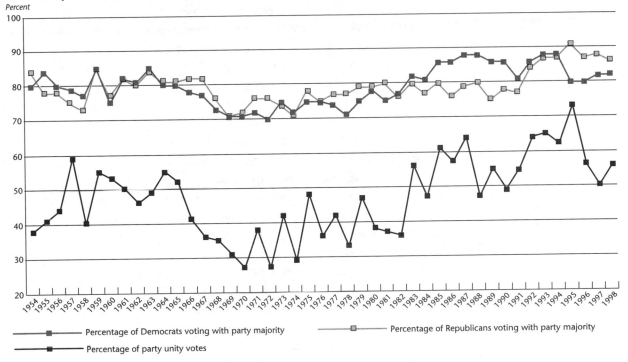

House of Representatives

Percent

Percentage of Democrats voting with party majority

Percentage of Republicans voting with party majority

Percentage of party unity votes

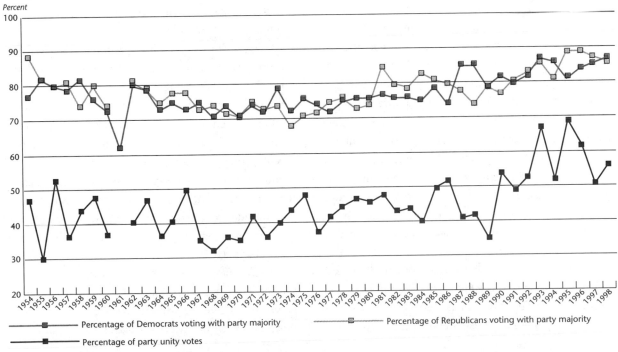

Senate

Percent

Percentage of Democrats voting with party majority

Percentage of Republicans voting with party majority

Percentage of party unity votes

Source: Norman J. Ornstein, Thomas E. Mann, and Michael J. Malbin, *Vital Statistics on Congress, 1997–1998* (Washington, D.C.: Congressional Quarterly, 1998), 210–213.

effect chose to tolerate higher transaction costs in order to reduce their conformity costs.

The degree of consensus within a party continues to affect how much authority party members are willing to delegate to party leaders. In the 1970s, for example, the Democrats strengthened the hand of their leaders in a variety of ways. The Speaker was given the authority to nominate all the Democratic members of the Rules Committee. He also was authorized to appoint temporary committees and special legislative task forces to deal with complex or controversial bills. At the same time, the Democratic Caucus (the organization of all House Democrats) reasserted its authority over committee organization, appointments, rules, and chairs. Once committee chairs became subject to election by secret ballot in the caucus, they lost much of the autonomy they had enjoyed since the New Deal.

Democrats could afford to strengthen their party's capacity to act collectively because the division between northern liberals and southern conservatives that had threatened from the beginning to split the New Deal coalition had faded. The ideological distinctiveness of southern Democrats had been undermined by the in-migration of northerners, industrial development, the movement of conservative whites from the Democratic into the Republican camp, and the Voting Rights Act of 1965, which brought African American voters into southern Democratic electorates. Thus there were fewer southerners, and among them fewer conservatives, in a more cohesive Democratic Party that saw smaller potential conformity costs in centralizing authority. House Democrats also tolerated stronger leadership after 1980 because they faced a hostile Republican president, Ronald Reagan, and from 1981 through 1987 a Republican-controlled Senate. By the 1990s congressional Democrats were more unified than they had been in decades.[29]

Republicans granted even more authority to their leaders when they took over the House in 1995. Unified by the party's Contract with America as well as by their shared conservative ideology, House Republicans made Newt Gingrich the most powerful Speaker since Cannon. At his behest, the Republican Conference (the Republican counterpart of the Democratic Caucus) ignored seniority in appointing committee chairs, ratifying without dissent the slate proposed by Gingrich. The Speaker also had a strong say in all the committee assignments, which he used to reward loyal junior members, and was given control of the House Administration Committee, which supervises management of the nonlegislative business of the House. The new majority party also adopted a rule limiting committee chairs to three two-year terms, reducing anyone's opportunity to build an independent committee domain.

House Republicans gave their leader an unusually strong hand to overcome their coordination and other collective action problems because they believed that keeping their promise to act on every item in the Contract with America within one hundred days of taking office was crucial to their and their party's future electoral fates. After accomplishing this feat, however, the party faltered in the 1995 showdown with Clinton over the budget, Gingrich's popularity plummeted, and during the 1996 election campaigns many Republicans sought to distance themselves from their leader.

By 1997 House Republicans' unity had frayed badly, and one faction mounted an attempt, soon aborted, to depose the Speaker. Gingrich hung on until Republican members, angry at the party's losses in the 1998 midterm election, forced him to resign—a pointed reminder that party leaders, as the majority's agents, are subject to dismissal if they do not satisfy their principals. Gingrich's eventual replacement, Dennis Hastert of Illinois, reflected the Republicans' need for a patient consensus builder to lead a divided party with only a narrow (223–211) majority. In Congress, strong party leadership is a consequence, not a cause, of party unity.

The decline and resurgence of congressional partisanship since the 1950s is evident in Figure 6–6. In both the House and Senate the proportion of "party unity" votes—those on which the party majorities took opposite posi-

Table 6–2 Party Committees and Leaders in the 106th Congress (1999–2000)

Republicans	Democrats
House of Representatives	
Speaker	
Majority Leader	Minority Leader
Majority Whip	Minority Whip
Conference (all Republicans)	Caucus (all Democrats)
Steering Committee	Steering Committee
Policy Committee	Policy Committee
National Republican Congressional Committee	Democratic Congressional Campaign Committee
Senate	
President Pro Tempore	
Majority Leader	Minority Leader
Assistant Majority Leader	Minority Whip
Conference (all Republicans)	Conference (all Democrats)
Policy Committee	Policy Committee
Committee on Committees	Steering and Coordination Committee
National Republican Senatorial Committee	Democratic Senatorial Campaign Committee
	Technology and Communications Committee

The success of House Minority Leader Richard Gephardt of Missouri rests on the trust of his Democratic colleagues that he will serve their individual reelection goals and the party's collective goal of restoring its majority in the House of Representatives. In 1996 and 1998 Gephardt helped Democrat Loretta Sanchez of California to prevail in her runs against former member of Congress Robert Dornan. In doing so, he appears to have won her enthusiastic support.

tions—fell off in the late 1960s and early 1970s when the parties were beset by internal divisions, then increased as the party coalitions become more homogeneous. The proportion of representatives and senators of both parties who voted with their party's majority on these party unity votes also dipped before rebounding to high levels in the 1990s. At the end of the decade, politics in both houses displayed the sharpest partisan divisions and highest levels of party unity in more than half a century. The House vote on the impeachment of Bill Clinton in December 1998 epitomized this trend; 98 percent of House Republicans voted for at least one article of impeachment, while 98 percent of House Democrats voted against all four articles.

Party Organization. The majority party in the House is led by the **Speaker of the House,** whose chief assistants are the **majority leader** and the majority whip (see Table 6–2 for a list of major party offices and organizations in the House and Senate). The structure of the minority party, the Democrats in the 106th Congress (1999–2000), is similar to that of the majority party but without the Speaker; the **minority leader** is its head. The party whips head up the whip organization—party members who form the communication network connecting leaders with other members. (The term **whip** comes from Great Britain, where the "whipper-in" keeps the hounds together in a pack during a foxhunt.) In addition to these official party committees, the Rules Committee is, in effect, an instrument of the majority party.

Party members give House party leaders resources for inducing members to cooperate when they are tempted to go their own way as free riders. These resources mainly take the form of favors the leaders may grant or withhold. For example, party leaders have a strong voice in all committee assignments (officially the province of the Steering Committees or, among Senate Republicans, the Committee on Committees), and they set the legislative agenda. Because a place on the agenda is a scarce resource, scheduling decisions determine the fate of many bills. Leaders also choose how much of their own time, energy, and organizational resources to devote to each legislative proposal. And they can help with reelection campaigns. Party leaders are therefore in a position to make it easier (or more difficult) for members to attain positions of influence, shape policy, and win reelection.

House party leaders are members' agents, however—not their bosses. They do not hire and fire party members; voters do, and so voters come first. Members, then, choose the style of leadership they believe will best serve their goals. Party leaders, who are elected or reelected to their position at the beginning of every Congress, are thoroughly, if informally, screened. They are members who have been around for a long time and whose styles, abilities, and flaws are well known. In the pre-Gingrich decades when Democrats held a majority of seats, they chose leaders, such as Thomas "Tip" O'Neill of Massachusetts (majority leader from 1973 to 1977), who were experts on procedure rather than policy and who cared more about building successful coalitions than about achieving specific legislative goals. But when the Republicans took over the majority in 1995, Speaker Newt Gingrich, as we saw earlier, pursued—with the full support of Republican members—a legislative agenda much more focused than the ones pursued by the Democratic Speakers before him.

For the minority party in the House, legislative leadership is less important because the party's legislative role is modest. Rather, leaders strive to keep up morale and establish a public record for the next election. They face an unhappy choice between cooperating with the majority, thus exerting some influence but getting little credit, and opposing and attacking the majority to position their party for future electoral battles. Their dilemma is sharpened when a president of their own party sits in the White House because the president has to cut deals with the majority to accomplish anything at all. As former minority whip, Gingrich managed to lead Republicans to majority status by abandoning a strategy of accommodation in favor of harsh partisan confrontation. After 1994 it was House Democrats who faced the daily choice of cooperation or confrontation.

Parties and Party Leaders in the Senate. Over the years the Senate has been slower than the House to develop formal leadership positions, and senators have never delegated as much authority to their leaders as have representatives. Senators initially saw themselves as ambassadors from sovereign states, and, as such, they could accept no less than equal rights with one another. In the years since, they have retained wide freedom of individual action because, with its smaller size, the Senate is able to get by without elaborate procedural shackles. (The Senate began with twenty-six members and did not reach one hundred until 1959; the House already had exceeded one hundred members by 1793.)

Under the Constitution, the vice president is the presiding officer of the Senate. The designated **president pro tempore** presides when the vice president is absent. But neither office has a real leadership role—after all, the vice president, who seldom presides, is not chosen by the Senate, and the president pro tempore, as the Latin suggests, is formally a temporary position. In fact, in the first few Congresses a new president pro tempore was elected every time the vice president was away.[30] In practice, no one led the Senate during the pre–Civil War period.

Parties formed in the Senate almost from the start, but party members were little inclined to delegate authority. The party caucuses did not take full control of committee appointments until 1846, after which they avoided intra-party conflicts over committee control by resorting to a strict seniority rule. Not until the end of the nineteenth century did senators concede the means to enforce party discipline—on procedural matters only—to party leaders.

Senate Minority Leader Thomas Daschle, Democrat from South Dakota, and Senate Majority Leader Trent Lott, Republican from Mississippi, appear to enjoy each other's company, which is fortunate since they spend much of their time conferring over the Senate calendar and resolving politically charged procedural disagreements between their political parties.

The positions of majority leader and minority leader were not formalized until 1913.

The power and influence exerted by Senate leaders have depended largely on their personal political skills and the extent of intra-party divisions. Lyndon Johnson, who led the Senate Democrats from 1953 until resigning to become vice president in 1961, exercised extraordinary influence over the Senate through skillful persuasion and manipulation. The resources at his disposal were no greater than those of other Senate leaders, but he used them to greater effect. Although no majority leader has since matched Johnson's fire or authority, others, such as Bob Dole, a Kansas Republican (served 1985–1986, 1995–1996), and George Mitchell, a Maine Democrat (served 1989–1994), have been skillful and effective majority leaders.

Party leadership in the Senate is more collegial and less formal than in the House. The minority party has greater influence in the Senate because so much of that body's business is conducted under **unanimous consent agreements** negotiated by party leaders. These agreements, which can be killed by a single objection, might govern, for example, the order in which bills are considered and the length of debate allotted to them. But unanimous consent agreements are only the most extreme example of the general rule: the capacity of House and Senate party leaders to lead depends largely on the willingness of party members to follow their leaders.

Other Groups in Congress. Although parties are by far the most important of Congress's coalitions, members have formed dozens of other groups, a few durable enough to have had permanent staffs until the new Republican House majority in 1995 banned the use of office allowances to pay staff salaries for member organizations. Some groups are explicitly ideological (Conservative Opportunity Society, House Progressive Caucus, Centrist Coalition, Mainstream Conservative Alliance). Others are based on demographics (Congressional Black Caucus, Hispanic Caucus, Caucus for Women's Issues). Bipartisan groups form around shared regional interests (Northeast-Midwest Congressional Coalition, Western Caucus, Coastal Coalition) and economic concerns (Steel Caucus, Textile Caucus, Travel and Tourism Caucus). Other groups focus on specific issues (Pro-Life Caucus, Pro-Choice Caucus, Heart and Stroke Coalition). The Congressional Friends of Animals Caucus fights for tighter regulation of livestock raising; the House Beef Caucus defends the livestock industry.

Such groups give members better access to information and allies on issues of special concern to them (or their constituents) that do not fit neatly into regular party or committee categories. They reflect the value of ready-made alliances in a system where success depends on building majority coalitions.

The Committee Systems

The committee systems of the House and Senate are the second organizational pillar upholding the institutional power of Congress in the federal system. Although committee power has at times been used to frustrate party majorities and leaders, committees are ultimately subject to the majority party, and the committee and party systems are closely integrated and mutually dependent. House committees, like House party leaders, are more powerful than their counterparts in the Senate, again reflecting the need for tighter organization in the larger body.

Evolution of Congressional Committees. The committee systems are the end product of more than two centuries of institutional evolution. The first Congresses delegated authority to committees sparingly. Instead, the House would turn itself into a Committee of the Whole (sitting as a committee, the House operates under a more flexible set of rules), frame a piece of legislation, elect a temporary committee to draft the bill, then debate and amend the bill line by line. After reassuming its guise as the House, it would vote on final passage.

From the start, this process was intolerably cumbersome. One early member, Fisher Ames of Massachusetts, likened it to trying to make a delicate etching with an elephant's foot.[31] Thus the House began to delegate more and more work to permanent committees. Ten were in place by 1809, twenty-eight by 1825. Transaction costs were further reduced by having committees appointed by the Speaker rather than elected. As the Speaker emerged as leader of the majority party, appointments became a partisan affair, and choice committee assignments became rewards for party loyalty and bargaining chips in campaigns for the Speakership.

The Senate was slower to set up permanent committees. Despite their smaller numbers and lighter workload, senators found they were spending too much time on electing a new committee to draft each bill, and the Senate began to accumulate standing committees. The initial twelve were established in 1816; by 1841 there were twenty-two. The Senate also was slower to delegate legislative action to committees and has never gone as far in this direction as the House.

After the Senate's parties assumed the right to make committee assignments, seniority became the criterion for selecting committee chairs: the office was awarded to the majority party member with the longest term of service on the committee. The seniority rule avoided two unwelcome alternatives: election, which would have led to divisive, time-consuming intra-party squabbles, and appointment by party leaders, which would have given the leaders more power than senators thought desirable or necessary. In technical terms the Senate's seniority rule reduced transaction and conformity costs.

Types of Committees. The **standing committees** of the House and Senate—those that exist from one Congress to the next unless they are explicitly disbanded—embody Congress's division of legislative labor (Table 6–3). Standing committees have fixed jurisdictions (that is, they always deal with the same legislative topics) and stable memberships, both of which facilitate specialization. Once appointed, a member in good standing cannot be forced off a standing committee unless his or her party suffers large electoral losses. That fate overtook some Senate Republicans after the 1986 election and some House Democrats after the 1994 midterm. Party ratios on committees generally match party ratios in the House and Senate. When a party has a narrow overall majority, however, it usually gives itself somewhat larger committee majorities, and it always gives itself extra seats on the most important committees. The job security associated with standing committees gives committee members both the motive and the opportunity to become knowledgeable about policy issues under their committee's jurisdiction. Expertise brings influence—other members defer to the judgment of committee experts they trust—and therefore a chance to make a real difference in at least one area of national policy.

Although committee membership is generally stable, changes occur when legislators seize the opportunity to move up to the committees deemed more important and desirable than the others. At the top of the heap in both chambers are the money committees—Ways and Means and Appropriations in the House, Finance and Appropriations in the Senate—because their activities are so central to Congress's main source of power in the federal system, its control over the budget. The House and Senate Budget Committees share some of this prestige. Seats on the Senate Foreign Affairs and Judiciary Committees also are in demand because of the Senate's special authority over treaties and diplomatic and judicial appointments. In the House the powerful Rules Committee, which controls the flow of legislation from committees to the floor, is especially attractive. Among the least desirable committees are those dealing with the internal administration of Congress, particularly its members' ethics; many members feel uncomfortable sitting in judgment on their colleagues.

Committee assignments are made by party committees under the firm control of senior party leaders and are ratified by the party membership. Members pursue committee assignments that allow them to serve special constituent interests as well as their own policy and power goals. For example, Agriculture (House and Senate) attracts members from farm states, and Armed Services (Senate) and National Security (House) attract members from regions with large military installations.

Because party leaders want to keep their followers in office, they are responsive to arguments that a particular

Table 6–3 The Committees of the 106th Congress

	Party Ratio	Number of Subcommittees
House of Representatives		
Standing Committees		
Agriculture	27R:23D	5
Appropriations	34R:26D	13
Banking and Financial Services	29R:25D	5
Budget	24R:19D	-
Commerce	28R:23D	5
Education and the Workforce	25R:20D	5
Government Reform and Oversight	24R:20D	7
House Oversight	6R:3D	-
International Relations	26R:21D	5
Judiciary	20R:15D	5
National Security	30R:25D	5
Resources	27R:23D	5
Rules	9R:4D	2
Science	25R:21D	4
Small Business	19R:16D	4
Standards of Official Conduct	5R:5D	-
Transportation and Infrastructure	40R:33D	6
Veterans' Affairs	16R:13D	3
Ways and Means	23R:16D	5
Select Committees		
Permanent Select Committee on Intelligence	9R:7D	2
Select Committee on China	5R:4D	-
Senate		
Standing Committees		
Agriculture, Nutrition, and Forestry	10R:8D	4
Appropriations	15R:13D	13
Armed Services	10R:8D	6
Banking, Housing, and Urban Affairs	10R:8D	5
Budget	12R:10D	-
Commerce, Science, and Transportation	11R:9D	7
Energy and Natural Resources	11R:9D	4
Environment and Public Works	10R:8D	4
Finance	11R:9D	5
Foreign Relations	10R:8D	7
Governmental Affairs	9R:7D	3
Judiciary	10R:8D	6
Labor and Human Resources	10R:8D	4
Rules and Administration	9R:7D	-
Small Business	10R:8D	-
Veterans' Affairs	7R:5D	-
Special and Select Committees		
Select Committee on Ethics	3R:3D	-
Select Committee on Intelligence	10R:9D	-
Special Committee on Aging	10R:8D	-
Special Committee on the Year 2000 Problem		
Joint Committees		
Joint Economic Committee	12R:8D	-
Joint Library Committee	6R:4D	-
Joint Printing Committee	6R:4D	-
Joint Committee on Taxation	6R:4D	-

assignment will help a member win reelection. Moreover, when members are assigned to the committees that best serve their personal and political interests, they will take committee work more seriously, making a larger contribution to their party's overall performance. The danger is that committees may become stacked with members whose views do not represent those of their party's majority. By and large, party leaders have managed to avoid this problem by judicious distribution of assignments, especially to the committees whose jurisdictions are most important to the party. A party's committee members are, like party leaders, the party's agents, and party majorities use their ultimate control over committee assignments to keep their agents responsive to the party's desires. For example, the House Democrats' committee on committees, the Steering Committee, has sometimes listed on a blackboard various measures of party loyalty next to applicants' names when deciding which members to place on important committees.[32]

Most committees are divided into subcommittees, many of which also have fixed jurisdictions and stable memberships. Like full committees, subcommittees serve Congress as a whole by encouraging specialization and, at the same time, reward members who develop expertise with special influence over their own small piece of legislative turf. Both committees and, in the Senate, subcommittees come with staffs of experts to help members do their work. Most committee staffers report to committee and subcommittee chairs; the ranking minority members also control a much smaller set of staff assistants.

In addition to the standing committees, Congress also forms special, select, joint, ad hoc, and conference committees. In theory, most **special committees** and **select committees** are appointed to deal with a specific problem and then disappear. A good example was the Senate's Select Committee on Secret Military Assistance to Iran and the Nicaraguan Opposition, formed in 1986 to investigate the Reagan administration's secret sale of arms to Iran and its use of the profits to support right-wing Nicaraguan

rebels despite a congressional ban on such aid. This committee issued its report a year later and disbanded, but some special and select committees sometimes last through many Congresses—for example, the Senate's Special Committee on Aging has been around since 1961.

Joint committees are permanent committees composed of members from both chambers; the committee leaderships rotate between the chambers at the beginning of each newly elected Congress. Joint committees gather information and oversee the executive but do not report legislation. One joint committee oversees the Library of Congress, the Botanical Garden, and public statuary; another (Printing) oversees the Government Printing Office and the arrangement and style of the *Congressional Record*, which publishes all of the speeches and debates on the floors of the House and Senate. In the House the Speaker occasionally appoints **ad hoc committees** to handle bills that are particularly sensitive (the 1989 congressional pay raise, for example). **Conference committees** are appointed to resolve differences between the House and Senate versions of bills (see section "Making Laws" in this chapter). The committees and subcommittees of the 106th Congress are listed in Table 6–3.

Committee Power. A century ago House committees were dominated by the Speaker, who appointed committee members and chairs. The revolt against Speaker Cannon in 1910 effectively transferred control over committees to committee chairs, who, under the altered rules, owed their position to seniority, not loyalty to their party or its leaders. By the 1950s both chambers were run by a handful of powerful committee chairs who could safely ignore the wishes of party majorities. Conservative southern Democrats, continually reelected from one-party strongholds, chaired the most powerful committees and cooperated with Republicans to thwart policies supported by a majority of Democrats, especially in the area of civil rights. The most notorious example was Howard W. Smith, a segregationist Virginia Democrat who used his position as chairman of the House Rules Committee during the 1950s to stop civil rights bills. The rules allowed chairs to run committees like dictators, and some of them did.

In 1959 frustrated younger liberals formed the Democratic Study Group (DSG) to take on the conservatives, hoping that they could make up in numbers what they lacked in institutional clout. Over the next decade the DSG grew large enough to take over and revitalize the Democratic Caucus. The most important changes occurred after the 1974 election, when the public reaction to the Watergate scandal brought seventy-four new Democrats, eager for action and disdainful of seniority, into the House. At their instigation, the Democratic Caucus adopted a rule that forbade any individual from chairing more than one committee or subcommittee; this way, many more members could enjoy this privilege. Committee members and the caucus, rather than chairs, assumed control over committee rules, budgets, and subcommittee organization. Committee nominations were transferred from Democrats on the Ways and Means Committee, who had held this authority since the revolt against Cannon, to the caucus's own Steering Committee.

The caucus itself elected committee chairs by secret ballot (secrecy removed the threat of retaliation). In 1975 the caucus actually deposed three committee chairs, underlining the new reality that the party's majority, not seniority, would now have the final say in who runs committees.

These changes produced a more fragmented and decentralized committee system in which fully half of the Democrats in the House chaired a committee or subcommittee. Although members benefited individually, they found it more difficult to act collectively. The simultaneous strengthening of the Speaker's authority, described earlier, logically complemented these changes. The party leaders may have found the task of coordination more difficult, but they also were given more tools (for example, control of nominations to the Rules Committee) to carry it out. The net effect was a strengthened party capacity for collective action.

The new Republican majority that took over the House in 1995 revised committee rules to ensure that the legislative agenda outlined in its Contract with America would move swiftly to enactment. The new rules gave committee chairs greater control over subcommittees by authorizing them to appoint all subcommittee chairs and control the work of the majority's committee staff. But committee chairs themselves now had to report to the Speaker and were limited to three consecutive terms. All these changes gave the Republican majority more control over its committees than any House majority had exercised since the early years of the twentieth century.

Jurisdiction. In the House does international trade policy fall within the jurisdiction of the Commerce Committee or International Relations Committee? Should education programs for veterans be handled in the Senate by Veterans' Affairs or by Labor and Human Resources? Where does something like energy policy, which affects virtually every aspect of American life—transportation, environment, the economy, international trade, national defense—fit? And making matters even more complicated, such technical issues are overlaid with political issues. Committees and subcommittees compete for jurisdiction over important policy areas, but the supply of legislative turf is always insufficient to meet the demand. Thus it is not surprising that the House and Senate have altered the number and jurisdictions of their committees from time to time, nor is it surprising that such changes have been highly contentious.

Within Congress, the constant pressure to multiply standing committees and subcommittees arises out of the increasing complexity, volume, and scope of legislative business and members' desires to serve as committee and subcommittee chairs, especially now that Congress is populated by career politicians seeking their own pieces of the action. Inactive committees are hard to kill off. For example, the Senate maintained a Committee on Revolutionary Claims (requests for payment of bills incurred during the American Revolution) until 1920, when it pruned its standing committees back from seventy-four to thirty-four. Many of the disbanded committees had not met in years, but their chairs clung to them because committees came with staff and office space. The cutbacks were achieved only by giving individual senators their own clerks and offices.

Since the 1920s the House and Senate have trimmed their committee systems several times, notably in the Legislative Reorganization Act of 1946, which sharply reduced the number of standing committees in both chambers (from thirty-three to fifteen in the Senate, from forty-eight to nineteen in the House). The act also rearranged committee jurisdictions to reduce the overlap and confusion and to make the House and Senate systems more similar. Reductions were achieved by consolidation, however, so many former committees simply became subcommittees. The most recent committee changes occurred in 1995, when the victorious House Republicans abolished three standing committees and made other modest alterations in committee jurisdictions.

The political problem with trying to distribute committee jurisdictions more sensibly (at one time in the Senate, seventeen committees and forty subcommittees had some jurisdiction over energy policy) is that changes redistribute power and upset long-established relationships among committee members, administrative agencies, and interest groups. Nevertheless, Congress must rationalize jurisdictions occasionally, or the emergence of new issues will lead to turf battles, overlapping jurisdictions, uneven workloads, and confusion. Recent Democratic leaders sought to cope with these problems by using **multiple referrals**—that is, sending bills, in whole or piece by piece, to several committees at the same time or in sequence. For example, a banking reform bill introduced in the House in the 102d Congress (1991–1992) went first to Banking, Finance, and Urban Affairs, then to Energy and Commerce, then to Agriculture, then to Judiciary, and finally to Ways and Means.[33] Rules adopted by the Republicans after 1994 do not allow the Speaker to assign the same bill to more than one committee at a time but permit sequential and split referrals.

The Money Committees. The "power of the purse" has inspired the most contentious jurisdictional fights. In the earliest years of government, revenue and spending bills were handled by Ways and Means in the House and Finance in the Senate. Then, during the 1860s, the spending power was transferred to a separate Appropriations Committee in each house to help deal with the extraordinary financial demands of the Civil War. Other committees in both houses later broke the Appropriations Committees' monopoly on spending, and by 1900 authority over national finances was spread among nearly twenty House and Senate committees. In the House this devolution of authority was not such a great impediment to action when the chamber was dominated by powerful Speakers, but a few years after the revolt against Cannon the Republican House majority underlined its commitment to parsimony by restoring the Appropriations Committee's monopoly. The Senate followed suit in 1922.

Since then, legislative spending has been a two-step process in each chamber. In step one, the committee with jurisdiction over a program *authorizes* expenditures for it, and, in step two, the Appropriations Committee *appropriates* the money—that is, writes a bill designating that specific sums be spent on authorized programs (sums that need not and often do not match the amounts authorized). For some important programs expenditures take the form of **entitlements,** which designate specific classes of people who are entitled to a legally defined benefit. Social Security and Medicare payments and military pensions are examples. Congress must spend whatever it takes to cover those who are eligible for entitlements—unless it changes the eligibility standards or the amounts to which the eligible are entitled.

After 1921 the money committees took on the institutional task of protecting congressional majorities from the collective damage that the pursuit of individual electoral goals threatened to impose. In the House the powerful Appropriations Committee used its authority to keep members' desires for locally popular projects (such as dams, highways, and harbor improvements) and programs (such as housing, urban renewal, and police equipment) from pushing up taxes or deficits to politically intolerable levels. Tax legislation emerging from Ways and Means was routinely granted a **closed rule** (forbidding members to propose or vote on amendments—changes in wording—to a bill being considered for final passage on the floor of the House) to prevent a scramble for revenue-draining tax breaks for local firms.

Budget Reform. By the early 1970s the ability of the money committees to enforce collective self-control had been seriously eroded. The committee reforms had weakened committee leaders, and a move toward congressional "openness"—doing more business in public—made it harder for individual members to resist the temptation to promote locally popular projects of dubious worth. Inhibitions against offering floor amendments to fiscal legislation fell by the wayside, and members became adept at finding ways to circumvent the normal budgetary process to finance their pet programs.

At about the same time, an important external constraint on congressional spending also ceased to work properly. Congress had come to rely on the president to impound—refuse to spend—some of the funds authorized and appropriated by Congress in order to keep spending totals from reaching unacceptable levels. But President Richard Nixon turned this authority against Congress, impounding funds to subvert the spending priorities of its Democratic majorities. In 1972, for example, he refused to spend $9 billion in clean-water funds and terminated many agricultural programs.[34] Nixon even impounded appropriations passed over his veto. His action posed a fundamental challenge to the House and Senate as institutions as well as to their Democratic majorities.

Congress responded with the Budget and Impoundment Control Act of 1974. The act subjected presidential impoundment authority to strict congressional control. More important, it revamped Congress's budgetary process with the goal of making impoundment unnecessary. Among other things, the act established a Budget Committee in each chamber to oversee the coordination

of taxing and spending policies. It also instituted procedures and timetables for setting budget targets, supervising the committees' decisions on revenues and spending, and reconciling the tax and spending bills enacted by Congress with the targets. The system was designed to compel members to vote on explicit levels of taxation, expenditures, and deficits, thereby taking direct responsibility for the fiscal consequences of the many separate decisions made during a session.

Despite Congress's good intentions, the reformed budget process proved entirely incapable of preventing the huge budget deficits produced by budget politics during the Reagan and Bush administrations. Orderly budgeting fell victim to the intense partisan conflict between the Republican presidents and congressional Democrats over budget priorities. Presidents Ronald Reagan and George Bush sought to keep taxes low; congressional Democrats sought to protect popular domestic spending programs. Since both low taxes and spending for popular programs proved politically irresistible, the budget was left unbalanced. No amount of reform, then, could have prevented the massive budget deficits of the 1980s and early 1990s because nothing can force Congress to follow the rules it makes for itself. Procedures are chosen to produce desired outcomes; when the rules stand in the way of desired outcomes, ways always can be found around them. Congressional leaders simply ignored the formal budget process when it proved unable to resolve budget conflicts in a way they found satisfactory.[35]

Attempts to reduce the deficit by procedural devices failed repeatedly until both sides developed the political will to support a precarious agreement. The negotiations that produced the Budget Enforcement Act of 1990, a package of tax increases and program cuts designed to reduce the projected deficit by some $500 billion over five years, exemplified budgeting under a government divided between the parties. It consisted of improvised deals worked out in charged, high-level negotiations between the president and congressional leaders. Congress and the administration, both under Democratic control after the

Figure 6–7   Congressional Staff, 1891–1997

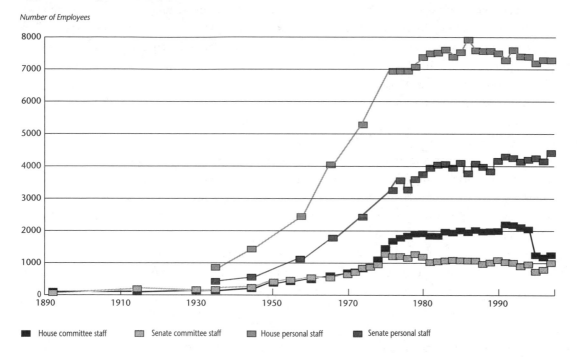

Number of Employees

Legend: House committee staff · Senate committee staff · House personal staff · Senate personal staff

Source: Norman J. Ornstein, Thomas E. Mann, and Michael J. Malbin, *Vital Statistics on Congress, 1997–1998* (Washington, D.C.: Congressional Quarterly, 1998), 135, 139.

1992 election, made further inroads into the deficit in 1993 with another round of tax increases and spending cuts intended to reduce the deficit by another $500 billion between 1994 and 1998.

Still, the budget did not come into balance, requiring yet another round of budget confrontations and negotiations, stretching from 1995 to 1997—and this time between a Republican Congress and a Democratic president. The agreement became possible when the booming economy produced a bonanza of tax revenues, making it much easier to accommodate the desires of both sides. By 1998 the economy had produced so much in new tax revenues that the budget was in surplus, and budget politics turned, at least temporarily, to the happier task of choosing among tax cuts, additional spending for government programs, or paying down the national debt. But politics continues to dominate process, and the formal budget rules control the action only insofar as they do not prevent congressional majorities from doing what they want.

Congressional Staff and Support Groups

In addition to relying heavily on its committee system, Congress has sought to cope with its expanding workload by adding staff (see Figure 6–7) and specialized research agencies. Staff doubled between the mid-1950s and the late 1970s (with most of the growth in personal staff); the numbers then remained stable until 1995, when House Republicans reduced House committee staffs by 30 percent. The cuts, however, left them with much larger committee staffs than they had had when they were in the minority; the staffers who lost their jobs were all on Democrats' payrolls.

Personal staff assistants manage members' offices in Washington and back in the state or district. They also draft bills, suggest policy, prepare position papers, write press releases, handle casework for constituents, deal with lobbyists, and negotiate with other staff on their boss's behalf. Almost any political or legislative chore short of casting formal votes in committee or on the floor can be delegated to staff assistants. Committee staff are deeply involved in all legislative activities; they organize hearings and investigations, research policy options, attend to legislative details, and negotiate with legislators, lobbyists, and executive branch officials on behalf of the party faction on the committee that employs them.

Members receive additional help in gathering and processing information from several specialized research agencies. The General Accounting Office (GAO) audits and investigates federal programs and expenditures, probing for waste, fraud, and inefficiency. The Congressional Research Service (CRS) gives Congress access to a highly professional team of researchers.

Expert advice on complex technological issues—such as air pollution control, converting defense industries to civilian work, and the health effects of dietary supplements and vitamins—are provided by the Office of Technology Assessment (OTA). This particular kind of advice is sorely needed by a legislature having very few members with any kind of scientific or engineering background.

The Congressional Budget Office (CBO) and the GAO are the most important congressional agencies. Created as part of the 1974 budget reforms, CBO provides Congress with the economic expertise it needs to make informed fiscal decisions and to hold its own in conflicts with the president's Office of Management and Budget (see Chapter 7). Among its tasks are economic forecasting and economic policy analysis. Although CBO was mainly designed to serve the collective institutional needs of Congress, it also serves members individually; it will, on request, provide analyses to let members know how various budget alternatives would affect their home states and districts.

By using the expert advisers within committee staff and congressional support agencies, members of Congress do not have to take the word of experts from the executive branch or interest groups, who cannot be expected to impart unbiased information. Although officially bipartisan, the support agencies are the most valuable to the majority party in Congress when the other party controls the executive branch. Indeed, it was no accident that a Democratic Congress created OTA and CBO (and initiated a major expansion of CRS) during the Nixon administration or that Republicans replaced the CBO director when they took control of Congress in 1995.

Making Laws

Congress's rules and structures—the parties and committee systems—are designed to enable majorities to make laws. At every stage of the many routine hurdles a bill must clear to become law, individual and collective (usually partisan) political interests shape the action (see Figure 6–8). The lawmaking process presents opponents of a bill with many opportunities to sidetrack or kill the legislation. It is considerably easier, then, for members to stop bills than to pass them. Although the regular legislative procedures are now regularly circumvented by party leaders trying to enact important and controversial bills in circumstances of intense partisan conflict and divided government,[36] an examination of these procedures will complete the picture of how ordinary legislative politics works.

Introducing Legislation

Only members may submit legislation to the House or Senate. Many proposals originate outside Congress—from the executive branch, interest groups, constituents—but they must have a congressional sponsor to enter the legislative process. The process itself is largely routine and routinely political. Some bills carry (informally) their au-

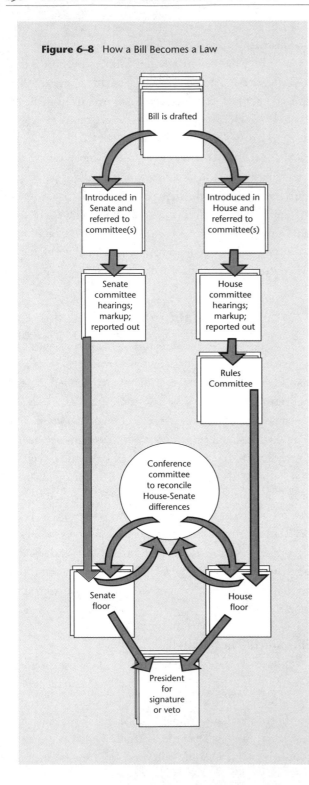

Figure 6–8 How a Bill Becomes a Law

thors' names; the Immigration Reform Act of 1986 is known as the Simpson–Mazzoli law after its chief sponsors, Republican Alan Simpson of Wyoming in the Senate and Democrat Romano Mazzoli of Kentucky in the House. The Balanced Budget and Emergency Deficit Control Act of 1985 is called the Gramm–Rudman–Hollings act after Republican senators Phil Gramm of Texas and Warren Rudman of New Hampshire and South Carolina Democrat Ernest Hollings. Even whole programs may be named after their authors. For example, the government helps college students finance their education through Pell grants, named after Democratic senator Claiborne Pell of Rhode Island. Personal credit for what is, after all, a collective act of Congress (one vote is never sufficient and rarely necessary to accomplish anything) is a valuable commodity. Proponents of bills try to line up cosponsors both to build support (by sharing credit) and to display it (increasing the chances for legislative action). Most important bills are introduced in the House and Senate at the same time so the chambers can work on them simultaneously.

The parties and the president (with the cooperation of congressional friends) also use legislative proposals to stake out political positions and to make political statements. Republican presidents Reagan and Bush regularly introduced proposals they knew were "dead on arrival" to establish a record that their party could run on in the future. So do members of Congress.

Assignment to Committee

After a bill is introduced, it is assigned a number (preceded by *H.R.* in the House, *S.* in the Senate) and referred to a committee. Even the number assigned can make a political point. In 1995 Republicans gave top billing to items from their Contract with America; *H.R. 1* was assigned to a bill applying federal labor and safety standards to Congress and *S. 1* to a bill limiting the federal government's ability to compel state and local governments to carry out policies without providing the money to pay for them. Most bills are routinely assigned to the appropriate committee; complex bills are sometimes referred to several committees, and controversial bills are occasionally handled by temporary ad hoc committees appointed for that single purpose. The Speaker makes the nonroutine decisions in the House, manipulating the committee process to assure more friendly or expeditious treatment of legislation important to the majority party. In the Senate, party leaders negotiate agreements to settle disputed referrals.

Once a bill has been referred to a committee, the most common thing that happens next is: nothing. Most bills die of neglect—and are meant to die of neglect—in committee. Many more bills are introduced than Congress has time to deal with. Some bills are introduced "by request," meaning the introducer was doing someone—a constituent or campaign contributor—a favor by offering the bill but has no further interest in its fate. Bills introduced by the minority party to score political points or embarrass the majority are deliberately buried. Like party leaders, committee chairs and their allies strive to avoid situations in which their party colleagues might have to cast potentially embarrassing votes. If the committee decides on further action, the bill may be taken up directly by the full committee, but more commonly it is referred to the appropriate subcommittee.

Hearings

Once the subcommittee decides to act, it (or the full committee) may hold hearings, inviting interested people—from the executive agencies, from interest groups, from academia, from almost anywhere—to testify in person or in writing about the issue at stake and proposals to deal with it. In a typical recent two-year Congress, the Senate held about 1,200 hearings, the House about 2,300. Hearings may be orchestrated to make a record for (or against) a particular proposal, to evaluate how a program is working, or simply to generate publicity—for committee members as well as issues. Committees can investigate almost anything, including the White House or Congress itself. Senate committees also hold hearings to evaluate

During the 105th Congress (1997–1998), the Senate Governmental Affairs Committee held public hearings on the Clinton administration's campaign fund-raising practices both to embarrass the president and vice president and to generate publicity for the committee's chairman, Republican Fred Thompson of Tennessee. Thompson was believed to have presidential ambitions of his own.

judicial, diplomatic, and senior administrative appointments.

Hearings also provide a formal occasion for Congress to monitor the administration of the laws and programs it enacts. The heaviest duty falls on the Appropriations subcommittees in the House, for government agencies have to justify their budget requests to these panels every year. Congress often is criticized for shirking its duty to oversee the administration of laws. After all, if carried out, comprehensive oversight would be a tedious, time-consuming, politically unrewarding chore. Instead, members of Congress set up administrative procedures that give affected interests an opportunity to protest damaging bureaucratic policies and decisions. In this way, members can confine their oversight to those areas of administration where the political stakes are demonstrably high. Members operate more like firefighters than police, waiting for fire alarms to go off before taking action rather

Here Senate Banking Committee members gather to mark up banking legislation. The Senate, with its tradition of full participation, does more work in full committee, less in subcommittee.

than patrolling the streets looking for crime.[37] By relying on people affected by administrative decisions to alert it to problems, Congress, in effect, puts a big bumper sticker on bureaucrats that says, "How am I driving? Call 1-800-Congress" (see Chapter 8).

Reporting a Bill

If the subcommittee decides to act on a bill (and often it does not), it marks it up—that is, drafts it line by line—and reports it to the full committee. The full committee then accepts, rejects, or amends the bill. With the exception of important and controversial bills, committees usually defer to subcommittees; otherwise, they lose the benefits of a division of labor.

Much of the coalition building that produces successful legislation takes place as subcommittees and committees work out the details of bills. No one wants to waste time on a bill that has no chance of passing—unless political points could be scored such as when a Democratic Congress sent Republican president George Bush a campaign finance reform bill he was certain to veto. If a bill cannot attract solid support from at least the majority par-

ty committee members (and perhaps minority party members as well), its chances on the House or Senate floor are slim indeed. But if amendments, compromises, and deals can build a strong committee coalition for a bill, its chances on the floor are very good. The committee system, then, also divides the labor of coalition building.

The written report that accompanies every bill reported out of committee is the most important source of information on legislation for members of Congress not on the committee and for other people in government, including the agencies and courts that have to implement and interpret the law once it is passed. These reports summarize the bill's purposes, major provisions, and changes from existing law. They also summarize the arguments for and against the bill.

Scheduling Debate

When a committee agrees to report a bill to the floor, the bill is put on the House or Senate calendar—a list of bills scheduled for action. Each house has different calendars for different types of bills. In the House, noncontroversial bills are put on the Consent Calendar or Private

Calendar to be passed without debate. Such bills also may be dealt with expeditiously under a suspension of the rules, which waives almost all of the formalities to allow swift action. Most legislation passed by the House follows one of these routes.

Controversial or important bills are placed on the Union Calendar (money bills) or House Calendar (other public bills). The committee reporting such bills must ask the Rules Committee for a **rule,** a resolution that specifies when and how long a bill will be debated and under what procedures. The rule may permit amendments from the floor (**open rule**), only certain amendments (**restricted rule**), or no amendments (closed rule). Majority party leaders use restricted or closed rules to keep unwanted amendments off the agenda, both to protect their party's members from casting embarrassing votes and to keep legislative packages from unraveling. Closed rules help to solve the majority's prisoner's dilemmas; many proposals that would not be enacted piece by piece because different members would defect on different sections can win if they are voted on as packages. As partisan competition became more intense during the 1980s, Democratic House leaders used restricted or closed rules to maintain control of the floor agenda (see Table 6–4). Republicans objected strenuously but, after taking over in 1995, resorted to restrictive rules themselves to prevent Democrats from hindering the Republicans' promised speedy action on proposals set forth in the Contract with America.

If the Rules Committee holds hearings on a rule, interested members may express their views on the legislation. After hearings, a bill may be granted a rule or it may be denied a rule entirely or until the originating committee has revised it to the Rules Committee's satisfaction. Once the Rules Committee grants a rule, it must be adopted by a majority vote on the floor. When floor action on a bill is constrained by its rule, the House majority has, in fact, consciously chosen to constrain itself. Sometimes the House kills a bill by voting against the rule rather than against the bill itself. In 1994, for example, the House rejected a rule for a bill to elevate the Environmental Protection Agency to cabinet status because the bill did not require the new department to consider the economic costs and benefits of new environmental regulations. The House's action killed the legislation.

The Senate has no equivalent of the House Rules Committee or, indeed, any rules limiting debate or amendments. Thus the leaders of both parties routinely negotiate unanimous consent agreements to arrange for the orderly consideration of legislation. Unanimous consent agreements are similar to a rule from the House Rules Committee in that they limit time for debate, determine which amendments are allowable, and provide for waivers of Senate rules. In the absence of a unanimous consent agreement, anything goes.

Table 6–4 Open and Restrictive Rules, 95th–104th Congresses (1977–1997)

Congress	Total Rules Granted	Open Rules Number	Open Rules Percent	Restrictive Rules Number	Restrictive Rules Percent
95th, 1977–1978	211	179	85	32	15
96th, 1979–1980	214	161	75	53	25
97th, 1981–1982	120	90	75	30	25
98th, 1983–1984	155	105	68	50	32
99th, 1985–1986	115	65	57	50	43
100th, 1987–1988	123	66	54	57	46
101st, 1989–1990	104	47	45	57	55
102d, 1991–1992	109	37	34	72	66
103d, 1993–1994	104	31	30	73	70
104th, 1995–1996	151	86	57	65	43

Source: Roger H. Davidson and Walter J. Oleszek, *Congress and Its Members,* 6th ed. (Washington, D.C.: CQ Press, 1998), 232.

Note: Democrats claim that Republicans misclassified rules in the 104th Congress, thereby overstating the frequency of open rules.

There is no limit on how long senators can talk or on how many amendments they can offer. Individuals or small groups can even **filibuster**—hold the floor making endless speeches so that no action can be taken on the bill or anything else—to try to kill bills that the majority would otherwise enact. And breaking a filibuster is difficult. Under Senate rules an extraordinary three-fifths majority of the Senate membership (sixty votes) is required to invoke **cloture,** which allows an additional thirty hours of debate on a bill before a vote is finally taken.

Filibusters were used most notoriously by conservative southern senators in their rear-guard action against civil rights laws a generation ago, but senators of all ideological persuasions now use the tactic. In fact, filibustering has become much more common in recent years, rising from an average of only one filibuster per Congress in the 1950s to more than twenty-five per Congress in the 100th–103d Congresses (1987–1994).[38] Senate Republicans, then in the minority, used it to kill a number of Bill Clinton's initiatives during the 103d Congress (1993–1994), including his economic stimulus package, a proposal to raise fees for grazing cattle on federal lands, a package of campaign finance reforms, a bill to bar members of Congress from accepting gifts from lobbyists, and a bill to forbid employers from permanently replacing workers who go on strike for higher pay. After 1994 Senate Democrats found new affection for the tactic; a record fifty cloture votes were taken in the 104th Congress, of which 18 percent were successful, the lowest rate ever.[39]

Even the threat of a filibuster can stop action on legislation because Senate leaders dislike wasting time on bills not likely to pass. With filibustering now so routine, the new reality is that the support of sixty senators is needed to pass any controversial piece of legislation. Under Senate rules, a few members can tie the Senate up in knots by refusing to consent to limited debate on a bill. Senators, then, must depend to a considerable degree on mutual restraint and bipartisan cooperation to get their work done. When cooperation breaks down, the Senate is immobi-

The longest speech in the history of the Senate was made by Strom Thurmond of South Carolina. Thurmond, a Democrat who later became a Republican, spoke for twenty-four hours and eighteen minutes during a filibuster against passage of the Civil Rights Act of 1957. This display of stamina was no fluke; Thurmond was still serving in the Senate during the 106th Congress (1999–2000) at age ninety-six.

lized. Senators thus buy lower conformity costs at the price of higher transaction costs.

Debate and Amendment

In the House the time for debate is divided equally between the proponents and opponents of a bill. Each side's time is controlled by a floor manager, typically the committee or subcommittee chair and the opposing ranking member. If amendments to a bill are allowed under the rule, they must be germane (pertinent) to the purpose of the bill; extraneous matters, known as **riders,** are not allowed. Debate on amendments usually is restricted to five minutes for each side. The House often debates bills as a Committee of the Whole because acting in the guise of a committee the House is less encumbered by formal procedures. For example, a quorum—the number of members who must be present for the House to act officially—is 100 rather than the usual majority of 218, and the gavel is wielded by a member chosen by the Speaker. The House must revert back to itself, however, to vote on legislation.

Floor debates do not change many minds because politicians are rarely swayed by one another's eloquence. Debates are for public consumption: to make arguments that members will use to justify their vote to constituents and others; to shape public perceptions through the media; to guide administrators and courts when they apply and interpret the legislation; to stake out partisan positions; to show off. More important, formal floor debates serve to legitimize policy. Whatever deals and compromises went into building a legislative coalition, whatever the real purposes of its supporters, they have to make a case that the proposed action would serve the public interest. The opposition has equal time to argue against the action. Occasionally, public justification assumes historic proportions such as in 1991 when ninety-four senators and more than three hundred representatives took the floor to explain their positions on U.S. intervention in the Persian Gulf.

Floor action does more to shape legislation in the Senate than in the House. Because unanimous consent is required to limit Senate debate (except when cloture is used to end a filibuster), members are free to spend as much time as they like debating a bill. Unlike in the House, few conflicts are resolved in committee or subcommittees; senators do much more legislating on the floor, offering amendments or complete alternatives to the bill reported by the committee. Senate amendments need not even be germane; important bills are sometimes passed as amendments—or riders—to completely unrelated bills. For ex-

ample, in 1994 when the Senate passed a bill elevating the Environmental Protection Agency to cabinet status—the same bill the House killed by voting down the rule—it also inserted into the text an amendment that would have reauthorized the 1974 Safe Drinking Water Act. Unrestrained floor debate is the fullest expression of the Senate's individualistic, participatory ethos. It also provides a prominent forum for the articulation of any social interest that catches the fancy of even one senator.

The Vote

Members of Congress are ever alert to the political implications of votes on important bills. The fate of legislation often is decided by a series of votes rather than a single vote. For example, opponents of a measure may propose "killer" amendments, which, if passed, would make the bill unacceptable to an otherwise supportive majority. In addition, opponents may move to recommit the bill—that is, to send it back to committee for modification or burial—before the final vote. And, on occasion, members may try to straddle an issue by voting for killer amendments or to recommit but then voting for the bill on final passage when these moves fail. Sophisticated observers have little trouble picking out the decisive vote and discerning a member's true position, but inattentive constituents may be fooled.

How do members of Congress decide how to vote? Political scientist John Kingdon sought to find out by asking them. They revealed that, along with their own views, the opinions of constituents and the advice of knowledgeable and trusted colleagues have the strongest influence on their decisions. Often they are aware of what their constituents want without anyone having to tell them. At other times, they rely on letters, phone calls, faxes, e-mail, editorials, and polls to get a sense of what people think. Even on issues where constituency opinion is unformed, members try to anticipate how constituents would react if they were to think about the issue. The idea is to cast an *explainable vote,* one that can be defended publicly if it is brought up by a challenger in some future campaign. Not every vote has to please the people who hire and fire members of Congress, but too many "bad" votes can expose a member to the charge of being out of touch with the folks back home.[40]

In general, members have reason to listen to anyone who can supply them with essential information: political information about how constituents and other supporters will view their actions and technical information about what the legislation will do. They also have reason to weigh the views of anyone who can help or hinder them in winning reelection, advancing their careers in Washington, and having an impact on policy. Constituents' views count the most because they have the most direct control over members' careers, but the views of interest groups, campaign contributors, and party leaders also shape decisions, especially on issues of little concern to constituents.

Most constituents know little and care little about most of the issues members vote on. The minority of the public that does pay attention varies from issue to issue. The relevant constituency opinions are those held by people who care, pay attention, and are not securely in the other party's camp, for their support will be affected by how the member handles the issue. In other words, the politically relevant interests on most issues are special interests. For that reason, in Congress intense minorities often prevail over apathetic majorities. One example: opponents of gun control, led by the National Rifle Association, have stopped or weakened gun control legislation many times over the years despite widespread public support for stronger regulation of firearms.

Trusted colleagues strongly influence voting decisions because legislators cannot possibly inform themselves adequately about all the matters they must vote on. They depend instead on the expertise of others, most often members of committees (usually from their own party) with jurisdiction over the bills outside their own specialties. Members say that lobbyists, executive branch officials, party leaders, congressional staff, and the news media influence their decisions much less than do con-

stituents and colleagues. Groups representing special interests are deeply involved in congressional policy making, but their direct influence is not strongly felt at this point in the legislative process; effective groups work through constituents and colleagues (see Chapter 13, Interest Groups).

And how influential is the president when the votes are finally cast? Occasionally presidents have been able to win against the odds by persuading wavering members of their party to stick with the team or by cutting special deals with pivotal members. For example, in 1993 President Clinton's successful appeals to party loyalty were crucial to his razor-thin budget victories (218–216 in the House, 51–50 in the Senate, where Vice President Al Gore's vote broke a tie); no Republican in either chamber would support the budget because it included tax increases. Essential, too, were the bargains made to modify the bill to satisfy reluctant Democrats.[41] On most votes, however, the administration's wishes are by no means paramount.

The same is true of the wishes of party leaders. Senate leaders exert little formal influence at this or any other stage of the legislative process. House leaders use their much more formidable powers at earlier stages and through control of the agenda. The majority party's leaders may, if they wish, do much to frame the choices that House members face. But their job is to construct legislative packages that party members are comfortable supporting. If they are successful, no persuasion is necessary. If they fail, few members are likely to put party loyalty ahead of constituents' views.

In the House, votes may be cast by voice, but at the request of at least twenty members a recorded "roll-call" vote is taken. Members vote by inserting a small plastic card into one of the more than forty stations scattered about the House floor and pressing yea, nay, or present (indicating they were on the floor for the vote but did not take a side). Senators simply announce their votes when their names are called from the roll of members rather than record it by machine.

LOGIC OF POLITICS

PORN FOR CORN

The conference committee charged with working out differences between the House and Senate versions of the fiscal 1992 appropriations bill for the Interior Department faced a typical problem and came up with a classical solution. The House had voted to increase the very low fees stock raisers pay to graze their animals on public land by more than 400 percent over a four-year period. The Senate, which overrepresents sparsely populated western states, opposed this provision.

In the meantime, the Senate had, in its Interior Department Appropriations bill, adopted language proposed by Republican senator Jesse Helms of North Carolina forbidding the National Endowment for the Arts (NEA) from spending federal money "to promote, disseminate, or produce materials that depict in a patently offensive way sexual or excretory activities or organs." Majorities in both chambers probably opposed censoring NEA grants, but they also realized it was politically risky to go on record as permitting taxpayers' money to fund anything that might smack of pornography.

The conference committee struck a bargain: the House delegation would vote to drop the grazing fee increase if the Senate delegation would vote to drop Helms's provision—an exchange of "porn for corn," as it was quickly labeled. The conference bargain held on the floors of the House and Senate. Helms tried to put the restrictions back in the appropriations bill, but western conservatives feared the resurrection of the grazing fee increase if they broke the deal and refused to go along with him.[1]

"Porn for corn" is a definitive example of doing politics: conservative western ranching interests made common cause with the liberal urban arts community though they scarcely shared common purposes.

1. Phillip A. Davis, "After Sound, Fury on Interior Bill Signifies Nothing New," *Congressional Quarterly Weekly Report,* November 2, 1991, 3196.

In Conference

Once passed, a bill is sent to the other chamber for consideration (if some version has not already been passed there). If the second chamber passes the bill unchanged, it is sent to the White House for the president's signature or veto. Routine legislation usually follows this route, but controversial bills often pass the House and Senate in different versions, so that the two bodies have to reconcile the differences in the versions before the bill can leave Congress.

This reconciliation is the job of a conference committee. Each house appoints a conference delegation that includes members of both parties, usually from among the standing committee members most actively involved for and against the legislation (if a conference committee is not appointed, as sometimes happens, the bill dies). The size of the delegation depends on the complexity of the legislation. The House delegation to the conference handling the 1,300-page Clean Air Act amendments of 1990 consisted of 130 representatives from eight different committees. The Senate got by with a delegation of nine from two committees. But the relative size of the delegations is not important, for each chamber votes as a separate unit in conference, and a bill is not reported out of conference to the House and Senate until it receives the approval of majorities of both delegations.

Conference committees are supposed to reconcile differences in the two versions of a bill without adding or subtracting from the legislation. In practice, however, they occasionally do both. Conference committees generally exercise the widest discretion when the two versions are most discrepant (see box "Porn for Corn" for an amusing example of conference maneuvering—and of how politics is done).

Once conferees reach agreement on a bill, they report the details to each chamber. A conference report is privileged—that is, it can be considered on the floor at any time without going through the usual scheduling process. The divisions in conference committees normally reflect the divisions in the chambers they represent, so majorities assembled in conference can usually be reproduced on the House and Senate floors. If both chambers approve the report, the bill is sent to the president.

Sometimes one or both chambers balks and sends the conferees back to work, perhaps with instructions about what to change. If differences cannot be reconciled, the bill dies. This outcome is unusual, however; when a proposal has attracted enough support to make it this far and members face a choice to take it or leave it, they usually take it. This situation strengthens the hand of the committees that originally reported the legislation because the conference delegates are normally drawn from these committees and the conference gives them a chance to have the last word.

To the President

Upon receiving a bill from Congress, the president has the choice of signing the bill into law; ignoring the bill, with the result that it becomes law in ten days (not counting Sundays); or vetoing the bill (also see Chapter 7, The Presidency, where the veto process is explained more fully). If Congress adjourns before the ten days are up, the bill fails because it was subject to a **pocket veto** (the president, metaphorically, stuck it in a pocket and forgot about it). When presidents veto a bill, they usually send a message to Congress, and therefore to all Americans, that explains why they took such action.

Congressional override of a presidential veto requires a two-thirds vote in each chamber. If the override suc-

ceeds, the bill becomes law. Success is rare, however, because presidents usually can muster enough support from members of their own party in at least one chamber to sustain a veto. When a head count tells presidents that an override is possible, they hesitate to use the veto because the override would expose their political weakness. Of the 453 regular vetoes cast between 1945 and 1996, only 46 were overridden. Presidents also exercised 310 pocket vetoes, none of which could be overridden, over the same period.[42]

Presidents often prevail without having to resort to a veto because members of Congress are reluctant to invest time and effort in legislation that will die on the president's desk. The exception is when congressional majorities want to stake out a position on a prominent issue to score political points. The veto, then, is a major weapon in the presidential arsenal; presidents can threaten to kill any legislative proposal they find unsatisfactory, usually leaving Congress with no choice but to cut presidents in on deals.

A Bias against Action

Emerging from this review of the process and politics of congressional lawmaking is one central point: it is far easier to kill a bill than to pass one. Proponents of legislation have to win a sustained sequence of victories—in subcommittee, in committee, in Rules (in the House), in conference, on the floors of both chambers (repeatedly), and in the White House—to succeed. Supporters of a bill have to assemble not one but a series of majority coalitions. Opponents need win only once to keep the bill from going forward. To be sure, a way can be found around every legislative choke point; Congress has special procedures to circumvent regular procedures when they prevent adamant majorities from getting their way or when Congress needs to act swiftly. But use of extraordinary procedures requires more attention and effort than legislative leaders usually are able to invest except on the most crucial legislation, such as the annual budget.

Dead bills, however, always can be revived and reintroduced in the next Congress. Indeed, it is not at all unusual for many years to lapse between the initial introduction of a major piece of legislation and its final enactment. Proposals for national health insurance have been on the congressional agenda for more than fifty years (only Medicare, applying exclusively to the elderly, has passed so far). Defeats are rarely final, but neither are most victories; the game is by no means over when a law is enacted. The real impact of legislation depends on how it is implemented by administrators and interpreted by the courts (see Chapter 8). And laws always are subject to revision or repeal later by Congress. That victories or defeats almost always are partial and conceivably temporary contributes a great deal to making politics—cooperation in the face of disagreement—possible. Politicians recognize that taking half a loaf now does not mean they cannot go for a larger share in the future.

Evaluating Congress

Americans hold contradictory views about their national legislature. In the abstract, most people approve of the Constitution's institutional arrangements. Any proposals for change advanced by constitutional scholars and reformers are ignored by virtually everyone else. And Americans generally like their own representatives and senators. Most members receive high approval ratings from constituents, and most win reelection even when the public professes to be thoroughly fed up with national politics and the politicians of one or both parties. But Congress as it operates and its members as a class are rarely appreciated. Sometimes large majorities of Americans assign their Congress a failing grade (Figure 6–9). The low point in congressional approval occurred in the early 1990s and coincided with an unusually high level of turnover in congressional seats.

The public's general disdain for Congress reflects the low repute garnered by politicians as a class. Habitual contempt for politicians arises from the nature of politics

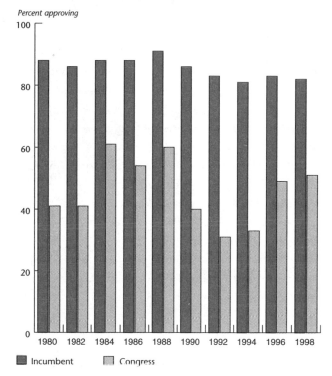

Figure 6–9 Approval Ratings of Congress and One's Own Representatives, 1980–1998

Percent approving

■ Incumbent   □ Congress

Source: American National Election Studies.

itself. Americans use politics as a vehicle for social decisions even when they share no consensus about the best course of action. Politics, then, inevitably requires compromises and trades, the results of which leave no one fully satisfied. The alternative to compromise—stalemate—is often equally scorned by a public more inclined to view legislative gridlock as a product of partisan bickering than of intractable conflicts among legitimate values, interests, and beliefs. In reality, Congress's difficulty in deciding on a budget, reforming the health care system, or dealing with an array of social problems (poverty, crime, education, urban decay) reflects the absence of any public consensus on what should be done about these issues. The only consensus is that national leaders, in failing to act, have failed to do their job.

Congress's poor reputation also arises from the very nature of pluralism. In pluralist politics, adamant minorities frequently defeat apathetic majorities because the minorities invest more of their political resources—votes, money, persuasive efforts—in getting their way. Indeed, the ability of pluralist systems to weigh the intensity of preferences as well as to count heads is viewed as a major advantage because it means that groups tend to win when they care most and lose when they care least. But it also means that "special interests" often win out over general interests, leaving members of Congress perpetually open to the charge of violating the public trust.[43]

During the 1980s and 1990s Congress's reputation also suffered from recurrent ethics scandals, including those involving such powerful leaders as Democratic Speaker Jim Wright (forced to resign in 1989 over a shady book deal), Republican Speaker Newt Gingrich (fined and reprimanded in 1997 for lying to the House Ethics Committee), Ways and Means chairman Dan Rostenkowski (jailed for mail fraud in 1996), and Senate Finance Committee chairman Bob Packwood (resigned in 1995 to avoid expulsion for sexual harassment). More broadly, the House bank overdraft scandal of 1992 and the publicity that followed about other congressional perks—gyms, beauty parlors, and limousines—fueled widespread scorn for Congress and helped Republicans overthrow forty years of Democratic rule in 1994.

All of these sources of public disdain for members of Congress represent conditions to be coped with rather than problems that can be solved. Senators and representatives cannot avoid making political deals, representing conflicted publics, or paying special attention to intensely held views. And not all of them will resist the many opportunities for corruption that come with the job. Thus members of Congress as a class are never likely to be revered by the public for any length of time.

Still, public approval of Congress does vary in response to how it seems to be doing its job. The public prefers bipartisan agreement to partisan bickering, cooperation with the president over conflict between the branches, and, most of all, successful public policies. For example, in early 1998, on the heels of the 1997 balanced budget agreement between Clinton and the Republican Congress and against a background of a booming stock market and unemployment and inflation rates down to levels not seen since the 1960s, public approval of Congress in the Gallup Poll reached 57 percent, up nearly thirty points from its low in 1992. But when Congress engaged in a highly partisan battle over impeaching Clinton for perjury and obstruction of justice in his attempt to cover up his sexual dalliance with a White House intern, its level of public approval fell sharply. In present-day politics, intense partisan conflict is far more common than bipartisan cooperation, so most of the public is likely to find fault with Congress most of the time.

Despite all its faults, perceived or real, the U.S. Congress remains the most powerful and independent legislature in the world. It has retained its power and independence for both constitutional and institutional reasons. The Constitution not only granted the House and Senate extensive legislative powers, but also provided the basis for electoral independence from the executive. Congress's formal legislative powers and electoral independence would have been of little avail, however, had members not created effective institutional devices for acquiring information, coordinating action, managing conflict, and discouraging free riding. By developing the party and committee systems and securing the assistance of numerous staff and specialized research agencies, members of Congress have given themselves the organizational means to carry out, and thus to retain, their constitutional mandate. But their task is rarely easy or the way smooth, for the Madisonian system that Congress epitomizes erects formidable barriers to collective action, and the range and complexity of contemporary political conflicts continually test Congress's fundamental ability to do politics successfully.

Key Terms

ad hoc committee / 190

casework / 172

closed rule / 193

cloture / 200

conference committee / 190

entitlement / 192

filibuster / 200

gerrymandering / 167

joint committee / 190

logrolling / 175

majority leader / 185

minority leader / 185

multiple referral / 192

open rule / 199

pocket veto / 204

political action committee / 169

pork barrel legislation / 175

president pro tempore / 186

proportional representation / 165

restricted rule / 199

rider / 200

rule / 199

select committee / 190

seniority rule / 180

Speaker of the House / 185

special committee / 190

standing committee / 188

ticket-splitting / 170

unanimous consent agreement / 187

whip / 185

Suggested Readings

Arnold, R. Douglas. *The Logic of Congressional Action*. New Haven: Yale University Press, 1990. Explains how congressional leaders can manipulate the rules to overcome electorally induced free riding when they want to enact policies that impose short-term or concentrated costs in order to achieve longer-term or diffuse benefits.

Cox, Gary W., and Mathew D. McCubbins, *Legislative Leviathan: Party Government in the House*. Berkeley: University of California Press, 1993. Lucid explanation of the logic that undergirds the House party organizations; makes a strong case that congressional parties are more powerful than most observers have assumed.

Fenno, Richard F., Jr. *Home Style: House Members in Their Districts*. Boston: Little, Brown, 1978. Fenno's close personal observation of House members' interactions with their constituents produces a wealth of insights about how representation actually works.

Jacobson, Gary C. *The Politics of Congressional Elections*. 4th ed. New York: Longman, 1997. A comprehensive look at congressional elections.

Mayhew, David R. *Congress: The Electoral Connection*. New Haven: Yale University Press, 1974. Classic analysis of how electoral incentives shape almost every aspect of congressional organization and behavior.

Rohde, David W. *Parties and Leaders in the Postreform House*. Chicago: University of Chicago Press, 1991. Explains the decline and resurgence of party unity in the House over the past several decades, with special attention to how the reforms of the 1970s fostered greater partisanship.

Chapter 7

THE PRESIDENCY

⭐ *What happened historically to transform the president from the "chief clerk" of the government (Abraham Lincoln's description) to a formidable politician whose preferences always must be taken into account?*

⭐ *Theodore Roosevelt called the presidency "the bully pulpit," and all modern presidents seek the public's support for their policies. But does their ability to sway public opinion really help them in dealing with other politicians in Washington?*

⭐ *Does the growth of the "institutional presidency" risk transforming America's executive into an isolated, imperial office?*

⭐ *What does the current era of divided party control of government imply for the president's ability to exercise national leadership?*

In the 1990s two presidents found themselves at loggerheads with an opposition-controlled Congress over the next year's budget. Eventually the critical moment arrived: each president had to decide whether to deal with Congress or to confront it. Either way, the president would find himself navigating a political minefield sown by the opposition party. In the first instance the president's plan goes awry and veers sharply toward failure. In the second it takes an arduous path but one that leads to success. Both presidents control the same constitutional leverage—the threat to veto unacceptable legislation—but with far different consequences for both national policy and their political careers.

Failure

In the late fall of 1990 President George Bush sat uncomfortably in front of a TelePrompTer, waiting to deliver a prime-time appeal to the American people. In the face of a mounting budget deficit that would soon trigger draconian cuts across government services, he was unveiling a deficit-reduction plan of increased taxes and reduced spending that more closely resembled the preferences of congressional Democrats than those of his fellow Republicans. His speech omitted any reference to the current Republican mantra—cut capital gains taxes. It even included a tax hike for wealthy (mostly Republican) taxpayers.

Ironically, Bush had worked hard to reach this unenviable position. To get budget negotiations moving he had had to sacrifice a promise made earlier to the American voters that he would hold the line on taxes. Indeed, the Democrats had insisted that the president retract his 1988 campaign slogan, "Read my lips, no new taxes," before they would sit down with him to talk about raising taxes.

Having campaigned in 1988 on the slogan "Read my lips, no new taxes," President George Bush was hunted down by reporters in 1990 after he conceded a tax increase in negotiations with congressional Democrats. When reporters caught the president jogging one morning and baited him with his contradiction, he yelled, "Read my hips." In the national news story that followed, the president's response was reported as an expression of his disregard for his promises.

Bush had tried to minimize the political fallout by slipping the language "tax-revenue enhancements" into a press release listing topics open to negotiation. Moreover, for months he had refrained from publicly criticizing the Democratic Congress lest he drive its members away from the bargaining table. Facing this predicament, he began his television address, feigning enthusiasm for the budget compromise. No wonder his appeal was brief and tepid, without impact on the country or Congress. In fact, his solicitation of the public's help—"Tell your congressmen and senators you support this deficit-reduction agreement"—did little to abate the avalanche of mail opposing the legislation.

Congressional Republicans had been largely ignored in developing the budget compromise; they were a minority, and an inflexible one. As a result, they were uncommitted to the plan, fearful that in the upcoming congressional election they, as members of the president's party, would be held responsible by their constituencies for the tax increases. Many Republicans began to complain publicly that their president had sold out to the opposition. Some congressional Democrats also criticized the budget compromise—for cutting social programs too deeply. On the floor of the House of Representatives the package of tax-

es and spending, which had taken months to stitch together, quickly unraveled amid partisan charges and countercharges.

With congressional Republicans in open revolt, President Bush faced a dilemma. He could allow the prevailing law to kick in and automatically reduce the deficit by means of severe across-the-board cuts in discretionary spending. Or he could return to the negotiating table in pursuit of stronger Democratic support that would lead to an even less palatable compromise. Considering the bickering among his advisers, this was not an easy call. He opted for the latter, probably out of fear he would be blamed for sudden reductions in popular federal programs.

As soon as the new package was signed, President Bush left town to repair his relations with congressional Republicans by helping in their reelection campaigns. "God, I'm glad to be out of Washington," the president told voters and darkly referred to Democrats as "America's biggest and most entrenched special interest." He explained away recent events by claiming the budget had been "held ransom" by Congress. In the future, he vowed, he was "absolutely going to hold the line on taxes."[1] Vows or no vows, his fellow Republicans were skeptical. One described the White House strategy this way: "They're going to sign off on the budget deal, then try to pin it on the Democrats, say George Bush didn't do it and expect the voters to believe this whole budget was an immaculate conception." Republican congressional candidates also were uneasy. Of the hundred or so who had filmed campaign commercials with Bush earlier in the fall, only a few used them. Many candidates canceled the president's planned visits to their districts, and some of those who needed his presence to raise campaign funds nonetheless stayed in Washington on "pressing business." Some candidates even expressed open hostility: one House Republican incumbent, in the president's presence, asked his audience, "Why did this President, last May, decide that the issue he had run on and won on now had to be laid on the table as a point of negotiations? We're talking about his pledge on taxes."[2]

By all objective indicators, Bush's strategy failed. The president's approval rating dropped from the mid-seventies to the mid-fifties in the weeks leading up to the midterm congressional elections. When the voters had their say, the Democrats added nine seats to their House majority. As for President Bush, his about-face on taxes would continue to haunt him in his losing reelection campaign against Bill Clinton.

Success

Five years later Bush's failure remained fresh in the minds of congressional leaders contemplating another budget deal with the president. This time, however, Congress was controlled by Republicans and a Democrat, Bill Clinton, occupied the White House. The fact that Clinton had defeated the Republican president Bush in part by re-

By Mark Streeter. Copyright 1995. Courtesy Savannah Morning News

minding voters about his failure to keep his "no new taxes" promise was lost on no one. Here was an opportunity for payback. Congressional Republicans, led by House Speaker Newt Gingrich and Senate Majority Leader Bob Dole, declared they would make President Clinton accommodate them just as congressional Democrats had "worked over" President Bush.

Nothing about President Clinton's first two years in office suggested he could stand up to pressure. His all-too-frequent willingness to compromise had forced even loyal staffers to wonder what he stood for.[3] Confronting the newly installed Republican Congress in early 1995, Clinton appeared clearly overmatched. As the Republican majorities busily enacted their "Contract with America" legislative agenda, President Clinton's standing in Washington and the nation probed new depths. In February House Speaker Gingrich delivered his own unprecedented "State of the Union" address to a live national television audience. In April, attempting to recapture center stage, President Clinton scheduled a rare prime-time news conference. Only one network showed up, and the president was asked whether people in Washington and across the nation still paid attention to him. Bristling, Clinton asserted, "The president is relevant here."[4]

By fall, a Republican budget axing many favored Democratic programs had reached the final stages of congressional passage. Clearly, President Clinton still had not demonstrated the validity of his "relevance." More specifically, he had failed to moderate the deep cuts in social spending contained in the Republican budget. He also had failed to stave off a massive tax cut that favored wealthier constituents. As they approached the endgame, Republican leaders believed they held a card that would trump any threat of a presidential veto: they had attached their spending and revenue legislation to a debt-ceiling bill the federal government needed to meet its payroll and entitlement obligations. The president would have to accept the whole package or shut down the government. Bush had flinched at a much less stark choice in 1991; surely this weak president would too. "I think the president will be forced to move toward us," predicted Republican John Kasich, chairman of the House Budget Committee. "At the end of the day he will explain why he made our program reasonable while signing our program."[5]

On November 13, however, Clinton vetoed the barebones budget, denouncing its "deep and unwise cuts," and prepared the nation for a government shutdown. "If America has to close down access to education, to a clean environment, to affordable health care, to keep our government open," Clinton asserted, "then the price is too high." He then added, "Yes, to balancing the budget. No, to the cuts." One White House aide confided to a reporter that the president was "prepared to fight all winter" on this issue. Two days later 800,000 federal workers were sent home. They would not return to their jobs for six days.

Media polls immediately detected that public opinion had swung to the president's side. When asked whether the president should have vetoed the budget, 56 percent of respondents in a *Wall Street Journal* poll said yes, and only 36 percent said no. Asked to assess Clinton's leadership, 49

percent of the public agreed that he was "a strong leader and standing up for what he believes in." By comparison, Gingrich and Dole received 33 percent and 30 percent approval ratings, respectively.[6] The president's arguments were repeated in national television commercials sponsored by the Democratic National Committee, which had budgeted $1 million a week for ads that ran through early 1996.

Republican leaders backed off temporarily, agreeing to interim funding to give negotiations a chance to resume. In early December Congress sent Clinton another budget bill, which he promptly vetoed. The president adhered to his public strategy of appearing moderate in his demands but eager to veto "radical" Republican legislation. Worried that the president's stand was "very risky," Donald Fowler, chairman of the Democratic National Committee, cautioned the White House that its strategy would succeed only "if the public gets the impression Republicans are intransigent."[7] As if following a script, the president soon appeared on television characterizing the Republican posture as "an exercise of raw, naked power."

After weeks of fruitless negotiations, the government shut down again. By mid-January both sides were facing the specter of government default on its debts. A weary Speaker Gingrich came out of one long negotiating session "close to exhaustion" and conceded to a reporter that the president and his team "were tougher than I thought they would be. . . . They have less flexibility than I thought they would have. Our strategy failed." Over the next few weeks Republican leaders backed off a sevenyear balanced budget commitment and more than half of the tax cuts they had passed three months earlier. By February, Republican and Democratic negotiators had agreed to fund the government for the next year at reduced levels. Few programs were eliminated, and mutually acceptable savings were achieved by broadly scaling back discretionary domestic spending.

On strictly budgetary terms, both sides found features of the February agreement they could point to with satisfaction. Politically, however, Clinton and the Democrats had won a significant victory. The president had reestablished his presence in Washington and recaptured the attention of the American public. His approval rating, instead of plunging after each government shutdown, rebounded to a level that made reelection in 1996 conceivable. Meanwhile, Republican leaders Gingrich and Dole saw their fortunes sink. The previous September, a Gallup straw poll pitting Clinton against the Republican Party's eventual nominee, Bob Dole, had found the Republican ahead by five percentage points. Six months after the budget confrontation, the president held a commanding twelve-point lead he would never relinquish. By standing up to the Republican Congress with the veto and direct appeals to the American public, Bill Clinton had rescued his presidency.

The differences between Bush's and Clinton's performances were subtle but consequential. Each threatened the veto; each sought the support of the American public. Clinton managed to extract full advantage from these assets, while Bush enlisted them maladroitly and, in the end, found himself, a Republican president, sponsoring what was essentially a Democratic plan. The starkly different outcomes of these two political struggles illustrate an important theme of this chapter: the occupants of the presidency are given no more than an opportunity to make a difference. Whether presidents succeed or fail depends on luck—that is, things beyond their control such as the actions and preferences of others—and their skill as politicians.

In his classic treatise *Presidential Power and the Modern Presidents,* Richard E. Neustadt poses the problem confronting every occupant of the White House: the Constitution guarantees the president little more than a role as the chief clerk of the government.[8] Congress, the constitutional kingpin, requires only the president's acquiescence—hardly more than a signature—to achieve its goals. Abraham Lincoln, one of America's greatest presidents, would have agreed with Neustadt's observation. "Chief clerk" is precisely the phrase he used to describe his duties. Successful presidents, however, are able to con-

Using the pen with which President Lyndon Johnson had signed the Medicare law in 1965, President Bill Clinton vetoed the congressional budget bill on December 6, 1995, and announced to the network cameras, "Today I am vetoing the biggest Medicare and Medicaid cuts in history, deep cuts in education, a rollback in environmental protection and a tax increase on working families. With this veto, the extreme Republican effort to balance the budget through wrongheaded cuts and misplaced priorities is over."

vert their relatively modest "clerkship" responsibilities into real leadership—leadership that has less to do with the authority of the office than with the president's political skill. Such skill, as the Bush and Clinton experiences illustrate, explains the difference between success and failure.

In this chapter we explore why the presidency's constitutional authority often falls short of that required for real leadership, as well as what twentieth-century presidents have done to strengthen their hand and improve their prospects for success. We begin with the Constitution, for it was the Framers, in their deep-seated ambivalence toward an independent executive, who mandated that presidents be *leaders* yet gave them the tools to be no more than *clerks.*

The Presidency in the Constitution

Long after the Framers of the Constitution left Philadelphia, the British historian Lord Acton wrote what became a famous line: "Power tends to corrupt and absolute power corrupts absolutely." His words capture precisely the problem that preoccupied most of the Framers as they designed the presidency: how much power could they safely cede to the office? Up to a point, presidential authority offered the nation efficiency and decisiveness in its collective undertakings—qualities sorely missing under the Articles of Confederation. Beyond that uncertain, critical point, however, presidential authority threatened tyranny, in large part because a branch consisting of a single office would lack the internal checks present in factionalized legislatures. Some saw solution in a plural executive, but this odd idea attracted little support. Perhaps memories of how indecisively and incompetently congressional committees had administered the Revolutionary War were still fresh in their minds.

The Convention delegates finally resolved the problem—at least to the satisfaction of the majority who enacted Article II—by withholding unessential authority from the office and, whenever they could, by legislating checks on executive prerogatives. Warily, the Framers avoided granting the president explicit administrative authority. They even limited the president's appointment power by requiring the Senate's endorsement of nominees. The president's one clear legislative authority, the veto, was understood to be a negative instrument that would poorly serve a president bent on usurping power. As for the chief executive's military and diplomatic authority, they sought the benefits of an executive able to act with dispatch, yet they also sought to harness that authority lest some future president use it unwisely.

The sections that follow assess the president's constitutional duties and authority as executive, legislator, diplomat, and commander in chief. But, taken together, these separate duties do not add up to the forceful character of the modern presidency. Unlike Congress whose authority derives directly from the Constitution, the modern presidency is rooted in subsequent congressional delegations of authority and presidential assertions of "inherent" authority. Beyond the formal powers of the office is its singular high visibility, allowing presidents to take full advantage of the twentieth-century development of mass communications to shape and mobilize public opinion.

The President as Chief Executive

The Framers' deep ambivalence about the kind of executive they wanted is reflected in Article II's rambling provisions for the office. Compared with Article I's detailed development of the structure and powers of Congress, Article II is long on generalities and short on matters where detail is required. It begins by stating, "The executive Power shall be vested in a President of the United States of America." But, instead of proceeding to define this power, the article abruptly shifts to a lengthy description of the qualifications for office, means of election, succession, and compensation.

Not until Section 2 does the Constitution confer any real administrative authority. It states that the president may appoint the officers of government "by and with the 'Advice and Consent of the Senate'"—that is, by a majority confirmation vote. Yet, not content with this check on the president's discretion, the Framers immediately qualified this authority by adding, "but the Congress may by law vest the Appointment of such inferior officers, as they think proper, in the President alone, in the Court of Law, or in the heads of Departments." On the subject of direct administrative authority, Section 2 is more revealing in what it leaves unsaid. It declares simply that from time to time the president may "require the opinion, in writing, of the principal officers in each of the executive departments." Then, as if fully addressing the president's appointment and administrative authority, the Constitution, in Section 3, admonishes the president to "take care that the laws be faithfully executed."

But where are the administrative tools presidents need to carry out this mandate? Conspicuously missing is any provision for executive departments or their administrative heads who later would constitute the president's cabinet. Perhaps the Framers should be applauded for leaving the structure and work of administrative departments wholly to the discretion of future Congresses, to be determined in pace with the nationalization of public policy. This omission, however, obviated any serious consideration of the president's administrative controls. Had the Framers actually created at least some of the easily anticipated "inferior officers" mentioned in the Constitution, clear executive controls might have emerged as well. The Framers could have given the president the authority to propose budgets, oversee spending, supervise personnel, and even countermand administrative decisions. These were, after all, among the familiar routine duties of eighteenth-century executives just as they are for present-day senior administrators, including the president. Instead, in allowing Congress to create the executive branch, the Framers also gave that body the prerogative to establish and subsequently modify what, if any, role the president would play as chief executive.

The president's missing administrative authority was particularly troublesome when one issue arose: the removal of presidential appointees from office. Indeed, in 1867 an impeached President Andrew Johnson came within one vote of being removed from office by the Senate for dismissing his secretary of war in direct violation of the Tenure of Office Act, enacted by Congress over Johnson's veto. Today Congress no longer prevents presidents from dismissing executives they have appointed to administer federal agencies. Yet important exceptions can be found at "independent" regulatory agencies such as the Food and Drug Administration and the Federal Reserve Board where presidents appoint officers for fixed terms.

Until the twentieth century, presidents found themselves ill-equipped to intrude into administrative practices and thus rarely did so. Instead, Congress exercised oversight of the bureaucracy by assigning its committees and subcommittees jurisdictions that matched those of the federal departments. Presidents stayed in the background and, except during national crises when they acted on their authority as commander in chief, seldom contested congressional control over the executive departments. To the degree the presidents of that era sought to influence policy, they generally did so informally through their political appointees who ran agencies and departments. They also, on occasion, issued formal instructions called **executive orders.** An executive order has the force of law until the president or a successor retracts it, Congress nullifies it, or a federal court rules it unconstitutional. Not until 1907 did the government bother to retain and catalogue executive orders by publishing and assigning them consecutive numbers. By 1999 presidents had issued over 13,000 executive orders.

The vast majority of executive orders arise from the authority and responsibilities explicitly delegated to the president by law. Most frequently they are enlisted to establish executive branch agencies, modify bureaucratic rules or actions, change decision-making procedures, and give substance and force to statutes. For example, the Pendleton Act of 1883 inaugurated the civil service system for federal employees by converting about 10 percent of the federal workforce from political patronage to merit appointment based on examinations. This law also authorized the president to issue executive orders extending civil service to other classes of employees. Over the next half-century, presidents issued executive orders that shifted hundreds of thousands of employees into the civil service system.

A much smaller class of executive orders is based not on some explicit congressional delegation but on presidents' assertions of authority implicit in the **"take care" clause.** Not until the twentieth century did presidents begin seriously to entertain the notion that this general language might give them more authority than their predecessors had claimed. Theodore Roosevelt (1901–1909) was the first to subscribe to this expansive view of the office. "The most important factor in getting the right spirit in my administration," wrote Roosevelt, reflecting on his term, "was my insistence upon the theory that the execu-

Sampling of President Clinton's Use of Executive Orders, 1997–1999

March 1997   Required government agencies to issue guns only after safety locks had been incorporated and forbade foreigners to buy handguns if they had been in the United States less than ninety days.

Banned the use of federal funds in any attempt to clone humans.

June 1997   Created a permanent management advisory board for the Internal Revenue Service.

July 1997   Ordered that all documents twenty-five years or older containing national security information be reviewed for declassification by April 2000.

August 1997   Clarified and reinforced the right of religious expression in civil branch agencies.

Banned smoking in most executive branch buildings.

September 1997   Directed federal agencies to use existing programs to help communities refurbish waterfronts and improve water quality in selected rivers.

Created a commission to study managed health care.

February 1998   Applied the patient's "bill of rights" to all federal health programs.

Created a White House council to coordinate efforts to fix the Y2K (year 2000) problem.

March 1998   Established a national task force on Employment of Adults with Disabilities.

May 1998   Extended federal workforce affirmative action guidelines to cover sexual orientation.

June 1998   Directed federal agencies to avoid any action that would degrade the condition of coral reef ecosystems within U.S. waters.

July 1998   Directed all federally licensed gun dealers to post a youth safety notice stating that "misuse of hand guns is a leading contributor to juvenile violence."

August 1998   Created a new presidential council on food safety.

February 1999   Extended the life of the president's Information Technology Advisory Committee to continue advising the administration on technological developments and assist the president in carrying out the requirements of the 1998 Next Generation Internet Research Act.

March 1999   Incorporated the Arms Control and Disarmament Agency into the State Department.

April 1999   Called up reservists for active duty in the Kosovo conflict.

tive power was limited only by specific restrictions and prohibitions appearing in the Constitution or imposed by Congress in its constitutional powers."[9]

This doctrine bears some resemblance to the general authority extended to Congress by the "necessary and proper" clause (Article I, Section 8)—an "elastic" authority Congress invoked frequently during the twentieth century to broaden its sphere of action (see Chapter 6). The big difference, however, is that Congress's authority is explicitly stated ("Congress shall have Power . . ."), whereas the president's "take care" might strike some readers as merely a job description. In lawsuits challenging presidents' broad use of executive orders, federal courts have at times interpreted this authority as clearly justifying a president's action; at other times they have regarded presidential claims based on this clause as just smoke and mirrors.

The President as Legislator

The Constitution gives presidents only a modest role in the legislative arena. They may call Congress into special session (used little since the modern Congress is nearly always in session) and, most important, veto laws passed by Congress. Presidents also are called on to report "from time to time" to Congress on the state of the Union.

Yet modern presidents, acting on the expectations of the public, the media, and their parties, attempt to direct American policy by promoting a legislative agenda with Congress. In addition to their few constitutional tools, modern presidents rely heavily on their ability to mobilize public support and thereby gain the attention of the elected politicians who sit in the House and the Senate.

State of the Union Address. The State of the Union address, a minor constitutional responsibility found in Article II, Section 3, epitomizes the president's intended

During his 1999 State of the Union address, President Clinton saluted two black heroes, Rosa Parks from the civil rights era and Chicago Cubs slugger Sammy Sosa.

"clerkship." Until the early twentieth century, presidents routinely satisfied this obligation by conveying their messages to Congress by courier. There, the presidential communiqué was read inaudibly by an officer of Congress to an inattentive audience more interested in socializing after a long adjournment. Today, however, sophisticated broadcast communications have transformed the State of the Union address into a "prime-time" opportunity for presidents to mold public opinion and steer the legislative agenda on Capitol Hill. The influence presidents derive from this event depends in large part on the susceptibility of politicians in Washington to the political breezes presidents can stir up in the country.

With this in mind, today's presidents "stage" their presentations and punctuate them with props and the introduction of "American heroes," appealing as much to television viewers as to the lawmakers on hand. In 1999 Bill Clinton decorated his State of the Union address with appearances by Chicago Cub slugger Sammy Sosa and civil rights legend Rosa Parks. Meanwhile, the media tracked the number of standing ovations and breaks for applause

THE VETO GAME

The veto game begins with the president and Congress at odds over a change in government policy (the status quo). If the two sides can agree on a change, a new policy will be created. If they continue to disagree and the president vetoes Congress's preferred policy, there is no change and the status quo prevails. (It is assumed the congressional majority is too small to muster the two-thirds support needed for a veto override.) Within this context, three scenarios are possible:

Scenario 1: The president and Congress have sharply different policy preferences.

This scenario depicts the simplest situation—and the only one that might actually end in a veto. Congress passes legislation changing the status quo. The president prefers the status quo, refuses to compromise, and simply vetoes the new legislation Congress has passed.

Anticipating this outcome, Congress may not even bother to create the legislation. When President Ronald Reagan (1981–1989) announced early in his first term that he would welcome legislation weakening certain provisions of the Clean Air Act, environmentalists in Congress knew that any attempt to strengthen the law during his tenure was doomed to failure. For the next eight years, then, the House Commerce subcommittee dealing with the environment occasionally held hearings but did not take action. The president's tacit veto trumped any real efforts to strengthen policy.

Scenario 2: Congress favors a more drastic change in policy than does the president.

In Scenario 2 both Congress and the president want a change in the status quo, with Congress favoring a more drastic change than the president. If Congress passes a law incorporating its preferences, the president will veto the bill since the administration favors the status quo more than the change Congress advocates. Nevertheless, Congress does not have to capitulate and precisely meet presidential demands. It only has to alter the original legislation enough to make the proposed policy marginally more attractive to the president than the status quo. Since the president's policy preferences are better served by signing than vetoing, the bill will become law.

When President George Bush (1989–1993) announced he would welcome a modest strengthening of the Clean Air laws, he shifted the game from Scenario 1 to Scenario 2. By stipulating early the provisions the bill would have to contain to win his signature, including a ceiling of $20 billion in new federal obligations, he was trying to signal precisely where the compromise should be. The Democrats immediately went to work on new legislation, but they did not confine themselves to the changes the president had proposed. After all, they only had to provide him with a bill that he found marginally more attractive than current policy. In the end, the Democratic House and Senate passed a stronger bill than the president had wanted, and Bush reportedly spent almost the full ten days vacillating between a veto and a signature. Finally, Bush pronounced the legislation barely acceptable and signed into law the 1990 revision of the Clean Air Act. The president's temporizing and carping reflect how well congressional Democrats squeezed all they could from the president.

Scenario 3: The president favors a more drastic policy change than does Congress.

In Scenario 3 the president and Congress swap places. The president favors a more drastic policy change than does Congress. Congress wants to change public policy as well, but by far less than does the president. Thus Congress can confidently pass its preferred legislation and expect the president to sign it since the bill goes further in meeting the president's goal than does the status quo. In this situation the veto is worthless; Congress's preferences are enacted into policy.

In 1983 President Reagan sent Congress a budget calling for a 10 percent increase in defense spending. The Democratic-controlled House agreed to only a 4 percent increase. When asked about the lower figure at a news conference, the president hinted that he might have to veto such a bill. The Democrats, however, quickly turned the tables. On hearing of Reagan's comment, a Democratic leader retorted that the president had better be careful, for the next time the House might just lower the increase to 2 percent! President Reagan grudgingly signed the 4 percent increase. More often than not, presidents who find themselves in this position are liberals promoting new social programs. Perhaps this finding accounts for the comparatively infrequent use of the veto by Democratic presidents (see Figure 7–1).

These simple illustrations of veto policies reveal much about the role of the veto in presidential leadership. In the first instance, the veto allows the president to single-handedly preserve the status quo. In the second, it prescribes the kind of compromise that allows both sides to agree. In the third, the veto proves worthless in pushing Congress where it does not want to go.

and conducted immediate post-speech polls to gauge the president's persuasiveness with the American public.

The Veto. Perhaps the president's most formidable tool in dealing with Congress is the veto. The Framers, ever alert to opportunities to introduce "checks and balances," were already familiar with the concept of an executive veto; it was exercised by most state governors. Unlike the president's administrative powers in Article II, Section 2, the Constitution defines the veto authority quite precisely. (See section "Making Laws" in Chapter 6, where the veto process is described in detail.) The sequence of decisions described in the Constitution's veto provisions can at times elicit high-stakes strategizing both in the White House and on Capitol Hill as each side tries to calculate how the other side might respond. As explained in the box "The Veto Game," whether the veto offers the president great or little influence over public policy depends on how close the president's policy stance and that of Congress are to the status quo.

Over the past half-century, presidents have averaged fewer than ten vetoes a year. The record belongs to Republican president Gerald Ford. Though he served less than one full term (from August 1974 until January 1977), Ford vetoed sixty-six bills (Figure 7–1). In the 1976 election he campaigned on his veto record, claiming that only a Republican in the White House would stand between hard-earned taxpayer dollars and the "spendthrift" Democratic Congress. Only twelve of Ford's vetoes were overridden, even though the Democrats commanded large majorities in both the House and the Senate. Thus Ford won many of the battles, but he lost the war—the election.

The Framers frequently referred to the veto as a "negative"—an appropriate characterization of this inherently conservative instrument. The veto allows presidents to block Congress, but it does not allow them to substitute their own policy preferences. Moreover, unlike most negotiating settings where each side must agree to a joint outcome, Congress acts first. As the veto game reveals

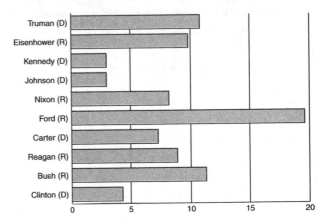

Figure 7–1 Average Number of Vetoes per Year of Legislation, Truman–Clinton Administrations

Source: Charles Cameron, *Veto Bargaining: Presidents and the Politics of Negative Power* (New York: Cambridge University Press, 1999), Table 2.3.

(see box), presidents' vetoes are reactive—take it or leave it—which limits their ability to shape policy.

The President as Head Diplomat and Commander in Chief

National security and foreign affairs were special concerns of delegates to the Constitutional Convention—concerns largely arising from the young nation's dismal experiences both at home and abroad under the Articles of Confederation. Ironically, it was a domestic uprising in 1786 by disgruntled Massachusetts farmers led by Daniel Shays that had exposed the Confederation's inability to provide national security. With the national government unable to act, public order was restored only after private funds were donated to finance a local militia.

Head Diplomat. The Confederation government, consisting of little more than a legislature, also found it difficult to transact foreign affairs. Even routine duties, such as responding to communications from foreign governments, proved to be an ordeal. To promote commerce, the states had tried to fill this vacuum, but European merchants and governments were able to pit one state against

POLITICS ⟶ POLICY

The Brief Life of the Line-Item Veto

Presidents who are confronted with omnibus legislation containing numerous unrelated parts must decide whether to sign or veto the entire bill. Frequently, thanks to logrolling, such legislation includes tax breaks or spending measures that benefit one or more narrow constituencies. In 1996 the Republican Congress, seeking to restrain these special-interest expenses, enacted the Line Item Veto Act. The act allowed the president, within five days of signing a bill into law, to reject spending provisions and tax breaks that affected less than a hundred persons or entities. Congress can repass these provisions with a simple majority vote, but the president can veto them as well, requiring Congress to override with a two-thirds vote.

In 1997, the first year the line-item veto was in effect, President Clinton used it to strike eighty-two items out of eleven bills. He claimed he saved the nation about $1 billion by eliminating narrow tax breaks, a special provision to help New York finance its Medicaid program, and local military construction projects. In June 1998 the Supreme Court, in a 6–3 decision, struck down the line-item veto as violating the Constitution's separation of powers doctrine. The Court reasoned that the Line Item Veto Act authorized the president to change a law passed by Congress into one whose text had not been voted on by either house of Congress or presented to the president. Thus the majority opinion ruled that the law was unconstitutional.

Source: Andrew Taylor, "Few in Congress Grieve as Justices Give Line-Item Veto the Ax," *CQ Weekly*, June 27, 1998.

another in a ruinous competition for markets and trade. A single executive would enjoy an inherent advantage over Congress in conducting foreign policy. With some misgivings, then, the Framers provided the president with broader authority to transact diplomatic affairs than they had found desirable on the domestic front.

From the outset, President George Washington interpreted the Constitution's provision "to receive Ambassadors and other public Ministers" to mean that he alone could decide whether the United States would recognize a new government and, accordingly, "receive" its ambassadors. The howls of protest in Congress that greeted this interpretation were echoed in that chamber a century and a half later when President Harry Truman recognized the state of Israel.

The most important constitutional limitation on the president's leadership in foreign affairs is the requirement that a two-thirds majority of the Senate ratify treaties. At times, the Senate has rebuffed a president's leadership by rejecting a treaty negotiated by the White House. Perhaps the most famous exercise of the Senate's ratification authority occurred at the close of World War I when it rejected the peace treaty that contained provisions for President Woodrow Wilson's brainchild, the League of Nations. Overall, however, this reservation of authority has proven less consequential than the Framers probably assumed.

To sidestep treaty rejections, presidents routinely negotiate **executive agreements** which are exempt from Senate ratification. Unlike a treaty, an executive agreement cannot supersede U.S. law, and it remains "in force" as long as the parties find their interests well served by it. In 1940 President Franklin Roosevelt employed such an agreement to circumvent a Senate (and a public) adamant about staying out of war in Europe. Under the agreement, the still-neutral United States supplied England with naval escorts to help British vessels fend off attacks from German submarines. Other historic executive agreements include the postwar Yalta (1944) and Potsdam (1945)

In April 1999 President Clinton speaks with the press about administration policy in the Balkans as his most senior military and foreign policy advisers stand by. Secretary of State Madeleine Albright is joined by Secretary of Defense William Cohen and the chairman of the Joint Chiefs of Staff, Gen. Henry Shelton. With his back to the camera is Samuel Berger who, as national security adviser, appears to be performing his assigned role as coordinator across the departments.

agreements among the Allies on the occupation of Germany and the future of Europe. Several decades later, various strategic arms-limitations agreements between the United States and the Soviet Union were negotiated as treaties but implemented as executive agreements when they failed to muster the necessary two-thirds endorsement in the Senate. In 1998, a slow year on the diplomatic front, the United States entered into agreements with Poland to assist in developing and modernizing that country's civil aviation structure; with China to establish a consultation mechanism to strengthen maritime safety; with Madagascar to consolidate, reduce, and reschedule certain debts owed to the United States and many others. Executive agreements, not treaties, are a mainstay of the nation's international relations.

Commander in Chief. The Constitution declares the president to be **commander in chief** of the nation's armed forces. This notion was a very difficult one for the Framers, and it remains so today. One Convention delegate, troubled by this grant of power, proposed limiting the military to no more than five thousand members, provoking Gen. George Washington to quip sarcastically that the Constitution also should limit invading armies to three thousand troops.[10] His point made, the Framers settled on a different kind of check to the president's powers as commander in chief: only Congress can declare war.

Yet the broad license this authority grants the president cannot be denied. President Abraham Lincoln suspended the writ of *habeas corpus* within six months of the Confederate firing on Fort Sumter in 1861, thereby allowing the Union Army to detain civilians suspected of spying or even just publicly opposing the war effort. He did not consult Congress before acting. Lincoln also approved a naval blockade of southern ports, extended voluntary military enlistment to three years, increased the size of the army and navy, and authorized the purchase of materials, all without congressional approval or even appropriation. Later, Lincoln justified his actions to Congress by

Figure 7–2 U.S. Post–Cold War Military Engagements

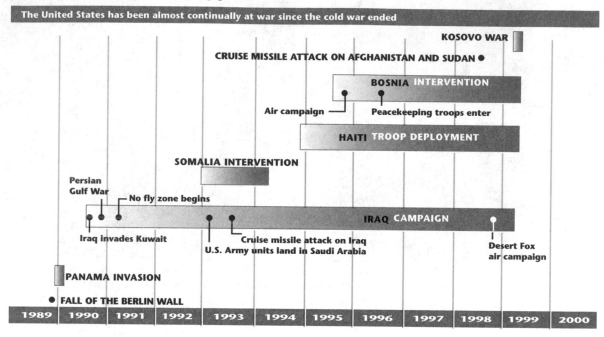

The United States has been almost continually at war since the cold war ended

KOSOVO WAR

CRUISE MISSILE ATTACK ON AFGHANISTAN AND SUDAN ●

BOSNIA INTERVENTION

Air campaign ─── Peacekeeping troops enter

HAITI TROOP DEPLOYMENT

SOMALIA INTERVENTION

Persian Gulf War

No fly zone begins

IRAQ CAMPAIGN

Iraq invades Kuwait

Cruise missile attack on Iraq
U.S. Army units land in Saudi Arabia

Desert Fox air campaign

PANAMA INVASION

● FALL OF THE BERLIN WALL

| 1989 | 1990 | 1991 | 1992 | 1993 | 1994 | 1995 | 1996 | 1997 | 1998 | 1999 | 2000 |

Source: Adapted by permission of Dow Jones, Inc. via Copyright Clearance Center, Inc. (1999) Dow Jones and Company, Inc. All Rights Reserved Worldwide.

relying exclusively on his authority as commander in chief: "The executive found the duty of employing the war power, in defense of the government, forced upon him." "Whether strictly legal or not," he added, these measures "were ventured upon . . . trusting, then as now, that Congress would readily ratify them."[11]

The idea that presidents have the military at their disposal—at least in the short run—remains unchallenged. And Congress's authority to declare war is, in most respects, a hollow check. Neither the Korean War (1950–1953) nor the Vietnam War, which began over a decade later, was ever declared. In 1973 Congress sought to carve out new authority for itself by enacting the War Powers Act over President Richard Nixon's veto. The act requires the president to inform Congress within forty-eight hours of committing troops abroad in a military action. Moreover, the military action must end within sixty days unless Congress approves an extension. But neither the

law's constitutionality nor its effectiveness in limiting the president's military authority has ever been tested. Presidents have continued to take military action without informing Congress—witness Reagan's 1983 invasion of Grenada, Clinton's deployment of U.S. troops to Somalia in 1993 as part of a United Nations peacekeeping force, and the participation of American forces in the North Atlantic Treaty Organization's 1999 action against Yugoslavia. In fact, since 1989 the United States has been almost continually at (undeclared) war somewhere in the world (Figure 7–2). While members of Congress may question presidents' policies, Congress as an institution has not challenged their authority to order an extended military engagement without a declaration of war.[12] After all, does it really want to unwittingly strengthen the resolve of the nation's enemies, further endangering troops in combat?

Although the administrative, military, diplomatic, and

legislative authority conferred on the president by the Constitution sounds impressive, the sum of the separate mandates does not equal the modern presidency. Overall, the Framers envisioned a diminutive executive—one that is a far cry from the modern office. Today's presidents occupy center stage in Washington, even when their own party does not control Congress. Yet the presidency, in the early years and now, possesses the same basic constitutional mandate. So what has changed? A brief look at the nineteenth-century presidency, as an extension of the constitutional model, will reveal the extent of the office's transformation during the twentieth century.

The Nineteenth-Century Presidency

During the Republic's first century, presidents typically assumed a small role in keeping with the Framers' modest expectations. In fact, in fulfilling their constitutional responsibilities, they had a greater effect on the welfare of their political party than on the nation or public policy.

LOGIC OF POLITICS

Lincoln and His Cabinet

Upon taking office in 1861, Republican president Abraham Lincoln confronted a nation threatening to dissolve. He also had to contend with a weak, young Republican Party composed of politicians who only recently had coalesced for the sole purpose of defeating the majority Democratic Party. To keep the party coalition together, Lincoln filled his cabinet with Republican leaders, even some of his rivals for the presidency.[1] Secretary of the Treasury Salmon Chase and Secretary of State William Seward, Lincoln's principal rivals for the presidential nomination, strongly disliked each other, but their support within the party and Congress kept both in Lincoln's cabinet.

Other cabinet officials of lesser stature but with impeccable political credentials were Pennsylvania's corrupt party boss and senator Simon Cameron who was forced to resign the post of secretary of war, and Maryland Republican Party leader Montgomery Blair who oversaw the patronage-rich Post Office Department. Blair's presence in the cabinet proved critical as he muscled the Maryland state legislature to defeat narrowly a motion calling for Maryland to secede from the Union.

Perhaps the most formidable cabinet member of all was the brusque Edwin Stanton, Cameron's replacement as secretary of war and a leader of the "war Republicans" in Congress. At times this gave him a veto over policy. "Stanton and I have an understanding," Lincoln wrote a friend, "if I send an order to him which cannot be consistently granted, he is to refuse it. This he sometimes does."[2] Thus by surrendering control over large blocks of the executive branch to these self-interested, strong-willed politicians, President Lincoln succeeded in keeping the fragile Republican majority in Congress behind the unpopular Civil War.

1. David Herbert Donald, "Lincoln, The Politician" in *Lincoln Reconsidered: Essays on the Civil War Era* (New York: Random House, 1956).

2. David Herbert Donald, *Lincoln* (London: Jonathan Cape, 1995), 334.

Because the occupants of the White House did not play a leadership role in formulating domestic policy, their accomplishments were mostly limited to their responses to wars, rebellions, and other national crises.

On a day-to-day basis, filling vacancies in a growing federal bureaucracy was a burdensome, time-consuming presidential task. Throughout the nineteenth century, all federal employees—from the secretary of state to the postmaster in Cody, Wyoming—were appointed directly by the president or one of his agents. Large chunks of presidents' daily calendars were devoted to interviewing job seekers, listening to their party sponsors, and signing appointment letters. And because party colleagues in Congress and national party committees expected their nominees to be appointed, presidents were able to derive little political advantage from the appointment authority. Rather, it was a thankless task, befitting a clerk. "For every appointment," President Grover Cleveland observed ruefully, "I make one ingrate and ten enemies." Presidents took special care, however, in appointing their cabinets. After all, these department heads represented important factions and interests of the president's party that had to be served if he hoped to win renomination and election and enjoy his party's full support in Congress.

The Era of Cabinet Government

Nineteenth-century presidents routed all matters related to administration and policy through the appropriate department secretary. When a president had a question about a policy, needed clarification on complaints or rumors about an agency head's performance, or was seeking advice on whether to sign or veto a bill he consulted his cabinet. Indeed, the nineteenth-century department heads who made up the cabinet routinely performed much of the work now carried out by the president's staff.

A strong cabinet, however, did not make for a strong president. Cabinet appointees, who were resourceful, in-

dependent, and frequently ambitious politicians, could not be expected to subordinate their own welfare to that of the president. An adviser to President Warren G. Harding (1921–1923) may have only slightly exaggerated a basic truth in remarking, "The members of the cabinet are the president's natural enemies."[13] Thus a pattern of intersecting interests characterized president–cabinet relations: presidents selected their department heads for their political assets such as their strength with a particular wing of a political party in Congress or with the electorate. Those who joined the cabinet, however, were likely to pursue their own political and policy objectives and, perhaps incidentally, the administration's. The result was a partnership based not on loyalty but on reciprocity: cabinet members helped the president achieve his political goals, and, through the cabinet appointment, he afforded them opportunities to pursue theirs.

The modern cabinet has lost much of its luster as an attractive political office. Control over policy and even department personnel has gravitated to the White House. Consequently, where ambitious politicians in the nineteenth century saw cabinet service as a steppingstone to the White House, modern politicians are more likely to view cabinet service as a suitable conclusion to a career in public service.

Parties and Elections

Nineteenth-century politicians generally attached as much importance to the political party that controlled the president's appointment pen for patronage jobs as to the particular individual who occupied the Oval Office. Presidential elections were the focal point for the national parties' efforts; after all, whichever party won the presidency won the federal patronage. Moreover, in this era before election reforms allowed voters privacy and the opportunity to cast their vote easily for candidates from different parties, the party that won the presidential contest locally almost invariably won control of other national, state,

REGULAR REPUBLICAN TICKET,

Except for Register of Deeds.

FOR PRESIDENTIAL ELECTORS.

AT LARGE.

THOMAS TALBOT, of Billerica. STEPHEN SALISBURY, of Worcester.

BY DISTRICTS.

1. WARREN LADD, . . . of New Bedford.		6. GEORGE W. MORRILL, . of Amesbury.
2. THEODORE DEAN, . . . of Taunton.		7. CARROLL D. WRIGHT, . of Reading.
3. JOHN FELT OSGOOD, . . of Boston.		8. JAMES RUSSELL LOWELL, of Cambridge.
4. MARTIN BRIMMER, . . . of Boston.		9. JOHN C. WHITIN, . of Northbridge.
5. SAMUEL C. LAWRENCE, . of Medford.		10. W. B. C. PEARSONS, . of Holyoke.
	11. RICHARD GOODMAN, . . of Lenox.

FOR GOVERNOR,

ALEXANDER H. RICE,

OF BOSTON.

FOR LIEUTENANT GOVERNOR,

HORATIO G. KNIGHT, . . of Easthampton.

For Secretary of the Commonwealth,   For Treasurer and Receiver General,

HENRY B. PEIRCE, of Abington. | CHARLES ENDICOTT, of Canton.

For Auditor,   For Attorney General,

JULIUS L. CLARKE, of Newton. | CHARLES R. TRAIN, of Boston.

For Representative to Congress,

WILLIAM CLAFLIN, - - - of Newton

For Councillor,

HARRISON TWEED, ... of Taunton

For Register of Deeds,

JOHN H. BURDAKIN, . . . of Dedham

For County Treasurer,

C. C. CHURCHILL, ... of Dedham

For Clerk of Courts,

ERASTUS WORTHINGTON, . . of Dedham

For County Commissioner,

GALEN ORR, ... of Needham

For Commissioner of Insolvency,—to fill vacancy,

GEORGE W. WIGGIN, . . . of Franklin

For Senator,

JOSEPH E. FISKE, ... of Needham

For Representative to the General Court,

EDWARD I. THOMAS.

Until the 1890s, Americans voted with paper ballots supplied by party workers or printed in newspaper advertisements. The voter simply took the ballot to the voting desk and publicly submitted it. On this 1876 ballot for the Republican ticket of Rutherford B. Hayes and his vice-presidential running mate, William Wheeler, the voter voted for all Republicans from president down to the lowly register of deeds. Because this method of voting made ticket splitting so difficult, the success of candidates for state and local offices was tied to the fortunes of their party's presidential candidate.

Table 7–1 Newspaper Coverage of Congress and the President, 1824–1876

Election Year	Percentage of Political News Devoted to	
	President	Congress
1824	43	57
1830 (midterm)	40	60
1840	98	2
1850 (midterm)	16	84
1860	76	24
1870 (midterm)	19	81
1876	70	30

Source: Samuel Kernell and Gary C. Jacobson, "Congress and the Presidency as News in the Nineteenth Century," *Journal of Politics* 49 (November 1987), 1016–1035.

Note: Percentages based on total column inches devoted to Congress (including members and committees) and the president (including cabinet and presidential candidates) by daily newspapers in Cleveland, Ohio, 1824–1876.

and local offices on the ticket. As a result, the political party that won the presidency almost always took control of Congress as well.

Presidential candidates were the engines that pulled the party train. A look at the coverage of the president and Congress by daily newspapers in Cleveland, Ohio, from 1824 to 1876 reveals just how specialized the president's role was during the nineteenth century (Table 7–1). In total coverage (measured in column inches) presidents (or presidential candidates) moved to center stage in presidential election years and receded into the background during midterm election years when they were not on the ballot. In 1840, 98 percent of all stories covered the president and only 2 percent dealt with Congress. Ten years later, in a midterm election year, nearly the opposite was true. Unlike today when presidents dominate the television network evening news, in the nineteenth century they received little news coverage. Congress, not the government's chief clerk, held the spotlight.

At the national party nominating conventions, presidential candidates usually were valued a great deal more for their widespread popular appeal and willingness to distribute patronage according to party guidelines than for their policy pronouncements.[14] As a result, candidates with little experience in government frequently enjoyed an advantage over established politicians who might be associated with a particular faction of the party or who, as an officeholder, had taken a controversial position on divisive national issues. National military heroes—Andrew Jackson, Zachary Taylor, and Ulysses S. Grant, and a number of generals who were nominated but lost—made fine presidential candidates. But for most of those who won, leadership ended on election day and glorified clerkship began.

What, then, does the nineteenth-century presidency say about the modern presidency? It is a reminder that the Constitution does not thrust leadership on the president, but it also hints at the potential for the future presidency to assume a much larger role. The presidents of this era may have adhered to the Framers' expectations of a diminutive office, but they also found that this singular office enjoys a competitive advantage over other national politicians in attracting the public's attention. The specialized role that nineteenth-century presidents played as the focal point for national campaigns harbingered the institution's development as a source of national political leadership in the twentieth century. As we shall see in the next section, when the national government's role as supplier of public policy expanded (both in absolute terms and in comparison with that of the states), presidents assumed important administrative responsibilities. This new policy role combined with national visibility to transform them into formidable political figures who rarely relinquish center stage in the nation's political affairs.

Emergence of the Modern Presidency

By any measure the national government has grown enormously during the twentieth century. Hundreds of government functions once left exclusively to the states and local communities are now administered in Washing-ton. Other activities that once resided beyond the scope of any government are the routine concerns of some federal agency. Rules and crop subsidies administered by the U.S. Department of Agriculture (USDA) enter into farmers' decisions about how much of which crops to plant; the Occupational Safety and Health Administration regulates the working conditions of farm hands (everything from the availability of toilets to exposure to unsafe chemicals); the Securities and Exchange Commission regulates the farm commodities markets which establish the price farmers will be paid for their crops; and a USDA agency inspects food processing and distribution facilities. (Chapter 8, The Bureaucracy, surveys in more detail the growth of the federal government during the twentieth century.) Also in this era of rapid growth, civil service rules replaced patronage. And what were the implications of this growth for the presidency? Virtually all of the legislation that created these programs contained language mandating new tasks for the president.

Growth of Administrative Responsibility

Given the conspicuous absence in the Constitution of any real administrative authority for the president, it was by no means obvious that the growth of the national government would enhance the president's control over public policy. Congress could have kept the president at bay, as it often did in the nineteenth century, by insisting that executive agencies report directly to congressional oversight committees. But as the obligations of government mounted, oversight began to tax Congress's time and resources and interfere with its ability to deliberate new policy. So, instead of excluding the president from administration, Congress found its interests best served by delegating to the White House a sizable share of administration and the policy discretion that went with it. Actually, Congress had no choice; it must delegate decisions to presidents if programmatic objectives are to be achieved. And therein lies real opportunities for presidents to influence public policy.

Delegation. "Let anyone make the laws of the country, if I can construe them," President William Howard Taft (1909–1913) once remarked.[15] By delegating to the president and the appointed executive branch the discretion to decide how best to implement and adjust policy in order to achieve its objectives, Congress shares its lawmaking powers with the president. Delegation has grown commensurately with government. As early as 1950, a survey found that over 1,100 public laws delegated discretionary authority to the president.[16] If such a survey were undertaken today, the number would, of course, be far larger.

In writing public laws and fine tuning them through the legislative language that accompanies annual appropriations, Congress can choose to delegate a little or a lot. If it opts for a little, the result might be rigid policies that fail to respond to changing conditions or the effects of policies. If, however, Congress delegates too much discretion to the executive, it may surrender control over important implementation decisions that could alter the intent of the legislation. In 1980 Congress erred in that direction when it passed the Paperwork Reduction Act, designed, as its name implies, to reduce the forms ("red tape") clogging the federal bureaucracy and irritating citizens. Soon after entering office, President Ronald Reagan, acting on his delegated power to implement the act, enlisted it to block congressionally mandated regulations he did not like.

At times, Congress delegates less from programmatic necessity than to gain political advantage. When legislators agree on the goals of a bill but disagree on its specifics, they may deliberately swathe its intent in vague language—thereby delegating broad authority to the executive branch—to secure majority support. At other times, members of Congress may find political advantage in delegating to the president broad responsibility for policies that might have politically unattractive outcomes. In such instances, legislators "pass the buck" and hope to avoid blame. In the 1970s, for example, the principle that endangered species should be protected aroused far less controversy than any particular plan to achieve it. To

Contemplating the shock that his successor, Gen. Dwight Eisenhower, would experience in the Oval Office, President Harry Truman remarked, "He'll sit here and he'll say, 'Do this! Do that!' And nothing will happen. Poor Ike—it won't be a bit like the Army. He'll find it very frustrating."

avoid negative repercussions, Congress delegated to the U.S. Fish and Wildlife Service the discretion to establish criteria for classifying species as "endangered" and "threatened." When the agency listed the northern spotted owl as an endangered species and limited the logging industry's access to Oregon's old-growth forest, the industry vented its anger at the agency and President Bush—not Congress. Not only did members of Congress escape retribution, but they also won some credit for subsequently softening the economic blow by passing a law that permitted the industry to harvest fallen trees.

Budgeting. When they formulate and send to Congress the annual budget for all federal programs, presidents are carrying out one of their most important "clerical" tasks. Yet it also offers them an opportunity to set the spending priorities of the federal government. In fact, this authority exists because Congress long ago insisted that presidents assume responsibility for the government's bookkeeping.

OMB director Franklin Raines presents the president's 1999 budget proposals to the House Budget Committee. This presentation kicks off the budgetary process in Congress, which ends in October with passage of the next year's appropriations and tax legislation.

Until the 1920s, agencies sent their budget requests directly to the House Appropriations Committee, which held hearings, determined appropriations, and passed them on to the chamber for a vote and then over to the Senate for its consideration. During this process, no one formally solicited the president's views. But when the flow of department and agency budgets began to congest the legislative process, Congress passed in 1921 the Budget and Accounting Act which gave the president responsibility for compiling budgets from the executive departments and submitting them to Congress as a single package. Here, then, Congress found itself strengthening the president's role in national policy making.[17]

The president's annual budget, submitted to Congress on the first Monday in February, represents months of assembling and negotiating requests from the agencies to bring them into conformity with the president's policy goals and proposed spending ceiling. Some years, the president's budget has sailed through Congress with minimal changes. Other years, congressional leaders have quickly pronounced the president's budget "DOA" (Dead

on Arrival), written a wholly "congressional" budget, and dared the president to veto it. As we saw at the outset of this chapter, presidential and congressional budgets can differ so much that compromise becomes a test of political will.

The president's budget provides Congress with valuable technical and political information. Running into hundreds of pages, it supplies congressional committees with economic forecasts, projected tax revenues, baseline spending estimates for each department broken down by program, and other essential information for formulating spending and taxation legislation. Politically, the budget represents the president's "opening bid" in negotiations over how much the government should spend on particular programs and where the revenue will come from. From the early 1980s until the late 1990s, annual deficits forced politicians in both branches to concentrate on spending cuts or tax increases, either of which were bound to displease the beneficiaries of retrenched programs or taxpayers. When the president made the first move in his budget, Congress could shed some of the political costs associated with cutting back on popular programs. In 1997, however, President Clinton turned the tables on Congress. He sent a budget to Capitol Hill that targeted savings on Medicare, but shied away from identifying cuts to achieve the savings. The Republican-controlled budget committees first denounced and later pleaded with administration officials to pinpoint where they would like the cuts to be made. The president had effectively passed the buck; Congress, facing the next deadline on the budget calendar, was forced to increase premiums and reduce benefits to bring the program's budget into conformity with the blueprint for balancing the budget.

Presidential Assertions of Authority. Through delegation, Congress has "pushed" work—and, with it, significant discretionary authority—toward the presidency. Presidents have sought to pull authority into the White House as well. Sometimes their efforts take the form of unilateral assertions of authority, but these moves meet with only mixed success since they are based merely on claims that Congress and the courts might reject. The rest of this section describes how three presidents, decades apart, tried to extend their authority by centralizing administration. In each case, the president sought to reroute the flow of information within the executive branch or between it and Congress.

The first case arose, appropriately, during the administration of President Theodore Roosevelt, the first president to dedicate himself to refashioning the executive branch and exerting control over administration. In 1902 Roosevelt issued an executive order prohibiting all federal employees from communicating with Congress "either directly or indirectly, individually or through associations, to solicit an increase of pay or to influence or to attempt to influence in their own interest any other legislation." His handpicked successor, William Howard Taft, extended the so-called **gag rule** to cover "congressional action of any kind" and barred employees from responding to congressional requests for information except as authorized by their department heads.[18]

Congress rapidly rejected these presidential efforts to centralize power by passing sweeping legislation that prohibited anyone from interfering in communication between federal employees and Congress. Given its vested interest in learning about problems within the bureaucracy that agency heads might try to conceal, Congress does, from time to time, reinforce the free flow of information from the bureaucracy, most recently in the Whistleblower Protection Act (1989) which protects employees who report waste and corruption to Congress.

The second case of presidential assertion occurred in 1939 when Franklin Roosevelt approached the same goal but somewhat differently and with greater success. Citing his statutory responsibility to prepare the annual budget, the president, through an executive order, required that all department communications to Congress possibly affecting future budgets first be cleared as consistent with

the president's policy by the Bureau of the Budget (today's Office of Management and Budget, or OMB). Unlike the gag rule, Roosevelt's order has endured, and today **central clearance** is a standard procedure for bureaucrats heading to Capitol Hill to give testimony.[19] This innovation has strengthened the president's hand in national policy, but not because it prevents agencies from communicating their policy differences with the president to Congress. (In fact, Congress can easily probe agency representatives when they testify at congressional hearings.) Rather, it prevents these officials from casually expropriating the president's endorsement for their legislative initiatives. Central clearance also alerts the White House early to attempted end runs in which an agency might seek more money and statutory authority than the president favors.[20]

In the third and more recent case, the president enlisted the mechanisms of central clearance for quite a different purpose. Elected in 1980 on a promise "to get the government off the backs of business," President Reagan, upon entering office, issued an executive order instructing all federal agencies to submit any new regulations or rules to OMB for a cost-benefit analysis. The reduced heft of the *Federal Register*, which lists proposed regulations, offers evidence of his success at curbing new rules; between 1980 and 1987 it shrank from 87,000 pages a year to fewer than 50,000.[21] Angered by this mechanism to block enforcement of various laws, the Democratic-controlled House voted to cut off funding for the OMB agency that administered regulatory reviews. The Senate entertained legislation to reorganize this presidential agency and subject the officer who administered oversight to Senate confirmation. After negotiations, Congress and the White House informally agreed that OMB would relax its clearance rules and Congress would withhold legislative action.

In these three cases, the further the presidents reached, the stronger the resistance from those whose own prerogatives were invaded by the innovation. The gag rule lasted less than a decade, and although both forms of central clearance introduced by Roosevelt and Reagan have become accepted procedure, they are exercised within negotiated bounds and are subject to numerous legislated exceptions. Congress has signaled clearly that a president who seeks to extract too much control from these practices is likely to lose them.

Emergence of the Institutional Presidency

Delegation creates opportunities for presidential leadership, but it also means more work. As the government has grown, and with it the president's duties, the presidency has evolved from a single individual assisted by a small retinue of aides to a fully developed institution. Thomas Jefferson's staff numbered fewer than a dozen, two or three of whom were clerks who spent most of their time copying letters, receiving visitors, and running errands.[22] When Franklin Roosevelt entered the White House more than 130 years later, the president's staff had grown to about fifty, but it remained loosely structured and tightly centered on the needs of the president. Despite the heavier workload, the presidency as an institution had changed very little.

In 1937 the President's Committee on Administrative Management, also known as the Brownlow Committee, concluded in its detailed analysis of the state of the presidency that "the president needs help." Likening the president to the chief executive officer of a large corporation, Louis Brownlow, one of a new breed of progressive public administration reformers, called for the creation of an organization dedicated to helping the occupant of the Oval Office. The president was like the CEO of a major corporation, Brownlow claimed, and required the same kinds of authority, expertise, and information afforded modern executives in the business world.

The recommendations in the Brownlow report ignored the plain fact that the Constitution withholds the kind of authority the presidency would need to command the federal bureaucracy as if it were a business. The president's fundamental constitutional predicament was not lost on Congress, however. When a delighted President Roosevelt forwarded Brownlow's recommendations to Capitol Hill for enactment, he was rebuffed. Congress, still angry over FDR's ill-fated attempt to pack the Supreme Court (described in Chapter 9), refused to act on the report. Not until some two years later did it agree to most of the Brownlow proposals.

Thus the institutional presidency was born and christened the Executive Office of the President (EOP). At first, it housed five "new" presidential agencies, two of which were and remain significant assets: the Bureau of the Budget, which Roosevelt moved from the Treasury Department by executive order, and the White House Office, the president's personal staff system.[23] The White House Office was vital to FDR, who frequently bemoaned his inability to elicit advice from and give orders to the departments except through the cabinet secretaries. In frustration, he sometimes compared himself to "a power plant with no transmission lines." His enlarged staff would help him transact daily business with the cabinet departments. The Brownlow report called for six loyal "Assistants to the President," who would perform their duties with "a passion for anonymity." But what began as six now exceeds five hundred, none of whom appears to crave anonymity.

Executive Office of the President. Over the years the Executive Office of the President has served as a suitable home for those agencies the president or Congress would like to keep in the shadow of the White House. Typically the ten agencies that, together with the White House Office, make up EOP work far more closely with the president and the White House staff than they do with each other (see Figure 7–3). In performing classic staff functions, these agencies gather information either from the executive branch (OMB and National Security Council) or from the broader policy environment (Council of Economic Advisers and Council on Environmental Quality) and help to maintain the organization itself (Office of the

Figure 7–3 The Institutional Presidency, 1997

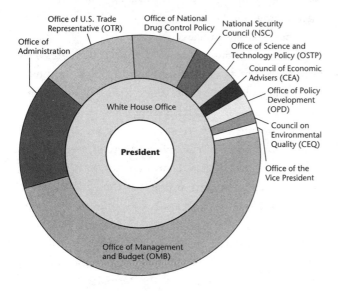

Source: Annual Budget of the President, 1997.
  Note: The White House Office and other Executive Office of the President offices are scaled to size.

Vice President and the Office of Administration). With no programs to administer, these agencies do not require the services of a field staff outside of Washington.

The most important of the presidential agencies is the Office of Management and Budget. Staffed by accountants, economists, and tax lawyers, OMB creates the annual federal budget, monitors agency performance, compiles recommendations from the departments on **enrolled bills** (bills that have been passed in identical form by both houses of Congress), and administers central clearance.

Another important agency within EOP is the National Security Council (NSC). Its statutory responsibility appears modest: to compile reports and advice from the State and Defense Departments and the Joint Chiefs of Staff and to keep the president well informed on international affairs. Yet the national security adviser, who heads this presidential agency, has at times assumed a role conducting foreign policy close to that traditionally associat-

ed with the secretary of state. The president's OMB director and national security adviser spend as much time working with the president as any cabinet heads or other staff advisers.

White House Office. While the EOP has, despite its growth, retained its original form as a collection of separate, independently staffed agencies near the president, the White House Office (WHO) has grown in both numbers and complexity (Figure 7–4). What began as a small, informal group of aides has evolved into a large, compartmentalized, multilayered bureaucracy. Richard Nixon (1969–1974) assembled the largest staff at almost 650 (Figure 7–4). It probably would have continued to grow had the Watergate scandal that drove Nixon from office not sent some Nixon aides to federal prison and turned the size of the White House into a campaign issue. Moreover, Congresses since then, most controlled by opposition parties, have reined in staff growth through budgets and legislative language limiting the president's ability to borrow staff from other agencies. The present-day White House staff has leveled off at about 400.

In its early years the organization of the White House varied according to the working styles of the presidents.

Figure 7–4 White House Office Staff, Coolidge to Clinton

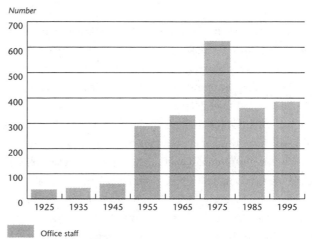

Source: Lyn Ragsdale, *Vital Statistics on the Presidency, Washington to Clinton*, rev. ed. (Washington, D.C.: Congressional Quarterly, 1998), Table 6–1.

President Dwight Eisenhower's passion for golf, when combined with his limited number of legislative initiatives, left him exposed to criticism that he installed Sherman Adams as his chief of staff so that he could devote himself to his favorite game.

In the last two decades, however, the staff organization has jelled into a small bureaucracy whose organization transcends administrations and whose offices are occupied by policy and political specialists. Presidents Franklin Roosevelt and Harry Truman favored a collegial management style in which they personally supervised their staffs. Roosevelt resisted the notion of fixed staff assignments; instead, he fostered competition by giving aides duplicate tasks or projects. Aware that the president might already have been briefed on a subject, or soon would be, FDR's aides undertook their assignments with the special diligence, not to be outdone. Truman preferred more cooperative relations among his staff. He conducted a meeting each morning with ten to twelve of his "senior" staff to receive reports and give out assignments. Later presidents tried to emulate FDR's and HST's collegial management styles but typically with less success.

Perhaps reflecting his military background, President Dwight Eisenhower introduced a more orderly and hierarchical organization to the White House. His assistants had fixed routines, job titles, and middle-level supervisors. On top, running the day-to-day activities of this still small (about two hundred) and only partially formed bureaucracy, was a chief of staff. Democratic critics derided this new approach to staffing as one that would do the president's work for him. Ike's successors, John Kennedy and Lyndon Johnson, reverted to the informal, president-run staff structure. But, Richard Nixon, who had served eight years as Eisenhower's vice president in close proximity to Eisenhower's staff, reinstated the formal chief of staff model. For years, then, these alternative styles, or models, of staff organization were enlisted according to the president's party affiliation.

When Democrat Jimmy Carter (1977–1981) assumed office, the pattern continued but only for a while. Carter, perhaps uncharacteristically for a former submarine commander, returned to the Democratic collegial, president-administered staff organization. But he immediately ran into problems. After coming under heavy criticism, even from Democrats, for being disorganized and failing to formulate a consistent legislative program, Carter sacked five of his cabinet secretaries who did not get along with the staff and reorganized the White House with clear lines of authority flowing from a strong chief of staff.

Carter's successors have not looked back. The chief of staff has become a fixture in the White House. More generally, specialists performing specific routine tasks have replaced yesterday's generalists who depended on their president for assignments. Reflecting the more sophisticated division of labor, office and job titles have become attached to names, and organization charts have become standard issue so that staff members can identify where

Figure 7–5   Clinton White House Staff Organization

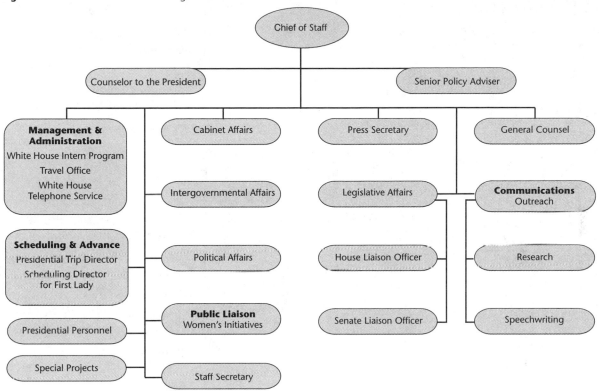

they belong within the organization (see Figure 7–5).

With its clear organizational lines, fixed assignments, and a loyal and enthusiastic staff, the White House staff system should run like a well-tuned engine. The facts, however, belie the expectations. Every recent president has experienced serious staffing problems that have erupted into public controversy, if not scandal. Many aides are motivated as much by interest in advancing a particular cause or policy agenda as by a desire to serve the president. This tendency is reinforced from outside as key constituencies press for one of their own to be on the staff. "Everyone in the White House has a constituency," complained senior Reagan aide Michael Deaver.[24] In 1978 a Carter aide who sided with his Jewish constituency's op-

position to the sale of airplanes to Saudi Arabia called a press conference and resigned in protest.[25] More often, staff will discreetly "leak" information supporting their preferences to the press. (The strategy of leaks is taken up more fully in Chapter 14, The News Media.)

Most of the president's staff arrives at the White House fresh from the presidential campaign. They not only typically come to Washington lacking the experience that will serve them best in their new positions, but they also come from a setting—the campaign—that actually rewards behavior that may be counterproductive once the candidate becomes president. Rather than seek compromise on a controversial policy with members of Congress, campaign aides in the White House might wrongly

the president's position when they prefer some other, and deflect those who want something from the president. With these difficult, unpleasant duties in mind, Nixon chief H. R. Haldeman called his position the "Official Son of a Bitch." Because chiefs of staff make enemies who ultimately seek revenge, most leave Washington with their reputations in tatters. Musing in his memoirs about how reporters ferreted out scandal in the unauthorized sale of arms to Iran, Donald Regan, President Reagan's second-term chief of staff, rankled at the job's vulnerabilities: "Because of my position, and because in a sense I was the only game in town, I was sought after by these excited men and women. The President was inaccessible on his mountaintop."[26]

Through delegation and the successful assertion of authority, modern presidents are thoroughly enmeshed in administration of the government's vast bureaucracy. Aided by an elaborate presidential staffing system, they have after two centuries become the chief executive the Constitution advertised. Yet, they still do not sit at the controls and pull the levers of government. The fundamental dilemma facing presidents remains: they have too little authority to satisfy expectations for their performance. Their success depends on their skill as politicians—that is, their ability to enlist their limited authority to persuade others in Washington to accommodate their preferences.

Modern Presidential Selection

Presidents are products of the system that selects them. Thus the waves of reform that have swept over the presidential nominating process since the 1970s go a long way toward explaining recent trends in presidential lead-

advise the president to stand firm on constituency commitments and appeal for public support, even when reasonable accommodations are available.

Staff members also commonly view their positions at the White House as way stations to lucrative careers. Consequently, they may have a greater stake in the outcomes of decisions and making their mark on policy than in respecting the integrity of the organization's procedures designed to inform presidents and advance their preferences. As staff members compete with others inside and outside the White House for influence, the tenets of orderly organization begin to crumble. Often, by the end of a four-year term, the staff has been largely reconstituted.

Probably no one in Washington suffers from a greater imbalance between power and legitimacy than the president's chief of staff. The chief of staff has to make other staff do things they prefer not to do, such as conform to

THE ELECTORAL COLLEGE
Where the Big States Hold the Cards

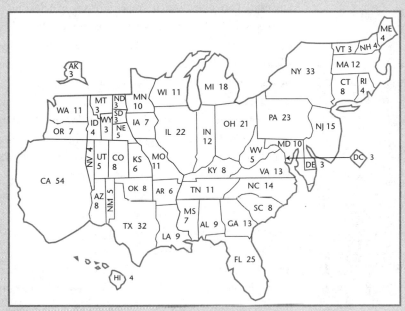

The States in Proportion to Their Electoral Votes

The Constitution's formula for allocating electoral votes to each state is simple: number of senators + number of representatives = number of votes in electoral college. This formula heavily favors the populous states, which not only have a lot of electoral votes, but, following a rule adopted by all states except Nebraska and Maine, award all their state's electoral votes to the candidate receiving the most votes. This winner-take-all rule means that California with its fifty-four electoral votes, New York with thirty-three, Texas with thirty-two, and Florida with twenty-five largely decide the winner. Based on the 1990 Census, the ten most populous states in the nation control 257 out of the 270 electoral votes needed to elect a president.[1] By contrast, the thirteen least populous states have only forty-six electoral votes—fewer than those held by the largest state, California.

White House hopefuls plan their campaign stops accordingly, heavily crisscrossing the vote-rich states, often at the expense of the vote-poor ones. Whether conservative or liberal, presidential candidates can ill-afford to avoid addressing the problems of these large, highly urban states.

An ongoing criticism of the electoral college system is that a candidate can win a plurality of the popular vote nationally but still not be elected because of failure to gain a majority in the electoral college. This happened to presidential candidates Andrew Jackson in 1824, Samuel J. Tilden in 1876, and Grover Cleveland in 1888. Jackson and Cleveland succeeded, however, in their next runs for the office. More typically, the electoral vote merely exaggerates the margin of victory of the winner of the popular vote. In 1992, for example, Bill Clinton won 43 percent of the popular vote but 68.7 percent of the electoral vote.

1. The allotment of House seats by state, and therefore electoral votes, will be adjusted after the 2000 Census.

From the 1940s to the 1970s the Democratic Party balanced northern presidential nominees with southern vice-presidential nominations to appeal to the divergent political views of Democratic voters in these regions, especially on the race issue. Despite the sometimes bitter relations between the candidates and their staffs, in 1960 Massachusetts-born John Kennedy was compelled to team up with Texan Lyndon Johnson to strengthen his bid for the South. An August 1960 campaign stop in Amarillo, Texas, was one of their few joint appearances. In fact, most of the time these candidates ran separate campaigns in different parts of the country, with little coordination between them. At the bottom of photo is Lyndon Johnson's wife, Lady Bird Johnson.

ership styles. Until these reforms, America's political parties nominated presidential candidates largely as they had done since Andrew Jackson introduced national nominating conventions in the 1820s. Delegates chosen mostly from the ranks of the state party organizations assembled

at their national convention every four years to nominate presidential and vice-presidential candidates. The parties also adopted a platform on national issues.

Heading the delegations were state party leaders whose efforts were vital to the party's success in the fall election. Thus they had an important say in selecting the parties' standard-bearers. With an eye toward the all-crucial vote in the electoral college (see box), these leaders favored candidates from vote-rich states who also commanded broad support across regions and key party constituencies. For years, Democratic leaders paired a southern vice-presidential candidate with a "national" Democrat to create a "balanced" ticket. The selection process favored politicians who came from states laden with electoral votes and who had established national reputations in Washington.

The state party "bosses" could play such a large role because they controlled their state delegations, even to the extent of allowing southern leaders to exclude minority voters from serving as delegates. With the onset of reforms, however, state party leaders lost power, and both the delegate and candidate selection processes became more open and democratic. With this development, different kinds of presidential aspirants, who had stood little chance with state party leaders in control, now found their prospects greatly improved.

Reforms. In the 1970s the Democratic Party adopted a series of delegate selection reforms that required state parties to open up their delegate selection process. (These reforms are examined more fully in Chapter 12, Political Parties.) To implement the reforms, many state legislatures chose to hold presidential primary elections to select convention delegates while others kept their caucuses but opened them to participation by all party members. To demonstrate their openness, state organizations were required to ensure that minorities, women, and young adults were well represented in delegations. Since most officeholders are white males over thirty, these rules meant that many of them would no longer be attending the convention. From 1960 to 1980 the percentage of Democratic senators attending their party's convention fell from 68 to 17; that of representatives fell from 45 to 11.[27]

Other reforms effectively shifted nomination of the presidential candidates from the convention to the presidential primaries and caucuses. Revised rules in both political parties bound delegates selected in primaries and caucuses to their declared candidate at least on the first ballot at the convention.[28] Whereas in 1960, 20 percent of Democratic delegates and 35 percent of Republican delegates were committed to a particular candidate, by 1980 these figures had grown to 71 and 69 percent, and by 1996, to about 85 percent for both parties.[29]

Added together, these reforms ended the reign of the nominating convention as a forum where party leaders selected the party's standard-bearer from the ranks of politicians mostly based in Washington. In its place arose a multiphase popularity contest with low entry barriers. Of the many more candidates who began to show up, few would have stood a chance under the old convention arrangements, and campaigning began much earlier. Some of these long-distance runners, many "outsiders," won their party's nomination and the presidency. Others did well enough to ruin the chances of the more conventional "insider" candidates.

Outsiders. Outsider status is less a matter of living outside Washington than of one's standing within the party or government establishment. But what exactly is the establishment? That definition is left to the candidate and the voters. Minnesota Democrat Eugene McCarthy was very specific in 1968: the establishment was President Lyndon Johnson. Ronald Reagan was less precise; he denounced the "bumbling bureaucrats" and "spendthrift politicians" who occupied the "puzzle palaces along the Potomac." Generally, the outsider strategy plays better when a candidate is competing against a front-runner who occupies a credible "insider" position. In 1984 Democratic senator Gary Hart of Colorado could not have

Capitalizing on the national visibility he gained conducting televised hearings into organized crime in the early 1950s, Democratic senator Estes Kefauver won virtually every presidential primary he entered in 1952. Yet, largely because of a suspect reputation among the party leaders, he managed to get no closer than the vice-presidential nomination in 1956. Here, during an Albuquerque, New Mexico, campaign stop, the Tennessean tries to form a coalition with the American Indian community, by donning a headdress over his trademark coonskin cap.

campaigned effectively on his ambiguous platform of "new ideas" and being "less beholden" had not his adversary, former vice president Walter Mondale, been so conspicuously "more beholden" to the "old ideas" of the Democratic establishment.

During the prereform era, the parties occasionally welcomed to their front ranks the likes of Gen. Dwight Eisenhower, an irresistible candidate whose fame rested on his nonpolitical career as chief of Allied forces in Western Europe in World War II. But more often candidates were drawn from the ranks of mainstream politicians. "Outsiders," even if they were members of Congress, did not stand a chance. By the time Jimmy Carter came to Washington in 1977, outsiders no longer were being shunted aside. In fact, three of the last four presidents—Carter (1977–1981), Reagan (1981–1989), and Clinton (1993–2001), all governors—are the first twentieth-century presidents to assume the Oval Office without any experience in Washington. "We came to Washington as outsiders . . . we left as outsiders," noted Carter in his memoirs.[30] The selection reforms thoroughly altered presidential recruitment.

Another class of presidential candidates boasts even stronger credentials as outsiders. These candidates have never held public office, but they possess the requisite resources—ample television exposure, political action committees (organizations authorized by law to collect money and make campaign contributions to candidates), and either a private fortune or a lucrative fund-raising list. Contending with an attractive "insider," Senate Majority Leader Bob Dole, magazine publisher Steve Forbes advertised heavily in the 1996 presidential campaign, spending $38 million of his own money. And he ran strongly until his poor organization and weak appeal to southern Republican primary voters ended his candidacy.

The advantages that the reformed selection process confer on outsiders are perhaps best illustrated by Bob Dole's effort during the 1996 primaries to disassociate himself from Washington. In a tearful announcement, the Senate majority leader resigned his seat of twenty-seven years, took off his tie and unbuttoned his collar, and asked voters to regard him no longer as senator but simply as "citizen Dole."[31]

Going Public

The presidential selection system is a kind of strategic environment that enhances certain skills and resources while penalizing others. In addition to their direct effects on candidates' fortunes, selection reforms have shaped the kinds of presidents elected by influencing the career decisions and styles adopted by potential candidates. As a result, presidents who reach the White House fresh from an extended and successful stint of campaigning, first to win the nomination and then the election, will not hesitate to go public—that is, to entrust their leadership in Washington to their ability to strike a responsive chord in the country.

Outsiders and the Public. Outsider presidents approach their leadership differently than, say, a longtime senator or another politician who enjoys the trust and good will of party leaders in Washington and the party's core constituency groups across the country. For one thing, they often are less knowledgeable about and less skilled in the practice of quiet diplomacy and bargaining that allow Washington's diverse community of politicians to maintain comity and reach agreement on mutually acceptable public policy. Nor do these new-styled presidents, who were self-reliant in their efforts to win the White House and therefore have few obligations to their political party, feel as compelled as Washington insiders to accommodate fellow partisans in Congress. Instead, they are free to adapt their policy stances to shifts in public opinion.[32] When frustrated congressional Republicans carped during President Clinton's first term that the president was stealing their legislative program by endorsing both welfare reform and a balanced budget, they were tacitly acknowledging the flexibility available to outsiders to break with their own party's long-standing commitments.

Presidents who engage in public relations to sustain their leadership regard their prestige as the currency of power. However gratifying personally, public approval is a resource whose cultivation and expenditure must be coolly calculated. For example, President Clinton's consistently high approval rating throughout 1998 almost certainly rescued him from the ignominy of being the first president to be removed from office. Had the American public abandoned the president, as many Republicans thought it would, the outcome of the Senate impeachment trial

President Clinton Talks His Way Out of a Jam

When the Monica Lewinsky scandal broke into the head-lines the week before President Bill Clinton's 1998 State of the Union address, many politicians and pundits predicted that his presidency was doomed. If the charges were true, how could he possibly weather it out until the end of his presidency? The first polls went into the field within twenty-four hours and immediately recorded a five percentage point drop in his job performance rating. The first victim of the crisis appeared to be his nationally televised address to the nation. A near consensus immediately formed that he should cancel it, and those who wanted it delivered insisted he change the subject from the state of the nation to explaining his behavior and apologizing to the American people. Instead, the president lived up to his nickname "The Comeback Kid" (born after his success in the scandal-plagued 1992 presidential election) by delivering an articulate and widely acclaimed message about his goals for the nation. Immediately the polls surged, and, despite an extraordinary number of adverse political developments culminating in his impeachment, his popular support hovered steadily in the vicinity of 70 percent.

A CBS/*New York Times* poll of the same respondents a few days before and after Clinton's address revealed the speech's effects on viewer opinions (see figure). According to the poll, the speech hurt the president with no one; from 92 to 98 percent of those who approved of Clinton before the speech continued to do so afterward. The president's detractors who viewed the speech responded enthusiastically. More than half of the Democratic disapprovers switched to approval, and, even more surprising, about a third of the Republican disapprovers did so as well. Even many of the respondents who said they did not see or hear

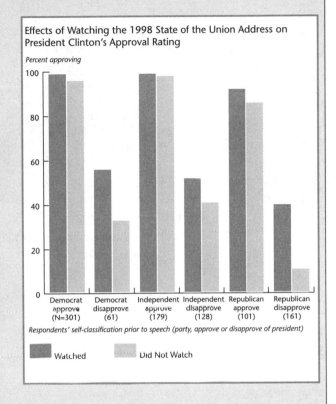

Effects of Watching the 1998 State of the Union Address on President Clinton's Approval Rating

Percent approving

	Watched	Did Not Watch

Respondents' self-classification prior to speech (party, approve or disapprove of president)

Democrat approve (N=301), Democrat disapprove (61), Independent approve (179), Independent disapprove (128), Republican approve (101), Republican disapprove (161)

the speech shifted to approval. Whether this result reflected the halo of favorable press in the aftermath of Clinton's "home run," as some news reports called it, or the effects of listening to the assessments of friends and colleagues who did watch the president, could not be determined from this survey.

Source: Samuel Kernell, "The Challenge Ahead for Explaining President Clinton's Public Support," *PRG Report* 21 (spring 1999) : 2.

OUTSIDER PRESIDENTS
Taking Problems to the People

One could hardly find a better illustration of the outsider's tendency to go public than the following colloquy between House Speaker Thomas P. "Tip" O'Neill Jr. and President Jimmy Carter during a 1977 pre-inauguration briefing in Plains, Georgia:

O'Neill: Mr. President, I want you to understand something. Some of the brightest men in America are in this Congress of the United States. Don't make the mistake of underestimating them. . . . We want to work together, but I have a feeling you are underestimating the feeling of Congress and you could have some trouble.

Carter: I'll handle them just as I handled the Georgia legislature. Whenever I had problems with the Georgia legislature, I took the problems to the people of Georgia.[1]

Two months later they were having the same conversation but in public. "It upsets me when they say, 'we'll bring it to the people,'" the stentorian white-haired Speaker declared. "That's the biggest mistake Carter could ever make."[2]

1. Sidney Blumenthal, "Marketing the President," *New York Times Magazine,* September 13, 1981, 22.
2. Hedrick Smith, "Congress and Carter: An Uneasy Adjustment," *New York Times,* February 18, 1977, B16.

might have been different. Instead, buoyed by a strong economy and adroit cultivation of public support, Clinton maintained the public's approbation and his job.

Because outsider presidents rest their leadership in Washington on their popular support in the country, the day-to-day business of governing at times resembles a campaign. Early in 1997, when asked by campaign-weary reporters why President Clinton maintained such a heavy travel schedule after his reelection, an aide explained: "Clinton has come to believe that if he keeps his approval ratings up and sells his message as he did during the campaign, there will be greater acceptability for his program. . . . The idea is that you have to sell it as if in a campaign."[33]

At no time have governing and campaigning so resem-

bled one another than in early 1999 when the Senate deliberated the president's removal from office. With the charged impeachment proceedings serving as an uninviting backdrop for the annual State of the Union address, many members of Congress publicly and privately advised President Clinton to cancel or postpone the event. Ignoring this advice and Republicans' chilly reception in the audience, Clinton delivered a critically acclaimed speech. Then, instead of dutifully retreating to the White House to await the Senate's verdict, he immediately took his legislative program on the road. During the next three weeks he logged nineteen separate appearances outside Washington. By going public at this unlikely moment, Clinton succeeded in drawing the contrast between his attentiveness to the "business of the American people" and

Figure 7–6 Presidential Addresses, 1929–1995 (Yearly Averages for First Three Years of First Term)

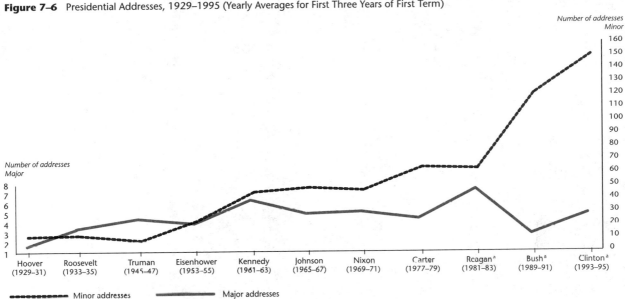

Sources: Data for Hoover, Roosevelt, Truman, Eisenhower, Nixon, and Carter are from William W. Lammers, "Presidential Attention-Focusing Activities," in *The President and the American Public,* ed. Doris A. Graber (Philadelphia: Institute for the Study of Human Issues, 1982), Table 6–1, 152. Data for Kennedy, Johnson, Reagan, Bush, and Clinton are from *Public Papers of the Presidents* series. See also Samuel Kernell, "The Presidency and the People: The Modern Paradox," in *The Presidency and the Political System,* ed. Michael Nelson (Washington, D.C.: CQ Press, 1984), 242.
Note: To eliminate public activities inspired by concerns of reelection rather than governing, only the first three years have been tabulated. For this reason, Gerald Ford's record of public activities during his two and one-half years of office has been ignored.
a. Includes television addresses only. With radio included, Reagan averaged twenty-four addresses per year.

the Senate's preoccupation with the impeachment trial that a majority of the public opposed.

But modern presidents do not reserve political travel and speaking for dire moments; they tend to return to a campaign footing whenever they want to improve the prospects of success for themselves and their policies. The steady growth of public speaking and presidential travel is evidence of this trend in going public.

Public Addresses. Today, presidents devote a great deal of their time, energy, and staff to taking their messages directly to the American people. The most dramatic way of going public, prime-time television addresses, originated with President Franklin Roosevelt's "Fireside Chats," nationally broadcast radio addresses during the depression and World War II. Every president since has continued the practice.

Direct addresses may be the most dramatic and effec-

tive way to influence public opinion, but they also can hurt the president if overused. Aware of this risk, recent presidents have held their major television addresses in check (Figure 7–6). Presidents and their media advisers worry that the public's attentiveness corresponds inversely to the number of appeals. In private correspondence Franklin Roosevelt said as much: "The public psychology . . . [cannot] be attuned for long periods of time to the highest note on the scale. . . . People tire of seeing the same name, day after day, in the important headlines of the papers and the same voice, night after night, over the radio."[34] Moreover, in recent years the television networks have grown increasingly reluctant to accommodate presidential requests for prime time to address the nation.[35] (Chapter 14 examines the effects of cable television on presidents' declining audience shares and the networks' growing reluctance to provide presidents with

prime-time access to the airwaves.)

Presidents also take their messages to the public through appearances at graduation exercises, union conferences, and the conventions of trade and professional associations where they can address the specific concerns of a particular constituency. Figure 7–6 reveals that these less visible, minor addresses have provided an attractive venue for the explosion in presidential talk: Reagan, Carter, and Nixon used these forums, on average, four times more often than Truman, Roosevelt, and Hoover. President Bush managed to double these already high levels of targeted addresses; during his first three years in office he made, on average, a minor address every three days. Clinton did Bush one better: he delivered a minor address nearly every other day during his first three years in office.

Travel. Presidential foreign and domestic travel, which typically has different political purposes, has increased sig-

nificantly in the past half-century (Figure 7–7). Eisenhower was the first president to travel extensively around the country.[36] Not until Reagan and Bush, however, did presidents spend a month away from Washington each year. Bush even broke the two-month mark in 1991, despite getting off to a late start because of the outbreak of the Persian Gulf War in January.

International political travel by presidents increased most sharply during the late 1960s. Eisenhower's 1959 "goodwill tour" around the world is generally recognized as the first international presidential travel for which favorable publicity appeared to be the primary consideration. Later presidents favored the idea as well. Presidents Carter and Bush, who enjoyed their greatest policy successes in foreign affairs, traveled extensively. By the end of his third year in office, Bush was so conspicuously absent on overseas travel that his critics—especially his opponent in the next election, Bill Clinton—found a large segment

Figure 7–7 Days of Political Travel by Presidents, 1929–1995 (Yearly Averages for First Three Years of First Term)

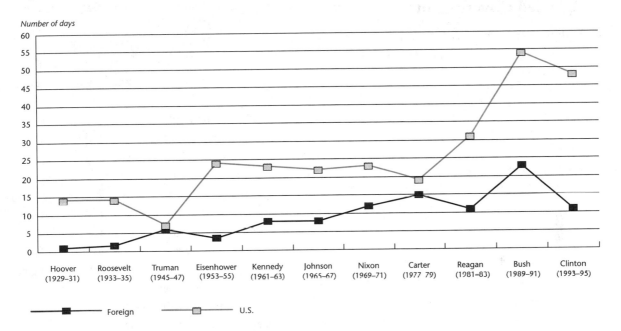

Number of days

| Hoover (1929–31) | Roosevelt (1933–35) | Truman (1945–47) | Eisenhower (1953–55) | Kennedy (1961–63) | Johnson (1965–67) | Nixon (1969–71) | Carter (1977 79) | Reagan (1981–83) | Bush (1989–91) | Clinton (1993–95) |

Foreign — U.S.

Sources: Data for Hoover, Roosevelt, Truman, Eisenhower, Nixon, and Carter are from William W. Lammers, "Presidential Attention-Focusing Activities," in *The President and the American Public,* ed. Doris A. Graber (Philadelphia: Institute for the Study of Human Issues, 1982), Table 6–5, 160. Data for Kennedy, Johnson, Reagan, Bush, and Clinton are from *Public Papers of the Presidents* series. See also Samuel Kernell, "The Presidency and the People: The Modern Paradox," in *The Presidency and the Political System,* ed. Michael Nelson (Washington, D.C.: CQ Press, 1984), 244.

  Note: To eliminate public activities inspired by concerns of reelection rather than governing, only the first three years have been tabulated. For this reason, Gerald Ford's record of public activities during his two and one-half years of office has been ignored.

of the public agreeing with them that the president was not paying enough attention to the nation's business. Under pressure to focus on domestic issues, Bush postponed a trip to Asia in late 1991, ostensibly to keep tabs on the Democratic Congress.

President Clinton had a special reason to travel extensively in the United States: as the first president since Nixon to win the office without a majority of the popular vote, Clinton was in effect continuing his campaign for the presidency. By the 1996 election he had averaged a visit to California, with its fifty-four electoral votes, every six weeks. In fact, Clinton has taken the presidency outside Washington more than most observers and pundits ever thought possible. Every fourth day or so during his first three years in office, the president was traveling somewhere around the country. (And during the approximately twenty days a month he stayed in Washington, he made heavy use of video conferencing.) Acting on lessons learned from his predecessor, George Bush, Clinton spent relatively little time traveling abroad during his first term, especially in the early months of his presidency when the recession remained a prime concern. Taken together, the statistics on Clinton's travel portray a president who, in contrast to his predecessors thirty and forty years ago, is far more personally involved in public relations and who recognizes that his success ultimately depends on his public support.

Modern Presidents and Divided Government

The twentieth century has been kind to presidents. Important administrative discretion has shifted from Capitol Hill to the White House, delegated by a Congress in danger of becoming overwhelmed by the plethora of responsibilities the national government has assumed. In response, presidents have acquired impressive institutional resources to cope with their expanded management responsibilities. Their hollow constitutional mandate notwithstanding, late twentieth-century presidents have finally become the "chief executive" advertised in the Constitution.

Equally important, early twentieth-century electoral and civil service reforms liberated presidents from the obligations of party service and allowed politicians more interested in policy than patronage to compete for the White House. Recent reforms of the presidential nominating system have, for better or worse, further loosened presidents' ties to other politicians within their political party.

The rapid evolution of the office both administratively and politically has prepared it well for the arrival of divided party control of the presidency and Congress. Of the twenty-seven Congresses since the end of World War II, in seventeen at least one chamber has been controlled by the president's opposition party. (Chapter 11, Voting, Campaigns, and Elections, considers the various causes of divided government.)

And how do modern presidents deal with an opposition Congress? Many have pulled decisions into the White House through the use of executive orders and central clearance, as well as careful screening of appointees to head federal agencies to ensure that administrators loyal and responsive to the president are in place. When dealing with Congress, presidents may enlist other unilateral assets such as the veto or solicitation of public support to try to force congressional compliance. The veto offers presidents a clear, self-enforcing means of asserting their preferences and explaining them to the American people. It represents, as Alexis de Tocqueville first observed in 1836, "a sort of appeal to the people," which modern presidents have not been shy about invoking against an opposition Congress.[37]

With the help of mass communications, presidents are able to appeal more directly for the public's support. These efforts may take the form of applied pressure—"Write, e-mail, or phone your member of Congress"—or more subtle pressure by rendering a policy position so publicly attractive that opposition members of Congress decide to hop on the bandwagon. In January 1999, in the face of Republican proclamations of a major tax cut, President Clinton used his State of the Union address to call for devoting most of the budget surplus to saving Social Security. After temporizing briefly, Republican congressional leaders took up the mantra and removed $70 billion of the savings from a targeted tax cut. Even when presidents fail in their public efforts to move an opposition Congress, they still may succeed in generating issues favoring the party in the next election.

At the outset of this chapter, we saw both Presidents Bush and Clinton use the tools at their disposal—the veto (or at least its threat) and public relations—in budget showdowns with Congresses controlled by the opposition party. The results, however, were quite different, whether measured by the final budgets or the success of these presidents in their next election. These cases serve as a reminder that despite the enlarged scope and authority of the modern office, presidential leadership remains uncertain, problematic, and ultimately dependent on the president's skills as a politician. The office may be vastly different from the one the Framers envisioned, but it remains tethered to its limited constitutional mandate.

Key Terms

central clearance /229

commander in chief /221

enrolled bill /231

executive agreement /220

executive order /215

gag rule /229

"take care" clause /215

Suggested Readings

Fisher, Louis. *The Politics of Shared Power: Congress and the Executive.* 4th ed. College Station: Texas A&M University Press, 1998. Considering that the subject is the distribution of formal authority between the presidency and Congress, this book is surprisingly readable. Fisher shows that the Framers left many interesting gaps in defining relations between these branches. Two hundred years later, some still have not been filled in.

Kernell, Samuel. *Going Public: New Strategies of Presidential Leadership.* 3d ed. Washington, D.C.: CQ Press, 1997. The author develops more fully the argument summarized here that modern presidents are more inclined to engage in public relations in seeking influence in Washington.

Milkis, Sidney M., and Michael Nelson. *The American Presidency: Origins and Development, 1776–1998.* 3d ed. Washington, D.C.: CQ Press, 1999. This popular text offers a thorough and highly readable historical treatment of the presidency.

Neustadt, Richard E. *Presidential Power and the Modern Presidents: The Politics of Power from Roosevelt to Reagan.* 4th ed. New York: Free Press, 1990. This is *the* classic statement of the leadership predicament confronted by all presidents. Originally published in 1961 and in print ever since, this book is a touchstone for anyone aspiring to understand the American presidency.

Woodward, Bob. *The Agenda: Inside the Clinton White House.* New York: Simon and Schuster, 1994. A lively and apparently accurate portrayal of life inside the early Clinton White House. It is not a pretty picture.

Chapter 8

THE BUREAUCRACY

⭐ *Who controls the bureaucracy? The president? Congress? The courts? No one?*

⭐ *How can the government grow while the bureaucracy shrinks?*

⭐ *Why do efforts to make government agencies more accountable lead to the proliferation of red tape?*

⭐ *Why does every president want to reform the bureaucracy but almost all fail?*

In September 1997 the Senate Finance Committee held hearings on the tactics used by the Internal Revenue Service (IRS) to collect federal income taxes. Some of the witnesses were IRS agents, carefully screened from sight, with their voices disguised electronically so they could avoid agency retaliation for blowing the whistle. The agents shocked committee members and taxpayers alike with their tales of horrific abuses: small errors escalating into ordeals lasting years, costing fortunes, and breaking up marriages; rogue agents knowingly violating the law and harassing innocent taxpayers to boost their own case statistics.

Eyebrows went up even further when agency statistics revealed that the IRS had been stepping up audits of vulnerable low-income taxpayers while cutting back on audits of high-income taxpayers who could afford lawyers and accountants to fight back. The agency also was charged with rewarding agents and managers who processed the most cases and brought in the most additional tax money, violating a 1988 law expressly forbidding

such criteria. It was the classic tale of an incompetent bureaucracy out of control—and the public's least favorite one at that. As one victim testified, "The IRS is judge, jury, and executioner—answerable to no one."[1] Outraged senators gave the acting IRS commissioner a thorough tongue-lashing. He apologized profusely, promised reform, suspended some district-level managers, and ordered the rest to root out and punish abuses.

An IRS run amok fit the popular stereotype of bureaucracies and offered an irresistible target for congressional umbrage. And the abuses exposed plainly were outrageous. But how much blame should fall on the IRS specifically or on "bureaucracy" in general? After all, the elected politicians in Congress and the White House created the IRS, finance and oversee its activities, and write the tax laws it is supposed to enforce. Moreover, only a few years earlier congressional critics had been attacking the IRS for not going after tax cheats aggressively and for not auditing enough cases. Should they be surprised when the agency steps up enforcement and tries to

Eating their cake and having it too, Congress writes a complex tax code, instructs the IRS to do better in catching tax cheats, and then publicly berates the agency for victimizing taxpayers. Here Senate Finance Committee chair William Roth, a Republican from Delaware, addresses witnesses who told tales of bureaucratic callousness during the 1997 televised Senate hearings on the IRS. Democratic senator Daniel Patrick Moynihan of New York is seated at left.

meet the demand for greater efficiency by processing a higher proportion of easier cases? Republicans had complained for years that low-income taxpayers were abusing the Earned Income Tax Credit. Should they be outraged when the IRS shifts its attention to low-income earners who claim the credit? Congress itself reduced the agency's budget and staff at the same time it was making the tax code ever more convoluted. If tax laws are so complex that they defy consistent interpretation and application, it is hardly the IRS's fault. And what about the nearly 20 percent of taxpayers who fail to pay what they owe voluntarily and the estimated $200 billion in taxes due that goes unpaid every year? Is it any surprise that IRS agents charged with collecting taxes from an often-reluctant citizenry come to view the people they deal with not as customers but as potential tax cheats? Finally, there was nothing accidental about the timing of the Senate hearings. Some Republican leaders hoped to use the unpopularity of the IRS to build public support for replacing the entire federal tax structure with a flat tax (one rate, no deductions) or a national sales tax.

This more nuanced take on the IRS story reveals some of the complex issues and questions raised by the modern federal **bureaucracy.** The roots of the bureaucracy are found in the Constitution where it authorizes Congress to make laws and the president to see that they are faithfully executed. Presidents necessarily delegate their duty to their agents in the executive branch. In the nation's earliest years these agents delivered the mail, collected the customs duties (taxes on imported goods) and excise taxes (on alcohol and luxuries) that were to finance the new government, prosecuted violations of federal laws, and managed relations with foreign nations. Surely the Framers did not envision anything like today's 102,000-strong IRS or the rest of the federal establishment, comprising some 2,000 departments, bureaus, agencies, and commissions which employ some 2.8 million nonmilitary personnel. But as we shall see in this chapter, the modern bureaucracy mirrors in a very direct way the pluralistic nature of American politics and society. Every new agency has been brought into being by a unique configuration of political forces and reflects in its mandate and organization the attempt of a successful policy coalition to preserve its victory through institutional design. The remarkable variety of arrangements adopted to administer government policies is largely a product of the endless search by Congress and the White House for ways to maximize the potential political benefits and minimize the potential political costs each time they decide to exercise and delegate their authority. The end product is the extravagantly diverse collection of entities that now compose the federal bureaucracy.

The Development of the Federal Bureaucracy

The Framers viewed the executive as the necessary source of "energy" in government, but questions of administration received remarkably little attention at the Constitutional Convention, and the Constitution itself said little about how the executive branch was to be organized. As we saw in Chapter 7, it did authorize the president, with the advice and consent of the Senate, to appoint ambassadors, Supreme Court justices, and heads of departments and other senior executive branch officials. Congress was left with the task of establishing executive departments and determining how they would be staffed.

From the beginning, Congress was wary of delegating too much power to the executive. The colonial experience with the king's governors and other royal officials was too fresh. And the Continental Congress's attempt to do without executive departments by setting up congressional committees to make all administrative decisions had proven quite impractical. Delegate John Adams, for one, "found himself working eighteen-hour days just to keep up with the business of the 90 committees on which he served."[2]

Modest Beginnings: The Dilemma of Delegation

With these experiences in mind, the First Congress began its work on the executive branch by reestablishing the departments that had existed under the Articles of Confederation: Treasury, Foreign Affairs (quickly renamed State), and War. Congress also authorized the hiring of an attorney general to give the president and department heads legal advice. Until 1817, however, the position remained a part-time job held by a succession of lawyers who maintained private practices. The larger departments were soon subdivided into a few more specialized offices, later called bureaus. For example, by 1801 the Treasury Department was dividing its work among units headed by a commissioner of revenue who supervised tax collection, a purveyor in charge of buying military supplies, and an auditor who, among other duties, oversaw the operation of lighthouses. It also included a General Land Office to deal with the sale of public lands.[3]

Congress readily agreed that each executive department should be headed by a single official responsible for its operations. There was far less consensus, however, about whether department heads were primarily responsible to Congress or the president. The Constitution itself was not clear on the matter; presidents appointed senior officials, but appointments were subject to senatorial approval (see Chapter 7). One crucial issue was whether presidents could dismiss officials without the consent of the Senate. The First Congress gave the president the sole right of removal, but only narrowly; Vice President John Adams cast the tie-breaking vote in the Senate.[4] The issue came up again during the Jackson administration (1829–1837) and later during Reconstruction (1867–1877) before it was finally settled in the president's favor: officials held their jobs at the pleasure of the chief executive, not Congress. This being said, many lower-level federal jobs such as local postmaster were, by the Adams administration, effectively controlled by Congress. When the president turned to its members for advice on appointments in their states and districts, they had quickly assumed their advice would be followed.

The dismissal controversy was one of many instances in which Congress faced the familiar dilemmas of delegation. The advantages of delegating authority to a unified executive that could energetically and efficiently implement the laws passed by the Congress were clear. But the potential drawback was equally clear: executives might energetically and efficiently pursue ends contrary to those desired by congressional majorities. Recognizing this drawback, Congress from the beginning sought ways in which to maintain agencies' responsiveness to Congress, thereby balancing the president's power to hire and fire agency officials. Its primary tool, it found, was its authority to establish executive branch agencies and set their annual budgets.

The executive struggled with the same dilemma. Even the skimpy government of the Federalist period (1789–1801) was too large to be managed by the president and his cabinet secretaries without delegating authority to subordinate officials. Thus they also faced a standard principal–agent problem: how to assure that agents acting ostensibly on their behalf would faithfully carry out official policies. As the nation has grown and the range of federal activities has expanded, so has the challenge of keeping appointed officials responsive to elected officials, just as elected officials are, in their turn, supposed to be responsive to the citizenry. As we shall see in this chapter, the various ways in which the government has tried to meet this challenge have had enduring consequences for the modern bureaucracy.

The Federalist Years: A Reliance on Respectability

For many decades the federal government had few responsibilities, and so it was small. In fact, George Washington (1789–1797) had so few staff that he occasionally called on his cabinet chiefs to take dictation, making them secretaries in a less exalted sense.[5] In 1792 the number of federal civilian employees stood at about 780; by the time Thomas Jefferson took office in 1801, the bureaucracy had grown to only 2,120. But how could such a small government serve a population that exceeded five million at the time? Most governing was done by state and local bodies.

Indeed, only a small fraction of federal employees worked in the capital city, where they were actually outnumbered by members of Congress until the 1820s. Yet Washington and his successors still had to deal with the problem of delegation, heightened during the early days of the Republic by the long distances and primitive communications between the capital and the states and cities where federal policies were administered.

During this period most federal government workers, laboring far from their bosses in the capital, were occupied with delivering the mail and collecting duties and taxes. The potential for corruption was considerable. President Washington believed that popular support for the young national government depended on honest and competent administration. Thus he sought to appoint civil servants of character and ability who were respected by their communities—in other words, men of superior education, means, family, and local reputation. The problem of delegation was to be met, in the first place, by choosing the right sort of people as agents. Other techniques also were used to ensure honest administration. Officials sometimes were required to post bonds of money or property that they would forfeit if they failed to perform their duties. Customs and alcohol tax collectors received a share of the proceeds from the sale of goods they seized from smugglers, giving them a financial incentive to detect and thwart smuggling. Heavy fines were imposed for giving or taking bribes.[6]

President Washington's efforts to establish an honest, competent federal civil service largely succeeded. Although presidents remained free to dismiss officials at will, an informal custom of tenure during good behavior emerged and remained in place until the 1820s. Political criteria were applied to the initial appointment, with presidents favoring people from their own party. But, once appointed, civil servants could count on keeping their jobs as long as they performed adequately. Indeed, it was not uncommon for officials to pass positions on to their sons or nephews.[7] This practice, consistent with Federalist notions of government by the respectable gentlemen, was contrary, however, to the democratic spirit that eclipsed Federalist views during the early decades of the nineteenth century.

Democratization of the Civil Service: The Spoils System

The most prominent spokesman for this democratic spirit, President Andrew Jackson (1829–1837), argued that public offices held as, in effect, private property would "divert government from its legitimate ends and make it an engine for the support of the few at the expense of the many." Moreover, "the duties of all public officers are, or at least admit of being made, so plain and simple that men of intelligence may readily qualify themselves for their performance."[8] In other words, when it comes to governing, no experience necessary. Jackson thus advocated **rotation in office**; officials would serve in positions for a short, fixed period, then move on to something else, perhaps in government, but more often returning to private life. The idea was to democratize the civil service along with the rest of the political system.

The democratic ideal of rotation in office meshed with the practical need of party organizations for ways in which to inspire and reward the activists they relied on to mobilize the expanding mass electorate (see Chapter 12). Who better deserved appointment to public office than the men who had proved their mettle by helping their political party to triumph? Debating the issue of tenure in office in 1835, Sen. William Marcy of New York assured himself a place in the history books by celebrating "the rule, that to the victor belong the spoils of the enemy,"[9] and giving the **spoils system**—the practice of allowing the winning party to dispense government jobs—its name. Once government jobs became a primary resource for maintaining party machines, members of Congress developed an even keener interest in influencing appointments to federal offices in their states and districts. Ironically, rotation in office and the spoils system, meant to democratize administration, led instead to its bureaucratiza-

Introduced by their member of Congress in return for past political support, job seekers, hats in hand, approach the president for positions in his administration. Before passage of the Pendleton Act in 1883 many government jobs were filled by patronage.

tion. Bureaucratic organization arises when leaders attempt to solve the huge problems of coordination and delegation raised by many forms of large-scale collective action. The characteristic features of bureaucratic institutions, delineated more than a century ago by the German sociologist Max Weber, are:

- A hierarchical structure of authority in which commands flow downward and information flows upward (for coordination and control)

- A division of labor (to reap the advantages of specialization in taking on complex tasks)

- A consistent set of abstract rules regarding what is to be done and who is to do it (for coordination among specialists, control over subordinates, and uniformity of action in each position regardless of who holds it)

- Impersonality, treating everyone in the same category the same regardless of who they are as individuals (for consistency and impartiality)

• A career system, with appointment and advancement by demonstrated merit, and often considerable job security (to create incentives for loyal and effective performance)

• Specified goals toward which the collective action is aimed (unlike, for example, economic markets, in which individuals and firms have goals—making money—but the market as a whole does not).

The model bureaucracy is, in short, a purposive machine with interchangeable human parts. Centralized control is exercised over large numbers of people performing complex social tasks, greatly amplifying the power of whoever sits at the top of the hierarchical pyramid. The classic example is an army, with its clear chain of command from the five-star general at the top down to the lowliest buck private at the bottom. Most modern business corporations, government agencies, even spiritual enterprises such as the Roman Catholic Church, also have organized themselves bureaucratically for more effective central control over collective pursuits. But whatever its advantages, bureaucratic organization imposes heavy conformity costs on both bureaucrats and the people they deal with in return for reducing transaction costs and agency losses (see Chapter 1).

American bureaucracies, like American political parties, arose more from expedience than from conscious design. The Jacksonians had no intention of erecting new bureaucratic structures, but the spoils system created administrative problems that begged for bureaucratic solutions. Under the old system run by long-tenured, gentlemanly civil servants, administration had been relatively personal, informal, and idiosyncratic. Officials had had time to accumulate a great deal of personal knowledge about the matters that came before them and to establish stable working relationships with other officials. The prospect of permanent employment in return for a job well done, together with the ethos of the class from which most officials came, had inspired honesty and efficiency.

By contrast, the spoils system, with its widespread "rotation in office," was fraught with the dangers of incompetence and corruption. Jackson, no less than Washington, sought honest, efficient government, recognizing that the continued success of his party depended on delivering it. The means his administration adopted to cope with the defects of the spoils system yielded a bureaucracy. Jobs became more specialized and clearly defined so that novices could quickly master and perform them. Administrative jurisdictions and responsibilities were spelled out in greater detail to avoid confusion and conflict among people who would be in office only for a short time. Hierarchies became more formal and elaborate, with new procedures designed to monitor and control agents whose honesty and efficiency could not be assumed and who had no long-term stake in how they performed their jobs. Officials kept meticulous records of their actions, which were subject to audit by a separate set of specialists. Government became more impersonal.[10]

The complex arrangements needed to ensure control quickly bred the kind of "red tape" for which bureaucracies are legendary. In 1836, for example, the House Ways and Means Committee blamed the Treasury Department's excessive workload on an accounting system that required the concurrence of no fewer than five officers—the treasurer, the auditor, the comptroller, a secretary, and the registrar—for all receipts of funds and expenditures. "The result of the reciprocal checks here established," the committee noted, "is that no money can be received or paid out without the agency of these five separate offices, involving the labor of one or more clerks in each."[11] When senior officials place the desire to monitor agents ahead of efficiency (in this case by arranging for them to monitor each other) chronic bureaucratic sluggishness is the result.

Civil Service Reform

Under Jackson, the federal administration did not become fully bureaucratized in the Weberian sense; the principle of rotation in office precluded the development of government service as a career with job security and advancement based on merit. Only after the Civil War (1861–1865) were the calls to adopt this additional component of bureaucracy finally heard. The pressure arose from the continuing quest of citizens and reformers for honesty and efficiency in government. The emerging industrial economy was raising new problems of administration that a civil service composed of short-term amateurs was poorly suited to address. More important, financial scandals, particularly during Ulysses S. Grant's administration (1869–1877), fueled attacks on the spoils system and prompted political support for civil service reform.[12] Perhaps the most dramatic incident was the exposure of the Whiskey Ring (see box). And last but not least, civil service reformers also were helped by their pivotal position as a swing constituency in an era of close two-party competition.

Defenders of the old system did not give up easily, however, and reforms that protected officials from political firing and imposed merit criteria for hiring and advancement were extended only gradually over federal appointees. The most compelling argument for reform was the assassination of President James Garfield in 1881 by a demented job seeker incensed at having been denied a patronage appointment. The ensuing revulsion against the spoils system led in 1883 to passage of the Pendleton Act, the basis of the modern civil service. The act itself put only 10 percent of federal jobs under the merit system, but it authorized the president to extend coverage by executive order. Presidents from Grover Cleveland on did exactly that, although, ironically, for the crassest of partisan motives. Each president about to relinquish office to the other party extended civil service protection to thousands of his own patronage appointees. By the time Franklin Roosevelt became president in 1933, 80 percent of federal workers were included in the merit system.[13]

Not all was well, however; the merit system bred its own set of agency problems. Rotation in office may have

THE WHISKEY RING

During the Grant administration, a group of revenue officials, all political appointees, conspired with distillers to evade taxes on distilleries on a massive scale. The conspirators, dubbed the "Whiskey Ring," included Gen. John McDonald, collector of internal revenue in St. Louis, the initial center of the conspiracy, as well as collectors and their subordinates in Chicago, Milwaukee, and San Francisco. Other co-conspirators were the chief clerk of the internal revenue division of the Treasury Department in Washington and Gen. Orville Babcock, President Grant's private secretary.

A small group of honest officials led by Secretary of the Treasury Benjamin Bristow exposed the conspiracy in May 1875. When the dust settled, forty-seven distillers, sixty rectifiers (who set the alcohol content of distilled spirits), ten wholesale dealers, and eighty-six of the Treasury Department's field agents were facing indictment. In all, 230 indictments were handed down. Of these, about a hundred defendants pleaded guilty, twenty were convicted, and a dozen fled the country. Babcock was acquitted with the help of Grant, who mistakenly thought he was innocent and made a deposition in his behalf for his trial. Grant later named Babcock inspector of lighthouses. Meanwhile, Bristow was forced from Grant's cabinet.

Source: Leonard D. White, *The Republican Era: A Study in Administrative History, 1869–1901* (New York: Macmillan, 1958), 372–374.

left the government short on experience and efficiency, but it had kept officials in close touch with the lives of ordinary citizens and responsive to the elected politicians who appointed them. Some proponents of a professional civil service naively thought it would turn government agencies into efficient, politically neutral tools subject only to the will of policy makers in Congress and the

On July 2, 1881, Charles Guiteau, outraged because Republican Chester A. Arthur lost the 1880 presidential election and therefore Guiteau's chance for a patronage job, shot the election winner, Democratic president James A. Garfield, in a Washington train station. Garfield died on September 19. The public uproar over the incident galvanized support in Congress for civil service reform.

An Expanding Government

Despite dramatic changes in *how* the government operated after Jackson, *what* the government did changed very little. The number of federal officials grew along with the population, but they continued to perform the same limited set of tasks assigned during the Federalist period: collecting duties and taxes, delivering the mail, disposing of public lands in the West, granting patents, managing relations with foreign nations and Native Americans, and maintaining a small army and navy. The federal establishment began small and stayed that way for decades because most Americans wanted it that way. Cheap, limited government was part of the democratic creed professed by disciples of Jefferson and Jackson, and any attempts to expand the federal domain met firm resistance in Congress. After establishing the Departments of War, State, and Treasury in 1789 and carving a Department of the Navy out of War in 1798, Congress went for more than fifty years without adding a single new cabinet-level department.

After the Civil War, however, the federal government began expanding its activities and personnel, and that trend, with a few exceptions, has continued to the present day. As Figure 8–1 reveals, federal employment grew steadily but not very steeply (except during World War I) from the 1870s until the New Deal period, when the rate of growth began to increase. World War II produced a dramatic surge in the size of the federal workforce that was only partially reversed afterward. Since then, the number of civil servants has continued to trend upward, but, as a proportion of the population, the federal workforce has been shrinking since the 1950s (Figure 8–2). The federal government has not been shrinking in any other sense, however. As we will see in the rest of this chapter,

White House. Career bureaucrats, however, inevitably develop their own personal and institutional interests, and the rules designed to protect them from political retaliation make it difficult to punish them for shirking. They become the reigning experts in their bureau's procedures and policy domains, magnifying the problems of hidden action (principals unable to observe what agents are doing) and hidden information (agents knowing things that principals do not) inherent in principal–agent relationships (see section "Delegation" in Chapter 1). Moreover, they can easily develop perspectives quite different from people outside of government. Organized into unions, bureaucrats form a potent political force. These problems are compounded by a constitution that compels Congress and the president to share, and compete for, control over administration; the agents can play their multiple principals off against one another. The political attempts to come to terms with these problems have produced much of the complexity and diversity characterizing the administrative units added to the federal government over the past century.

Figure 8–1 Federal Civilian Employment, 1816–1997

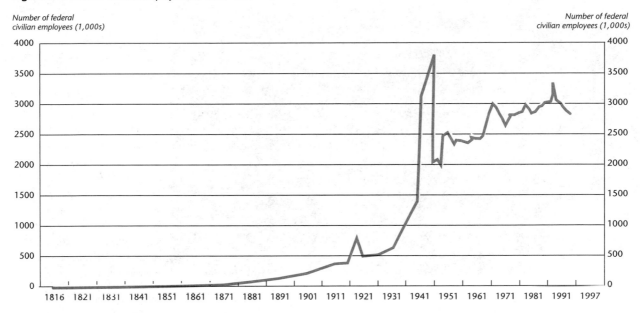

*Number of federal
civilian employees (1,000s)*

*Number of federal
civilian employees (1,000s)*

Sources: Harold W. Stanley and Richard G. Neimi. *Vital Statistics on American Politics, 1997–1998* (Washington, D.C.: CQ Press, 1998), 255–256; data for 1997 from
<http://www.opm.gov.feddata/factbook/1998/98FB-03.htm>.

Figure 8–2 Federal Civilian Employment Per Capita, 1821–1997

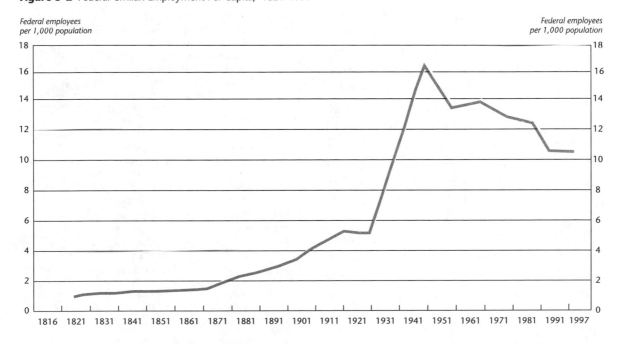

*Federal employees
per 1,000 population*

*Federal employees
per 1,000 population*

Sources: Calculated by the authors from Harold W. Stanley and Richard G. Neimi, *Vital Statistics on American Politics, 1997–1998* (Washington, D.C.: CQ Press, 1998),
255–258 and 353; data for 1997 calculated by the authors.

In the summer of 1997 federal workers moved into Washington's newest federal building, the largest to be built in half a century. According to one estimate, it contains as much space as a 150-story skyscraper. With great irony (and perhaps some hypocrisy), the new structure was named after Ronald Reagan, a politician who bashed the bureaucracy with special zeal.

politicians have found ways to expand the government's activities without expanding its workforce.

The Cabinet

Agencies that rise to the department level and gain a seat in the president's cabinet receive no special powers or privileges. Presidents can and do invite whomever they choose to serve in their cabinets regardless of whether they head a department. Over the years, however, political entrepreneurs have fought vigorously to confer departmental status on the agencies that administer policies affecting their constituents. They do this in part for a leg up in the competition for scarce resources and in part for symbolic recognition of the political centrality of their concerns. Each addition to the roster of cabinet-level agencies represents and helps to sustain the political triumph of a particular coalition. The history of the cabinet thus provides a concise, if incomplete, picture of the succession of social and economic interests that have become powerful enough to command this level of political recognition (Table 8–1).

Table 8–1 Origin of Cabinet-Level Departments, 1789–1988

1789	War, State, and Treasury (The attorney general, a part-time appointee, sat in on cabinet meetings as well.)
1798	Navy (split off from War)
1849	Interior
1870	Justice (Office of the Attorney General was established in 1789 and elevated to department status in 1870.)
1889	Agriculture (established in 1862 but not elevated to cabinet status until 1889)
1903	Labor (established as the Bureau of Labor in Interior in 1884; achieved cabinet status as the Department of Labor and Commerce in 1903; split from Commerce in 1913)
1903	Commerce (established as part of the Department of Labor and Commerce; split from Labor in 1913)
1947	Defense (combined War, Navy, and new Air Force Departments; initially called the National Military Establishment; renamed Defense in 1949)
1965	Housing and Urban Development
1966	Transportation
1977	Energy
1979	Health and Human Services (formerly Health, Education, and Welfare, 1953–1979)
1979	Education (established as a free-standing subcabinet department in 1867; placed in Interior a year later; eventually ended up in Health, Education, and Welfare, from which it split when raised to cabinet status)
1988	Veterans Affairs

Source: Compiled by the authors.

The Earliest Departments. Until 1849, Treasury, State, Navy, and War stood alone as cabinet-level departments. They were joined that year by the Department of the Interior, whose creation represented a major political victory for members of Congress from the western states. These westerners wanted the government to pay more attention to their constituents' concerns: public lands, natural resources, and Native American affairs. Its creation also was symbolic as well as practical acknowledgment of the continental expansion of the United States.

The Department of Justice achieved cabinet status in 1870 after Congress, in response to the Civil War, Reconstruction, and the problems created by the growth of industry, expanded the government's role in law enforcement. Among other things, the department took over all of the government's legal work, thereby ending the expensive practice of letting each department hire its own lawyers and allowing the ruling party to centralize the processing of patronage appointments of judges, U.S. attorneys, and U.S. marshals. The head of the Justice Department, the attorney general, has been a key political figure in most administrations. In 1961 President John Kennedy, recognizing the very sensitive nature of the office, entrusted it to his brother, Robert Kennedy.

Clientele Agencies. The Departments of Agriculture (1889), Labor (1903), and Commerce (1903) represented a new type of government agency altogether. Unlike the existing departments which served general social purposes, each of the new departments was established to serve the particular **clientele** indicated by its title: farmers, labor unions, and business. In seeking department-level status, these clienteles were represented by sophisticated interest groups which lobbied intensely on their behalf (organized labor successfully insisted on the separation of "its" department from Commerce in 1913). The demand for such clientele agencies reflected the emerging national market economy and the industrial revolution's legacy of increasingly distinct economic interests.

With the advent of the new industrial economy, information became a valuable resource. Thus in their early years all three departments worked particularly hard to gather and disseminate the kinds of technical information needed by their clients. The Department of Agriculture helped farmers by sponsoring experiments; collecting, testing, and distributing new plants and seed varieties; and gathering crop and market statistics. Labor settled industrial disputes and looked out for workers' welfare, but also conducted economic research through its Bureau of Labor Statistics. Commerce sought to make American business more prosperous and competitive internationally by, among other activities, gathering and publishing commercially useful data. The Census Bureau came under its jurisdiction.

The Military Establishment. The Department of Defense (1947) was a legacy of the Second World War and the emergence of the United States as an international superpower. Until World War II the United States had maintained a very modest military establishment, except in times of war. Indeed, until the twentieth century state militias were the main sources of trained soldiers for wartime duties; the colonial experience had convinced Americans that large standing armies were tools of oppression. In 1796 the American army numbered 3,300, climbing to only 16,200 by the eve of the Civil War. During the war it expanded to more than 1 million, but a few years later it was back under 25,000. The army grew to 3.7 million during World War I but fell to 214,000 in 1920 and to 135,000 by 1932. Shifts in naval strength were less dramatic but followed a similar pattern.[14]

The enormous military machine assembled to fight World War II—8.3 million soldiers, a 2,800-ship navy, an air corps of 2.4 million men, and 80,000 planes—also quickly shrank after 1945, but it remained much larger than in the prewar period. With the onset of the cold war, it was expected to remain large indefinitely.[15] For U.S. military and civilian leaders, World War II was instructive: only with a unified command of all military forces could the government coordinate the land, sea, and air opera-

The Pentagon, said to be the world's largest office building, is the only U.S. government departmental headquarters located outside the District of Columbia.

tions essential for modern warfare. In 1947 Congress, acting on this knowledge despite considerable resistance (the navy in particular resented losing full-fledged departmental status), subordinated the Departments of the Army, Navy, and Air Force to a single cabinet-level Department of Defense, headquartered in a five-sided building across the Potomac River from Washington. From then on, the Pentagon became the symbol of the large, expensive military responsibilities assumed by the United States as a world power.

Extension of the Federal Domain. Established in 1979, the Department of Health and Human Services (HHS) embodies another major transformation in the government's role. HHS, like its predecessor, the Department of Health, Education, and Welfare (HEW), is an umbrella department containing numerous social welfare agencies and programs that have their roots in the New Deal and its aftermath. The establishment of HEW in 1953 by a Republican administration and Congress was a pivotal political statement: the Republicans had finally accepted the legitimacy of the federal government's expanded role in

providing for the economic welfare of Americans; their party would not repeal the New Deal but only manage it more efficiently. The creation of HEW also was a Republican ploy to reduce the autonomy of officials appointed by the Democrats during the New Deal.

The remaining three departments also consolidated expansions of the federal domain while making pointed political statements. The Department of Housing and Urban Development (HUD) embodied the commitments of the Kennedy and Johnson administrations to reviving inner-city neighborhoods and solving urban housing problems. HUD also was linked to the civil rights movement. President Kennedy campaigned for the department in part so he could appoint Robert C. Weaver as its head, thereby seating the first African American in the cabinet. It was President Lyndon Johnson, however, who finally made the appointment after he convinced Congress to authorize HUD in 1965.

The new Department of Transportation became home to all the agencies established piecemeal over the years to promote the different forms of transportation:

highways, air carriers, railroads, sea transport, and, later, urban mass transit. These agencies often had worked at cross purposes—for example, the agency responsible for locating new highways would labor in ignorance of the plans of the agency responsible for locating new airports. The department was created in 1966, again at the instigation of President Johnson, who sought better coordination of the plans and policies for the various interlocking transportation modes. Congress agreed, but only after carefully limiting the department's authority over federal spending for transportation projects. Members were not about to reduce their own influence over a domain so rich in "pork."

The Department of Energy embodied another effort to coordinate policy, this time for sources of energy (coal, oil, natural gas, atomic, hydroelectric, geothermal, solar). Its establishment in 1977 was President Jimmy Carter's political response to the energy shortages of the early 1970s, a declaration of his administration's commitment to assuring the nation adequate supplies of the energy essential to modern American life.

The Symbolism of Cabinet Status. The creation of the Departments of Education in 1979 and Veterans Affairs in 1988 was almost entirely symbolic. By pushing through the legislation that established a cabinet-level Department of Education, Carter kept his promise to the teachers groups whose support had been crucial to his bid for the White House. The elevation of the Veterans Administration to the Department of Veterans Affairs and to cabinet status was, among other things, a belated symbolic bow to veterans of the long, contentious Vietnam War as well as an effort by the Republican Reagan administration to woo the veteran vote. Neither department came with much in the way of new programs. Education took over programs and bureaus from HEW and other agencies; Veterans continued to do what it had done as an independent executive agency. Symbolism, then, played a major role in the creation of both departments. Proponents of the departments also hoped that cabinet status would

Table 8–2 Cabinet Department Staff and Budget, 1996

Department	Personnel (thousands)	Budget (billion dollars)
Agriculture	106.5	52.5
Commerce	34.8	3.8
Defense	749.5	258.3
Education	4.6	30.0
Energy	17.1	14.5
Health and Human Services	59.5	339.5
Housing and Urban Development	10.9	27.5
Interior	67.9	6.7
Justice	117.3	14.3
Labor	15.8	30.5
State	24.1	5.2
Transportation	64.2	39.8
Treasury	140.4	379.3
Veterans Affairs	243.3	39.3

Source: Bureau of the Census, *Statistical Abstract of the United States: 1998* (Washington, D.C.: Government Printing Office, 1998), 341, 353.

strengthen each department's interests in the battle for government's limited resources, including the president's attention. But symbolism cuts both ways, to be sure. Republican leaders since Ronald Reagan have sought unsuccessfully to dismantle the Department of Education because of its largely Democratic clientele.

Some divisions of present-day departments are as prominent as the departments themselves—for example, the Federal Bureau of Investigation, or FBI (Justice), the Census Bureau (Commerce), the National Park Service (Interior), and the U.S. Coast Guard (Transportation). Of the departments, the big spenders are Defense, HHS with its Medicare program, and Treasury which pays the interest on the public debt (see Table 8–2). Altogether the executive branch departments account for about 63 percent of the civilian government workforce and about 79 percent of the more than $1.7 trillion the federal government spends annually. The rest is accounted for by a host of agencies which, for a variety of calculated political reasons, have been placed outside the mainline departments.

Non-Cabinet Agencies

The expansion of the federal government has not been confined to cabinet-level executive departments. Since the Civil War, Congress and the president have created an additional set of administrative bodies to make and carry out national policy. Most fall into one of three general categories: independent executive agencies, regulatory agencies, and government corporations.

Independent Executive Agencies. Executive agencies are placed outside departments for one of several reasons, all political. Presidents promoting new initiatives that demand quick action may want to avoid placing bureaucratic layers between them and the responsible agency. For example, President Kennedy kept his cherished Peace Corps out of the stodgy and unsympathetic State Department. When the Soviet Union launched its space vehicle *Sputnik* in 1957, the National Aeronautics and Space Administration (NASA), established in 1958, was the administrative response. Its status as an independent executive agency reflected both the space program's urgency and the politicians' desire to keep it in civilian hands. NASA proved to be a brilliant organizational success, fulfilling President Kennedy's audacious dream of landing a man on the moon by 1969. Agencies also may report directly to the president to enhance the agency's prestige (for example, the Environmental Protection Agency, a candidate for cabinet status during the Clinton administration) or effectiveness (the Federal Emergency Management Agency, which, as we saw in Chapter 3, coordinates federal responses to natural disasters—occasions for conspicuous displays of presidential leadership).

In keeping with the president's role as commander in chief, the Central Intelligence Agency, U.S. Arms Control and Disarmament Agency, and Selective Service System all report directly to the president. Their independent status is intended, in part, to keep important defense-related activities—intelligence gathering, arms control negotiations, and the draft—under predominantly civilian control.

The independent executive agencies, as organizations,

look much like the divisions within regular executive departments. They typically are headed by presidential appointees, subject to Senate approval, who serve "at the pleasure of the president"—meaning the president can dismiss them at any time. One example is the Social Security Administration, which has a budget larger than any department but Treasury ($358.4 billion in 1997) and was part of HHS until 1995. The Veterans Administration was an independent executive agency before it was elevated to the Department of Veterans Affairs in 1988. The United States Information Agency (USIA) was also independent until 1997, when Republican Jesse Helms of North Carolina, chairman of the Senate Foreign Relations Committee, insisted that, for economy's sake, it be put under the State Department.

Independent Regulatory Commissions. Unlike the independent executive agencies, independent regulatory commissions are designed to maintain their independence from the president and the executive departments. Congress adopted the commission form of administration to cope with new problems of delegation. The emergence after the Civil War of an industrial economy with a national market gave rise to economic dislocations and disputes on a scale too wide to be managed, as in the past, by local authorities. As a result, the railroads and steel, oil, and banking industries became targets for national regulation. But Congress could not and did not want to do the regulating itself; the issues were too many, too technical, too dynamic, and too fraught with political conflict. Some of its constitutional authority "to regulate Commerce . . . among the several States" (Article I, Section 8) had to be delegated—and in a way that allowed far more administrative discretion than Congress was accustomed to granting to executive agencies. The regulatory commission represents Congress's attempt to hedge against the potential political costs of delegation by restricting the influence of presidents and party politics on regulatory decisions. Table 8–3 lists the most important independent regulatory agencies.

Typically, independent regulatory commissions are run

Table 8–3 Independent Regulatory Agencies

Agency	Year Established	Term of Service	Service at President's Discretion?
Commodity Futures Trading Commission (CFTC)	1975	5	No
Consumer Product Safety Commission (CPSC)	1972	7	No
Equal Employment Opportunity Commission (EEOC)	1965	5	Yes
Federal Communications Commission (FCC)	1934	7	No
Federal Deposit Insurance Corporation (FDIC)	1933	6	No
Federal Election Commission (FEC)	1975	6	No
Federal Maritime Commission (FMC)	1961	5	No
Federal Reserve System (Fed)	1913	14	Yes
Federal Trade Commission (FTC)	1914	7	No
National Labor Relations Board (NLRB)	1935	5	No
National Transportation Safety Board (NTSB)	1966	5	Yes
Nuclear Regulatory Commission (NRC)	1975	5	No
Postal Rate Commission (PRC)	1970	6	No
Securities and Exchange Commission (SEC)	1934	5	Yes

On occasion, Congress does give the president greater than normal authority over regulatory bodies. Some agencies are governed by commissioners who serve at the president's pleasure. Other agencies, such as the Food and Drug Administration and the Occupational Health and Safety Administration, are ordinary bureaus housed in executive departments and are subject to the normal executive authority. Congress, however, is not without means for keeping these agencies at least as responsive to it as to the president. But sometimes it chooses not to. A major reason for delegating authority to an independent agency is to avoid direct responsibility for unpopular decisions. In 1887 Congress set up the now-defunct Interstate Commerce Commission to regulate the railroads in part because any decision made about shipping rates would likely anger some politically potent interest. The Postal Rate Commission takes the heat for increases in postage rates. The most striking case, however, is the Federal Reserve Board, which makes decisions of enormous consequence for the entire economy (see box "Insulating the Fed"). In this case and in others, an agency's independence helps to insulate the president and Congress from the political fallout from unpopular decisions, explaining why both have been willing to accept this form of administration.

Over the years, the government's regulatory reach expanded in roughly three waves. The first, which swept in during the late nineteenth and early twentieth centuries, was regulation of the railroads (Interstate Commerce Commission), trusts (Federal Trade Commission), and monetary system (Federal Reserve System). The second,

by boards of commissioners (usually five in number) who conduct their decision making by majority rule rather than by single directors. The commissioners are appointed by the president, with the consent of the Senate, to serve fixed, staggered terms of no less than five years. Terms are staggered so presidents cannot stack the deck in their favor by new appointments; terms of five or more years ensure that service exceeds any single presidential term. In most cases the president cannot dismiss appointees without cause—evidence of some sort of malfeasance—and therefore cannot simply replace commissioners whose decisions are displeasing. Appointments are bipartisan, with no party permitted to have more than a one-vote majority. In theory, this keeps presidents from loading the agency up with their own partisans, but, in practice, they always can find someone in the other party who shares their regulatory goals.

LOGIC OF POLITICS
INSULATING THE FED

Sometimes the task given an independent regulatory commission is such a hot potato that members of Congress, the president, and even lobbyists maintain a hands-off policy. When the task is the very sensitive one of setting a nation's economic course, the logic of insulating the commission from political pressures makes imminent sense. The Federal Reserve System, popularly known as the Fed, is the most independent and powerful of the regulatory commissions. Its main responsibility is to make monetary policy.

The decisions handed down by the Fed influence the country's supply of credit and level of interest rates, which in turn affect the rates of inflation, unemployment, and economic growth. During periods of economic recession and high unemployment, the Fed buys securities from banks, increasing the banks' reserves so that they have more money to loan. Interest rates then fall, stimulating investment that leads to faster economic growth and job formation. This makes everyone happy. When a booming economy and low unemployment bring (or sometimes even threaten) inflation, the Fed puts on the brakes by selling securities, which reduces the supply of money banks can loan, thereby raising interest rates. Profits fall, investment declines, the economy slows, and some people lose their jobs. This does not make everyone happy.

Federal Reserve Chairman Alan Greenspan

Members of the Fed's Board of Governors are appointed by the president to a single fourteen-year term. The board's chair, who dominates its deliberations and is appointed for a renewable four-year term, is one of the most influential people in government. During the long economic expansion and stock market boom of the 1990s, the financial community scrutinized Chairman Alan Greenspan's every comment for omens about the future of interest rates, and every hint of an increase brought a sharp (but often temporary) drop in the price of stocks and bonds.

All members of the Federal Reserve Board serve at the pleasure of the president, but presidents do not try to exert authority over the Fed because they do not want responsibility for its decisions. Neither does Congress, which even allows the Fed to finance itself through its own investments. Politically insulated, the Fed is left alone to take the heat for the painful steps needed to protect the nation's economy. Even when the president and Congress are genuinely unhappy with the Fed's actions, they dare not do much beyond grumbling about it because any real action to curb the Fed might spook the financial markets.

Source: Jeffrey E. Cohen, *Politics and Economic Policy in the United States* (Boston: Houghton Mifflin, 1997), 215–221.

Figure 8–3 The Growth of Federal Regulation, 1940–1998

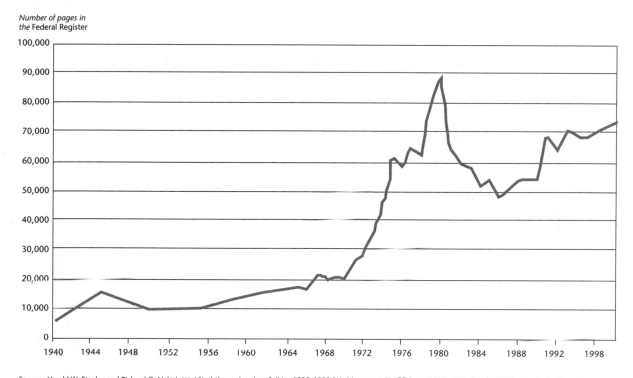

*Number of pages in
the* Federal Register

Sources: Harold W. Stanley and Richard G. Nelmi, *Vital Statistics on American Politics, 1997–1998* (Washington, D.C.: CQ Press, 1998), 258; data for 1998 compiled by the authors from the 1998 *Federal Register.*

also economic in focus, occurred during the 1930s as part of the Roosevelt administration's response to the depression. The government assumed responsibility for, among other things, the integrity of the banking system (Federal Deposit Insurance Corporation), the stock market (Securities and Exchange Commission), and labor relations (National Labor Relations Board). The third wave, occurring in the 1960s and 1970s, extended federal regulation on behalf of consumers (Consumer Product Safety Commission), motorists (National Transportation Safety Board), the environment (Environmental Protection Agency, Nuclear Regulatory Commission), and civil rights (Equal Employment Opportunity Commission).

The third wave did the most to expand the scope of regulation (see Figure 8–3). The dramatic growth in regulation during the 1970s, as measured by the number of pages in the *Federal Register* (which publishes all administrative rules that have the force of law), was followed by a drop in the 1980s after the deregulation of the transportation and telecommunications sectors and the 1981 arrival of the Reagan administration, which was ideologically hostile to regulation.

Variations in the structure, duties, and procedures of independent regulatory agencies, as of all other government agencies, stem from the politics of their creation. Agencies embody the objectives, strategies, and uncertainties of the coalitions that bring them into being. Because the parties making up these coalitions have different objectives, agencies often are given potentially incompatible missions. For example, the Interstate Commerce Commission was supposed not only to regulate railroads in the public interest, but also to ensure they remained profitable. Interests opposed to regulation sometimes lose the battle over creating an agency but win the war by strangling it with "fragmented authority, labyrinthine procedures, mechanisms of political intervention, and other structures that subvert the bureaucracy's performance and open it up to attack."[16] In other words, unresolved political conflicts may be built into an agency's structure, where they will continue to play themselves out in a new venue.

Government Corporations. When Congress puts the government in the business of delivering the kinds of services usually provided by private corporations, it sometimes imitates the corporate form of administration as well. Like private corporations, government corporations are typically run by a chief executive officer, or CEO, under the supervision of a board of directors or commissioners. The boards are chosen in the same manner as members of regulatory commissions. Government corporations can buy and sell property, lend and borrow money, and sue or be sued like any other business. Congress, however, may put any constraints it chooses on their organization or activities.

Besides the U.S. Postal Service, the most important of the government corporations are the Tennessee Valley Authority and the National Railroad Passenger Corporation, or Amtrak. The TVA was created in 1933, during the New Deal, to develop electric power, water transportation, and agriculture in the Tennessee Valley area, which at the time was poor and economically backward. Amtrak, launched in 1970, represents Congress's effort to maintain intercity rail passenger service, which had been dying out for want of investment and competition from air, bus, and auto travel. The U.S. Postal Service actually predates the Constitution; it was established in 1777 by the Second Continental Congress. Known then as the Post

Office Department, it was for much of its history the largest government agency delivering the most familiar government service. It also was a major source of congressional patronage during the heyday of patronage-based party politics in the latter decades of the nineteenth century (see Chapter 12). But politics did not promote efficiency or innovation, and by the post–World War II economic expansion, the system's inadequacies had become quite evident. The agency was radically reorganized as a government corporation in 1970.

Indirect Administration. Over the past half-century, federal spending in real (inflation-adjusted) dollars has increased by 600 percent, and federal programs and activities have mushroomed. Yet the federal workforce has scarcely grown at all (Figure 8–1), and, indeed, as a proportion of the population (and total labor force) it has been falling for more than forty years (Figure 8–2). How can this be? The answer, as we saw in Chapter 3, is that many federal policies and programs are administered by someone else—mostly the states. Major social welfare programs such as Medicaid and Temporary Assistance for Needy Families are administered by state governments. State and local agencies also carry out some of the federal government's regulatory work, such as enforcing air pollution rules and occupational health and safety standards. By delegating administrative duties to state and local government agencies, Congress is able to add programs, which voters like, without increasing the federal bureaucracy, which voters do not like.

The federal government also contracts extensively with private nonprofit organizations to implement programs. For example, in the 1970s the Labor Department's Youth Incentive Entitlement project was administered entirely by the Manpower Demonstration Research Corporation, a private nonprofit corporation set up just for this purpose. More than 80 percent of the federal government's scientific research funds are administered by nonfederal institutions, including universities, research laboratories, and think tanks.[17] Contracting, then, is another way in which the federal government can take on more tasks without hiring more personnel. For politicians, the payoff can be significant. They can claim credit for reducing the size of the federal bureaucracy without reducing popular programs and services. President Clinton made just such a claim during his successful 1996 reelection campaign.

Who Controls the Bureaucracy?

The more things elected representatives want the government to do, the more discretionary authority they must give to administrators. In recent years the proliferation of government agencies and programs has led critics to charge that Congress has abdicated its authority to the president, to an out-of-control bureaucracy, or to the clients the agencies serve.[18] The charges deserve to be taken seriously. Congress, in fact, has delegated a wide range of tasks to the executive branch, often with only the vaguest guidelines on how authority is to be exercised. In 1914, for example, Congress authorized the Federal Trade Commission to enforce laws against "unfair methods of competition . . . and unfair or deceptive acts or practices" without defining what these methods, acts, or practices were. At times, government agencies and programs have served private interests almost exclusively; the history of the Department of Agriculture is littered with examples. Regulatory commissions have sometimes served as the handmaidens of the interests they are supposed to regulate in the public interest. Until the mid-1970s, for example, the Civil Aeronautics Board fought valiantly to protect the major airlines from competition. Congress, though, often pays little attention to what its bureaucratic agents are doing; administrative oversight is not a high priority (see Chapter 6). This being said, congressional majorities have found many ways in which to delegate authority to the executive branch without abdicating control. Legislators are fully aware of principal–agent dilemmas (though they do not think of them in those terms) and have strategies to cope with them.

Methods of Congressional Control

Congress operates from a position of overwhelming strength in its relationship to administrative agencies. It creates and empowers them by ordinary legislation, and it can eliminate or change them in the same way. Most agencies require new budget appropriations every year to continue functioning. Congress also has a say in who is appointed to head departments and bureaus. Indeed, some programs are set up with the explicit understanding that a particular individual will or, in some cases, will not be chosen to run it. Any president who wants an agency to thrive will choose appointees who can get on well with the agency's handlers in Congress. As a result of these *indirect methods of control*, bureaucratic agents recognize that, at some level, the very existence of their agency (and jobs) depends on at least the toleration of their congressional principals even when the principals seem to be paying no attention to what they are doing (see box "William Clay's Revenge").

Congress also deploys more *direct methods of control* to keep its bureaucratic agents in line. Among them are:

• Hearings and investigations, in which bureaucrats are called before subcommittees to explain and defend their decisions, and outsiders are sometimes invited to criticize them. The 1997 Senate hearings on the IRS are an example. Most agencies must testify annually about their activities before the House Appropriations subcommittee that has jurisdiction over their budgets.

• Mandatory reports, in which Congress requires executive agencies, even the president, to report on programs. For example, under an antidrug bill passed in 1986 the president is required to submit a report every March 1 on whether certain nations where illegal narcotics are produced or transshipped have "cooperated fully" with U.S. efforts to stem the drug traffic. Countries not certified as cooperating face a cutoff in U.S. aid.

• **Legislative vetoes,** which allow one or both houses of Congress (sometimes even individual House and Senate committees) to veto by majority vote an agency's poli-

WILLIAM CLAY'S REVENGE

In 1996 the Social and Behavioral Sciences Division of the National Science Foundation (NSF) awarded a $174,000 grant to two political scientists, Sandy Maisel of Colby College and Walter Stone of the University of Colorado, to study the recruitment of congressional candidates. Maisel and Stone were particularly interested in learning why qualified and promising potential candidates often failed to run. They began their study by asking local observers in two hundred congressional districts across the country to identify potentially viable House candidates, whom they would then interview about what shaped their decisions to run or not run for Congress.

House members soon learned that a couple of professors were nosing around their districts, asking why more and better candidates did not run for Congress. They were not pleased. Most displeased was William Clay, a longtime Democratic representative from Missouri. Clay was not worried about potential opponents; he had always won election by overwhelming margins. But it was rumored he hoped to pass his seat on to his son, a state senator, and he was furious that someone was stirring up potential rivals.

At Clay's request, Jerry Lewis, a California Republican, offered an amendment to an appropriations bill reducing NSF's 1998 budget by exactly $174,000 as punishment for funding the study. Even some of the agency's strongest supporters joined the criticism, notably George Brown, a California Democrat. Here is what they had to say on the floor of Congress during debate of the amendment:

Mr. BROWN of California. . . . This matter . . . has been brought to my attention very forcibly by a number of my friends and colleagues across party lines here in the House. I have been torn by the need to make a decision as to what is happening here. Let me explain why. Generally speaking, I support good peer reviewed social science research by the National Science Foundation.

Mr. LEWIS of California. I know the gentleman does.

Mr. BROWN of California. In this particular case, Mr. Chairman, I think there was the most inept foresight with regard to the impact of a research grant that I have ever seen. I think that we do need to send a message to the National Science Foundation that on issues of great delicacy, which they should have perceived this would be, there needs to be some action to prepare the proper attitude within Members of Congress for this sort of thing. This was not done in this particular case.

I hope that the action that the gentleman contemplates will convey the message to the National Science Foundation that while we support good research, including good social science research, we think that there should be some good judgment displayed over there in setting the groundwork for such items that may turn out to be controversial with Members of Congress.

Mr. LEWIS of California. I believe the gentleman has capsulized my intent. A message is really my intent.

Mr. CLAY of Missouri. Mr. Chairman, I rise in support of the gentleman's amendment. . . . I have been very supportive down the years of the National Science Foundation. But this particular kind of incident has caused me to have second thoughts about the wisdom of all the grants that they have been permitting.

If there is one thing we do not need in this country, it is . . . more people to run for Congress than presently run for Congress. . . .

The amendment was adopted by voice vote. Message sent—loud and clear.

Source: *Congressional Record*, July 16, 1997, H5323.

cy proposals. Although the Supreme Court in 1983 declared the legislative veto unconstitutional because it violates the separation of powers, Congress continues to enact legislative vetoes, and agencies continue to send decisions to Congress for prior approval, knowing that Congress has other sanctions at its disposal if they do not.

• Committee and conference reports, which often instruct agencies how Congress expects them to use their "discretion." Though not legally binding, bureaucrats ignore such instructions at their peril.

• Inspectors general, with independent offices (outside the normal bureaucratic chain of command) in virtually every agency, who audit its books and investigate its activities on Congress's behalf.

• The General Accounting Office, with a staff of more than five thousand, which audits programs and agencies and reports on their performance to Congress.

A variety of *procedural devices* also are available to Congress for monitoring and controlling bureaucrats. Congress may not have the capacity to specify what bureaucrats are to do, but it can tell them how they have to do it. The broadest procedural requirements are found in the Administrative Procedures Act (APA) of 1946, which covers all rule making by government agencies unless an agency's legislative authorization specifies otherwise.

Congress normally regulates by delegating broad grants of authority to regulatory agencies and letting them fill in the details by making rules. These rules have the force of law, just as if Congress itself had enacted them. When an agency wants to make a rule, it first must give public notice in the *Federal Register*, outlining the proposed rule, disclosing the data and analysis on which it is based, and inviting written comments from the public. Public hearings may be held as well. The agency then responds to the public comments in compiling the rule-making record, which will be needed to justify the agency's decision if it is challenged in federal court.

These procedures serve several purposes. For one thing, they make rule making a public act, observable by

members of Congress and anyone else who may be interested. They also give members of Congress—and agency officials—advance notice of the political fallout that any particular regulation would produce, allowing them to avoid political trouble. When the Federal Trade Commission proposed rules in 1982 requiring more complete disclosure of funeral costs and used car defects, undertakers and used car dealers protested loudly. Members of Congress, who were quickly reminded just how many undertakers and car dealers they had in their districts and how influential they were, forced the agency to back down.[19] In other words, the APA sets up a fire alarm mechanism that alerts members of Congress when delegated authority is being exercised in a way that might hurt them politically. In effect, it recruits interested outsiders to monitor the activities of bureaucratic agents on Congress's behalf.

When it chooses, Congress can fine-tune procedures to guarantee a desired balance of interests in regulatory policy making. For example, the National Environmental Policy Act of 1969 requires federal agencies, as well as many other public and private entities, to consider what effects all major undertakings (construction projects, landfills, dredging schemes, and so forth) might have on the environment and to prepare environmental impact statements specifying the environmental effects of proposed projects and their alternatives. The act also gives private citizens legal **standing** to bring suit in federal court to challenge the adequacy of impact statements and, indirectly, the proposals they were intended to justify. Standing enables environmental groups and their lawyers to enforce compliance through the courts, assuring that environmental interests will not be ignored. In the 1970s Congress even gave some agencies budgets to pay the costs for **intervenor** groups to participate in the rule-making process. The Federal Trade Commission, for example, was required to pay the costs of appearances by groups seeking to persuade the commission to regulate advertising on children's Saturday morning television programs.[20]

Rules and Regulations

Federal Register

Vol. 64, No. 105

Wednesday, June 2, 1999

This section of the FEDERAL REGISTER contains regulatory documents having general applicability and legal effect, most of which are keyed to and codified in the Code of Federal Regulations, which is published under 50 titles pursuant to 44 U.S.C. 1510.

The Code of Federal Regulations is sold by the Superintendent of Documents. Prices of new books are listed in the first FEDERAL REGISTER issue of each week.

DEPARTMENT OF AGRICULTURE

Animal and Plant Health Inspection Service

7 CFR Part 301

[Docket No. 96–016–24]

RIN 0579–AA83

Karnal Bunt Regulated Areas

AGENCY: Animal and Plant Health Inspection Service, USDA.

ACTION: Final rule.

SUMMARY: We are adopting as a final rule, with changes, an interim rule that amended the Karnal bunt regulations by modifying the criteria for classifying regulated areas and by modifying the classification of restricted areas. The interim rule required that a bunted wheat kernel be found in or associated with a field within an area before that area would be designated as a regulated area. The interim rule also established separate restricted areas for seed and for regulated articles other than seed. The actions taken in the interim rule were necessary because tests currently available for use in identifying spores do not allow us to differentiate between small numbers of Karnal bunt spores and the spores of an as yet unnamed, but widely distributed, ryegrass smut. The interim rule had the effect of removing some areas in Arizona and California from the list of regulated areas and relieving restrictions on the movement of grain and other regulated articles from additional areas in Arizona, California, New Mexico, and Texas.

EFFECTIVE DATE: June 2, 1999.

FOR FURTHER INFORMATION CONTACT: Mr. Mike Stefan, Operations Officer, Domestic and Emergency Operations, PPQ, APHIS, 4700 River Road Unit 134, Riverdale, MD 20737–1236, (301) 734–8247.

SUPPLEMENTARY INFORMATION: Karnal bunt is a fungal disease of wheat (*Triticum aestivum*), durum wheat (*Triticum durum*), and triticale (*Triticum aestivum* X *Secale cereale*), a hybrid of wheat and rye. Karnal bunt is caused by the smut fungus *Tilletia indica* (Mitra) Mundkur and is spread by spores, primarily through the movement of infected seed. In the absence of measures taken by the U.S. Department of Agriculture (USDA) to prevent its spread, the establishment of Karnal bunt in the United States could have significant consequences with regard to the export of wheat to international markets. The regulations regarding Karnal bunt are set forth in 7 CFR 301.89–1 through 301.89–14.

In an interim rule effective on April 25, 1997, and published in the **Federal Register** on May 1, 1997 (62 FR 23620–23628, Docket No. 96–016–19), we amended the Karnal bunt regulations by modifying the criteria for classifying regulated areas. We required that a bunted wheat kernel be found in or associated with a field within an area before that area would be designated as a regulated area. In that interim rule, we also modified the classification of restricted areas by establishing separate restricted areas for seed and for regulated articles other than seed.

We solicited comments concerning the interim rule for 60 days ending June 2, 1997. We received 13 comments by that date. They were from five State agricultural agencies, three associations representing grain growers and processors, a food corporation, a grain handler, a wheat grower, and a scientific society. One of the commenters fully supported the interim rule as written. The remaining 12 commenters expressed concerns or made suggestions regarding certain aspects of the interim rule, although 8 of those commenters did offer their support for the changes contained in the interim rule. The issues raised by those 12 commenters are discussed in detail below.

Comment: The definition of *infestation (infected)* in § 301.89–1 of the regulations states that an area is infected if any stage of the fungus *Tilletia indica* (Mitra) Mundkur is present. Section 301.89–3(e) lists several criteria that are used to classify regulated areas, with the classification of regulated areas being based on the discovery of bunted kernels. If the

discovery of bunted kernels is now the criterion on which an area is regulated, rather than the detection of spores, should the definition of *infestation (infected)* be modified to reflect that change?

Response: If the discovery of bunted kernels was the sole criterion on which an area's regulatory status was based, it would be appropriate to modify the definition of *infestation (infected)* as suggested by the commenter. However, § 301.89–3(e) still provides for the designation of regulated areas based on the detection of spores in a field when that field is found to be associated with grain at a handling facility containing a bunted wheat kernel. Therefore, it would be inaccurate to base the definition of *infestation (infected)* only on the detection of bunted kernels.

Comment: Is the designation of regulated areas in § 301.89–3(f) valid only for the 1996–1997 crop production year? Since those regulated areas differ from those regulated in the 1995–1996 crop year, will the 1996–1997 regulated areas be modified for the 1997–1998 crop year? If so, what criteria will be used to define those areas?

Response: We do not intend to update the list of regulated areas in § 301.89–3(f) on a "crop year" basis as envisioned by the commenter. Rather, we will continue to amend the list of regulated areas when the situation warrants, removing areas from the list when we determine that it is no longer necessary to regulate them to prevent the spread of Karnal bunt and adding new areas to the list based upon the detection of Karnal bunt. The criteria used to define regulated areas are found in § 301.89–3.

Comment: In § 301.89–3(d), we would suggest that State plant regulatory officials be included in the written notification of the designation of an area as a regulated area. It is vital that State and Federal agencies interact closely with industry on this issue.

Response: Paragraph (d) of § 301.89–3 deals with the temporary designation of a nonregulated area as a regulated area. Because the movement of regulated articles from the temporarily designated regulated area will be subject to the regulations, the written notification is directed to the person most immediately affected by the designation of an area as a regulated area, i.e., the owner or person in possession of the land or, in the case of

---

How, then, do we reconcile this picture with news clips of members of Congress portraying themselves as enthusiastic bureaucracy bashers on the principle that "no politician ever lost votes by denouncing the bureaucracy"?[21] They are, in fact, the principal architects of the bureaucracy, and its design generally suits the political purposes of the congressional coalitions that create and sustain its various components. It is no accident that the division of responsibilities among agencies in the executive branch tends to mirror the division of legislative turf in the congressional committee and subcommittee systems. This is not to say, however, that Congress has exclusive control over administration. The president and the federal courts also have a major say, and Congress itself is subject to pressure from interest groups, the media, and constituents on how it deals with administrative issues. Moreover, the fragmented political system can give agencies considerable room to maneuver in pursuit of their own ends.

The President and the Bureaucracy

The president, who as the chief executive is charged by the Constitution with seeing that the laws are faithfully executed, sits officially atop the bureaucratic hierarchies of the executive branch. The heads of departments and other executive agencies and their immediate subordinates—the undersecretaries, assistant secretaries, bureau chiefs—serve at the president's pleasure, as do members of some of the governing boards, commissions, foundations, institutes, and public corporations that make up the rest of the executive branch. With their duty to implement laws, power to appoint senior government officials, and other congressionally conferred grants of authority, presidents have enormous administrative responsibilities. The institutional realities, however, impose formidable barriers to presidential influence—let alone control—over the sprawling federal bureaucracy.

The Powers of Appointment and Approval. Presidents pursue their policy goals by appointing senior officials loyal to them and their ideas. For example, Ronald Reagan's appointment in 1981 of conservatives Anne Gorsuch Burford to head the Environmental Protection Agency and Michael Connolly as general counsel to the Equal Employment Opportunity Commission resulted in sharp reductions in these agencies' regulatory activities.[22] Congress, however, may not be content to sit on the sidelines, and presidents may find their influence diluted. Indeed, if enough members of Congress oppose the objectives of the president's appointees, they can force the agency back into line. Both Burford and Connolly eventually resigned under heavy congressional and public criticism for failure to carry out their agencies' mandates.

Senatorial Approval. Presidential appointments require Senate approval, and senators make the most of their authority. Rarely does the full Senate reject a nominee, but it is not unusual for an appointment to be withdrawn after an unfavorable committee vote or, earlier, after unfavorable publicity during a hearing on the appointment. In 1993 President Clinton had to withdraw his first two nominations for attorney general, corporate lawyer Zoë Baird and then federal judge Kimba Wood, when the media reported that both had employed illegal immigrants for household duties. Also in 1993 he withdrew the nomination of Lani Guinier to head the Civil Rights Division of the Justice Department when she came under fire for academic writings arguing that majority rule deprived minorities of a fair share of political power. Many nominations are not even made because presidents anticipate Senate opposition and decide the fight is not worth the political resources it would take to win. Senators also use the approval process to extract promises from appointees about what they will or will not do in office, further limiting administrative discretion.

In addition to satisfying the Senate, the president may have to satisfy the clientele groups who care intensely about who heads "their" agency or risk alienating the groups and weakening the agency. Thus the secretary of labor needs the nod of the AFL-CIO, at least if the presi-

When the Republican leadership in the Senate blocked confirmation of President Bill Clinton's nomination of the openly gay James Hormel to serve as ambassador to Luxembourg, the president took advantage of his constitutional authority to make appointments during a congressional recess and named Hormel to his post in June 1999. Recess appointments expire automatically at the end of a two-year Congress, which is when Hormel's appointment might have ended in any event since Clinton will leave office in 2001.

dent is a Democrat; the chair of the Federal Reserve Board must measure up on Wall Street; and the head of the National Institutes of Health must have the respect of the academic and research communities. Clientele groups of the president also may benefit from the appointments process. Indeed, presidents often use appointments as symbolic payoffs to important factions in their party's electoral coalition. In 1993 Bill Clinton took extraordinary pains to assemble an administration that "looked like America," insisting on racial, gender, and geographic di-

versity; his third and successful nominee for attorney general, Janet Reno, also was a woman. In making appointments for any reason, however, the president also must weigh competence; policy expertise may not be essential, but no president wants to be embarrassed by appointees too ignorant or unskilled to manage their agencies' business.

Some presidents, notably Richard Nixon and Ronald Reagan, have tried to ignore other criteria in order to stack their administrations with personal or ideological loyalists, but with only partial success. Sheer numbers pose a serious problem. Because presidents are responsible for filling more than four thousand positions, they must rely on the advice of others and an imperfect screening process to fill most of the slots. They also must accept the fact that most appointees will be total strangers to them. In short, the president as principal can make only limited use of the power of appointment to guard against political losses.

Once appointed, even initially loyal officials tend to "marry the natives," becoming agents of their departments or bureaus rather than maintaining their role as agent of the president. Political appointees typically serve short terms—about two years—and often are unfamiliar with the rules, programs, and political relationships of the organizations they lead. To avoid disastrous mistakes, let alone to achieve anything positive, they need the candid advice and active cooperation of permanent civil servants. In return, they can offer effective advocacy of their agency's interests in the battles waged over programs and resources within both the administration and the Congress.[23] In doing so, they may come to identify with the success of their agency rather than with that of the president, and thus pursue more programs and larger budgets—or defend programs and budgets from cuts—without regard for how their agency fits into the administration's overall program. Department and bureau heads also wield powers delegated directly to them by Congress, allowing them to bypass the president and further promote their independence of the president and dependence on Congress.

Mechanisms for Presidential Supervision. In an attempt to gain some control over the far-flung activities of the federal bureaucracy, presidents have built up their own supervisory bureaucracy in the Executive Office of the President (analyzed more fully in Chapter 7). The president's primary control instrument is the Office of Management and Budget (OMB), which oversees agency budgets and rule making and assembles the annual budget for all government agencies that the president is required to submit annually to Congress. The budget process allows presidents to emphasize their own priorities and policy goals. When Congress ignores presidents' recommendations—and it frequently does so—presidents may use the veto to nudge that recalcitrant body closer to their own budget preferences, as President Clinton did in 1995 (see Chapter 7).

For bureaucrats, favorable treatment in the president's budget is worth pursuing—so they have an incentive to keep the White House happy. But this inherently political relationship works two ways: the White House is much more likely to get its way if it can persuade political appointees and permanent civil servants that their best interests are served by doing what it wants. Because presidents do not hold undisputed authority over the executive branch, bargaining or indirect manipulation through mobilized interest groups or congressional allies is often more effective than issuing orders.[24]

The Courts and the Bureaucracy

The third main branch of government, the judiciary, also shares authority over the bureaucracy. The United States inherited the common law principle that the government, no less than individual citizens, is bound by law. Under this principle, a dispute between the government

Twice in late 1995 nonessential federal government services were halted when President Bill Clinton and Congress could not agree on spending legislation for fiscal 1996 (which began on November 1). Here, on November 14, a U.S. Immigration and Naturalization Service officer turns people away from the INS office in New York City, one of the busiest in the country.

and a private individual over whether the government is acting according to law—that is, a statute duly passed by Congress and signed by the president—comes before the courts as a normal lawsuit. The judge treats the government as any other party to a lawsuit, granting it no special status whatsoever. The development of American administrative law has been strongly influenced by this tradition. Judicial review of administrative decisions is taken for granted; regulatory commissions and agencies have, from the beginning, been constrained by the courts' defense of individual rights.

Expansion of the government's regulatory activities, particularly during the New Deal, put a host of bureaucratic agencies in the business of making rules and applying them—that is, agencies were authorized to make general rules, just like a legislature, and to adjudicate individual cases under them, just like a court. Federal courts

REGULATING TOBACCO

The Food and Drug Administration (established in 1906 as the Agriculture Department's Bureau of Chemistry and given its present name in 1931) is charged with regulating the food, drug, and medical device industries to ensure the safety and effectiveness of their products. For its first ninety years the agency ignored tobacco, claiming it was neither a food nor a drug nor a medical device. In 1996, however, at the instigation of the Clinton administration, the FDA issued a set of rules regulating the sales and marketing of tobacco and intended to reduce teenage smoking. It justified regulating tobacco as a drug by pointing to the accumulation of "clear and compelling evidence that nicotine is extremely addictive, that consumers use tobacco products because they are addicted" and that the industry had intended its products to exploit smokers' nicotine addiction.[1]

The tobacco industry challenged the regulations in court on the grounds that Congress had not given FDA the authority to regulate nicotine as a drug. Administration lawyers countered that Congress had not explicitly forbidden regulation either, and federal agencies routinely issue new rules in response to new threats to public health—as with AIDS, for example—without getting fresh permission from Congress. In August 1998 a three-judge panel of the 4th U.S. Circuit Court of Appeals sided, 2–1, with the tobacco industry; the two Reagan appointees made up the majority and the lone Clinton appointee dissented. The court determined that the FDA had tried to "stretch the [Food, Drug, and Cosmetic Act of 1938] beyond the scope intended by Congress" and accepted the industry's argument that if FDA did have jurisdiction over tobacco, it would have no choice under its mandate but to ban tobacco altogether as a demonstrably unsafe product.[2]

The administration appealed the decision to the Supreme Court, which agreed in April 1999 to hear the case of *FDA v. Brown and Williamson Tobacco Corp.* The Court will have to decide whether congressional silence on the issue (despite FDA's many requests that Congress weigh in) should be taken as denial of FDA's authority or as acquiescence to it. What the Court hears in the sound of silence may revise the criteria for constitutionally valid delegations of congressional authority.

Instead of appealing the decision, the Clinton administration could have asked Congress to settle the matter by explicitly giving the FDA authority to regulate tobacco. But Republican congressional leaders were not fond of the idea. When FDA first proposed to regulate tobacco in 1995, House Speaker Newt Gingrich said it had "lost its mind"—and even if public pressure had forced Republicans to act, they were certain to place narrower limits on FDA's authority than the administration wanted.[3] Meanwhile, the tobacco industry tried to reduce pressure to empower the FDA by arguing that it already had agreed to similar limits on marketing to teens as part of the settlement in a multibillion dollar lawsuit brought by a coalition of state governments to recover their tobacco-related medical costs.

1. "Court to Make FDA–Tobacco Decision," April 26, 1999 <http://www.nytimes.com/aponline/w/AP-Court-Tobacco.html> (April 26, 1999).

2. Allan Freedman, "FDA Jurisdiction over Tobacco Thrown into Doubt by Ruling," *Congressional Quarterly Weekly Report*, August 22, 1998, 2286–2288.

3. Ibid., 2286.

maintained appellate jurisdiction over both sets of activities, hearing appeals on rules as well as their enforcement, and court decisions gradually imposed a set of procedural standards that Congress eventually codified in the Administrative Procedures Act.

Under the APA, any agency dealing with individual cases like a court must act like a court—that is, it must hold hearings conducted by neutral referees (now called administrative law judges). Parties may be represented by counsel, with written and oral testimony and opportunities for cross-examination. Decisions handed down by the agency must be issued in writing and justified on the evidence in the record. Those that violate these procedures can be challenged and overturned in federal court. An agency that wants its judgments sustained must carefully follow administrative due process.

Over the years the federal courts have come to interpret the APA as requiring almost as much procedural care in making rules as in deciding cases. Courts have elaborated on and formalized the APA's notice and hearings requirements and now insist on a comprehensive, written justification backed by a complete record of all information and analysis that went into an agency's decision. The APA allows courts to invalidate rules only if they are "arbitrary and capricious," which would seem to give agencies wide latitude. Yet in the 1960s and 1970s the courts used judicial review "to create and impose on agencies a huge body of administrative law which was so complex and demanding that it allowed judges to strike down new agency rules whenever they pleased."[25] The courts were particularly interested in the highly contentious and highly technical areas of regulation of the environment, health, and safety. Soon regulatory agencies adapted, however, by overwhelming the courts with reams of data and analysis, both to convince the judges they had made the most scientifically defensible choice and to make it more difficult for judges lacking technical expertise to say otherwise. The courts have since backed off a bit, but they still play a major role in shaping regulatory decisions.

Congress may, of course, rewrite the law if the courts invalidate rules that solid House and Senate majorities want to see implemented. Yet any change must negotiate the usual congressional obstacle course, which, as we saw in Chapter 6, is by no means easy, particularly if the president prefers the court's position. Congress does rectify both judicial and administrative decisions it does not like, but only under major provocation.

Bureaucratic Autonomy

Although subject to the authority of Congress, the president, and the courts, bureaucrats are by no means always kept on a short leash. Indeed, the 1997 IRS hearings revealed bureaucrats out of control and responsible to no one, or at least no one who was, in turn, responsible to the voters. The reality is that some agencies operate with substantial autonomy, while others are carefully monitored by their multiple principals. The ability of agencies to expand their autonomy—that is, to use their discretionary authority as they think best—depends on a variety of circumstances, not least of which are the political skills of individual bureaucrats.

It is neither surprising nor necessarily a bad thing that government agencies strive for autonomy. Most of them are staffed by specialists who devote their entire careers to a narrow area of public administration. The U.S. Forest Service hires and trains professional foresters who make a career of managing America's national forests; the FBI recruits and trains a special kind of law enforcement officer; the Centers for Disease Control recruit health care professionals who become specialists in combating infectious diseases. During long service in such agencies, people develop a strong sense of what their agency is supposed do and how it is supposed to do it—that is, they absorb its **bureaucratic culture.** Political scientist James Q. Wilson defines an organization's culture as its "persistent, patterned way of thinking about the central tasks of and human relationships within [the] organization. Culture is to an organization what personality is to an individual.

The U.S. Forest Service, which maintains the nation's 152 national forests, enjoys a reputation for professionalism and independence. The agency has achieved this standing despite the fact that 90 percent of its revenue traditionally comes from logging permits. A less professional organization might favor logging and forget conservation.

Like human culture generally, it is passed on from one generation to the next. It changes slowly, if at all."[26]

Bureaucrats imbued with their agency's culture come to dislike interference from outsiders ignorant of the problems, practices, and political environment they know so intimately. They also tend to value their agency's programs and services more highly than outsiders might and thus seek the resources and the freedom to carry out their missions in the way they believe is best. On the whole, then, there is nothing undesirable about having agencies staffed with people who have a strong sense of professionalism and confidence that their work is important and that they know best how to do it. A nation would not want its army and naval officers, for example, to think any

other way. The problem is that the very conditions that give an agency high morale and a strong sense of mission may encourage it to seek independence from political control.

Bureaucrats as Politicians

As partisans of their agencies and missions, bureaucrats are necessarily politicians. Indeed, the Weberian notion of civil servants who act as neutral instruments for implementing the policies chosen by their elected superiors has never taken hold in the United States. Agency officials operate in a world of competition for scarce resources, often intense conflicts among interests and values, and multiple bosses (principals). Scholars have proposed a variety of motives, in addition to the desire for autonomy, that might account for bureaucratic behavior. These motives include a desire for larger budgets, more subordinates, and greater authority; the chance to do some good; a stable, predictable environment; and career security and advancement. But whatever the goals, they can only be achieved through politics: mobilizing supporters, gathering allies, negotiating mutually beneficial deals with other politicians, keeping in touch with people whose cooperation is needed, adapting to the realities of power.

The political environment of most government agencies, as we have seen, is occupied by the House and Senate members of the subcommittees handling agencies' authorizing statutes and budgets, committee and subcommittee staff, the political appointees who head agencies, the White House (especially its Office of Management and Budget), the interest groups affected by agency activities, and the federal courts. Occasionally the news media and the broader public also show up on the radar screen.

Even though bureaucrats serve in the executive branch under the president, their most important political relationship is usually with Congress. Congress controls the organization, authority, budgets, and staffing—indeed, the very existence—of departments and bureaus. Although presidential appointees rarely stay in their agencies more than a few years, members of Congress and senior committee staff are in for the long haul, as are the interest groups that play an important role in Congress's political environment. Keeping Congress happy often means keeping interest groups happy.

Politically astute bureaucrats carefully cultivate members of Congress and their staffs. The principle is simple, though following it is sometimes far from simple: do things that help members to achieve their goals and avoid doing things that have the opposite effect. Along the way, establish a reputation for competence and frugality. No one whose job relies on voters is going to defend bureaucratic ineptitude or malfeasance. Keeping in touch, usually through congressional staff, also is crucial. Politicians and bureaucrats live in an uncertain, ever-changing world. Good information is a scarce and therefore valuable commodity (see Chapter 6). Information about their own activities is one political resource bureaucrats have in abundance. A regular exchange of intelligence helps both sides anticipate consequences and reduces the incidence of unpleasant surprises. Shrewd bureaucrats are responsive to informal suggestions as well as legislative mandates; they can take a hint. In short, bureaucrats prosper by convincing their congressional principals that they are good and faithful agents—never easy where hidden action and hidden information abound.

The survival of bureaucrats, like that of other politicians, also depends on having an appreciative constituency. Some agencies acquire organized constituencies at the moment of birth—the interests who lobbied them into existence. As noted, the clientele-oriented Departments

of Agriculture, Labor, and Education fall into this category, as well as the Federal Maritime Commission (shipping interests) and the Environmental Protection Agency (environmental groups). Other agencies have to organize supporters themselves. An early secretary of commerce, for example, helped to found the U.S. Chamber of Commerce. Many of the groups that now lobby on behalf of programs for the handicapped, mentally ill, and other disadvantaged people were brought into being through the efforts of government officials in social service agencies (for other examples, see Chapter 13, Interest Groups).[27] Agencies that service politically feeble clienteles—such as the Bureau of Prisons (federal criminals) and the Agency for International Development (foreign countries)—inevitably suffer in the struggle for political attention and resources. In addition to their constituencies, government agencies also try to cultivate broad public support, and most have public relations offices devoted to publicizing their activities (see box "NASA on Mars").

Savvy bureaucrats design and manage their programs in ways that enhance political support in Congress. If feasible, programs produce widely distributed local benefits even when their primary purpose is to produce diffuse national benefits. For example, defense spending buys a diffuse national good—protection from potential enemy nations—but also helps the local economies where the money is spent. Aware of this aspect of military procurement, Pentagon officials protect weapons programs by making sure their components are produced in as many states and districts as possible. The program that built nearly one hundred B-1 bombers, at a cost of more than $200 million each, employed subcontractors in forty-eight states and more than three hundred congressional districts.[28]

Bureaucrats also target benefits to key members of Congress. For example, from 1965 through 1974 a disproportionate share of grants for water and sewer facilities under a program administered by HUD went to the districts of members of the subcommittees that dealt with

NASA ON MARS

The National Aeronautics and Space Administration (NASA) runs the U.S. space program, an expensive enterprise ($14 billion in 1996) that has no direct impact on the lives of most Americans. When the end of the cold war also brought an end to space competition with the Russians and large federal deficits put severe pressure on NASA's budget, the agency realized it needed to cultivate broad public support to win continued funding for its programs. Its strategy: do everything possible to encourage ordinary citizens to share in the excitement of space exploration.

The 1997 *Mars Pathfinder* mission was a superb example. The Mars landing and the first pictures transmitted to Earth were televised to the world. In keeping with their public relations "mission," NASA scientists gave the robot-ic exploration vehicle (Sojourner) and the rock formations it examined evocative or folksy names (Yogi, Scooby Doo, Stimpy, Moe, Half Dome). They also created a splendid Web site that offered daily updates on the mission in the form of photographs, scientific data, Martian weather reports, and a chat room where people could exchange ideas with mission scientists.

The mission and the Web site (which logged more than 220 million hits over one four-day period in August 1997) were very popular, helping to revive NASA's political fortunes after some expensive failures. As a result, Congress ended up appropriating more money than the president had requested for NASA's fiscal 1998 budget.

NASA's Web site: <http://www.nasa.gov>

the program and of conservatives who otherwise might have voted against the program out of philosophical opposition to federal spending.[29] To sweeten such deals, bureaucrats make sure members of Congress have an opportunity to take credit when local projects or grants are announced. They also try to stay in close touch with the organized interests active in their policy domains in order to anticipate and possibly head off political problems. The interest groups, for their part, naturally want to maintain cordial relations with "their" agencies as well.

Iron Triangles, Captured Agencies, and Issue Networks

The politics of program administration gives bureaucrats, members of Congress, and organized interest groups powerful incentives to form mutually beneficial alliances to manage policy in their areas of specialization. When successful, these alliances become the **iron triangles** made much of by political scientists a generation ago: narrowly focused subgovernments controlling policy in their domains, out of sight or oversight of the full Congress, the president, and the public at large. The classic examples operated in the areas of agriculture, water, and

A POLITICALLY UNTOUCHABLE BUREAUCRAT
J. Edgar Hoover of the FBI

The career of J. Edgar Hoover, director of the Federal Bureau of Investigation (FBI) from 1924 until his death in 1972, reveals just how much power and independence a politically astute bureaucrat can amass. Officially, the FBI is a subunit of the Justice Department. Its director is subordinate to the attorney general and serves at the pleasure of the president. How then did Hoover manage to hold onto his job for forty-eight years even though his conflicts with the various attorneys general and the eight different presidents under whom he served would have ended in the firing of anyone else?

Taking over an agency notorious for its corruption, political favoritism, and incompetence, Hoover turned it into a professional, disciplined, technologically advanced, and efficient anticrime force—and then did everything he could to make sure the public would always see it as such. One of his innovations, the famous "Ten Most-Wanted List," still generates news reports of FBI triumphs whenever suspects on the list are captured. Hoover also cooperated with the journalists and radio, movie, and television producers who made FBI agents the heroes of their stories. He remained wary, however, of the crime-fighting activities—enforcing drug laws and attacking organized crime—in which the bureau might not succeed and which might invite corruption. Indeed, for years Hoover denied that organized crime even existed.

Hoover also cultivated and served two clienteles. First, the FBI served local police departments, which consulted, among other things, its Central Fingerprint Repository and National Automobile Altered Number File. Second, the bureau fueled and championed the cause of people who thought the United States was swarming with subversives bent on destroying the American way of life. In the eyes of many Americans, any criticism of Hoover or the FBI carried the taint of disloyalty. Hoover also used the bureau to gather highly personal information about politically prominent individuals who might cross him. That way, the information could be selectively shared with those in power and leaked to cooperative members of Congress or friendly reporters.

Although presidents from Franklin Roosevelt to Richard Nixon would have happily fired Hoover, the potential political cost was never worth the potential political gains. So, they had to live with him. He used his autonomy to run the FBI like a personal fiefdom, and he illegally harassed organizations and leaders he found politically objectionable, keeping a separate set of secret records on the projects so that his and the FBI's lawbreaking would not be discovered. In the early 1960s, although formally under the supervision of Robert Kennedy (at right in photo), the attorney general and brother of President John Kennedy (left), Hoover ran his agency without much regard for the wishes of either Kennedy. Threatening to leak embarrassing information on civil rights leader Martin Luther King Jr., Hoover "persuaded" the Kennedys to authorize phone wiretaps on King, which unleashed massive FBI surveillance of the civil rights leader. Hoover's attempt to discredit King was probably his most egregious abuse of power.

Source: Jack H. Knott and Gary J. Miller, *Reforming Bureaucracy: The Politics of Institutional Choice* (Englewood Cliffs, N.J.: Prentice-Hall, 1987), 190–192.

The U.S. Department of Agriculture was created in 1862 to introduce agricultural technologies to the nation's farmers. Over the years the department has assumed many other tasks, from expediting international trade to administering food stamps. In recent years one of its most visible activities has been educating the nation on nutrition. Here Dan Glickman, secretary of agriculture in the Clinton administration, unveils a new "food pyramid" for children that prescribes daily consumption of the various food groups.

public works, where the active players shared concentrated benefits.[30] The broader public, excluded from the process, paid the diffuse costs.

Similarly, the politics of regulation allows the regulators to be "captured" by the very interests they were instituted to regulate. Once Congress establishes a regulatory agency in response to some threat to the public welfare—whether it be railroad monopolies, dangerous or quack medicines, or impure processed food—the agency's dealings are not with the unorganized public, whose attention turns elsewhere because the government is supposed to be taking care of the problem, but with the industries it regulates. Because industries have an enormous economic stake in how they are regulated, they become the primary source of political pressure on the regulators. Ironically, the regulated sectors also are the primary repository of the expertise needed to regulate effectively. Thus the regulatory agency, typically underfunded and understaffed, may come to rely on firms in the very sector under its care for the information, and sometimes even the personnel, it needs to regulate them. Add to this the routine legislative mandate that the agency maintain the economic health of the industries it regulates and the story is complete: regulators become the allies, if not agents, of the sector they regulate. At times, for example, the Food and Drug Administration catered to drug companies; the Interstate Commerce Commission (ICC) ended up at the beck and call of established firms in the trucking industry; and the Civil Aeronautics Board (CAB) protected the major airlines from competition.

In reality, iron triangles and captured agencies survive only as long as the costs they impose on everyone are small enough to avoid attracting serious attention from political entrepreneurs in Congress or the White House scouting for popular issues to champion. For example, the ICC and the CAB no longer exist; the CAB was abolished in 1985, and ten years later the ICC, by then more than a hundred years old, was finally put to rest. The reason: the sectors they once regulated are now governed by the marketplace. In the name of economic efficiency and lower prices for consumers, a cross-party coalition that included both executive branch officials and Congress cooperated to deregulate airline fares and routes in 1978 and the railroad and trucking industries in 1980. In the early 1960s one congressional coalition forced the FDA to impose much tougher standards for proving the safety and efficacy of new drugs. The 1990s, however, saw another coalition make it ease up again on the grounds that delays in approval of new drugs also hurt the public health.

Members of Congress learned from these experiences

REINVENTING GOVERNMENT

In 1993, just six weeks after taking office, President Bill Clinton assigned his vice president, Al Gore, the job of overseeing a review of the federal government with the goal of cutting, consolidating, and reshaping. The project, initially called the National Performance Review (NPR), was renamed the National Partnership for Reinventing Government in 1998 and given the slogan "America @ Its Best." In launching the program in 1993, the Clinton administration staged one of its more successful "photo-ops": Presi-

dent Clinton and Vice President Gore standing beside forklifts of government forms and regulations against the backdrop of the White House.

In 1998 Donald F. Kettl, senior fellow at Washington's Brookings Institution, found the fifth anniversary of NPR an appropriate time to take stock of the Clinton administration's efforts and to grade its performance. Here is a slightly abbreviated version of his report card:

The Fifth-Year NPR Report Card

Category	Grade	Comments
Downsizing	B	Accomplished the goal, but planning to match downsized workforce with agency missions was weak.
Identifying objectives of government	D	The NPR sought in 1995 to focus on what government *should* do—but the effort evaporated as the Republican threat faded.
Procurement reform	A	Fundamental transformation of procurement system. Some vendors complain, but the system is far more efficient than it was.
Customer service	B+	Great progress in some agencies, but major failures in others—notably the IRS.
Disaster avoidance	B–	Substantial efforts in many agencies, notably Federal Emergency Management Agency. Spectacular failures in others, notably IRS. The big test: the Y2K problem.
Political leadership	C+	Consistently strong leadership from the top but inconsistent below. Federal workers have gotten mixed signals.
Relations with Congress	D	Efforts to develop legislative support for NPR initiatives have, with the exception of procurement reform, been weak and ineffective. Support from Congress: poor.
Improvements in citizen confidence in government	C	The steady slide in public trust and confidence in government has ended, but that has more to do with a healthy economy than improved government performance.
Effort	A+	No administration in history has invested such sustained, high-level attention to management reform efforts.
OVERALL GRADE	B	Substantial progress made over first five years, but much more work lies ahead. Successive administrations will have little choice but to continue the NPR in some form.

Source: Donald F. Kettl, "Reinventing Government: A Fifth-Year Report Card," CPM 98-1, Center for Public Management, Brookings Institution, Washington, D.C., September 1998, Table 1, 2–5.

and designed new regulatory procedures to prevent the capture of agencies such as EPA (see the discussion of "standing" earlier in this chapter). The proliferation of self-proclaimed public interest groups in the 1960s also altered the political environments of many agencies, leaving them no option but to negotiate a far more complex, open, and conflict-ridden configuration of political forces (see Chapter 13). Thus scholars now talk of policy domains shaped by **issue networks**—amorphous, ever-changing sets of politicians, lobbyists, academic and think-tank experts, and public interest entrepreneurs such as Ralph Nader—rather than iron triangles.[31]

Agencies have had to adapt. The Interior Department's Bureau of Reclamation, once focused exclusively on building dams and irrigation works in the arid west, has become far more responsive to environmental and recreational interests. The Department of Agriculture now pays attention to nutrition and other consumer concerns as well as to the needs of agribusiness. Today's Environmental Protection Agency considers the economic as well as environmental effects of its decisions. But agencies do not always find it easy to adapt because new missions may go against the culture of an agency. For example, the U.S. Army Corps of Engineers, which for two centuries had been damming rivers, dredging harbors, and draining wetlands, was not eager to make cleaning up toxic wastes and protecting threatened ecosystems a high priority. But when the political environment changes, government agencies have little choice but to change as well.

Reinventing Government?

The Clinton administration took office in 1993 with a promise to "reinvent government." Indeed, every modern president has viewed the federal bureaucracy as a problem that needs fixing; Clinton's effort was distinguished by its focus on how well bureaucratic services are delivered. Vice President Al Gore headed the administration's National Performance Review, which sought ways to "cast aside red tape," encourage entrepreneurial administration that "put customers first," decentralize authority to "empower those who work on the front lines," and in general, produce "better government for less" with a reduced workforce.[32] Not to be outdone, the Republican House freshmen elected in 1994 sought not merely to reinvent government but also to disinvent it. Republicans proposed abolishing the Departments of Commerce, Energy, Education, and Housing and Urban Development, terminating many of their programs and bureaus and distributing the remainder to other departments.

Proposed at a time when the public's disaffection with government was widespread (see Chapter 10, Public Opinion), both the Republican and Democratic initiatives were imbued with political logic. Making government work like a business that depends on keeping customers happy has obvious appeal. So does getting rid of obsolete and wasteful programs and agencies. Yet, despite some success in improving the performance of several agencies and reducing the number of federal employees, the Clinton administration recognized that its goal of an efficient, customer-friendly bureaucracy was still a long way off. One need look no further than the 1997 IRS hearings for confirmation. And House Republicans, though slashing some agency budgets and terminating a few programs, failed to eliminate any major agency, let alone whole cabinet departments. The fact is that the federal bureaucracy is hard to reform and still harder to prune because its actions and structure have a political logic of their own.

The Logic of Red Tape

Red tape—labyrinthian procedures, layers of paperwork (in quadruplicate!), the demand for strict adherence to form—does not flourish by accident. It proliferates because it helps principals to control and monitor their agents (the goal of the Administrative Procedures Act) and because it helps agents to demonstrate to their principals that they are doing their jobs correctly. Many rules and procedures are adopted to assure fair or at least equal treatment of each citizen by preventing unaccountable, arbitrary behavior. For example, federal agencies procuring goods and services from the private sector are bound by an elaborate set of requirements imposed on them by Congress:

> The essential rules are that all potential employers must be offered an equal opportunity to bid on a contract; that the agency's procurement decision must be objectively justifiable on the basis of written specifications; that contracts awarded on the basis of sealed bids must go to the contractor offering the lowest price; and that unsuccessful bidders must be offered a chance to protest decisions with which they disagree.[33]

The *Federal Acquisition Regulation,* which spells out these rules, runs more than six thousand pages long. Bureaucrats have a strong incentive to follow the rules, for there is only one safe answer— "I followed the rules"— when a member of Congress asks pointedly why a favorite constituent did not get the contract.[34] By the same logic, bureaucrats like to have rules to follow. Detailed procedures protect as well as constrain bureaucrats, so red tape is frequently self-imposed.

Empowering bureaucrats on the front lines of service delivery may increase efficiency and even customer satisfaction, but it also may make it easier for bureaucrats to go astray. Each time an agency does go astray, Congress tends to write more elaborate procedures and add another layer of inspectors and auditors to keep it from happening again. Thus *red tape often springs directly from Congress's desire to control administration.* As a result, although Congress rails against red tape in general, it views attempts to reduce the controls that generate red tape with suspicion. Successful efforts could reduce its ability to monitor and influence administration, a risk congressional majorities have been reluctant to accept, especially when the other party holds the White House.

Reformers seeking bureaucratic efficiency also may run into several other problems. Efficiency stems from using resources in a maximally productive way, but any assessment of efficiency must be based on measures of output. The output of many agencies, however, defies measurement. Diplomats in the State Department are supposed to pursue the long-term security and economic interests of the nation. How do we measure their "productivity" in this endeavor? Complicating matters even more, agencies sometimes are assigned conflicting objectives. Is the IRS supposed to maximize tax compliance, requiring tough enforcement, or customer service, requiring flexible, tolerant enforcement? Effective enforcement and effective customer service are not the same thing.

Because an agency's degree of success in accomplishing its vaguely defined ends is often impossible to measure, bureaucrats focus instead on outputs that can be measured: reports completed, cases processed, meetings held, regulations drafted, contracts properly concluded, forms filled out and filed. These means become the ends because they produce observable outputs for which bureaucrats can be held accountable. The result is yet more red tape. The notorious bureaucratic focus on process rather than product arises from the reality that, unlike private businesses, government agencies have no "bottom line" to measure the success or failure of their enterprise.

The Bureaucratic Reward System

Conflicting goals and the lack of a bottom line hardly inspire the creative, "entrepreneurial" government envisioned by the Clinton/Gore National Performance Review. Entrepreneurs take risks proportionate to prospective rewards. Civil servants, by contrast, seldom profit personally from their attempts to make agencies more productive or customer-friendly. And if bold new approaches end in failure, they can count on being blasted in the media and in Congress. Bureaucrats are famously cautious for a good reason: a mistake is much more likely than a routine to set off a fire alarm in Congress. If an alarm does sound, the routine, rather than the bureaucrat, gets the blame.

The merit system rewards conscientious, long-term service; it does not encourage entrepreneurial risk-taking.

Congress could, of course, decide to give agency managers more authority to hire, promote, reward, redeploy, or fire staff personnel on the basis of their performance. But doing so would mean reducing the civil service protections put in place for well-considered political reasons: to avoid a partisan spoils system and to preserve congressional influence over administration.

The Clinton administration's plans for reinventing government inevitably included proposals to reduce bureaucratic waste and improve policy coordination by consolidating overlapping agencies and programs. Every president since Franklin Roosevelt has sought to do the same. And indeed, it is easy to find examples of duplication, confused lines of authority, and conflict among the government's multifarious activities. Basic scientific research, for example, is funded by the National Science Foundation; the National Institutes of Health; the Departments of Energy, Agriculture, Defense; and NASA. The National Park Service, the U.S. Forest Service, the Bureau of Land Management, and the Fish and Wildlife Service all manage public campgrounds. Responsibility for developing water resources is spread over five separate agencies. The government both supports the price of tobacco to keep tobacco farming profitable and tries to discourage smoking. One agency subsidizes the lumber industry by building logging roads into national forests; another tries to curb it to protect endangered species. And the list could go on.

This duplication would all seem senseless if government pursued a coherent set of interrelated goals, but it does not. Government pursues overlapping, conflicting, or disconnected goals in response to the diverse demands Americans place on it. Each agency and each program reflect the coalition of forces that brought it into being and that now form its political environment. Different coalitions want different things and design different administrative institutions to get them. As two observers of the bureaucracy noted, "Executive branch structure is, in fact, a microcosm of our society. It reflects the values, con-flicts, and competing forces to be found in a pluralistic society."[35]

In short, then, the problem of bureaucracy is not bureaucracy but politics. It is not impossible to reform, reinvent, streamline, or shrink the administrative leviathan, but it is impossible do so without changing power relationships among interests and institutions. Deregulating the bureaucracy and empowering front-line bureaucrats would make agencies more efficient, but it also would make them less accountable to elected officials. Consolidating and rationalizing bureaucratic authority would reduce duplication, confusion, and expense, but it also would create losers whose interests or values would no longer enjoy undivided institutional attention. As we have seen in this chapter, the federal bureaucracy is an expression of American democracy's luxuriant institutional and social pluralism as well as, ironically, its deep suspicion of political authority. It thus changes only as its larger political and social environment changes.

Key Terms

bureaucracy / 248

bureaucratic culture / 273

clientele / 257

Federal Register / 263

intervenor / 267

iron triangle / 276

issue network / 280

legislative veto / 265

red tape / 280

rotation in office / 251

spoils system / 251

standing / 267

Suggested Readings

Downs, Anthony. *Inside Bureaucracy.* Boston: Little Brown, 1967. A comprehensive theory of bureaucracy from a nontechnical but "economic" perspective.

Light, Paul C. *Thickening Government: Federal Hierarchy and the Diffusion of Accountability.* Washington, D.C.: Brookings, 1995. How and why bureaucratic layers have multiplied and how this makes government agencies less accountable to elected officials and less effective in performing their tasks.

Seidman, Harold. *Politics, Position, and Power: The Dynamics of Federal*

Organization. 5th ed. New York: Oxford University Press, 1998. How politics shapes bureaucratic organizations and practices.

Shapiro, Martin. *Who Guards the Guardians? Judicial Control of Administration.* Athens: University of Georgia Press, 1988. A lucid and informative account of court–agency relations since the New Deal.

Skowronek, Stephen. *Building a New American State: The Expansion of National Administrative Capacities, 1877–1920.* Cambridge: Cambridge University Press, 1982. Classic account of the development of the modern American bureaucracy, focusing on the civil service, the army, and agencies regulating the economy.

Waterman, Richard W. *Presidential Influence and the Administrative State.* Knoxville: University of Tennessee Press, 1989. Case studies from the Nixon, Carter, and Reagan administrations of presidential efforts to implement policies via the bureaucracy.

Wilson, James Q. *Bureaucracy: What Government Agencies Do and Why They Do It.* New York: Basic Books, 1989. If you read only one book on the bureaucracy, it should be this one.

Chapter 9

THE FEDERAL JUDICIARY

☆ *How can a democracy like ours justify endowing nine unelected judges with the authority to nullify state and national laws that were enacted by elected representatives?*

☆ *All federal judges—from the district courts to the Supreme Court—are appointed for life and are independent of one another. How can the federal judiciary be expected to dispense justice consistently and equitably?*

☆ *Is the judiciary truly, as Alexander Hamilton argued in* **The Federalist,** *"the least dangerous branch" of government?*

☆ *In what ways is the judiciary susceptible to the same pressures of politics and national opinion that affect the elected branches?*

☆ *If the Supreme Court "guards" the Constitution, who guards the guardians?*

By 1800 the same national leaders who had led the nation through the Revolution and reorganized the government under the Constitution had divided into two warring camps—the ruling Federalist Party, led by John Adams and Alexander Hamilton, and the Democratic-Republican opposition, led by Thomas Jefferson and James Madison. Once allies, these two groups now despised and feared one another. Each believed that the future of the Republic rested on its party's victory in the presidential election of 1800. Consequently, the electoral campaign of 1800 was one of the most vitriolic in American history.

Both sides indulged in negative campaigning, but the Federalists excelled at it; they attacked Jefferson as the devil incarnate. In political pamphlets and letters to the editor the Federalists called Jefferson an "infidel" and "atheist," a darling of the French Revolution who looked favorably on use of the guillotine, a proponent of majority rule (and thus apt to pursue a course that would destroy the republican Constitution), a philanderer, and—perhaps the ultimate insult for a politician—a "philosopher." The author of one pamphlet added that Jefferson was not even a very good philosopher—perhaps adequate for a college professor but certainly not president. The attack finally dredged bottom in charging that Jefferson had written a "textbook" on American government that promoted abstract ideas and "hooted at experience." In short, the Federalists did not care one bit for Jefferson and his Democratic-Republican colleagues and appeared ready to do whatever was needed to stop them and save the Republic.

John Marshall (1755–1835) had never sat on the bench before his installation on the Supreme Court. Moreover, his legal education was limited to reading Blackstone's Commentaries *with his father and to three months of lectures by George Wythe at the College of William and Mary in 1780. Marshall's formidable powers of reasoning and leadership in unifying his colleagues behind unanimous decisions were complemented by an amiable disposition and "some little propensity for indolence."*

Toward the end of the campaign both sides sensed that Jefferson could not be stopped, but neither appeared to anticipate the magnitude of the Democratic-Republican victory. Not only did the party walk away with the electoral college vote, but it also took control of Congress. It was not clear who had been elected president, however, because of a quirk in the Constitution's rules on counting presidential and vice-presidential votes (a problem corrected by the Twelfth Amendment in 1804). The tally showed Jefferson and his vice-presidential running mate, Aaron Burr, with the same number of electoral votes. The election, then, had to be settled by the House of Representatives, which was still controlled by the outgoing Federalists.

During the weeks between the election and the House vote, rumors swirled across the nation, inspiring talk of conspiracies. Would the Federalist Congress ignore the Constitution's technical glitch and ratify Jefferson's victory, or would it somehow exploit this opportunity to deny the White House to this free-thinking radical? One scenario had the Federalists contriving a tie vote in the House, a development that would have taken the presidential election beyond circumstances anticipated by the Constitution. Another scenario had President Adams stepping down at the end of his term and Secretary of State John Marshall assuming caretaker control of the executive branch until a new presidential election could be called.[1] And yet another option, which clearly lay within the Constitution's provisions and was perhaps more seriously considered, had the Federalists electing Aaron Burr president as the lesser of two evils.[2] None of these options appeared feasible, however. Thus, after weeks of strategizing and perhaps a little soul searching, the Federalist Congress ratified the nation's choice, and Jefferson became the third president of the United States.

Had the peaceful transfer of power not occurred in this first real test of the new Republic, the election of 1800 *might* have weakened the Constitution permanently. Failure here would have put the Constitution's integrity in doubt and left future politicians in the (prisoner's) dilemma of deciding whether to abide by the rules or renege before the other side could. But the Federalists did not capitulate altogether. They enlisted a risky fallback strategy and thereby triggered a different kind of constitutional crisis. The unanticipated outcome was a reconfiguration of power among the branches of government, including the Supreme Court.

Setting the Stage for Judicial Review

As they prepared to vacate office, the Federalists enacted the Judiciary Act of 1801. The law, designed to protect the Constitution against perceived Democratic-Republican schemes, sharply raised the number of district and appeals courts and conveniently created new judgeships for aspiring Federalists.[3] Moreover, President Adams nominated and the Senate quickly confirmed Marshall's appointment to the Supreme Court to fill the vacant position of chief justice.

At this point, the story turns from grand strategies of contending partisan armies to the personal foibles and ambitions of politicians—in other words, it begins to resemble a soap opera. President Adams needed help processing the flurry of last-minute Federalist judicial appointments and so asked his new chief justice to stay on for a brief time as secretary of state. According to Jefferson, Adams was still signing appointment commissions at nine o'clock the evening before his departure from office. Apparently, in the rush to make way for the new administration Marshall left on his desk a stack of signed and sealed justice of the peace commissions for the District of Columbia. The departing Federalist Congress had created these five-year positions to reward loyal Federalists. The next day Marshall, as chief justice of the United States, delivered the oath of office to the new president, his archrival Thomas Jefferson.

Later, on discovering or being advised (the lore is inconsistent on this point) that some of the commissions had not been delivered but were lying around the office, Jefferson ordered that they be withdrawn. These commissions were the least of the Federalists' worries, however.

After the inauguration the Democratic-Republicans derided the judiciary as a "hospital of decayed politicians" and made clear their intention to repeal the Judiciary Act as soon as their Congress opened the following December.[4] Jefferson expressed his party's sentiment: the Federalists had "retired into the Judiciary as a strong hold . . . and from that battery all the works for republicanism are to be beaten down and erased by fraudulent use of the constitution."[5] With the convening of Congress, the stage was set for an epic partisan battle in which the Democratic-Republicans controlled the presidency and (narrowly) both chambers of Congress, and the Federalists controlled the federal judiciary.

But could Congress abolish courts and thereby remove life-tenured judges? With repeal of the Judiciary Act imminent, Federalist politicians began urging Marshall to prepare to defend the Federalist bulwark by ruling recision unconstitutional. This strategy presupposed, of course, that the Supreme Court possessed such authority. In private, Federalist strategists also urged their recently appointed judges to ignore Congress until the Marshall Court came to their rescue.

On February 3, 1802, by a 16–15 vote, the Senate voted to repeal the Judiciary Act and eliminate the Federalist judges' offices. All but one Democratic-Republican voted for repeal, and all Federalists voted against it. The House passed the repeal bill a month later with but a single Democratic-Republican holdout, and Jefferson promptly signed it into law.[6] The Supreme Court already had decided that it would not or could not resist repeal, but Jefferson and his allies had to wait until the Court's next session in 1803 to learn this. Marshall had not caved in, however. Early in 1803 the Court delivered two decisions that, considered together, represent a masterful political maneuver. On March 2, 1803, the long-anticipated showdown on the repeal of the Judiciary Act fizzled for the Federalists as the Court ruled in *Stuart v. Laird* that Congress had the authority to reorganize the judiciary.[7] The Federalist barricade had been dismantled; the Democratic-Republican victory was complete. The Federalist Party would never again win control of the presidency or either chamber of Congress.

Although the young Constitution survived the election of 1800, the partisan confrontation surrounding the Judiciary Act, the Federalists' late-night machinations on the eve of Jefferson's inauguration, and the Democratic-Republicans' resolute resistance, these events led to a significant constitutional development. Six days before the *Stuart* decision, the Court had issued another decision that was viewed by politicians as more of a partisan slam at Democratic-Republicans than anything to do with constitutional principle. William Marbury and several other Federalists who had been denied their justice of the peace commissions nearly two years earlier appealed to the Supreme Court to issue a **writ of mandamus** to force Secretary of State James Madison to do his duty and deliver the commissions.

Based on the facts of the case, *Marbury v. Madison* did not seem to be the ideal vehicle for establishing "new" authority for the Court. Not only did the issue border on the trivial, but Chief Justice Marshall was himself deeply entangled in the dispute; his oversight, after all, had caused the problem in the first place. Moreover, a casual inspection of Marshall's options suggests that this was a terrible case for a weak Court to face. If the Court decided in favor of Marbury and ordered Madison to deliver the commissions, Marshall could reasonably assume that it would be ignored. (No administration official had even bothered to appear before the Court to defend Jefferson's decision.) There was even talk in the Democratic-Republican press of impeaching the justices if they decided in Marbury's favor. Such a ruling, then, invited disaster for the long-term health of the federal judiciary. But if Marshall ruled against Marbury, the Court would appear to be kowtowing to the Democratic-Republicans and confirming the judiciary's subordinate position. Faced with this dilemma, Marshall found a solution that not only extricated the Court from its predicament but also established an important principle for the future.[8]

After lecturing the administration on the validity of Marbury's claim, Marshall ruled that, nonetheless, the Court lacked the authority to compel the commission's delivery. By refusing to hear the case, Marshall managed to back away from a confrontation he could not win and to assert new judicial authority. The Judiciary Act of 1789 which had authorized the Supreme Court to hear such cases was itself unconstitutional, Marshall reasoned, because the *Constitution* already specified the Court's original jurisdiction and it could not be changed by an act of Congress.[9] The correctness of this reading of the Constitution is less impressive than Marshall's argument that the Court had the right to issue this ruling in the first place.

Table 9–1 Federal, State, and Local Laws Declared Unconstitutional by the Supreme Court, by Decade, 1789–1998

Years	Federal	State and Local
1789–1799	0	0
1800–1809	1	1
1810–1819	0	7
1820–1829	0	8
1830–1839	0	3
1840–1849	0	9
1850–1859	1	7
1860–1869	4	23
1870–1879	7	36
1880–1889	4	46
1890–1899	5	36
1900–1909	9	40
1910–1919	6	118
1920–1929	15	139
1930–1939	13	93
1940–1949	2	58
1950–1959	5	60
1960–1969	16	149
1970–1979	20	193
1980–1989	16	162
1990–1998	19	49
Total	**143**	**1,237**

Sources: Lawrence Baum, *The Supreme Court,* 6th ed. (Washington, D.C.: CQ Press, 1998), 201, 203; Kenneth Jost, *The Supreme Court Yearbook, 1996–1997, 1997–1998* (Washington, D.C.: Congressional Quarterly, 1998, 1999), 20, 21.

"It is emphatically the province and duty of the judicial department *to say what the law is,*" Marshall wrote for the unanimous Court. He added, "If then the courts are to regard the constitution; and the constitution is superior to any ordinary act of the legislature; the constitution, and not such ordinary act, must govern the case to which they both apply."[10]

The strategic beauty of this decision lay in the fact that it did not force the other political actors to do anything to affirm the Court's authority. It only required the Court to refuse to act in Marbury's behalf. Marbury and the other plaintiffs walked away without their commissions, and Jefferson and the Democratic-Republicans went about their business confident that the Federalist bench had at last been tamed. What Marshall had done, however, was to place on the books a strong argument in favor of **judicial review,** a phrase referring to the Court's authority to judge whether acts of Congress (and the states) violate the requirements of the Constitution. This decision did not in itself alter the Court's place among the separated branches of government, but it opened the door.[11]

Although the Court claimed the authority to review the constitutionality of acts of Congress as early as 1803, portions of only two federal laws had been declared unconstitutional by 1860. The frequency with which the Court struck down federal legislation remained low throughout the late nineteenth century, but surged during the 1920s and 1930s. Judicial review then began to recede to nineteenth-century levels over the next two decades (Table 9–1). In the 1960s an activist Court once again took a hard look at federal and state laws alike.

Three Eras of the Court

These trends in the Court's activism coincide with three distinct "issue eras" in its history. In each era the most important cases that came before the Court embodied a particular set of unresolved questions about interpretation of the Constitution. These questions concerned nation–state authority, government regulation of the economy, and civil rights and liberties. As the controversy surrounding each issue developed, the federal judiciary confronted an upwelling of cases in which it asserted its preferences over those of other national and state officials.

Nation versus State

During the first and least active of these issue eras (up to the Civil War), the unresolved jurisdictional boundaries between the national and state governments were at the heart of the judiciary's most significant cases. Under Mar-

shall's leadership, the Court favored national authority when it conflicted with states' rights. Reasoning that the national government had been approved directly by the citizenry in special ratification conventions, Marshall maintained that the national government's legitimacy was both independent of and superior to that of the individual states.

One of Marshall's historic decisions embodying this doctrine came in 1819 in *McCulloch v. Maryland,* a case that was, like *Marbury,* rooted in party conflict.[12] When in power, the Federalist Party had created a nationally chartered bank and appointed party members to administer it. Showing their displeasure, several Democratic-Republican-controlled state governments, including Maryland, sought to tax the national bank out of existence. In the *McCulloch* decision, Chief Justice Marshall, speaking for the Court, issued the famous declaration that "the power to tax involves the power to destroy." Thus state taxation of federal property or its activities was unconstitutional. But first Marshall dealt with an even more fundamental issue. The state had argued that in the absence of any provision in the Constitution explicitly authorizing Congress to charter a national bank, the national government had exceeded its authority. To this, Marshall responded that the necessary and proper clause (Article I, Section 8) gave Congress a broad mandate: "Let the end be . . . within the scope of the constitution, and all means which are appropriate, which are plainly adapted to that end, which are not prohibited, but consist with the letter and the spirit of the constitution, are constitutional."

Despite its Federalist leanings, the Marshall Court could not establish for all time the explicit powers of the state and national governments. Marshall died in July 1835, and at the end of that year President Andrew Jackson selected Roger Taney to serve as the next chief justice. Jackson favored Taney largely because of his advocacy of states' rights, and, true to his reputation, Chief Justice Taney led the Court away from the national supremacy doctrine Marshall had crafted. Taney's effort culminated in *Dred Scott v. Sandford* (1857), which, as we found in Chapter 4, brought the nation to the brink of war.[13] In addition to ruling that escaped slaves in the North had to be returned to their owners, Taney's majority opinion held that federal laws outlawing slavery north of the Mason–Dixon line (as in the Missouri Compromise) unconstitutionally infringed on settlers' territorial rights to self-government and private property.[14]

The overwhelming public outcry against Taney's reasoning left the Court seriously discredited. *Dred Scott v. Sandford* took on issues that were too important and divisive to be decided by judicial fiat, said the critics. In the end, the enduring problems of states' rights and slavery had to be settled by war rather than by legislation or litigation. The defeat of the Confederacy in the Civil War signaled a decisive triumph for federal over state government.

After the Civil War, the Fourteenth and Fifteenth Amendments were ratified and Congress passed laws that committed the Court to review state laws when they ran counter to national statutes. The Court was not bound to support the federal government in every dispute, but it was obliged to devote more attention to policies emanating from the lower levels of government. Thus after 1860 the decisions striking down state and local laws increased markedly (see Table 9–1). Oliver Wendell Holmes Jr., one of the most distinguished Supreme Court justices of the early twentieth century, observed, "I do not think the United States would come to an end if we lost our power to declare an Act of Congress void. I do think the union would be imperiled if we could not make that declaration as to the laws of the several States."[15]

Regulating the National Economy

The major issue during the second distinct era of judicial review, from the end of the Civil War to the 1930s, was the government's regulation of the economy. Although the Civil War had settled the supremacy issue in favor of the national government, the actual scope of government powers at both levels remained uncertain. With the rapid industrial expansion after the war, Washington and state capitals alike came under increasing pressure to regulate monopolies and to provide new services to the citizenry. Most such demands were brushed aside, but some, such as regulation of the railroads, proved politically irresistible. Invariably, whenever a state or, infrequently, the national government enacted a regulatory policy, it quickly found its way onto the docket of the unsympathetic Court.

By the late nineteenth century, a constitutional tradition had developed that served to shield business from economic regulation. The Framers had considered the right to private property to be fundamental, equated with liberty. Indeed, it was the economic problems caused by the flaws in the Articles of Confederation that brought them together in Philadelphia in the first place. Marshall shared the Framers' commitment to property, and during hard economic times the Court vigilantly protected the integrity of contracts against state efforts to annul them on behalf of debtors. Marshall wrote in one decision, "the people of the United States . . . have manifested a determination to shield themselves and their property from the effects of those sudden and strong passions to which men are exposed."[16]

After the Civil War the Court generally maintained its historical sympathy for property rights. The Fourteenth Amendment was adopted in 1868 with the intent of protecting newly freed slaves from the repressive actions of the former Confederate states. The amendment said, in part, that no state shall "deprive any person of life, liberty, or property, without due process of law." As we saw in Chapter 4, the nineteenth-century Supreme Court discovered little basis in the due process clause to shield African Americans from disfranchisement and segregation. It did, however, find ample justification for protecting railroads and other businesses from regulation. To invoke the due process clause, it had to define corporations as "persons," which it did without reservation.

The Supreme Court did not deliver a pro-business decision in every case, however. It consistently upheld state

Figure 9–1 Number of Economic and Civil Liberties Laws (Federal, State, and Local) Overturned by the Supreme Court, by Decade, 1900s–1990s

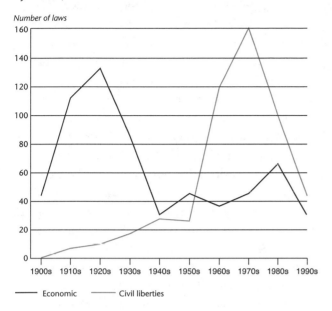

Number of laws

Economic ——   Civil liberties ——

Source: Lawrence Baum, *The Supreme Court,* 6th ed. (Washington, D.C.: CQ Press, 1998), 213. *Note:* Civil liberties category does not include laws supportive of civil liberties. The figures for the 1990s are based on the actual numbers for 1990–1996, multiplied by 1.43 to create a ten-year "rate" for that decade.

prohibitions against the sale of alcohol and occasionally upheld state regulation of businesses "affected with the public interest."[17] But this last criterion was filled with ambiguity, and it prevented the Court from settling on a consistent doctrine. Consequently, the states continued to test the boundaries of permissible regulation, and the early twentieth-century federal courts were inundated with these cases.

The Court's track record in work hour regulation is one example. In *Lochner v. New York* (1905) the Court struck down a New York law restricting the work hours of bakers to a maximum of ten hours a day or sixty hours a week.[18] Laws "limiting the hours in which grown and intelligent men may labor to earn their living," the majority declared, "are mere meddlesome interferences with the rights of the individual." Three years later, however, the Court upheld an Oregon statute limiting the workday of

female workers.[19] Nine years later still, the Court disregarded *Lochner* altogether to uphold an Oregon law limiting to ten hours the workday of any person working in a "mill, factory, or manufacturing establishment."[20]

During the 1920s the Supreme Court became decidedly more conservative and with unprecedented vigor struck down laws regulating business in state after state. Figure 9–1 shows a steady rise in the number of economic measures overturned under the due process clause, reaching a peak of 133 from 1920 to 1929.[21] These decisions won the Court the enmity of many elected officials who found that the justices obstructed their efforts to respond to the demands and needs of their constituents.

After the great stock market crash of 1929, the nation plummeted into a deep economic depression. State and federal governments responded with numerous emergency economic reforms, many of which the Court narrowly affirmed. Yet, as the depression lingered on and the government's intervention in the economy became more substantial, the Court majority turned against regulation. From 1934 to 1937 the Court, still made up of justices who had been appointed before the depression, struck down twelve statutes enacted during President Franklin Roosevelt's first term. These included laws creating emergency relief programs, controlling the production of coal and basic agricultural commodities, regulating child labor, and providing mortgage relief, especially to farmers.

Earlier, the Civil War had ended slavery and rendered moot the Dred Scott decision. In this era of economic turmoil, resolution of the impasse required a direct confrontation between the Supreme Court and the elected branches of government. Shortly after his landslide reelection in 1936, President Roosevelt proposed a plan for revamping the judiciary. Part of it was the famous (or infamous) **Court packing plan.** Ostensibly the plan was intended to alleviate the backlog of cases on the Court's docket by allowing the president, among other things, to appoint an additional Supreme Court justice for every sitting justice over the age of seventy. With the opportunity to name as many as six new justices to the high bench,

Congressional attempts to curb child labor by taxing the items produced were repeatedly rebuffed by the Supreme Court in the early twentieth century.

Roosevelt could ensure himself a Court majority sympathetic to his New Deal programs. Public reaction to the idea was generally negative, and the legislation failed in Congress. Ultimately, however, victory went to Roosevelt. With a 5–4 decision in a case about wage and working conditions regulations in Washington State, the Court began to uphold the same type of economic regulations it had been rejecting for the past two years.[22]

The Court's about-face started when one justice changed his mind. Owen Roberts's famed "switch in time that saved nine" allowed the Court to bend to the emerging national consensus that recovery required the government's active management of the economy. In the years after the Court packing crisis, President Roosevelt sealed the Court's retreat from economic policy by filling vacant seats on the bench with appointees who were committed to the New Deal. He had many opportunities: between 1937 and 1941, seven members of the Court either died or retired. Only Roberts and Harlan Fiske Stone, whom Roosevelt raised to chief justice, remained. The justices, now more in tune with the elected branches' thinking about the government's role in the economy, began to pay attention to a different set of issues—civil rights and civil liberties.

The Rise of Civil Rights and Civil Liberties

The third era of judicial review began in earnest in the 1950s and 1960s. During this period the Court's main object of concern was the relationship between the individual and government. The broad scope of this new direction was surveyed in Chapters 4 and 5; here we are interested in why the Supreme Court went in this particular direction.

A number of historical reasons for this development have been proposed, and all of them may be true. For example, the rise of totalitarian regimes in Europe and the horrors of World War II may have caused jurists to reflect more critically on the preservation of personal freedoms in the United States. Black troops returning from the war

THE COURTS AND MENTAL HEALTH
How Far Should an Activist Judge Go?

The Supreme Court's decision in *Roe v. Wade* (1973) legalizing abortion has been at the center of heated debates over the legitimate limits of judicial activism for more than two decades. Yet *Roe* hardly describes the sum total of policy making by the federal courts. Consider the case of *Wyatt v. Stickney* decided in 1971 by district court judge Frank M. Johnson Jr.[1] *Wyatt* concerned conditions in Bryce Mental Hospital of Tuscaloosa, Alabama. Built in the 1850s, Bryce was a massive institution that housed more than five thousand patients, including substantial numbers of geriatric and other patients with no diagnosis of mental illness. The barnlike dormitories were poorly ventilated and posed a serious fire hazard. The residents lived in appalling conditions. As one eyewitness recounted, "Human feces were caked on the toilets and walls, urine saturated the aging oak floors, many beds lacked linen, some patients slept on floors, archaic shower stalls had cracked and spewing shower heads. . . . Most of the patients were highly tranquilized and had not been bathed in days. All appeared to lack any semblance of treatment. The stench was almost unbearable."

Contemplating the plight of these patients, Judge Johnson ruled that for the state to confine patients to Bryce without the guarantee of adequate treatment, first, violated the Fourteenth Amendment's mandate forbidding states from depriving "any person of life, liberty, or property, without due process of law," and, second, broke the Eighth Amendment's prohibition against "cruel and unusual punishment." Finding the conditions at Bryce to be unconstitutional, Johnson then identified the constitutional standards of adequate treatment that the state was required to meet. Johnson's treatment standards were impressive in their detail. He not only established the minimum ratio of staff to patients, but also set guidelines for

the ratio of toilets to patients as well as for the water temperature of hospital dishwashers.

Johnson's decision initiated a period of close court supervision of Alabama's mental health institutions that lasted nearly fifteen years. By the end of that time, the number of patients in Bryce had decreased by roughly half, and the practice of simply "warehousing" the mentally ill without treatment had been discontinued. But not all of the consequences of court-ordered reform were intended, or beneficial. As the director of the American Psychological Association observed, "Judge Johnson's order was interpreted as saying you can't hold these people prisoner; you either have to give them treatment or let them go. And they said, 'Fine, we'll let them go,' and they did in vast numbers." An increased number of mentally ill individuals were discharged directly onto the streets where they, needless to say, received no treatment at all.

The *Wyatt* example raises hard questions about judicial activism and the role of the courts as policy makers. Does the fact that mental hospitals responded to Judge Johnson's exhaustive (and expensive) list of standards by releasing patients suggest that judicial restraint would have been a better approach? If Judge Johnson had exercised judicial restraint, what would have become of the thousands of patients originally suffering at Bryce? More generally, can we say that judges are well suited to reform the administration of mental institutions? If not, who should make these decisions?

Source: Factual material for this discussion was drawn from Jack Bass, *Taming the Storm: The Life and Times of Judge Frank M. Johnson, Jr., and the South's Fight over Civil Rights* (New York: Bantam, 1993), 277–303.

1. *Wyatt v. Stickney,* 334 F. Supp. 1341 (1971).

expected their lives to be better than before, and they were joined in their search for a better quality of life by the large numbers of African Americans who migrated from the South to the industrial cities of the North. There, they created a community that no longer would allow the nation to ignore segregation in the South and racial discrimination elsewhere. Before winning victories in Congress, civil rights proponents found a Supreme Court willing to support their cause.

The three eras reviewed here are historic not only because they represent periods of sharp disagreement between the Court and the elected branches, but also because they led to major changes in the country. Certainly during the modern era, relations between the independent judiciary and the national legislature have not erupted into the kinds of constitutional confrontations just surveyed. Once the Court left the policy arena of economic regulation, it removed a major source of friction between these institutions. They continue to adjust to one another's decisions, but their actions and reactions occur in a much narrower field of public policy. The Supreme Court still engages in judicial review as indicated in Table 9–1 by the comparatively large number of federal and state laws invalidated. But for the most part these issues have been at the fringes of national policy and consequently render it less threatening to the President, Congress, and the national majorities they represent.

The Structure of the Federal Judiciary

The United States has more than seven hundred federal courts, but only the Supreme Court is explicitly mentioned in the Constitution (see Article III). The Framers knew more would be needed, but unable to resolve a disagreement over whether to create a separate federal judiciary or have the state courts oversee the initial trials and lower-level appeals, they agreed to defer the decision and let Congress create "inferior" courts as the need arose. Congress promptly did so by means of the Judiciary Act

of 1789. Of the various types of courts Congress has created over the years, those of most interest here are **constitutional courts,** which are vested with the general judicial authority outlined in Article III.[23] These lower-level courts, designed to handle litigation, exercise the same power of judicial review available to the Supreme Court. In this sense, the entire federal judiciary serves as agents of the Supreme Court. The courts examine the merits of a case, weigh them against prescribed Supreme Court doctrine, and presumably arrive at approximately the same decision the Supreme Court would have rendered had it heard the case.

Chapter 6 describes how Congress delegates work to specialized committees and sizable staffs to deal with the myriad issues and policies it handles. Much the same story is told for the modern presidency in Chapter 7; a large, highly specialized White House staff helps to monitor the hundreds of executive branch agencies. As with these other institutions, the Supreme Court's effectiveness also rests on delegation—in this instance, on its success in persuading, by the strength of its opinions, the lower federal judiciary to implement its policies.

The federal judiciary is organized as a three-layered pyramid (Figure 9–2). At its base are ninety-four **district courts** staffed by 632 judges. Every state has at least one district court and the three largest states—California, New York, and Texas—have four. These trial courts deal with three kinds of cases: criminal, which are instigated by indictments initiated by the local U.S. attorney; civil, in which both the plaintiff bringing the suit and the defendant are private parties contesting an alleged violation of civil law (such as a dispute over contractual obligations or patent infringement); and public law, in which a private party typically charges a government agency with acting illegally or failing to carry out its statutory responsibilities.

Above the district courts are thirteen **courts of appeals,** administered by 179 judges. Eleven separate geographic regions, or "circuits," cover the fifty states; a twelfth is assigned to the District of Columbia. The thir-

Figure 9–2 The Federal Court System

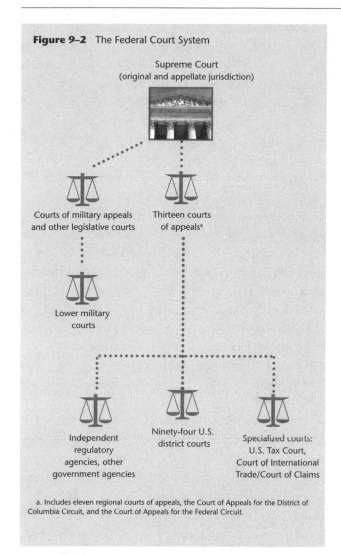

Supreme Court
(original and appellate jurisdiction)

Courts of military appeals and other legislative courts

Thirteen courts of appeals[a]

Lower military courts

Independent regulatory agencies, other government agencies

Ninety-four U.S. district courts

Specialized courts: U.S. Tax Court, Court of International Trade/Court of Claims

a. Includes eleven regional courts of appeals, the Court of Appeals for the District of Columbia Circuit, and the Court of Appeals for the Federal Circuit.

In 1998 the Supreme Court was called upon to resolve a dispute between New York and New Jersey over which state "owned" Ellis Island. Situated at the mouth of the Hudson River, the island served from 1891 to 1954 as the port of entry for millions of immigrants from Europe. Much to the disgust of New Yorkers, the Court ruled that part of the island belongs to New Jersey.

teenth, called the United States Court of Appeals for the Federal Circuit, has a nationwide jurisdiction and deals mostly with federal policies. Usually sitting as three-judge panels, these courts review district court decisions.

The Supreme Court is the court of final appeal. Under its appellate jurisdiction, the Court may hear cases appealed from the lower federal courts or directly from the highest state courts when an important constitutional question is in dispute. Through these channels, the Court receives the bulk of its work. Article III also gives it original trial court jurisdiction in all cases "affecting Ambassadors, other public Ministers and Consuls, and those in which a State shall be a Party." This constitutional quirk required the Supreme Court in 1998 to hear a dispute between New York and New Jersey over which state "owned" Ellis Island, which is located at the mouth of the Hudson River. Original jurisdiction cases always have accounted for a small part of the Court's work—only about 160 in two hundred years.

The Supreme Court's lofty position at the apex of this network of federal courts suggests far greater control over the administration of justice in America than in fact exists. Contrary to the clean lines of authority depicted in Figure 9–2, the judicial system is anything but a tightly supervised hierarchy. Rather, it is a decentralized organization, physically dispersed across the nation and administered at every level by independent, life-tenured judges.

The Supreme Court's success in fostering coherence among the lower federal courts largely determines whether the judiciary realizes its status as a coequal branch of government. Unlike the presidency, which delegates to the Office of Management and Budget oversight of the bureaucracy, or the House and Senate, which delegate to committees responsibility for drafting legislation, the Supreme Court possesses few administrative controls over the lower courts. The Court depends heavily on the lower courts behaving like loyal agents in deciding thousands of cases annually.

The Limits of Administrative Control

If the federal judiciary were a true hierarchical organization, the Supreme Court would enjoy a relationship with the district and appeals courts far different from what it actually has. Like the CEO of a major corporation it would routinely supervise and give orders to its subordinate units. When policy questions arise, especially those having implications for the organization, subordinates would seek guidance from their superiors. They would be motivated to do so by the knowledge that making the wrong choice might result in an unfavorable merit review, demotion, or even dismissal, while the right choice might be rewarded with a bonus and promotion.

None of these techniques is available to the Supreme Court in seeking responsiveness from the district and appellate courts. Instead, the life tenure of judges, which insulates the Court from the other branches, also insulates judges from each other. Only Congress can remove a federal judge and then only for serious offenses—not for incompetence or policy disagreement with the Supreme Court. Moreover, the Supreme Court cannot distribute the caseload to the lower courts: the distribution of cases depends on geographical jurisdictions and decisions by litigants as to which court or judge they would prefer to have hear their case.

Even when the Supreme Court disagrees strongly with a lower court's decision, it cannot countermand the decision. One of the litigants has to appeal the decision before the Court can assume jurisdiction. An example of the Court's inability to exercise complete control over its docket is found in the case study that opened Chapter 4, Civil Rights. Once the Piscataway school district agreed to settle the affirmative action lawsuit with one of its teachers, the case became moot and was removed from the Supreme Court's calendar. As a result, the Court lost its only opportunity of the 1997–1998 term to rule on the constitutionality of affirmative action.

The Supreme Court also may have difficulty enforcing implementation of its decisions in the lower courts. Outright resistance to Supreme Court decisions by lower-court judges is unusual but does occur. Declaring that the Court had "erred," an Alabama federal judge in 1983 upheld prayer in the public schools, in spite of the Court's prohibition of the practice.[24] In a capital punishment case in 1993 an appellate judge kept granting a stay of execution despite the Supreme Court's rejection of the defendant's appeal; it had to send down an order barring any more delays.[25]

More commonly, policy differences occur when lower-court judges take advantage of ambiguities arising from the particular facts of a case or in Supreme Court doctrine to avoid complying with the higher court's preferences. This is precisely what happened in the aftermath of *Brown v. Board of Education*.[26] When the Court ordered public schools to desegregate with "all deliberate speed" instead of setting a deadline, it unwittingly invited segregationist federal judges throughout the South to move at a snail's pace.

Yet the Supreme Court is not helpless. It can reverse lower-court decisions when it disagrees; even the threat of reversal should deter deviations from Court doctrine. After all, a reversal represents a "defeat" for a judge, and those who suffer frequent reversals damage their professional reputations as jurists. Fearing reversal, most judges probably temper their rulings to bring them into sufficient conformity with established doctrine to withstand litigants' efforts to persuade the Supreme Court to review the rulings. Nonetheless, reversal remains an imperfect sanction. Some judges may be willing to risk a few reversals to defend strongly held views.[27]

Managing the Caseload: Strategy and Tactics

The huge caseload of the federal judiciary means that the risk of reversal may not be so great. The district courts handle approximately 45,000 criminal and 200,000 civil cases a year. The Supreme Court, by contrast, decides fewer than 100 cases annually, or about 1 percent of the appeals it receives (Figure 9–3). Most of the reviews of district court decisions are handled by the appeals courts, which average about 45,000 cases annually. Thus this intermediate level of the judiciary—and not the Supreme Court—oversees the district courts' compliance with prevailing doctrine, allowing the Supreme Court to act as a "general staff or selective formulator of policies."[28]

In 1925 when the number of appeals had begun to grow at an alarming rate, the Supreme Court persuaded Congress to change the rules granting access to a hearing by the Court. Over the years these rules have been strengthened in favor of giving the Court greater discretion to choose the cases it reviews. Instead of having a right to "their day in court," litigants must file a **writ of certiorari,** requesting that the Court order a lower court to send it the records of the trial in question. By means of this device, the Court gained control over its caseload since the vast majority of the cases arrive by this route. Indeed, the Court has managed to cut in half the number of cases it hears annually, despite a six-fold increase in the number of requests.

Discretionary control over its caseload solved only part of the Court's problem, however. From the 7,500 or so certiorari requests it receives each year, how does the Court decide which 100 to review? The only rule governing case selection is that four of the nine justices must favor hearing a case for a certiorari petition to be granted.

Figure 9–3 Supreme Court Caseload, 1950–1998

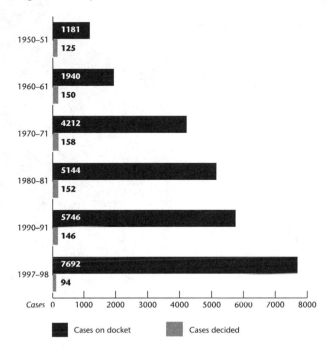

Source: Administrative Office of the Courts, Supreme Court Public Information Office.

Unlike Congress and the president, whose staffs number in the thousands, the Supreme Court is not attended by a large bureaucracy to help it cull through the piles of petitions and find cases that satisfy its criteria. Each justice is permitted to hire up to four clerks, usually graduates of the country's most prestigious law schools, who spend a year or two at the Court. To deal with the petitions, the clerks form a "cert pool" to review them and make recommendations to the justices. Because the opportunity to hear cases is limited, justices take a hard, strategic look at each one before promoting it with their colleagues. Do the facts of the case allow for the Court to arrive at a "clean" decision that will guide the lower courts? More important, will the justice's preference stand a chance of garnering the five votes necessary to win if the case is heard on its merits? If not, a justice who otherwise would

This 1885 Puck *magazine cartoon calls for Congress to relieve the Supreme Court's congested docket. Relief would come later with reforms giving the court the writ of certiorari.*

want to hear a case will pass on it for fear of allowing the majority to establish even more firmly a policy he or she opposes.[29] Thus deciding whether to hear a case is itself a major decision—and one fraught with political strategy. After all, as Chief Justice William Rehnquist acknowledged, "There is an ideological division on the Court, and each of us has some cases we would like to see granted, and on the contrary some of the other members would not like to see them granted."[30]

Because justices want to weigh in on cases in which they feel the lower courts have made an error, cases granted certiorari have a good chance of being overturned, and in a typical year almost two-thirds are. Justices also look for cases they can use to resolve ambiguities and conflicting lower-court decisions. Recognizing that the Court has a strong stake in maintaining standards and coherence within this highly decentralized organization, justices tend to carefully scrutinize those cases coming from district and appeals courts where the judges have poor reputations for following Supreme Court doctrine. The liberal

Ninth Circuit Court of Appeals in San Francisco has in recent years been overturned more often than any other circuit. As a result, the present Supreme Court, with its conservative leanings, is nearly twice as likely each year to grant petitions arising from this circuit. During the 1996–1997 and 1997–1998 terms, the Supreme Court heard forty-six cases from the Ninth Circuit and overturned all but five of its decisions.[31]

In selecting cases for resolution, the justices economize by paying close attention to what others tell them. In addition to the plaintiff (or prosecutor in criminal cases) and defendant, the Court allows interested parties—interest groups, businesses, and government agencies, among others—to submit **amicus curiae** (friend of the court) briefs arguing that a certiorari petition be granted or denied. Just as interest groups testify before Congress in hearings, business, government, and other groups "testify" before the Supreme Court in these briefs. Of all the interested parties, the most important and prolific is the federal government itself. Through the office of the

Chief Justice William Rehnquist, who served as a law clerk for Justice Robert Jackson (served 1941–1954), meets with his clerks to discuss pending cases.

solicitor general the administration lets the Court know which cases it thinks are important.

The anecdotal record has long acknowledged that the presence of amicus curiae briefs from prestigious sources increases a case's chances of being accepted by the Court. One systematic analysis of the Supreme Court's decision to grant or reject certiorari found that the solicitor general had supported a hearing in about half of the cases the Court accepted.[32] And in controversial cases—defined as those cases in which lower courts disagreed or amicus curiae briefs had been filed on both sides of the issue—the Court's decision to hear a case followed the solicitor general's recommendation more than 95 percent of the time.

At first glance, these figures appear to indicate that the solicitor general dictates the Court's agenda. A more subtle process is probably at work, however. In looking for cases they hope will persuade the Court to adopt a doctrine to their liking, the government and interest groups

tend to submit amicus curiae briefs in those cases they think will catch the eye of the Court. In this way, they actually help the Court identify the most important cases for that session.

The Strategy of Making Doctrine

Like the management of other decentralized organizations, the Supreme Court has sought to exercise control and to cope with the ever-growing caseload by establishing standard operating procedures prescribing how lower courts within the organization should decide cases. But because the Court does not directly supervise its agents, it tries to direct lower courts through its decisions on cases. In rendering decisions, the Court is prescribing guidelines for district and appeals judges to use when they try similar cases. These prescriptions are called **judicial doctrine.** Lower-court judges welcome doctrine not only because it makes their jobs easier, but also because it allows them to estimate how far they can diverge from the Supreme Court's preferences before they run the risk of being reviewed and overturned.

Judicial doctrine assumes two forms: procedural and substantive. Procedural doctrine governs how the lower courts should do their work. Substantive doctrine, which is more akin to policy making, guides judges as to which party in a case should prevail. Sometimes the two doctrines clash, such as when the Court decides to change current policy—for example, a search and seizure doctrine—but doing so requires a repudiation of existing precedents that the lower courts have dutifully followed.

Stare Decisis *and Other Procedural Doctrines. Stare decisis,* Latin for "let the decision stand," is long-established Supreme Court doctrine that directs the lower courts (as well as the Supreme Court itself) to follow established precedent in deciding current cases. Generally, precedents are earlier decisions, such as *Griswold v. Connecticut,* that establish a new substantive doctrine—in this case, the implicit right of privacy (see Chapter 5). Especially at the appellate stages of a case, the plaintiff's and the defendant's lawyers invoke precedents that support their positions. To the extent that they follow *stare decisis,* the lower courts find it easier to extend the Supreme Court's preferences. The Court, in turn, is freer to monitor decisions closely and thereby to address unresolved issues pressing for a decision.

Even when followed conscientiously, *stare decisis* cannot strictly determine the outcome of every case; new and unusual circumstances arise for which existing doctrine offers little guidance. Or the doctrine may be ambiguous, perhaps reflecting uncertainty or disagreement among members of the Court as to what the policy should be. Or, as happens frequently, the facts of a case may bring two doctrines in conflict.

The ability to interpret doctrine and apply precedents to specific cases is an important skill. Among other things, a judge must decide whether the particulars of a given case bring it within the domain of a particular precedent. Judges who develop strong reputations for writing convincing opinions that influence the way other judges think about comparable cases—that is, their opinions assume value as precedent.

Other procedural doctrines identify who may initiate cases in federal court and under what circumstances. Only litigants who are directly and adversely affected by the action in dispute have the right, or *standing,* to bring the case to court. Established doctrine instructs judges to ignore constitutional questions if other considerations are sufficient to govern the outcome of the case. And if the circumstances that gave rise to a case have changed or render the outcome moot, then the case should be dismissed rather than judged hypothetically. One of the most important procedural doctrines establishes a boundary of federalism within the judiciary: only those cases in

After inflaming white southerners with the Court's ruling in Brown v. Board of Education *in 1954 and other groups throughout the country with liberal civil liberties rulings, Chief Justice Earl Warren became a target of a grassroots impeachment campaign. In this 1963 photo he accepts impeachment literature while passing picketers. No Supreme Court justice has ever been removed by impeachment.*

the state courts that raise a constitutional question at the outset—such as a civil liberty protected by the Bill of Rights—may be appealed to the federal judiciary after a loss in the state courts.

Substantive Doctrine. As the Supreme Court selects and decides cases, it is less interested in simply "seeing justice done" in a particular instance than in identifying standards and general characteristics of cases that will allow a decision to be applied to government policy as well as to future cases. Some issues lend themselves better than others to this form of policy making. One issue that did not was obscenity. The Supreme Court agonized for years over how to define obscenity, one of the few kinds of speech that does not enjoy First Amendment protection. The effort led one exasperated justice to exclaim, "I know it when I see it!" By contrast, the clear standards for protection of the accused's right to avoid self-incrimination enunciated in the *Miranda* decision (see Chapter 4) allowed the lower courts to apply those standards easily, which they did.

Every Supreme Court decision contains two elements essential to creating doctrine. The first is the vote that decides the case in favor of one of the parties. The second is the opinion, a statement or set of statements in which the majority explains the rationale for its decision in such a way as to create doctrine (that is, make policy) and the minority, if there is one, explains why it dissents.

A unanimous Court decision, simply because it is less likely to be reversed in the future, creates more compelling precedent than a case decided by a 5–4 vote. After the justices express their views on a case and vote tentatively on the outcome in a private conference, the chief justice (if voting with the majority) assigns one of the majority the task of drafting an opinion. The task is not insignificant; actions may speak louder than words, but for the Supreme Court its actions are its words. The author of an opinion gives voice to the majority position and, in doing so, strongly influences the shape that judicial policy takes.

Once the majority opinion is drafted, it often becomes the focus of prolonged internal bargaining as the writer attempts to persuade the other justices that its legal arguments are correct. The author of the opinion generally writes with the aim of maintaining the decision's core support as well as appealing to dissenters who might be converted. In 1954 Chief Justice Earl Warren used his considerable powers of persuasion to coax reluctant justices to abandon their disparate positions over school desegre-

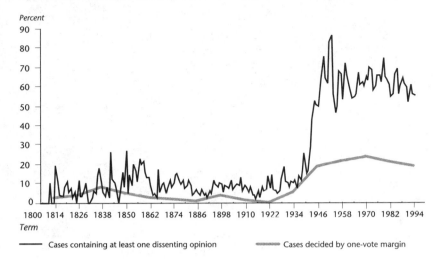

Figure 9–4 Percentage of U.S. Supreme Court Cases Containing at Least One Dissenting Opinion and Percentage Decided by a One-Vote Margin, 1800–1994 Terms

——— Cases containing at least one dissenting opinion   ▬▬▬ Cases decided by one-vote margin

Data Sources: Lee Epstein and Jack Knight, *The Choices Justices Make* (Washington, D.C.: CQ Press, 1998), 24; Lee Epstein et al., *The Supreme Court Compendium*, 2d ed. (Washington, D.C.: Congressional Quarterly, 1996), Table 3–2.

gation to forge a unanimous opinion in *Brown v. Board of Education.*

Successful persuasion has its costs, however. Generally, to persuade colleagues to maintain or shift their positions the drafter must change the opinion's language and perhaps blur its message, allowing each member of the majority to find language in the opinion he or she can agree with. Thus reluctant justices joined Warren's opinion in *Brown* on the condition that he not specify a time schedule for school desegregation. The consequences, we found in Chapter 4, were anything but slight. The failure to set a deadline opened the door for dilatory tactics as southern school boards first resisted and then engaged in token desegregation and for years tied up enforcement with litigation. The price of broad support among the justices may be vague, imperfectly enforced doctrine.

The prevalence of nonunanimous and closely divided decisions is a modern development, but what accounts for the trends displayed in Figure 9–4? For one thing, until passage of the Judiciary Act of 1925, which gave the

The current Supreme Court is considered collegial, yet it, like other recent Courts, has decided many cases by very narrow margins. From left to right: Clarence Thomas, Antonin Scalia, Sandra Day O'Connor, Anthony M. Kennedy, David H. Souter, Stephen G. Breyer, John Paul Stevens, William H. Rehnquist, and Ruth Bader Ginsburg.

Supreme Court greater control over its caseload, the Court had to decide far more cases than it considers today. Obligated to review many lower-court decisions with which it agreed, the Court before 1925 produced a large number of unanimous opinions. As the Supreme Court has freed itself to focus on cases that contain important, unresolved policy issues, the proportion of controversial cases has risen dramatically.

Two other influences have been at work as well. First, the Court stopped contesting the authority of Congress and the president to regulate economic activity and began applying the Bill of Rights to state—not just federal—actions. That the justices would not march in unison toward this new body of judicial doctrine was not surprising. The second influence has been the somewhat regular alternation of party control of the White House—a pattern largely absent in the late nineteenth and early twentieth centuries. In the next section we shall see that an impor-

tant result of this political development has been a more heterogeneous Supreme Court. Democratic and Republican presidents have taken turns appointing liberals and conservatives to the high bench. In 1999 the Supreme Court had seven Republican appointees and two Democratic appointees.

The decision about the rationale on which to base an opinion may be more consequential for future cases than the decision itself. More often than not, justices reach different conclusions about cases; after all, the easy cases with precedents providing clear guidance tend to be resolved by a lower court. And even when justices vote together on the resolution of a case, they may have different reasons for doing so.

Because all justices wish to influence future decisions, each has an interest in opinion writing. A justice who disagrees with the majority of the Court may elect to explain why in a **dissenting opinion.** A justice who has

Figure 9–5   Concurring and Dissenting Supreme Court Opinions, 1800–1994

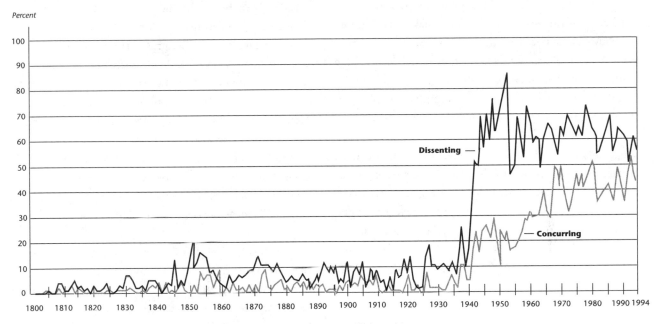

Percent

Source: Lee Epstein, et al., *The Supreme Court Compendium,* 2d ed. (Washington, D.C.: Congressional Quarterly, 1996), Tables 3 2 and 3–3.

unique reasons for supporting the majority may choose to write a **concurring opinion.** Concurring and dissenting opinions allow justices to provide their interpretations of what the majority opinion means. While only the majority opinion counts as the Court's final decision in any given case, dissenting and concurring opinions may nonetheless influence reactions to the majority's position, providing guidance for the application of the majority's reasoning to future cases.

The number of dissenting opinions has, of course, paralleled the growth of nonunanimous decisions, and the proportion of cases containing concurring decisions has increased as well (Figure 9–5). As the Court has devoted its attention more exclusively to policy making, individual justices have taken the opportunity to express themselves.

Influence of the Elected Branches

Judicial review combined with life tenure would appear to deal the federal judiciary a strong hand in asserting its policy preferences over those of Congress and the presidency. Indeed, Table 9–1 revealed that the Supreme Court does not shy away from its prerogative to rule laws unconstitutional. Today's Court also devotes a large share of its caseload to statutory interpretation—that is, resolving disputes about what the laws mean and how they should be administered. By one count, the Court delivered 374 such rulings from 1986 through 1990. At times, it will even recommend changes in law that will produce more desirable results.[33] Unquestionably, the judicial branch is an active participant that the other branches must take into account in formulating national policy. On closer inspection, however, the federal judiciary appears to lack the kinds of internal resources that would allow it to be a powerful, autonomous policy maker. The limited veto authority offered by judicial review, the huge caseload, the lack of enforcement authority, and even the life tenure of all of its members, reveal it to be an organization ill designed to formulate and implement public policy. This is the way it should be in a democracy.

When Hamilton described the judiciary as the least dangerous branch, he was not referring to its organizational weaknesses. Nor was he attributing special virtues to its members. Rather, he was reassuring delegates to the state ratifying conventions that the judiciary had been given less power than Congress or the president. Not only do the elected branches have the authority to make and enforce policy, Hamilton might have added, they also have the wherewithal to prevent the judiciary from drifting too far afield from majority opinion in the country.

Despite the Constitution's formal provisions for the separation of powers, Congress and the president do have ways of bringing judicial policy into alignment with their preferences. They range from the rarely enlisted yet potentially formidable constitutional prerogatives to the day-to-day maintenance tasks of filling judicial vacancies and creating new courts to handle a growing caseload.

Constitutional and Statutory Control

Several provisions of the Constitution equip Congress and the president to rein in a Supreme Court when they disagree. Article III allows Congress to set the jurisdiction of the Court and to create lower courts. The Constitution is silent on the size of the Supreme Court which means the Framers implicitly gave this authority to Congress. During the nineteenth century, Congress did, in fact, add to and subtract from the number of justices, but since 1869 the number has been set at nine. At times, when one of the political parties has captured control of the White House and Congress, it has expanded the size of the lower judiciary as a way of creating vacancies that can be filled with sympathetic judges.[34] The net effect of this practice is to bring the judiciary into closer alignment with changes in national opinion.

When all else fails, Congress may move to amend the Constitution (Article V). The Fourteenth Amendment's declaration that "all persons born or naturalized in the United States . . . are citizens of the United States" was designed to invalidate the Court's claim in *Scott v. Sandford* that African Americans cannot be U.S. citizens. After repeated failures to persuade the Supreme Court that the Constitution does not forbid an income tax, Congress sent to the states the Sixteenth Amendment legalizing the personal income tax once and for all. The states ratified it in 1913.

The historical rarity of these attempts does not mean they are altogether irrelevant to these institutions' relations. Their existence reminds justices that they cannot long impose a radically different interpretation of the Constitution and their role within it, without facing sanctions from the elected branches. In 1937 President Roosevelt lost the Court packing battle, but he achieved his objective of stopping the Supreme Court from meddling in his New Deal economic recovery policies. The conservatives on the Court were confronted with the stark reality of the superior authority of the elected branches, and they nimbly began undoing precedents they had asserted only a few years before. Shortly thereafter, the Four Horsemen—the apocalyptic nickname given to the conservative justices who voted in unison against Roosevelt's policies—left the bench: one died and three retired.[35]

Statutory responses to disagreeable Supreme Court decisions are, by contrast, routine. One study found that from 1967 through 1990 Congress averaged a dozen new laws a year explicitly designed to reverse or modify a federal court ruling. Moreover, about half of all Supreme Court decisions that involved interpretation of federal law became the specific subject of congressional hearings.[36]

One area in which congressional oversight has been especially rigorous is civil rights. In 1980 the Supreme Court ruled that before electoral rules that diluted the political impact of a racial minority could be judged violations of the 1965 Voting Rights Act, the plaintiff had to demonstrate that the laws not only had an adverse "effect" but also were enacted with the "intent" to discriminate against minorities.[37] Because some of the local laws in question had been on the statute books for a half-century or more, proving intent was sometimes impossible. In 1982, when Congress renewed the Voting Rights Act for another seven years, it added language stating that plaintiffs need only demonstrate vote dilution to challenge local electoral laws. In 1991, with the enactment of new civil rights laws, Congress overrode nine Supreme Court decisions.

Sometimes Congress and the president attempt to control judicial policy by enacting laws that strip jurisdiction from federal courts. For example, Congress passed a law in 1996 making it easier to deport criminal immigrants. At the same time, it removed the courts' authority to review, and thus delay, these administrative decisions. Two years later, however, an appeals court ruled that Congress may not strip immigrants of their constitutional right to a court hearing. This decision remains open to a final Supreme Court determination.[38]

Institutional Resources

Aside from the Constitution's checks and balances, each branch of government has internal assets and liabilities that help to define its influence with the other branches. We already have examined the effect of the judiciary's decentralized structure on the Supreme Court's ability to influence the other branches. Two additional contributing factors are the Court's lack of enforcement authority and the president's own "judicial bureaucracy," the hundreds of prosecutors in the Department of Justice who routinely bring cases to the judiciary and therefore have a say in defining its agenda.

Absence of Judicial Enforcement. In 1974 President Nixon refused to release Oval Office recordings of private conversations to the special prosecutor investigating the variety of misdeeds known as the Watergate scandal. When the two sides went to court, the Supreme Court, by an 8–0 vote, rejected Nixon's claim of executive privilege and instructed him to turn over the tapes to the special prosecutor, which he did.[39] The contents of the tapes led directly to his resignation. Had he defied the Court—and the press speculated that he might—Congress would have taken the next step and decided whether his refusal constituted grounds for impeachment.

The absence of enforcement authority has allowed Congress and the president at times to ignore Supreme Court rulings. In *Immigration and Naturalization Service v. Chadha* (1983) the Court declared the one-house **legislative veto** unconstitutional, upsetting established procedures between Congress and the executive branch.[40] The case itself concerned a minor issue, the deportation of a man who had overstayed his student visa, but its implications were potentially far-reaching. The legislative veto dates back to 1932, when Congress and the president agreed to provisions that since then have been included in more than two hundred public laws, including the War Powers Act. These provisions allow either one or both houses of Congress to pass a resolution to reject an executive action. Although *Chadha* technically voided this mechanism, the departments still abide by these legislative vetoes. And Congress and presidents have good reasons for favoring this approach. In essence, it allows Congress to turn over some lawmaking responsibilities to the executive branch. The bureaucracy can design policies to implement the laws, while Congress need not fear that the policies will drift too far away from congressional intent. Presidents realize that Congress is more willing to relinquish control when it knows it has a way to rescind it. In effect, the elected branches have overruled the Supreme Court's constitutional verdict "by open defiance and subtle evasion."[41]

Department of Justice. The federal government, represented primarily by the Department of Justice, is by far the most frequent and most important litigant in the federal court system. Indeed, the structure of the department parallels that of the federal courts, giving it the power (and efficiency) to press for legal action at all levels of the federal court system. The head of the department, the attorney general of the United States, can pick and choose cases and venues—in other words, courts—where the Justice Department is most likely to win and, more important, create precedent for its legal position on an issue.

The department includes the U.S. attorneys, one for each of the ninety-four federal judicial districts. They are responsible for bringing cases to district court on behalf of the federal government and deciding which criminal investigations to prosecute and which civil suits to pursue. Because they engage in more litigation at the district court level than anyone else, U.S. attorneys play a major role in determining the docket of the lower federal courts. They have a fair degree of discretion in selecting cases, but they are not completely independent. Nominated by the president and confirmed by the Senate, U.S. attorneys are formally authorized to serve for four years, but they may be reappointed indefinitely or removed early at the pleasure of the president.

The Department of Justice has six legal divisions: Antitrust, Civil, Civil Rights, Criminal, Environment and Natural Resources, and Tax. Each division is headed by an assistant attorney general who supervises the litigating activities of the U.S. attorneys. Presidential appointment and department supervision guarantee that U.S. attorneys serve as dutiful agents in enlisting the court system to pursue the kinds of cases the administration wants to emphasize. For example, in 1996, after a number of black churches had been firebombed, President Clinton announced a special effort to find and prosecute the culprits. Over the next six months, several cases were prosecuted in federal court. Conversely, when the same year California passed an initiative intended to legalize the use of marijuana for medicinal purposes, the U.S. attorneys

As Bill Clinton's attorney general, Janet Reno (left) appears to be the government's chief lawyer, but, in fact, she administers the federal government's varied law enforcement activities from overseeing the FBI to enforcing public laws. One of her subordinate offices is that of the solicitor general, Seth Waxman, who represents the Clinton administration in its dozens of filings with the Supreme Court each session.

stayed clear of prosecution, despite the Justice Department warning that possession of marijuana remained a federal crime.[42]

The decision to appeal government cases to the U.S. Courts of Appeals as well as the appeal itself is handled by one of the Department of Justice's six legal divisions, depending on the content of the case. Subsequent appeals to the Supreme Court, regardless of case content, are handled by the Office of the Solicitor General. Supported by a staff of about twenty-five attorneys, the solicitor general carefully selects only a few key government cases for appeal to the Court. This reputation for restraint creates a high level of credibility for the solicitor general with the Court. Just as interest groups' amicus curiae briefs may alert the Court to significant cases, the solicitor general's endorsement of a certiorari request sends a reliable signal of a case's importance. The result is a close relationship between the Court and the solicitor general—so close, in fact, that some Court watchers call it the "tenth justice."

The office's record of success before the Court speaks for itself.[43] While only a little more than 1 percent of all appeals are heard by the Court, the solicitor general's success rate in gaining the Court's review hovers between 70 and 80 percent. And on these cases, the Court adopts the solicitor general's position about 70 percent of the time.

The special relationship the solicitor general enjoys with the Court rests in part on this office's professional independence from other political actors. Although they remain subordinate to the attorney general and serve at the pleasure of the president, solicitors general historically have been given some latitude to pursue cases without being mere "mouthpieces" for the administration.[44] In fact, solicitors general have sometimes retained their offices after a change in administration and parties—Erwin Griswold, for example, was solicitor general under both Presidents Johnson and Nixon.

Judicial Recruitment

The Constitution provides that all federal judges shall be nominated by the president with the "advice and consent" of the Senate (Article II, Section 2). Traditionally, the president has deferred on district court nominations to the preferences of the senators from the state in which the court is located. Appointments to the courts of appeals and Supreme Court, however, tend to be more presidential and less collegially reliant on the Senate's "advice" than are lower-court appointments. In fact, judicial nominations represent the veto game in reverse. The president nominates, and the Senate accepts or rejects. This shared responsibility provides politicians in these institutions with their best chance to influence the policies flowing from the federal judiciary. Moreover, it guarantees that the president and Senate will carefully consider the nominee's political views. From the earliest days of the Republic, the president and Congress have appreciated the mer-

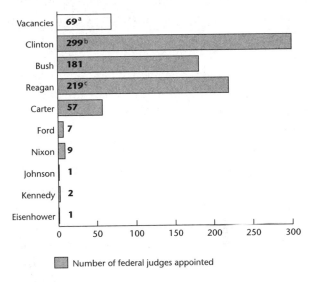

Figure 9–6 Presidential Imprint on the Federal Bench

Number of federal judges appointed

Source: Alliance for Justice.
Note: Article III judges serve on the Supreme Court, circuit, district, and International Trade Court.
   a. As of June 1, 1999.
   b. Presidential nominations as of January 1, 1999.
   c. Chief Justice William Rehnquist is counted as a Reagan appointee.

its of appointing like-minded colleagues to the federal judiciary. As we saw in the opening to this chapter, the outgoing Federalists understood this as early as the 1790s, when they stuffed as many of their partisans as possible into this branch before vacating the presidency and Congress. Two hundred years later so too did George Bush and Bill Clinton, each of whom appointed members of their own party 90 percent of the time.

In picking judicial nominees, presidents and Senate sponsors also have a stake in selecting individuals with strong professional credentials. Most nominees, for example, are practicing attorneys or sitting judges. Other things being equal, quality appointments will more effectively represent the president's views on the high bench. Moreover, less than stellar résumés may open the way for senatorial and other opponents who can claim to disapprove of the nominee not because they disagree with his or her views but because of a desire to appoint only the best-qualified candidates with impeccable records. When Justice Abe Fortas resigned from the Court in 1969, Richard Nixon nominated southerner Clement Haynsworth to replace him. Although Haynsworth was judicially well qualified, the Senate rejected him because he had participated in cases in which he may have had a financial interest. In early 1970 Nixon selected another southerner, G. Harrold Carswell. Senate Democrats successfully attacked Carswell's lackluster career in his state's court system. There should be room for mediocre justices, argued Sen. Roman Hruska of Nebraska, Carswell's exasperated Republican supporter, because "all Americans, even the mediocre members of society, deserve to be represented" on the Court. But this argument did not prove to be compelling, and Carswell failed to be elevated to the Supreme Court.

Presidential Appointments. Historically, nominations to the district courts have concerned the senators from the state where the court is located more than the president. Consequently, modern presidents delegate the task to those senators in a practice known as **senatorial courtesy**—one of the last vestiges of the patronage era of American politics. Because the courtesy of such appointment power is extended only to senators of the president's party, this practice goes a long way toward explaining why the nominations so heavily favor members of the president's party.

During the Reagan administration, the executive branch began to take a more active interest in district court appointments. Reagan's attorney general oversaw the compilation of the short list of possible nominees and interviewed the leading candidates to ascertain their conservative credentials. Bush and Clinton continued careful presidential scrutiny, although both also solicited the views of the relevant senators.

Presidents traditionally have taken greater personal interest and enjoyed more discretion in filling vacancies to the appeals courts. Senatorial courtesy has never formally applied to these appointments, probably reflecting the greater policy importance of these judges as well as the impracticality of vetting a nominee with all of the senators from those states encompassed by the court. Nine western states, for example, fall within the jurisdiction of the Ninth Circuit Court of Appeals.[45] Presidents have generally relied on the Department of Justice to screen candidates for the courts of appeals. President Jimmy Carter, however, departed from this tradition, creating a U.S. circuit judge nominating commission with panels in each circuit designed to recruit judicial nominees from a broader spectrum of the population. While the nominating commission ostensibly aimed at removing politics from the selection process, "merit" hardly seemed to be the defining characteristic of the commission's selections: 82 percent of Carter's appointments at this level were Democrats of a markedly liberal bent.[46] President Reagan dismantled the commission and returned control of the selection process to the Justice Department.

Nominees to the Supreme Court, the highest federal tribunal, receive the full attention of the president, the Senate, and the many constituencies whose interests are affected by judicial decisions. A president's impact on the composition of the Court depends on the frequency with which vacancies arise. During the first three years of the Nixon administration, four vacancies occurred, but none during Jimmy Carter's four years in the White House. President Reagan made four appointments, and Bush and Clinton made two each.

When a vacancy occurs, the president enlists several criteria in choosing a nominee. Understandably, in appointing an individual to a lifetime position of such importance, presidents try to guess how the nominee will vote on the controversial issues of the day—especially those issues that concern the president's supporters. Yet, predicting a future justice's votes has at times proved to be a highly unreliable science. One never knows how the particulars of a case will affect a justice's thinking. Also, suddenly insulated from political pressure, elected officeholders who join the Court may shed political positions that had more to do with their roles as representatives than with their sincere preferences.

One way of reducing uncertainty is to select nominees from the president's party—and, in fact, more than 90 percent of all nominees to the Supreme Court have shared the president's party affiliation. Another is to interview potential nominees carefully and subject their work to intensive examination. Sandra Day O'Connor, for example, was interviewed twice by administration officials and once by President Reagan before her nomination was announced.

Presidents also may regard a vacancy as an opportunity to reward a political ally or personal associate. President Franklin Roosevelt appointed Alabama senator Hugo Black to the Court in recognition of Black's strong support for the New Deal and the Court packing plan. Few anticipated that this Alabama politician, who had once belonged to the Ku Klux Klan, would become one of the Supreme Court's most ardent civil libertarians. But perhaps the most famous example of all is President Eisenhower's nomination of Earl Warren, the governor of California, to serve as chief justice, reportedly as reward for the crucial support Warren's delegation provided Eisenhower's nomination at the 1952 Republican convention. Eisenhower later regretted his choice of Warren as well as that of another justice, William Brennan, both of whom proved too activist and liberal for Eisenhower's taste. Asked if he had made any mistakes as president, Eisenhower, it is widely reported, responded, "Yes, two, and they are both sitting on the Supreme Court."[47]

Presidents also may use appointments to buttress and build political alliances. Historically, an appointee's region of origin was an important criterion. More recently, presidents have focused on the religion, sex, and race of nominees in an effort to build support with constituencies who might be pleased to have one of their own appointed to the Supreme Court. Just as Louis Brandeis broke the anti-Semitic barrier to the Court earlier in the century, Thur-

Toles © 1991 The Buffalo News. *Reprinted with permission of Universal Press Syndicate. All Rights Reserved.*

good Marshall was the first African American on the Court, and Sandra Day O'Connor the first woman. The fact that Marshall was a liberal activist appointed by a Democrat and O'Connor was a conservative appointed by a Republican suggests that presidents can make these symbolic gestures to constituencies without jeopardizing their policy goals.

Senate Confirmation. Once the president has named someone to fill a judicial vacancy, the Senate Judiciary Committee schedules confirmation hearings so that it can make a recommendation to the full chamber. When the same party controls the presidency and Senate, these nominations sail through the chamber with only cursory examination. But when the opposition controls the Senate, as has happened in thirteen of the last twenty-five Congresses, the process of scrutinizing the nominee often becomes highly political and deliberative. Although only six Supreme Court nominees have been rejected (or withdrew their nominations) during the twentieth centu-

SENATE CONFIRMATION
Another Kind of Veto Game

Under the Constitution, the president nominates candidates to the federal judiciary and the Senate confirms or rejects them. This sequence reverses the veto game described in Chapter 7 in which Congress proposes legislation and the president either endorses or vetoes it. In this game it is the Senate that confronts a "take it or leave it" decision that limits its opportunity to shape the result. For the Senate, the trick is to have presidents incorporate its preferences into their judicial nominations. But how can such a compromise occur when the proposal is a person?

President Bill Clinton's dealings with the Republican Senate after the election of 1994 demonstrated two possible solutions. Clinton accommodated the Senate by nominating moderate judges whose views were acceptable to its conservative majority. An alternative solution was to assemble a "package" of nominees that would allow Republicans to name some appointments in exchange for confirmations of others. President Clinton has been reluctant to do this, however, largely because Republicans wanted conservative jurists who were bound to stir up heated opposition from some of Clinton's core constituencies.

Nonetheless, in 1999 Republican senator Orrin Hatch of Utah, chairman of the Senate Judiciary Committee, persuaded the president to negotiate such a deal. Entering mid-June with seventy-two vacancies in the federal judiciary and forty-two Clinton nominations awaiting Senate action, Hatch's committee had yet to conduct its first confirmation hearing for 1999. In the meantime, Hatch was promoting Republican Ted Stewart, conservative head of Utah's Department of Natural Resources, for a vacancy to the federal district court in Salt Lake City. With a wink and a nod, Hatch suggested that were Clinton to nominate Stewart, the committee would go to work processing the president's pending nominees.

For nearly two months President Clinton hesitated. If he agreed, the Senate might clear dozens of pending nominees. But then he would lose the opportunity to fill the Utah vacancy with someone who shared his views on environmental policy. Worse, the president might anger environmentalists who adamantly opposed Stewart's nomination and had been publicly pressuring Clinton to reject Hatch's overture. Clearly, the Stewart nomination would be costly and the president had to be sure he would get something in return. But could he assume that Hatch would, or even could, safely usher many of his nominees to their seats on the federal bench?

The deal with Hatch represented a political minefield. How many pending nominees would Republicans allow through the committee in exchange for Stewart? Once Stewart's name was sent up, would Hatch, who had urged the president's removal during the impeachment trial earlier in the year, renege and play the president as a sucker? Clearly, a successful deal required the president and Hatch to navigate around a potential prisoner's dilemma. Beyond this, Clinton had to wonder about the fate of his nominees on the Senate floor even with the committee's endorsement. Republican Senate majority leader Trent Lott already had groused that Hatch's committee had been too generous with Clinton's nominations over the years. Would Stewart sail through confirmation while the Republican Senate (perhaps with Hatch's private complicity) refused to bring the president's nominees to a vote?

In mid-June the president decided time was running out and he had to make a move. In a phone conversation, Hatch and Clinton agreed to proceed in small, cautious steps that would allow each to avoid a potential double-cross. The president discreetly initiated the routine FBI check and submitted Stewart to the American Bar Association for its assessment. In return, the Senate Judiciary Committee on June 17 held its first hearing on eight of Clinton's judicial nominees. Two weeks later the deal finished up when the president announced his intent to nominate Stewart, and Hatch announced his committee's goal to clear for Senate vote at least ten of Clinton's pending nominees.

"He said"/"she said" assumed new dimensions in 1991 when Clarence Thomas, nominated to replace Justice Thurgood Marshall on the Supreme Court, was confronted with an accuser at the Senate Judiciary Committee hearings on his nomination. Coworker Anita Hill accused Thomas of sexual harassment. As one network executive said of the televised hearings, it was one of the few times daytime viewers of the soap operas did not complain about their programs being interrupted.

ry, three of these have occurred since 1969 when Republican presidents tried to get judicial conservatives past a Senate controlled by Democrats.

Toward the end of a president's first term the process of Senate confirmation may become so deliberative that nothing much happens until the senators learn whether the president will be returning for another term. In 1996, a presidential election year, the Republican Senate set a record in confirming none of President Clinton's nominees for the appellate court and only seventeen for the district court. Three years later, with the president facing possible removal from office, the Senate confirmation process once more came to a halt. In fact, not until mid-June 1999 did Senate confirmation hearings resume, and then only after President Clinton and Senate Judiciary Committee chairman Orrin Hatch, Republican from Utah, cut a political deal (see box "Senate Confirmation: Another Kind of Veto Game").

The president's announcement of a nominee usually triggers responses from a variety of interest groups whose policy preferences will be affected by who sits on the bench. From civil rights organizations to industrial lobbyists, many interest groups are affected by Court decisions and thus want to influence the Senate's decision. The height of interest group activity came in 1987 during the confirmation battle over Supreme Court nominee Robert Bork. Liberal interest groups, convinced that Bork would make the Court more conservative, mounted a massive campaign against his confirmation that supplemented personal lobbying of senators with direct mailings, newspaper advertisements, and press conferences. This effort cost an estimated $12–$15 million, an unprecedented amount to influence a Senate confirmation. These liberal organizations overwhelmed Bork's poorly organized conservative supporters. Largely because of their efforts, Bork's nomination was defeated, 58–42.

In 1991 liberal groups again mounted a vigorous attack against Bush nominee Clarence Thomas after a colleague,

Table 9–2 The Changing Composition of the Supreme Court, 1953–1999

1953	1961	1969	1977	1981	1992	1999
Hugo Black 1937-FDR	Hugo Black 1937-FDR	Hugo Black 1937-FDR	William J. Brennan Jr. 1956-DDE	William J. Brennan Jr. 1956-DDE	Byron R. White 1962-JFK	William H. Rehnquist* 1972-Nixon
Stanley Reed 1938-FDR	Felix Frankfurter 1939-FDR	William O. Douglas 1939-FDR	Potter Stewart 1958-DDE	Potter Stewart 1958-DDE	Harry A. Blackmun 1970-Nixon	John Paul Stevens 1975-Ford
Felix Frankfurter 1939-FDR	William O. Douglas 1939-FDR	Earl Warren 1953-DDE	Byron R. White 1962-JFK	Byron R. White 1962-JFK	William H. Rehnquist* 1972-Nixon	Sandra Day O'Connor 1981-Reagan
William O. Douglas 1939-FDR	Tom C. Clark 1949-HST	John M. Harlan 1955-DDE	Thurgood Marshall 1967-LBJ	Thurgood Marshall 1967-LBJ	John Paul Stevens 1975-Ford	Antonin Scalia 1986-Reagan
Robert H. Jackson 1941-FDR	Earl Warren 1953-DDE	William J. Brennan Jr. 1956-DDE	Warren E. Burger 1969-Nixon	Warren E. Burger 1969-Nixon	Sandra Day O'Connor 1981-Reagan	Anthony Kennedy 1988-Reagan
Harold Burton 1945-HST	John M. Harlan 1955-DDE	Potter Stewart 1958-DDE	Harry A. Blackmun 1970-Nixon	Harry A. Blackmun 1970-Nixon	Antonin Scalia 1986-Reagan	David H. Souter 1990-Bush
Fred M. Vinson 1946-HST	William J. Brennan Jr. 1956-DDE	Byron R. White 1962-JFK	Lewis F. Powell Jr. 1972-Nixon	Lewis F. Powell Jr. 1972-Nixon	Anthony Kennedy 1988-Reagan	Clarence Thomas 1991-Bush
Tom C. Clark 1949-HST	Charles E. Whittaker 1957-DDE	Abe Fortas 1965-LBJ	William H. Rehnquist 1972-Nixon	William H. Rehnquist 1972-Nixon	David H. Souter 1990-Bush	Ruth Bader Ginsburg 1993-Clinton
Sherman Minton 1949-HST	Potter Stewart 1958-DDE	Thurgood Marshall 1967-LBJ	John Paul Stevens 1975-Ford	John Paul Stevens 1975-Ford	Clarence Thomas 1991-Bush	Stephen G. Breyer 1994-Clinton

Note: Black type indicates that the justice was appointed by a Republican president. Colored type indicates that the justice was appointed by a Democratic president.
* President Reagan named Rehnquist chief justice in 1986.

Anita Hill, leveled sexual harassment charges against him. In the nationally televised hearings, which kept audiences glued to their sets, an indignant Thomas defended his reputation. In the end, the Senate confirmed his nomination by 52–48, the narrowest margin in U.S. history.

Confirmation authority limits the Senate to exercising a veto. It can either accept the president's candidate or leave the judgeship vacant hoping the president's next candidate will be more acceptable. During Bill Clinton's second term the Republican Senate adopted the latter course. At the beginning of 1998 one-tenth of all federal judgeships were vacant. In the liberal Appeals Court for the Ninth Circuit, which Republicans have targeted for conservative appointments, the vacancy rate had reached a third.[48]

The confirmation "veto" offers an opposition-controlled Senate more influence than the number of rejected nominees would indicate. Presidents, calculating the prospects of defeat of a nominee, usually forgo the battle and potential embarrassment of defeat and opt for someone whom the administration and the Senate find acceptable. Occasionally, the president and the Senate committee negotiate a "package" of nominations so that both sides get some of the judges they prefer.[49] Whatever the Senate's indirect influence, one can reasonably conclude that partisanship and ideology represent primary considerations in nomination and confirmation of federal judges. Because judges do in fact make policy, it is fitting that the president and Congress take their ideology into account and understandable that they would prefer judges who agree with their own political views. Indeed, with some exceptions, the judges appointed by Democratic presidents tend to vote in a liberal direction, and those appointed by Republican presidents tend to be conservative.[50]

This observation implies that the party that wins the White House receives, if the opportunity arises, the chance to shape the policies of the Supreme Court. And because Supreme Court justices serve for life, presidents' imprints may continue long after they have left office. When one party dominates the presidency, the cumulative impact on judicial policy can be great. As Republicans returned to the White House in 1953 for the first time in two decades, they encountered a Supreme Court wholly appointed by Democrats Roosevelt and Truman. But by the time President Eisenhower left office in 1961, Republican appointees constituted a majority of the membership (see Table 9–2). Since Lyndon Johnson left office in 1969, the Democrats have appointed only two justices. Although national conservative politicians have been quick to take the Court to task for "coddling" criminals and "undermining" religion, Republican presidents have selected three times as many Supreme Court justices as Democrats since 1953. Unsurprisingly, during these years the Court has assumed a more conservative posture on many policy issues.

The Federal Judiciary in National Policy Making

The question that arose in Chapter 5, Civil Liberties, rears its perplexing head again here: how appropriate is it that unelected, life-tenured judges are able to decide on the constitutionality of acts of Congress? This arrangement does violate the democratic principle of majority rule, but it met the Framers' broader concerns that they create a balanced political system in which competing interests check one another. Majorities, we saw in *Federalist* No. 10, are just as capable of exploiting their control of government to pursue their own interests and exploit the powerless as are kings and other unelected rulers. Through the Constitution's separation of powers and checks and balances, the Framers appear to have planned for the judiciary to be part of the Constitution's balancing act.

It remains unclear, however, whether the Framers really intended for the Court to possess judicial review, especially over national policy. While carefully stating the powers of Congress and, to a lesser extent, the presidency, the Framers left unstated the potentially enormous power of judicial review. An assessment of the impact of judicial review on the balance of power with the elected branches is especially important for understanding the role of the modern Supreme Court because it has been more inclined to exercise this authority during the past several decades than at any other time in history. Had there not been judicial review, the modern Court no doubt would still play a prominent role in formulating national policy; Congress might well have delegated to the federal judiciary a substantial role in protecting individual liberties. Moreover, much of the important work of the modern Supreme Court involves interpreting public laws rather than weighing their constitutionality—an activity that does not require judicial review. Clearly, however, the authority to rule unconstitutional and thereby void state and federal laws, presidential actions, and bureaucratic regulations is unmatched in the powers given the other branches. It appears to make the Court the guardian of the Constitution.

But who is to guard the guardian? Does not this seemingly absolute authority violate the republican principle of balance as much as it does the democratic principle of majority rule? This chapter has identified several sources of limitations on the absoluteness of judicial review. They are found in other provisions of the Constitution, in the internal, organizational weakness of the federal judiciary, and in the various subtle ways Congress and the president can redirect judicial doctrine. Together they prevent the Court from long straying too far from national opinion.

The constitutional amendment process offers one certain way to countermand the Court's ruling of unconstitutionality, but the process is difficult and thus rarely employed. The Constitution also empowers Congress to alter the size (and therefore the ideological complexion) of the Court as well as change its jurisdiction, but these ploys have been attempted even less frequently. Perhaps the rarity with which Congress has resorted to these difficult constitutional remedies reflects its ability to achieve adequate responsiveness through easier and less-controversial means.

To enforce its policies, the judiciary depends on the compliance of other institutions. In the face of concerted opposition—whether from school districts bent on segregation or Congress and presidents wanting to preserve a legislative veto—the Court may have a difficult time changing public policy. Moreover, Congress can effectively nullify an adverse judicial decision by writing a new public law that addresses the Court's concern or achieves the same goal in a somewhat different way. As we found in Chapter 3, the Supreme Court may rule that Congress cannot order local sheriffs to administer federal gun control procedures, but the ruling does not prevent Congress from tying such compliance to the eligibility of states and their communities for federal grants. Finally, the fact that presidents appoint justices and that Congress may expand the number of district courts allow the elected branches to pull a straying Court back into the mainstream of opinion.

As for judicial review and the long shadow cast by *Marbury v. Madison,* they have allowed the modern Supreme Court to stake out a large role in those areas of public policy, such as the Bill of Rights, where the Constitution appears to give it special license to intervene. The doctrine of judicial review has worked because it does not foreclose effective responses from the other branches. Moreover, the Court's decisions, just like those emanating from the other branches, come and often go. Rarely are they final.

Key Terms

amicus curiae /298	judicial review /289
concurring opinion /303	legislative veto /305
constitutional courts /294	senatorial courtesy /308
court of appeals /294	solicitor general /299
Court packing plan /291	*stare decisis* /299
dissenting opinion /302	writ of certiorari /297
district courts /294	writ of mandamus /288
judicial doctrine /299	

Suggested Readings

Baum, Lawrence. *The Supreme Court.* 6th ed. Washington, D.C.: CQ Press, 1998. An up-to-date introduction to all facets of the Court's structure and procedures, including a thorough discussion of judicial recruitment and approaches to decision making.

Brest, Paul, and Sanford Levinson. *Processes of Constitutional Decision-making.* 3d ed. Boston: Little, Brown, 1992. A detailed introduction to the structure and function of the federal court system emphasizing the important policy-making opportunities enjoyed by lower-court judges.

Carp, Robert A., and Ronald Stidham. *The Federal Courts.* 3d ed. Washington, D.C.: CQ Press, 1998. A classic introduction to the federal court system, with an examination of the different eras of judicial review in Supreme Court history.

Epstein, Lee, and Jack Knight. *The Choices Justices Make.* Washington, D.C.: CQ Press, 1997. A fine demonstration of the value of thinking strategically about the judiciary.

McCloskey, Robert, and Sanford Levinson, eds. *The American Supreme Court.* 2d ed. Chicago: University of Chicago Press, 1994. An "insider's" view of the politics of the Supreme Court drawn from internal memoranda and interviews with former Court law clerks.

Rosenberg, Gerald N. *The Hollow Hope: Can Courts Bring about Social Change?* Chicago: University of Chicago Press, 1991. One of the few books to carefully examine the effects of Court decisions on public policy.

Woodward, Bob, and Scott Armstrong. *The Brethren: Inside the Supreme Court.* New York: Simon and Schuster, 1979. Not only highly readable, but generally regarded as an accurate fly-on-the-wall report of the inner workings of the Supreme Court.

Chapter 10

PUBLIC OPINION

⭐ *Do politicians and other policy advocates invest heavily in trying to move public opinion to their side because people's views are so easy to manipulate or because they are so difficult to manipulate?*

⭐ *Polls often present conflicting evidence about the public's opinions on political issues. When can we believe polling results and when should we be skeptical?*

⭐ *Can stable and coherent public opinion arise from a population that often is uninformed about basic political facts and lacks consistent political views?*

⭐ *How accurately can we predict Americans' political views by knowing their age, race, sex, religion, or education?*

During his successful 1992 campaign for the presidency, Bill Clinton promised to overhaul the American health care system. It was a popular promise because, at the time, health care costs were skyrocketing and unemployment was rising. Millions of Americans feared losing their health insurance if they lost their jobs. But when Clinton tried to fulfill his campaign promise, a Democratic Congress refused to pass the necessary laws. Why? Did Congress, by its inaction, ignore the public's demand for health care reform? Or did its rejection of Clinton's proposal accurately represent public opinion? Indeed, did ordinary citizens have meaningful opinions on the issue, or were their expressed views just the echoes of slick propaganda campaigns mounted by self-serving interests opposed to reform? That the answer to all these questions may be yes introduces us to the cru-

cial but complicated role of public opinion in American politics.

Polls published in the first half of 1994 portrayed a public in which 72 percent believed the country was having a health care crisis; 62 percent thought that most people were not satisfied with the quality of their health care; 86 percent believed that most people were not satisfied with the cost of their health care; and 71 percent would be disappointed if Congress did not reform the health care system. The proposed changes attracting the most public support were to extend health insurance to every American and to ensure that health insurance could never be lost or canceled for any reason (in both cases, 82 percent thought the goal was "very important"). A plurality also supported a requirement that employers pay most of the cost of health insurance (44 percent, compared with 42 percent who thought employers should be required only to make insurance available to employees).[1]

So, the public was ready for a major overhaul along the lines of the Clinton administration's proposal, which included permanent, universal coverage and a requirement that employers pay 80 percent of the cost of health insurance, right? Wrong. The same polls showed that

- 50 percent opposed President Clinton's plan, while only 42 percent favored it;
- 62 percent thought Clinton's plan would "create another large and inefficient government bureaucracy";[2]
- 78 percent were satisfied with the quality of their own health care;
- 48 percent were satisfied with the cost of their own health care (47 percent were not satisfied);
- 34 percent thought the quality of health care would decrease under Clinton's plan, while only 11 percent thought it would increase;
- 57 percent thought they would pay more for health care under Clinton's plan, while only 11 percent thought they would pay less;
- 61 percent wanted more debate, with action delayed until the next Congress, while only 34 percent wanted Congress to act right away.[3]

According to the polls, then, Americans thought there was a health care crisis but wanted to delay action, favored the main features of Clinton's reform package separately but not together, wanted the government to guarantee health care for all but balked at setting up the administrative machinery to do it, and were satisfied with their own health care arrangements but thought most other people were not.

Polls were not the only source of information on public opinion, to be sure. Members of Congress received countless letters, e-mails, phone calls, and faxes from constituents. Interest groups with a major stake in the health care system—doctors, hospitals, insurance companies, labor unions, large corporations, small business owners,

In 1993 the health insurance industry targeted key congressional districts—especially those served by members of the House Ways and Means Committee—for television ads featuring "Harry and Louise," a fictitious couple whose conversations dwelled on the bureaucratic nightmare likely to arise from President Bill Clinton's health care reform proposals. The ads proved effective in sapping early congressional enthusiasm for health care reform.

drug manufacturers, the American Association of Retired Persons, and many, many more—bombarded Congress with their conflicting versions of what "the people" wanted.

As the debate heated up, interest groups spent millions of dollars on propaganda aimed at bringing people to their side, for none of the players in the politics of health care reform treated public opinion as settled. Although it is true that opinion polls taken around the time of the 1992 election found widespread support for a major overhaul of the health care system, this consensus did not guarantee public backing for any particular reform. The administration, represented most prominently by the president's wife, Hillary Rodham Clinton, campaigned around the country in an attempt to build public support for the complex, comprehensive reorganization plan devised by its team of health policy experts.

The plan's opponents attacked many of its features in a wide variety of forums. The health insurance industry ran television ads and small business owners rallied against the plan's requirement that employers pay most of the cost of insuring their workers, claiming it would drastically reduce the number of people they could afford to hire. Congressional leaders from both parties chimed in with a barrage of criticisms and alternative proposals. The effectiveness of these attacks showed up in the public's growing ambivalence toward health care reform and sharply diminished support for Clinton's plan. In August 1993, 57 percent had said they generally supported the plan, while 31 percent opposed it; by July 1994 only 37 percent supported it and 49 percent opposed the plan.[4] In the end, the Clinton administration's most ambitious policy initiative collapsed because most members of Congress concluded that inaction would do them less political damage than any other option they could agree on.

What Is Public Opinion?

The effort that went into probing and shaping opinions during the political battles over health care reform attests to the importance of public opinion in American politics. But what is public opinion? The simplest definition, proposed more than thirty years ago by the eminent political scientist V. O. Key Jr., is that public opinion consists of "those opinions held by private persons which governments find it prudent to heed."[5] According to this definition, every government, democratic or otherwise, has to pay attention to public opinion in some fashion. Democracies differ from other forms of government in terms of which private persons governments find it prudent to heed (potential voters and those who can sway potential voters) and the main reason it is prudent to do so (an election is coming). In the United States, basic constitutional guarantees—regular elections, broad suffrage, freedom of speech and press, freedom to form and join political organizations—allow citizens to express their views freely and compel government leaders to take the public's opinions into account if they want to keep their jobs. These guarantees also make it both possible and essential for political leaders and policy advocates to try to shape and mobilize public opinion on behalf of their causes.

The origins of these guarantees predate the Constitution, and American public opinion has from the beginning been treated as a political force to be alternatively shaped, mollified, or exploited. The object of *The Federalist* was to sway educated public opinion in favor of the Constitution, but national ratification was secured only when its supporters bowed to the widespread demand that a bill of rights be added (see Chapter 2). In the first years of the Republic, leaders of the nascent parties quickly established newspapers to promote themselves and their policy proposals and to attack the ideas and character of their opponents. The highly partisan press they created continued to give form and voice to public opinion throughout the nineteenth century. Ever mindful of the public's concerns, politicians on the make routinely sought to squeeze political advantage from whatever issue excited the people, be it hysteria about the supposed machinations of secret societies, which led to brief success for the Anti-Masonic Party in the 1830s, or hostility to Irish Catholic immigrants, which did the same for the American or "Know-Nothing" Party in the 1850s (see Chapter 12).

The leaders of movements dedicated to the abolition of slavery, prohibition of alcoholic beverages, suffrage for women, and the end of the spoils system (see Chapters 8, 12, and 13) labored mightily to mold public opinion (through pamphlets, speeches, demonstrations, sermons, editorials, magazines, novels, and plays) and then to serve as agents for its political expression. Any incident that inflamed public sentiment was fair game for exploitation. Enforcement of the Fugitive Slave Law, for example, led to incidents that regularly outraged northern communities, helping abolitionists to win converts and silence op-

SCIENTIFIC POLLING

The basic techniques for measuring public opinion are simple in concept, if often difficult to carry out in practice. Select a random sample of the population in question, ask the people in the sample some appropriate questions about their views, and count up their answers.

The larger the sample, the more closely the sample's answers will approximate the answers the pollster would get if everybody in the population could be asked. As the sample gets larger, however, the rate of improvement in accuracy declines; it makes little sense to use a sample size larger than 1,200–1,500 people. With numbers in this range, researchers can be confident that, nineteen times out of twenty, the sample's division on a typical question will fall within three percentage points of the entire population's division. For example, if 45 percent of the respondents in a poll of 1,500 people say they approve of how the president is doing the job, chances are nineteen in twenty that the actual level of approval throughout the whole U.S. population falls somewhere between 42 percent and 48 percent. Strange as it may seem, a sample of 1,500 mirrors a population of 250 million just as accurately as it would a population of 10,000, and a sample of 15,000 would not be markedly more accurate than a sample of 1,500.

A truly random sample of any population is rarely feasible, however, because there is no single directory where

everyone is conveniently listed and so can be given a perfectly equal chance of being selected, which is what strict random sampling requires. Most commercial polls are conducted over the phone and so cannot reach the 6 percent of the population without phones. Not everyone selected is willing to answer questions, and people who refuse differ systematically from the people who answer the pollster's questions (on average, refusers have less money, education, and political knowledge). Methods have been developed to adjust for these problems, but they work imperfectly, so no poll is completely free of the biases they introduce.

Another potential problem with interpreting polls lies in the questions, which respondents may not always understand or may not answer accurately by, for example, offering an opinion on an issue they have never given a moment's consideration. Even the most carefully designed question is subject to some measurement error because the fit between the words and concepts used in questions and how people actually think about issues is never perfect. Properly conducted polls with well-designed questions are nonetheless far less subject to distortion than any other method of measuring public opinion.

ponents. Then, as now, interest group entrepreneurs sought to mobilize public opinion as a weapon in the policy wars, threatening electoral retaliation against leaders who refused to support their cause.

Modern efforts to measure, shape, and exploit public opinion have spawned two linked industries. One is devot-

ed to sounding the public's views on an endless array of issues, and the other to marketing ideas, policies, and politicians. Before the advent of scientific polling, politicians had to gauge public opinion haphazardly, relying on information supplied by editorials, pamphleteers, local leaders, spokespersons for social causes, party activists, and sometimes even less-conventional sources. According to one congressman who served in the 1930s, "This might sound odd, but myself and many other members of Congress that I knew, used to get a lot of ideas on how the general public felt by reading the walls in bathrooms in towns and cities that we were in."[6] Self-selected, perhaps angry, with axes to grind, such sources were of doubtful reliability. Even open expressions of public sentiments, such as marches, rallies, and riots, could not be taken at face value, for they said nothing about views of the majority that stayed home. Not until well into this century were the tools for systematically investigating the opinions of ordinary people developed.

Today, public opinion is most commonly measured by asking questions of a carefully selected sample of adults (see box "Scientific Polling" and box "Straw Polls" which describes some pitfalls of alternative techniques for measuring public opinion). From modest beginnings in the

STRAW POLLS

Newspapers and magazines had taken "straw polls" for a hundred years before the advent of scientific polling. The term refers to tossing straws in the air to see which way the wind is blowing. The *Harrisburg Pennsylvanian* sponsored the first known newspaper poll in 1824, correctly predicting that Andrew Jackson would win the popular vote in the presidential election. The polling techniques varied, but all allowed the respondents to select themselves. Sometimes readers were invited to clip facsimile ballots from the paper, fill them out, and send them in, or they were mailed postcards that they were asked to complete and return.

The *Literary Digest*, a popular magazine, had used the postcard method successfully to forecast the presidential winner in every election from 1920 to 1932. In 1936, it again sent out 10 million postcard ballots to names and addresses taken from telephone books, voter registration lists, club rosters, and lists of automobile owners and mail order customers. The returned cards split 57 percent for Alf Landon, the Republican candidate, to 43 percent for Franklin Roosevelt, the Democratic president running for a second term. On election day Roosevelt defeated Landon, 62 percent to 38 percent, winning every state but Maine and Vermont.

How did the *Literary Digest* get it so wrong? First, their sample was badly biased for an election that, unlike the previous contests, divided the electorate strongly along economic lines. During the Great Depression, telephones and cars were luxuries that many Americans could not afford; those who could afford them were far more likely to favor Landon and the Republican Party. Second, the respondents selected themselves. Only 22 percent of those who were sent the postcard ballot responded. The kinds of people who respond to mail surveys are not typical; they tend to have more education, more money, and more ardent political views. Finally, the postcards were sent out too early (September) to pick up any late-breaking trends. Meanwhile the fledgling Gallup Poll, following more sophisticated sampling principles and drawing on a much smaller sample, accurately predicted Roosevelt's landslide victory.

Modern professional polls avoid the pitfalls of straw polling, but the resort to nonscientific sampling is still common. The White House reports mail counts ("the mail is running 5 to 1 in favor of the president's position"); members of Congress claim to know the public mind from responses to questionnaires inserted into their newsletters; CNN invites watchers to call a 900 number (at $.50 a call) to register their views on issues and reports the results. In all such polls, the respondents select themselves. The samples are therefore subject to severe bias and the results are completely unreliable as measures of public opinion.

1930s, opinion polling has grown into a huge industry producing an endless stream of information about the public's views on almost any conceivable matter. Every president since Jimmy Carter (1977–1981) has had an in-house pollster taking regular readings of the public's pulse. In just one year, 1993, the Clinton administration spent nearly $2 million to monitor public opinion, taking three or four polls and conducting three or four focus groups (described in Chapter 11) every month.[7]

Efforts to shape and channel public opinion have grown apace. As presidents have become more reliant on grassroots public support for winning policy battles, the line between campaigning and governing has blurred. Early in 1997, when campaign-weary news reporters asked Clinton's press secretary why the president maintained such a heavy travel schedule even after winning reelection, he replied, "Campaigns are about framing a choice for the American people. . . . When you are responsible for governing you have to use the same tools of public persuasion to advance your program, to build public support for the direction you are attempting to lead."[8]

The president has no monopoly on the "tools of public persuasion." Virtually all large modern institutions—government agencies, political parties, corporations, universities, foundations, religious bodies, and so on—employ public relations specialists whose job is to present the organization in the best possible light. Interest and advocacy groups of all kinds issue reports and exposés, publish newsletters and magazines, jostle for space on the op-ed pages of newspapers, and promote their causes through ads in the mass media. Opponents of Clinton's health care proposals spent a reported $60 million on television commercials alone.[9]

Institutions also promote the *expression* of public opinion. Pollsters articulate public opinion by the very process of measuring it. A 1997 survey on issues raised by the threat of global warming discovered that 60 percent of Americans were apparently willing to pay an additional $.25 per gallon for gasoline to reduce hydrocarbon emis-

E-MAIL TO THE RESCUE

In 1998 the Federal Deposit Insurance Corporation, regulator of the banking industry, proposed a new "Know Your Customer" policy that required banks to monitor their customers' transactions and report to federal agents activity that might indicate money laundering. As required by law when contemplating new regulations (see Chapter 8), the FDIC invited public comment on the proposal.

The public's reaction to the prospect of the government using banks to snoop into private financial affairs was resoundingly negative. Between December 1998 and March 1999, the FDIC received an unprecedented 257,000 comments on the proposal. Eighty percent, or about 205,000, arrived by e-mail. Only about fifty comments favored the proposal. In the face of such massive and unanimous protest, the FDIC quickly backed down. FDIC chairwoman Donna Tanoue attributed the reversal to "the nature and volume [of the comments]. When consumers get excited about an esoteric bank regulation, we have to pay attention. Certainly it's been an enlightening chapter for the FDIC."

It also is a significant chapter in the emergence of a new venue for mobilizing and expressing public opinion. Because it is such a cheap and easy way to communicate, e-mail is subject to heavy discounting by its recipients, but the FDIC's reaction shows that e-mail can make up in quantity what it lacks in quality.

Source: Rebecca Fairley Raney, "Flood of E-Mail Credited with Halting U.S. Bank Plan," *New York Times*, March 24, 1999, <http://www.nytimes.com> (March 24, 1999).

sions, a level of support that came as a surprise to people on both sides of the policy debates.[10] Policy advocates routinely take polls hoping to demonstrate that the people are on their side, and they do not always resist the temptation to choose questions that will elicit the "right" responses, a subject discussed later in the chapter. Organized efforts to mobilize citizens to write, call, protest, or otherwise express their views to political leaders also are common. The banking industry, for example, got many of its customers to protest vigorously when Congress contemplated withholding income tax from interest earnings, killing the move (see Chapter 13). In 1999 another proposed banking policy was scotched by a deluge of e-mail (see box "E-Mail to the Rescue"). Firms specializing in organizing or, according to their critics, counterfeiting outpourings of "grassroots" sentiment are now available for hire by anyone.

Modern techniques for molding or measuring public opinion have contributed to the nationalization of American politics. Earlier strategies for gauging and shaping opinion depended on institutions such as newspapers and party organizations whose primary focus was local. The relevant publics were those of specific cities, towns, counties, and, to a lesser extent, states; national opinion emerged only as an aggregate of diversely measured local opinions. The advent of scientific polling has made it possible to measure and therefore to treat public opinion as a national phenomenon. National polls probe issues of national concern, raising their visibility in the minds of politicians, the news media, and the public alike. Organized efforts to shape public opinion have taken on national dimensions as well. To be sure, politicians who hold their jobs by the grace of local electorates maintain an abiding interest in local opinion (ask any member of Congress), but the institutional forces that shape local opinion have themselves become national in scope.

The Origins of Public Opinion

Public opinion attracts all this attention because of its effect on political behavior, most notably voting, which is the main, sometimes the only, political act of the great majority of ordinary citizens. Like the vote, public opinion has its political effect as an aggregate phenomenon,

but, also like the vote, it is no more than the sum of its individual parts. To make sense of public opinion, we need to understand the basis of individual opinions.

Attitudes

Where do the individual opinions that collectively constitute public opinion come from? Most scholars who study public opinion believe that expressed opinions reflect underlying attitudes. Basically, an **attitude** is "an organized and consistent manner of thinking, feeling, and reacting with regard to people, groups, social issues, or, more generally, any event in one's environment."[11] An attitude thus combines feelings, beliefs, thoughts, and predispositions to react in a certain way. For example, a person's attitude toward the Republican Party might include feelings ("I trust the Republicans"), beliefs ("the Republican Party is against high taxes"), and an inclination to answer "Republican" to a pollster's question about which party handles the economy better. When invited to state an opinion or cast a vote, people respond in ways that express the underlying attitudes evoked by the choice they face.

Individuals differ widely in the attitudes they bring to bear on political choices. Some people have an elaborate set of informed, organized, internally consistent attitudes that allow them to understand, evaluate, and respond to almost any political phenomenon that catches their attention. Such people are unusual, however. Most people have more loosely structured sets of political attitudes, not necessarily consistent with one another or well informed by facts and concepts. And some people's attitudes are so rudimentary that they offer little guidance in making sense of or responding to political phenomena. People also differ in how strongly they hold attitudes. Some are intensely partisan—the "rock-ribbed Republicans" and "yellow-dog Democrats" (who would vote for a yellow dog if it were a Democrat) of political lore (for further discussions of partisan attitudes, see Chapters 11 and 12). Others maintain attitudes that are far more tentative and open to modification by new information or ideas. Individuals thus vary widely in how they form opinions and make political choices, and the forces that shape public opinion work in different ways on different people.

Ideologies

Elaborately organized sets of political attitudes often take the form of political **ideologies.** In theory, ideologies promote consistency among political attitudes by connecting them to something greater, a more general principle or set of principles. In practice, ideologies often combine attitudes linked more by coalitional politics than by principle. The ideological labels commonly used in American politics are **liberal** and **conservative.** Over time, the meanings of these labels change, reflecting shifts in the clusters of issue positions adopted by rival sets of political leaders, who, like other people centrally involved in politics, routinely use ideological categories to simplify the complexities of political life.

In American politics today, liberals typically favor using government to reduce economic inequalities, champion the rights of disadvantaged groups such as racial minorities and women, and tolerate a more diverse range of social behaviors. They prefer a smaller defense establishment and usually are less willing to use military force in international politics. They believe that the rich should be taxed at higher rates to finance social welfare programs. Conservatives distrust government and have greater faith in private enterprise and free markets, but they are more willing to use government to enforce traditional moral standards. They favor a larger military and more assertive pursuit of national self-interest. Conservatives advocate lower taxes, particularly on investment income, to stimulate growth and to restrict the government's capacity to finance social welfare programs. But these two sets of attitudes are by no means the only logical ways to combine political views. Most libertarians would minimize government regulation of both social and economic behavior and oppose any military involvement except direct de-

fense of U.S. territory. But the standard combinations approximate current party alliances, with most liberals in the Democratic Party and most conservatives in the Republican Party.

Although *liberal* and *conservative* are used constantly in public discussions of politics and are familiar to everyone active in politics, these terms do not guide the political thinking of most citizens, nor do the opinions most people express fall neatly into one ideological category or the other. When asked to place themselves on a scale from very liberal to very conservative, about half the people classify themselves as liberals or conservatives; of the rest, about a quarter position themselves in the middle and another quarter do not place themselves at all.[12] Those who do place themselves on the scale tend to take positions on issues that are consistent with their chosen location, but a substantial minority take positions inconsistent with it. About half the adult population can apply the terms *liberal* and *conservative* correctly to political issues and figures, but only about one in five uses these terms spontaneously to explain their own opinions on parties and candidates.[13] Ideological labels may be indispensable to politicians and pundits, but most citizens get by without them and feel no obligation to be consistently liberal or conservative.

Adopting a liberal or conservative pattern is not the only way people organize their political attitudes. Some studies suggest that a person's political attitudes reflect a small number of **core values,** such as individualism, support for equal opportunity, moral traditionalism, or opposition to big government. A favorable attitude toward Republicans might reflect the values of individualism and opposition to big government. Attitudes that arise from the same core value will be in harmony, but, because most people maintain more than one, attitudes also can conflict.[14] Psychologists have found that people are uncomfortable holding inconsistent attitudes and tend to change one attitude or the other to reduce inconsistency when they become aware of it. Often, however, people remain blissfully unaware of inconsistencies among their attitudes, keeping them in separate mental compartments so they are not brought to mind at the same time by political figures and events. A citizen who dislikes "big government" but favors stricter regulation to protect consumers, workers, and the environment is by no means unusual.

Acquiring Opinions

Where do the attitudes that underlie political opinions come from? In one way or another, attitudes derive from experience. Most often, however, the experience is indirect, interpreted and passed along by families, schools, friends, opinion leaders, and the mass media. Children who grow up in families that talk about politics absorb political beliefs and values, just as they absorb other beliefs and values imparted by the people who raise them. Schools transmit political knowledge and values deliberately when they teach about the Declaration of Independence and the Constitution or conduct classroom elections; they also teach politics informally through the way teachers and other school officials resolve conflicts and exercise authority. Later, peer groups—friends, fellow students, coworkers—become sources of political ideas and information. The news media supply a steady stream of information and commentary that shape people's thinking about politics. The books, movies, and television shows of the mass media convey political ideas and values in ways that engage people's emotions as well as their intellect. Movie offerings run the gamut from the idealistic *Mr. Smith Goes to Washington* to the cynical *JFK, Primary Colors,* and *Wag the Dog.* **Political socialization,** as the process of acquiring political attitudes is known, takes place during childhood and young adulthood, but new experiences can alter attitudes at any stage of life.

Because political attitudes are learned, different experiences produce different perspectives on politics and different degrees of political sophistication. Generally, people tend to develop more complex, richly informed attitudes when the cost of doing so is lower or the payoff is higher. Individuals raised among politically active people, or who

In 1998 "Wag the dog" entered America's political vernacular after a movie by that title told the story of a president who succeeded in deflecting public attention from a sex scandal by staging a mock war in Albania. The movie's uncanny similarities to the situation President Bill Clinton found himself in a year later—war in Kosovo (Albania's neighbor) and a White House sex scandal—left him defending his policies as critics and news reporters repeatedly invoked the movie's title. In this scene from Wag the Dog, actor Dustin Hoffman, producer of the mock war, envisions a scene from his political pageant.

spend more years in school where they are exposed to political concepts and information, or whose jobs put them in touch with political affairs on a regular basis, are more likely to develop elaborate and well-informed political views. Most people, however, live in social settings where political ideas, events, and personalities are far down on the list of things people talk about or care about, so they have neither the opportunity nor the incentive to develop sophisticated political attitudes.

Although we learn political attitudes, the social environment does not rigidly program us to accept a particular view of politics. People are perfectly capable of modifying or rejecting what they are taught, and almost everyone is exposed to competing ideas and perspectives.

Moreover, life hands out experiences that can reshape political ideas. People who are out of work for the first time, or run the bureaucratic maze of paperwork and regulations necessary to start a small business, or see how much the government takes out of their first paycheck, or try to keep a toxic waste incinerator out of their neighborhood may well revise their attitudes toward government and politics in light of their new experiences. When political attitudes do not "work," when they no longer seem to give adequate guidance for understanding and acting, we change them.

Although attitudes are certainly influenced by personal experiences, they are by no means dominated by them. For example, most people base evaluations of the president's economic performance on their beliefs about the national economy, not on their own family's economic fortunes. Recall that large majorities thought that the health care system was in crisis even though their own medical arrangements were satisfactory. The perception that public schools are failing or crime is rampant creates a potent political issue even when most people are satisfied with their own local schools or feel safe in their neighborhoods. Indeed, when people rely solely on their own circumstances to make political judgments, it often is because they are unaware of what is happening more broadly and so have no other information to go on. Because politics is primarily about the provision of collective goods, and ordinary citizens can achieve political ends only through collective action, it is logical that political opinions would reflect attitudes arising more from collective than from personal experiences. For example, people can be unemployed for any number of reasons, but whatever the reason, their economic future is brighter when unemployment stands at 5 percent rather than 10 percent, and it therefore makes sense to use national rather than personal unemployment to judge the president's management of the economy.

Widely shared experiences give rise to the political ideas and opinions that are passed along by various agents

After nearly four decades away from their country, Cuban exiles have never forgotten their homeland or abandoned public rallies as a means of reminding the American public and politicians of their cause. At a 1996 rally this youngster is learning the techniques of the protest craft from his father.

of political socialization. The experiences of slavery, segregation, and continuing racial prejudice have given many African Americans a view of politics that leads them to express greater support for government programs aimed at integrating schools, workplaces, and neighborhoods than is typical among whites. Millions of working people who were helped by Franklin Roosevelt's New Deal during the Great Depression developed an abiding loyalty to the Democratic Party. Some experiences fix political thinking for generations; it took a hundred years for white southerners to move beyond political attitudes forged in the Civil War and Reconstruction. Collective political attitudes and beliefs of this sort are grounded in experience, but not necessarily direct experience. Rather, they arise from how families, politicians, journalists, historians, storytellers, songwriters, moviemakers, and artists interpret events. Competing versions of experience underlie much of the diversity of political opinions both within and between social groups.

Information

Most Americans, most of the time, pay little attention to politics because they have little practical reason to do so. As a result, people's opinions on issues often appear to be both uninformed and unstable. Numerous polls have found the public to be surprisingly ignorant of basic political facts, concepts, and issues. A sampling of questions illustrating typical levels of public information on political matters is shown in the box "The Public's Political Knowledge." The percentages listed reveal that large majorities know some basic facts about the presidency and can identify major political figures such as the vice president and their state's governor. Smaller majorities know something about government institutions, such as the Supreme Court's authority to pass on the constitutionality of legislation or the president's power to appoint federal judges, and they understand basic political facts such as which party is more conservative. But more detailed policy questions and lower-level political figures go unnoticed by most of the public. In 1998, for example, only one American in nine could identify William Rehnquist as chief justice of the United States.

The box also reveals that knowledge of political facts varies with the availability of free information about them. People are most aware of leaders and events on the front page and the nightly television news. Less newswor-

thy figures and issues go largely unrecognized. The difference in recognition of Newt Gingrich (60 percent) and Thomas Foley (26 percent) during their respective terms as Speaker of the House is instructive. Although both held the same formal position, Gingrich, as point man for the Republican "revolution" initiated in 1994, figured more prominently in the news, so more people could identify him. The other source of free information on items in the list is the basic high school civics course.

Ignorance does not necessarily prevent people from expressing opinions; pollsters can get as many as one-third of the people they interview to offer opinions on entirely imaginary issues.[15] Uninformed opinions are not very stable, however. The same person asked the same question at different times may well give different answers. When a sample of citizens was asked in both January and June of 1980 whether the United States should take a more cooperative or more confrontational stance toward the Soviet Union, only 45 percent gave the same answer both times, even though 30 percent would be expected to do so by chance alone.[16]

Answers may be affected by even minor changes in question wording. Public support for U.S. involvement in the wars in Korea and Vietnam was sharply higher if the word *communist* appeared somewhere in the question.[17] More recently, public support for President Clinton's decision to send American troops to Bosnia to help implement the 1995 peace treaty looked rather different depending on how the question was asked. An ABC News poll posed it this way:

Clinton said now that a Bosnia peace treaty has been signed, he's sending 20,000 U.S. troops there as part of an international peacekeeping force. Do you support or oppose sending 20,000 U.S. troops to Bosnia as part of an international peacekeeping force?

Asked this way, 39 percent supported Clinton's decision, and 57 percent opposed it. The Gallup Organization used a different wording:

THE PUBLIC'S POLITICAL KNOWLEDGE

- 95 percent knew the length of the president's term (1989)
- 89 percent knew the meaning of "veto" (1989)
- 89 percent identified **Al Gore** as the vice president (1998)
- 75 percent knew which party had a majority in the House of Representatives (1996)
- 73 percent identified the governor of their state (1989)
- 72 percent knew which party had a majority in the Senate (1996)
- 67 percent knew the Supreme Court decides if laws are constitutional (1992)
- 67 percent could identify **Boris Yeltsin** as president of Russia (1996)
- 60 percent could identify **Newt Gingrich** as Speaker of the House (1998)
- 58 percent knew the Republicans are the more conservative party (1992)
- 58 percent knew that the president appoints federal judges (1992)
- 57 percent knew what an economic recession is (1989)
- 52 percent knew each state has two U.S. senators (1978)

- 52 percent knew what the Fifth Amendment is (1989)
- 46 percent knew that the first ten amendments are called the Bill of Rights (1989)
- 34 percent could name the current secretary of state (1978)
- 30 percent knew that the term of a U.S. representative is two years (1978)
- 26 percent could identify **Thomas Foley** as Speaker of the House (1992)
- 25 percent could identify both senators from their state (1989)
- 25 percent knew that the term of U.S. senators is six years (1991)
- 20 percent could name two First Amendment rights (1989)
- 11 percent knew that **William Rehnquist** was chief justice of the United States (1998)
- 2 percent could name two Fifth Amendment rights (1989)

Sources: 1996 and 1998 entries are from the 1996 and 1998 American National Election Studies; other entries are from Michael X. Delli Carpini and Scott Keeter, *What Americans Know About Politics and Why It Matters* (New Haven: Yale University Press, 1996).

Now that a peace agreement has been reached by all the groups currently fighting in Bosnia, the Clinton administration plans to contribute U.S. troops to an international peacekeeping force. Do you favor or oppose that?

Asked this way, 46 percent supported the move, and 40 percent opposed it. The use of the word *contribute* as opposed to *sending* and leaving out the number of troops evidently made the difference.[18]

Because wording can influence responses, poll questions are sometimes formulated to elicit maximum support for the views advocated by their sponsors. Sophisticated users of polling data recognize that polls always provide a *mediated* take on public opinion and pay close attention to the details of sampling and question wording when interpreting them.

Framing

Social scientists have argued for years about whether unstable survey responses mean that many people's expressed opinions are not anchored in relevant attitudes or that survey questions are too crude to gauge attitudes accurately.[19] Although there are elements of truth in both views, the most important source of instability in a person's expressed opinions is probably **ambivalence.** Particular issues may evoke attitudes and beliefs that pull in opposite directions. When that happens, the response to a pollster's questions depends on which considerations come to mind first and seem most weighty. And that depends on the context: recent events, the mention of particularly potent symbols (such as the word *communism* in questions on Korea and Vietnam), or questions that have come earlier in the survey.

Some people might believe the poor deserve government help, but they also might detest welfare cheats. Thus these people might well respond differently if asked about their views on "government programs to help the poor" rather than "welfare programs" (see the box "Public Opinion and Welfare Reform," page 339). They also might respond differently depending on whether earlier questions brought to mind hungry kids or welfare queens. Or they might respond differently depending on whether last night's TV documentary focused on homeless families or welfare scams. In other words, their responses are shaped by the considerations most recently brought to their attention because they think of them first.[20] The context frames the question, and the frame determines which attitudes govern the response.

Framing explains how both the mass media and political campaigns can affect people's expressed political opinions. The messages sent by the media and the candidates do not have to change underlying attitudes to change expressed opinions. All they have to do is frame the issue in a way that draws out one response rather than the other. Studies have shown that the content of TV news programs affects the standards people use to evaluate presi-

Standing at the microphone in May 1999, Democratic representative Carolyn McCarthy of New York urges House Speaker Dennis Hastert to open discussions on gun safety legislation. In 1993 her husband was killed and her son injured by a gunman on a New York commuter train. Speaking about her own tragedy, she is able to convey a personal message that attracts the public's attention and gives her message special credibility in depicting the urgency of gun control.

dents; people who have watched stories about a particular problem give greater weight to the president's performance on *that* problem in forming their overall evaluation of the president's performance.[21] Simply by covering some issues and ignoring others, the news media help to define the political agenda, influencing which considerations are in the foreground when citizens make political judgments. Political campaigns, as we shall see in the next chapter, do not set out to change people's political views, but to bring to the forefront attitudes that favor their candidate. In the 1992 presidential campaign when George Bush tried to make "character" the issue while Bill Clinton insisted that the issue was the economy, each was trying to frame the choice in a way that favored his cause.

From this perspective, we can understand why the answers to pollsters' questions about health care reform in 1994 seemed inconsistent. Different questions evoked different frames, putting different beliefs and attitudes into play. Most people believed the current system had serious shortcomings even if their personal arrangements were adequate. Many families would face financial disaster if they lost coverage and had serious medical problems. Because universal, portable coverage would ease that worry and extend a basic necessity to everyone, large majorities responded favorably when asked if they supported these goals. But in 1994 most Americans also doubted the government's ability to do anything right, so support for health care reform dried up when pollsters' questions raised issues of cost, quality, and restrictions on the choice of doctors and treatments. Framed in terms of ends, health care reform drew broad public support; framed in terms of means, it did not.

Is Public Opinion Meaningful?

If large segments of the public are politically ignorant, hold inconsistent views, and can be manipulated by varying the words or context of questions, how can public opinion play its assigned role in democratic politics, which is to guide and constrain elected agents? The answer is that, despite the deficiencies uncovered by survey research, public opinion continues to play a crucial and effective part in American politics because a variety of formal and informal political institutions give it shape and force. And public opinion is meaningful because, although individual opinions may be badly informed and unstable, *aggregate public opinion*—the sum of all individual opinions—is both stable and coherent.

Stability of Aggregate Public Opinion

The evidence for the stability of aggregate public opinion is impressive. When there is no obvious reason to expect change, the distribution of opinion tends to be highly stable. One study examined more than a thousand poli-

Figure 10–1   Public Opinion on Health Spending, 1971–1987

Are we spending too much, too little, or about the right amount on improving and protecting the nation's health?

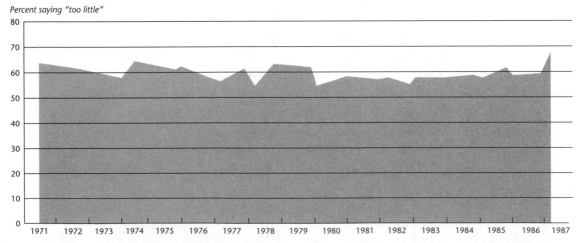

Percent saying "too little"

Source: General Social Survey, National Opinion Research Center, University of Chicago.

Figure 10–2   Public Support for Integrated Schools, 1942–1985

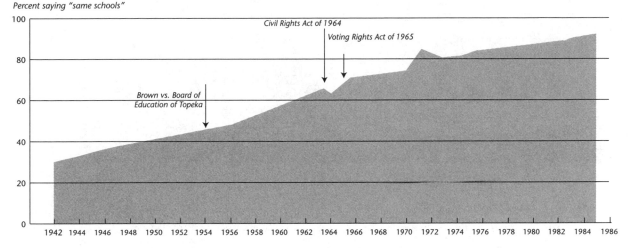

Do you think white students and (Negro/black) students should go to the same schools or separate schools?   (Asked of whites only.)

Percent saying "same schools"

Source: Harold W. Stanley and Richard G. Niemi, *Vital Statistics on American Politics, 1997–1998* (Washington, D.C.: CQ Press, 1998), Table 3–17.

cy questions asked in identical form at least twice in surveys conducted between 1935 and 1990. In a majority of cases there was no appreciable change in the public's responses between surveys, and nearly half of the changes that did occur were modest. On some questions, aggregate public opinion has not changed for several decades. Figure 10–1 illustrates the striking stability of aggregate public opinion on whether the government is spending too little on health care.

More important, when substantial changes occur, they reflect intelligible historical trends or responses to changed conditions. For example, public support for integrated schools grew between 1942 and 1985 as public policy and public sentiment turned against racial segregation (see Figure 10–2).[22] Likewise, support for greater spending on national defense rose in the late 1970s and early 1980s, responding to crises in Iran and Afghanistan and President Ronald Reagan's leadership on the issue but then declined once the government had increased military spending (see Figure 10–3; note the brief upward tick

in 1991 at the time of the Gulf War). In aggregate, then, public opinion appears both consistent and intelligible.[23]

Other studies have detected broad cyclical changes in public opinion across a range of issues, with opinion swinging back and forth between liberal and conservative "moods." The inevitable shortcomings of both the liberal and conservative approaches to government eventually make the opposition's ideas more attractive. Experience with conservative policies moves public opinion in a liberal direction, while experience with liberal policies makes the public more conservative.[24] For example, the liberal expansion of the welfare state in the 1960s under Lyndon Johnson eventually led to the conservative tax revolts of the late 1970s and early 1980s and the election of Reagan, a conservative Republican, as president. The growing economic inequalities produced by the policies of Reagan and his successor, George Bush, revived, at least temporarily, public support for government programs to improve the economic well-being of the less affluent, helping to elect Bill Clinton. Changes in mood bring about

Figure 10–3   Public Opinion on Defense Spending, 1960–1993

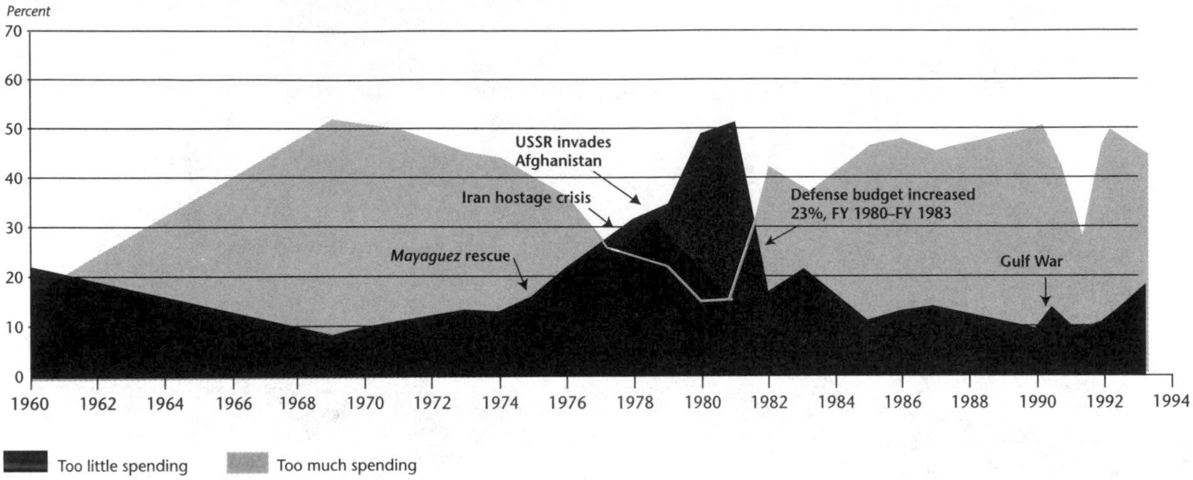

Percent

Legend:
- **Too little spending** (dark)
- **Too much spending** (gray)

Source: Harold W. Stanley and Richard G. Niemi, *Vital Statistics on American Politics, 1997–1998* (Washington, D.C.: CQ Press, 1998), Table 3–22.

changes in policy, as candidates more in tune with the new mood win office and many of the holdovers adapt to survive. After Reagan's victory in 1980, congressional Democrats had to adapt and they did—by joining Republicans to cut income taxes and social welfare spending.

Aggregate opinion also varies in coherent ways over the shorter term. The president's level of public approval varies from month to month with economic conditions and international events. Bush's presidency offers a striking example. His level of approval in the Gallup Poll reached a record 83 percent in early 1991 in appreciation of his skillful handling of the Gulf War, but continuing high unemployment and slow economic growth over the next eighteen months, along with Bush's inability to "get it," brought it down to 32 percent. **Aggregate partisanship**—the proportion of poll respondents labeling themselves Republicans or Democrats—also shifts with changes in economic conditions, political events, and presidential approval. Popular presidents presiding over growing economies and successful foreign policies enhance their party's strength among voters; failed policies, foreign and domestic, undermine it.[25] In aggregate, then, public opinion does not move erratically or unintelligibly.

When it is not stable, its movements can usually be explained by real-world events and circumstances.

Opinion Leadership

How can stable and coherent public opinion arise from unstable and incoherent individual opinions? Part of the answer lies in the aggregation process itself. When survey responses are added together, **measurement errors** (from the mismatch of survey questions with the attitudes they are supposed to measure) and random individual changes tend to cancel one another out; therefore, the average remains the same if circumstances remain the same. The more important part of the answer lies in the division of labor between the minority of the public that is attentive and informed and the much larger majority that is neither. A small segment of the public forms opinions by paying close attention to political events and issues. The uninformed and inattentive majority forms opinions by taking cues from members of this attentive segment. In aggregate, public opinion is given rationality and coherence by these **opinion leaders.**[26]

Opinion leadership arises naturally as people respond to different incentives. The widespread ignorance of political facts and issues does not mean that most Americans are dunces. Indeed, in an important sense political ignorance is rational. It takes time and energy to become informed. Political issues and processes often are exceedingly complicated, and even the most devoted student of politics cannot hope to master them all. Most citizens, on most political questions, receive no tangible payoff from becoming better informed. People are unlikely to improve either U.S. policy or their own lives by developing a better understanding of the Kosovo conflict. The same goes for health care policy. Better information holds no promise of a better outcome because the views of any single individual are so unlikely to be decisive. It makes sense to gather information about options when we get to make the decision (what kind of car to buy), but not when our influence on the choice is effectively nil (what kind of helicopters the Marines should buy).

Suppose we do want to participate in politics, if only in a small way, by voting or by responding to a public opinion poll. Or suppose friends are discussing politics. If we want to join in, we need to adopt some positions on the issues. But how do we know which side of an issue to favor, and why, without investing the time and effort to learn about it? If we are like most people, we rationally ride free on the efforts of others, following the cues given by people we consider informed and whose biases we know. They may be people we know personally—friends, relatives, or coworkers who pay special attention to politics; community activists; or leaders in our places of worship. They may be public figures—political leaders, TV or radio personalities, and newspaper columnists. Organizations such as the Sierra Club, the Roman Catholic Church, and the National Organization for Women also may be sources of cues. Thus instead of learning about an endless variety of complicated political issues, all we have to learn is whose attitudes reliably match or contradict our own and then follow their cues. Their biases need not match ours for the cues to be useful; sometimes we can determine what we are for by noting who is against it, and vice versa.

Conservative radio host Rush Limbaugh led the surge in talk radio during the early 1990s. He was especially noted for his unrelenting attacks on President Bill Clinton. In a short time, Rush Limbaugh emerged as a prominent referent, allowing the public to figure out where they stood on an issue according to his endorsement.

Cognitive shortcuts of this sort are available because interested people and groups have a stake in gathering and disseminating political information. Some folks find politics as fascinating as others do baseball and enjoy being recognized by friends as political mavens. But most people who traffic in political information do so to be more effective in their pursuit of power and policy goals. The activities and biases of information specialists usually reflect their institutional roles. Tobacco company officials need to know everything that is said about the dangers of second-hand smoke to counter these claims and defend corporate profits. The American Cancer Society's staff seeks out and publicizes information emphasizing the damage tobacco does to the nation's health and health care budgets. Officials at Common Cause, a public interest lobby, investigate and publicize campaign contributions from political action committees (PACs) to justify its proposals to reform the campaign finance system. Newspaper columnists and radio talk show hosts are paid to express opinions on political issues. Professional politicians and those with political ambitions also need to master issues and be prepared to discuss them. A pluralist political system breeds—and depends on—opinion leaders of many kinds.

The sources of opinion leadership differ from issue to issue, just as the audience for policy differs from issue to issue. Many political issues go unnoticed except by distinct **issue publics**—subsets of the population who are better informed than everyone else about the issue because it touches them more directly and personally. Farmers pay attention to farm programs; retired people (and their doctors) keep tabs on Medicare policy; research scientists monitor National Science Foundation budgets and rules. Citizens committed to a moral cause, such as protecting animal rights, banning abortion, or protecting civil liberties, form issue publics for policies affecting their cause. Most policy domains are of concern only to issue publics, so it is usually their opinions, not mass opinion, that matter to politicians. Together, opinion leaders and issue publics are the main conduits of public opinion in a pluralist political system. They apply most of the routine pressures felt by government officials engaged in the day-to-day making of public policy on the countless matters dealt with by the federal government. By the same token, their interest makes them the targets of most organized attempts to sway and mobilize public opinion for political ends.

Aggregate public opinion, then, is given its coherence and focus by opinion leaders, typically based in institutions, whose knowledge, ideas, proposals, and debates define the positions and options from which ordinary citizens adopt their expressed views. This conclusion does not mean that public opinion is routinely manipulated by self-serving elites (although there is no shortage of attempts to do so); pluralist competition usually denies any particular opinion leader a monopoly. Opinion leaders maintain their leadership status only if people choose to

follow them. Even though the news media focused on the scandals plaguing Bill Clinton during his second term as president, the public proved quite capable of ignoring the "scandal" frame in evaluating his performance as president (see box "Framing Bill Clinton").

The aggregate stability of popular views reveals that, in an often confused and poorly articulated way, people do have a real basis for the opinions they express. They do not respond to opinion leaders randomly, but in ways that are consistent with the values and notions about politics they have accumulated during their lives. Cognitive shortcuts would be of no value if they did not bring people somewhere near the destination they would have reached by taking the longer path.[27] Opinion leaders, therefore, lead by expressing the political sentiments of those who follow them. This is why politicians, who are fully aware of how fickle and poorly informed people's expressed opinions may be, still think twice about going against the polls. Aggregate opinion is meaningful, and aggregates are what count when a politician is running for reelection or trying to get a bill passed.

The Content of Public Opinion

Political opinions reflect people's underlying values and beliefs about how the world works. This fact is no less true of second- or third-hand opinions than of original opinions because core values and beliefs influence the choice of cue-givers. Americans share a broad consensus on basic political values that puts real limits on what is politically possible. Yet within these bounds, Americans find plenty to disagree about. Consensus on the basics makes politics—defined here as reaching agreement on a course of common, or collective, action despite disagreement on the purposes of the action—*possible;* disagreement within this general consensus makes politics *necessary.*

Consensus on the System

Opinion polls find that almost every American supports the institutional underpinnings of modern democ-

LOGIC OF POLITICS

FRAMING BILL CLINTON

Allegations of sexual and financial improprieties plagued President Bill Clinton throughout his administration, and the public came to take a dim view of his honesty and morals. Yet as controversy intensified in January 1998 with published accusations of sexual involvement with a White House intern, Clinton's Gallup poll job approval rating reached 69 percent, the highest level of his administration, and stayed near that mark for months afterward. Many Americans evidently made a sharp distinction between Clinton as a person—they maintained serious doubts about his morals—and his policies—they rewarded him for a robust economy, a balanced federal budget, and declining rates of crime, welfare dependency, and unwed motherhood. In doing so, they ignored the frame presented by the news media's obsessive coverage of the scandal (as well as of earlier allegations of campaign finance improprieties), responding in-

stead to conditions in which they had a more direct personal stake: jobs, inflation, and crime.

Clinton's continuing high level of public approval through 1998 and into 1999 did not stop the Republicans in Congress from trying to remove him from office via impeachment, but it did prevent them from succeeding. With large majorities of Democratic and independent voters opposed to the Republican effort, Democrats in Congress found it politically easy to oppose impeachment and block conviction. Congressional Republicans faced a more difficult choice: heeding the two-thirds of the general public who opposed impeachment, or heeding the two-thirds of Republican voters (and three-quarters of Republican activists) who wanted Clinton removed. All but a handful sided with their core partisan supporters.

---

racy: the right of every citizen to vote; the freedom to speak, write, and work with others for political goals; the right to due process and equal treatment by courts and other government agencies. Although each of these principles was once controversial (see Chapters 4 and 11), opposition to them has now virtually disappeared from public life. Large majorities also favor a capitalist economy, defined as one in which businesses are privately owned, free markets allocate goods, people choose their own occupations, and incomes depend on the market value of

services rendered. No one with serious aspirations to political leadership attacks democracy or free enterprise.

When it comes to the practical application of these abstract values, however, consensus breaks down. When a poll taken in 1940 asked a sample of Americans, "Do you believe in freedom of speech?" 97 percent said yes. When those who said yes were asked, "Do you believe in it to the extent of allowing fascists and communists to hold meetings and express their views in the community?" 76 percent said no. In 1940, the year these questions were

Americans strongly support equal opportunity but typically reject policies designed to promote equal outcomes. Consequently, public opinion in America has found large differences in personal income to be an acceptable social condition. The many homeless people in America are all too aware of these preferences. Soup kitchens like the one shown here feed hundreds of homeless people every day.

posed, war was raging in Europe, and both fascism and communism loomed as serious threats. But even in calmer times, many people who say they favor First Amendment rights would deny them to people with unpopular views. Polls taken in the mid-1970s found 82 percent agreeing that "nobody has the right to tell another person what he should or should not read," but also 50 percent agreeing that "books that preach the overthrow of the government should be banned from the library."[28] When the abstract value of free expression comes up against the more tangible matters of national security or social order, free expression does not always come out on top. It is therefore important to note that free speech and

other democratic values find stronger support among the minority of Americans who specialize in politics; those who play the political game are more supportive of its rules.[29]

Other basic political values are similarly hedged. Large majorities say they favor free enterprise and dislike government meddling in the economy, but majorities just as large back laws regulating businesses in order to protect the environment or the health and safety of workers and consumers. Again, people who pay more attention to politics are more likely to recognize the implications of one position for another and to offer more consistent sets of opinions. But almost everyone holds political values and beliefs that can clash. Forced to choose, people have to consider tradeoffs; sometimes, political conflict and compromise go on right in their own heads.

At one level, the values of democracy and capitalism are not compatible. Democracy treats people as equals and permits majorities to rule. Capitalism extols liberty, not equality. It distributes its rewards unequally and leaves crucial economic decisions (what products to produce, what jobs to offer, where to build factories) in the hands of individuals and private corporations, whose goals are profits. The fear that democracy would bring economic ruin by allowing popular majorities to despoil the wealthy minority was a central motive behind the Constitution's elaborate avoidance of direct popular rule. But the fear proved to be groundless because Americans have come to make sharp distinctions about the kinds of equality they consider appropriate. Just about everyone favors political equality. Support for equal opportunity is at least as strong: statements such as "everyone in America should have an equal right to get ahead" and "children should have equal education opportunities" are accepted almost without dissent when posed in opinion polls.[30] Americans also support equal pay for equal work and generally oppose discrimination against any class of persons (women, racial minorities, and homosexuals) in the workplace.

Very little popular support exists, however, for mandating equal outcomes. Asked whether, under a fair econom-

Figure 10–4 Public Confidence in Government, 1964–1998

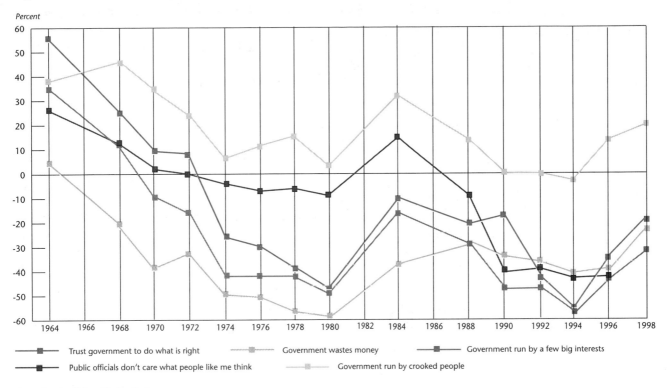

Trust government to do what is right — Government wastes money — Government run by a few big interests

Public officials don't care what people like me think — Government run by crooked people

Source: American National Election Studies.

Note: The entries are the percentage of respondents expressing confidence in government minus the percentage expressing a lack of confidence in government on each question. The questions are:

1. How much of the time do you think you can trust the government in Washington to do what is right—just about always, most of the time, or only some of the time? ("Always" or "most of the time" minus "some" or "none of the time.")

2. Do you think that people in government waste a lot of money we pay in taxes, waste some of it, or don't waste very much of it? ("Some" or "not much" minus "a lot.")

3. Would you say that the government is pretty much run by a few big interests looking out for themselves or that it is run for the benefit of all? ("Benefit of all" minus "a few big interests.")

4. Please tell me if you agree or disagree with this statement: Public officials don't care what people like me think. ("Disagree" minus "agree.")

5. Do you think that quite a few of the people running the government are crooked, not very many are, or do you think hardly any of them are crooked? ("Hardly any" or "not many" minus "quite a few.")

ic system, all people would earn about the same or people with more ability would earn higher salaries, 7 percent chose the first option, 78 percent the second.[31] Nor is there much support for affirmative action programs intended to remedy past discrimination against women or racial minorities by putting them first in line for jobs and school admissions. When asked whether "ability determined by test scores" or special treatment "to make up for past discrimination" should govern decisions on jobs and college admission, overwhelming majorities choose test score ability.[32] The result is that Americans, renowned

since Alexis de Tocqueville's day for their egalitarian social and political values, tolerate huge differences in wealth among individuals and groups.

Politicians: A Suspect Class

Americans approve overwhelmingly of the U.S. political system and its symbols; pride in the Constitution and the flag are nearly universal. They are far less pleased, however, with the people they elect to run the system. Criticizing the government is a national pastime with a pedigree longer than baseball's, but the public's distrust of government and its practitioners has deepened markedly over the past several decades. Figure 10–4 traces the public's growing cynicism about government through a set of questions that have been asked repeatedly in the biennial American National Election Studies. Far more than in the 1950s and 1960s, Americans are now inclined to believe that public officials are crooked and that the government wastes tax money, cannot be trusted to do what is right, is run by a few big interests for their own benefit, and does not care about ordinary people.

The most common explanation for these trends is that the conflicts over civil rights and the Vietnam War in the 1960s, followed closely by the Watergate scandal that drove a president from office (note the sharp drops in 1974), led to a more critical press and a disillusioned public. Confidence revived somewhat with the economy in 1984, but later problems, including a stagnant economy during the Bush administration (1989–1993), large federal budget deficits, assorted political scandals such as the House bank scandal of 1992, high crime rates, and a pervasive sense that the United States was moving in the wrong direction, have kept public distrust of government high.

One result has been widespread public support for measures to curb politicians: term limits for legislators, constitutional amendments compelling Congress to balance the budget, national referenda in which voters would be allowed a direct say in making laws by putting them on a national ballot. A large part of the appeal of Ross Perot, who won 19 percent of the vote as an independent presidential candidate in 1992 (but then fell to 8 percent in 1996), was his image as a champion of political reforms intended to make elected officials more accountable to ordinary people. Any popular sentiment as widespread as this is bound to find political sponsors. Indeed, part of the Republicans' strategy for taking control of Congress in the 1994 elections was a promise to act on constitutional amendments to impose term limits and a balanced budget. In Figure 10–4 three of the confidence measurements reached their lowest points in 1994, evidence of the anger at government that Republicans both

fanned and exploited to win Congress. Confidence in government rebounded with the booming economy and balanced federal budget during the second Clinton administration but still remains far below what it was in the 1950s.

Public Opinion on Issues

Popular agreement on the fundamentals of representative democracy does not translate into agreement on every important policy area. In each of three broad domains—the economy, societal morality, and foreign policy—the central issues have consistently generated wide divisions of opinion. It is crucial to understand how these differences split the public, for these factions form the raw material from which political leaders try to construct majority coalitions. When the public is divided in different ways on different issues and lacks consensus on what issues are most important, strategies for assembling and maintaining party coalitions become more difficult to conceive and execute.

Economic Issues. Although Americans believe fundamentally in capitalism, almost no one believes that private businesses should be completely unregulated or that the things people value should be allocated exclusively by an unfettered free market. Political conflict occurs over how far the government should go in regulating business and redressing market-driven economic and social inequalities. Historically, the trend has been toward an ever-larger government role in managing economic affairs, with notable expansions in the 1930s under Franklin Roosevelt's New Deal policies and in the 1970s with new laws to protect consumers and the natural environment (see Chapter 8). Today, government action to enhance economic welfare usually enjoys broad public support. At the same time, people are less than enthusiastic about paying the costs of "big government" in the form of higher taxes and greater bureaucratic regulation. Programs that serve the middle class attract the most support; programs that serve the poor are on shakier political footing.

More specifically, large majorities typically support stable or increased government spending for programs that serve (or will eventually serve) nearly everyone: Social Security (pensions for the disabled or retired), Medicare (medical care for retirees), and unemployment insurance (cash for people laid off from jobs). Social Security is so popular that politicians call it "the third rail of American politics—touch it and you die" (referring to the high-voltage rail from which subway trains draw their power). Other individual government programs designed to improve health and welfare also command broad support—with a few revealing exceptions (see box "Public Opinion and Welfare Reform" which lists some typical poll results and illustrates how such opinions can affect major policy decisions).

By and large, Americans seem to support a wide range of economic and social welfare policies that commonly are classified as liberal. But when it comes to principles, as opposed to programs, Americans are much more likely to think of themselves as conservatives. Majorities also

POLITICS → POLICY

PUBLIC OPINION AND WELFARE REFORM

The public is broadly supportive of major social spending programs—except those that evoke the wrong frames. Consider the public's responses to the following question: "Should spending on the following programs increase, decrease, or stay the same?"

	Increase	Stay the Same	Decrease
Social Security (1993)	46%	46%	8%
Improving and protecting health (1993)	74	18	8
Improving the education system (1993)	69	25	6
Welfare (1993)	17	26	57
Assistance to the poor (1993)	65	23	12
Food stamps (1996)	11	42	47
Solving problem of the homeless (1996)	58	31	11
Aid to college students (1996)	53	38	9
Research on AIDS (1996)	56	33	11

Only a tiny minority wants the government to spend less on Social Security, health, education, college loans, the homeless, and AIDS research than it is now doing. Programs whose names evoke the wrong symbols, however, enjoy much less support. Here, for example, 57 percent would reduce spending on "welfare," although 65 percent would increase spending on "assistance to the poor"—overlooking the fact that welfare is assistance to the poor. This is a clear example of framing. Most Americans think government should help the poor, but the word "welfare" conjures up images, however unfair, of lazy people living off the sweat of the taxpayers. Charity is a virtue, but so is self-reliance, and poverty issues can be framed in terms of either one.

Images and frames matter. In 1996 the Republican Congress sent Bill Clinton a welfare reform bill that cut back on federal assistance to poor people. Among other things, the bill imposed a time limit on welfare eligibility for the first time since the adoption of the original assistance program in the 1930s. It also slashed the food stamp program, which apparently shares welfare's negative connotations (see the entry for food stamps in the table). The bill was opposed by most congressional Democrats, but, facing reelection, Clinton signed it anyway because it was widely supported by a public that had applauded his previous campaign promise to "end welfare as we know it."

Source: 1993 data are from the General Social Survey, reported by Robert S. Erikson and Kent L. Tedin in *American Public Opinion*, 5th ed. (Boston: Allyn and Bacon, 1995), 89; 1996 data are from the 1996 American National Election Study.

agree with conservative politicians who say that taxes are too high, that the government wastes a lot of money, that bureaucrats are too meddlesome, and that people ought to take care of themselves rather than depend on government handouts. The poll findings on health care reform, discussed at the beginning of this chapter, show how conflicting liberal and conservative stances can leave public opinion ambivalent on major policy issues. Majorities responded as liberals when asked about the goals of health care reform but as conservatives when asked about the means.

Social and Moral Issues. Politics is about the distribution of goods, which can be moral as well as material. The great struggles to abolish slavery, achieve votes for women, prohibit alcohol, and end racial segregation were driven largely by moral rather than economic considerations. Today, social and moral issues produce some of the most heated political controversies. Questions about abortion, religion in public life, and the rights of women, ethnic and racial minorities, immigrants, and homosexuals make up an important part of the political agenda. These issues raise conflicting considerations that are difficult to reconcile, not only between opposed groups, but for individuals in their own minds.

In modern times abortion is the best-known example. Since the Supreme Court handed down its *Roe v. Wade* ruling in 1973, thereby overturning state laws making abortions illegal, the abortion issue has become a defining one for a whole political generation. The public debate has been dominated by groups with starkly opposing positions. At one extreme are those who want the law to forbid abortion as murder; at the other are those who object to any restriction on a woman's right to abort. Neither of these positions commands a majority, although more favor no restriction (42 percent in 1998) than favor a total ban (12 percent).[33] For most people, the answer is, "It depends."

Aggregate public opinion on abortion is both highly consistent and acutely sensitive to how the issue is framed. Figure 10–5 shows the trends in responses to one

set of questions posed almost yearly by the Gallup Poll since 1965. After an initial increase in support for legalized abortion (coinciding with *Roe v. Wade*), aggregate opinion has changed very little. Large majorities think abortion should be legal if the pregnancy resulted from rape or would endanger the woman's health or if there is a strong chance of serious birth defects. The public is much more evenly split on whether abortion for financial or family reasons should be legal. Other ways of wording the questions produce a similar spread.

Unlike the activists on both sides, most Americans are torn on the issue. Majorities agree that "abortion is murder" (62 percent) and "morally wrong" (61 percent) but think that a woman should be allowed to have an abortion if she wants to and her doctor agrees to it (61 percent) and oppose a constitutional amendment outlawing abortions (70 percent). Perhaps the best expression of the average person's view is summed up by an option offered by one poll on the issue: "I personally feel that abortion is morally wrong, but I also feel that whether or not to have an abortion is a decision that has to be made by every woman for herself"; 78 percent agreed.[34]

Abortion is the kind of issue that defies political resolution because the wide disagreement on values leaves little space for agreement on action. It generates intense feelings among minorities on both sides who tolerate nothing less than full support for their position. Intense feelings are, moreover, far more prevalent among political activists (some of whom are activists *because* of their intense feelings), and they are most common among the minority that would forbid abortion entirely. Ordinary citizens are much less certain about how the issue should be resolved and remain uncomfortable with either extreme. Thus exploitation of the issue politically is a delicate undertaking.

In preparing for the 2000 presidential election, moderate Republican leaders sought to drop the right-to-life plank from the Republican platform (see Chapter 12) in order to widen the party's appeal, especially to well-educated women. They met stiff resistance, however, from

Figure 10–5 Public Opinion on Abortion, 1965–1996

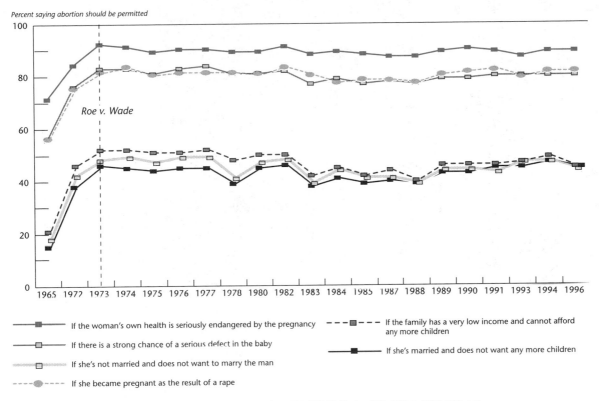

Percent saying abortion should be permitted

Roe v. Wade

——■—— If the woman's own health is seriously endangered by the pregnancy

- - -■- - - If the family has a very low income and cannot afford any more children

——□—— If there is a strong chance of a serious defect in the baby

——■—— If she's married and does not want any more children

·····□····· If she's not married and does not want to marry the man

- - - -●- - - - If she became pregnant as the result of a rape

Source: Harold W. Stanley and Richard G. Niemi, *Vital Statistics on American Politics, 1997 1998* (Washington, D.C.: CQ Press, 1998), Table 3–16.

conservative Christians who were Republicans primarily because the party was committed to banning abortion. The dilemma for Republican presidential aspirants is that a firm "pro-life" stance helps in Republican primaries but makes it harder to win the general election.

Americans take conservative positions on most other social issues, but in practice their views are often balanced by considerable respect for individual freedom. Formal prayer in public schools, banned by Supreme Court decisions in the early 1960s, receives overwhelming public support. Likewise, very large majorities take strong "law and order" positions, favoring capital punishment for murderers and opposing the legalization of drugs such as marijuana and cocaine. In 1990, 86 percent of those with an opinion wanted to outlaw "burning or destroying the American flag as a form of political protest."[35] Few support unrestricted access to pornography. Social conservatism grew during the 1990s as problems of crime, drug abuse, single-parent families, and welfare dependency became the focus of political attention. Yet the public remains leery about using government to impose traditional moral standards on private citizens. Most people (about 80 percent) believe that homosexuality is immoral, but a majority (57 percent) thinks homosexual relations between consenting adults should be legal.

Foreign Policy. Because most foreign policy issues are remote from everyday experience and few people pay sustained attention to foreign affairs, public opinion on for-

In March 1999 the National Albanian American Council followed standard procedure in trying to drum up public support for the Clinton administration's policy in Kosovo, where U.S. air crews had joined those from other NATO countries in expelling the Yugoslav forces from the province. The Albanian Americans staged their rally at Lafayette Park, across the street from the White House and not far from the offices of the network news bureaus.

eign policy is particularly responsive to opinion leadership. The president is the most important opinion leader on foreign policy, but presidential influence varies according to whether other opinion leaders—rival politicians, foreign policy experts, and news commentators—agree or disagree with the White House.[36] Since World War II large majorities have supported an active international role for the United States, but backing for particular policies has been much more variable.

Until the breakup of the Soviet Union at the end of 1991, the cold war conflict between the United States and the Soviet Union framed both public and elite thinking on foreign affairs. The avowed U.S. objective of "containing" the Soviet Union to prevent the expansion of communism enjoyed broad public acceptance, but the public did not agree on all of the actions taken in the name of containment. Both the Korean and Vietnam Wars lost popular support as casualties mounted.[37] Later, majorities opposed proposals by the Reagan and Bush administrations to give military assistance to the Nicaraguan contras in

their civil war against the avowedly socialist Sandinista government. In all of these cases, public divisions reflected in a very direct way the divisions among opinion leaders. In general, opinion on whether to take a tougher or more conciliatory approach to dealing with the Soviets varied with U.S. perceptions of Soviet behavior: events like the Soviet invasion of Afghanistan in 1979 to prop up a threatened communist regime made a tougher line more popular, whereas arms control agreements and summit meetings between the United States and the Soviet Union during the cold war years made conciliation more popular.[38]

National leaders have reached no new consensus on a guiding framework for U.S. foreign policy during the post–cold war period, and so neither has the public. The war against Iraq to liberate Kuwait in 1991 attracted widespread public support even before its stunning success because Iraq's invasion threatened the U.S. economy (by putting the Persian Gulf oil supply at risk) and America's closest ally in the region, Israel. But the Clinton adminis-

Vietnamese demonstrators in southern California use the February 1999 Vietnamese New Year celebrations to protest a store owner's decision to hang a portrait of Ho Chi Minh, once communist leader of Vietnam, in his window. The protestors are waving the national flag of the former South Vietnam.

tration had great difficulty building popular support for policies aimed at resolving conflicts in Somalia, Bosnia, Haiti, and Kosovo, partly because the administration itself was vague about what was at stake for the nation in these conflicts and partly because other opinion leaders opposed the Clinton administration's policies.

Effects of Background on Public Opinion

People's opinions on specific issues reflect the knowledge, beliefs, and values they have acquired over their lifetimes. The public's various points of view often represent differences in background, education, and life experiences. When polling data are analyzed, these differences show up in the way opinions vary with demographic characteristics such as race, ethnicity, sex, income, education, region, religion, and age. Politicians pay close attention to group differences because they determine feasible coalition-building strategies.

Race and Ethnicity

The sharpest differences of opinion between major groups in U.S. politics occur between African Americans and whites, and the biggest gap is on issues related to race. Unlike in the past, a large majority of white Americans now reject segregation and support equal opportunity for all races, but they disagree with blacks on what, if anything, should be done about the lingering effects of racial discrimination. A 1992 survey asked respondents if they favored preferences for minorities in college admissions and in hiring and promotion decisions. Blacks supported admissions quotas 70 percent to 23 percent (the remaining 7 percent were undecided), while whites rejected them by 71 percent to 24 percent; blacks supported hiring and promotion preferences 53 percent to 41 percent, while whites rejected them by 83 percent to 13 percent.[39] African Americans also are more likely than whites to favor greater government action to provide jobs, health care, and other government services. But they are less supportive of defense spending. Finally, 44 percent of blacks oppose the death penalty for murder compared with only 16 percent of whites.

These contrasting views reflect the profoundly different perceptions and life experiences of blacks and whites in American society. African Americans, along with numerous other minority groups—Hispanics, Native Americans, and Asian Americans of diverse national origins—share a history of discrimination based on race; many have experienced discrimination first-hand. Whites tend to think that legal equality has now been achieved and that any special effort to overcome the effects of past discrimination is unfair to whites. Blacks also tend to have lower incomes than whites and so are typically more favorably disposed toward government efforts to improve economic welfare. Their greater propensity to oppose the death penalty reflects skepticism, based on bitter historical experience, about the fairness of the criminal justice system toward black defendants.

On all of these issues, the views of African Americans are closer to the positions taken by the Democratic Party, and blacks vote overwhelmingly Democratic. As a result, they are a crucial part of the Democratic coalition. Only twice since World War II has the Democratic presidential candidate won more of the white vote than the Republican candidate (Lyndon Johnson in 1964 and Bill Clinton in 1996); every other Democratic victory (Harry Truman in 1948, John Kennedy in 1960, Jimmy Carter in 1976, and Bill Clinton in 1992) has depended on huge majorities among African Americans to offset narrower Republican majorities among whites.

Other minority groups show distinctive patterns of issue opinion and voting behavior, but in most instances these patterns reflect the group's economic status rather than particularly ethnic views. Hispanics tend to have lower incomes and so favor more extensive government services and the Democratic Party; Asian Americans tend to have higher incomes and so are economically more conservative and more Republican than Hispanics. But there are enormous differences within these broad categories in the ethnic backgrounds and economic status of

subgroups. Hispanics include Cuban Americans, Puerto Ricans, Mexican Americans, immigrants from the nations of Central America, and people whose roots in the Southwest go back centuries. Asian Americans include people of Korean, Japanese, Chinese, Vietnamese, Philippine, and Laotian extraction, some further divided into different eras of immigration and regions of origin. Generalizing about group opinions is risky, although one pattern seems to hold: ethnic minorities do express strong and distinctive political views on issues directly affecting their groups. Cuban Americans are deeply concerned about U.S. policy toward Cuba. Opposed to any softening of the official U.S. hostility toward Cuban leader Fidel Castro, Cuban Americans favor Republicans, who generally take a harder line against the dictator. Mexican Americans are far more likely than other groups to oppose the denial of public education and health care to undocumented immigrants, a view that brings them closer to the Democrats.

Sex

On most kinds of issues, the sexes think alike, but on some things they do not. Women are consistently less inclined than men to support the use of violence in foreign and domestic policy. For example, they are more likely to oppose military involvement in foreign conflicts, to support arms control negotiations, and to back gun control and less likely to demand the death penalty for murderers. The differences between the sexes on such issues can be quite large, twenty percentage points or more. By smaller margins, women have more favorable attitudes toward social welfare spending and regulations designed to protect the environment, consumers, and children.[40] The reasons for these differences are still a matter of debate. What is known is that they have created a "gender gap" in recent electoral politics, with women more supportive than men of the Democratic Party and its candidates. In 1996 Bob Dole defeated Bill Clinton among men, 44 percent to 43 percent, but Clinton won the women's vote, 54 percent to 38 percent, and hence the election.[41]

It is interesting to note that women and men do not

differ very much on sex-related issues. Both show high levels of support for women and men having an equal role in society and politics. Men are slightly more supportive of abortion rights than are women.

Income and Education

The politicians who designed the Constitution thought the most enduring political conflicts would pit the poor against the rich. Surveys find abundant evidence that opinions differ among income classes, but the differences are modest compared to those found in most other modern industrial nations. People with lower incomes are more inclined to support spending on government services helpful to people like them: Social Security, student loans, food stamps, child care, and help for the homeless. People with higher incomes are notably less enthusiastic about government spending on social programs or taxing higher incomes at higher rates. Economic self-interest easily explains these differences: people getting more of the benefits tend to see greater merit in social programs than do those paying more of the costs.

On non-economic issues, however, higher income groups tend to be more liberal than lower income groups. This difference has less to do with income than it does with education. People in higher income groups tend to have more years of formal education, and the more education people have, the more likely they are to take the liberal side on issues such as abortion, homosexual rights, equality of the sexes, freedom of speech, and minority rights.

Religion

Religion has played an important role in American political life since the founding of the first colonies. A large majority of Americans profess a religious affiliation, and more people belong to religious groups than to any other kind of organization. Religious beliefs shape values, including many of the values people pursue through political action. The movements to abolish slavery, prohibit alcohol, extend civil rights to African Americans, end the war in Vietnam, and ban abortion have all been strongly imbued with religious ideals.

Differences in religious beliefs often underlie differences in political opinions. Not surprisingly, religious beliefs influence opinions on more social issues than economic issues. People who are secular (no religious preference), Jewish, or belong to one of what scholars call the mainline Protestant denominations, such as Episcopalians, Presbyterians, and Congregationalists, tend to be more liberal on social issues. Evangelical Protestants, such as Baptists and Pentecostals, tend to be very conservative. Roman Catholics, who form the largest single denomination, fall in between, but only on average; a wide variety of social views are supported by various organizations within the Catholic church. Regardless of religious affiliation, the more active people are in religious life, the more socially conservative they are likely to be.

Beginning with the Reagan administration, the Republican Party has made a concerted effort to win the support of evangelical Protestants and other religious conservatives, with a good deal of success. While the country as a whole was electing Bill Clinton in 1992, George Bush won the vote of Protestant evangelicals 62 percent to 26 percent. Christian conservatives have become so large and active an element in the Republican coalition that they now dominate the party organization in many states. The risk for the party is that their prominence may alienate affluent and educated social liberals who would otherwise be attracted by Republican economic policies.

Other demographic divisions of opinion are worth noting. Younger voters tend to be more liberal than their elders on social and economic issues. City dwellers are more liberal than residents of suburbs, small towns, or rural areas. People living near the coasts tend to be more liberal than people living in the South, Midwest, or mountain states, but regional differences of this kind have been on the decline. White southerners once stood out starkly from the rest of the population in their opposition to inte-

People who live in the country have less to fear from neighbors with guns than do apartment residents in urban centers. Many rural Americans also enjoy hunting, a popular pastime. It is not surprising, then, that both public and congressional enthusiasm for gun control is closely correlated with urbanization.

gration, but the gap has almost entirely disappeared. The fading of regional differences is yet another sign of the growing nationalization of American politics.

Differences of opinion among major social groups constitute the raw material of electoral politics. Candidates and parties trying to win elections have no choice but to piece together coalitions out of the material at hand. When the American public is divided across a range of issues, as it is today, electoral coalitions are difficult to assemble and even more difficult to maintain. The more affluent voters tend to be economic conservatives but social liberals; voters with more modest incomes combine economic liberalism with social conservatism. Social issues have given Republicans a wedge to split the Democratic coalition by appealing to the social conservatism of voters who, on economic issues, think like Democrats. Democrats have countered by using issues such as abortion rights and gun control to woo highly educated voters (particularly women) whose economic interests place them closer to the Republicans. Because there are more voters with modest than with ample incomes, Democratic candidates usually like campaigns to focus on economic issues, while Republican candidates want to talk about "family values" and law and order.

This description of political cleavages is too simple, however. One major polling organization analyzing public opinion on a wide variety of political values and attitudes found no fewer than ten distinct clusters of like-minded citizens, with the center just as divided as the left and right ends of the spectrum. Race, income, education, occupation, sex, religion, and age all contribute to distinct patterns of political values and beliefs.[42] It is easy to see how a coalition built on one issue can fall apart when the frame switches to another.

Public Opinion: A Vital Component of American Politics

The vast network of organizations engaged in measuring or trying to influence public opinion attests to its crucial influence in American politics. But it also underlines the reality that public opinion's influence is rarely simple or unmediated. Individual opinions become public opinion only when aggregated, and organizations and leaders do the aggregating. Polling organizations reveal and express public opinion even as they measure it. Politicians and other policy advocates give it shape, focus, and force through their efforts to persuade and activate citizens to support their causes. The mass media report and interpret the collective political experiences that become the material basis for individual opinions. Opinion leaders provide the cues that the rationally ignorant majority uses as shortcuts to forming its opinion. Individual opinions, although rooted in personal values and experiences, are both shaped by and expressed through leaders and institutions.

Leaders and institutions do not, however, control public opinion. People choose which leaders to follow and which messages to heed according to the values and beliefs they accumulate over a lifetime. Their assessments of parties, issues, candidates, and other political phenomena, derived from personal observations and life experiences as well as from families and friends, retain a strong practical component, reflecting real interests and needs. For most people, basic political orientations, whether a reflection of an ideology, a few core values, or simple preference for a party, are quite resistant to change. The raw individual material that goes into the construction of public opinion is not particularly malleable, and neither, therefore, is aggregate opinion. Candidates, policy advocates, and anyone else whose political goals require public support (or at least acquiescence) have little choice but to work within the formidable if often hazy constraints imposed by public attitudes. They succeed, if at all, by framing the choice favorably rather than by changing minds. This is clearest in the electoral context, which is the subject of the next chapter.

Key Terms

aggregate partisanship /332   **attitude** /323
ambivalence /329   **cognitive shortcut** /333

conservative /324   **liberal** /324
core values /324   **measurement error** /332
framing /329   **opinion leader** /332
ideology /324   **political socialization** /325
issue publics /334

Suggested Readings

Asher, Herbert. *Polling and the Public: What Every Citizen Should Know.* 4th ed. Washington, D.C.: CQ Press, 1998. A nontechnical primer for citizens who wish to become smarter, more critical consumers of polls and the media stories that report them.

Brody, Richard R. *Assessing the President: The Media, Elite Opinion, and Public Support.* Stanford: Stanford University Press, 1991. The public's rating of the president is shaped by the economy, international crises, political scandal, the news media, and politicians.

Page, Benjamin I., and Robert Y. Shapiro. *The Rational Public.* Chicago: University of Chicago Press, 1992. Mass public opinion responds in reasonable ways to national political events and experiences.

Sniderman, Paul M., and Edward G. Carmines. *Reaching Beyond Race.* Cambridge: Harvard University Press, 1997. A cleverly designed survey using computer-assisted telephone interviews examines what white Americans say about race when they face no risk of appearing racist.

Stimson, James A. *Public Opinion in America: Moods, Cycles, and Swings.* 2d ed. Boulder, Colo.: Westview Press, 1998. Broad trends in public opinion on a wide range of policy issues, or public "moods," both shape and reflect broad trends in national policy. At the most general level, government policies do respond to public preferences.

Zaller, John. *Nature and Origins of Mass Opinion.* New York: Cambridge University Press, 1992. Four simple axioms about how people respond to political information generate a rich variety of models of how public opinion shifts in response to events and to elite persuasion.

Chapter 11

VOTING, CAMPAIGNS, AND ELECTIONS

☆ *If Americans universally cherish the right to vote, why do so many neglect to exercise it?*

☆ *What difference does it make who votes and who does not?*

☆ *Why is political party identification, which many Americans discount, still the best single predictor of how people will vote?*

☆ *If attentive and informed voters are likely to be turned off by negative advertisements, why do campaigns pour so much money into running them?*

☆ *Why have policy makers found it so difficult to agree on a satisfactory campaign finance system?*

When Bill Clinton moved into the White House in 1993 he had big plans. As a presidential candidate he had promised, among other things, to get the economy moving and to overhaul the health care system. Yet a little more than two years later, both his economic stimulus package and his health care proposals were dead. "The era of big government is over," conceded Clinton. Then, bowing to the political winds, he promised to cooperate with the new Republican Congress by proposing spending cuts that would balance the budget by 2002. What happened? The 1994 elections, in which voters responded to the Clinton administration's first two years by giving Republicans full control of Congress for the first time in forty years, are what happened. Clinton got the public's message and changed his.

The Republicans who took over Congress in 1995 talked revolution: slashing budgets, programs, and taxes and abolishing entire executive departments along with agencies such as the National Endowment for the Arts (NEA). But eighteen months later not only were the NEA and the Departments of Commerce, Education, and Energy still standing, but Congress had caved in to Clinton on the budget, voted to raise the minimum wage, and enacted modest health insurance reforms. What happened this time? The 1996 elections were on the horizon, and opinion polls were making it clear that the radical proposals backed by revolutionary rhetoric had alarmed the public. Moreover, Clinton had won the budget showdown in late 1995 (see Chapter 7), boosting his own popularity (and reelection prospects) and sending that of House Speaker

Newt Gingrich plummeting. Congressional Republicans had little choice but to adopt more moderate policies if they hoped to retain control of Congress. They got the public's message and changed theirs.

As these examples illustrate, elections forge the main link between public opinion and government action in the United States. They not only prompt elected officials to take voters' views into account when they make policy choices but also provide a reason for citizens to form opinions on issues and candidates. For candidates, public opinion serves as the raw material of electoral politics. As we saw in Chapter 10, Americans are divided on a broad range of political issues. Often, the divisions do not form consistent patterns; different groups come together on different issues. The challenge for each candidate is to find ways to persuade voters of disparate and often conflicting views to agree on a common action, which is to vote for the candidate. Building coalitions—getting people to agree on action in the absence of agreement on the purposes of the action—is what pluralist politics is all about, and it is as fundamental to electoral politics as it is to governing. The challenge for voters is to figure out which candidates will best serve their interests and represent their values. The way voters and candidates attempt to meet these challenges is the subject of this chapter. First, however, we will review the logic of elections and their historical development in the United States.

The Logic of Elections

Democracy in America is representative democracy. James Madison, in defending the Constitution in *Federalist No. 10*, adopted the term *republic* to emphasize the distinction between democracy as eighteenth-century Americans saw it and the proposed new system:

The two great points of difference between a democracy and a republic are: first, the delegation of the government, in the latter, to a small number of citizens elected by the rest; secondly, the greater number of citizens, and greater sphere of country, over which the latter may be extended.

The sheer size of the new nation made self-government by direct democracy impossible. If the American people were to govern themselves at all, they would have to do it indirectly, through the delegation of their authority to a small number of representatives. But delegation raised the unavoidable danger, immediately acknowledged by Madison, that representatives might use their authority to serve themselves rather than the people they are supposed to represent: "Men of fractious tempers, of local prejudices, or of sinister designs, may, by intrigue, by corruption, or by other means, first obtain the suffrages [votes], and then betray the interests of the people."

As noted in Chapter 1, any delegation of authority raises the possibility of betrayal. Whenever we engage someone to act on our behalf, we face the risk that they will put their interests ahead of ours. Worse, it is often difficult to tell whether they are faithful agents because we cannot see what they do or know why they are doing it. The problem of delegation has no perfect solutions. One effective, if *imperfect,* solution adopted by representative democracies is to hold regular, free, competitive elections. Elections work to ameliorate the delegation problem for several reasons. First, they give ordinary citizens a say in who represents them. Second, the prospect of future elections gives officeholders who want to keep (or improve) their jobs a motive to be responsive agents. And third, elections provide powerful incentives for the small set of citizens who want to replace the current officeholders to keep a close eye on representatives and to tell everyone else about any malfeasance they detect.

Elections do not guarantee faithful representation; indeed, many Americans today do not feel faithfully represented (see Figure 10–4, p. 337), even though the United States holds more elections for more public offices than any other nation in the world. But the absence of regular, free, competitive elections does guarantee that ordinary citizens will not be faithfully represented. Competitive elections in which virtually all adult citizens are eligible to vote are the defining feature of modern democratic governments.

Nineteenth-century itinerant American artist George Caleb Bingham sometimes depicted local campaign scenes. In fact, Bingham was as much politician as painter. An ardent supporter of Whig candidate William Henry Harrison in the 1840 presidential election, Bingham gave speeches and painted banners. He also was elected to the Missouri legislature (on his second attempt) and later served as state treasurer. In "County Election" citizens line up to declare their votes publicly. Although the painting offers a stylized and benign image of democracy in early America, the inebriated voter toward the end of the line being helped to the poll serves as a reminder that this painter-politician also had the sensibilities of a realist, to be expected of someone who once had been narrowly defeated for election.

The Right to Vote

The practice of selecting leaders by ballot arrived in North America with the first settlers from England. So, too, did the practice of limiting suffrage. Every colony imposed a property qualification for voting, and many denied the franchise to Catholics, Jews, Native Americans, and freed black slaves. No colony allowed women to vote.

Many of these restrictions survived the Revolution in-

tact; only about half of the free adult male population was eligible to vote at the time the Constitution was adopted. The story since that time has been the progressive, if sometimes frustratingly slow, extension of the franchise to virtually all adult citizens (defined as people who have celebrated their eighteenth birthdays) not in prisons or mental institutions. Every expansion of suffrage had to overcome both philosophical objections and resistance rooted in the mundane calculations of political advantage. The triumph of (nearly) universal adult suffrage reflects the powerful appeal of democratic ideas, combined with profound social changes, the struggles of dedicated activists, and the perpetual scramble of politicians for votes.

Wider Suffrage for Men

The property qualifications and other restrictions on voting brought over from England in colonial times reflected the basic social realities there. Most adults were poor, illiterate, and dependent; they were servants, tenants, hired hands, or paupers. Members of the upper-class minority—wellborn, prosperous, and educated—took for granted their own right to share in governing. They were not about to risk the existing social order, which served them so well, by extending voting rights to people whose interests might be better served by changing it. The trip across the Atlantic took some of the bite out of the property qualifications. Land was easier to acquire and far more evenly distributed in the colonies than in England, so a larger proportion of adult males qualified to vote. In the more fluid colonial communities, restrictions often were enforced laxly if at all. By the revolutionary period any "respectable" man—meaning white, Protestant, and gainfully employed—was, in practice, allowed to vote in many places.[1]

The Revolutionary War exerted a powerful influence on the demands to enlarge the franchise. The rallying cry against England of "no taxation without representation," initially a demand for home rule, also implied that anyone who paid taxes should have the right to vote. Men who risked their lives in the fight for independence felt entitled to full political citizenship regardless of wealth. More important and more long-lasting, the ringing pronouncements in the Declaration of Independence that "all men are created equal" and enjoy unalienable rights to "Life, Liberty, and the pursuit of Happiness" and that governments derive "their just powers from the consent of the governed" left little ground for denying voting rights to any citizen.

Still, universal suffrage for (white) men was not fully achieved until the 1840s in the wake of the triumph of Jacksonian democracy. The rear guard defense of suffrage restrictions rested on traditional arguments: people without a stake in the social order should not have a say in governing it. If every man were allowed to vote, the votes of those dependent on the wealthy for their livelihoods—employees, tenant farmers, servants, and apprentices—would be controlled by their patrons, enhancing the power of the rich. If, to avoid such untoward influence, a secret ballot were used, the more numerous poor might support unscrupulous demagogues promoting schemes to redistribute wealth. It boiled down to this: only the independent and virtuous were fit to govern, and the best evidence of independence and virtue was being a property-holding, white, Protestant male.

Gradually, however, this view lost ground to the argument for political equality implicit in the Declaration of Independence. The franchise was not extended everywhere at the same time, but eventually it took on an irresistible political dynamic. (The Framers, prudently avoiding a contentious issue, had left it up to the states to decide who could vote.) As the right to vote slowly spread to all taxpayers, to militiamen, and, informally, to any white male when local officials did not bother to enforce restrictions, opposition to universal male suffrage became a political liability. The more democratic the electorate, the more politically suicidal it was to oppose more democracy, as the Federalists found out too late. The French observer Alexis de Tocqueville noted with his usual clarity:

There is no more invariable rule in the history of society: the further electoral rights are extended, the greater is the need of extending them; for after each concession the strength of the democracy increases, and its demands increase with its strength. . . . Concession follows concession, and no stop can be made short of universal suffrage.[2]

Suffrage for Women

As Tocqueville correctly observed, the democratic logic that justified giving the vote to all white men did not

Despite success in some state legislatures, the suffragist movement never lost sight of the need for a constitutional amendment that would guarantee women everywhere the right to vote. The movement worked, then, to build public support throughout the nation and spur Congress to send an amendment to the states. Marches on Washington were one weapon in the suffragist movement's campaign arsenal.

stop there; it also nurtured demands that all adult citizens, regardless of race or sex, be eligible to vote. For more than a century, race, sex, and the institution of slavery interacted to complicate suffrage politics. The women's suffrage movement grew directly out of the antislavery movement, sharing its underlying ideals and some of its activists. Suffragists felt betrayed when the Civil War amendments (formally, if not in practice) enfranchised the newly freed black men but not women. The largely successful effort by white southerners to purge blacks from the electorate after the end of Reconstruction (see

Chapter 4) raised a major barrier to giving women the vote. Southern whites opposed any action that might focus national attention on repressive local electoral practices. As one Mississippi senator candidly put it in the 1880s, "We are not afraid to maul a black man over the head if he dares to vote but we can't treat women, even black women, that way. No, we'll allow no woman suffrage. It may be right, but we won't have it."[3]

The resistance to women's suffrage was gradually overcome by a combination of social change—the expansion of education for both sexes, the entry of women into the

With so many young men and women serving and dying in the war in Vietnam, the movement to lower the voting age to eighteen met with only token resistance in the state legislatures. The Twenty-sixth Amendment was ratified in 1971. Twenty years later, presidential candidates were appearing on MTV.

Suffrage for African Americans, Young Americans

Despite ratification of the Civil War amendments, the effective extension of the vote to blacks and other minorities came much later, again as a result of social changes and the political incentives they produced. The story, crowned by the landmark Voting Rights Act of 1965, is told in Chapter 4.

The most recent expansion of voting rights—the Twenty-sixth Amendment (1971), which lowered the voting age of citizens to eighteen years—also was a political move, one provoked by the Vietnam War. The idea appealed to antiwar activists because young people were so prominent in their movement. Politicians who supported the war also endorsed the amendment because it enfranchised the troops fighting in Vietnam. The movement echoed the logic advanced after the Revolutionary War that those who risk their lives on the battlefield ought to have a voice in governing the nation they are defending.

Consider, though, what consequences did *not* ensue from the formal expansions of suffrage. The propertyless did not despoil the propertied. Votes for women did not immediately transform electoral politics in any measurable way: no distinctive pattern of women's voting was evident until the 1980s, following a steep increase in the proportion of single working women in the electorate. The only discernible consequence of granting eighteen-year-olds the right to vote has been a decline in turnout. The Fourteenth and Fifteenth Amendments did not prevent a century of racial discrimination at the polls. Only the Voting Rights Act quickly and effectively achieved its goals. The democratic idea has yet to reach its logical limits, however. Some activists have proposed enfranchising children over age twelve and noncitizen residents, even those

workforce outside the home—and political need. Western territories (later states) were the first to grant women the right to vote, not because places like Wyoming and Utah were hotbeds of radical democracy but because women were expected to vote for "family values" in raw frontier communities. The campaign for suffrage sometimes took on nativist overtones, proposing to use women's votes to uphold Anglo-Saxon civilization; indeed, many suffragists did not object to the literacy tests, poll taxes, and other devices designed to keep the "wrong" sorts of people out of the electorate. As women's suffrage grew at the state and local levels, politicians competing for women's votes naturally supported further expansion. Once party politicians sensed an irresistible trend, they scrambled to make sure their side was not stigmatized for standing in the way. Only southern Democrats held out to the bitter end; fears for their goal of maintaining white supremacy trumped everything else.[4] The Nineteenth Amendment to the Constitution, adopted in 1920, finally guaranteed women everywhere the right to vote.

illegally in the United States. In contemporary America, "no taxation without representation" implies a remarkably inclusive franchise.

Who Uses the Right to Vote?

Most Americans agree that the right to vote is the very essence of democracy. On Memorial Day and other holidays the nation honors the soldiers who have fought and died for that right. If the right to vote is so valuable, then, why do millions of Americans choose not to?

It might seem paradoxical that many people who think that the right to vote is worth dying for do not bother to go to the polls. But this reality is not paradoxical at all: it is inherent in the logic of elections. The benefits of elections—in both the broad sense of maintaining democratic accountability and in the narrower sense of electing a preferred candidate—are collective benefits. People enjoy these payoffs even if they have not helped to produce them by voting. It makes perfect sense for citizens to insist on the right to vote, for it gives leaders a reason to care about people's interests, opinions, and values. But it makes equal sense not to bother voting if the only purpose in voting is to influence leaders. After all, the likelihood that any single vote will influence anyone or anything is minute. Totaled up, votes are decisive; individually, they count for next to nothing. Why then spend the time and energy required to go to the polls if individual participation, or its absence, makes no difference in the outcome of the election? The real question is not so much why millions of Americans do not vote, but why millions of Americans forgo free riding and *do* vote.

The same logic applies to gathering information about the competing candidates and parties if a person chooses to vote. There is no point in investing time, energy, or money in becoming better informed about electoral options because the payoff for casting the "right" vote—for the candidate who would, in the voter's view, do the best job—is for all practical purposes nil. If there is no real chance that a vote will be decisive, it is of no consequence whether the vote is right or wrong. Ignorance, like abstention, is rational.

Followed to its logical conclusion, this idea would lead to the collapse of electoral politics and thus to the collapse of democracy: no voters, no accountability, no consent of the governed. In practice, however, these free-rider problems are overcome, but they are overcome quite imperfectly and in ways that have important consequences for how American democracy actually works.

The share of eligible voters who go to the polls has varied widely over American history (turnout patterns are traced in Chapter 12). The most dramatic change has been the decline in voter turnout since 1960. In recent presidential elections, little more than half the eligible electorate has bothered to register and vote; in 1996 it was less than half. These variations in turnout pose the questions we address in this section: Who votes, why, and to what effect? Why has turnout fallen, and does it matter?

Individual Factors Affecting Turnout

A great deal of research has gone into figuring out who votes, who does not, and why. The state of the art is represented by the work of political scientists Steven Rosenstone and John Mark Hansen; their findings are partially summarized in Table 11–1.[5] The entries in the table indicate the difference a particular factor makes in the likelihood of voting (with the effect of the rest held constant). For example, other things being equal, turnout in midterm elections (when people vote for senators and representatives but not the president) is twenty-seven percentage points higher for the most educated as compared with the least educated. In presidential elections turnout among the oldest citizens is twenty-nine points higher than among the youngest citizens.

Age and education have the strongest influence on voting, but many other things affect turnout as well. Blacks and Hispanics are less likely to vote (taking all other factors into account), as are people who live in southern states or states bordering the south. People with deeper roots in their communities (longer-time residents, home-

Table 11–1 Influences on Voter Turnout

	Presidential Elections	Midterm Elections
Demographic Characteristics		
Income	15.8	4.6
Education	16.6	27.0
Age	29.0	25.7
Black	−4.4	−8.5
Mexican American and Puerto Rican	−5.7	−9.3
Lives in southern state	−16.3	−9.8
Lives in border state	−6.1	−8.4
Social Involvement		
Years in community (logarithm)	10.7	23.3
Church attendance	15.1	10.2
Homeowner	7.5	10.2
Currently employed	2.1	
Psychological Characteristics		
Internal efficacy	2.9	
External efficacy	10.6	8.2
Evaluation of Parties and Candidates		
Strength of party identification	10.6	17.5
Affect for a party	11.4	
Cares which party wins presidentail election	6.4	
Cares which party wins congressional elections		20.7
Affects for presidential candidate	5.6	
Mobilization by Parties and Campaigns		
Contacted by a party	7.8	10.4
Close presidential election	3.0	
Gubernatorial election	5.0	
Open House seat		3.7
Unopposed House seat		−4.0
Toss-up House election		6.0
Legal Organization of Elections		
Voter registration closing date	−5.6	
Literacy test (blacks)	−16.0	
Poll tax (blacks)	−10.2	
Periodic registration (blacks)	−11.6	
Voting Rights Act (blacks)	26.4	
Voting Rights Act (whites)	9.5	

Source: Steven J. Rosenstone and John Mark Hansen, *Mobilization, Participation, and Democracy in America* (New York: Macmillan, 1993), 130–131.

Note: Data for presidential elections cover 1956 through 1988; date for midterm elections cover 1974 through 1986. Table entries are the differences in turnout rates between the highest and lowest values taken by each variable, controlling for the effects of the other variables. For income, it is the difference between people in the highest (top 4 percent) and lowest (bottom 16 percent) of five income groups; for education, it is the difference between people with some college and people with no more that an eighth-grade education. For age, it is the difference between the oldest and youngest citizens. Party affect is measured by the absolute value of the sum of positive comments about the first party and negative about the second minus the sum of positive comments about the second party and negative comments about the first (responses to questions about what respondents liked and disliked about the parties); affect toward presidential candidates is measured equivalently. The voter registration closing date indicates the number of days prior to the election that one can last register to vote. Voting Rights Act is coded 1 if respondent lived in a state covered by the Voting Rights Act in 1986 or 1972, 0 otherwise.

owners, church members, and people with jobs) are more likely to go to the polls, as are individuals with greater confidence in their own ability to understand and engage in politics (internal efficacy, as it is known in political science) and to influence the decisions of government (external efficacy). Turnout also is higher among people with stronger partisan views and electoral preferences and those who live in areas with active parties and competitive campaigns. Finally, turnout is higher where legal barriers to registration are lower.

Why is sex missing from this list of influences on voting? Other things being equal, the voting rates for men and women are about the same. Also absent are measures of trust in government and beliefs about government responsiveness; the cynical and distrusting are as likely to vote as everyone else. This point contradicts a popular explanation for the decline in participation—that it results from the dramatic increase in public cynicism and mistrust since 1960.[6]

The explanation for these patterns is straightforward. Voting and other forms of political participation, such as contributing money or time to campaigns, writing letters to elected officials, and attending political meetings, incur costs but produce benefits. People participate when they can meet the costs and appreciate the benefits. Those with money, education, experience, free time, and self-confidence find it easier to meet the costs, while those with a greater psychological stake in politics—from a concern with issues, a sense of obligation to carry out their duty as citizens, or a strong interest in parties or candidates—receive

The elderly vote. Free time, a distaste for taxes, and dependence on government retirement programs render the elderly a highly vigilant, issue-oriented electorate whom politicians approach with some fear and great care.

greater benefits (also mainly psychological) from participation. Voting, therefore, is rational for the millions of individuals for whom the personal satisfaction derived from doing their duty or expressing themselves at the polls outweighs the typically modest cost of going to the polls.

Institutional Factors Affecting Turnout

Differences in participation cannot be explained completely by individual differences in resources and psychological involvement, however. The institutional context—for example, variations in registration laws—affects turnout equally. The more onerous the registration requirements, the higher is the cost of voting. In the decades after the Civil War southern states adopted devices such as poll taxes, literacy tests, and the requirement that voters re-register periodically to discourage African Americans from voting. But after the Voting Rights Act of 1965 banned literacy tests and authorized

the Justice Department to oversee voter registration in states with a history of flagrant racial discrimination, voting among blacks (and whites, too) increased sharply. Still, the effects of old practices linger on. Even with the end of formal and informal restrictions on voting and the advent of two-party competition in their region, southerners are notably less likely to vote than Americans who reside elsewhere.

Social circumstances also play a crucial part in stimulating turnout. Social connections create personal incentives to participate when, for example, coworkers take note of who is performing their citizen's duty to vote. These connections also provide plenty of free information through casual conversation touching on politics. Even more significant, however, are the deliberate efforts of political activists of all kinds to get people to vote. Often, people participate because they are asked, a fact that has never been a secret to politicians. The desire to win elections has inspired extensive efforts by candidates, parties, interest groups, and other campaigners to get their potentially free-riding supporters to show up at the polls.

The assorted demographic and institutional influences on voting produce an electorate in which wealthy, well-educated, older white people are overrepresented and the poor, uneducated, young, and nonwhite are underrepresented. Unequal resources are only part of the reason. The other is that people with social advantages are more likely to be mobilized by parties, interest groups, and campaign organizations. Political leaders deploy their scarce resources efficiently, targeting the people who are cheapest to reach and likeliest to respond. In other words, they go after people like themselves (educated and relatively affluent), people already aggregated and identified by membership in voluntary associations, and people whose social characteristics already incline them to participate. "Thus," in the words of Rosenstone and Hansen, "the pressures that political leaders face to use their own resources most effectively build a class bias into their efforts to mobilize."[7]

Variations in Turnout over Time

If these factors explain variations in participation among individuals, what accounts for variations in turnout over time? More specifically, why has turnout declined by more than ten percentage points since 1960 (see Figure 12–1, page 394)? The decline has been especially puzzling to scholars because voter registration laws have been eased and educational attainment has risen—two trends that should have increased turnout. But they have not done so because their effects have been more than offset by contrary trends. Rosenstone and Hansen's analysis of the forces contributing to changes in turnout is summarized in Table 11–2.

Easier registration and increased formal education have had a positive effect on turnout, but other changes have had the opposite effect. For example, extending the franchise to eighteen-year-olds reduced the turnout percentage by enlarging the pool of eligible voters with the age group least inclined to vote—citizens younger than twenty-five. Turnout also has declined because fewer people have deep community roots, feel politically efficacious, or feel strongly about parties and candidates.

The major reasons for the decline, however, are institutional: a decline in mobilization by parties, candidates, and groups such as labor unions. Fewer people are voting in part because fewer people are being asked to vote by neighborhood activists working for parties or candidates. Most candidates and parties have replaced labor-intensive door-to-door campaigns with money-intensive television and direct-mail campaigns. Moreover, because media campaigns are so expensive, parties and others are concentrating scarce resources on the tightest races, thereby reducing attempts to mobilize voters in the rest. The fading of the civil rights movement diminished efforts to get African Americans to register and vote. And the decline of the labor movement has eroded the unions' traditional grassroots campaigning, although in the late 1990s labor leaders sought, with some success, to reverse this trend. In short, turnout is directly affected by the activities of political entrepreneurs pursuing office or policy. When

Table 11–2 Sources of Decline in Voter Turnout between the 1960s and 1980s

Change	Effect on Percentage Change in Turnout between 1960s and 1980s	Percentage of Decline in Turnout Explained
Easing of voter registration laws	+1.8	
Increased formal education	+2.8	
A younger electorate	–2.7	17
Weakened social involvement	–1.4	9
Declining feelings of political efficacy	–1.4	9
Weakened attachment to and evaluation of political parties and their candidates	–1.7	11
Decline in mobilization	–8.7	54
Net change in voter turnout	**–11.3**	**100**

Source: Steven J. Rosenstone and John Mark Hansen, *Mobilization, Participation, and Democracy in America* (New York: Macmillan, 1993), 215.
   Note: The first column lists the net contribution of each change in electoral conditions to changes in the turnout rate between the 1960s and 1980s; the second column indicates the proportion of the total change in turnout over this period accounted for by each factor.

their goals and tactics change, so does the level of electoral participation.[8]

The decline in voting turnout is much more pronounced among those whose participation is most dependent on outside stimulation: the poorest and least-educated citizens. In general, the smaller the electorate, the greater is its upper-class bias. Logically, a biased electorate should produce biased policy because politicians naturally cater to the people whose votes control their futures. In confronting the budget deficit, for example, Congress was more willing to cut social welfare programs benefiting poor people (food stamps, job training programs, and aid to families with dependent children) than to cut social welfare programs benefiting the politically active middle class (Social Security and Medicare). Even so, the systematic evidence suggests that the policy preferences of voters and nonvoters are usually not very different and that few, if any, election results would change if every eligible person voted.[9] Such evidence has not, however, kept poli-

LOGIC OF POLITICS
THE MOTOR VOTER LAW

YES ( )   NO ( )   3.   If you are not registered to vote where you currently live, would you like to register to vote here today?

Tens of millions of eligible Americans do not bother to vote in national elections. This rampant free riding inspires chronic editorial hand-wringing and numerous projects for boosting turnout. Any attempt to raise turnout through legislation, however, automatically becomes a partisan issue. Politicians believe, despite evidence to the contrary, that higher turnout favors Democrats.[1]

The National Voter Registration Act of 1993, popularly known as the motor voter law, is a case in point. Enacted over Republican opposition, the law requires states to allow citizens to register to vote when applying for or renewing their drivers' licenses, to register by mail, or to receive mail registration forms and assistance in filling them out at state welfare offices. It also forbids states to purge voters from the rolls for failing to vote. The purpose of the bill is to increase turnout by making registration easy—in other words, by reducing the cost to the citizen.

Republicans attacked the proposal in Congress and later in the courts as, in the words of Republican senator

Paul Coverdell of Georgia, "a classic example of a bully government placing an extreme financial burden on our states."[2] Their real concern, however, was not the unfunded mandate (see Chapter 8), but the prospect of hordes of new Democratic voters. Ironically, the law's effect so far has favored Republicans; the regions with the largest increases in registration under the law have been Republican strongholds in the South and West.

The motor voter law added millions to the voter rolls, and analysts suggest that it has the potential to increase turnout by as much as ten percentage points.[3] But voting participation was actually lower in the presidential and midterm elections held after the law took effect (1996 and 1998) than in the two elections immediately before. Many of the new registrants apparently have not yet voted, indicating that the cost of registering was not what was keeping them from the polls. Because national turnout varies over time with circumstances having nothing to do with registration laws, it will take several election cycles to learn whether the motor voter law really leads to greater participation in elections.

1. Benjamin Highton and Raymond E. Wolfinger, "The Political Implications of Higher Turnout" (paper presented at the annual meeting of the American Political Science Association, Boston, September 3–6, 1998).

2. Alan Greenblatt, "Court Rejects 'Motor Voter' Case, But the Battle Isn't Over," *Congressional Quarterly Weekly Report*, January 27, 1996, 232.

3. Benjamin Highton and Raymond E. Wolfinger, "Estimating the Effects of the National Voter Registration Act of 1993," *Political Behavior* 20 (June 1998): 79–94.

cies designed to raise turnout from provoking partisan squabbles (see box "The Motor Voter Law").

How Do Voters Decide?

Casting a vote is making a prediction about the future—that electing one candidate will produce a better outcome in some relevant sense than electing another candidate. To make such a prediction, a voter has to choose the standards for "better" and "relevant" and then determine which candidate best meets the standards. These choices are made under conditions of considerable uncertainty, and, because the likelihood of casting a decisive vote is so tiny, people find it makes little sense to put much effort into acquiring information that might reduce uncertainty. Thus they economize by using simple cues as cognitive shortcuts and by relying heavily, if selectively, on the free information delivered by the news media, campaign advertising, and their own experience to inform their predictions.

One way to predict the future is to look at the past. Voters may treat an election as a referendum on the incumbent's or majority party's performance in office. Has the current agent done an adequate job of serving their values and interests? One simple rule is to vote for incumbents who have performed well. The question then becomes performance on what? The answer depends on the office and the circumstances. Presidents seeking reelection often are held accountable for the national economy—the rates of inflation, unemployment, and economic growth. Economic problems probably cost Jimmy Carter and George Bush their jobs, while a strong economy contributed to Ronald Reagan's reelection in 1984 and to Bill Clinton's in 1996. Presidents also may be reviewed for their conduct of foreign policy. Dwight Eisenhower's success in ending the war in Korea helped assure his reelection in 1956; Carter's inability to obtain the release of the U.S. diplomats held hostage by Iran damaged his reelection chances in 1980. The performance of representatives and senators, by contrast, is often measured by their success in providing services and projects for their states and districts or in casting acceptable votes in Congress (see Chapter 6). But some voters hold the president's party as a whole responsible, casting their congressional votes according to how well they think the administration has governed. Many of the voters who were upset with President Clinton in 1994 took it out on Democratic candidates for Congress.

How can voters assess performance efficiently? Personal experience supplies a good deal of politically relevant information. Looking for a job, shopping at the supermarket, or trying to get a mortgage to buy a house teaches people about unemployment, inflation, and interest rates. Taking out a student loan or applying for veterans' benefits teaches something about government programs. Millions of retired Americans are keenly aware of the size of their monthly Social Security checks. The threat of a military draft certainly raised the political consciousness of college age Americans during the Vietnam War. Those without direct experience with certain issues learn about them through the news media. For example, crime became a bigger public issue in the 1990s than it had been a decade earlier—even though the crime rate had actually declined—because the news media put greater emphasis on crime in the 1990s.

Another strategy for predicting which candidate will be the more satisfactory agent is to compare the future policy options they represent. By the positions they take on issues, by their overall ideological stances, or by their party affiliation, candidates offer a choice among alternative national policies. Which policy positions matter? The answer depends on the voter and the circumstances. For voters with strong views on abortion, any difference between candidates on this issue may be enough to settle their choice. **Single-issue voters** also coalesce around causes such as gun control (its most adamant opponents) and environmental protection (its most adamant proponents). Instead of a single issue, other voters may consider bundles of issues, choosing, say, between the expectations of lower taxes and more generous social spending.

Rivals for the White House or the perfect Republican ticket? Approaching the 2000 presidential primary season, many Republican strategists believed that the nomination of Elizabeth Dole as vice president on a ticket headed by Texas governor George W. Bush offered the party its best chance to retake the White House. Dole, a former cabinet official and experienced campaigner, would make a strong bid for the "women's vote" which Republicans had failed to attract in recent presidential elections.

The times also may determine which issues become important to voters. Civil rights became critical in the 1964 election when the Republican candidate, Sen. Barry Goldwater of Arizona, voted against the 1964 Civil Rights Act. What to do about Vietnam dominated voter opinion while American soldiers were fighting there. And crime and illegal immigration were hot-button issues in 1994.

The news media and the campaigns supply plenty of free information about candidates' positions on the issues and policy promises. But voters cannot take the information at face value, for candidates have an incentive to misrepresent themselves to win votes. Voters can deal with this problem by taking cues from opinion leaders (see Chapter 10). In electoral politics, opinion leadership is often formalized through endorsements. A candidate supported by the National Abortion and Reproductive Rights Action League, the Reverend Jesse Jackson, and the Sierra Club is certain to have rather different policy objectives from one endorsed by the Christian Coalition, the National Rifle Association, and the National Taxpayers Union.

Voters also make predictions based on the candidates' personal characteristics. One set of personal considerations includes qualities such as competence, experience, honesty, knowledge, and leadership skills. Another set includes characteristics such as sex, race, ethnicity, age, and place of residence. The rationale for such criteria is straightforward. Voters cannot anticipate all the problems and issues that will come up after the election, nor can they easily monitor the behavior of their elected officials. Much of what these officials do is out of public sight, and much of the information they act on is unknown to their constituents. Under these circumstances, using personal criteria makes a great deal of sense. A candidate's demographic features give voters clues about his or her personal values. Voters feel that people who are like them in some tangible way are more likely to think and act as they would in the same circumstances. A candidate's competence and character give clues about how far he or she can be trusted to do the right thing even when no one is watching.

The most important information shortcut voters use

to make predictions is **party label.** A large majority of voters continue to take their cues from party, even though popular attitudes toward parties as institutions tend to range from indifference to outright hostility.[10] The party label provides useful information for both **performance voting** (vote for the "ins" when one thinks the government is performing well; vote for the "outs" when one thinks it is performing poorly) and **issue voting** (the typical positions of Republicans and Democrats differ in predictable ways on many issues). Most voters drastically simplify their electoral evaluations and decisions by developing a consistent bias in favor of the candidates of one of the major parties, making the party label the most influential "endorsement" of all.

Party identification, as this attitude is called, is the best single predictor of the vote in federal elections and is therefore a central focus of modern electoral research. Since the 1950s a biennial survey, the American National Election Study, has asked scientifically selected samples of the American public a set of questions probing the strength and direction of their partisanship. Respondents are first asked, "Generally speaking, do you usually think of yourself as a Republican, a Democrat, an independent, or what?" Those who answer "Democrat" or "Republican" are then asked, "Would you call yourself a strong Democrat (Republican) or a not very strong Democrat (Republican)?" Those who answer "independent" or something else are then asked, "Do you think of yourself as closer to the Republican Party or the Democratic Party?" Answers to these questions locate respondents on a seven-point scale: strong Democrats, weak Democrats, independents leaning Democratic, pure independents, independents leaning Republican, weak Republicans, and strong Republicans. This scale serves as the standard measure of a respondent's party identification.

Party identification has proven to be a strong predictor of the vote in any election in which candidates run under party labels. In 1996, for example, about 95 percent of the strong partisans voted for their own party's presidential candidate; weaker partisans were less loyal, and pure inde-

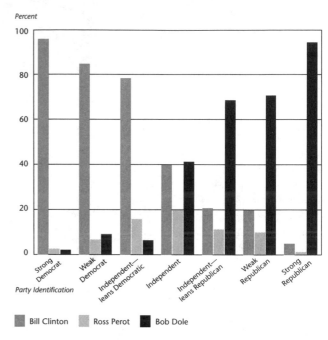

Figure 11–1 Party Identification and Presidential Voting, 1996

Source: American National Election Study, 1996.

pendents split their votes evenly between the two major party candidates. The weaker a survey respondent's partisanship, the more likely he or she was to vote for third party candidate Ross Perot (see Figure 11–1).

The connection between party identification and vote choice varies over time but is always quite powerful. Figure 11–2 shows that in elections from 1952 through 1996, typically about three-quarters of presidential voters were self-identified partisans supporting their party's candidate. The proportion defecting to the opposing party's candidate ranged from 7.6 percent to 24.1 percent, and the proportion voting for independent or third party candidates varied from less than 1 percent to 15.3 percent. Usually, less than 10 percent are pure independents who say they favor neither party. Still, there are enough independents and partisan defectors to keep party alone from determining who wins or loses presidential elections.

Party identification is subject to varying interpretations, but they are complementary rather than mutually exclusive. The researchers who initiated the voting studies in the 1950s viewed party identification as a psychological phenomenon. Voters who were willing to label themselves Democrats or Republicans identified with the party in the same way they might identify with a region or an ethnic or religious group: "I'm a New Yorker, an Irish Catholic, and a Democrat." The party preference was, literally, an element of an individual's personal identity, either rooted in powerful personal experiences (best exemplified by the millions who became Democrats during the Great Depression) or learned, along with similar identifications, from family and neighborhood (see Chapter 10). So interpreted, identification with a party was thought to establish an enduring orientation toward the political world. Voters might defect if they had strong enough reactions to particular candidates, issues, or events that ran counter to their party identification. But once these short-term forces were no longer present, the influence of party identification would reassert itself and they would return to their partisan moorings. For most citizens, only quite powerful and unusual experiences would inspire permanent shifts of party allegiance.[11]

Another interpretation emphasizes the practical rather than psychological aspects of party identification. People think of themselves as Democrats or Republicans because they have found, through past experience, that their party's candidates are more likely than those of the other party to produce the kinds of results they prefer. Past experience is a more useful criterion than future promises or expectations because it is more certain. Party cues are recognized as imperfect, and people who are persuaded that a candidate of the other party would deal more effectively with their concerns vote for that candidate. If cumulative experience suggests that candidates of the preferred party are no longer predictably superior in this respect, the party preference naturally decays.[12] According to this interpretation, partisanship can change gradually in strength or direction without the psychological

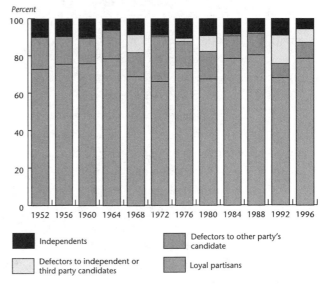

Figure 11–2 Partisan Voting in Presidential Elections, 1952–1996

Percent

Independents

Defectors to independent or third party candidates

Defectors to other party's candidate

Loyal partisans

Source: American National Election Studies

upheaval associated with revising one's personal identity.

But, again, these interpretations are not mutually exclusive. A party might be just a shorthand cue for some voters, but a source of personal identity for others. Cumulative practical experience with leaders and policies might well strengthen or weaken an individual's sense of identification with a party. Conversely, gut feelings about the parties may simply be the brain's efficient way of storing the results of cumulative experiences, providing a shortcut to action (deciding how to vote) without further cognitive effort. However interpreted, party remains for a large majority of voters a default cue: unless there is a compelling reason to do otherwise, vote for the candidate of the preferred party. Although the proportion of strong partisans has diminished somewhat since the 1950s (see Chapter 12), most voters continue to identify themselves as Republicans or Democrats, and partisan preferences, while by no means immutable, are among the most stable of political attitudes.

Election Campaigns

If voters are short of information and uncertain about what criteria to apply to the choice, the candidates and their allies are only too happy to help them out. Experienced campaigners are fully aware of voters' reliance on free information and cognitive shortcuts, and they concoct strategies for winning votes accordingly. Each campaign responds to voters' tendencies to rely on free, easily absorbed information by emphasizing selected facts and cues aimed at getting at least a plurality of voters to prefer its candidate to the others and to take the trouble to express that preference at the polls on election day. The choice among strategic options depends on what the candidate and campaign staff believe will work in *this* contest in *this* year with *this* electorate. Campaigns are intensely pragmatic, opportunistic affairs, highly variable because they must adapt to circumstances that are highly variable—the office in question, whether the contest is a primary or general election, and current political events and issues. Nonetheless, all competitive campaigns have features in common because they face many of the same challenges.

The Basic Necessities: Candidates and Messages

The basic necessities are a candidate, a message, and a way to inform voters about both. A **candidate** is a person who can be portrayed as sufficiently qualified and trustworthy for the job. Achieving this status is not as simple as it sounds. Members of the House of Representatives often run unopposed because no one is willing to take them on in the primary or general election. Even more often members run against candidates so lacking in political experience, talent, temperament, or background that voters do not consider them seriously as viable choices. Sometimes, although less frequently, senators are equally lucky: Sen. Robert Dole of Kansas, for example, was opposed in 1986 by a candidate who reportedly abhorred advertising and large crowds.[13] Guess who won? Presidential contests, however, usually attract plenty of political talent.

Variations in the quality of House and Senate candidates reflect the rational strategies of people interested in successful political careers. Politically ambitious people with the skills, resources, and experience to be effective candidates hesitate to try to move up the political ladder unless they have a good prospect of success, for defeat will stall, and may even end, a career in electoral politics. Unless conditions are promising—the incumbent is in political trouble, the seat is open, a strong partisan tide favors their party—the strongest potential candidates stay out, leaving the field to weaker competitors. Even the pool of presidential candidates may be affected by expectations: when President George Bush seemed unbeatable in 1991 after the Gulf War triumph, some prominent Democratic presidential prospects decided not to run, leaving room for Arkansas governor Bill Clinton, to move to the front of the pack.

Getting Out the Message. The **message** is the answer to the voter's question: Why should I vote for this candidate rather than another? It tells voters why, *in their terms,* this particular candidate is their best choice. Messages are shaped by candidates' theories about the political beliefs, perceptions, values, and responses of different segments of the electorate. Uncertainty is so pervasive and good information about voters is so valuable that campaigns invest heavily in research—if they can afford it.

Presidential campaigns can afford it, and they display the full range of possibilities. They run hundreds of opinion surveys and conduct numerous **focus group** sessions in which a small number of ordinary citizens are observed as they talk with each other about political candidates, issues, and events. Presidential campaigns use focus groups to test their general themes as well as the specific advertisements promoting the themes. They monitor the effects of campaign ads and events with tracking polls that sample citizens' views on a continuing basis to measure changes in responses. In 1988 there was nothing accidental about the Bush campaign's relentless attacks on the Democratic opponent, Michael Dukakis, for being "soft on crime." Nor was it simple intuition in 1992 that made

Clinton's campaign manager, James Carville, put up the now-famous sign reminding himself and the rest of the staff of their campaign's most powerful theme: "the economy, stupid." Nor was there anything mysterious about Clinton in 1996 endlessly repeating the vow to protect "Medicare, Medicaid, education, and the environment." In each case, the campaign's research told it that these messages were winners.

These examples illustrate something else about campaign messages: they are chosen opportunistically. Slow economic growth during the Bush administration handed the Clinton campaign in 1992 a powerful, ready-made theme, and the campaign really would have been stupid not to make the most of it. Clinton's questionable candor about his draft record, experimentation with marijuana, and alleged extramarital adventures handed the Bush campaign its central theme: Bill Clinton was too untrustworthy to be president. Bob Dole took advantage of the aura of scandal permeating the first Clinton administration to make the point again in 1996.

James Carville (aka "the ragin' Cajun") was chief strategist for Democratic presidential candidate Bill Clinton in the 1992 campaign. Here he is shown (left) working the phones at the campaign's national headquarters in Little Rock, Arkansas, the day before the election.

The same strategy is applied to congressional races. The House bank scandal (Chapter 6) gave House challengers a powerful message for their 1992 campaigns: vote the self-serving deadbeats out. The controversial hearings in 1991 over the nomination of Clarence Thomas to the Supreme Court provided another stick. Anita Hill's accusations that Thomas had sexually harassed her were handled clumsily by a committee of middle-aged men, who, many women thought, "just didn't get it." The result was that a candidate's sex became an important shorthand cue for many congressional voters in 1992.

Candidates work hard to convey the message that they do "get it," that they understand and care about the concerns of their fellow citizens. Like other job seekers, candidates prepare glowing résumés highlighting the credentials, experience, and accomplishments that qualify them for the job. But they also try to show that, regardless of their backgrounds, they share some common ground with voters of all sorts. Patrician Yale graduate George Bush advertised his fondness for pork rinds and bass fishing to connect with ordinary folks. The plaid shirts worn by former Tennessee governor Lamar Alexander symbolized his distance from the Washington establishment during his 1996 campaign for the Republican presidential nomination. Clinton's impromptu saxophone jams showed that he could be just one of the gang. It is a robust appetite for votes, not food, that leads candidates to eat bagels and lox at a corner deli in a Jewish neighborhood in the morning, black-eyed peas at an African American church at lunch, and green chili enchiladas at a Mexican American fiesta in the evening. The implicit message is empathy: "Though I may not be one of you, I appreciate your culture and understand your special needs and concerns, so I can serve effectively as your agent."

Actions intended to symbolize a candidate's concerns do not always work as planned, however. In 1972 the

Eating a tamale on the campaign trail represents a small, insignificant bid by a candidate for attention from the Hispanic community. In 1976 President Gerald Ford, campaigning for reelection in San Antonio, bit into his tamale with the husk on and seemed to convey to his bemused Hispanic audience that he was not sure what he had done wrong. This first-class gaffe made it on network news and onto the list of famous Ford blunders.

Democratic candidate, Sen. George McGovern of South Dakota, displayed his ignorance rather than appreciation of Jewish culture when he ordered milk to go with his kosher hot dog while campaigning in a Jewish neighborhood in Queens, New York. Handed a tamale while campaigning among Mexican American voters in San Antonio in 1976, Gerald Ford took a vigorous bite out of the inedible corn husk wrapper, a gaffe that made all the network news broadcasts. During the 1988 presidential campaign, Michael Dukakis reaped widespread ridicule, not enhanced credentials on defense issues, when news broadcasts showed him peering out dolefully from under an ill-

fitting helmet while riding on an army tank.[14] In all three instances, the action conveyed a message quite opposite to the one intended. Campaign advisers may want to display their candidates as all things to all people, but the human material often proves recalcitrant.

Acquiring and maintaining a public image appropriate to the office sought is a particular challenge for presidential candidates, who are subject to intense scrutiny by both their opponents and the news media over many months of campaigning. Most presidential primaries now take place so early in the election year—thirty-one states selected convention delegates before the end of March 2000—that campaigns begin shortly after the midterm election, if not earlier. In years with crowded primary fields (as of June 1999 twelve Republicans were officially in the race for the 2000 nomination) aspirants have to fight for attention and to make sure that they rather than their opponents or skeptical reporters shape their public images. Candidates blessed with famous names (in 2000 Gov. George W. Bush of Texas, son of a former president, and Elizabeth Dole, wife of the 1996 Republican candidate, Bob Dole) and ample money (Bush and multimillionaire Steve Forbes) enjoy a distinct advantage in these endeavors, but front-runners also become all the other candidates' favorite targets. Early caucuses and primaries often decide the nominees well before the party conventions, leaving many months for opponents and the media to pour over every facet of their lives and careers.

Televised debates are another special challenge for presidential candidates trying to convey the message that they are the right person for the job. For clear front-runners, especially those not fully comfortable in front of television cameras, the risks of damaging missteps during a debate outweigh the potential gains from winning it. But the media and public now expect debates, so there is no graceful way to avoid them. For challengers and candidates behind in the polls, the nationally televised debates offer a chance to share equal billing with the leader and to make up lost ground before the largest audiences of the campaign. Independent candidate Ross Perot, for example, made the most of his opportunity in 1992, stealing the first debate from Bush and Clinton with his folksy style and populist rhetoric, thereby giving his candidacy a major boost.[15]

Debates demand considerable preparation—cramming and rehearsal—as much to prevent embarrassing lapses in knowledge and misstatements as to score points. Predictably, the leading candidates focus on avoiding mistakes and tend to stick with their tried and true campaign themes while deflecting their opponents' efforts to shake things up. Running behind in 1996, Bob Dole went on the attack, charging Clinton with destroying Americans' faith in their government: "[Y]ou have thirty some in your administration who have been investigated or in jail or whatever, and you've got an ethical problem. . . . I'm not talking about private, we're talking about public ethics."[16] Clinton countered with a neat (and no doubt prepared) variation on the "Medicare, Medicaid, education, and the environment" theme, declaring loftily that "no attack ever created a job or educated a child or helped a family make ends meet. No insult ever cleaned up a toxic waste dump or helped an elderly person."[17]

Debates rarely cover new campaign ground, but they remain popular among the press and public because they show the presidential candidates up close under sustained pressure. Candidates for the House and Senate occasionally participate in debates, but incumbents often duck debates to deny their obscure opponents free publicity and the opportunity to upstage them.

Negative Campaigning. Campaign messages emphasizing one candidate's personal suitability for the job invite rebuttals from the other side. **Negative campaigning,** pointed personal criticism of the other candidate, is thus a normal if sometimes ugly component of the electoral process—and an effective one. As one Democratic consultant explained: "People say they hate negative campaigning. But it works. They hate it and remember it at the same time. The problem with positive is that you have to run it again and again to make it stick. With negative, the poll numbers will move in three or four days."[18] Cam-

paign professionals distinguish between accurate comparative ads that highlight differences between the candidates (fair) and strictly personal attacks of dubious accuracy or relevance (unfair), although voters may not always appreciate the distinction. Negative ads exploit voters' justifiable skepticism given the dangers and uncertainties inherent in the delegation of authority to powerful agents. Research suggests that negative ads do inform people about the candidates but also make them less enthusiastic about voting for any candidate.[19]

As negative campaigns have proved effective, candidates have sought to erect defenses against them. In 1988 Bush campaign adviser Lee Atwater created a series of attack ads that succeeded in branding Dukakis, who began the campaign unfamiliar to most voters, as a far-out liberal, soft on crime and weak on defense. Four years later, Clinton's strategists, determined to prevent a similar fate for their candidate, organized a rapid response team that blanketed the news media with forceful rebuttals of every charge made by Bush or his supporters, often on the same day charges were made. They also replied swiftly to negative television ads. For example, within forty-eight hours of the broadcast of a spot criticizing Clinton's tax record as Arkansas governor, the Clinton campaign produced, tested with a focus group, revised, and aired their own spot that included some text from the Bush ad with "UNTRUE" stamped across it.[20] The idea was to counter negative messages before they could sink in. Candidates also may try to preempt attacks. For example, Democratic senator Patrick Leahy ran an ad in 1986 warning his Vermont constituents, "Oh boy, it's going to get knee deep around here. Dick Snelling [his opponent] has hired some famous dirty tricksters to foul the airwaves with a big bucks, political smear campaign. . . . Do we really have to go through this in quiet, sensible Vermont?"[21]

Negative or not, campaign ads are rarely subtle, for their targets are the rationally ignorant, marginally involved voters who have not already made up their minds—not the informed political sophisticates or the confirmed partisans for whom the information provided

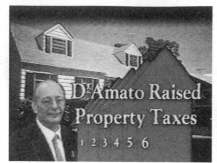

(Source: "Decades," Schumer for Senate, Producer/consultant: Morris, Carrick & Guma)

In the 1998 New York State Senate race between Democrat Charles Schumer and the Republican incumbent Alfonse D'Amato, television viewers were pummeled with negative campaign ads. ANNOUNCER: "D'Amato raises property taxes six times. D'Amato requires government workers to kick back salaries. D'Amato takes hundreds of thousands in speaking fees from special interests. D'Amato rebuked by Senate Ethics Committee. D'Amato conducts partisan hearings on Hillary Clinton. D'Amato votes with Gingrich to cut Medicare. D'Amato votes to cut Head Start, student loans and against school standards. D'Amato opposes campaign finance reform. D'Amato: Too wrong for too long." D'Amato lost the election.

by campaigns is superfluous. As one campaign consultant put it:

The voters have a lot more important things on their minds than political campaigns. . . . Most of the people we are trying to reach with our message don't think about [campaigns] at all until late October. They don't read all the news magazines, the *Wall Street Journal,* and two local dailies. They don't watch CNN and C-Span. They watch "Wheel of Fortune," and they think about politics and campaigns less than five minutes a week.[22]

Simplicity, repetition, exaggeration, and symbolism (images of home, hearth, neighborhood, and flag) are therefore the staples of political advertising.

In the end, though, a successful campaign comes down to several basics. Its goal is to win a majority of votes, not every vote. Planners begin by figuring out who is certain to support the candidate, who is up for grabs, and who is certain to support the opponent. The central clue here, at least for general elections, is the voter's party identification. The campaign is designed to appeal to the first two groups, but especially the second if, as is usually the case, the first does not amount to a majority. Campaign staff find out where the swing voters live, what they care about, and what their mood and concerns are this year. Then campaign strategists find a way to frame the

choice—establishing what the election is about—that underlines the candidate's strengths and plays down his or her weaknesses. In doing so, they develop a simple, coherent campaign theme that explains both why the candidate should be elected and why the opponent should not. Finally, they repeat the theme ad nauseam to reach the crucial late-deciding voters who pay almost no attention to politics. None of these things, however, can be accomplished without money.

The Other Necessity: Campaign Money

No matter how qualified the candidate is or how powerful the message, neither will count for much if voters never hear about them. Thus the third requirement of a competitive campaign is an effective way to communicate with voters. For most of America's history, party organizations and newspapers were the chief conduits for political propaganda. Parties organized marches, rallies, and picnics; supplied the speakers; did the door-to-door canvassing of potential voters; and distributed pamphlets, broadsides, and posters bearing the campaign message. The campaign itself was a team affair, agitating for the election of all of the party's candidates, although the spotlight usually was on the top of the ticket.

Eventually, however, things changed. Patronage-based party organizations declined and television gained popularity as a campaign medium (see Chapter 12). As a result, parties gradually lost their central role in campaigns, to the point that today campaigns are largely the province of individual candidates and their personal organizations. Candidates assemble their own campaign teams, raise the funds, hire the consultants and technical specialists, and design and execute their own individual campaign strategies, sometimes with the help of their national or local party organizations, but often without it.

All of these activities cost money. Modern campaigns for federal office are unavoidably expensive. There is simply no way for most candidates to organize and plan a campaign, do research, develop and package a message, and get that message out to potential voters on the cheap. Genuine electoral competition that gives voters a choice of agents and gives the winners an incentive to remain faithful (lest they be replaced) requires that candidates raise and spend money—lots of it. In 1998, for example, the eighty-four House candidates in highly competitive elections—defined as races in which the winner received 55 percent or less of the major party vote—spent an average of more than $1 million each. Senate candidates in competitive races typically spend much more, although the total varies with the size of the state's population. In 1994 Democratic senator Dianne Feinstein of California spent $14.4 million to eke out a narrow victory over her Republican challenger, Michael Huffington, who spent almost $30 million, largely from his own deep pocket. Presidential elections are in a class by themselves, with total spend-

Campaigning for Congress in 1938 in Crossville Tennessee, Walter Faulkner followed the standard practice of his day: passing through towns and hamlets, attracting an audience with loudspeakers attached to his car, and "pressing the flesh."

ing in the hundreds of millions of dollars for the major party nominees.

Regulating Campaign Money. Taxpayers partially finance presidential campaigns, but a great deal of the money spent on them, and all of the money spent on House and Senate elections, comes from private sources. Privately financed elections inevitably raise two related problems for American democracy. First, democracy demands political equality: one person, one vote. But because money is distributed very unequally, its role in electoral politics threatens democratic equality. Second, privately financed elections raise the suspicion that elected officials will serve as agents of their contributors rather than of their constituents. The dilemma, then, is that meaningful elections require money, but the pursuit of money can subvert the very purpose of elections.

Efforts to resolve this dilemma through regulation have enjoyed limited success. Prior to the 1970s, campaign money was effectively unregulated. Congress had, from time to time, passed limits on contributions and spending, but the limits were easily circumvented and never enforced. The Corrupt Practices Act of 1925, which placed unrealistically low limits on spending in congressional elections, was in force more than four decades, but no one was ever prosecuted under the act. It was easy to circumvent the limits legally, and, anyway, the law contained no enforcement mechanism. This casual attitude toward campaign money faded with the spread of candidate-centered campaigns and the rise of broadcast campaigning, both of which quickly drove up the costs. Higher costs accelerated not only the demand for campaign money but also the fear that the winners would favor contributors over constituents.

Congress's response was the Federal Election Campaign Act of 1971, extensively amended in 1974. FECA provided partial public funding for presidential campaigns and required full public reporting of and strict limits on all contributions and expenditures in federal elections. The Supreme Court, in *Buckley v. Valeo* (1976), upheld the reporting requirements and contribution limits (to prevent "corruption or the appearance of corruption") but rejected spending limits on the ground that they interfered with political speech protected by the First Amendment.[23] Presidential candidates, however, could be required to abide by spending limits as a condition of receiving public funds for their campaigns. Also in *Buckley* the Court overturned, again on First Amendment grounds, ceilings on how much of their own money candidates could spend on their campaigns and on how much anyone could spend to agitate for or against candidates independently of candidates' campaigns. A 1996 Court decision gave party organizations the right to unfettered independent spending as well.[24] Concerned that spending limits were choking off traditional local party activity in federal elections, Congress liberalized FECA in 1979, amend-

ing the act to allow unrestricted contributions and spending for state and local party-building and get-out-the-vote activities. Funds for these activities are commonly called **soft money.**

Broadly speaking, campaign finance operates through two parallel systems. Money going directly to candidates is subject to limits on the size of contributions and full public disclosure of sources.[25] Presidential candidates who accept public funds also must observe spending limits. But money raised and spent outside of the candidates' campaigns—the party's soft money and money raised by groups to pay for independent campaigns and issue advocacy (promoting candidates under the guise of promoting a position on a policy issue)—is lightly regulated and not subject to limits. In practice, this means that any citizen who wants to invest any amount of money in campaign activities can find a legal way to do so.

The Flow of Campaign Money. The money flowing through both campaign finance systems has outpaced inflation since the adoption of FECA. At first, the candidates' system accounted for by far the greater part of campaign money, but recently the second system has grown explosively. In 1996 soft money spending by the major parties totaled $271.5 million, an increase of more than 300 percent over 1992. Indeed, it was the scramble for soft money that turned the White House into a bed-and-breakfast for generous Democratic donors in 1996 and led to the campaign finance investigations that bedeviled Bill Clinton during his second term as president. Today, then, much more money is spent outside the official, publicly financed general election campaigns for president than is spent in them. Both 1996 presidential campaigns were limited to spending $61.8 million on the general election, but much of the $700 million that passed through the hands of the two parties was raised and spent by their presidential contestants.

Spending in House and Senate campaigns also has continued to grow since FECA took effect, rising by an average of about 7 percent (in inflation-adjusted dollars) from

SOFT MONEY

The story of how campaign finance reform led to the flood of "soft money" in presidential election campaigns exemplifies the partisan conflicts, dilemmas, and unanticipated consequences that vex campaign finance policy. The Democrats' defeat in the 1968 presidential election between Republican Richard Nixon and Democrat Hubert Humphrey left the party $9 million in debt and worried about falling further behind in an escalating financial arms race with the Republicans. As a result, congressional Democrats embraced reform proposals that would limit campaign spending and finance presidential campaigns with public funds. Republicans, however, saw no reason to bail out the Democrats or sacrifice their own financial advantage. Although President Nixon promised to veto any bill providing for public financing of campaigns, Congress passed the Federal Election Campaign Act (FECA) anyway in 1971. Nixon signed the bill only after Congress agreed to delay public financing of presidential campaigns until 1976. In 1974, just as the Watergate scandal, in which campaign finance abuses figured prominently, was reaching its climax, another wave of campaign finance reform hit Congress, this time in the form of amendments to FECA. After Nixon resigned in August 1974 to avoid impeachment, his successor, Gerald Ford, who also opposed public financing of campaigns, reluctantly agreed to sign the FECA amendments, conceding that "the times demand this legislation."

Use of the new system in the 1976 elections exposed an unanticipated problem. To meet spending limits, the presidential campaigns focused on mass media advertising to take advantage of its efficiencies and maintained tight central control of all other campaign activity to avoid violating the law. State and local parties had little chance to participate, and the absence of the familiar paraphernalia of grassroots campaigns—bumper stickers, lapel buttons, yard signs—was widely noted and lamented. To preserve a role for local parties and grassroots activists in presidential campaigns, Congress in 1979 amended FECA to permit state and local parties to raise and spend money on party building, voter registration, and get-out-the-vote activities. No limits were placed on contributions or expenditures for these purposes, and, until the law was amended again in 1988, the sums involved did not even have to be reported to the Federal Election Commission. These funds were nicknamed "soft money" to distinguish them from the tightly regulated "hard money" governed by the public funding system. Permissive interpretations by the Federal Election Commission and the federal courts since 1979 of what constitutes "party building" have allowed presidential candidates to raise and spend unlimited sums under the legal fiction that they are merely helping to fertilize the grassroots. Consequently, presidential campaign finance is almost as wide open now as it was before the reforms of the 1970s. Partisan disagreements continue to keep Congress from reforming the system, and perhaps only a new scandal the magnitude of Watergate will break the logjam.

Sources: Dollar Politics, 3d ed. (Washington, D.C.: Congressional Quarterly, 1982), 8–24; Frank J. Sorauf, *Inside Campaign Finance* (New Haven: Yale University Press, 1992), 147–150.

In the Clinton years the White House was for a short time the most expensive bed and breakfast in America. Clinton and his fellow Democrats rewarded the most generous contributors to the party with a stay in the Lincoln Bedroom.

one election year to the next. In 1998 the average House campaign spent nearly $500,000 and the average Senate campaign about $3.5 million. Both supply and demand have driven campaign spending up. The supply of contributions continues to grow because the stakes represented by the election are so great. Decisions made by the federal government affect every aspect of American economic and social life, so there is no shortage of incentives for trying to influence who gets elected and what the winners do in office. In the 1990s the tight battle for majority control of Congress also stimulated heavier investment in campaigns. And demand is continually keeping pace with supply. Candidates' appetites for campaign funds continue to grow because the cost of developing an effective message and getting it out to voters continues to climb.

House and Senate spending averages mask the huge variation in the amounts available to individual congressional candidates. Some candidates raise and spend mil-

lions, while others have to make do with almost nothing. The differences result from strategic choices made by contributors and candidates. Congressional candidates in search of campaign money can tap four basic sources: individuals, political action committees (PACs), their own pocketbooks, and party organizations. House candidates typically receive about half their funds from private individuals and get about 40 percent from PACs; another 8–9 percent comes out of their own pockets. Direct party contributions amount to no more than 1 percent of their funds, but the parties also help out with significant amounts of **coordinated** and **independent** campaign spending. Party committees make coordinated expenditures in behalf of candidates for activities such as polling, producing ads, and conducting research on the opposition. Independent expenditures go for campaign activities (mainly advertising) that are not supposed to be coordinated in any way with the candidate's campaign. Senate candidates raise relatively more from individuals (about 70 percent) and less from PACs (about 25 percent) and receive more help in the form of coordinated and independent spending by their parties.

All types of contributors, with the possible exception of the candidates themselves, distribute their funds strategically. They avoid wasting resources on hopeless candidacies, preferring instead to put their money behind their favorites in races they expect to be close, where campaigning and therefore campaign spending might make a difference. Contributors also favor likely winners whose help they might need after the election. In practice, then, congressional incumbents, usually safe—or at worst in tight races for reelection—have the least trouble raising campaign funds. How much they actually acquire depends in good part on how much they think they need; the safer they feel, the less they raise and spend.

Challengers to incumbents, however, have a great deal of trouble raising money unless they can make a persuasive case to contributors that they have a serious chance of winning. But few challengers manage to do so in any election year. Because races tend to be closer when the advantages of incumbency do not apply, candidates for **open seats** are usually in a much better position to raise funds. Contributors correctly see open contests as their best opportunity for taking a seat from the other party. As a result, average campaign spending varies sharply according to the kind of candidate (Figure 11–3). Incumbents typically outspend challengers by a wide margin, while candidates for open seats often are even better financed than incumbents.[26]

Does it matter how much candidates are able to raise and spend? The short answer to this complex question is it matters only to the degree that a lack of money prevents candidates from getting their messages out to voters. Campaign money has little to do with the results of general elections for president, and this was true even before public funding put the major party candidates on a roughly equal financial footing. These candidates always are at

least adequately financed, and the media transmit so much free information about presidential candidates that the balance of resources is irrelevant. What matters is how voters respond to the competing campaign messages.

Campaign money does matter in presidential primaries, where rationally ignorant voters cannot rely on the party label as a default cue and so need to know something about the candidates. Well-known candidates have a leg up, but lesser-known contenders, to have any chance at all, need to get the attention of voters, which almost always requires spending substantial sums of money. Held in February at the beginning of the primary season, the Iowa caucuses and New Hampshire primary once gave unknowns such as Jimmy Carter (1976) and Bill Clinton (1992) an opportunity to parlay relatively inexpensive early successes into fund-raising bonanzas for later primaries. But with so many states now holding primaries in March, candidates have little time to exploit unexpected success and cannot compete effectively without raising a great deal of money before the election year begins. In 1999 George W. Bush's strong early lead in the polls helped boost his already formidable fund-raising capacity to the

Figure 11–3 Candidate Type and Campaign Spending in House Elections, 1978–1998

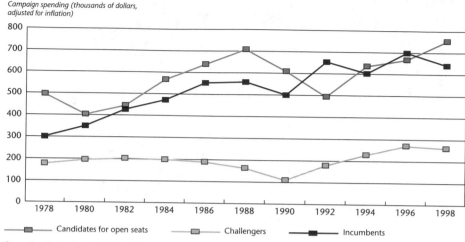

Campaign spending (thousands of dollars, adjusted for inflation)

Source: Compiled by the authors from Federal Election Commission data.

point where, by June, he had a commanding financial lead over every rival save the self-financed Steve Forbes. Most of the other candidates had fallen well short of their fund-raising goals, leaving their prospects for competing effectively in grave doubt.

In House and Senate races, money—specifically, the lack of it—is frequently decisive. Typically half of Senate incumbents and 70–80 percent of House incumbents win by default because their opponents spend too little money to make a race of it. In a candidate-centered electoral system, voters tend to reject candidates they know nothing about and support those they recognize. In the elections held from 1980 through 1998 an average of 92 percent of House voters and 97 percent of Senate voters recognized the incumbent's name. Awareness of their challengers was much less common; over the same period only 52 percent recognized the House challenger's name and 77 percent the Senate challenger's name. Challengers who do not improve substantially on these averages have no chance of winning, and few can do so without heavy campaign spending. Campaign spending has little effect on awareness of incumbents because voters already are familiar with them before the campaign begins.[27]

Campaign money, then, is much more important to challengers (and obscure candidates of any kind) than it is to incumbents or other well-known candidates. In House elections the more challengers spend, the more likely they are to win, but few spend enough to be competitive (Figure 11–4). In elections from 1984 through 1998, a majority (58 percent) of challengers spent less than $100,000, and every single one of them lost. As spending increases, so does the likelihood of winning. Curiously, though, the opposite appears true for incumbents. They are much more likely to spend at high levels, yet the higher their spending, the more likely they are to lose (see Figure 11–5).

This surprising fact is a byproduct of the strategies pursued by contributors and candidates. The more threatened incumbents feel, the more they raise and spend, but the additional effort does not fully offset the threat that provokes it. For incumbents, then, spending lavishly is a sign of electoral weakness that is ultimately registered at the polls. For challengers, higher spending is a sign, as well as a source, of electoral strength. Challengers with better prospects (attractive candidates with potentially effective messages) are able to raise more money, and the more they spend, the more professional their campaigns,

Figure 11–4 Challengers' Spending and Success Rates in House Elections, 1984–1998

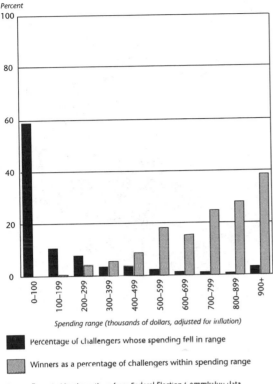

Spending range (thousands of dollars, adjusted for inflation)

Percentage of challengers whose spending fell in range

Winners as a percentage of challengers within spending range

Source: Compiled by the authors from Federal Election Commission data.

Figure 11–5 Incumbent's Spending and Success Rates in House Elections, 1984–1998

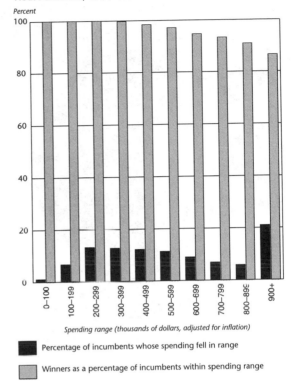

Spending range (thousands of dollars, adjusted for inflation)

Percentage of incumbents whose spending fell in range

Winners as a percentage of incumbents within spending range

Source: Compiled by the authors from Federal Election Commission data.

the more voters they reach, and the more support they attract. Challengers do not have to outspend incumbents to win. Indeed, fewer than one-quarter of the successful House challengers in the past decade spent more than the incumbent they defeated; on average, they spent $278,000 less. They simply have to spend enough to make their case. When both candidates spend enough money to mount full-scale campaigns, the content of the campaigns, not the balance of resources, determines the outcome.

How Are Campaign Funds Spent? Once candidates have raised campaign money, they have to decide how to spend it, unless, like many congressional incumbents, they face such feeble opposition that they are free to stash it away for some future contest. No one is certain about the most

effective way to use scarce campaign resources. The most commonly expressed view is that "half the money spent on campaigns is wasted. The trouble is, we don't know which half."

Because a fundamental goal of every campaign is to reach voters with the candidate's message, it is no surprise that in the 1992 House and Senate elections the largest expense was advertising, with television and radio ads leading the way (Figure 11–6). Senate campaigns make heavier use of broadcast advertising, while House campaigns use more "persuasion mail." The reason is efficiency. Media markets in large metropolitan areas may include as many as thirty House districts (Greater New York). Thus House candidates opting for broadcast advertising have to pay for a station's entire audience, not just

Figure 11–6 House and Senate Campaign Expenses, 1992

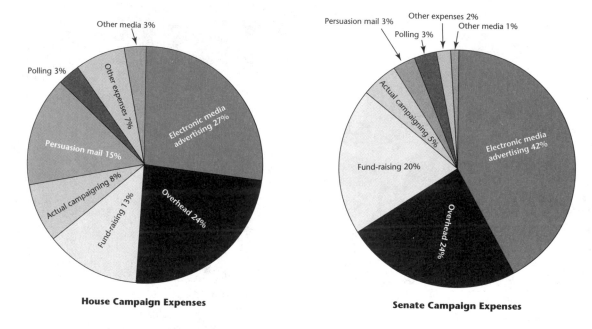

House Campaign Expenses

Senate Campaign Expenses

Source: Based on data reported by Dwight Morris and Murielle P. Gamache in *Handbook of Campaign Spending: Money in the 1992 Congressional Races* (Washington, D.C.: CQ Press, 1994), tables 1–5, 1–6.

that fraction living in the target district. Mailings, by contrast, can be targeted precisely to district residents. Still, House campaigners with enough money often use television even where it is inefficient because it is the only way to reach many potential voters and avoids the risk of campaign brochures being tossed out as "junk mail."

Only a small proportion of funds is spent on traditional campaigning—speeches, rallies, soliciting votes door-to-door, and shaking hands at the factory gate. Yet these activities remain a major part of every campaign because candidates hope to extend their impact far beyond the immediate audience by attracting news coverage. Campaigns display considerable imagination in coming up with gimmicks that will gain free media exposure; indeed, campaign professionals work so hard for it that they prefer to call it "earned" media. One particularly brave House challenger even traveled with a large pig to under-

line his opposition to the incumbent's "pork barrel politics" (see Chapter 6). What local TV station could resist the visuals? Another tactic is running paid ads designed to provoke controversy. The ensuing news coverage then spreads the message to an audience much larger than the one originally exposed to the ad.

In pursuing favorable news coverage, presidential campaigns are in a class by themselves. Indeed, modern presidential campaigns are basically made-for-TV productions. Candidates tolerate grueling travel schedules, participate in countless carefully staged events, and compose pithy "sound bites"—short comments designed to be excerpted for broadcast, such as George Bush's "read my lips, no new taxes" in 1988—to get their messages on the news and out to the voters. The celebratory post-convention bus tour taken by the Clintons and Gores in 1992 is a successful example; it brought out large, exuberant crowds, generating a good deal of positive media coverage both nationally and in the states visited. Presidential candidates also exploit soft news and entertainment shows. In 1992 Bill Clinton, a master of the talk-show format, appeared on *Donahue,* the *Arsenio Hall Show, Larry King Live,* and MTV's *Rock the Vote* as well as *Good Morning America* and *Today.* Meanwhile, Ross Perot announced his independent candidacy on *Larry King Live* and appeared on King's talk show and others throughout his campaign. The folksy billionaire also broadcast lengthy "infomercials"—essentially his own talk shows—featuring simple graphics illustrating his ideas about the economy.

When it comes to media coverage, the rich get richer and the poor get ignored. The best-funded campaigns (for president, or hotly contested Senate seats) get the most attention from the news media. Poorly funded candidates may be desperate for news coverage because they cannot afford to buy air time, yet the very fact of their poverty makes them look like sure losers and therefore not worth covering. Campaigns that must depend on the news media to get their messages out invariably fail.

A large share of congressional campaign funds goes for expenses not directly connected to reaching voters (Figure 11–6). For example, nearly a quarter of the money is spent on overhead—staff salaries, office and furniture rental, computers and other equipment, telephone calls, travel, legal and accounting services, and the like. Fundraising is another major expense, particularly for Senate candidates who spend 20 percent of their money on just raising more money. Because of their larger constituencies, Senate candidates usually have to raise bigger sums than House candidates, but FECA contribution limits compel them to raise it in the same size chunks.

Incumbents and nonincumbents have somewhat different spending patterns. Often, weak opposition leaves incumbents free to spend relatively less on reaching voters or not to spend the money at all. Nonincumbents spend about two-thirds of their funds on activities designed to reach voters directly; incumbents spend a little

During the 1996 reelection campaign, President Bill Clinton and running mate Al Gore repeated their successful 1992 postconvention bus tour by taking a two-day bus trip through the Midwest. The contrasts with the 1938 Faulkner campaign pictured earlier in this chapter are many, but "pressing the flesh" and "stump speeches" remain popular campaign techniques largely because the audience includes members of the news media.

less than half of their funds for such purposes. In 1992 House incumbents actually gave away 6 percent of their campaign money, sometimes to local charities, but mostly to their party and to other candidates. Members aspiring to leadership positions now routinely cultivate support by passing campaign money on to less-secure colleagues; some even form their own PACs for this purpose.

Where Are Campaign Funds Spent? Presidential candidates invest heavily in television advertising, the most efficient way to reach an electorate of nearly 100 million people. In 1992, for example, Clinton, Bush, and Perot together spent more than $100 million on television time. But *where* is the investment best spent? Given the design of the electoral college (described in Chapter 7), it is strategically sensible for presidential campaigns to focus on states with large numbers of electoral votes rather than the national electorate. Whoever wins the most popular votes in a state, except for Maine and Nebraska, gets all of its electoral votes no matter how narrow the margin of victory.[28] The object of a presidential campaign, then, is to piece together enough state victories to win at least 270 electoral votes.

The usual strategy is to concentrate on states that polls indicate could go either way and that are populous enough to be worth winning and to ignore states that are locked up by either side. On occasion, however, a campaign will put some effort into states that the other side is expected to win as a way of making the opposition use up some of its resources of time and money defending its base. In 1996 the Clinton campaign conceded most of the South and mountain West to Dole and invested relatively little in the Northeast where Democratic support was solid. The campaign focused instead on the large industrial states of the upper Midwest and on the top prize, California. But it also invested heavily in Florida, forcing Dole to defend (unsuccessfully) a state that had gone Republican in the previous seven presidential elections. The Dole campaign first targeted the upper Midwest, shifted to the mid-Atlantic states (New Jersey, Pennsylvania), and finally, in desperation, moved on to California, in each case failing to overcome Clinton's lead in the polls. The campaigns' allocation of television ads exemplified their targeting strategies. Between April 1 and September 29, 1996, the Clinton campaign ran 55,721 spots in thirty-eight states, but 45 percent of them were shown in just five states: Florida, Michigan, California, Ohio, and Pennsylvania. The Dole campaign broadcast a similar number of ads and also put 45 percent of them into just five states; four duplicated Clinton's top five, with Tennessee replacing Michigan as the fifth.[29]

Money and Elections: Policy Issues

Perhaps now it is clearer why the dilemma noted at the beginning of this discussion of campaign money is so thorny. Elections are supposed to keep agents responsive by making them compete with other would-be agents for the votes needed to win and hold their jobs. This does not require that every election be hard fought, but it does require that officials anticipate serious competition if they serve constituents poorly. Serious electoral competition is expensive because informing voters about alternatives is expensive. The costs are met by gathering large sums of money from people and groups whose values and interests may differ from those of voters, raising the suspicion that elected officials will be more responsive to contributors than to voters, undermining the purpose of elections and, eventually, democracy. The evidence for the claim that campaign money buys influence and that elected officials ignore voters to please donors is actually quite tenuous (see Chapter 13, Interest Groups). No one denies that money buys **access**—the politician's ear—but what else it buys is a question still much in dispute among academic researchers.

Still, the news media and self-proclaimed public interest lobbies have convinced most Americans that campaign donations buy, in addition to White House hospitality and golf dates with congressional leaders, specific policy favors. The democratic dilemma posed by the campaign finance system has grown more acute with the rise in campaign spending, and major changes in the system are proposed in Congress after every election. Since adoption of FECA more than two decades ago, however, none has succeeded. Some popular reform proposals are based on a misunderstanding of electoral politics. For example, most Americans are convinced that campaigns have become too expensive and would like to impose ceilings on campaign spending. But if the goal is competitive elections, the greater problem is that a large number of campaigns are too poorly funded to give voters even a modestly informed choice. Moreover, unless the spending limits are quite high, they will help incumbents at the expense of challengers (see Figures 11–4 and 11–5).

Another reform suggested would democratize congressional campaign finance by forbidding large donations and banning PACs, forcing candidates to finance their campaigns with small contributions from private individuals. This reform runs aground on a standard free-rider problem, however. Because a candidate's victory benefits all who desire it whether or not they contribute to the campaign, and because no single small contribution will affect the outcome or buy access to the victor, it is impossible for most candidates to raise enough money in small donations to conduct a competitive campaign. Recognizing this, reformers have proposed a standard solution: financing campaigns with tax dollars. In their view, elections untainted by special-interest contributions are a public good that citizens should compel themselves to purchase just as they pay for national defense. The precedent is the system for financing presidential campaigns (ignoring, for the moment, soft money and independent spending).

For many who support the idea, publicly financed congressional elections have another advantage: candidates could be required to accept spending limits in return for public funds for their campaigns. But again, unless the limits are high enough, this scheme would hurt challengers, reducing electoral competition. Yet if every campaign gets enough money to be truly competitive, the system will be expensive, with tens of millions of tax dollars spent on many candidates who have no serious prospects of winning. Moreover, any method of public finance would have to accommodate primary elections and third party or independent candidacies. So far, the idea of extending public funding to congressional candidates has made little headway because the public does not support

the move. Opponents have succeeded in characterizing public funds as "welfare for politicians," a frame that combines two widely unpopular referents.

The ultimate barrier to a more egalitarian campaign finance system, however, is the First Amendment as currently interpreted by the Supreme Court. Even if campaigns were fully funded by tax dollars and private contributions to candidates prohibited, people and organizations would remain free to spend all the money they could gather on independent campaigns supporting or attacking candidates. Moreover, we can be certain that many of the people and groups who now send dollars to candidates would merely redirect their funds into independent campaigns if the law closed off other avenues of participation. Organized labor's unregulated $35 million "voter education" campaign against selected House Republicans in 1995–1996 is one indication of what to expect (see box "Educating Voters"). Because no one believes that the justices will change their minds any time soon, some reformers, including Richard Gephardt of Missouri, the Democratic House minority leader, proposed in 1997 amending the Constitution to allow Congress to impose "reasonable" spending limits on everyone. The amendment went nowhere that year, but the idea is likely to be around as long as the campaign finance impasse remains.

Despite widespread agreement among politically active people that the campaign finance system is flawed in one way or another, fundamental changes are unlikely because there is no consensus on what would count as an improvement or how to achieve it. Changes likely will come only in the form of ever more inventive campaign finance practices. But this is not necessarily a bad thing: if the campaign finance system is far from egalitarian, it is remarkably pluralistic. People espousing a wide variety of interests and values take part in financing campaigns, and no single point of view predominates. Promising candidates with potentially effective messages usually can find financial allies, and therefore elected officials can anticipate electoral trouble if they get out of touch or out of

EDUCATING VOTERS

The Republican takeover of Congress in 1995 inspired a vigorous counterattack by the AFL-CIO, an alliance of labor unions that are core components of the Democratic coalition. In April 1995 the AFL-CIO initiated direct-mail and broadcast campaigns against selected House Republicans for allegedly voting against workers' interests. The effort was later expanded into a $35 million campaign targeting sixty-four House Republicans for defeat. The campaigns were highly effective against first-term Republicans, reducing their vote totals by an average of about four percentage points, but not against the much smaller proportion of more senior Republicans who were targeted. Had it not been for the AFL-CIO's campaign, seven of the twelve Republican freshmen who lost probably would have survived. The campaign failed, however, to achieve its goal of returning control of the House to the Democrats because the party had fielded too few challengers with the experience and resources to take advantage of the boost provided by the unions' effort.

What makes the campaign especially significant is that the money spent on it was completely unregulated. The AFL-CIO did not have to report the expenditures to the Federal Election Commission because the ads carefully avoided explicitly endorsing or opposing particular candidates. They maintained the legal fiction that their purpose was to educate union members and the general public about national issues. Voters were merely told who opposed the interests of old people, working people, students, and the environment (and, in some cases, who did not) and were left to draw their own conclusions. These "voter education" campaigns had the added advantage that, unlike contributions to parties or candidates, they could be paid for out of union dues. Republicans cried foul and tried to throw up legal roadblocks, but their own allies—Newt Gingrich's GOPAC and the Christian Action Network—had pioneered the strategy and won the court cases that confirmed its legality. So long as ads do not explicitly tell people how to vote, the Supreme Court regards them as pure exercises of free speech protected from regulation by the First Amendment.

Source: Gary C. Jacobson, "The Effect of the AFL-CIO's 'Voter Education' Campaigns on the 1996 House Elections," *Journal of Politics* 61 (February 1999): 185–194.

line with the people who elected them. Money is important because candidates need it to reach voters, but the voters still have the last word.

The Logic of Elections Revisited

Despite all the problems with U.S. elections, they work remarkably well to preserve American democracy. Regular, free, competitive elections guard the nation against the dangers that inevitably arise when citizens delegate authority to governments. Elections allow citizens, as principals, to pick their agents and to fire and replace those whose performance falls short. The threat of replacement provides elected officials with a powerful incentive not to go astray. Elections also create incentives for entrepreneurs and organizations to solve the free-rider and coordination problems that beset citizens acting as collective principals. Aspiring leaders and their political allies compete for votes by keeping an eye on officials and informing citizens about their shortcomings, paying the information costs that individual citizens would not rationally pay. Similarly, by getting out the vote on election day they turn citizens who might otherwise rationally abstain from casting a ballot into voters. They also bear much of the cost, through polling and focus groups, of keeping track of what citizens want from their agents in government, again making up for the lack of rational incentives for individual political expression. But all of these activities cost money, and the campaign finance system presents its own set of agency problems that are not easily solved.

Elections also induce candidates and campaigns to help solve the massive coordination problem faced by millions of voters trying to act collectively to control or replace their agents. By offering competing frames for the voting decision, they clarify and focus the electoral choice to the point where rationally ignorant voters can manage it. Candidates' opportunistic choice of issues puts voters' concerns on the agenda and helps make election results intelligible: in 1992, for example, the issue really *was* the economy. When candidates form relatively stable coalitions with other would-be leaders—that is, combine into political parties—they narrow the choices to a manageable number, often as few as two. Indeed, party labels simplify voters' choices across offices and over a series of elections. They also allow voters to hold elected officials collectively responsible for their performance in office. In other words, elections create strong links between public opinion and government action. But they do so only because politically ambitious people have found it serves their own purposes to engage in the activities that forge the links. One durable institutional byproduct of political ambition pursued under American electoral rules, the party system, is the subject of the next chapter.

Key Terms

access / 378

candidate / 364

coordinated spending / 372

focus group / 364

independent spending / 372

issue voting / 362

message / 364

negative campaigning / 367

open seat / 373

party identification / 362

party label / 362

performance voting / 362

single-issue voters / 360

soft money / 370

Selected Readings

Campbell, Angus, Philip E. Converse, Warren E. Miller, and Donald E. Stokes. *The American Voter.* Chicago: University of Chicago Press, 1976. First published in 1960, this seminal survey-based study of American voting behavior presents the classic psychological theory of party identification. It is still essential reading for every student of American politics.

Downs, Anthony. *An Economic Theory of Democracy.* New York: Harper and Row, 1957. The seminal theoretical work explaining how electoral and party politics reflects rational strategies of candidates and voters.

Fiorina, Morris P. *Retrospective Voting in American National Elections.* New Haven: Yale University Press, 1981. Survey-based study supporting the Downsian theory of party identification as a running tally of positive and negative experiences with the parties' performance in government.

Lupia, Arthur, and Mathew D. McCubbins. *The Democratic Dilemma: Can Citizens Learn What They Need To Know?* New York: Cambridge University Press, 1998. The answer, according to the theory and experimental evidence reported in this book, is a clear yes; despite "rational ignorance," people use freely available cues to make reasoned choices among candidates.

Miller, Warren E., and J. Merrill Shanks. *The New American Voter.* Cambridge: Harvard University Press, 1996. Sequel to *The American Voter,* with an emphasis on generational changes in patterns of turnout and partisanship since the New Deal.

Popkin, Samuel L. *The Reasoning Voter: Communication and Persuasion in Presidential Campaigns.* 2d ed. Chicago: University of Chicago Press, 1994. How voters use "gut reasoning" and information shortcuts to decide how to vote in primary and general elections for president.

Rosenstone, Steven J., and John Mark Hansen. *Mobilization, Participation, and Democracy in America.* New York: Macmillan, 1993. The most prominent and intractable question in American politics is why voting turnout has declined over the last thirty years. Rosenstone and Hansen offer the closest thing we have to an answer that is actually supported by evidence.

Republican comic book, 1956

Chapter 12

POLITICAL PARTIES

☆ *If the first generation of leaders elected under the Constitution rejected political parties on principle, why did they create them anyway?*

☆ *Why does a nation as diverse as the United States sustain only two major parties?*

☆ *Today national party conventions merely certify the winners of primary elections instead of choosing the presidential nominees, as they did in the past. So why do the parties continue to hold these gatherings?*

☆ *Ninety percent of Americans claim they always vote for the person best suited for the job, regardless of party. How can it be, then, that political parties are healthier than ever?*

In the 1998 gubernatorial election Minnesota voters rejected two well-known candidates with long party pedigrees, Democrat Hubert Humphrey III and Republican Norm Coleman, and elected instead Jesse Ventura, a flamboyant former professional wrestler. Ventura ran as the candidate of the Reform Party, a legacy of Ross Perot's forays into presidential politics. Like Perot's surprisingly strong showing in 1992 (19 percent of the votes, the largest share for any candidate without a major party base in more than a century), Ventura's stunning victory seemed to be yet another sign of the public's growing disillusionment with the traditional parties. Indeed, to listen to the American public is to conclude that the party system in the United States is on its last legs. More than 90 percent of Americans claim they always vote for the person they think best suited for the job, regardless of party.[1] A majority believe that "parties do more to confuse the is-

sues than to provide a clear choice on the issues."[2] Only 39 percent favor a continuation of the current two-party system rather than having candidates run as individuals without party labels (35 percent) or forming new parties that could effectively challenge the Democrats and Republicans (26 percent).[3]

By contrast, anyone who looks at how people vote, who wins elections, and how the nation is governed would have to conclude that the two major parties rarely have been healthier. A large majority of voters are willing to identify themselves as Republicans or Democrats, and, of these partisans, a large majority vote loyally for their party's candidates. Jesse Ventura notwithstanding, rarely does a candidate win state or federal office without a major party nomination. Moreover, party remains the central organizing instrument in government.

The wide gap between people's opinions about and behavior toward political parties has deep roots in American history. None of the politicians who designed the Constitution or initially sought to govern under it thought parties were a good idea—including the very people who unwittingly created them. Even in their heyday, parties never lacked articulate critics or public scorn. Still, parties began to develop soon after the founding of the nation and, in one guise or another, have formed an integral part of the institutional machinery of American politics ever since. The chief reason for their longevity is that the institutions created by the Constitution make the payoffs for using parties—to candidates, voters, and elected officeholders—too attractive to forgo. American political parties represent the continuing triumph of pure political expedience.

Although expedience explains the existence of the parties, the activities that maintain them contribute to successful democratic politics in unforeseen ways. Indeed, the unintended consequences of party work are so important that most political scientists agree with E. E. Schattschneider who said, "Political parties created democracy and modern democracy is unthinkable save in terms of parties."[4] Parties recruit and train leaders, foster political participation, and teach new citizens democratic habits and practices. Beyond that, they knit citizens and leaders together in electoral and policy coalitions and allow citizens to hold their elected agents collectively responsible for what the government does. They also help to channel and constrain political conflicts, promoting their peaceful resolution. Finally, parties organize the activities of government, facilitating the collective action necessary to translate public preferences into public policy (see Chapters 6 and 7). In short, political parties make mass democracy possible.

This chapter examines the origin and development of national parties in the United States, as well as what parties are, why and how they were invented, and how they have evolved. Parties, as we shall see, are the products of a compelling political logic, emerging from the strategic acts of politicians and citizens pursuing their political goals within the framework of institutions established by the Constitution.

The Constitution's Unwanted Offspring

The Constitution contains no mention of political parties. During the nation's founding, parties were widely considered to be dangerous to good government and public order, especially in republics (see box, "No One Wanted to Party"). In such an intellectual climate, no self-respecting leader would intentionally set out to organize a political party.

The pervasive fear of parties reflected both historical experience and widely held eighteenth-century social beliefs. Factional conflict brought to mind the bloody religious and political wars of England's past and the internal strife that had destroyed the classical republics in Greece, Rome, and Italy. Society was viewed ideally as a harmonious whole, its different parts sharing common interests that all wise and honest authorities would dutifully promote. (Pluralism, though implicit in Madison's defense of the Constitution in *The Federalist,* was not yet on the intellectual horizon.) People in authority saw themselves as agents acting on behalf of the whole community; any organized opposition was therefore misguided at best, treasonous at worst. Accepting the same perspective, rivals justified their opposition by imagining that those in power were betrayers of the community's trust. When the leaders of the new government took the steps that led to the creation of the first political parties, they did not expect or want party competition to become a permanent feature of American politics. Rather, their aim was to have the common good—their version, naturally—prevail and their opponents consigned to oblivion. The first parties were created as strictly temporary expedients.

Expedient they were, but temporary they were not. Disdained by all, parties nonetheless flourished. The First Amendment's guarantees of freedom to speak, write, and

NO ONE WANTED TO PARTY

In the early years of the United States, conventional wisdom inveighed against political parties. Benjamin Franklin spoke out against the "infinite mutual abuse of parties, tearing to pieces the best of characters."[1] In *Federalist* No. 10 James Madison called them a species of "faction," which, by definition, holds intentions "adverse to the rights of other citizens, or to the permanent and aggregate interests of the community." George Washington used his Farewell Address to "warn . . . in the most solemn manner against the baneful effects of the Spirit of Party, generally,"[2] and his successor, John Adams, averred that "a division of the republic into two great parties . . . is to be dreaded as the greatest political evil under our Constitution."[3] Even Thomas Jefferson once declared, "If I could not get to heaven but with a party, I would not go there at all."[4]

1. Richard Hofstadter, "The Idea of a Party System," in *After the Constitution: Party Conflict in the New Republic*, ed. Lance Banning (Belmont, Calif.: Wadsworth, 1989), 20.

2. Nobel E. Cunningham, ed., *The Making of the American Party System: 1789 to 1809* (Englewood Cliffs, N.J.: Prentice-Hall, 1965), 16.

3. Hofstadter, "Idea of a Party System," 20.

4. Richard Hofstadter, *The Idea of a Party System: The Rise of Legitimate Opposition in the United States, 1780–1840* (Berkeley: University of California Press, 1970), 123.

assemble ensured that party activities would be legal. Beyond that, the framework of institutions established by the Constitution created powerful incentives for undertaking the activities that created and sustained parties. The design of the Constitution also had a profound effect on the *kind* of parties that developed. The party system

has changed in important ways over the years as political entrepreneurs have adapted parties to new purposes and opportunities, but the basic features that reflect the constitutional system have reappeared in every period.

Incentives for Party Building

The political incentives that spawned parties are transparent. In any system where collective choices are made by voting, organization pays. When action requires winning majorities on a continuing basis in multiple settings, organization is absolutely essential. The Constitution's provisions for enacting laws and electing leaders therefore put a huge premium on building majority alliances across institutions and electoral units. Parties grew out of the efforts of political entrepreneurs to build such alliances and to coordinate the collective activity necessary to gain control of and use the machinery of government.

To Build Stable Legislative and Electoral Alliances. The first American parties appeared in Congress when leaders with opposing visions of the national future began competing for legislative votes. Passing legislation requires majority support in the House and Senate. Anyone wanting to get Congress to act has to identify enough supporters to make up a majority, arrange a common course of action, and then get the supporters to show up to vote. To control policy on a continuing basis, legislative leaders find it advantageous to cultivate a stable group of supporters because durable alliances sharply reduce the transaction costs of negotiating a winning coalition on each new proposal. They also need to build alliances that cross institutional boundaries, incorporating the presidency as well as members of the House and Senate, as all three institutions have a hand in lawmaking.

Legislative alliances are by necessity coalitions. Given the diversity of American society, which Madison delineated in *Federalist* No. 10 (see Chapter 2), it is impossible for stable alliances of any appreciable size to be built solely on shared interests or values. Rather, alliances require coordination; the participants have to agree to cooperate

Congressional party leaders recognize that their words and actions send signals to voters and create issues that affect the success of all candidates who wear the party label. Here House Republican leaders (left to right) J. C. Watts Jr. of Oklahoma, Dennis Hastert of Illinois, and Dick Armey of Texas prepare their remarks before meeting the press on March 25, 1999, on the Capitol steps.

on action even though they have different, even conflicting reasons for doing so. Holding diverse coalitions together takes continuing political effort, for participants cooperate only as long as it serves their purposes. The sustained organizational effort needed to keep legislative coalitions working in harmony produces legislative parties.

Organized competition for votes in Congress leads directly to organized competition for votes in congressional elections. Coalitions vying for majority status need to recruit like-minded candidates and work to elect them; successful legislative alliances in Washington depend on successful electoral alliances in the states and districts. The organizational work required to negotiate and maintain electoral alliances expands legislative parties into electoral parties.

The presidential selection rules also offer powerful incentives for building electoral alliances across districts and states. The Constitution assigns selection of the president to the electoral college or, if no candidate wins a majority of electors, to the House of Representatives. Many early observers expected the House to make the choice most of the time, believing that sectional jealousies would keep a majority of electors from uniting behind a single candidate. In fact, sectional rivalries and the competing ambitions of the larger states were constant sources of political friction. The incentives embodied in the rules for selecting the president provide a powerful counterweight to sectionalism, however. If an alliance can recruit and elect people pledged to one candidate in enough states, it can win the presidency. The alternative is to stack the House of Representatives with enough supporters to make the alliance's choice prevail should no candidate win a majority in the electoral college. In either case, the problem is to sustain cooperation among numerous politicians, often with competing purposes and interests, across great distances. To the degree that the effort succeeds, the result is a national party organization.

To Mobilize Voters. No matter how well organized, electoral alliances fail if they cannot get enough people to vote for their candidates. The competition for votes motivates alliance leaders to attract voters and get them to the polls on election day. In the early days of the Republic, electioneering followed traditional forms. The custom of political deference to one's "betters" had by no means died with the Revolution. The natural agents of a harmonious society were thought to be its most prominent and successful members, and a community's interests were assumed to be safest in the hands of those with superior breeding, education, and experience in public affairs. Restrictions on suffrage were common (see Chapter 11). Those who could vote made their preferences known orally and in public, a practice that encouraged deference to the local gentry. The elections themselves were decided largely on a personal basis; contests, if they arose, were between individuals backed by their personal followings. In such circumstances, open pursuit of political office was thought to be unseemly, and campaigns had to be conducted on the sly, through friends and allies. This is not to say that election campaigns were unknown; after all, the techniques of soliciting support and rounding up votes had been known for centuries because elections had been held for centuries. But they were techniques designed for small communities with even smaller electorates that, for the most part, took their cues from local worthies.

After the adoption of the Constitution, property and other qualifications for (white male) voting were progressively reduced or eliminated, and the egalitarian spirit of the frontier gradually eclipsed the habits of deference, even in the older states. As the size of the electorate increased, so did the task of identifying and attracting supporters and getting them to show up at the polls. Whoever could win over these new voters would enjoy a distinct political advantage. The networks of leaders and activists assembled to mobilize electoral support became the first party organizations.

To Develop New Electoral Techniques. Once organized, electoral parties initiated new relationships between voters and elected leaders. The personal appeals and services that candidates had used to win the support of their neighbors since colonial times did not disappear, but they were, by themselves, inadequate for reaching a much larger, dispersed, and anonymous electorate. Party organizers turned to mass communications—newspapers, pamphlets, public letters, and printed speeches—designed to excite voters with emotional appeals on issues. The temptation to press hot buttons was irresistible when campaigns sought to persuade politically unsophisticated and uninvolved people that they had a stake in the election and a compelling reason to vote. Anyone trying to mobilize citizens to vote also has to overcome their tendency

"Get out the vote" drives, conducted here using Spanish-language campaign literature, are among the oldest party strategies in America. At election time the national Democratic Party organizes these drives among those core supporters who chronically turn out to vote in low numbers—among them, Hispanics and African Americans.

to ride free, for a party's victory is a collective good that people get to enjoy whether or not they vote (see Chapter 11). Since the beginning, then, much of the work of campaigns has been aimed at overcoming, by one means or another, the free-rider problem.

To Use Party Labels and Enforce Collective Responsibility. Voters need a way to distinguish among candidates for the many offices filled by election. Party labels offer a serviceable shorthand cue that keeps voting decisions cheap and simple—as long as the labels are informative. The more accurately a candidate's party label predicts what he or she will do in office, the more useful it is to voters and the more voters will rely on party cues in making their choices. In addition, the more voters rely on party cues, the more valuable party labels are to candidates. Would-be leaders adopt one of the existing political identities in order to benefit from the electorate's cue-taking

This 1884 Republican poster explains to voters why they should vote Republican. High tariffs supported working families because they kept products made by cheap foreign labor out of country. With protection, the factories hum (compare smokestacks), food is on the table, and mom does not yell at the kids. Note also the prominence given party labels during the nineteenth century.

habits. Local candidates join national party alliances even though local political divisions may have no logical relation to the issues that national parties fight about.

Once they have adopted the party label, however, politicians have a personal stake in maintaining the value of their party's "brand name," which may require subordinating their own views and ambitions to the party's welfare and reputation. Party labels allow voters to reward or punish elected officials as a group for their performance in office. If voters do not like what the government is doing and want to "throw the rascals out," they have an easy way to identify the rascals: they are members of the majority party. The threat of collective punishment gives the majority party a strong incentive to govern in ways that please voters.

Basic Features of the Party System

Parties developed, then, not because anyone thought they were a good idea, but because the institutional structures and processes established by the Constitution made them too useful to forgo. Their obvious value to elected leaders competing for policy, to candidates competing for office, and to voters in search of cognitive shortcuts to voting decisions has guaranteed that their practical virtues would be rediscovered by every political generation. Parties have not always taken the same form, to be

LOGIC OF POLITICS

THIRD PARTY BLUES

Third party and independent candidates have a hard time with the winner-take-all electoral system. Even with considerable popular backing, these candidates may get few votes if their supporters believe they cannot win and pull the lever instead for one of the major party candidates. For example, many voters who preferred independent Ross Perot (center in photo) in 1992 but believed—correctly—that he could not win, voted for Bill Clinton (right) or George Bush (left) in an effort to keep their least favorite candidate from winning. By arguing that "a vote for Perot is a vote for Bush," the Clinton campaign attracted Perot supporters whose top priority was replacing Bush. The Republicans made exactly the same pitch to voters who preferred Perot to Bush but Bush to Clinton. Only voters whose disdain for both major party candidates exceeded their desire to elect the lesser of two evils stuck with Perot. In the end, then, only those third parties (or independent candidates) that manage to supplant one of the two reigning parties as a viable option in voters' minds gain rather than lose support from strategic voters. The last time this occurred on a national scale was 1856, when the Republicans surged ahead of the Whigs, who were fatally split over the slavery issue.

Third party and independent candidates can be influential despite their electoral futility, however. The policies and ideas they promote may survive them through adoption by one, sometimes both, of the major parties. For example, many of the regulatory innovations sought by the Populist Party in the 1890s became part of the Democrats' New Deal after 1932. George Wallace's 1968 campaign theme of law and order soon found its way into many Republican campaigns. And the legislative term limits advocated by Perot ended up in the Republicans' 1994 "Contract with America." Third party movements thus contribute to the evolution of the major party coalitions even as the winner-take-all electoral system takes its inevitable toll.

sure; there is more than one way to arrange for collective action in American politics. But some features reappear in every historical party system because they reflect the basic constitutional structure of American government. These features include competition between two major parties made up of decentralized, fragmented party coalitions that are maintained by professional politicians.

Two-Party Competition. During the first few Congresses, national leaders gradually divided into two major camps, initiating a pattern of two-party competition that has continued, with a few temporary exceptions, to this day. Americans tend to think of a **two-party system** as normal, but most modern democracies have more than two parties. It is, in fact, quite remarkable that a people sharply divided by region, religion, race, and ethnicity, not to mention social beliefs and economic interests, could fit into as few as two major political camps. But this pattern has continued for a very compelling reason. In any election where a single winner is chosen by plurality vote (whoever gets the most votes wins), there is a strong tendency for serious competitors to be reduced to two because people tend to vote strategically. If their favorite party's candidate has no chance to win, they turn to the less objectionable of the major party candidates who does have a chance to win (see box, "Third Party Blues"). Office seekers, aware of this pattern, usually join one of the two competitive parties rather than pursue office as independents or third party nominees.

This logic is sufficiently compelling that, at most, only an election or two is required after the disruption of old party alliances and the appearance of new party coalitions for voters to narrow the viable choices down to two. To survive, a party must win or place; show is no better than out of the money. Competition for survival, not to mention victory, puts strong pressure on party leaders to assemble broad coalitions, extending the party's hand to the voters ready to give up on their first choice. Any idea promoted by a third party that proves to be popular with voters is subject to poaching by one, sometimes both, of the established parties. Thus incentives to expand electoral coalitions also help to reduce the number of parties to two.

Elections in the United States have almost always been winner-take-all affairs, so the rules have continually worked to reduce the viable options to two. An alternative kind of electoral system—**proportional representation,** under which a party receives legislative seats in proportion to its share of votes—is used in many European democracies. This system helps to preserve smaller parties because votes for their candidates are not wasted, but it has never been tried in the United States on any significant scale. Once two-party competition was in place, both parties had a stake in preserving electoral rules that discriminate against third parties.

Strictly speaking, the winner-take-all logic applies only within a given electoral unit (a single congressional district or state, for example); it does not require that the same two sides face each other in every electoral unit. But for purposes of electing a president, the entire United States works as a single electoral unit. The contest for the presidency became so central to electoral politics that it shaped party competition for lesser offices as well.

Decentralized, Fragmented Party Coalitions. Another reason the two-party pattern endures is that federalism fragments the political system. Historically, national parties have been assembled from diverse state and local political factions concerned chiefly with the vibrant politics of their states, counties, or cities. The decentralized policy-making system allowed these local parties to work together to elect national leaders while going their own way on matters closer to home. National leaders were able to maintain diverse, unwieldy coalitions because many of the factions within them had little contact with one another except when choosing the party's presidential candidate. Indeed, since the beginning the major parties have been diverse, unwieldy coalitions, ready to fly apart unless carefully maintained. Skillful management and the compelling need to hold them together for any chance at office have usually, but by no means always, kept the parties from self-destructing.

Professional Politicians. At the time the Constitution was adopted, political leadership was the prerogative of successful and prominent men who viewed service in public office as a temporary duty that fell to members of their class. As organization became essential to winning public office, political power flowed into the hands of people with the skills to build networks of party workers, manage alliances of local leaders, and mobilize voters on election day. Personal wealth, education, and status were still advantages, but they no longer were essential. Of those attracted to party politics, many were ambitious people who latched onto the party as a vehicle for personal advancement; opportunism made no small contribution to the emergence of political parties.

Eventually, the variety and frequency of elections generated by the multilayered federal system made party management a full-time job in many places. To maintain the electoral machinery, party managers had to attract resources and reward the efforts of party workers. Thus **patronage**—jobs, offices, government contracts, business licenses, and so forth—grew in importance. By the 1840s, when they were fully developed, parties had become ends in themselves to the thousands of local politicos who depended on them, one way or another, for their livelihood. That dependence ended in the late nineteenth and early twentieth centuries, however, when reforms largely destroyed the patronage-based party organizations. Today, full-time professionals manage the parties, and the activists are mainly amateurs who volunteer their time.

The Development and Evolution of the Party Systems

The historical development of parties reveals how they were shaped by politicians' strategic reactions to the opportunities and challenges posed by the Constitution. Scholars have identified a sequence of five (possibly now six) distinct historical party systems. Each system derives its special characteristics from its epoch's society, economy, and technology, as well as the goals and tactics of political leaders. But common strategic responses to ongoing institutional incentives unite them all.

The first party system (1790–1824) illustrates the logic that led to the creation of national parties. Institutional innovation in the second party system (1824–1860) set parties on their basic organizational course. The full flowering and then decline of party machines under Progressive assault characterized the third (1860–1894) and fourth (1894–1932) party systems. Each of these party systems also was defined by its distinctive pair of rival coalitions, but the coalitional aspect of American parties is clearest in the creation and erosion of the party coalitions of the fifth party system (1932–).

The First Party System: The Origin of American Parties

The American party system was born in the first few Congresses as leaders with opposing views on national political issues sought to have their views prevail. Alexander Hamilton, secretary of the Treasury in George Washington's administration, proposed an ambitious and controversial set of measures designed to foster economic development and to give propertied interests—financiers, wealthy merchants, and manufacturers—a stake in the new Republic. His program was opposed by other prominent leaders, notably James Madison and Thomas Jefferson, who saw no constitutional basis for the federal government doing any such thing. They thought Hamilton's ideas favored New England over other regions and threatened the well-being of the small farmers and tradesmen who made up a majority of the citizenry. The two sides also disagreed on foreign policy: Hamilton and his allies wanted strong ties with England, while Jefferson's group leaned toward France.

Hamilton's pursuit of votes in Congress led him to create what was, in effect, a legislative party. Although he was not a member of Congress, "Hamilton was involved much in the manner of a modern floor leader, caucusing with members, trying to round up votes, and helping to schedule legislation."[5] His ambitious effort to enact his proposals led him to cultivate a stable group of allies willing to cooperate on a continuing basis. Hamilton and his allies were labeled "Federalists," a name deriving from their earlier support for ratification of the Constitution and their endorsement of a strong national government.

Members of Congress who opposed Hamilton's policies gradually coalesced under the leadership of Jefferson and Madison. Protesting the alleged aristocratic pretensions (or intentions) of Hamilton's group, they styled themselves Republicans. Members of this party also were called Democratic-Republicans until the 1820s, when they became known simply as Democrats. Today, the Democratic Party is the oldest political party in the world.

American Political Parties 1789–1996

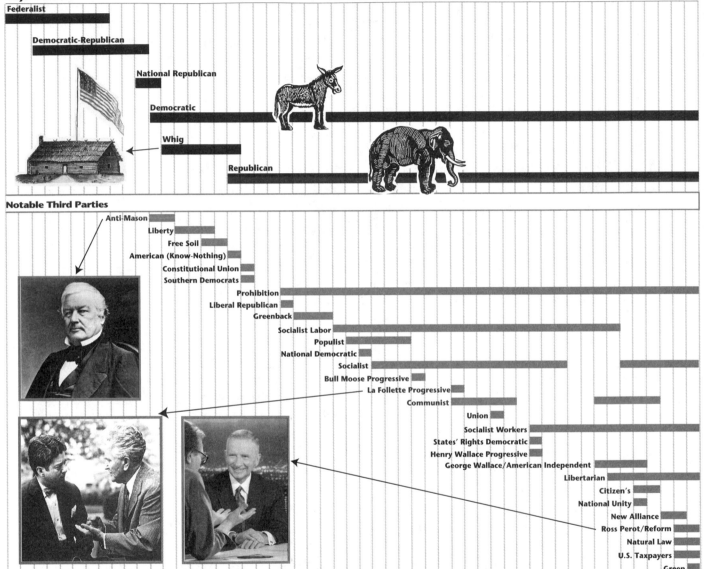

Note: Throughout U.S. history there have been more than 1,500 political parties. For this chart Congressional Quarterly editors have selected those parties that achieved national significance during presidential election years. The spaces between the rules on this chart indicate the election year only. For example, the Constitutional Union Party and the Southern Democrats were in existence for the 1860 election only and were gone by 1864. Similarly, the Green Party first fielded a presidential candidate in 1996.

As the Federalists continued to roll up legislative victories, the Democratic-Republicans realized they needed more votes in Congress if they were to prevail. That meant getting more like-minded people into Congress, which meant recruiting and electing candidates. Because senators were chosen by state legislatures, national leaders began to pay attention to state elections as well. The Federalists recognized the same realities and reached the same conclusion. The two groups began to compete in elections.

The presidential election required the parties' attention as well, for the Federalists—Hamilton, acting in Washington's name, and John Adams as Washington's successor—had demonstrated the importance of controlling the presidency as well as Congress. The Constitution had left it up to the states to decide how to select their presidential electors. A number of selection procedures were tried—most commonly popular election, selection by the state legislature, or some combination of the two. In 1800, for example, five of the sixteen states chose electors by popular vote, and state legislatures made the choice in the others. The Framers expected the electors to be prominent local men who would deliberate with others from their states before deciding how to cast their votes.[6]

Challenging Adams for the presidency in 1800, Jefferson and his Democratic-Republican allies realized that these deliberations could be short-circuited if they recruited and elected a majority of electors pledged to support Jefferson. By reaching out to local political leaders who were potential electors and to the growing mass of voters who chose the electors and state legislators, Jefferson successfully patched together an alliance of state and local factions, which led to a historic victory for his Democratic-Republicans and the ousting of the Federalists. In another innovative maneuver intended to rally voters to their cause, the Democratic-Republicans wedded organization to a controversial issue. They attacked the Alien and Sedition Acts, enacted by the Federalists in 1798 to stifle political criticism, as a frontal assault on republican government itself. Their tactics were adapted to an expanding electorate:

Party spokesmen . . . exploited every available agency of mass communication: official papers such as petitions against governmental measures, public circular letters from congressmen to their constituents, newspapers, pamphlets, handbills, private letters which circulated among leading figures, and personal contacts and word-of-mouth communications.[7]

It is no accident that the Democratic-Republicans did the innovating: the history of party building is largely a story of the "outs" finding new ways to become the "ins." Successful methods are then imitated by the losers. The Federalists tried with uneven success to duplicate the Democratic-Republicans' organizational efforts. They were hampered, however, by their nostalgia for deferential politics, the feeling that "better" people like them were by right the natural leaders, which left them uncomfortable making popular appeals to an increasingly egalitarian electorate.

With the pledging of electors, presidential candidates replaced individual electors as the object of the voters' decisions. The practice of pledging therefore went a long way toward democratizing the choice of president. In doing so, it strengthened the president's hand within the constitutional system as an executive chosen by the people and beholden to them, not other politicians.

The first parties were by no means the elaborate national organizations that emerged a generation later. One eminent historian has characterized them as "loose collections of provincial interests. . . . Highly local, evolving from rivalries within towns and cities, counties and states, they appealed to an electorate without firmly anchored, hereditary loyalties."[8] Both parties' coalitions were unstable, lacking even uniform names. In fact, any loyalty felt by politicians or voters did not extend much beyond the immediate issue or election.

When their pro-British leanings put them on the wrong side in the War of 1812, the Federalists faded as a national force. In the aftermath of the party's collapse, politicians and informed observers hoped that party

Figure 12–1   Voter Turnout, Presidential and Midterm Elections, 1789–1998

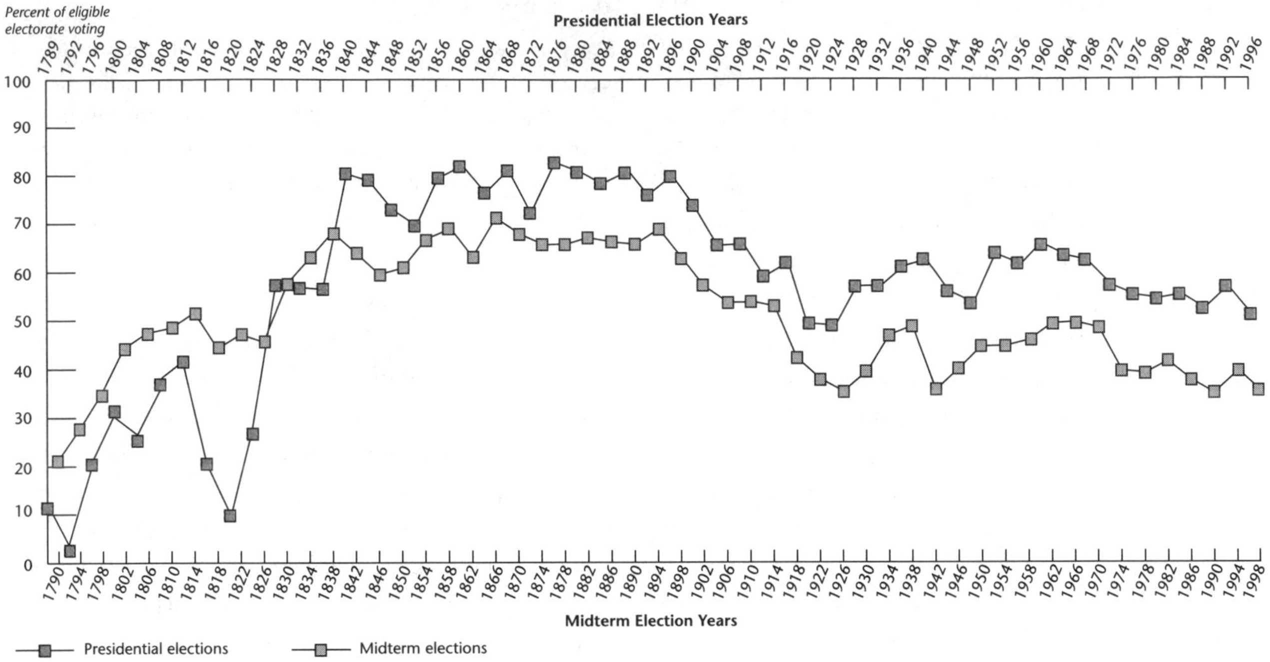

Sources: Harold W. Stanley and Richard Niemi, *Vital Statistics on American Politics, 1997–1998* (Washington, D.C.: Congressional Quarterly, 1998), Figure 1–1. Data for 1998 are from the Center for the Study of the American Electorate, news release, November 5, 1998.

competition—and therefore parties—would disappear. The idea that organized opposition would or should be a permanent part of American national politics was still unorthodox. Nevertheless, the first parties accurately presaged future developments.

The Second Party System: Organizational Innovation

By the second decade of the nineteenth century the Democratic-Republicans had eclipsed the Federalists nearly everywhere. James Monroe crushed the Federalists' last presidential nominee in 1816 and was reelected without significant opposition in 1820. The Monroe years were so lacking in party conflict that the period was dubbed the Era of Good Feelings. But the end of party conflict did not mean the end of political conflict; it only meant that political battles were fought out within the re-

maining party. Without the need for unity to win national elections, party networks fell apart. Personal and factional squabbles reemerged to replace party conflict in most states. One immediate consequence was a dramatic falloff in voter participation: turnout among eligible voters dropped from more than 40 percent in 1812 to less than 10 percent in 1820—eloquent testimony to the parties' crucial role in mobilizing voters (see Figure 12–1).

Party competition revived with a fight for the presidency. Under the first party system, the parties' congressional **caucuses** (members assembled with their allies to make party decisions) had nominated presidential candidates—a natural development because electoral competition had begun as an extension of party competition in Congress. This method became a problem, however, when the Federalists dissolved, leaving almost everyone in Congress a nominal Democratic-Republican. With one party so dominant, whoever picked its nominee effectively picked the president. The caucus, then, could have its way as long as there was a general consensus among its members on the nominee, as in the case of Monroe. Without a consensus, the caucus lost influence and legitimacy.

In 1824, after Monroe, no fewer than five serious candidates—all of them Democratic-Republicans—sought the presidency. The congressional caucus nominated William Crawford, who came in dead last. Andrew Jackson, hero of the Battle of New Orleans, won the most popular and electoral votes but a majority of neither. John Quincy Adams came in second, and House Speaker Henry Clay came in third. (The remaining candidate, John C. Calhoun, withdrew early and was elected vice president instead.) Because no candidate received a majority of electors, the election was thrown into the House of Representatives. There, Clay gave his support to Adams, who, upon taking office, made Clay his secretary of state—at the time the holder of that office was assumed to be first in line for his party's nomination in the next presidential election.

Jackson's supporters were outraged that a "corrupt deal" had denied "Old Hickory" his rightful place in the White House. A shrewd New York politician, Martin Van Buren, recognized in that outrage the opportunity to build a new political coalition. Unlike many political leaders of the time (Adams and Jackson among them), Van Buren valued parties and party competition. His experience in New York as leader of a faction that was, for all practical purposes, a political party in close competition with another party of sorts, predisposed him toward party politics as inevitable and useful. Moreover, Van Buren thought that a national party along the lines of the old Jeffersonian coalition would have the best chance of containing the most explosive issues of the day, particularly slavery. Van Buren put the case for such a party like this:

We must always have party distinctions and the old ones are the best. . . . Political combinations between inhabitants of the different states are unavoidable & the most natural & beneficial to the country is that between the planters of the South and the plain Republicans of the north. The country has once flourished under a party thus constituted & may again. It would take longer than our lives (even if it were practicable) to create new party feelings. . . . If the old ones are suppressed, geographical divisions founded on local interests or, what is worse prejudices between free and slave holding states will inevitably take their place.[9]

With Jackson as the focal point, Van Buren assembled a political network that became the Democratic Party. Central committees set up in Washington and Nashville, Jackson's hometown, promoted the formation of state organizations, which in turn promoted Jackson clubs or committees in towns and counties. Aided by a nationwide chain of newspapers established to support the cause, Van Buren and Jackson used this organizational pyramid to spread propaganda that kept Jackson and the "wrong" done him in the public consciousness. Local politicians, recognizing Jackson's popularity as a vehicle for their own ambitions, rallied voters with meetings, marches, barbecues, and hickory pole raisings.[10]

Supporters of President Adams had no choice but to put together a network of their own. Adams detested parties and had sought during his administration to build a coalition incorporating all factions of the old Democratic-Republican and Federalist parties. He did nothing himself to cultivate electoral allies. Yet his backers, in the process of nominating electors and candidates for other offices and working to get people to vote for them, created what amounted to an Adams party. As one historian has put it, "just by standing for reelection Adams brought a national party into being."[11]

National Conventions. Jackson's smashing victory in 1828 was, among other things, a powerful lesson in the value of political organization. The 1832 election, which he also won handily, featured the first **national party conventions.** Actually, the Anti-Masonic Party had held a convention in 1831, and Jackson's loosely organized opponents, calling themselves National Republicans, had convened a small national gathering that year as well. But the

One of the most spectacular campaign gimmicks was the great ball stitched together for Whig William Henry Harrison's presidential campaign in 1840. Made in Allegheny County, Maryland, of buckskin and carrying a long rhymed message, the ball was rolled through the state by costumed mountain boys. The gimmick was the origin of the phrase "keep the ball rolling."

Democratic convention that met in Baltimore to renominate Jackson in 1832 is considered the original full-scale national party convention.

The national convention was promoted as a more democratic alternative to the discredited congressional caucus, allowing much broader popular participation in making presidential nominations. But it also was an eminently practical device for solving problems of conflict and coordination that stand in the path to the White House. The convention was the occasion for assembling, and later refurbishing, the national party coalition. It provided a forum for doing the politicking that convinced diverse party factions to agree to rally behind a single presidential ticket—without necessarily agreeing on anything else. It also was a giant pep rally, firing up the party troops for the contest to come.

The Democrats held a national convention again in 1836, this time to nominate Van Buren as Jackson's successor. Jackson's leading opponents meanwhile had organized themselves as the Whig Party, a name borrowed from British political history that had come to symbolize

opposition to royal tyranny, which "King Andrew" Jackson's opponents were fond of alleging. A fractious coalition promoting national development but united primarily by their hostility to Jackson, the Whigs did not hold a national convention, but instead attempted to divide and conquer by running three regional candidates. Their plan was to combine their strength behind the strongest candidate in the electoral college or, failing that, to throw the election into the House.

When that strategy flopped in 1836, the Whigs turned to a ploy that won the party its only two presidential victories: nominating a popular military hero without known political coloration and obscuring party divisions by not writing a platform. The Whig nominee in 1840 was William Henry Harrison, hero of the Battle of Tippecanoe (fought against a confederation of Native American tribes in 1811) and extolled as a rough-hewn man of the people. He defeated Van Buren in a contest that moved party competition to an entirely new level—but whether higher or lower is still a matter of debate.

The 1840 campaign extended organized two-party competition to every state in the nation, framing not only the contest for president, but competition for offices at all levels of government. Competition inspired unprecedented efforts to involve and mobilize ordinary voters, turning political campaigns into the most exciting spectacles the era offered. As one historian of the period observed:

Those tens of thousands of men and women who attended the mammoth Whig festival at Nashville in 1840; those untold millions who carried torches, donned uniforms, chanted slogans, or cheered themselves hoarse at innumerable parades and rallies; those puffed-up canvassers of wards, servers of rum, and distributors of largess; and all those simple folk who whipped themselves into a fury of excitement and anxiety as each election day approached, were thrilling to a grand dramatic experience, even a cathartic experience. There was no spectacle, no contest, in America that could match an election campaign.[12]

In effect, the parties solved the problem of free riding endemic to mass electorates by making participation exciting and fun. One sign of their success was a dramatic increase in turnout (see Figure 12–1, p. 394). In 1824 only 27 percent of the eligible electorate (adult white males) had bothered to vote. When Jackson was elected in 1828, turnout rose to 57 percent, and it stayed at about that level for the next two presidential contests. In 1840 fully 80 percent of the eligible voters took part.[13] More striking evidence of the crucial role of parties—and party competition—in making mass democracy a reality could scarcely be imagined.

Participation in the hoopla surrounding the presidential contest bred strong feelings of party loyalty among many voters. The emotional ties and bonds of loyalty developed in the heat of battle became powerful forces to keep the parties intact even when the inevitable strains that beset such diverse coalitions threaten to break them up.

The Spoils System. Parties on the rise always attract opportunists. The politicians who had flocked to Jackson's banner or joined his Whig opponents were not, for the most part, altruists; rather, they carried on the party work because they were ambitious for an office or other favors. These motives are neither surprising nor appalling. Parties pursue a collective good: victory for their candidates and policies. All who prefer the winner benefit from the party's victory whether or not they contribute to it. Thus, without some prospect of private reward as well, the free-rider problem would have left parties stillborn. The men who worked to elect Jackson or Harrison took as their right the spoils of victory—mainly government jobs, but also contracts to supply goods and services to the government or special projects from which they might profit.

The pursuit of political spoils intensified party competition and put a heavy premium on winning. For better or worse, party entrepreneurs proved themselves willing to "rise above" principle if that was the price of winning. On the positive side, putting victory ahead of principle made parties open and inclusive. For a time, broad national coalitions helped manage the dangerous intersectional conflict over slavery and other divisive issues. The high stakes also inspired imaginative efforts to mobilize the first mass electorate in history. On the negative side, the desire to win contributed to corruption, moral myopia regarding slavery, and public cynicism about the honesty and motives of politicians. In either case, the Democrats and Whigs of the second party system set the pattern for the future: every successful American party has cared more about winning elections than about furthering a consistent set of principles.

Indeed, principled conflict is often a threat to party coalitions. Established party politicians put unity first because their careers depend on it, but voters have no such stake and may care very deeply about the positions a party takes on controversial issues. The Whigs and the Democrats built coalitions around differences on economic policy. The Whigs favored a national bank, high tariffs to protect U.S. manufacturers, and federally sponsored public works; the Democrats rejected the bank and the activist economic role it implied and advocated low tariffs to benefit farmers. Both parties were badly split by the slavery issue. Leaders tried to keep slavery off the political agenda, but, as feelings intensified, this proved impossible, and the second party system began to fall apart. For the first and only time in U.S. history, a third party emerged to supplant one of the two dominant parties.

The Third Party System: Entrepreneurial Politics

The Republican Party, organized in 1854 as a coalition of antislavery forces, is unusual only in the success of its challenge to the two-party establishment. Third parties have arisen time and again, but most have failed to attract enough of a following to become more than obscure

THE ANTI-MASONIC PARTY

The above plate represents "a poor blind candidate," taking the oath of an entered apprentice mason. He is divested of all clothing but a shirt, drawers, and one slipper; he kneels before the masonic altar on his naked knee, with a halter round his neck, and a hoodwink over his eyes; his left arm and breast are also bare: and in this humiliating posture he receives his oaths from the "worshipful master," wherein he binds himself to keep all masonic secrets, under the penalty of having his throat cut, his tongue torn out, and his body buried in the ocean. He is then taught the sign, grip, and word of that degree, and is presented with a little sheepskin apron, told he must wear it with the flap up, and that it is more honorable than the Star and Garter, or any other order that could be conferred upon him, except is a masonic lodge! and that it had been worn by kings, princes, and potentates, who were not ashamed to wear it. He is finally permitted to put his clothes on, and *thank the worshipful master, wardens, and brethren, for the honor they had conferred upon him!*

The Anti-Masonic Party arose during the late 1820s in western New York during a period of disconcertingly rapid social and economic change. The Masons were a secret fraternal organization with a largely upper-class membership. Charges that a Mason had kidnapped and murdered a local dissident who had revealed the order's secrets and then used political clout to cover up the crime provoked a frenzy of public outrage. Agitators denouncing the Masons as a monstrous elite conspiracy against republican government found a ready audience among poor farmers. The movement also attracted religious enthusiasts eager to join a crusade against sin as manifested in slavery, intemperance, and urban life. For a time in the early 1830s, the Anti-Masons formed the primary opposition to the Democrats in parts of New England and the mid-Atlantic states. In 1831 the party held the first national convention, nominating William Wirt for president. Wirt won only a single state (Vermont), but the party managed to elect two governors and win fifty-three House seats.

The party was so successful in achieving its initial purpose of destroying Freemasonry that it soon lost its main rallying point. In New York, for example, the number of Masonic lodges dropped from 506 to 48 in six years. Most of its leaders and adherents eventually joined the Whigs, with profound consequences for that party.

Antimasonry left Whigs a legacy of egalitarianism and evangelism. Antimasonic leaders . . . were much more willing to rabblerouse and organize lower class voters than patrician National Republicans had been. . . . Antimasonic voters among the Whigs remained moralistic crusaders susceptible to isms, and they imparted to Whiggery a Sabbatarian, protemperance, and antislavery spirit in the North that shaped national and state campaigns and often did more than economic issues to define the Whigs.[1]

1. Michael F. Holt, *Political Parties and American Political Development from the Age of Jackson to the Age of Lincoln* (Baton Rouge: Louisiana State University Press, 1992), 111.

refuges for the disaffected. On a few occasions, however, third parties have managed to shake up the system, leaving notable traces in party politics long after they have disappeared. The Anti-Masonic Party and the American (Know-Nothing) Party are examples from the pre–Civil War era. Both sprouted in periods of economic distress and social crisis, originating as anti-parties—movements of "the people" against corrupt and compromising party regulars. As soon as they showed a capacity to win elections, however, they attracted opportunists seeking to jump-start political careers. For some ambitious men, the protest party was a way station to a position of leadership in a major party. Anti-Masons joined the Whigs; Know-Nothings joined the Republicans.

The Republican Party was organized in opposition to the Kansas-Nebraska Act (1854), which overturned limits on the extension of slavery to the territories enacted earlier in the Missouri Compromise of 1820 and the Compromise of 1850. It drew leaders and followers from two earlier antislavery parties, as well as the Know-Nothings, antislavery Whigs, and dissident Democrats. Its adopted name laid claim to the mantles of both the Jeffersonian Republicans and the National Republicans who had backed Adams against Jackson.

Although founded on the slavery issue, the Republican Party was by no means a single-issue party. It also appealed to business and commercial interests (elements of the old Whig coalition) by promising a protective tariff and a transcontinental railway and to farmers by promising free land for homesteading. On only its second try, the party elected a president, Abraham Lincoln. His victory over divided opposition in 1860 triggered the South's secession from the Union and then the Civil War, from which the Republicans emerged as the party of victory and union. For the next generation the party sought to retain its ascendancy by appealing variously to patriotism, national expansion, and laissez-faire capitalism, and by distributing pensions to Civil War veterans and protective tariffs to manufacturers.

The end of Reconstruction in 1876 restored local control to southern politicians (see Chapter 4) and left the revived Democratic Party an equal competitor for national power. Democrats benefited from overwhelming majorities in the South, where the Republicans were despised as the party of the enemy. The Democrats also had pockets of strength in the border states (heavily settled by southerners), among immigrant groups in urban northern areas (especially German Lutherans and Irish Catholics), and in the west.

Party Machines. Party organizations reached their peak of development during the third party system. Patronage—jobs, contracts, development rights, zoning favors—generated by the rapid growth of industrial cities provided the capital; party entrepreneurs provided the management. The classic **party machines** were built on simple principles of exchange: party politicians provided favors and services to people throughout the year in return for their votes on election day. They found an eager market for their offerings among the growing population of poor immigrants whose basic needs—shelter, food, fuel, jobs, and help in adapting to a new and bewildering country—were far more pressing than any concern for party programs or ideologies. One such party politician was George Washington Plunkitt, who, thanks to such exchanges, thrived during the heyday of New York City's Tammany Hall Democratic machine at the turn of the century (see box, "The Wisdom of George Washington Plunkitt").

The party machine worked like this: to win elections, the party amassed legions of grassroots workers to blanket precincts and neighborhoods. In return for their services, workers received patronage jobs or other personal benefits from their victorious party. The party also used its control of municipal offices to obtain the support of far less needy citizens.

As a kind of political Santa Claus, the boss could reward with low tax assessments the contractors who had been "good," and he could leak plans to widen Ann Street to friendly real-estate operators who could speculate without gambling, and he could give Mrs. Higgins's boy Mike a job in the police court. He who

THE AMERICAN PARTY (KNOW-NOTHING)

The American Party began life as the Order of the Star Spangled Banner, organized in 1849 in New York. Its members, sworn to secrecy, replied to inquiries about its rituals and aims by saying, "I know nothing about it." The Know-Nothings, as they came to be called, were united by their hostility to immigrants—especially Roman Catholics—and to the reigning Democrat and Whig

politicians who refused to nominate only native-born American Protestants for public office. They initially entered politics by secretly backing sympathetic candidates of the major parties. Then, in 1855, they went public as the American Party.

The party grew rapidly by fanning anti-Catholic bigotry among native Protestants, making immigrants scapegoats for the economic and social dislocations of the time. (In the cartoon Irish and German immigrants are "stealing" the ballot box and with it American elections.) It also picked up factions of the Whig coalition as it fell apart over the slavery issue. The party appealed to people disgusted with the corruption and compromises of the regular party politicians. In the mid-1850s Know-Nothings won governorships in California, Connecticut, Delaware, Kentucky, Massachusetts, New Hampshire, and Rhode Island, and elected five senators and forty-three members of the House.

For a brief time, the Know-Nothings outstripped the Republican Party in the contest to replace the moribund Whigs as the Democrats' major opposition. But they too soon split over slavery. In 1856 the party chose former president Millard Fillmore, signer of the notorious Fugitive Slave Law, as its presidential nominee, pleasing the southerners but alienating northerners, many of whom defected to the Republican candidate, John C. Fremont. Fremont finished second to the victorious Democrat, James Buchanan. Fillmore came in third with 21 percent of the popular vote—the most ever for a third party presidential candidate, but still third. Within a short time most of the northern Know-Nothings—leaders as well as followers—had been absorbed by the Republican Party, which in return took on an anti-Catholic, nativist tinge in many states. Although Abraham Lincoln opposed Know-Nothingism, he owed his nomination in 1860 to former Know-Nothings in the Republican Party who hated his chief rival, William Seward, even more than they did him.

Source: Michael F. Holt, *Political Parties and American Political Development from the Age of Jackson to the Age of Lincoln* (Baton Rouge: Louisiana State University Press, 1992), 123–125.

giveth could taketh. A bad-mouthing saloon keeper might be visited by a health inspector who would enforce a long-forgotten ordinance; a disloyal banker might find city deposits removed to a competitor's vault.[14]

The late nineteenth-century party machines represented the culmination of trends reaching back to the Jacksonian era. Politics had become a full-time profession for

thousands of individuals. Those who took it up were mostly "men of slender social distinction, whose training came not from the countinghouse or the university, but from the street gang, the saloon, the fire department, the political club."[15] Winning local elections was the paramount goal of party professionals; issues, programs, and candidates (national as well as local) mattered only insofar

THE WISDOM OF GEORGE WASHINGTON PLUNKITT

There's only one way to hold a district: you must study human nature and act accordin'. . . .

To learn real human nature, you have to go among the people, see them and be seen. I know every man, woman, and child in the Fifteenth District, except them that's been born this summer—and I know some of them, too. I know what they like and what they don't like, what they are strong at and what they are weak in, and I reach them by approachin' at the right side.

George Washington Plunkitt dispensing advice from the New York County Courthouse bootlack stand.

For instance, here's how I gather in the young men. I hear of a young feller that's proud of his voice, thinks he can sing fine. I ask him to come around to Washington Hall and join our Glee Club. He comes and sings, and he's a follower of Plunkitt for life. Another young feller gains a reputation as a baseball player in a vacant lot. I bring him into our baseball club. That fixes him. You'll find him workin' for my ticket at the polls next election day. . . . I rope them all in by givin' them opportunities to show themselves off. I don't trouble them with political arguments. I just study human nature and act accordin'. . . .

* * *

What tells in holdin' your grip on your district is to go right down among the poor families and help them in the different ways they need help. I've got a regular system for this. If there's a fire in Ninth, Tenth, or Eleventh Avenue, for example, any hour of the day or night, I'm usually there with some of my election district captains as soon as the fire engines. If a family is burned out I don't ask whether they are Republicans or Democrats, and I don't refer them to the Charity Organization Society, which would investigate their case in a month or two and decide they were worthy of help about the time they are dead from starvation. I just get quarters for them, buy clothes for them if their clothes were burned up, and fix them up until they get things runnin' again. It's philanthropy, but it's politics, too—mighty good politics. Who can tell how many votes one of these fires brings me? The poor are the most grateful people in the world, and let me tell you, they have more friends in their neighborhoods than the rich have in theirs.

* * *

Another thing, I can always get a job for a deservin' man. I make it a point to keep track of jobs, and it seldom happens that I don't have a few up my sleeve ready for use. I know every big employer in the district and the whole city for that matter, and they ain't in the habit of saying no to me when I ask them for a job.

Source: William L. Riordan, *Plunkitt of Tammany Hall: A Series of Very Plain Talks on Very Practical Politics* (New York: Dutton, 1963), 25–28.

as they could help or hinder that goal. National parties were contentious alliances of local party organizations competing for patronage. Votes were sought wherever they were available by whatever means worked.

The Progressive Attack. Party machines were regularly attacked as corrupt and inefficient and party politicians as incapable of imagining, let alone implementing, solutions to the many problems created by the growth of large industry and national markets. Reformers, working almost entirely from within the two-party system, sought to destroy the party machines by depriving party leaders of the capacity to reward followers. Eventually, they succeeded.

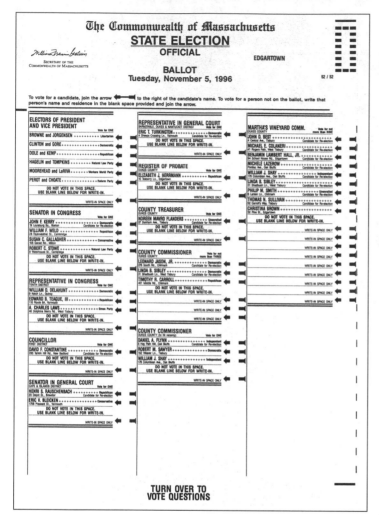

The most important changes were introduced during what is now called the Progressive Era—the decades just before and after the turn of the twentieth century, overlapping the end of the third party system and the beginning of the fourth. The most important reforms were the civil service, the **Australian ballot,** and **primary elections.**

After passage of the Pendleton Act in 1883, reformers began to replace the spoils system with a civil service system in most jurisdictions. Under the spoils system, the winning party filled appointive government jobs with its faithful workers, firing everyone who had not worked for

the ticket. The civil service system turned government jobs into professional careers. Appointment and advancement depended on merit (typically, performance on a competitive examination), not political pull, and civil servants could not be fired except "for cause"—failing to do their jobs or committing crimes (see Chapter 8). As more government jobs were brought under civil service, the rewards for party work and therefore the number of party workers shrank.

Another reform associated with the Progressive Era was the secret ballot. Prior to the 1890s each party produced its own ballots (listing only its candidates), which were handed to voters outside the polling place (see Chapter 7, p. 225). Because party ballots were readily distinguishable, voters were unable to keep their choices to themselves or easily vote a **split ticket**—that is, vote for candidates of different parties for different offices—for this required manipulating several ballots. The system invited corruption and intimidation; party workers could monitor voters and reward or punish them accordingly. Thus between 1888 and 1896, 90 percent of the states adopted the Australian ballot, named for its country of origin. The new ballot, still in use today, was printed by the government, listed candidates from all parties, and was marked in the privacy of a voting booth. This change made it much more difficult for parties to exchange favors for votes, for it left no (legal) way for the party to know if voters had kept their side of the bargain.

With adoption of the Australian ballot, the government became involved in party nominations, for someone had to determine officially which parties and names would be listed on the government-produced ballot. Laws were passed to regulate party nominating conventions and, later, to allow a party's voters to nominate candidates through primary elections. Strong party machines were still able to dominate primaries, but as party organizations were weakened by other changes, primaries deprived them of a crucial political re-source: the ability to control access to elective public office by controlling nominations.

Progressives advocated, and in many places achieved, other reforms intended to detach local politics from national politics on the grounds that "there is no Republican or Democratic way to pave a street." At the local level, elections were made officially "nonpartisan" and held separately from federal elections. States also adopted laws requiring would-be voters to register before election day (to reduce the possibilities of fraud) and to pass literacy tests (unlike the old party-produced ballots, the Australian ballot could be used only by literates). Professional city managers were hired to run cities like business corporations, and urban services were "taken out of politics" by putting them under the control of independent boards. At the national level, a constitutional amendment, ratified in 1913, took the choice of U.S. senators from the state legislatures and gave it to the voters, eliminating the party politics that had governed the selection of senators.

Although ostensibly aimed at rooting out corruption and cleaning up

In Waco, Texas, and throughout the one-party South in the early twentieth century, Progressive Era reforms introducing the nominating primaries and nonpartisan local elections produced a profusion of candidates bereft of party labels. Note the absence of party labels in these 1938 campaign posters.

electoral politics, progressive reforms also were designed to enhance the political clout of the "right" kind of people—educated middle- and upper-middle-class folks like the reformers themselves—at the expense of poor urban immigrants and their leaders "of slender social distinction." Stricter voter registration laws discriminated against the poor and uneducated. Literacy tests had the

same effect and were used widely in the South to disenfranchise blacks.

Progressive reforms were adopted to varying degrees in almost every state. And on the whole they worked, weakening or destroying party machines and preventing their resurrection. Where the progressive agenda was most fully achieved, parties became little more than empty shells, existing mainly to help the state government administer elections. Until recently, for example, official party organizations in California were not allowed to endorse candidates in primary elections. Vigorous party organizations did survive, though, in some places, often for many years. For example, a tightly controlled Democratic machine ran Chicago until the 1970s. Over the long run, however, progressive reforms deprived state and local party organizations—the basic building blocks of national parties—of much of their political power.

The Consequences of Progressive Reforms. These changes had several important consequences for electoral politics. First, turnout declined. Tighter registration laws, the Australian ballot, and literacy tests discouraged voting. With fewer jobs and favors to reward the party workers, fewer people were willing to do the work that wedded voters to the party and got them to vote. According to Figure 12–1, from the Civil War to the 1890s about 80 percent of the eligible electorate voted in presidential elections. By the 1910s turnout had fallen to around 60 percent. It fell further when women were enfranchised in 1920 and the number of eligible voters doubled. It has not risen much above 60 percent in any election year since. Many women initially ignored politics as "men's business," and women's turnout levels—which today surpass men's—took a half-century to pull even. Turnout declined most among poor and uneducated people, the very citizens most dependent on parties for incentives to vote. (For more on turnout, see Chapter 11).

The reforms also began to shift the focus of electoral politics from parties to candidates. When party organizations controlled nominations and voters chose between whole party tickets, political careers were bound tightly to parties. With the advent of the Australian ballot and primary elections, these bonds weakened. Candidates could win nominations with or without the party's blessing by appealing directly to voters; they could campaign separately from the party's team because voters could now split their tickets more easily. The full flowering of candidate-centered electoral politics had to await the de-

velopment of new communication technologies—mainly television and computerized direct mail—but the seeds were planted by the progressive reforms.

By altering the incentives to perform party work, reforms also contributed to changes in the demographics and goals of party organizations. Traditional party organizations were built on material incentives attractive to working-class people; consequently, parties concentrated on winning elections to keep the material benefits flowing. As their resource base shrank, patronage-based parties were supplanted by party organizations made up of middle-class people inspired by nonmaterial incentives—devotion to a particular candidate, issue, or ideology—for whom a party victory was often less important than the success of their preferred candidate or issue positions.

Paradoxically, the Progressive Era left the Republicans and Democrats organizationally weaker but more entrenched than ever. Once considered private groups, parties were now treated by the law in many states as essentially public entities charged with managing elections. Regulations tended to privilege the two major parties and discriminate against new parties and independent candidates. Moreover, the advent of primary elections encouraged dissidents to work within the established parties because outsiders could now compete for control of the party's machinery and name. Why should malcontents buck the long odds against winning under a new party label when they could convert an established party to their cause? No new party came close to challenging either of the major parties in the twentieth century, but those parties suffered some convulsive changes as the result of challenges from within.

The Fourth Party System: Republican Ascendancy

From the end of Reconstruction in 1876 until 1896, the third American party system settled into place, and the Republicans and Democrats competed on nearly even terms. In 1896 the Democrats reacted to a severe economic downturn by adopting the platform of the People's Party, or Populists, a party of agrarian protest against high

POLITICS → POLICY

THE WHITE PRIMARY

After the end of Reconstruction in 1876 white southerners sought to protect white supremacy and racial segregation by keeping African Americans out of the electorate. One tactic used to circumvent the constitutional ban on racial discrimination in voting was the so-called white primary (see Chapter 4). With the Democratic Party enjoying a near monopoly in most southern states until the 1960s, the only real contest was in the primary election.

A Supreme Court decision in a 1921 case unrelated to race implied that Congress had no power to regulate primaries.[1] Segregationist legislatures saw the decision as an invitation to do in primaries what they could not constitutionally do in general elections: exclude blacks. In 1927, however, the Court overturned a Texas law barring blacks from Democratic primaries on the ground that it represented state action in violation of the equal protection clause of the Fourteenth Amendment.[2]

Texas countered by repealing the law and replacing it with a statute authorizing every state party executive committee to "prescribe the qualifications of its own members." The state's Democratic Party quickly decreed that only whites were eligible to vote in its primaries. In a 5–4 decision the Court overturned the new law too, concluding that by authorizing the parties to prescribe voter qualifications, the state had made them its agents and so was again, albeit indirectly, denying equal protection.[3] The state's racist legislature did not give up; instead, it repealed the law's authorizing clause, thereby allowing the Democratic State Convention, without official sanction, to declare itself a "private group" that only white persons could join. In *Grovey v. Townsend*, the Court agreed that the party had indeed acted as a private group, not an agent of the state, and therefore was not subject to the Fourteenth Amendment's strictures.[4]

This reasoning did not survive long, however. In a 1941 decision not involving race, the Court determined that primaries were "an integral part of the election machinery" and were thus subject to congressional regulation after all.[5] Following that precedent, the Court soon overturned *Grovey*, declaring that the constitutional ban on racial discrimination in voting "is not to be nullified by a state through casting its electoral process in a form which permits a private organization to practice racial discrimination in the election."[6] In taking this position, the Court acknowledged the reality that the parties, although retaining some attributes of voluntary private organizations, had long since become semi-official agents of government because of their central role in the electoral process. The attempt by Texas to exploit the private aspect of political parties to perpetuate racial discrimination thus helped to confirm their fundamentally public status.

1. *Newberry v. United States,* 256 U.S. 232 (1921).
2. *Nixon v. Herndon,* 273 U.S. 536 (1927).
3. *Nixon v. Condon,* 286 U.S. 73 (1932).
4. *Grovey v. Townsend,* 295 U.S. 45 (1935).
5. *United States v. Classic,* 313 U.S. 299 at 318 (1941).
6. *Smith v. Allwright,* 321 U.S. 649 at 661 (1944).

Source: Henry J. Abraham and Barbara A. Perry, *Freedom and the Court: Civil Rights and Liberties in the United States,* 7th ed. (New York: Oxford University Press, 1998), 370–374.

railroad rates and the gold standard, whose first presidential candidate had won five states in 1892. The Democrats nominated for president William Jennings Bryan, a candidate with strong Populist sympathies. Bryan and the Democrats proposed, among other economic innovations, to make silver as well as gold a monetary standard. The silver standard would increase the money supply, easing interest rates and therefore the pressure on debtors, which included most farmers and westerners. The Republican campaign persuaded many urban workers that the Democrats' proposals threatened their livelihoods ("sound" money backed by gold was the backbone of the financial system that sustained the industrial economy) and so converted them into Republicans. The reaction to the agrarian takeover of the Democrats left the Republicans with a clear national majority for the next generation; the new alignment is commonly designated the fourth party system.

The Republican Party ultimately lost its ascendancy to the Great Depression. Having taken credit for the prosperity of the 1920s with policies highly favorable to financial institutions and industrial corporations, the Republicans and their president, Herbert Hoover, were saddled with the blame for the economic devastation and high unemployment that followed the 1929 stock market crash. Franklin Roosevelt, the Democratic candidate, defeated Hoover in the 1932 election. Roosevelt's New Deal solidified a new coalition of interests that gave the Democrats a popular majority which, despite the coalition's slow demise since the 1960s, it retains—barely—to this day.

The Fifth Party System: The New Deal Coalition

Nothing illustrates the diversity of American party coalitions more strikingly than the **New Deal coalition**, which brought together Democrats of every conceivable background. It united white southern segregationists with northern blacks (very few southern blacks could vote), progressive intellectuals with machine politicians, union members and their families with the poorest farmers, Roman Catholics with Southern Baptists. These diverse groups agreed on only one thing—electing Democrats—while having very different reasons for wanting to do so.

Some were attracted by Roosevelt's New Deal policies, which, in tackling the depression's devastation, radically expanded the federal government's responsibility for, and authority over, the economic and social welfare of all Americans. The Wagner Act of 1937, known as organized labor's "bill of rights," cemented union support. Public works programs pulled in poor and unemployed citizens, including northern blacks (until then partial to the party

of Lincoln), and provided patronage for urban machines. Farm programs appealed to distressed rural voters. Progressive intellectuals applauded the federal government's expanded role in attending to the economic welfare of citizens. The adoption of the Social Security and unemployment insurance systems earned the gratitude of working people whose economic insecurity had been so painfully exposed by the depression.

Other groups were part of the Democratic coalition by tradition. Conservative southern whites were still expressing political identities forged in the Civil War. Roman Catholics, already disproportionately Democratic (a tinge of anti-Catholic nativism was a legacy of the Republicans' Know-Nothing heritage), had become overwhelmingly so in 1928, when the party chose Al Smith, the first of their faith to be nominated for president by a major party. They remained in part because the Democrats kept their pledge to repeal prohibition. As a movement, prohibitionism was largely Protestant, with clear anti-Catholic, anti-immigrant overtones. Jews in the cities of the East and Midwest also had supported Smith, in reaction to the rural and small-town Protestant bigotry his candidacy had provoked, and stayed with the Democrats under Roosevelt, an early and staunch enemy of Nazi Germany.

The opposing Republican coalition was a smaller, inverted image of the Democratic coalition: business and professional people, upper-income white Protestants, residents of smaller towns and cities in the Northeast and Midwest, and ideological conservatives. It was united by what it opposed: Roosevelt's New Deal programs and the greatly enlarged federal bureaucracy they engendered (see Chapter 8), which Republicans excoriated as unconstitutional, unwise, and un-American.

Erosion of the New Deal Coalition. The complexities of coalition politics aside, national electoral competition during the New Deal period was organized around a single question: Are you for or against the New Deal? As long as that was the question, the New Deal alignment held. But when new issues become the focus of electoral politics, the Democratic coalition began to unravel. The

Republicans enabled new issues to shape electoral politics by finally recognizing that the major New Deal programs were there to stay; a party in search of a national majority cannot cling forever to losing positions. When they finally regained the White House in 1952 (using the old Whig ploy of nominating a military hero, Dwight Eisenhower), it was not on a promise to repeal the New Deal, but to administer its programs more frugally. Once that question was settled, other issues could come to the fore.

The first and most important of these issues was civil rights for African Americans (discussed in detail in Chapter 4). As the Democrats became the party of civil rights, white southerners began to depart. Some became Republicans outright; others initially supported George Wallace's 1968 campaign as the candidate of the American Independent Party, then became Republicans; still others remained independents, voting for Republicans for president and Democrats for other offices. Wallace won five states, all in the deep South, but he also did well enough in other areas to prove that some civil rights policies, such as busing students out of their neighborhoods to integrate schools, had alienated working-class whites outside the South as well.

About the same time, the war in Vietnam also split the Democrats, largely along the fault lines of class. The party machine politicians and labor leaders whose blue-collar constituents supplied most of the soldiers generally supported the war, as did most southern Democrats. Opposition was led by liberal intellectuals and was most conspicuous on elite university campuses. New controversies over the bounds of acceptable social behavior deepened the split, as sexual freedom, pornography, abortion, women's rights, and gay rights became the stuff of politics.

Traditional Democratic constituencies also were divided over new economic initiatives. The Great Society programs enacted during Lyndon Johnson's presidency (1963–1969) lacked the broad appeal of the New Deal. The major New Deal programs—Social Security, unemployment insurance, and Medicare (a New Deal–type program, although not enacted until 1965)—serve politically active majorities. Great Society programs—housing subsidies, school nutrition programs, Head Start, food stamps, and Medicaid—serve a politically apathetic minority: the poor. For many working-class and middle-class Democrats, the New Deal was for "us," but the Great Society's War on Poverty was for "them." The costs of these programs weighed more heavily as economic growth slowed in the 1970s, increasing opposition to taxes. A new issue—environmental protection—also posed dilemmas for Democrats, pitting blue-collar jobs (or recreation activities) against the aesthetic and health benefits sought by middle-class environmentalists.

The Republicans, although less diverse than their rivals, could not avoid some serious divisions of their own. The conservative and moderate wings struggled for dominance from the New Deal period until the 1980s. Conservatives took over the national party in 1964, nominating one of their own, Sen. Barry Goldwater of Arizona, as president. Goldwater's vote against the Civil Rights Act of 1964 endeared him to southern segregationists but alienated moderates in his own party, as did his hostility to the core New Deal programs. His overwhelming defeat left the party temporarily in tatters. It quickly recovered, however, by taking advantage of the deep divisions within the old Democratic coalition to win five of the next six presidential elections.

Richard Nixon, Ronald Reagan, and George Bush built winning coalitions by combining affluent economic conservatives with middle-class and working-class social conservatives, particularly from what is called the New Christian Right. To attract economic conservatives, the Republicans declared war on taxation, regulation, and welfare; to win over social conservatives, they offered law and order, patriotism (opposition to the Vietnam War left Democrats vulnerable here), and "traditional family values," defined to mean a ban on abortion, promotion of prayer in public schools, and heightened concern for the civil rights of white males. But this coalition is not much more united than its Democratic counterpart. Many affluent economic conservatives are not attracted to the Christian

Battles between Vietnam War demonstrators and the Chicago police outside the 1968 Democratic national convention caused a revolt in the convention culminating in the removal of the Chicago mayor Richard J. Daley as a delegate. Not only did the last of the party machine mayors depart, but the turmoil stimulated the party to install reforms that have dramatically altered the way the political parties nominate their presidential candidates.

Right's social agenda and many social conservatives of modest means remain reluctant to expose themselves to the mercies of an unfettered free market.

Changing the Rules. Divisions within the parties' electoral coalitions during the 1960s were played out in intraparty battles that reshaped the parties as organizations. One major result was the progressive-style reform of presidential nominations. The Democrats' nominating practices had fallen into disrepute because many southern delegations were discriminating against black voters just recently activated by the civil rights movement. It was the Vietnam War, however, that triggered wholesale reform. When those Democrats opposed to U.S. American involvement in Vietnam sought to nominate an antiwar candidate in 1968, they found the diverse, arcane state procedures for selecting delegates to the national nominating convention a formidable barrier. Only fifteen states held primary elections, and, in some of them, support in primaries did not translate into convention delegates. Presidential primaries were merely venues for candidates to

show party bosses how electable they were. In Pennsylvania, for example, the antiwar candidate, Sen. Eugene McCarthy, won 72 percent of the primary votes, but Vice President Hubert Humphrey got 80 percent of Pennsylvania convention delegates. Because in most states, including Pennsylvania, party leaders chose the delegates, the convention itself was dominated by leaders from the larger states.

In 1968 the convention was still the quadrennial coming together of diverse and fractious state party organizations that it had been since the 1830s. Most party regulars were, by habit, loyal to their president, Lyndon Johnson, and his anointed successor, Humphrey. Meeting in Chicago, the Democrats nominated Humphrey while antiwar protests filled the streets outside the convention hall. When the demonstrations got out of hand, they were violently suppressed by the Chicago police on the orders of Mayor Richard J. Daley, boss of the strongest surviving party machine and a major Humphrey backer. The party's internal divisions, dramatized by the riots and exposed to the world on national television, doomed the Democratic ticket and led to the election of Richard Nixon as president.

To repair the Democratic coalition and restore the convention's legitimacy, a party commission (the McGovern-Fraser Commission) drew up a new set of criteria specifying that convention delegations had to be chosen in a process that was "open, timely, and representative." The state parties could comply in one of two ways. They could hold a primary election, the outcome of which would determine at least 90 percent of the state's delegation. Or they could hold local party caucuses open to all Democrats, who would select delegates to a meeting at the county, congressional district, or state level. These delegates would in turn elect delegates to the national convention. The easiest option was the primary, and most state parties have adopted it. In 1996 Democratic primaries were held in thirty-six states, including eighteen of the twenty most populous states.

In another change, the winner-take-all method of allocating delegates went out the window; instead, they were to be allocated proportionately according to the votes in the primary or the caucus. To meet the "representativeness" standard, delegations had to include more minorities, women, and young adults. Because most elected officeholders were white males over thirty, these rules meant that many of them could no longer attend the convention.

The Democrats' delegate selection rules created a whole new ball game. Previously, the party's supreme plum, its presidential nomination, had been conferred by party leaders who sought to pick a winner who would be obligated to them so presidential favors would come their way and who would help the whole party ticket on election day. Now the nomination goes to the candidate who can best mobilize support in primary elections.

The new process may be "fairer," as intended, but it has threatened other party goals, namely winning and governing. The candidate who most excites the activist minority who show up for primary elections (turnout is typically in the neighborhood of 20 percent) may not even be the best vote-getter among Democrats generally, let alone the broader electorate. For example, Sen. George McGovern, the 1972 nominee, was the choice of antiwar Democrats but no one else; he won only 38 percent of the general election vote, the worst showing for a Democrat since the New Deal realignment.

The system also allows outsiders with tenuous links to other Democratic leaders to compete. Jimmy Carter, an obscure one-term governor of Georgia, won the nomination and then the White House in 1976, but found it nearly impossible to work effectively with his party in Congress. Carter's lack of experience in the ways of Washington, and his lack of political ties to its movers and shakers, clearly handicapped his administration (see Chapter 7).[16] Responding to such problems, the Democrats altered their rules several more times to give party regulars more influence in the selection process. Prominent elected officials—governors, senators, and representatives—are now automatically among the convention delegates. These so-called **superdelegates** held 18 percent of the seats at the Democrats' 1996 convention.[17] Their presence has yet to make any difference, however, because every Democratic nomination since 1972 has been locked up in the primaries before the convention has even met.

The decisiveness of primaries has altered the purpose and meaning of national conventions. Conventions were once venues for state and local party leaders to renegotiate their complex coalitions and to choose a torchbearer around whom the troops could rally. Now, delegates belong to candidates, not party officials. Conventions no longer choose the party's candidate; caucus activists and voters in primaries do. The attention is not so much on renewing the party coalition and rallying the faithful as it is on presenting an attractive image and message to citizens watching the action at home on television. In this sense, conventions are still crucially important to parties, showing voters what sorts of people make up the party and what groups and causes they champion. A display of party unity still matters, not to energize activists, its

OPINIONS OF PARTY ACTIVISTS AND VOTERS ON THE ISSUES, 1996

		Democratic Delegates	Democratic Voters	Republican Voters	Republican Delegates
1. How would you describe your views on most political matters? Generally do you think of yourself as liberal, moderate, or conservative?	Liberal	43%	26%	7%	0%
	Moderate	48	50	40	27
	Conservative	5	19	50	70
2. Which comes closer to your view: government should do more to promote traditional values, or government should not favor one set of values over another?	Promote	27%	41%	44%	56%
	Not favor	66	53	51	33
3. Which comes closer to your view: government should do more to solve national problems, or government is doing too many things better left to business and individuals?	Do more	76%	46%	18%	4%
	Doing too much	12	47	78	91
4. When it comes to regulating environmental and safety practices of business, do you think the federal government is doing enough: should it do more, or should it do less?	Do more	60%	66%	37%	4%
	Do less	2	5	28	61
5. Is your opinion of the conservative Christian political movement known as the religious right favorable or not favorable?	Favorable	4%	26%	39%	55%
	Not favorable	91	53	42	23
6. Do you think children of illegal immigrants should or should not be allowed to attend public schools?	Should	79%	63%	46%	26%
	Should not	16	32	48	58
7. Do you favor or oppose the nationwide ban on assault weapons?	Favor	91%	80%	62%	34%
	Oppose	6	17	33	51
8. Do you think most government affirmative action programs in hiring, promoting, and college admissions should be continued, or do you think these affirmative action programs should be abolished?	Continued	81%	59%	28%	9%
	Abolished	13	27	61	78
9. Do you think organized prayer should or should not be permitted in the public schools?	Permitted	20%	66%	69%	57%
	Not permitted	74	31	27	27
10. Do you think making abortion illegal is the kind of issue you would like to change the Constitution for, or isn't abortion that kind of issue?	Is that kind	3%	22%	24%	34%
	Is not	96	71	69	57
11. These days, do you think it is necessary to have laws to protect homosexuals from discrimination in hiring and promotion, or don't you think it's necessary?	Necessary	72%	54%	27%	12%
	Not necessary	24	40	69	82

Source: New York Times/CBS News Poll, 1996 Democratic Delegate Survey, August 8–22, 1996.

Note: Percentages do not sum to 100 because respondents with no opinion are omitted.

earlier purpose, but to convince the public that the party has its act together and can be trusted to govern.

A party's self-display at its national convention is not without risk, however. Party activists often hold more extreme views on the issues of the day than do ordinary party voters, who may question whether the party actually represents their values and interests. The problem is illustrated in the box "Issue Opinions of Party Activists and Voters," which compares the views of voters who identify themselves as Republicans or Democrats with the respective parties' convention delegates in 1996. On almost every question, the opinions of convention delegates are more strongly polarized than those of their parties' voters. On a few issues, party delegates' views are miles away from those of supporters (Democrats on school prayer, Republicans on banning assault weapons). It is easy to understand why many voters would see the Republicans as too conservative and the Democrats as too liberal to represent their views reliably. The responses also show that Democratic and Republican voters differ on many issues as well, including scope of government activity, environmental protection, education for illegal immigrants, and affirmative action.

Consequences of Fractured Alignments. When issues arise that split the existing party coalitions, partisan identities weaken and the party label may not provide the information voters want. The fracturing of the New Deal alignments and the difficulty party politicians faced in reconstructing stable coalitions around new issues reduced the importance of party cues to voters. They became less certain about which political camp they belonged to. The consequences were abundantly evident in election and polling results.

Party line voting declined, and ticket splitting increased. As we saw in Figure 11–2 (page 363), party line voting in presidential elections declined between the 1950s and the 1970s. The same was true of House and Senate elections during this period: the proportion of voters who were party loyalists fell by more than ten percentage points between the 1950s and the late 1970s. While the proportion of loyalist

voters rose during the 1990s, it has not reached the level of the 1950s. Ticket splitting—casting votes for different parties' candidates for different offices—increased sharply over the same period (see Figure 12–2, p. 412). Clearly, party identification lost some of its influence on the vote as the New Deal coalition unraveled.

Voters became more indifferent to the parties. Political scientist Martin Wattenberg analyzed responses to four decades (1952–1992) of survey questions asking people what they liked and disliked about the parties. He found that, over time, the net sum of voters' comments about the parties became increasingly neutral (an even partisan balance of likes and dislikes) mainly because a growing share of respondents had nothing good *or* bad to say about either party (Figure 12–3, p. 413).[18] In 1952 far more voters gave responses that, when summed up, favored one of the parties than gave responses that were evenly balanced between the parties; by the 1970s neutrality was as common as partisan bias.

With voters substituting personal cues for party cues, the electoral advantage enjoyed by congressional incumbents grew. Incumbents got greater mileage from their name recognition advantage and assiduous delivery of services to constituents when fewer voters automatically rejected them because of their party affiliation. (For details, see section "The Advantages of Incumbency" in Chapter 6, p. 170.)

The electorate became more volatile. The Democrats' presidential vote dropped by 12 million between 1964 and 1968; the Republican vote dropped by 15 million between 1984 and 1992. In House contests, partisan vote swings became more variable across districts, making election results less predictable from one election to the next.[19]

Independent and third party candidates have increased their take. Between the beginning of the New Deal in 1932 and 1964, no minor party or independent candidate received more than 3 percent of the vote. Since then, three candidates in four races have exceeded that margin: George Wallace (14 percent in 1968), John Anderson (7 percent in 1980), and Ross Perot (19 percent in 1992, 8 percent in 1996).

Figure 12–2 Split Ticket Voting, 1952–1998

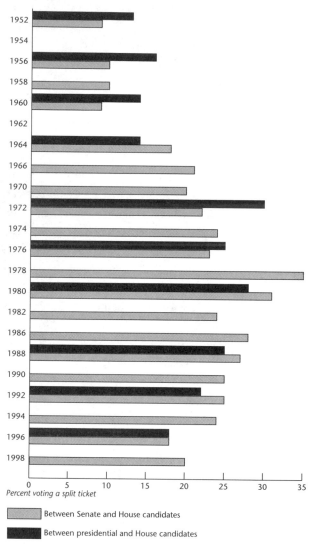

Percent voting a split ticket

Between Senate and House candidates

Between presidential and House candidates

Source: American National Election Studies.

Divided partisan control of governments has become common. American voters now regularly divide control of the White House and Congress between the parties (Table 12–1). Do they do it on purpose? Certainly, moderate voters might prefer **divided government,** for it allows each party to block the other's more extreme proposals and forces both parties to compromise when making policy.[20]

People who simply distrust politicians also might prefer to have the parties in a position to check one another. Despite this logic, there is little evidence that many people deliberately split their votes to achieve moderate policies or to make "ambition counteract ambition." Divided government is more likely a byproduct of voters applying different criteria for different offices, responding to the specific options in each contest, or making tradeoffs among their incompatible preferences (for low taxes but generous middle-class entitlements, for less regulation but more protection from environmental and market risks).[21] But even if few people deliberately vote for divided government, most are happy when they get it. In a survey taken shortly after the 1998 elections, 56 percent of voters preferred to have the presidency and Congress split between the parties, while only 24 percent preferred to have one party control both (the rest said it did not matter).[22] In more than half the states, voters in recent elections also have put different parties in control of the governor's office and at least one house of the state legislature.[23]

Media and Money. The weakening of party influence on voters was hastened along by technological changes and the growing availability of campaign resources—money, skill, activists—from sources other than political parties. The most important technological innovation was the advent of television as a campaign medium, but newer technologies, such as computerized direct mail and mass-produced campaign videos, have contributed as well. The electronic media have made parties less essential to candidates and voters alike. Ross Perot was able to conduct a surprisingly successful campaign in 1992 with no party at all behind him. (He did not organize the Reform Party until 1995.) Voters informed by the news media as well as by the candidates' electronic campaigns are offered cheap cues other than party labels to guide their decisions. News coverage of elections, not to mention campaign advertising, focuses on individual candidates and largely ignores parties, thus inviting voters to do the same.

Campaigns conducted on television and through direct

Table 12–1 The Growth of Divided Government, 1928–1998

Election year	President	House of Representatives	Senate
1928	R (Hoover)	R	R
1930	R (Hoover)	D	R
1932	D (F. Roosevelt)	D	D
1934	D (F. Roosevelt)	D	D
1936	D (F. Roosevelt)	D	D
1938	D (F. Roosevelt)	D	D
1940	D (F. Roosevelt)	D	D
1942	D (F. Roosevelt)	D	D
1944	D (F. Roosevelt)	D	D
1946	D (Truman)	R	R
1948	D (Truman)	D	D
1950	D (Truman)	D	D
1952	R (Eisenhower)	R	R
1954	R (Eisenhower)	D	D
1956	R (Eisenhower)	D	D
1958	R (Eisenhower)	D	D
1960	D (Kennedy)	D	D
1962	D (Kennedy)	D	D
1964	D (L. Johnson)	D	D
1966	D (L. Johnson)	D	D
1968	R (Nixon)	D	D
1970	R (Nixon)	D	D
1972	R (Nixon)	D	D
1974	R (Ford)	D	D
1976	D (Carter)	D	D
1978	D (Carter)	D	D
1980	R (Reagan)	D	R
1982	R (Reagan)	D	R
1984	R (Reagan)	D	R
1986	R (Reagan)	D	D
1988	R (Bush)	D	D
1990	R (Bush)	D	D
1992	D (Clinton)	D	D
1994	D (Clinton)	R	R
1996	D (Clinton)	R	R
1998	D (Clinton)	R	R

Source: Samuel Kernell, *Going Public: New Strategies of Presidential Leadership,* 3d ed. (Washington, D.C.: CQ Press, 1997), 47.
    Note: Colored type indicates divided government.

Figure 12–3 Comparative Party Evaluations, 1952–1996

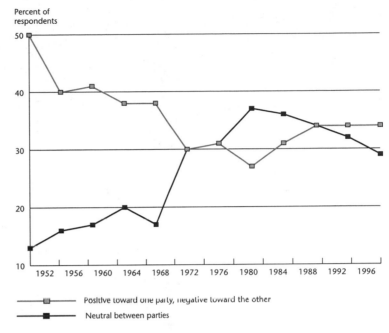

Percent of respondents

——■—— Positive toward one party, negative toward the other

——■—— Neutral between parties

Sources: Martin P. Wattenberg, *The Decline of American Political Parties, 1952–1992* (Cambridge, Mass.: Harvard University Press, 1994), 174; and personal communication, 1997.

mail are expensive, driving up the demand for campaign funds. The proliferation of candidate-centered campaigns also has driven up costs because such campaigns cannot operate with the economies of scale enjoyed by candidates working as a party team, communicating a common message, and sharing the cost of consultants, specialists, and advertising. But these changes would not have happened had the supply of money not risen to meet the demand. It did so because a growing economy provided the funds for people to invest in politics, and the expanding role of the government in their lives and businesses gave them more reason to do so.

The Survival (Revival?) of the Parties

Despite the forces working against parties, and despite the public's doubts about the value of parties in general, the Democratic and Republican Parties continue in many ways to dominate electoral politics. Indeed, the evidence in Figures 12–2 and 12–3 suggests a modest revival of partisanship among voters in the 1990s. Ticket splitting has returned to its levels of the 1960s, and voters have become slightly less neutral about the major parties. Parties have survived for the same reasons they came into being: elected officials, candidates, and voters still find them indispensable. The continuing importance of the parties within government is described in other chapters; their continuing value to voters and candidates is described here.

Partisanship Endures

Although fewer voters think of themselves as staunch partisans than was the case thirty years ago, most people are still willing to call themselves Democrats or Republicans, and, significantly, party affiliation remains the single best predictor of how people will vote. The distribution of partisan identities from 1952 through 1998, shown in Figure 12–4, is surprisingly stable despite the dramatic political events that occurred within that period. The proportion calling themselves independents has grown, but most independents are actually closet partisans leaning toward one of the parties and supporting its candidates as consistently as do weak partisans.[24] The proportion of "pure" independents grew from 6 percent in 1952 to 15 percent in 1976, but by 1998 was back down to 10 percent, and, because self-described independents are less likely to vote, their share of the electorate was actually only 6 percent. The proportion of strong partisans (combining both parties) declined between the 1950s and the 1970s but has since rebounded.

Figure 12–4 Party Identification, 1952–1998

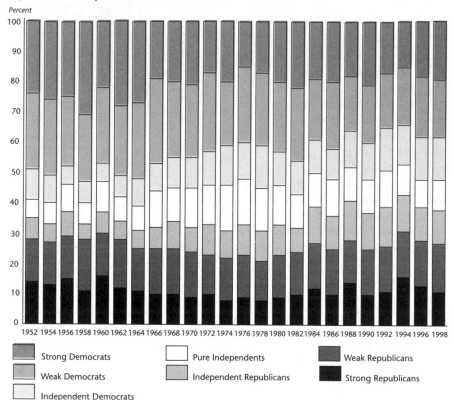

Source: American National Election Studies.

Party Differences

Voters may not think much of parties, but large majorities still admit to a party preference and use parties to guide their voting decisions. They do so because, despite the divisions within the party coalitions and regardless of how they feel about the parties, the party labels still carry valuable information about candidates.

In general, Republicans tend to favor a smaller, cheaper federal government; they advocate lower taxes, less regulation of business, and lower spending on social welfare. They would be more generous only to the Pentagon. Democrats are more inclined to regulate business in behalf of consumers and the environment and are more supportive of government programs designed to improve domestic welfare; they would spend less on national defense. Democrats are more concerned with "fairness" and

1996 PARTY PLATFORMS

This summary of the 1996 Democratic and Republican platforms reveals some of the differences between positions typically held by the parties. But very few voters learn of these differences by reading the platforms. Rather, they learn about the parties' positions through political news and campaign advertising.

	Democrats	**Republicans**
Abortion	The Democratic Party stands behind the right of every woman to choose, consistent with *Roe v. Wade.*	The unborn child has a fundamental individual right to life which cannot be infringed. We support a human life amendment to the Constitution.
Budget	President Clinton has put forward a plan to balance the budget by 2002 while living up to our commitments to the elderly and our children.	Republicans support a Balanced Budget Amendment to the Constitution, phased in over a short time and with appropriate safeguards for national emergencies.
Crime	We support the President's call for a constitutional amendment to protect the rights of victims.	Because liberal jurists keep expanding the rights of the accused, Republicans propose a constitutional amendment to protect victims' rights.
Discrimination	The Democratic Party has always supported the Equal Rights Amendment, . . . and to vigorously enforce the Americans with Disabilities Act. . . . When it comes to affirmative action, we should mend it, not end it.	We oppose discrimination based on sex, race, age, creed, or national origin and will vigorously enforce anti-discrimination laws. We reject the distortion of those laws to cover sexual preference. . . . We will attain our nation's goals of equal rights without quotas or other forms of preferential treatment.
Education	Today's Democratic Party will stand firmly against the Republican assault on education. Cutting education as we move into the 21st century would be like cutting defense spending at the height of the Cold War. We must do more to expand educational opportunity, not less.	. . . [T]he federal government has no constitutional authority to be involved in school curricula or to control jobs in the workplace. That is why we will abolish the Department of Education, and end federal meddling in our schools and promote family choice at all levels of learning.
Foreign Policy	We are committed to promoting democracy in regions and countries important to America's security, and to standing with all those willing to take risks for peace, . . . our allies, willing partners, the U.N. and other security organizations.	We oppose the commitment of American troops to U.N. "peacekeeping" operations under foreign commanders and will never compel American servicemen to wear foreign uniforms or insignia.
Guns	Today's Democratic Party stands with America's police officers. We are proud to tell them that . . . any attempt to repeal the Brady Bill or assault weapons ban will be met with a veto.	We defend the constitutional right to keep and bear arms.
Immigration	. . . [W]e call on all Americans to avoid the temptation to use this issue to divide people from each other. . . . [T]o bar the children of illegal immigrants from school . . . is wrong. . . .	Illegal immigrants should not receive public benefits, . . . and those who become parents while illegally in the United States should not be qualified to claim benefits for their offspring.
Language	We believe every American should learn English, . . . but we strongly oppose divisive efforts like English-only legislation. . . .	We support the official recognition of English as the nation's common language.
Taxes	Today's Democratic Party is committed to targeted tax cuts that help working Americans, . . . and we insist that any tax cuts are completely paid for, because we are determined to balance the budget.	American families are suffering from the twin burdens of stagnant incomes and near-record taxes. . . . In response to this unprecedented burden, we support an across-the-board, 15 percent tax cut to marginal tax rates.
Welfare	We know the new bill passed by Congress is far from perfect —parts of it should be fixed because they go too far. . . . Our job now is to make sure this welfare reform plan succeeds.	Because illegitimacy is the most serious cause of child poverty, we will encourage the states to stop cash payments to unmarried teens and set a family cap on payments for additional children.

Source: As summarized in Stephen J. Wayne, *The Road to the White House 1996* (New York: St. Martin's Press, 1997), 174–177.

Opinion polls conducted in 1998 found a healthy majority of the public opposing the impeachment of President Bill Clinton. Most Republicans, however, favored the step, as reflected in this October 1998 straight party-line Republican vote in the House to launch an impeachment inquiry. The vote revealed the sharp partisan divide in Congress—the sharpest since the 1950s.

equality, Republicans with letting free enterprise flourish. Republicans would ban abortion and allow official prayer in public schools; Democrats would not. Not all candidates adhere to their party's modal positions; some Republicans support freedom of choice on abortion, and some Democrats advocate large defense budgets. But the party label continues to distinguish candidates from one another on many issues with considerable accuracy. Indeed, in Congress party divisions are sharper and clearer now than they have been since the 1950s (see Chapter 6). Thus voters continue to use party cues, even if not as exclusively as in the past.

Changes in the Party Coalitions

The party coalitions of the 1990s still retain strong traces of the New Deal alignment (for example, lower-income voters are still more likely to be Democrats; higher-income voters Republicans), but they have undergone several crucial changes since the 1960s. In the 1950s white southerners were overwhelmingly Democratic, but they responded to the civil rights revolution by moving gradually but steadily into the Republican camp. A solid majority of white southerners now identify themselves as Republicans. African Americans favored Democrats even before the 1960s, but the magnitude of the Democratic advantage more than doubled in the 1960s and has remained huge since then.

Men have become more Republican, while women have not, creating the famous "gender gap" between the parties.[25] The Democratic advantage among Catholics has shrunk, and regular churchgoers of all religions have become relatively more Republican. Indeed, during the Reagan years the electorate as a whole became more Republican, less Democratic (see Figure 12–4, p. 414).

These changes in the party coalitions have been extensive enough to suggest that a sixth party system is now in place. Because the changes occurred gradually and at different times, the new system's starting date is unclear: some analysts propose 1968, others say 1980 or 1984. Whatever the timing, the most salient difference between the current and New Deal party systems is the Republican Party's increased strength, symbolized by its winning majorities in the House and Senate in three straight elections (1994, 1996, and 1998) for the first time since the fourth party system. Although Democrats maintain an edge in party identifiers, the Republican coalition includes more people with higher incomes and more formal education, so Republican identifiers vote at higher rates than do Democrats. The Democrats' advantage therefore is typically even smaller when the analysis is confined to voters. Because Republican voters also are somewhat more loyal to their party, electoral competition is evenly balanced in the current party system.

Modern Party Organizations

Despite the rise of television and other electronic campaign media and the advent of professional campaign consultants, parties are still useful to candidates as well as to voters. Party organizations have not disappeared; indeed, in some ways, they are in better shape now than ever before. Both national parties and many state organizations have become modern, businesslike enterprises with permanent offices, professional staffs, and relatively stable budgets.

Party organizations have been modernized for the same reasons they were created in the first place: they are an important, if no longer unrivaled, tool for pursuing political power by coordinating collective electoral action. A good deal of the impetus for state party modernization has come from the national party organizations. Although both major parties have had permanent national committees since before the Civil War, only since the 1970s have national organizations played a significant role in party politics. The Democrats began to nationalize their party structure when the various post–1968 reform commissions operating out of national headquarters imposed rules on state and local parties. But it is the Republicans who have led the way since then.

As always, the "outs" did the major innovating. The Watergate scandal and the economic recession that beset the second Nixon administration devastated the Republicans in the 1974 congressional elections and helped defeat Gerald Ford in 1976. Party leaders William Brock, Guy Vander Jagt, and Robert Packwood—chairmen, respectively, of the Republican National Committee and the party's House and Senate campaign committees—resolved to build their organizations into effective promoters of Republican candidates. The first thing they did was to raise money, lots of it. They perfected the new technique of computerized direct-mail fund raising, developing lists of people who were willing to send modest checks in response to regular solicitations to create a steady source of income for the party. Their growing success during the early 1980s, when they were raising 80 percent of their money through the mail in checks averaging less than $30, is documented in Figure 12–5, p. 418.

With the money coming in, the Republicans enlarged their organization staff and began to provide a host of services to their candidates. Today, they help candidates for federal office raise money, comply with campaign finance regulations, design polls, research opponents' records, put together lists of voters to contact, and design campaign strategy. They contribute a good deal of money directly to candidates' campaign war chests. In some years, they have conducted national campaigns for the entire party ticket. Republican candidates also are helped indirectly by the money and training the national party has contributed to state and local Republican organizations across the nation to strengthen the party at the grass roots. In addition, the campaign committees have stepped up efforts to identify, recruit, and train effective candidates for Congress and, in some instances, for state offices as well.[26]

The Democrats were shocked into a similar effort to expand the services offered by their national party committees when in 1980 they lost both the White House (to Ronald Reagan) and their Senate majority. They are still playing catch-up in fund raising, however, and therefore lag well behind in the help they can give their candidates (Figure 12–5). Even the shameless pursuit of soft party money that caused Bill Clinton and Al Gore so much embarrassment after the 1996 election did not raise enough for the Democrats to match the Republicans that year. Nonetheless, the Democrats do far more at the national level for their federal candidates than ever before in the party's history.

Although modern parties continue to play a major fi-

Figure 12–5 Party Spending and Contributions in Federal Elections, 1977–1998

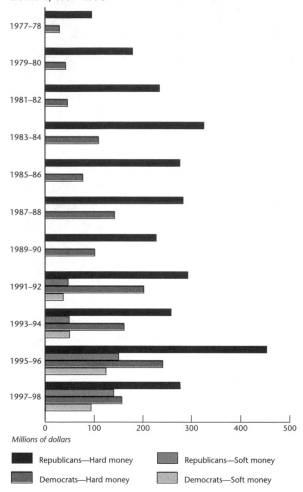

Millions of dollars

■ Republicans—Hard money   ■ Republicans—Soft money

■ Democrats—Hard money   ■ Democrats—Soft money

Note: Beginning in 1991, the parties were required to report soft money receipts and expenditures to the Federal Election Commission.

Rep. Kenny Hulshof, Republican from Missouri, sits in a television studio run by the National Republican Congressional Committee and produces satellite feeds to local news shows back in Missouri. His two-percentage-point margin of victory in the 1996 election made him an avid fan of Republican broadcast technology.

nancial and organizational role in electoral politics, they have clearly lost the near-monopoly they had on campaign resources until the mid-twentieth century. Candidates, rather than parties, are the focus of campaigns; the party's activities are aimed at helping individual candidates compete more effectively, not at promoting the party. According to political scientist John Aldrich, "A new form of party has emerged, one that is 'in service' to its

ambitious politicians but not 'in control' of them as the mass party [of the past] sought to be."[27]

Expediency Persists

American parties developed and have endured because they have proven so useful to politicians and voters attempting to act collectively within the institutional framework established by the Constitution. The federal system offers powerful incentives for organizing and expanding both legislative and electoral coalitions—that is, political parties—to win and exercise political power. For one thing, it rewards political entrepreneurs who can organize cooperative action across government institutions and electoral arenas. For another, it prompts voters to use party labels to simplify their decisions, giving politicians a reason to cooperate with party leaders to maintain the value of the party's "brand name."

Although the party coalitions have shifted periodically in response to new national issues and conflicts, leaving five—perhaps six—identifiable party systems, the basic pattern of competition between two broad, usually fractious coalitions has persisted. The two-party system arises from strategic voting in the winner-take-all competition for the presidency (and for all other federal offices as well) and has been strengthened by laws (mandating, for example, primary elections) that treat the parties as official components of the electoral machinery. Party coalitions remain fractious because party entrepreneurs pursuing majorities must combine diverse groups that are not by any measure natural allies, but these coalitions persist because party organizations remain decentralized, mirroring the decentralized institutions of American federalism.

Progressive Era reforms, followed by the development of new technologies of communication after the Second World War, weakened traditional party organizations and ended their monopoly control of campaigns, but parties continue to play a central role in electoral politics. Despite their expressed disdain for parties, voters still rely heavily on party cues in making their decisions because party labels continue to provide useful, cheap information about candidates. Party entrepreneurs, for their part, have simply redesigned party organizations to operate more effectively in today's media-based, candidate-centered electoral arena. They are walking down the trail blazed by Jefferson and Van Buren, and for the same reason: to elect those who share their views so that they may shape public policy to their liking.

Suggested Readings

Aldrich, John H. *Why Parties? The Origin and Transformation of Party Politics in America.* Chicago: University of Chicago Press, 1995. An astute theoretical and historical analysis of American parties that deepens and extends the approach taken in this text.

Chambers, William Nesbit, and Walter Dean Burnham, eds. *The American Party Systems: Stages of Development.* New York: Oxford University Press, 1967. Fascinating historical essays on American party development. The essay by Eric L. McKitrick explaining how partisan politics helped Abraham Lincoln and how its absence hurt Jefferson Davis during the Civil War is especially instructive.

Mayhew, David R. *Placing Parties in American Politics.* Princeton, N.J.: Princeton University Press, 1986. To understand why some states developed strong party organizations and others did not, read this book.

Polsby, Nelson W. *The Consequences of Party Reform.* New York: Oxford University Press, 1983. According to Polsby, the consequences have not been good.

Riordan, William L. *Plunkitt of Tammany Hall.* New York: Dutton, 1963. According to the subtitle, "a series of very plain talks on very practical politics, delivered by George Washington Plunkitt, the Tammany Philosopher, from his rostrum—the New York County Court House bootblack stand." Includes a good introductory essay on nineteenth-century party machine politics.

Sundquist, James L. *The Dynamics of the Party System*, rev. ed. Washington, D.C.: Brookings, 1983. Highly detailed study of historical party realignments; for those who prefer complex stories rather than simple ones.

Wattenberg, Martin P. *The Decline of American Political Parties, 1952–1992.* Cambridge, Mass.: Harvard University Press, 1994. Strongest statement of the "party decline" thesis based on analysis of public attitudes toward parties.

Key Terms

Australian ballot /402	**patronage** /391
caucus /419	**primary election** /402
divided government /412	**proportional representation** /390
national party convention /395	**split ticket** /402
New Deal coalition /406	**superdelegate** /409
party machine /399	**two-party system** /389

Chapter 13

INTEREST GROUPS

☆ *The number of interests represented in Washington has grown enormously over the past several decades. Has this development left "special interests" more powerful or less powerful?*

☆ *Most lobbyists are paid advocates of special interests. Why should politicians believe anything they say?*

☆ *Free riding should doom "public interest" lobbies. Why do so many emerge and thrive nonetheless?*

☆ *Do interest groups spawn government programs, or do government programs spawn interest groups?*

☆ *Do political action committees buy policy with their campaign donations? If not, what do they buy?*

On February 1, 1996, Congress swept away sixty-two years of telecommunications policy to make way for the information superhighway. Remarkably, the Telecommunications Act of 1996, mandating the most radical overhaul of the government's role in communications policy since 1934, passed both houses by huge bipartisan majorities. Near unanimity in Congress was not the result of any policy consensus within the telecommunications industry or among members of the public, however. Conflicts among regional telephone companies, long-distance service providers, cable television companies, local television and radio broadcasters, and the major networks had stifled action for years; meanwhile, the public had scarcely taken note of what was happening. Finally, though, push came to shove. Congressional leaders and the administration managed to broker a package of deals that satisfied the main con-

tenders, all of whom had become convinced that the status quo was no longer an option.

The stakes were enormous. The telecommunications sector accounts for more than $1 trillion annually, about one-seventh of the U.S. gross domestic product. Rapidly evolving technology had opened new opportunities and rendered the old regulatory regime obsolete. The major players all wanted to erase rules that had kept them from moving in on one another's businesses and to maintain barriers that had kept rivals out of theirs. Long-distance companies sought permission to compete with regional telephone companies for local service customers; the regional companies wanted to offer long-distance and video services. The cable television industry sought an end to regulation of the rates they could charge customers and permission to compete with regional telephone companies. Broadcasters wanted free access to a

President Bill Clinton signed the Telecommunications Reform Act at the Library of Congress on February 8, 1996. He used the occasion to showcase the V-chip, introduced as part of the landmark legislation. Installed in new sets, the chip would allow parents to block shows they consider too violent for their children.

new electromagnetic spectrum for high-definition digital broadcasting; media conglomerates wanted limits raised on the number and share of media outlets they could own. All wanted to be free to form whatever mergers or partnerships they thought might help them survive in the highly uncertain and competitive industry that telecommunications had become.

They were not the only interested parties. Internet providers and civil libertarians battled groups wanting to censor "cybersmut." President Bill Clinton pushed for a provision requiring new televisions to be equipped with a "V-chip," allowing parents to block objectionable TV shows. Consumer groups sought to limit deregulation and media concentration, which they asserted would lead to higher prices and narrower choices. No group interested in any aspect of telecommunications policy could af-

ford to ignore this rare legislative moment when everything seemed up for reconsideration.

With so much at stake, **lobbyists** descended on Capitol Hill in droves. They sponsored dueling academic studies, advertised heavily in newspapers and magazines read inside the Beltway, stepped up their already generous campaign giving, and brought local affiliates to Washington to lobby their representatives. They also formed shifting alliances with one another as deals were struck on different parts of the bill and sought through polls and other means to demonstrate broad public support for their positions. In one instance, lobbying firms representing the regional telephone companies contracted with vendors to purchase phone calls to 175,000 citizens who would then consent to have mailgrams sent to members of Congress in their names. The tactic backfired, however, when it came out that one of the vendors, falling short of its quota, had used people's names without their consent.[1] Public reaction seemed to be one big yawn; the legislation was so complicated and its effects so uncertain, even to industry insiders, that most people paid little attention. With the public uninvolved, the field was left to industry lobbyists; representatives of consumer groups won only vague assurances that the increased competition mandated by the bill would serve the public by bringing down prices and expanding services.

In the end, the high degree of uncertainty helped to win broad industry and thus congressional support for the final package because it was far from obvious who had won or lost. Every interest got at least part of what it wanted, and all at least avoided immediate economic damage. The main contenders recognized that the bill was only a first (though huge) step in the process of adapting regulatory institutions to the technological revolution in telecommunications; much of importance would be decided later by the Federal Communications Commission and the courts.[2] Yet in the months that followed the tune changed. When competition was slow to arrive, mergers created ever-larger telecommunications conglomerates. As telephone and cable charges continued to rise, critics charged that the public had been sold out. "During the debate on the communications bill," observed Republican senator John McCain of Arizona, "everyone was protected but the consumer."[3]

The story of telecommunications politics in 1996 introduces the central themes of this chapter. **Interest groups** and **lobbying** are inevitable and, indeed, essential components of modern democratic politics. They also are a continual source of problems for democracy. The American political system could not function without the endlessly busy work of organized interests and their representatives. Yet there has never been a time in American history when they have not been under attack from one quarter or another as threats to democracy itself. This chapter looks at why interest groups are both essential and problematic.

The Logic of Lobbying

The logic of lobbying is transparent. People who want to influence government decisions that affect their lives and welfare quickly recognize the advantages of banding together with others of like mind and asking astute and powerful friends to help out. Governments, for their part, have good reason to welcome lobbying—appeals from citizens and groups for favorable policies and decisions. Even officials in blatantly nondemocratic governments find life considerably easier if they have the support, or at least acquiescence, of the governed (ask any parent). They cannot estimate the costs and benefits of alternative actions without having some idea of how people will react to their initiatives. All governments also need the information, political as well as technical, that people and organizations outside the government are in the best position to provide—for a price. Where government positions of power are filled by competitive elections, elected officials try to accommodate people commanding electoral resources—votes, money, organization—that may affect

Effective lobbyists understand how government institutions work and enjoy warm personal friendships with the key institutional players. For one Washington lobbyist, however, "friendship" raises an ethics problem. Linda Daschle, former deputy administrator of the Federal Aviation Administration and wife of Senate Minority Leader Tom Daschle, Democrat from South Dakota, joined a Washington law firm as a lobbyist in February 1997. Under Clinton administration rules, senior officials must pledge not to lobby their former agencies for five years after leaving office, but they may lobby Congress. To avoid the appearance of any impropriety, Daschle took a personal oath to avoid lobbying the Senate because of her husband's position there.

their job security. And always and everywhere, at least a few government officials have been willing to trade favors for personal "gifts" of every imaginable sort.

Modern politics also breeds professional lobbyists. For the same reason they hire lawyers to represent them in court, people hire agents who are specialists to represent them before legislatures and executive agencies. Like courts, modern legislatures and bureaucracies are complex institutions bound by arcane rules, procedures, and customs. People wishing these institutions to act in their behalf are more likely to succeed if they are represented by agents who understand how the institutions work and enjoy warm personal friendships with the key institutional players.

Lobbying as a profession thus emerged with modern representative government and has flourished with the growing scope and complexity of government activities. But if interest groups and lobbying arise naturally with the development of representative institutions, so do doubts about their legitimacy. Their very presence, not to mention any political success they may achieve, raises the suspicion that "special interests" win at the expense of the "public interest." Even people who deny that the public interest can be defined objectively—such as many modern political scientists—often argue that successful lobbying subverts the basic principles of democratic equality and majority rule. Groups vary widely in how readily they can be organized for collective action, creating marked imbalances in the representation of social interests. Moreover, policy gridlock and political paralysis in the face of pressing national problems are commonly blamed on the cacophony of competing interests. For these reasons, organized political interests have been attacked and criticized as long as they have existed.

James Madison, with his usual cogency, captured the dilemma posed by politically active groups in his famous discussion of factions in *Federalist* No. 10. For Madison, factions were by definition pernicious, pursuing selfish aims contrary to the rights of others or to the public interest. As such, factions were, in Madison's view, a major threat to popular government: "The instability, injustice, and confusion introduced into the public councils" by the "dangerous vice" of faction "have, in truth, been the mortal diseases under which popular governments have everywhere perished."

Why then not just get rid of factions? Madison's answer was that factions could be eliminated only by "destroying the liberty which is essential to [their] existence . . . [or by] giving every citizen the same opinions, the same passions, and the same interests." He found the first cure "worse than the disease" because popular govern-

ment is supposed to protect liberty and the second impossible: "As long as the reason of man continues to be fallible, and he is at liberty to exercise it, different opinions will be formed."

Practically speaking, then, to maintain the freedoms specified in the First Amendment—to speak, publish, assemble, and "petition the Government for a redress of grievances"—a political system must tolerate factions even though they may be, as by Madison's definition, opposed to the public good. Political parties, interest groups, lobbyists, and peaceful political organizations of all kinds are, in effect, licensed by the Constitution and can be suppressed only by violating its principles.

If factions cannot be suppressed without subverting the very purpose of popular government, how can they be prevented from destroying the polity? As we saw in Chapter 2, Madison's solution was to divide authority among the federal institutions envisioned in the Constitution. The fragmentation of authority would prevent any single faction from dominating, and the nation's diversity would foster a wide variety of competing interests that could use this institutional machinery to thwart each other's selfish designs. Madison's solution to the problem of faction was, in other words, institutional and social pluralism. It was, characteristically, a solution firmly grounded in American realities.

The Origins of Interest Group Politics in America

Madison's discussion of factions, though abstract, was anything but academic. Organized attempts to influence government decisions have been a integral part of American politics since the nation's earliest days.

The Colonial Era

In the colonial era, merchants, manufacturers, and ethnic and religious minorities actively sought favorable policies from authorities in London as well as from colonial governors and assemblies. By the middle of the eighteenth century such groups had developed most of the techniques of persuasion still used today. Colonial interests submitted petitions to the government, hired agents to "handle the delicate work involved in extracting concessions from ministers and lesser bureaucrats," examined the voting records of legislators to identify prospective supporters, organized letter-writing campaigns, reminded legislators that a group's supporters were among their constituents, and formed logrolling coalitions with other interests.[4]

As the involvement of the British Parliament in colonial government deepened, American interests and their British allies learned to cultivate parliamentary leaders, as well as draft legislation and slip it into an opportune spot on the parliamentary calendar. They also bombarded members of Parliament with information and arranged for expert testimony, often planting questions to get the desired answers on the record. Then they lobbied members in person and in writing, at home and in London, "urging leaders to give active support and imploring less active ones at least to show up and vote."[5] Such **insider lobbying** by narrowly focused interests has been a familiar part of legislative politics in Anglo-American democracies ever since.

The eighteenth century also witnessed the invention of the **public interest lobby** using the outsider tactic of appealing to the general public for support of its goals. The chief innovator was the English radical John Wilkes, whose Bill of Rights Society promoted a general cause— the expansion of suffrage—rather than defend any particular interest. Disdaining the customary tactics of friendly persuasion, the Wilkesites attacked government officials.[6] Similar organizations appeared in the colonies, the best known of which was the Sons of Liberty. Among other subversive activities, this group threw the Boston Tea Party.

By the time of the American Revolution, a wide variety of politically active groups had emerged: merchants'

societies, chambers of commerce, religious sects, organizations pushing radical causes, groups interested in local improvements, ethnic societies, insurance societies, clubs with social and intellectual aspirations, workers' organizations, military and professional associations. Delegates to the Continental Congress—which at first was not much more than another private alliance of colonial interests— were treated to lobbying tactics used to this day. Among other things, they were lavishly wined and dined with "hogsheads of Madeira and port, . . . huge dinners of mutton and pork, duck and turkey, fools and tarts and jellies . . . served . . . on tables with white linen and bright with English silver" provided by people hoping to influence their decisions.[7]

Delegates to the Constitutional Convention were so accustomed to lobbying that they agreed to meet behind locked doors and to keep their deliberations secret until after the convention was over. No official record was kept "lest word of their intentions leak out and they become beset by a horde of citizens seeking to advance their own interests."[8] This was by no means the last time the public interest was best served by letting negotiations proceed out of the public eye.

The Early Republic

As Madison had anticipated, the political system established by the Constitution allowed "factions" to flourish. Political parties emerged almost immediately (see Chapter 12). Of the many coordinated efforts made to shape government decisions in the early decades of the Republic, most were directed at state and local governments since at that time they made most of the decisions important to citizens. By the 1830s organizations of all kinds formed an integral part of American life. French visitor Alexis de Tocqueville noted with astonishment the abundance and variety of organized groups in the United States: "In no country in the world has the principle of association been more successfully used, or applied to a greater multitude of objects, than in America. . . . There

Lobbyist Defined, Nineteenth-Century Style

1841. Historian James Silk Buckingham defined *lobbyists* as "agents, selected for their skill in the arts of deluding, persuading, and bribing members of legislative bodies."

1856. Poet Walt Whitman dismissed "lobbyers" as "crawling serpentine men, the lousy combings and born freedom sellers of the earth."

1873. A reporter for *The Nation* depicted the professional lobbyist as "a man whom everybody suspects; who is generally during one half of the year without honest means of livelihood; and whose employment by those who have bills before a legislature is only resorted to as a disagreeable necessity."

1875. Novelist John William De Forest in his novel *Honest John Vane* let out all the stops: "Men of unwholesome skins, greasy garments, brutish manners, filthy minds, and sickening conversation; men who so reeked and drizzled with henbane tobacco and cockatrice whisky that a moderate drinker or smoker would recoil from them as from a cesspool; men whose stupid, shameless boasting of their briberies were enough to warn away from them all but the elect of Satan . . . [and] decayed statesmen, who were now, indeed, nothing but unfragrant corpses, breeding all manner of vermin and miasma."

1888. Everit Brown and Albert Strauss's *Dictionary of American Politics* offered this definition: "*Lobby, The,* is a term applied collectively to men that make a business of corruptly influencing legislators. The individuals are called lobbyists. Their object is usually accomplished by means of money paid to the members, but any other means that is considered feasible is employed."

Source: Margaret Susan Thompson, *The "Spider Web": Congress and Lobbying in the Age of Grant* (Ithaca, N.Y.: Cornell University Press, 1985), 54–57.

is no end which the human will despairs of attaining through the combined power of individuals united into a society."[9]

Because most of these groups sought to achieve their ends without involving the government, they were not what we would call political interest groups, but many did have explicit political aims. Examples were the American Anti-Slavery Society (founded in 1833); the National Trades Union (1834), which lobbied for a ten-hour workday; and the American Temperance Union (1836), which lobbied for a halt to the sale of alcoholic beverages, or prohibition. Like Madison, de Tocqueville thought that such associations could be dangerous to public order and good government, but his observations convinced him that voluntary groups were essential to an egalitarian social and political system. In contrast to aristocratic nations led by powerful nobles able to undertake great public projects by themselves, "amongst democratic nations, . . . all citizens are independent and feeble; they can do hardly anything by themselves, and none of them can oblige his fellow-men to lend him their assistance. They all, therefore, become powerless, if they do not learn voluntarily to help each other."[10] The endorsement of interest group activity in politics by de Tocqueville was tempered by the same concern that had worried Madison—excessive factional conflict might destroy the political system, leaving liberty unprotected—but he remained on the side of those who believed that interest groups enhanced rather than threatened democracy. Later observers were not so sure. During the years of national expansion—geographic and industrial—after the Civil War, the scope of the federal government's activities expanded enormously, and so did the activities aimed at shaping its decisions. Among the most visible activities were those undertaken by the newly emerging, large-scale industrial corporations and trusts. The methods of their political agents, exposed by a generation of journalists and social critics known collectively as "muckrakers," tainted lobbying with an evil reputation it has never fully lived down (see box, "*Lobbyist* Defined").

PUCK.

THE BOSSES OF THE SENATE.

Joseph Keppler, one of the most popular political cartoonists of his day, pays tribute to the "Bosses of the Senate." By 1889 the Senate was known as the millionaires' club. The presiding officer was a Wall Street banker and its principal members represented the oil, lumber, railroad, insurance, silver, gold, utility, and manufacturing interests. Note that the "People's Entrance" is "closed."

Citizens outraged by political corruption formed new associations to agitate for reform. Over time, these groups succeeded in rewriting the rules of electoral and party politics and reorganizing government at all levels (see Chapters 8 and 12). These changes were part of a larger collection of innovations—child labor and wages-and-hours laws, regulation of railroads and other large-scale business enterprises, women's suffrage, the income tax—that were adopted during the late nineteenth and early twentieth centuries, a period historians now label the **Progressive Era.** The impetus for these innovations—as well as a good deal of the resistance to them—came from interest groups of every description. One of the

most remarkable, if temporary, successes was achieved by the Anti-Saloon League, which engineered the adoption of the Eighteenth Amendment. It prohibited the sale of alcoholic beverages in the United States from 1919 to 1933 when the amendment was repealed (see box, "The Anti-Saloon League," p. 428).

The groups that had so impressed de Tocqueville in the 1830s had been largely local and ephemeral. By the last decades of the nineteenth century, however, a growing number of permanent national associations had formed. The Civil War (1861–1865) spawned the Grand Army of the Republic, an organization of Union Army veterans that was transformed by entrepreneurial claims agents

THE ANTI-SALOON LEAGUE

The Anti-Saloon League, the most successful single-issue lobbying group in U.S. history, was the leading force behind adoption of the Eighteenth Amendment, which from 1919 until its repeal in 1933 prohibited the sale and transportation of "intoxicating liquors" (including beer and wine) in the United States.

For decades before the Anti-Saloon League was founded in 1896, numerous groups had advocated abstinence from alcohol and opposed the liquor traffic, but they had come and gone. Even a political party—the eponymous Prohibition Party—was on the temperance bandwagon, but the movement's political achievements were limited until the Anti-Saloon League took root.

The league's leaders, Purley Baker and Wayne Wheeler, were among the most astute politicians of their day. They put together an organization led by paid professional staff and supported by monthly subscriptions as well as large donations from wealthy benefactors. Working through preexisting organizations—mainly churches, but also local temperance groups—the league operated as the central coordinator of the movement's many components.

It focused strategically on a single issue—stopping the liquor trade; it took no political stance on any other issue. Tactically, the league concentrated on electoral politics with the simple goal of defeating "wets" and electing "drys." It monitored legislative votes and demanded writ-

ten pledges from aspiring candidates who wanted the league's support and did not have track records on the issue. The league did not care whether candidates themselves drank, only how they would vote on legislation restricting liquor sales. It established the value of its support by mobilizing sympathetic voters (largely through Protestant churches) and persuading them to cast votes based exclusively on the liquor issue: wets were punished at the polls. When the movement for prohibition went national, the league rallied constituents to send mail and petitions to Congress demanding action and even staged a march on Washington, attended by four thousand temperance advocates, to lobby for a constitutional amendment establishing prohibition.

Success, however, was the league's undoing. Because Prohibition lacked widespread public support in many areas, especially in the big cities, enforcement could be achieved only at great expense. But stringent enforcement would have made it even more unpopular. It finally fell victim to waning popular support and the Great Depression, which spurred demands for the jobs and taxes the liquor industry could offer. Prohibition was repealed on December 5, 1933, putting whiskey smugglers, like the one shown in the photo, out of business.

Source: Peter H. Odegard, *Pressure Politics: The Story of the Anti-Saloon League* (New York: Columbia University Press, 1928).

(lobbyists who made their living representing veterans trying to prove their eligibility for war pensions) into the largest interest group of its day. At its peak influence, one-fifth of total government revenue went to veterans' and widows' pensions.[11]

The proliferation of large-scale organizations also was an integral part of the industrial revolution. The emerging industrial economy, with its expanding national and international markets, bred large corporations, trusts and other complex financial structures, and numerous labor and farm organizations. An increasingly elaborate division of labor led to the formation of trade and professional associations; familiar groups like the American Medical Association, American Bar Association, and American Political Science Association got their starts during this period. Members of such groups were attracted mainly by the specialized services and enhanced status they offered, but, once organized and staffed, with a steady income from membership dues, the groups formed a permanent institutional base for attending to the political interests of members.

Interest Groups Defended

With the emergence of stable political associations as major players in national politics, scholars began to study interest groups. One result was the first systematic defense of their legitimate role in a modern democracy. The case was made most fully by political scientist David Truman in his influential book, *The Governmental Process,* published in 1951.[12] Truman viewed the proliferation of political interest groups as a natural and largely benign consequence of economic development. These groups formed spontaneously whenever shared interests were threatened or could be enhanced by political action. Modern industrial society, characterized by an ever more elaborate division of labor, became awash in interests and therefore in interest groups. As society became progressively more fragmented and variegated, so did the universe of associations.

Because groups were free to organize and participate in an open political system, the political process balanced competing interests, just as James Madison had promised. If established groups advocated policies that threatened the interests of other citizens, the threatened would organize to defend themselves. Demands provoked counterdemands, and so policies embodied the numerous compromises and tradeoffs necessary for building winning coalitions within and between political institutions. Aware that overreaching would stir opposition, established groups prudently moderated their demands in order to let sleeping dogs lie. Thus unorganized interests constrained active groups even when they were not represented by lobbies of their own.

Truman and other pluralist scholars also emphasized that the American political system was particularly conducive to pluralist politics. Its decentralized structure offered numerous points of access—political parties, congressional committees and subcommittees, the courts, the enormous variety of federal, state, and local governing agencies—where groups could bid for favorable policies. It also provided a set of political actors—elected officials—whose purposes were served by building broad-based coalitions and defending widely shared values. In this idealized conception, pluralist politics created a policy balance that reflected both the distribution of interests in society and the intensity with which they are pursued. Widely shared interests weighed in heavily because elections make numbers count; intensity entered the equation because the people who care the most about an issue are the most inclined to organize and act.

Clearly, then, this view of American pluralism did not embrace the customary disdain of "special interests" or "pressure groups" or "lobbies." Rather, interest groups were regarded as essential and valuable participants in the democratic politics of a modern industrial society. Without their participation, policy would be made in far greater ignorance of what citizens actually wanted from their government.

As a description of reality, this sunny conception of pluralism was open to some obvious criticisms. No one doubted that organized groups often were important political players; this was not at issue. But it was also undeniable that the groups most visibly active in politics did not, by any stretch of the imagination, form a balanced cross section of economic or social interests. Some interests, such as those of large industrial corporations, seemed to be vastly overrepresented; other interests, such as those of migrant laborers and the unemployed, were not represented at all. "The flaw in the pluralist heaven," as political scientist E. E. Schattschneider put it, "is that the heavenly chorus sings with a strong upper-class accent."[13] The readiest explanation for this bias was that organizational resources—money, information, access to authority, skill, bargaining power—are distributed very unequally across political interests. Thus when organizations invest in politics, the outcome will be biased in favor of groups supported by the affluent, informed, and powerful.

The Problem of Collective Action

A subtler but more cogent explanation for the observed bias in group representation lies in the way the incentives for collective action and the barriers to organization vary across different types of groups. The explanation, developed by the economist Mancur Olson in *The Logic of Collective Action* (1965), begins by pointing out that classical pluralists such as Truman were mistaken in assuming that people would form interest groups spontaneously to promote or defend shared interests.[14] Someone has to take on the work of organizing the group and finding the resources to keep it going. And to succeed, organizers have to overcome a standard collective action problem: most political interest groups pursue collective goods that, by definition, all group members would enjoy whether or not they helped to provide them. Rational self-interest leads to universal free riding, dooming the organization and the effort unless some way is found around this difficulty.

Some kinds of groups solve the problem far more easily than do others. Small groups are easier to organize than large groups because transaction costs are lower and the free-rider problem is less severe since free riders are more readily detected and subject to scorn and other social sanctions. Moreover, interests with a great deal at stake in a policy domain are more readily organized for political action than are people with little at stake. When prospective costs or benefits are large, so are incentives to invest in political action.

Similarly, when costs or benefits are diffused across many individuals, the effect on any one of them may be so small that it would not justify any effort to shape the policy. Oil producers, for example, have a much stronger incentive to invest in lobbying than do the people who buy gasoline. A decision that would change the price of gasoline by a few cents a gallon is a poor stimulus for action against the price increase by a single consumer, but its huge effect on oil company profits would justify a heavy investment by those companies in lobbying for the increase. Similarly, firms that benefit from a tax break have a much stronger incentive to invest in lobbying to retain the break than do taxpaying citizens who have to make up the lost revenue by an imperceptibly higher tax bill. Dairy farmers, to pick another example, have much more compelling economic reasons to finance the political effort to retain milk price supports than consumers have for financing efforts to eliminate them.

Group size and stakes often are inversely related, compounding the bias. For a few fortunate groups, a single member might have enough at stake to justify paying the entire cost of pursuing the group's collective interests. Exxon, for example, might find it profitable to invest in lobbying for repeal of price controls on gasoline even if it had to pay the entire cost of producing a benefit that would have to be shared with all gasoline producers. By contrast, many widely shared, diffuse collective interests will be poorly represented if those who share them behave rationally and remain free riders.

AARP: "GRAY POWER"

With its more than 32.4 million members, AARP (originally the American Association of Retired Persons, but now officially known by its acronym, which rhymes with harp) is the largest interest group in the United States. Nearly half of all Americans over fifty, or about one-fifth of the electorate, belong. AARP has more members than all the nation's labor unions combined; only the Roman Catholic Church has more.

Membership is attractive because for a mere $8 in annual dues (only $5 for the first year) members receive a bimonthly magazine, *Modern Maturity*, plus discounts on rental cars, hotels, airlines, and travel packages, and access to attractively priced health insurance and prescription drugs. Its Washington headquarters, housing a staff of eleven hundred, including forty-four policy specialists and twenty-two registered lobbyists, has its own five-digit zip code. In 1998 AARP took in $541 million in revenues and spent $483 million on programs and services, including $41 million on "legislation, research, and development," the lobbying expense category in its budget. AARP is the prime defender of Social Security and Medicare. In 1997 when AARP asked to hear from retirees what they thought about the federal government limiting Medicare coverage

of hospital outpatient services, it received thousands of responses. John Rother, AARP's chief lobbyist, happily shared the letters with lawmakers. AARP's effectiveness explains why retirees have been largely spared when Congress and the president have sought to reduce budget deficits.

Sources: Christopher Georges, "Old Money," *Washington Monthly*, (June 1992): 16–21; Susan Levine, "AARP Hopes That Boom Times Are Ahead," *Washington Post*, June 2, 1998, A1; Bill McAllister, "AARP Alters Name to Reflect Reality," November 18, 1998, A25; *AARP 1998 Financial Statements*, 5.

This analysis may explain why lobbies representing narrow economic interests predominate in Washington, but it raises a new question: why are there nonetheless so many vigorous lobbies claiming to speak for widespread, diffuse interests? Indeed, one of the most striking changes in the interest group universe over the past three decades has been the proliferation of organizations claiming to represent millions of citizens and to be devoted to some version of the public interest. This proliferation stems in part from the many people willing to contribute to

groups espousing causes they care about without worrying about whether or not their contribution will make any appreciable difference. Moral incentives, the personal satisfactions of active self-expression, trump the economist's concept of rationality for the millions of concerned citizens who send checks to groups pursuing environmental protection, political reform, a ban on abortion, animal rights, and a host of other social visions. These groups did not arise spontaneously through the action of concerned citizens; most were put together by enterpris-

With the growth of federal programs and regulation, lobbying has thrived as a profession. Because so many lobbyists practice their profession on Washington's K Street, it has become known as "lobbyist row."

est group in the United States by far—AARP—was formed to market insurance to senior citizens and thrives by providing members with a variety of selective benefits (see box, "AARP: 'Gray Power'"). Indeed, to a remarkable extent the interest groups that now throng the nation's capital are offshoots of organizations that exist for reasons other than political action.

Contemporary Interest Groups

The exact dimensions of the present-day interest group universe are unknown, but it is an expanding one. According to one recent estimate, the number of lobbying organizations has tripled in the last thirty years.[15] The 1995 edition of *Washington Representatives*, a directory of interest groups and lobbyists, had approximately 14,000 entries, more than double the number listed in the 1980 edition. The total included roughly 1,500 corporations, 2,100 labor unions and trade and professional associations, 2,200 advocacy groups (the fastest-growing category), 2,800 lawyers registered as lobbyists, 2,500 public relations consultants, and 250 think tank staff. About 4,000 groups are registered with the Federal Election Commission (FEC) so they can contribute funds to candidates for federal offices. These groups are the political action committees, or PACs, introduced in Chapter 11.

A large majority of active lobbying organizations are sponsored by institutions—corporations, unions, and professional associations—that exist for purposes other than lobbying. Also falling into this category are government entities—states, cities, counties, and their agencies—which are behind much lobbying activity. No fewer than forty-five California government bodies employ Washing-

ing activists supported by charitable foundations, wealthy individuals, or the government itself. Yet many are sustained by dues and small contributions from a large number of private citizens.

Other large organizations circumvent the collective action problem by offering inducements to join and contribute. Unions representing workers in firms with "closed shops" can require union membership (and the payment of dues) as a condition of holding a job. Attorneys join state bar associations in order to practice law; physicians join the American Medical Association to qualify for malpractice insurance and to receive the association's journal. And farmers seek membership in the American Farm Bureau Federation to receive the assistance of county farm agents. Groups that initially attract members by providing them with benefits, as most professional and trade associations do, may, once they are going concerns, invest some of their resources in pursuing collective benefits through political action. The largest inter-

HOW RALPH NADER GOT HIS START

Ralph Nader, the most successful of all public interest entrepreneurs, got an initial boost from an unlikely source. In 1965 Nader published a best-selling book, *Unsafe At Any Speed,* charging that the Chevrolet Corvair, General Motors's first American entry into the compact car market, was unsafe to drive. GM responded by hiring private investigators to pry into Nader's private life, presumably looking for dirt to discredit or silence him. When he discovered the spying, Nader sued GM, eventually settling out of court for $250,000. He used the publicity as well as the money the suit garnered to set up

the Center for the Study of Responsive Law, the first of his many consumer lobbies. Later he formed Public Citizen, a mass membership organization that funded enterprises such as the Tax Reform Research Group, Congress Watch, Health Research Group, Citizen Action Group, Litigation Group, Critical Mass (for nuclear power issues), and the national Public Interest Research Group (PIRG), the inspiration for numerous state-level PIRGs now active in consumer issues.

Source: James Q. Wilson, *Political Organizations* (New York: Basic Books, 1973), 322–323.

ton representatives. So do nearly one hundred colleges and universities, thirty-five Native American tribes, fifteen ethnic organizations, and seventy-eight religious denominations. Most advocacy groups also are the creatures of preexisting institutions. From abolition to temperance to civil rights to nuclear disarmament to the "right to life," churches and synagogues have provided the stable institutional base for organizing movements pursuing social and political change. Most of the self-designated public interest groups that have proliferated in recent decades initially were financed by patrons—philanthropic foundations, corporations, wealthy individuals, or the government itself—and many depend on continuing subsidies for a significant part of their budgets. The interests of welfare recipients, the mentally ill, children, and the homeless do not lack advocates even though such groups are not organized for collective action. Their cause has been taken up by lobbies representing the social service professionals (mostly government employees) who run the programs

that serve them. Even the flourishing public interest industry begun by longtime consumer advocate Ralph Nader got its start with the timely if unintended help of one of its initial targets (see box, "How Ralph Nader Got His Start").

Not every group depends on outside assistance for its resources. Prominent public interest groups such as Common Cause and Ralph Nader's various organizations are financed principally by membership dues and small donations, as are many of the large environmental lobbies, such as the Sierra Club, the National Audubon Society, and the Wilderness Society. These and other organizations have taken advantage of modern computer technology to solicit and maintain a mass membership and donor base through direct-mail appeals to current and prospective supporters. Because they depend on moral or purposive incentives—persuading people to invest in collective goods despite the temptation to free ride on the efforts of others—their memberships and budgets fluctuate with

LOGIC OF POLITICS

THE BLESSINGS OF ADVERSITY

Voluntary organizations that survive on dues and small contributions from a mass membership often do best when the political climate is worst. Such groups solicit most of their members and raise most of their money through direct-mail appeals, which are most effective when they invoke threats that make people angry or fearful enough to leave off free riding and join up or send another check. As one practitioner put it, "You've got to have a devil. If you don't have a devil, you're in trouble."[1] Devils are easier to find when power is in enemy hands. Thus, for example, membership in the National Rifle Association (NRA), a group adamantly opposed to any kind of gun control, grew rapidly during Democrat Jimmy Carter's administration (1977–1981), peaked in the early 1980s, then drifted downward from 1984 though 1991 when pro-gun Republicans Ronald Reagan (1981–1989) and then George Bush (1989–1993) sat in the White House. NRA growth revived with the election of gun control advocate Bill Clinton in 1992, then fell off again after the Republicans took control of Congress in 1995.[2]

For environmental groups the pattern was inverted. They received an enormous boost from the Reagan and Bush administrations. Their best (if unwitting) recruiters were James Watt, Reagan's first secretary of the interior, and Ann Gorsuch Burford, head of the Environmental Protection Agency, who made no bones about putting private economic interests ahead of environmental protection. The Sierra Club's membership rose from 181,000 in 1980 to 364,000 in 1985 and to 650,000 in 1992 and its budget more than quadrupled (from $9 million to $40 million). The National Audubon Society grew by 50 percent, adding 200,000 members to its rolls during the Reagan–Bush years, and other major environmental groups also grew rapidly. After 1992, however, with an environmentalist safely in the White House, membership in most of these groups stabilized or fell off. By 1998 the Sierra Club was down to 550,000; Greenpeace, which had peaked at 2.35 million members in 1990, claimed only 500,000 in 1998. A few smaller groups bucked the tide, particularly after the Republican congressional victories in 1994 gave them new "devils."[3]

1. Jeffrey M. Berry, *The Interest Group Society* (Boston: Little, Brown, 1984), 84.
2. Kelley Patterson, "The Political Firepower of the National Rifle Association," in *Interest Group Politics*, 5th ed., ed. Allan J. Cigler and Burdett A. Loomis (Washington, D.C.: CQ Press, 1998), 125–129.
3. Christopher Bosso, "Adaptation and Change in the Environmental Movement," in *Interest Group Politics*, 3d ed., ed. Allan J. Cigler and Burdett A. Loomis (Washington, D.C.: CQ Press, 1991), 613. Data for 1998 are from *The Encyclopedia of Associations*, 34th ed. (Detroit: Gale Research Company, 1999).

circumstances. They tend to grow when in opposition and shrink when sympathetic politicians are in power (see box, "The Blessings of Adversity").

Why Have Interest Groups Proliferated?

Several interacting factors have contributed to the rapid proliferation of interest groups since the 1960s. For one thing, the *social ferment* initiated by the civil rights movement inspired and instructed the stream of organizations that began agitating for social change in the decades that followed. Some groups led the opposition to the war in Vietnam; other organizations asserted the rights of women, gays, Native Americans, Hispanics, Asians, and the handicapped. Environmental and consumer groups emerged, along with the right to life and conservative Christian movements and animal rights organizations.

The list could (and no doubt will) go on. Organizers of social movements quickly imitate successful innovations, and each new group has been able to draw on the experience of its predecessors.

The clientele for such groups has come from a growing and increasingly *well-educated and affluent middle class,* people with a surplus of money or time to invest in causes that excite them strongly enough to discourage free riding. *Technological innovations*—computerized mass mailings, 800 numbers, fax machines, the Internet—have made it easier and cheaper than ever before for entrepreneurial leaders to establish and maintain organizations that have a large number of geographically scattered and socially unconnected members.

Successful groups inspire *opponents* as well as imitators. Corporate and business leaders whose interests were threatened by the political gains of environmental and consumer groups organized to defend themselves. Legislation that added to their regulatory burden and threatened the bottom line was a powerful stimulus to political action by industries and firms. Business leaders sought as well to beef up the intellectual case for their side by financing think tanks dedicated to promoting conservative ideas and policies—among them the Hoover Institution, the American Enterprise Institute, the Heritage Foundation, and the Cato Institute.[16]

The most important part of the dynamic behind the expanding interest group universe, however, has been the *encouragement of the federal government* itself. In addition to stimulating the organization of business interests, the growing scope of government activity has encouraged the proliferation of organizations in the nonprofit and public sectors:

The growth, during the twentieth century, of public schools, parks and forest preserves, agricultural research stations, public hospitals, and social welfare agencies of all kinds stimulated the creation of numerous professional associations made up of the providers of these new public services. *These groups often were created at the suggestion of public officials who realized the political value of organized constituents working to promote their programs from outside of government* (emphasis added).[17]

Prominent examples include business groups such as the U.S. Chamber of Commerce and the Business Roundtable, which were created under the leadership of secretaries of commerce in, respectively, the Taft and Nixon administrations; the American Farm Bureau Federation, which developed from a network of official advisory committees to the U.S. Department of Agriculture's county agents; and the National Organization of Women (NOW), a leading feminist organization. Indeed, the women's movement itself was jump-started by the government. In the early 1960s the Kennedy administration sponsored legislation that encouraged the creation of a Commission on the Status of Women in every state. Later, a series of conferences on women's issues were held, funded by both the state and federal governments. In 1966 some delegates to the annual meeting of State Commissioners on the Status of Women, frustrated by how their status as government officials limited their ability to take political action, sought a voice by founding the National Organization for Women.[18]

The federal government also has contributed to the proliferation of interest groups through the tax code. Many groups qualify as nonprofit organizations, which are exempt from most taxes, and donors may deduct contributions to some kinds of nonprofit groups from their taxable income. The government also subsidizes the mass mailings of nonprofit groups through special postal rates. These groups do face some restrictions on their political activity, however; they may educate, but they are not supposed to lobby openly or to engage in partisan electoral politics. The philanthropic foundations that fund many advocacy groups are themselves creatures of tax policy; rich people and families put their assets into foundations as a legal way to avoid income and inheritance taxes. Administrations also subsidize some politically favored organizations by hiring them to conduct studies or carry out specific projects. Groups thrive in good part because public policy has encouraged them to thrive.

Finally, although discussions of pluralist politics commonly assume that government programs emerge in response to interest group demands, in reality it often is the other way around: interests (and interest groups) arise in *defense of government programs*. Typically, groups benefiting from government programs get organized and active only after the programs are in place. For example, most of the potent groups defending the interests of elderly people emerged after the enactment of Social Security (1935), Medicare (1965), and the Older Americans Act of 1965; AARP did not become the five hundred-pound gorilla of American politics until these programs were in place to defend.

With or without the deliberate instigation of government officials, new policies create constituencies ripe for organization. People who adapt their plans to existing policies (on tax credits for capital investments, for example) develop a stake in continuation of the policies. And it is easier to mobilize people to defend what they already have than to pursue the more doubtful prospective benefits they do not yet enjoy—that is, the threat of loss is a more powerful spur to action than the hope of gain.[19] In general, the more the government does, the more incentives it creates for organized political action. For example, the Telecommunications Act of 1996 restructured a complex industry that accounts for one-seventh of the entire U.S. economy. It provoked intensive lobbying because its potential economic consequences were so numerous and so large.

Fragmentation and Specialization

The expanding interest group universe also reflects the fragmentation of old interests and the growing division of labor among groups sharing the same broad goals. New organizations form when new issues pull old groups apart; increasingly complex issues and fragmented policy processes force groups to specialize to be effective. Meanwhile, as links between diverse problems have become

more transparent, a wider range of organized interests has pushed into formerly isolated issue domains.

Farm policy, for example, was for many years the exclusive domain of the farm bloc, an alliance composed of a handful of interest groups (most notably the American Farm Bureau Federation), farm program officials from the U.S. Department of Agriculture, and members of Congress from the farm states who sat on the House and Senate agriculture committees and the appropriations subcommittees that handled farm programs. Today, more than two hundred organizations attempt to shape agricultural policy in a far more diffuse policy environment. Commodity groups (representing, for example, growers of wheat, cotton, corn, soybeans, rice, sugar beets, and peanuts, as well as producers of milk, honey, beef, chicken, and wool) have been joined by groups concerned with nutrition, food safety, international trade, food processing and distribution, environmental quality, farm credit, and the welfare of rural residents. A study of 130 of these groups found that only one in six pursued a broad agenda; the rest addressed only a narrow range of policy issues in their chosen niches.[20]

The environmental domain also has spawned a variety of specialized organizations. Some groups concentrate on specific issues: Ducks Unlimited, for example, focuses on saving wetlands; the Friends of the Earth specializes in Third World environmental problems; the Wilderness Society lobbies to protect and expand wildlands; and Greenpeace works to save the whales and other sea mammals. Other groups are tactical specialists: the Natural Resources Defense Council litigates; the Sierra Club educates and mobilizes its grassroots constituency in behalf of environmental causes; and the League of Conservation Voters is best known for its forays into electoral politics (see box, "The Return of the Dirty Dozen," p. 445). The niches filled by other environmental groups are expressed in their names: Grand Canyon Trust, National Park Foundation, Platte River Whooping Crane Trust, and Committee for Environmentally Effective Packaging.

Specialization responds not only to changes in the external environment but also to organizational imperatives. To survive, an interest group must convince its individual or institutional backers that their continued investment is worthwhile. To do so, it must distinguish itself from similar outfits competing for the same constituency by showing that its contribution is unique. Most groups survive by staking an exclusive claim to leadership and expertise on a particular subset of issues. To avoid mutually destructive poaching, potential competitors for the same constituency reach informal accommodations, deferring to each other's issue turf.

For over a century interest groups have reenacted this scene to show that their interest commands grassroots support. In this 1995 "media event" the U.S. Public Interest Research Group delivers to Capitol Hill petitions signed by 1.2 million citizens opposed to proposed congressional changes in environmental policy.

An interest group's health is not threatened by its opponents; indeed, as we saw earlier in this chapter, powerful opponents often invigorate a group. It is in greatest danger from similar groups appealing to the same supporters. This problem makes the formation of coalitions tricky. Groups often have to form alliances to succeed politically, but to be submerged in a coalition threatens the loss of a group's special identity. Thus many groups are reluctant to participate in coalitions and join them only on a temporary basis for specific purposes.[21] Nonetheless, groups with common interests—and no fear of losing their separate identities—do sometimes form new groups that are, in effect, standing coalitions. An example is the Consortium of Social Science Associations, whose members include the American Political Science Association, American Sociological Association, American Economic Association, American Anthropological Association, and a half-dozen other professional social science associations. This coalition was formed to combat the drastic cuts in funding for social science research proposed during the first year of the Reagan administration. More than a few of the organizations listed in *Washington Representatives* are coalitions of other groups that are

themselves representatives of institutions. There is even a National Association of Business Political Action Committees (NABPAC), representing about 120 business PACs that themselves represent corporations and trade associations. NABPAC advises its members on membership, fund raising, and candidates, and testifies in defense of PACs in congressional hearings on campaign finance legislation.

What Do Interest Groups Do?

What do all these interest organizations spend their time doing? For most, the first objective is not political influence but simple survival. Interest group leaders keep their organizations in business by cultivating and retaining patrons willing to pay the bills or supply other essential resources. This activity not only absorbs a great deal of time and energy, but also strongly shapes a group's political activity. Organizations that survive on small contributions from a mass membership, for example, have no choice but to focus on the issues that keep contributions coming in. Common Cause, which initially advocated a broad range of civic reforms, has spent much of its time in recent decades agitating for campaign finance reform because the issue always tops the list when members are surveyed at membership renewal time.

Lobbying groups that represent corporations and trade associations have to pass muster with executives or boards of directors who may have only a shaky understanding of political realities. As a result, group leaders may spend as much time explaining government to their patrons as they do explaining their patrons' interests to government officials. They also may spend more time engineering a consensus among patrons on what the group's policy goals should be than pursuing the goals themselves: "Representatives of the Peanut Growers Group . . . spent considerably more time agreeing on what they would contest in the 1985 farm bill than they did working to get it."[22] In short, interest group leaders and their constituents are involved in a principal–agent relationship, with all the familiar problems and challenges such relationships pose.

On a more mundane level, group officials must manage their offices—hiring and firing, assigning work, keeping staff productive and content. All of this work adds up; interest group officials spend a good deal of their time just keeping the organization going.

Insider Tactics: Trafficking in Information and Cultivating Access

Interest groups have proliferated in Washington in part because the federal government's expanded activities affect almost everything that people care about deeply, giving them plenty of reason to invest in political activities aimed at defending or extending their interests. But to do so they first must know when and how their interests are at stake, not always a simple matter in a world of complex issues and processes. Meanwhile, political decision makers, facing the same complex and uncertain world, are always hungry for information about the potential conse-

quences of different courses of action. The informational needs of politicians and interest groups create a basis for mutually beneficial exchanges. The importance of these exchanges was confirmed when officials from a representative sample of 175 organizations with Washington offices were asked to specify their most important activities: exchanging information topping the list, shown in Table 13–1.[23]

The information provided by interest groups is inherently suspect, of course, for, as government officials realize, it is intended not merely to inform but to persuade. Thus much of what goes on between lobbyists and government officials is aimed at establishing sufficient trust to permit mutually beneficial exchanges of information. For example, lobbyists spend a lot of their time just keeping in touch with the government officials—members of Congress, congressional staff, bureaucrats—who deal with their issues so they can know when their interests are at stake. Much of their work lies in responding to proposals or actions by other interests or government officials, and early warning often is essential to an effective response (see box, "Sharp Eyes"). Lobbyists gather intelligence by regularly reading newspapers and more specialized publications and talking to other lobbyists as well as to government officials. Keeping in touch facilitates cordial relations with the officials they might do business with someday. People are more inclined to listen to friends than strangers, but even mere acquaintance makes it easier to interpret, and therefore take into account, a lobbyist's pitch. Indeed, just being visible is important: *"You have to be seen.* Even if the legislators don't know who you are, if they see you often enough, they'll start to feel you belong."[24]

When an issue of concern to an interest group does arise, information is central to the effort that goes into persuading government officials to act as a lobbyist desires. Decision makers need two related types of information: technical and political. Congress, for example, cannot legislate clean air or water if it does not know how pollution is produced and how it might be reduced—tech-

Table 13–1   What Lobbying Groups Do

Activity	Percent Engaging in Activity
1. Testifying at hearings	99
2. Contacting government officials directly to present the group's point of view	98
3. Engaging in informal contacts with officials—at conventions, over lunch, and so forth	95
4. Presenting research results or technical information	92
5. Sending letters to members of the group to inform them about its activities	92
6. Entering into coalitions with other groups	92
7. Attempting to shape the implementation of policies	90
8. Talking with people from the media	89
9. Consulting with government officials to plan legislative strategy	86
10. Helping to draft legislation	85
11. Inspiring letter-writing or telegram campaigns	84
12. Shaping the government's agenda by raising new issues and calling attention to ignored problems	84
13. Mounting grassroots lobbying efforts	80
14. Having influential constituents contact their members of Congress	80
15. Helping to draft regulations, rules, or guidelines	78
16. Serving on advisory commissions and boards	76
17. Alerting members of Congress about the effects of a bill on their districts	75
18. Filing suit or otherwise engaging in litigation	72
19. Making financial contributions to electoral campaigns	58
20. Doing favors for officials who need assistance	56
21. Attempting to influence appointments to public office	53
22. Publicizing candidates' voting records	44
23. Engaging in direct-mail fund raising for the group	44
24. Running advertisements in the media about the group's position on issues	31
25. Contributing work or personnel to electoral campaigns	24
26. Making public endorsements of candidates for office	22
27. Engaging in protest demonstrations	20

Source: Kay Lehman Schlozman and John T. Tierney, *Organized Interests and American Democracy* (New York: Harper and Row, 1986), 150.

SHARP EYES

The executive director of a major trade association representing the petroleum industry noticed an announcement buried in the fine print of the *Federal Register*. The Federal Aviation Administration (FAA) was intending to issue new regulations that would require the pilots of noncommercial aircraft to file detailed flight plans. The FAA was responding to recent events: several noncommercial aircraft had gone down, and search and rescue efforts had been hampered by lack of information on the pilots' intended routes. But for the trade association director, the FAA's remedy was the petroleum industry's headache. He frantically phoned his group's members, asking them to pressure the FAA to set aside the regulation. Why? Once detailed flight plans were on record with the FAA, anyone using the open disclosure provisions of the Freedom of Information Act could learn where his member companies' planes were exploring for oil, gas, and minerals. The director's sharp eyes and rapid mobilization of his member industries prevented the loss of possibly millions of dollars in secret data to their competitors.

Source: Edward Laumann and David Knoke, *The Organizational State: Social Choice in National Policy Domains* (Madison: University of Wisconsin Press, 1987), 3.

nical information. The Environmental Protection Agency cannot carry out its mandate to assure the safety of a pesticide without a great deal of technical information on the dangers it poses. Many important policy questions are fiendishly complex; government officials, wishing to avoid disastrous, costly mistakes, welcome any information that reduces uncertainty and the likelihood of nasty surprises. Knowing this, interest groups provide volumes of technical information designed to show that their preferred course of action will produce superior results and that policies they oppose will fail, cost too much, or produce new disasters.

Lobbyists are aware that just being visible in the hallways of Congress is important. Keeping in touch with key members of Congress is even more crucial. Here lobbyists and reporters crowd the hall outside a meeting of the House Banking subcommittee where members are marking up legislation.

Political information tells politicians how the people they depend on for their jobs are likely to react to alternative policies. Lobbyists, not surprisingly, take pains to point out that actions they favor will please a politician's supporters and the actions they oppose will have the opposite effect.

Since politicians know that lobbyists are advocates, when can they trust a lobbyist's information? Only when both sides expect to have a continuing relationship. A lobbyist who needs a politician's good offices on a continuing basis must maintain credibility or go out of business. If information turns out to be misleading or inflicts political damage, its source will never be heeded again.

Lobbyists do have ways of increasing the credibility of their messages. One reason they arrange for scientists or scholars to testify at congressional committee hearings is to back technical claims with evidence from more neutral sources. Testimony also allows groups to put their case into the public record, contributing to the legislative history that will guide the interpretation of laws by courts and administrative agencies. Because arranging testimony

is costly for a lobbyist, it demonstrates to members of Congress that the group represented really does care about the issue under discussion. Testimony also is a way for lobbyists to show the people who pay their bills that they are doing their jobs. Often, the same representatives of a group show up at the same subcommittee hearings and give the same testimony year after year, not because they expect to be effective but because the activity fits their job description. They are sustaining the organization, if not the cause.

The credibility of political information is enhanced when a group mobilizes its constituency as a part of the lobbying effort. Supportive letters, e-mail, phone calls, telegrams, and faxes from the districts of key members of Congress reinforces the impression that a favorable vote is in their best interests. The banking industry's successful effort in 1982 to kill a provision in the tax law that would have imposed income tax withholding on the interest earned by bank accounts is a classic example (see box, "Banks and the Interest Interest"). A representative or senator who is skeptical of messages coming from some hired gun in Washington may be convinced by evidence that some constituents care enough to put time and effort into sending the same message.

Lobbying by informing requires *access;* persuasive information does no good if it does not reach decision makers. Politicians grant access to people who can help them achieve their own goals. These people are the representatives of politically important interests in their constituencies, the supporters who help finance their campaigns, the men and women who have provided valuable information or assistance in the past—in other words, the people who can help them do what they want to do more effectively. Indeed, successful lobbying is political persuasion

BANKS AND THE INTEREST INTEREST

The 1982 tax bill included a provision requiring banks and savings and loan associations to withhold 10 percent of their customers' interest and dividends, just as employers are required to withhold a portion of employees' wages. The idea was to get at tax cheats who failed to report interest income. Bankers hated the idea, because it caused administrative headaches and might discourage depositors. Acting on their members' concerns, the American Bankers Association and the U.S. League of Savings Institutions organized a full-dress lobbying campaign in which Capitol Hill was inundated with mail urging repeal of the provision; Senate offices counted between 150,000 and 300,000 letters and postcards on the issue. Although not usually regarded as a hotbed of populism, the banking industry had the advantage of routine monthly contact—the monthly statement—with everyone having an account, allowing it to get its message out quickly and cheaply. It carefully avoided correcting the widespread and mistaken assumption that the provision increased, rather than simply collected, taxes on interest and dividends (money withheld in excess of taxes owed would have been refunded after income tax returns were filed). In response, a panicky Congress quickly caved in and repealed the measure despite its bipartisan suppport from President Ronald Reagan and congressional leaders.

Source: Bill Keller, "Lowest Common Denominator Lobbying: Why the Banks Fought Withholding," *Washington Monthly* (May 1983): 32–39.

in its purest form: a lobbyist must get people to do what he or she wants them to do by convincing them that the action serves their goals.

Legislators and other government officials always have more things to do than they have time to do them. An interest group can encourage a sympathetic politician to spend time on its issue by making it cheaper (in time and staff resources) for the politician do to so. (See Table 13–1, p. 439, for some of the things lobbying groups can do to help politicians.) By helping officials plan legislative strategy, assemble legislative coalitions, draft legislation, organize hearings, and draft rules and regulations, lobbyists will not so much change minds as activate politicians already on their side by reducing the politicians' cost of getting involved.

Interest groups also can make the jobs of regulators and other bureaucrats easier. Congress usually writes general legislation, leaving decisions on the detailed rules and regulations up to the administrative agencies. The Administrative Procedures Act of 1946 requires that all such proposed rules and regulations be published in the *Federal Register* before they are promulgated and that public hearings be held on them if anyone objects (see Chapter 8). An important task of many group officials is to monitor the *Federal Register* for proposed rules that might affect their group's interests and to provide research and testimony in opposition or support.

For their part, regulators, hoping to avoid writing rules that get shot down by appeals to the courts or Congress, keep in touch with politically potent groups in the sectors they regulate. Often the relationship is formalized though the creation of advisory groups representing the relevant private interests, which can be consulted on a continuing basis. More than 875 such groups exist, including the Health Insurance Benefits Advisory Committee of the Department of Health and Human Services and the U.S. Department of Agriculture's Advisory Committee on Hog Cholera Eradication.[25] Again, the benefits are mutual. On the one hand, the interests represented on the advisory group have permanent access to decision makers, so their views are guaranteed a hearing. On the other hand, the regulators can get an early reading on the likely reaction to their proposals and maintain a conduit to the groups whose interests they affect. Interest group officials, sitting on the inside, develop a greater appreciation for technical, legal, and political grounds for regulatory decisions and may end up lobbying their own members to accept them.

Interest groups also can be valuable to bureaucrats as allies in dealing with the elected officials who control their budgets. During the cold war, for example, all three branches of the military mobilized civilian support groups to help fight the battles in Congress and, more important, with each other, for a larger share of the defense pie. The Navy League, Air Force Association, and Association of the U.S. Army lobbied vigorously for the programs and weapon systems sought by their respective services and against those of rival services. Each organization enjoyed the financial support of the defense contractors who proposed to build the weapons systems they advocated.

Outsider Tactics: Altering the Political Forces

The *insider* tactics just described depend on personal access to government officials and work through mutually beneficial exchanges between lobbyists and politicians. The *outsider* tactics employed by interest groups do not require any personal contact with politicians and may take the form of implicit or explicit threats—real pressure—rather than offers of mutually helpful exchanges. The strategy is to persuade politicians to act as the group desires by altering the political forces they feel obliged to heed.

One common tactic is use of the mass media to shape public opinion. Common Cause tries to generate support for its campaign finance reform proposals by assembling and publicizing reports on campaign contributions and spending. Think tanks regularly hold press conferences to bring attention to research reports on public issues. The Children's Defense Fund assembles and publicizes reports

on the growing level of childhood poverty to convince Congress to spend more on programs for poor children. Other groups try to get the media to buy their version of the public interest on, for example, the danger from pesticides or the incidence of breast cancer so that the threat of bad publicity will hang over the heads of politicians who oppose their demands.

Demonstrations—picketing, marches, sit-ins—are another time-honored outsider device. The principal techniques, around for centuries, were used by antislavery groups, suffragettes, and prohibitionists, but they were perfected in their contemporary form by civil rights groups in the 1950s and 1960s and have since been widely imitated by a host of social movements. Demonstrations are intended to focus public attention on the cause. Freedom marches in the South brought the issue of segregation—and the brutality of its defenders—into the homes of Americans everywhere through the then-fresh medium of television (see Chapter 4, Civil Rights). Demonstrations also may show the breadth of support for a cause. In the early 1970s opponents of the Vietnam War massed hundreds of thousands of demonstrators in Washington for this purpose. Civil disobedience—sit-ins and other demonstrations that openly violate the law—dramatizes the intensity of commitment; it is difficult to ignore a cause for which large numbers of people are willing to go to jail. Finally, demonstrations foster group solidarity—shared work and risk are powerful bonding agents—and thus may strengthen the organization.

Demonstrations are used most often by groups that do not enjoy insiders' access. They have become so common in Washington that, unless they are extraordinary in some way, the news media pay little attention. But an offbeat demonstration is still too good a story to pass up. In July 1993 reporters outnumbered the forty-five demonstrators, some claiming to have been abducted by space aliens, who picketed the White House to demand that President Clinton make "full disclosure of government UFO secrets and an open, public inquiry into the phenomena."[26]

Reports, news conferences, and demonstrations aimed

at putting issues on the agenda and compelling government officials to do something about them depend on media attention. If the news media ignore them, they fail. Private interests that wish to publicize their views without the uncertainties of relying on free coverage may, if they can afford the cost, buy advertising. Mobil Oil, for example, for many years bought a regular space on the op-ed page of the *New York Times* to express its views on public issues.

Insider and outsider strategies are not mutually exclusive, and groups may use either or both, depending on circumstances and opportunities. The banking industry employs top Washington professionals for its day-to-day insider lobbying, but in 1982 it adopted outsider tactics to fight tax withholding (see box, "Banks and the Interest Interest," p. 441). Most organizations, however, tend to specialize in one strategy or the other. Groups with money and expertise whose issues are narrow or nonconflictual usually take the insider route. Large groups whose issues are conspicuous and contentious are more likely to operate from the outside, relying on **grassroots lobbying,** a favorite tactic of such groups. For example, when the National Rifle Association wants to prevent new restrictions on firearms, its members shower Congress with letters, e-mail, faxes, and telegrams supporting its position. The intended message is that people who care enough to write on an issue care enough to vote for members of Congress according to their stance on the issue. Members of Congress discount patently stimulated mail—that is, hundreds of identically worded letters may count for less than a handful of spontaneous, original messages. Indeed, some supposedly grassroots efforts, particularly those run by firms specializing in the business, are so patently artificial that they are dismissed as "Astroturf campaigns."

This is not news to the organizations that use this tactic, so some contrive to make the process seem more personal and less mechanical. Using modern computer technology, some groups provide appropriate letters that vary in wording, typeface, and styles of stationery; members need only sign and mail them. Others ask members to use

Congress Must Choose: Big Tobacco or Kids?

The tobacco industry is counting on its friends in Congress to kill or water down tough legislation that would protect kids from tobacco addiction.

America's kids are counting on Congress to do the right thing in this important fight.

Tobacco vs. Kids. Where America draws the line.

CAMPAIGN for TOBACCO-FREE Kids™

To learn more, call 800-284-KIDS or visit our web site at www.tobaccofreekids.org.

The National Center for Tobacco-Free Kids
1707 L Street NW, Suite 800, Washington, DC 20036

© 1998, National Center for Tobacco-Free Kids

During the debate in 1998 on a bill to tax and regulate tobacco, this ad appeared in an issue of the CQ Weekly. It reminded members of Congress how challengers for their seats would portray a vote against the bill, which was supported by the ad's antitobacco sponsors. The tobacco industry hit back. Its $40 million television campaign in thirty of the nation's fifty top media markets attacked the bill as a big-government tax grab. The tobacco industry won; the bill did not pass.

their own words but to emphasize suggested themes. Members may be urged to write in longhand, even to use colloquial grammar, to make messages seem more authentic.

Outsider tactics differ from insider tactics because they impose real pressure, even threats—sometimes veiled, sometimes not—pushing politicians to act in ways they otherwise would prefer not to. Politicians, then, are far more resentful of **outsider lobbying** tactics than of insider ones. Indeed, such tactics can backfire when overdone; the pose of "standing up to pressure" has its political attractions, after all.

Litigation

Litigation is one tactic equally available to insiders and outsiders. Interest groups snubbed by lawmakers or regulators may seek redress in court, challenging hostile laws or regulations. This strategy is especially attractive to groups that can rest claims on constitutional rights and that do not have the political clout to influence elected politicians. During the 1940s and 1950s, when many African American citizens were effectively denied the right to vote and there was only limited public sympathy for their cause, civil rights groups used the courts extensively (see Chapter 4). People in jail or accused of crimes, unpopular religious minorities, and groups on the political fringe—none of whom are likely to be championed by officials who depend directly on voters for their jobs—have all found redress in court. But then so have General Motors, Exxon, and Microsoft. Despite the notable court victories of some groups on the margins of society, large corporations with deep pockets make the most frequent and effective political use of litigation.

Although about one-third of the Washington representatives of interest groups are lawyers, only a small proportion of interest groups list litigation as their predominant activity. Using the courts to good purpose often requires winning legislative battles in the first place. For example, environmental groups, notably the Environmental Defense Fund, have been able to use the courts effectively because the National Environmental Policy Act (1969) was deliberately designed to make it easy for private citizens to go to court to enforce environmental regulations (see the discussion of *standing* in Chapter 8).

Electoral Politics and Political Action Committees

Both outsiders and insiders use electoral politics to influence elected officials, but insiders offer electoral help, while outsiders more commonly threaten electoral harm. Groups unhappy with current policy always can try to replace the current decision makers with friendlier ones by recruiting and financing challengers, but this tactic is used mainly by partisan or ideological organizations. For example, GOPAC, chaired by Georgia Republican Newt Gingrich from 1986 to 1994 when he became House Speaker, nurtured the political careers of many of the Republican freshmen elected to the House in 1994. More typically, though, groups monitor and publicize the voting records of elected officials on their key issues. The idea is to identify friends and enemies so that campaign contributors and voters sympathetic to the group know which politicians to reward and which ones to punish (see box, "The Return of the Dirty Dozen"). Interest groups act most conspicuously in electoral politics, however, through political action committees.

As noted in Chapter 11, modern election campaigns are unavoidably expensive. Candidates who are not independently wealthy have to rely primarily on private individuals and political action committees to pay the bills. In their modern form, PACs are a creation of the Federal Election Campaign Act (FECA) of 1971 (as amended in 1974). FECA encouraged groups to form PACs by clarifying their legal status and specifying rules under which they could legitimately participate in financing campaigns; it also put the financial activities of PACs on the public record. To qualify as a *multicandidate committee* (the legal term for a political action committee), a PAC must raise money from at least fifty people and contribute to at least five candidates. The maximum contribution is $5,000 per candidate per campaign, which means, in effect, $10,000—$5,000 each for the primary and general election campaign (plus another $5,000 if there is a primary runoff in states where one is required when no candidate wins more than half

LOGIC OF POLITICS

THE RETURN OF THE DIRTY DOZEN

During the 1970s an environmental lobby, Environmental Action (EA), compiled and publicized a list of the "Dirty Dozen," twelve members of Congress who supposedly had the worst environmental records (according to EA's standards). The group shrewdly targeted members who were vulnerable as well as objectionable. In elections from 1972 through 1980, twenty-four of the fifty-two who made the list (some more than once)

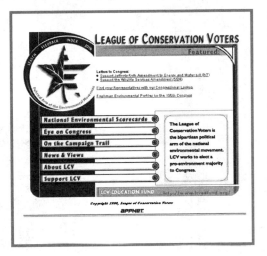

were defeated—a striking record when compared with the 90-percent-plus success rate of incumbents during the period. A consultant who worked on the campaigns claimed that the tactic "was very effective at making congressmen think twice about certain votes. There were numerous examples of members or their staff calling and saying, 'Is the congressman close to being on the list?' or 'Is this vote going to be used to determine the list?'"[1]

The group's later campaigns were less successful as it ran out of vulnerable targets, and it faded away. But another environmental alliance, the League of Conservation Voters (LCV), revived the tactic for the 1996 and 1998 elections, again with considerable success. Seven of the twelve

incumbents initially targeted in 1996 were defeated (three of them not until 1998), and nine of their "baker's dozen" of thirteen 1998 targets lost. Three of the 1998 losers were incumbents; four were representatives trying to advance to the Senate, one was a state legislator, and one was former representative Bob Dornan, who was trying to recapture the California district he lost in 1996. Like Environmental Action, LCV deliberately targeted close races where its investment—$2.3 million for field organizers, mailings, broadcast ads, and get-out-the-vote activities in 1998—had a reasonable chance of paying off. Its goals were both to defeat objectionable candidates and to demonstrate the perils of opposing environmental interests. The tactic's potential was underlined by Dornan's reaction to being listed. The flamboyant conservative, with a career LCV environmental support score of about 10 on a 100-point scale, said, "In my heart, I'm a Greenpeace kind of guy."[2]

1. Bill Keller, "The Trail of the Dirty Dozen," *Congressional Quarterly Weekly Report,* March 21, 1981, 510.
2. *League of Conservation Voters,* <http://www.lcv.org/dirtydozen/callahan_poststmt.htm> (June 3, 1999).

the votes cast). By contrast, individuals may contribute only $1,000 per candidate per campaign.

Growth of PACs. The number of PACs grew dramatically in the first decade after FECA was enacted but then leveled out at about four thousand in the mid-1980s (Figure 13–1). PAC contributions to candidates (Figure 13–2) grew in a similar fashion, increasing by 377 percent be-

tween 1974 and 1986, but by only 13 percent between 1986 and 1998 (adjusted for inflation). The sharp increase in PAC activity during the first decade under the Federal Election Campaign Act and the continuing financial importance of PACs since then are at the center of a lively controversy, for PAC generosity raises the obvious question: what do PACs get in return for their contributions?

Figure 13-1 Political Action Committees, 1974–1998

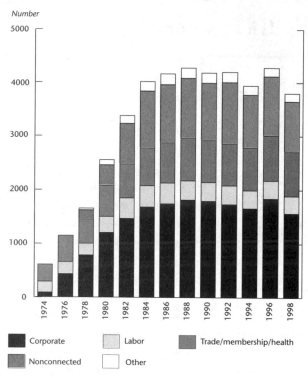

Source: Federal Election Commission.

Figure 13-2 Contributions by Political Action Committees, 1974–1998

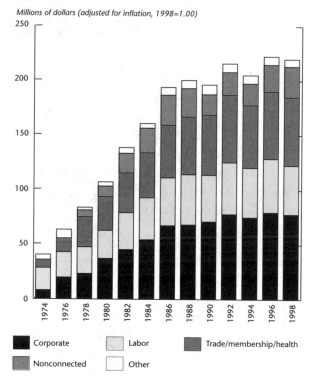

Source: Federal Election Commission.

Indeed, assaults on the legitimacy of interest groups now focus commonly on PACs.

The term *PAC* is applied to a very diverse set of organizations. The categories of PACs—labor, corporate, trade/membership/health, nonconnnected, cooperative, and corporation without stock—used by the Federal Election Commission in reporting financial activities merely hint at the variety. Some amount to little more than an entrepreneur with a mailing list; others are adjuncts of huge corporations or labor unions. Some pass out millions of dollars in every election cycle; others exist only on paper. Donations may be at the sole discretion of the PAC director or only after extensive input from the PAC's contributors. The goals of some are immediate, narrow, and self-interested; others pursue long-term objectives based on broad ideological visions. Most PACs just give money, but

a few also provide campaign workers, offer endorsements (who would not want to be regarded as a "friend of small business"?), produce advertising, advise on campaign strategies, get out the vote, and recruit and train candidates.

Although all PACs hope to influence public policy, they differ in how broadly or narrowly policy objectives are conceived and in strategies for reaching them. For many business corporations, labor unions, and trade associations, a PAC is simply an aid to traditional insider lobbying for narrowly focused economic interests. Money is given not so much to affect the outcome of the election as to gain access to and curry favor with the winner. PACs of this sort thus contribute to sure winners, to members of both parties sitting on committees dealing with legislation they care about, and to newly elected members after the election. Incumbents, already holding office and likely to retain it, naturally benefit.

At the other end of the spectrum are PACs with broad ideological agendas. Their goal is to maximize the number of seats held by people sympathetic to their views, changing policies by changing representatives rather than by persuading representatives to change policies. Thus they support promising nonincumbent candidates and concentrate their resources on close races, where the help is most likely to make a difference. Although such PACs may support friendly incumbents in tight races, they primarily adopt an outsider strategy. Examples are the Conservative Victory Committee on the right, and the Women's Campaign Fund and EMILY's List (both of which support pro-choice women) on the left.

Between the extremes are PACs that pursue both short- and long-term goals. When the Democrats controlled Congress, many business-oriented PACs supported incumbent Democrats who seemed certain to be reelected, switching to Republican challengers only when their prospects looked extraordinarily promising. Although most business groups are closer to Republicans ideologically, they were reluctant to risk access by offending Democratic incumbents when they ran the Congress. After Republicans took control after 1994, the short- and long-term goals of business PACs were more easily reconciled. Republican leaders threatened retaliation against PACs that continued to support Democrats.[27] Thus in 1994 Democrats received 54 percent of corporate PAC contributions to House candidates; in 1996 they received only 31 percent.

Some PACs also conduct independent campaigns for or against specific candidates, a practice that has become increasingly common in recent elections. For a campaign to be independent, it must not coordinate its activities with the candidate's campaign. The law does not limit independent expenditures, but they must be reported to the Federal Election Commission. In 1998, for example, 115 PACs spent a total of $9.3 million on independent campaigns for or against particular candidates, nearly twice as

Named by Roll Call, *the newspaper of Capitol Hill, one of the "50 most influential Washingtonians who work to elect Congressional candidates," Bernadette Budde is senior vice president of BIPAC, the bipartisan leadership PAC for the business-industry community. BIPAC not only donates directly to the campaigns of pro-business candidates, but also advises other corporate PACs on where to invest their contributions. It also defends PACs in congressional hearings on campaign finance reform legislation, lobbying, as it were, in behalf of lobbyists.*

much as in the previous midterm election cycle. Interest groups also may conduct "voter education" campaigns which are totally unregulated (their costs are not even reported to the FEC) so long as they do not explicitly recommend voting for or against a candidate. In 1996, for example, the AFL-CIO, the nation's leading labor organization, spent as much as $35 million on voter education drives aimed at defeating sixty-four House Republicans (conservative Christian organizations had pioneered the tactic).[28] Although still a relatively small component of campaign finance, PAC spending on independent and voter education campaigns could increase dramatically if the law is changed to further restrict PAC contributions to candidates. The Supreme Court has ruled that independent spending is protected by the First Amendment.

The PAC Dilemma. Interest groups in general and PACs in particular pose a dilemma. According to one view, PACs corrupt the entire legislative process, giving citizens "the best Congress money can buy" because members vote with an eye more to the interests of their PAC donors than to those of their constituents or the nation. PAC contributions buy votes and policy, period.[29] The evidence usually offered for this charge, however, is largely circumstantial or anecdotal. An investigative reporter or a campaign reform lobby such as Common Cause reveals that members supporting legislation desired by some interest group—milk producers, used car dealers, physicians, the banking industry, and the National Rifle Association are examples—got more campaign money from PACs representing the group than do members who oppose the legislation. Such evidence is inconclusive, however. PAC officials counter that they are merely helping to elect legislators who share their own conception of the public interest. It would be bizarre indeed if PACs distributed money randomly to friend and foe alike; no one should expect them to be that careless. The fact is, no simple matching of contributions to roll call votes or other activities can prove that PACs buy influence. More careful scholarly studies have found that PAC contributions exert, at most, only a modest effect on a legislator's decisions, most of which are shaped by party, ideology, and state or district interests. But on issues that attract little public attention and do not divide members along party or ideological lines, votes appear to reflect, in a modest way, prior PAC contributions. All things being equal, members of Congress favor interests that help finance their campaigns. But all things are not usually equal. Despite the many tales of members who vote to please financial backers or who demand money from lobbyists in return for help, there is little reliable evidence that policy is being bought wholesale by special interests.[30]

This is not to say, however, that PAC contributions do not have other effects on some members of Congress. Both members and PAC officials admit that, at minimum, contributions ensure access—a necessary if not sufficient condition for insider influence. Doors are open to lobbyists representing groups who have supported members' campaigns. Furthermore, roll call votes are by no means the only important decisions shaping legislation. Crucial choices are made before bills reach the floor, but little is known about how PACs influence the preliminary stages of the legislative process. One study did find, however, that PAC contributions stimulated committee activity in behalf of the PACs' legislative goals.[31] Interest groups are not likely to put much time, energy, and money into PAC activities without some perceived legislative payoff.

Still, there are some formidable barriers to PAC influence. Many important issues generate conflicts among well-organized interests, giving members access to PAC money no matter which side they take and thus freeing them to take whatever side is consistent with their personal or district preferences. Given the variety of sources of campaign money available to incumbents—private individuals and parties as well as the thousands of PACs—most should have little difficulty financing campaigns without putting their principles on the block. Furthermore, the point of campaigns is to win elections, not raise money. Campaign contributions are a means to an end—winning votes and elections—not the end in themselves. For incumbents, the marginal return on campaign spending is small; the prospective value, in votes, of even the maximum PAC contribution ($10,000) is tiny. Thus it makes no sense for a member, to please a PAC, to take a stand that produces even a small net loss of voter support. The sentiments of a member's constituents, when they can be estimated, far outweigh campaign contributions in determining roll call votes.

Finally, one fact, often overlooked, is that members of Congress are in a much stronger position to influence

PACs than PACs are to influence members of Congress. Like other forms of lobbying, the activities undertaken by PACs are largely defensive. They ignore invitations to fund-raisers at their peril because they risk losing access and putting the interests they represent at a competitive disadvantage. Yet for politicians, granting access is relatively cheap; it does not promise action, merely a hearing. Groups are thus "awash in access but often subordinate in influence."[32] PACs that cannot afford to say no or to offend members by funding their challengers are scarcely the powerhouses of legend.

It is important to remember that PACs are not themselves lobbying organizations, though lobbyists sometimes organize PACs to try to bolster the political clout of the interest groups they represent. In fact, PACs form a relatively small, quite specialized part of the interest group universe, and only a small portion of the money spent to influence politics passes through them. Most politically active interest groups do not form PACs at all. Rather, they use one or more of the other methods described in this chapter to influence politics. If PACs were to be abolished tomorrow, interest group politics would continue unabated.

Interest Group Politics: Controversial and Thriving

The charges levied against PACs are only the most recent variation on the enduring theme that special-interest lobbies subvert democracy and trample the public interest. Scholarly critics of mid-twentieth-century interest group politics emphasized two faults. The first was captured by Schattschneider's oft-quoted observation that in the pluralist heaven "the heavenly chorus sings with a strong upper-class accent"—that is, group representation is biased in favor of wealthy corporations and affluent individuals. The second was that rampant pluralism had let private interests abscond with public authority. The mutually advantageous "iron triangles" formed by interest groups, agencies, and congressional subcommittees allowed special interests to dominate their policy domains. Agencies established to protect the public rather than to serve a particular sector were soon captured by the very interests they were supposed to be regulating.

As we saw in Chapter 8, few observers today fret about iron triangles or captured agencies. The rise of public interest groups and the fragmentation of the interest group universe, as well as the ability of legislators to learn from past mistakes, broke up the iron triangles and liberated (or eliminated) the captured regulatory agencies. Public interest groups kept the spotlight on agencies and changed the political equation by promising political benefits (good publicity, a reputation as the defenders of citizens) to elected officials who pursued their version of the public interest and threatened political damage to those who did not. The organizational fragmentation of interest representation undermined old accommodations. The more than two hundred organizations active in agriculture policy, for example, cannot form stable, autonomous alliances with agencies and legislators.[33] Changes in the way Congress operates also contributed to the breakup of iron triangles. The legislative process has become more open and permeable; committee and subcommittee autonomy has declined, and influence over policy has become more widely distributed. There are simply too many potential players for stable subgovernments to persist.

The demise of iron triangles, however, has not ended the criticism of pluralist politics. The charge of class bias remains plausible. Some observers argue that despite the startling proliferation of lobbying organizations, the relative balance among competing interests has changed little; business organizations and other groups representing well-heeled interests still predominate. Even public interest groups represent largely upper-middle-class clienteles—well-educated people with enough discretionary income to indulge in expressive contributions to causes they deem worthy. The interests of poor people, welfare mothers, and the homeless may be represented, but only through the good offices of middle-class people and organizations presuming to speak for them.[34]

Although iron triangles no longer reign, the proliferation of groups that contributed to their demise has created problems of its own. The clamor of competing groups is blamed for policy gridlock because with many more active players, policy advocates find it harder to assemble winning coalitions. And with so many groups capable of vigorously defending themselves, some observers argue that it has become impossible to initiate any change that imposes concentrated costs to achieve general benefits even if the benefits greatly outweigh the costs.[35]

Examples of policy gridlock are plentiful. Health care reform is one; the long battle to reduce the budget deficits during the 1980s and 1990s is another. Although nearly everyone pays lip service to the ideal of a balanced budget, every spending program and every tax break are defended by organized beneficiaries, while deficit reduction, a diffuse collective good, inspires far less active organized support. Deficit reduction proved so difficult in part because any step in that direction offended some important interest, threatening immediate political retribution without producing compensating support from the broader public unaware or uncertain of the payoffs.

Yet if interest group politics produced only gridlock and maintenance of the status quo, then the airlines, airwaves, and trucking industry would never have been deregulated; major deficit-reduction packages would not have been enacted in 1990, 1993, and 1997; and tax reform would have failed in 1986. The success of the 1986 tax bill surprised almost everyone. As we saw in Chapter 6, few thought that a bill eliminating tax breaks to finance a general reduction in income tax rates would stand a chance. Nonetheless, it passed because congressional leaders fixed the legislative game to ensure that political wisdom lay in voting for reform.

The tax bill example raises a crucial point: the proliferation of interest groups has actually strengthened the hand of elected officials. Specialized, fragmented groups are more dependent on members of Congress or White House officials to build and lead legislative coalitions. Legislators control access, an essential commodity that is in ever greater demand because of the growing number of interest groups. As the real insiders, members of Congress are in the best position to know when particular interests are likely to be at stake—crucial information for lobbyists facing a political world fraught with uncertainty. Moreover, opposing groups often simply cancel one another out, leaving politicians free to pick and choose among interests according to their own personal or partisan beliefs. There are some obvious and important exceptions—not many elected officials are willing to cross AARP, for example—but most interest groups exercise little clout individually. Collectively, however, they remain enormously influential, for they are the main source of the technical and political information that shapes public policy.

Although James Madison would be astonished at the proliferation of organized "factions" in contemporary American politics, he would be the first to acknowledge the logic behind this development. The rules and institutions established by the Constitution, adapted to a drastically transformed society and economy, have made interest groups both inevitable and essential. Government distributes scarce goods and values, creating incentives for citizens to influence its decisions. Acting on their First Amendment rights, they exercise their freedom to combine and act together to pursue their interests and values through politics. The wider and the greater the impact of government decisions, the more diverse and intense is the level of interest group activity. Moreover, the more government does, the more officials need to know about the potential consequences of their choices. Elections make political information essential; complexity makes technical information essential. Modern American government could not function without the information supplied by organized interests.

Yet Madison also would be the first to recognize that factions continue to raise serious problems for American democracy. The interest group universe, though remarkably large and diverse, favors some interests at the expense of others. The resources needed to gain influence—money, access, and expertise—are distributed very unevenly. And some groups are able to overcome the barriers to collective action more easily than others. Narrow private interests thus often enjoy an advantage over broader ones.

These problems are somewhat mitigated by electoral incentives; candidates for public office rationally champion widely shared values and interests whether or not these have wealthy or well-organized advocates. The advent of many lobbying groups dedicated to some moral vision of the public good also has mitigated the problems just described. The institutional and social pluralism Madison thought would cope adequately with the "mischiefs of faction" has grown ever more luxuriant. This change has raised the specter of hyperpluralism and policy gridlock, but the fundamental source of policy stalemate is the public itself. Health care reform failed in 1994, not simply because interest groups lobbied it to death, but because no popular consensus emerged for any particular approach (see Chapter 10). Congress and the president found it difficult to balance the budget not simply because special interests defended every spending program and every tax break, but because there was no popular consensus on what combination of spending cuts and tax increases should be made to balance it (or, indeed, that balancing the budget was the most important goal of government). The conflicts among organized interests mirrored, and sometimes crystallized, divisions and uncertainties prevalent among Americans. To paraphrase Pogo, we have met the special interests, and they are us.

Key Terms

grassroots lobbying /443
insider lobbying /425
interest group /423
lobbying /423
lobbyist /422
outsider lobbying /444
Progressive Era /427
public interest lobby /425

Suggested Readings

Browne, William P. *Private Interests, Public Policy, and American Agriculture.* Lawrence: University of Kansas Press, 1988. A thorough case study of modern interest group politics focusing on the agricultural sector and showing how the proliferation of interest groups has transformed the once cozy, politics-shaping farm policies.

Herrnson, Paul S., and Ronald G. Shaiko, eds. *The Interest Group Connection: Electioneering, Lobbying, and Policymaking in Washington.* New York: Chatham House, 1998. Nineteen scholarly essays on interest group activity in Congress, the executive, the courts, and election campaigns.

Lowi, Theodore J. *The End of Liberalism: The Second Republic of the United States.* 2d ed. New York: Norton, 1979. Vigorous scholarly polemic arguing that private interest groups have taken control of bureaucratic agencies, allowing special interests to dominate policy making, thereby subverting democracy.

Moe, Terry M. *The Organization of Interests: Incentives and the Internal Dynamics of Interest Groups.* Chicago: University of Chicago Press, 1988. A critique and revision of Mancur Olson's seminal argument in *The Logic of Collective Action,* which asserts that political entrepreneurs and nonmaterial incentives often are able to solve the free-rider problem.

Olson, Mancur. *The Logic of Collective Action: Public Goods and the Theory of Groups.* Cambridge: Harvard University Press, 1965. Classic analysis of how the free-rider problem hampers organization for voluntary collective action and some of the ways it can be overcome.

Schlozman, Kay Lehman, and John T. Tierney. *Organized Interests and American Democracy.* New York: Harper and Row, 1986. A thorough account of Washington-based interest groups in the early 1980s. It concludes that the huge increase in the number of groups has not changed the balance of group power, for groups representing business interests still far outnumber their opponents.

Walker, Jack L., Jr. *Mobilizing Interest Groups in America: Patrons, Professions, and Social Movements.* Ann Arbor: University of Michigan Press, 1991. Emphasizes the role of patronage by government agencies and private foundations in organizing interests for collective political action.

Chapter 14

THE NEWS MEDIA

☆ *To what extent does the venerable label worn by the American news media as the "fourth branch" of government describe its modern role?*

☆ *Is political news a "mirror reflection" of politics in Washington, or is it better understood as a product of a political process?*

☆ *Which is the better source of news in the United States—newspapers or television?*

☆ *A news "leak" is rarely inadvertent. What advantages do politicians and others gain by leaking information to the press?*

Vietnam may have been the first "prime-time" war, but its vivid images could not match the high-tech display that transpired more than two decades later in the Persian Gulf. On the evening of January 16, 1991, television viewers throughout the world witnessed the live launching of Desert Storm, the code name for an attack on Iraq. The U.S.-led assault by a coalition of countries was sparked by Iraq's August 1990 invasion and annexation of neighboring Kuwait. American viewers did not learn about the outbreak of hostilities in the traditional way, from a presidential address, but from CNN's live coverage of the first bombs landing in Baghdad, the Iraqi capital.[1]

The opening moments of the war launched a forty-day display of cutting-edge technology by both the military and the broadcast media. American television viewers watched a laser-guided "smart" bomb enter an Iraqi mili-

tary warehouse through its chimney and then blow out the building's front door. In neighboring Israel, shortly after a live network interview with the Israeli defense minister, who insisted on wearing his gas mask in anticipation of an Iraqi attack, viewers worldwide saw the feared Iraqi SCUD missiles approaching their targets in Jerusalem. They also watched live as American Patriot missiles were launched in an attempt to intercept the SCUDs.

No less impressive was the modern satellite communications that instantaneously brought images of these events into homes throughout the world. Because of the media, the American public knew as much about what was happening in the Gulf as most key officials—even *very* high officials.[2] In the early days of the war President George Bush and his senior commanders relied on CNN's coverage from Baghdad to assess the impact of the war on Iraq and its leader, Saddam Hussein. The Pentagon,

Opening frame of one of CNN's live broadcasts from Baghdad during the 1991 Gulf War. CNN's coverage from both sides of the front to a rapt global audience made this truly a "television war" as none other.

however, was leery of having the press in the Gulf, fearing a small army of insistent reporters would get in the way and generally make themselves a nuisance. Even worse, they might inadvertently reveal troop locations and facilities, thereby assisting the Iraqi army. Military leaders also remembered how in 1968 the networks had declared the Tet offensive a total victory for North Vietnam, despite military indicators to the contrary.

Thus when troops were first dispatched to Saudi Arabia in August 1990, no news agencies had been allowed to accompany them. Only after the twenty-eight-nation containment operation, known as Desert Shield, was secure did the Pentagon allow the news media restricted access to the area. The military set up press pools—small groups of escorted reporters—to go to the front and gather news for the hundreds of journalists dispatched to the Gulf. Of the 1,400 journalists on hand, only 192 actually engaged in direct news gathering participated in any of these press pools.[3] Professional journalists, who prided themselves on

ferreting out the news and doing a better job of it than their colleagues, found themselves being spoon-fed identical second-hand information and then beaten by the wire services to filing a story. Most of them, then, were very unhappy about the little opportunity they had to compete for the attention of viewers and readers.

And there were other irritants. Without consultation, the military stipulated twelve categories of information that could not be reported without military approval, including details of major battle damage and casualties. The military's public affairs officers screened all written reports, videotapes, and photographs. Visits to troops, military installations, or the battlefront itself required special passes and military escorts. The war correspondents glumly found themselves reporting what the military told them.

A few journalists, undaunted by such tactics, tried to circumvent the military's monopoly of information by renting trucks and heading out to the desert on their own. A crew led by CBS reporter Bob Simon even managed to get captured by the Iraqis. The most notable escapee from military supervision was CNN's Peter Arnett, who remained in Baghdad and filed reports daily throughout the war. His most controversial broadcast, and one that confirmed the Pentagon's suspicions about the press's lack of self-regulation, was a live interview with Saddam Hussein in which the Iraqi leader charged that the allies had bombed an infant formula factory instead of an arsenal as claimed by the Pentagon. Clearly, Arnett was in no position to challenge Saddam's veracity, but many soldiers and ordinary citizens alike objected to Arnett giving the enemy leader rebuttal time on American television.

Tension between the press and government officials extends well beyond the military, however. In a democracy, where public opinion matters, government and elected officials must account for unfavorable news while continually seeking favorable publicity. In 1993, for example, critical press coverage of the FBI's fiery siege of a compound in Waco, Texas, occupied by a religious cult known as Branch Davidians sidetracked the careers of several senior officials who had coordinated the effort to disarm and arrest the group.

James Madison and his fellow Framers surely would have applauded this tension as in keeping with the spirit of "checks and balances." In fact, it closely resembles the strategy Madison endorsed in *Federalist* No. 51 of dispersing institutional authority in order to pit "ambition against ambition." That this relationship reflects the ethic that molded the Constitution is hardly coincidental. The Framers did, after all, explicitly provide in the First Amendment that "Congress shall make no law . . . abridging the freedom of speech, or of the press." In building a protective wall around the news media, the Framers allowed the press to exercise unfettered oversight over the actions of government officials. Indeed, the role of the press in mobilizing resistance to the British during the independence movement had established its credentials as a bulwark against tyranny. Later, Thomas Jefferson explained to a friend his rationale for listing freedom of the press at the beginning of his proposed Bill of Rights: "The basis of our government being the opinion of the people, the very first object should be to keep that right; and were it left to me to decide whether we should have a government without newspapers or newspapers without a government, I should not hesitate a moment to prefer the latter."[4]

Liberated at the outset from government regulation, the news media in America developed to its current state guided by entrepreneurs, new technologies, and market forces. The media are very much a political institution in their consequence, but they also are a profit-seeking industry in their operation. Thus one cannot fully understand their political role and effects without appreciating their dual character.

Development of the News Business

The news media are the organizations that gather, package, and transmit the news through some proprietary communications technology.[5] More than in other Western democracies, the news media developed in America as private business enterprises uncontrolled by government regulation or investment. In this setting, the production of news can be viewed in large part as the result of decisions made by economic entrepreneurs.

To characterize the news media as businesses does not impugn their integrity as suppliers of vital civic information. To the contrary, the influence of profit seeking has been in some respects highly democratic. Especially since the introduction of mass circulation and advertising, the news media have been in continual competition to increase the audiences for their news. The national broadcast networks, newspaper chains, public television and radio, and twenty-four-hour news programming on cable television all represent the kinds of entrepreneurial strategies that arise from such a pursuit.

Such strategies are strongly influenced by the era in which they are made. While editors of colonial newspapers shared the same desire to maximize profits as do modern media corporations, the constraints facing colonial actors were quite different from what they are today. The following sections will explore some of these factors—production technology, business organizations and practices, audience characteristics, and regulatory environments—and how they have evolved over time.

The Economics of Early Newspapers

In colonial times almost no one earned a living solely by publishing the news. Instead, most early newspapers were run by people in related businesses such as print shop owners and postmasters who ventured into the news business because their marginal printing and delivery costs made newspaper publishing a viable sideline.[6] Still, producing newspapers in the colonial era was an extremely expensive task. In fact, high **unit costs**—the costs of transmitting a news product to each consumer—characterized journalism in the United States until the mid-nineteenth century. Some of these costs stemmed from the nation's poor communications and transportation infrastructure. It was not unusual for newspapers to prominently feature "breaking news" that had occurred two months earlier. And poor transportation drove up distribution costs, making newspapers expensive consumer commodities throughout the colonies.

Perhaps the main source of high unit costs was the time-consuming, labor-intensive printing process. Every page had to be composed (in reverse) from individual pieces of metal type. And the act of actually printing a single impression on paper with a wooden, hand-cranked press required thirteen separate steps. The best printers of the day could only manage to print 240 impressions an hour. The printing process itself was characterized as "physically demanding work, repetitive and often dreary, usually carried on in uninviting, foul-smelling (urine was the preferred substance for soaking the leather covers of inking balls), and poorly lighted surroundings."[7]

By the mid-1770s approximately twenty-five weekly newspapers were serving the colonies. Some, such as the *Massachusetts Spy,* helped to whip up public support for independence; others opposed the notion. But this era's most significant medium of political communication was the pamphlet. During the Revolution Thomas Paine's famous pamphlet, *Common Sense* (1776), became an instant best-seller, more than 120,000 copies were sold in its first three months. Eventually, more than a half million copies were published.[8] The pamphlet was the preferred medium for good reason. More durable than newspapers, it could be passed easily from reader to reader. Where sufficient demand existed, in fact, commentaries or reporting that first appeared in a weekly paper would be republished in pamphlet form to allow wider circulation.[9]

With the emergence of the Federalist and Democratic-Republican Parties in the 1790s, commercial concerns redirected newspapers toward politics. Almost immediately the parties launched newspapers wherever they competed in order to advance their particular vision for the Republic. Objective reporting had little place in these party organs. Instead, their pages advocated party platforms, promoted candidates, and attacked the opposition.[10] These party-sponsored newspapers did not attract large audiences. According to one estimate, during the first few decades of the Republic the number of subscribers held steady at approximately four thousand, most of whom were likely voters.[11] The laws of supply and demand could not be defied for the long term, however; the papers had to be subsidized by the parties. And, when possible, party politicians turned to the government for subsidy in the form of printing contracts or appointment of newspaper editors as local postmasters.[12]

Thus newspaper publishers depended on their party sponsors. They knew that if their paper lacked sufficient partisan fervor, their sponsor might withdraw its subsidy. Moreover, the government subsidy also might disappear if the party lost the election. Consequently, the newspapers championed their party as if their survival depended on it—because it did.

Readers were more or less incidental to this relationship except that sufficient numbers were needed to justify the party's financial support. The press, then, to establish its independence from government, would have to break its financial dependence on the political parties. Many editors probably wanted to do so, not so much to justify the Framers' faith in the press as to place their businesses on a more secure financial footing. The fortunes of a political party were a poor basis for building a business.

The Penny Press and the Rise of Advertising

A larger audience was the main alternative to relying on a party subsidy. While parties were generally interested only in communicating with the party faithful, businesses had an incentive to reach a mass audience, thereby generating revenue and attracting advertisers. But market

Figure 14–1 Newspaper Circulation, 1830–1996

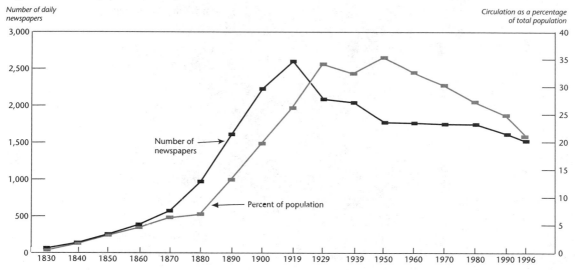

Number of daily newspapers

Circulation as a percentage of total population

Source: The figures for 1830 and 1840 are taken from Michael Schudson, *Discovering the News: A Social History of American Newspapers* (New York: Basic Books, 1978), 13–14; for 1850–1996, from Harold W. Stanley and Richard G. Niemi, *Vital Statistics on American Politics, 1997–1998* (Washington, D.C.: Congressional Quarterly, 1998), 163–164.

size depended on price, and that in turn on unit cost. Until some cheaper way to print newspapers could be found, these small businesses would be locked into low readership and party subsidies.[13]

Liberation began in the 1830s with the adaptation of steam power to printing and the development of faster, more reliable cylinder presses. These two technologies introduced dramatic economies of scale, allowing publishers to sell papers more cheaply, increase their audiences, and, in the process, split away from party sponsorship (see Figure 14–1). The *New York Sun* was the first paper to enlist this new technology, but not until several years later, in 1835 when its competitor the *New York Herald* opened its doors and followed suit, was the full potential for cultivating a mass readership realized.[14]

The *Herald* sold for a penny on the newsstand, while most of the competition was still wedded to six-cent, limited editions. Soon, the *Herald*'s readership was twice that of its nearest competitor and advertising revenues soared.

The success of the "penny press" depended on more than price, however. To attract new readers, the *Herald* and the dozen imitators that soon surfaced in the nation's larger markets expanded the realm of the news to include human interest stories and coverage of crime, business, and social events. Not only did the space devoted to party politics decrease, but coverage became muted so that papers could appeal to as diverse a readership as possible.[15]

Competition for a mass readership became even more intense at the end of the nineteenth century. Screaming headlines and sensational stories tempted newsstand browsers. Critics of these devices, many of whom worked for competing papers, derided these papers as "yellow journalism," a reference to the yellow ink in which the *New York World*'s comic strips were printed.[16] These criticisms impressed publishers around the country less than the huge circulations and profits megapublishers like Joseph Pulitzer and William Randolph Hearst were accumulating (see box, p. 459). From 1870 to 1900 the cir-

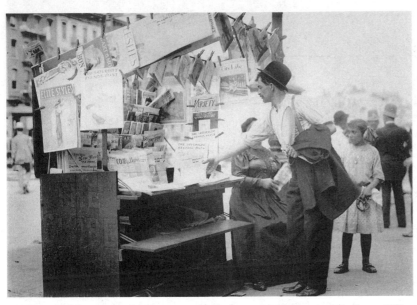

By the turn of the century, the American public had a wealth of print news media available.

culation of the nation's daily newspapers grew sixfold, from roughly two and a half to over fifteen million. By 1904 there were twelve million readers of Sunday papers.

As publishers established successful newspapers in one city, they would try to repeat their success elsewhere. The result was the emergence of the great modern newspaper chain. Building on the success they enjoyed after launching the *Detroit Evening News* in 1873, the brothers James and E. W. Scripps went on to establish newspapers in Cleveland, St. Louis, Cincinnati, and elsewhere. Scripps owned nine daily newspapers in 1900 and twenty-two in 1910. But it was Hearst who built the largest chain. By 1935 he owned twenty-four daily newspapers and sixteen Sunday newspapers from New York to Los Angeles. Indeed, at one point he could boast that nearly one in four people in the country read one of his newspapers.[17] Hearst bought his first paper to boost his political aspirations, and critics would charge that the same motivation accompanied every subsequent acquisition as well.

Like Hearst, newspaper publishers and editors discovered that their freedom from party control enabled them to influence public opinion and, in turn, national politics. And few were reluctant to assume their weighty civic responsibility as opinion leaders. The transformation of newspapers into instruments of mass communication meant that politicians frequently found themselves genuflecting to powerful editors and publishers.[18]

In many ways the period between 1883 and 1925 was the golden age of newspapers. They essentially held a monopoly over mass communication; national political news proceeded through their pages or not at all. Moreover, the publishers and editors who ran the chains relished the power their monopoly conferred. Reflecting the interests of a mass market, these newspapers took a decidedly populist view of America's national civic life at a time when few other institutions did. The most vivid demonstration of this medium's willingness to exercise its power came in 1898, when the Pulitzer and Hearst chains declared war on Spain. Shortly thereafter, Congress issued an official declaration of war. During the heat of jingoistic propaganda, the sales of the two New York papers soared to one and a half million copies a day. Citing the inflammatory rhetoric, one critic of the war dubbed the venture "Mr. Hearst's War." This sentiment was echoed by the prime minister of Spain who ruefully remarked that newspapers in America apparently had more power than the national government.[19]

Over the past half-century the extensive power of newspapers has eroded substantially. One need look no further than the declining circulation figures to appreciate the extent to which consumers have substituted radio and

A PROFILE: NEWSPAPER PUBLISHERS JOSEPH PULITZER AND WILLIAM RANDOLPH HEARST

Via different routes, publishers Joseph Pulitzer and William Randolph Hearst came to New York and competed fiercely for readers. From the innovations their rivalry fostered, the modern mass-circulation newspaper was created. Joseph Pulitzer arrived first. He had begun as a reporter for a German-language newspaper in St. Louis. After a brief stint in the state legislature, he decided his calling was that of crusading publisher. He bought a couple of ailing dailies, merged them into the present-day *St. Louis Post-Dispatch* and demonstrated that by expanding the market to the "common man," large dailies could be profitable.

With the purchase of the *World* in 1883, Pulitzer took his strategy to the most important testing ground in the nation, New York City, with its millions of recent immigrants who were not being targeted for marketing by the mainstream dailies.

William Randolph Hearst was named managing editor of the *San Francisco Examiner* in 1887 when he was only twenty-four years old. His father, George Hearst, a wealthy California investor and U.S. senator, had owned the newspaper for seven years. Eight years later, in 1895, the younger Hearst bought the *New York Journal* and challenged the *World*.

For a while, Hearst (like Pulitzer) became infatuated with holding public office. He served in the House of Representatives for two terms but gave it up to dedicate himself to "yellow journalism." Hearst's insatiable political ambition and megalomania were captured by actor, writer, and producer Orson Welles in his 1941 classic film *Citizen Kane* (see photo).

Both men used their newspapers to promote causes. Hearst's paper, like the man, was more flamboyant and erratic in its commitments. His political views vacillated from the radical left to the radical right. When he boosted Franklin Roosevelt for the Democratic Party nomination in 1932, he did so vigorously and with hyperbolic praise; his ardor was repeated a few years later when he turned against Roosevelt. Pulitzer, by contrast, employed his editorial pages (as well as the news articles themselves) to promote consistently liberal causes. Freedom of speech, personal liberty, and the excesses of "money power" were the staple of his commentaries.

In 1912 Pulitzer, in a bequest to Columbia University, established annual awards for achievements in journalism and letters. The coveted Pulitzer Prize is awarded annually on the recommendations of an advisory board at the Columbia School of Journalism.

In 1898 William Randolph Hearst's New York Journal *stirred war fever with its unsubstantiated charges that the Spanish had destroyed the U.S. battleship* Maine *in a Cuban harbor.*

television for newspapers. In 1920, the year of the first commercial radio broadcast, about 2,400 daily newspapers dotted the nation with a circulation encompassing 31 percent of the population. By 1990 one-third fewer newspapers circulated among less than one-quarter of the population. Over the same period the number of U.S. cities that had more than one newspaper dropped from 39 percent to less than 2 percent.[20] With the loss of their monopoly on the news, the formidable publisher barons—the Pulitzers and Hearsts—disappeared from the political landscape.

The Emergence of Broadcasting

In 1920 Westinghouse launched the nation's first commercial radio station, KDKA, in Pittsburgh. Within sever-

al years five hundred stations were broadcasting to an audience of two million. By 1930 just over 40 percent of all households owned radios.[21]

Although television technology was well understood by the 1930s, the television broadcast industry did not take root until the close of the Second World War in 1945. The 1950s witnessed astonishing growth, however, as the public embraced television as an essential home appliance. From 1950 to 1960 the number of local stations soared, and the television audience exploded from six to sixty million viewers, more than 88 percent of U.S. households.[22] By the end of the 1960s the penetration of televisions into America's homes was nearly complete. More households had televisions than indoor plumbing.

The broadcast media enjoyed several advantages over newspapers. For one thing, once a broadcast station was established (and its listeners had paid the initially high cost of buying radio or television sets), the cost of delivering the news was very low (and the cost of receiving it was nil). Speed was another asset of broadcast technology. While newspapers and broadcasters received much of

Figure 14–2 Households with Radios and Televisions, Cable TV, and VCRs, 1930–1995

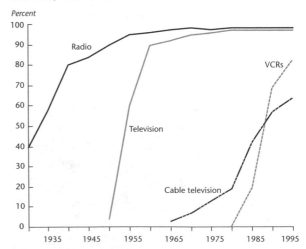

Sources: Historical Statistics of the United States: Colonial Times to 1970, Vols. 1 and 2 (Washington, D.C.: Government Printing Office, 1975), series R104, R105, and A335. Data for 1975 through 1995 are from Statistical Abstract of the United States (Washington, D.C.: Government Printing Office, 1996).

their news copy at the same time from the wire services, newspapers were constrained by their fixed publication schedule, whereas broadcast stations could update their reports throughout the day and even instantly. Finally, radio and especially television provided not only far greater immediacy and intimacy than newspapers but also greater credibility (see the section "Content" in this chapter, p. 464).

Despite its advantages, radio initially had little to do with civic affairs. During its first decade, most radio news took the form of brief on-the-hour announcements, which were welcomed by the newspapers since they believed readers would then turn to them for the "whole story." By the early 1930s, however, radio was beginning to take advertising dollars away from the papers and so was increasingly recognized as the competition. In 1933 the newspaper association organized a news boycott of radio. No longer could radio networks draw news from the papers or the wire services, which the newspaper industry effectively controlled. The boycott collapsed quickly, however, under pressure from advertisers and independent broadcasters. Within several years, any design by the print industry to keep radio broadcasting out of the news business was history.[23] As early as 1940 *Fortune* magazine survey reported that most respondents claimed to get their news mainly from the radio.

Television has continued this erosion of newspaper readership (Figure 14–3).[24] By the mid-1960s television had replaced newspapers as the preferred source of news. According to these trends, newspapers have been losing their audience at a clip of 1 percent or more each year.[25] By 1994, 72 percent of respondents were reporting that they got their news predominantly from television.

Facing a publication deadline, the Chicago Daily Tribune *took a chance on the 1948 presidential election result and got it wrong. This famous photograph of incumbent president Harry Truman, who had the last laugh on his opponent, Republican Thomas Dewey, tells the story.*

Other survey evidence suggests that the decline in newspaper readership will not be ending anytime soon. Two personal attributes traditionally associated with readership are age and education—that is, older and better-educated survey respondents consistently report stronger preferences for newspapers. One might think, then, that as American society ages and becomes better educated—both of which are occurring—Americans collectively will rely more heavily on newspapers. Yet, from the 1970s to the 1990s the percentage of survey respondents who reported reading the newspaper every day declined from 67 to 46 percent. Figure 14–4 reveals that the pattern between age and education with newspaper readership persists for the 1990s, but across every age and educational group the overall consumption of newspapers has declined. In some instances, this trend is pronounced.

Figure 14–3 Predominant News Source, 1959–1994

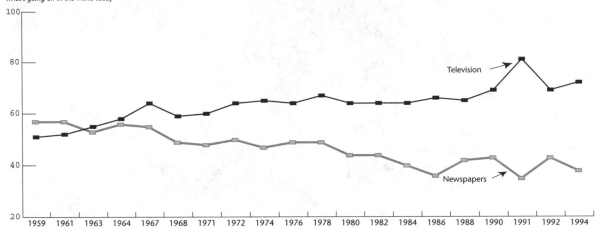

Percent identifying television or newspapers as the source for ". . . most of your news about what's going on in the world today"

Television

Newspapers

Source: Harold W. Stanley and Richard G. Niemi, *Vital Statistics on American Politics, 1997–1998* (Washington, D.C.: Congressional Quarterly, 1998), Table 4–5.

Figure 14–4 Declining Newspaper Readership, by Age and Education

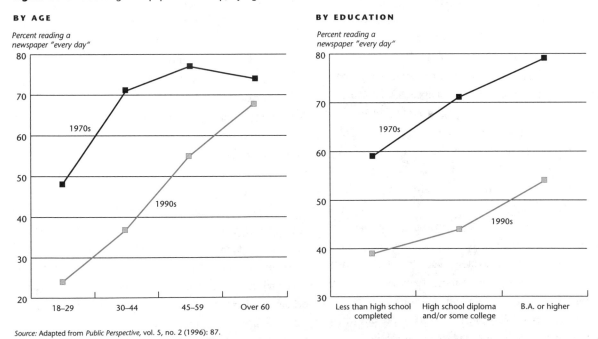

BY AGE

Percent reading a newspaper "every day"

1970s

1990s

18–29   30–44   45–59   Over 60

BY EDUCATION

Percent reading a newspaper "every day"

1970s

1990s

Less than high school completed   High school diploma and/or some college   B.A. or higher

Source: Adapted from *Public Perspective*, vol. 5, no. 2 (1996): 87.

Where 61 percent of young (under thirty), college-educated respondents in the 1970s claimed to read the paper daily, only 29 percent of the same group did so in the 1990s. The possible causes are many, ranging from the tripling of cable audiences to the growing cynicism about American politics that has dampened curiosity about public affairs.

Regulating the Broadcast Media

Unlike the newspaper industry, the broadcast industry caught the attention of government regulators. Within a few years of its inception, the profusion of radio stations was creating massive congestion problems across the radio spectrum. Stations were overcrowding desirable spots on the radio dial, causing signal interference and threatening to reduce this new medium to a tower of Babel.[26] Each station acting rationally was unable to solve this classic coordination problem. When the government became involved—to allocate stations and establish signal strengths—the door opened for more substantive regulation over programming and ownership of stations.

The Communications Act of 1934 declared the airwaves to be a public resource rather than private property.[27] Stations could be licensed to occupy a particular place on the radio spectrum, but the public retained ownership, and broadcasters were obligated to "serve the public interest, convenience and necessity." Although the law explicitly prohibited government censorship, it did not state precisely what this language required. Interpretation and implementation of Congress's intent were given to a new independent agency, the Federal Communications Commission (FCC).[28] It has, over the years, sought to preserve diversity of access to the airwaves through licensing and rule making.

Every eight years, radio and television stations must renew their licenses, giving the FCC an opportunity to review their programming. Although only a few licensees have failed to win renewal, the prospect of an embarrassing challenge obliges local broadcasters to include some public interest programming in their schedules. Over the years, the FCC also used its licensing mechanism to implement Congress's preference that a concentration of ownership be prevented. Initially, implementation took the form of a limit on the number of radio and television stations owned by an individual or corporation. With passage of the 1996 Telecommunications Act, however, Congress removed this limit. A company may own as many radio and television stations as it would like so long as it does not run afoul of FCC regulations intended to prevent domination of any local market.

More consequential for the day-to-day operation of broadcast stations is the set of "fairness" rules the FCC has promulgated over the years to ensure balanced coverage of controversial issues. The oldest of these rules, the *equal time* provision, required that a radio or television station make equal time available to all candidates for political office if it had sold or given time to one candidate. News reports and local talk shows were excluded from this provision, however. To avoid having to surrender time to a large number of candidates, stations typically gave no candidate any time, which, of course, wholly frustrated the public's interest in making informed voting decisions.[29] In 1987 the FCC acted to abolish the fairness doctrine altogether.[30] The emergence of the cable industry and the prospect of virtually unlimited programming in the foreseeable future had undermined the rationale for having such a doctrine in place.

News as a Consumer Product

In the early days of radio, scholars and others rejoiced at the coming age of an enlightened citizenry. They predicted that Americans would consume more news and draw it from a variety of sources, as if by triangulation they would gain a more accurate understanding of the true state of civic affairs.[31] As we discovered in Chapter 10, however, the availability today of virtually unlimited news programming has not yielded a better-informed citizenry.

Some news media compete for readers and viewers by offering news when it is "easier" for them to consume it. For many, the morning paper and morning coffee are inseparable. Other media compete by offering costly, but

Citizens are efficient news consumers. Many tune out political news most of the time but start paying closer attention as an election approaches. Others, such as President Lyndon Johnson, find their interests best served by high levels of daily news consumption.

Figure 14–5 Chicago's News Market

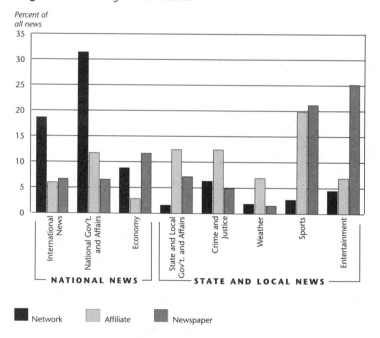

Source: Doris Graber, *Mass Media and American Politics,* 5th ed. (Washington, D.C.: CQ Press, 1997), 110–111. The study was conducted from June 1 to July 20, 1995. The news sources were ABC. CBS, and NBC national news (network); the local news of Chicago's three network affiliates (affiliate); and the Chicago *Sun-Times* and *Chicago Tribune* (newspaper). Because not all categories of news are included in this graph, the percentages across categories do not sum to 100 percent.

valuable, information. For example, some glossy, expensive magazines advertise that they hold the key to a winning investment strategy. Indeed, the modern news media offer consumers a wide array of content and form.

Content. One determinant of news content is the targeted **audience.** Because the television networks cater to a nationwide audience, they devote proportionately far more space to national and international stories than do their local affiliates, which concentrate on area events and personalities. For example, one study of the content of the news media in Chicago found that nearly half of local news programming was devoted to weather, sports, crime, entertainment, and obituaries, whereas less than 10 percent of the national news broadcasts touched on these subjects. These figures were reversed, however, on national topics such as politics and the economy.[32]

Another important determinant of news content is a medium's **carrying capacity**—the amount of information a particular communication technology can economically provide its audience. The more restricted a medium's carrying capacity, the more selective it must be in the kinds of information it offers (which also helps to explain the "division of labor" between the network and affiliate news bureaus). The carrying capacity of newspapers is much greater than that of the evening news programs of the television networks, but much less, of course, than that of an all-news cable channel. In fact, the front page alone of a typical daily newspaper contains more words than the script of the average evening news broadcast from the networks. A newspaper, then, can provide a broader array of news than the television networks and their local affiliates (see Figure 14–5 which breaks down coverage in Chicago of both national and state and local news).

Television may not offer the quantity available to a newspaper, but it does offer the immediacy and credibility captured by the adage "a picture is worth a thousand words." However sophisticated tape editors may be in selecting footage that conveys an intended message, the fact remains that television (and, to a lesser degree, radio) supplies the consumer with more "primary" data than is available in the newspaper. The video and sound images come straight from the source and allow the viewer to form his or her own interpretation of the news event. This advantage probably explains why for the past several decades survey respondents have consistently rated television news a more believable source than newspapers by margins of more than two to one.[33]

Television news stories are kept brief in part because of

the medium's limited carrying capacity, but also to minimize the cost to the marginally interested viewer in waiting for the next story. Television news editors select and present stories that are targeted to the tastes and sophistication of the "median viewer" and are framed in ways that make them more appealing and comprehensible. Along the way, abstractions and ambiguities give way to

POLITICS → POLICY

THE CRIME WAVE ON THE AIRWAVES

According to public opinion surveys in recent years, crime is one of the nation's most pressing problems, and, for many, it is only getting worse. A national survey in 1981 found 44 percent of respondents feeling "very safe" when they walked alone at night on the streets of their neighborhood. By 1997 the percentage giving this answer had fallen to 29. Other polls, asking a variety of questions about the public's fear of crime, yield similar trends.

By all objective indicators, however, actual crime is declining sharply and has been for some time. Between 1973 and 1995 federal crime statistics showed sharp declines for rape and burglary—both down 50 percent—and murder and robbery, both down by a quarter. Yet a 1995 survey found only 14 percent of respondents aware of this pronounced downward trend; 51 percent thought that crime had actually risen.

So why is there a discrepancy between how Americans feel about their personal safety and what crime statistics report they are experiencing? When one considers that two-thirds of respondents say they get their crime information from television—compared with 10 percent who report learning about crime from their own experience or that of a friend's—the answer begins to emerge. Between 1993 and 1996, when the national murder rate dropped 20 percent, network news coverage of crime soared 700 percent. Combined with the "if it bleeds, it leads" journalistic strategy of local television news, it is the crime wave on the airwaves that appears to have Americans fearing for their safety.

Source: Richard Morin, "The Airwave of Crime," *Washington Post*, August 18, 1998 (national weekly edition).

more concrete and simpler frameworks. Election campaigns are presented as "horse races" between two individuals rather than as contests between candidates who are committed to different policies. A failed public policy is attributed to the incompetence or malfeasance of individual officeholders rather than to the intractability of the problems the policy seeks to correct.[34]

While television may be fairly criticized as presenting a superficial, stripped-down representation of reality, there is evidence that for some news consumers, simpler is better. In one experiment, subjects who scored on pretests as relatively uninformed about apartheid in South Africa were found to learn more when exposed to television reports than when presented with newspaper accounts on the subject. The opposite pattern turned up for those subjects with high levels of prior information. For many of them, television only repeated what they already knew, whereas the newspaper coverage offered new information.[35] Apparently, in emphasizing new information rather than context, newspaper articles pose barriers to readers who do not already have a framework for acquiring and integrating information. This finding comports well with survey evidence that the better one's education, the more likely one is to rely on newspapers as the primary source of information.

Format. Newspapers have compensating advantages, however. Unlike a television set, a newspaper can be picked up and read at any time. Its greater carrying capacity, however, can be a mixed blessing. Readers who are highly selective in their news consumption face potentially high costs in searching through extraneous information to find the news that interests them. In recognition of this problem, newspapers organize news in ways that help readers locate those articles that interest them. Even the content of the articles themselves is structured to maximize reading efficiency. Using the "inverted pyramid" style of organization, reporters present the most important information—who, what, where, and when—at the outset so that readers can decide whether they are inter-ested in reading the entire article as its information becomes progressively more detailed.

Television newscasts are organized as a linear sequence of stories that the viewer cannot control, and the stories presented are generally much less developed and detailed than those found in newspapers. While television "pushes" stories at the audience, newspapers allow readers to skip around and "pull" out the stories they desire. Since the advent of cable television and home satellite dishes, however, viewers know that at the top of the hour they can always find the lead news stories by selecting CNN's *Headline News,* sports events by selecting ESPN, cartoons by choosing the Cartoon Network, and so on. Viewers also have some ability to control their viewing within a broadcast: prior to commercial breaks the news anchor previews upcoming stories, prompting the viewer to make an informed choice about whether to stay tuned or not.

The Politics of News Making

From 1962 until his retirement in 1981 Walter Cronkite anchored the *CBS Evening News.* During his tenure, public opinion surveys repeatedly found him to be one of the most trusted persons in the country. When Cronkite matter-of-factly closed each broadcast with his signature "And that's the way it is," the American public believed him. But is news reporting ever a simple, objective "mirror image" of reality?

Americans are accustomed to thinking about news—especially television news—in this way. But the jousting between soldiers and journalists during Desert Storm is a reminder that even momentous events come to viewers in a highly mediated form. Presumably, the soldiers and journalists each had their own vision of the "best" news viewers should receive. It is more accurate and suggestive, then, to think about news less as an objective record and more as one particular *representation* of facts and events.

Actually, most political news does not claim to report

events. One careful content analysis of two major newspapers found that barely 1 percent of politics-related news stories did so. Instead, almost all of the news examined derived from political talk intended to attract public notice. A quarter of all stories came from interviews and another 42 percent from press conferences and news releases. Altogether, individuals and organizations engaged in talk contributed two-thirds of all sources of political news.[36]

Political talk assumes many forms—from official declarations to press releases to "off the record" conversations with a reporter over lunch. Politicians undertake these activities because it is important to their success. As naturally garrulous as elected officeholders may appear on camera, political purpose lies behind all of their efforts to make news. They may be simply trying to garner favorable publicity or to build public support for their position on some issue. Frequently, the ultimate target of their efforts is not the public but other politicians in Washington. But whatever the strategy underlying their public utterances, they must in every instance persuade a reporter that what they have to say is worth transmitting to an audience.

Earlier chapters noted some of the many news-making activities undertaken with specific purposes in mind—activities such as publication of *The Federalist,* interest groups' Web sites and newsletters to their members, the selection of Birmingham and Selma as sites for major civil rights demonstrations, campaign advertising, and Rose Garden bill-signing ceremonies by presidents. In each of these instances, someone—James Madison in one instance, the Reverend Martin Luther King Jr. in another—made news in order to influence the preferences of the public and, ultimately, the positions of other leaders.

That the great majority of political news derives from talk does not necessarily diminish its status as news or its value to the audience. Much of what specialists and officials have to say is invaluable to a public trying to make sense of a particular set of facts. For example, a scientist publishes a paper offering a new explanation for acid rain; the chairman of the Federal Reserve Board interprets the latest economic indicators at a congressional briefing; the head of a local housing agency announces a critical shortage of shelters for the homeless. In deciding to portray the gravity of a problem and in selecting the information to disclose—including whether to disclose it at all and when—these experts and officials are using the news media to achieve some political purpose.

The fact that most news begins with talk reveals another distinguishing characteristic. Unlike television commercials produced by inspired Madison Avenue copywriters or academic journal articles hammered into submission by solitary professors, news does not spring forth as the product of a single actor or set of collaborators. Rather, it is the joint product of two independent actors, frequently competing with one another to define the story. As they engage each other in an enterprise of news making, they do so to achieve different and frequently incompatible goals. Politicians seek to influence the course of political events and thus want any news story to cast them and their positions on the issues in the most favorable light. Those in the business of reporting the news must keep a keen eye on their audience's interest in the proposed story and the willingness of their readers or viewers to rely on their news organization over that of a competitor. In doing so, reporters find it pays to demonstrate independence from their political sources so that the consumers of their work will appreciate their value in uncovering the real story and not simply passing along what politicians would like the public to know. The relationship between politicians and reporters, then, is built on a tension between reciprocity and competition. Occasionally, unhappiness over the other side's performance erupts publicly in charges and countercharges. Politicians typically complain that the news media are biased and uninformed; reporters may charge that they, or the news, are being manipulated.

In a very real sense, then, politicians and reporters

President Theodore Roosevelt has been generally credited with introducing the trial balloon to the presidency. He would try out an idea on a reporter, but if it backfired he would deny the story and denounce the reporter. In these early days of White House correspondents, the president held the advantage in the relationship.

engage in politics. In both this relationship and politics, as defined in Chapter 1, participants work cooperatively to achieve their own separate goals. The final product of their efforts—whether a public policy or a news story—reflects the ideal preferences of neither but is an acceptable course of action for both. The sections that follow look more closely at why and how politicians seek to influence the news, as well as the goals and techniques reporters and their news organizations bring to this relationship. We will then examine their strategic interaction —that is, the politics of making the news.

News Makers: Politicians and Public Officials

When politicians engage in news making they usually have one or both of two audiences in mind: the public or fellow politicians. Although elected officeholders are always on the lookout for ways in which to improve the public's estimate of their service, much of their news-making activity is really an attempt to communicate with other politicians rather than to merely grandstand before the public. The reason is simple: public statements can at times get their colleagues' attention and force a response when a private communication will not. In 1993 the leader of the congressional Black Caucus called a press conference to declare that just because almost all of its members were Democrats, President Bill Clinton should not take for granted the caucus's support for his proposed welfare reforms. Surely they had said this repeatedly to the president and his staff, but, by going public, they placed him on notice that to disregard their views might damage his support with the African American community. Similarly, when a president threatens publicly to veto legislation nearing a floor vote in Congress, the threat gains credibility by virtue of its publicity. If Congress were to pass the legislation anyway and the president did not follow through with a veto, he or she would suffer a damaged reputation both on Capitol Hill and with the public.

Every elected politician in Washington has a press secretary on staff to generate favorable news about the boss.

The president's press secretary probably has the biggest job of them all, befitting the importance of public opinion to modern presidential leadership. The institutions within which these politicians serve are designed to offer them numerous occasions to generate favorable news. Members of Congress can, among other things, conduct public hearings, publicly state their positions on issues on the floor of their chamber in front of C-Span's cameras, and insert speeches and press releases into the *Congressional Record*. Every time presidents step outside the White House they are trailed by the White House press corps, looking for a story in a presidential speech, an appearance in a elementary classroom, or even a foray into a department store to shop. In 1994 President Clinton lobbied Congress almost daily to pass his health care legislation, but his lobbying was not limited to phone calls, invitations to the White House, or instructions to his staff to work the corridors of Congress. The president devoted several days each week to traveling around the country and speaking on the need for health care reform. He and his advisers knew that presidential travel assured the network television coverage required for him to keep this issue in the news and before a reluctant Congress.

One venerable news strategy employed by politicians to transact politics with one another is the *trial balloon*. A politician "floats" a policy or some other idea with a reporter on the condition that the source of the story remain anonymous. If the story containing the proposal elicits a favorable response from others in Washington, the politician then publicly announces the proposal. Presidents often float trial balloons by persuading a member of Congress to propose a policy, allowing the president to gauge the political breezes before committing to a course of action.

Another discreet news-making strategy equally available to presidents, members of Congress, and lesser government officials is the news **leak.** This political term, listed in Noah Webster's 1832 American dictionary, arises when strategically consequential information is given to the news media on the condition that its source not be identified by name. The "leaker" may be targeting the communication to the public or to other politicians or both. The most common leaks involve a source saying something good about themselves or something bad about someone else.[37] An interesting variant that appeared more than once during the massive leaking that accompanied the recent Clinton White House sex scandal was the "inoculating" leak. Independent counsel Kenneth Starr, who was investigating the affair between the president and White House intern Monica Lewinsky, denied serving as the source of leaks and instead blamed the president's staff for releasing unfavorable information both to impugn his office and to minimize any future damage when the information became public. The president's lawyer, David Kendall, vigorously challenged this assertion, arguing instead that the independent counsel's office was engaged in an ongoing campaign of leaks (see box, "The Language of Leaks"). Indeed, earlier, in 1997, when the Senate was holding hearings on Clinton's campaign fund-raising practices, a representative of the White House literally "stood outside the hearing room door reminding reporters most of what they were hearing had already been reported because [Independent Council Starr] had leaked it months ago."[38]

Another class of leaks is even more ambitious than simply scoring points for oneself and against one's adversary. These leaks aim to trigger an action or response from others in Washington. On October 5, 1991, liberal staff members of the Senate Judiciary Committee opposed to the nomination of Clarence Thomas to the Supreme Court leaked part of Thomas's background check. It stated that a former Thomas employee, Anita Hill, had accused Thomas of making inappropriate sexual advances in the workplace. Hill had requested the confidentiality of the Senate Judiciary Committee, but once the story broke into national headlines, she agreed to appear on October 11 before the nationally televised Senate confirmation hearings. Four days later, the Senate narrowly confirmed Thomas's appointment to the Court.

THE LANGUAGE OF LEAKS

How do readers know a leak when they encounter it? The first telltale sign is that the reporter refers vaguely to an informant. Reporters prefer to identify their sources as accurately as possible to certify the authenticity of the information. But the specific, identifying language might have to be negotiated with the source who desires anonymity or may even wish to mislead readers into thinking another source provided the information, as in the inoculating leak. Sometimes reporters agree to this subterfuge, which means they intentionally mislead their audience in order to get the leak.

David Kendall

Kenneth Starr

The following leaks were identified in February 1998 by Clinton lawyer David Kendall in a complaint to the federal judge overseeing the performance of the Office of the Independent Counsel, headed by Kenneth Starr. The independent counsel and his staff were investigating the Clinton sex scandal involving White House intern Monica Lewinsky. The judge was sufficiently impressed that much of the information could only have come from Starr's office and thus launched an investigation into the leaks. Note in italicized phrasing the ambiguous language reporters enlist to identify their sources.

"Starr's investigators expect Lewinsky to invoke Fifth Amendment rights against self-incrimination. If she refuses to talk, Starr is likely to threaten a criminal indictment to impel her to cooperate, *people familiar with Starr's strategy* said Wednesday."

[*USA Today*, January 22, 1998]

"*Lawyers familiar with the content of some of the tapes* said that Ms. Lewinsky told of the President advising her that if anyone asked about the affair, she was absolutely to deny it. In another reported disclosure, Ms. Lewinsky told her friend that Mr. Jordan, the President's confidant, took her for a ride in his car and advised her that if she kept quiet, nobody would go to jail."

[*New York Times*, January 22, 1998]

"The tapes, *according to lawyers and others close to Mr. Starr's inquiry*, also quote Miss Lewinsky as saying that Mr.

Clinton and Mr. Jordan told her to lie about the relationship during her deposition in the Jones suit."

[*Washington Times*, January 23, 1998]

"*Sources close to Starr* describe a far different episode that dragged on mainly because Lewinsky insisted her mother be present. Although investigators did pressure her to cooperate, sources said, the onetime White House intern spent much of the time waiting for her mother to arrive . . . ."

[*Washington Post*, January 24, 1998]

"*People familiar with the investigation* said Starr is pursuing what investigators consider 'credible' indications that a Secret service agent or other member of the White House Staff saw Clinton and Lewinsky together under embarrassing circumstances."

[*Los Angeles Times*, January 26, 1998]

"However, Mr. Starr is balking at granting blanket immunity to Ms. Lewinsky until he is certain that she is a credible witness, lawyers involved in the talks say. . . . In past discussions with Mr. Ginsburg, *lawyers for Mr. Starr*, reflecting doubts about Ms. Lewinsky's reliability as a witness, have said she should take a polygraph exam before they will consider accepting her offer to tell them everything she knows. The difference over the timing of the polygraph exam has become a stumbling block to an agreement between the independent counsel and Ms. Lewinsky, *lawyers involved in the case* said today."

[*New York Times*, February 2, 1998]

"*One official involved in the discussions about whether Ms. Lewinsky would cooperate with the investigation* by Kenneth W. Starr, the Whitewater independent counsel, said prosecutors had set a deadline of Friday at noon for her lawyers to indicate whether she would talk to prosecutors. If the deadline passes without a deal, the official said, Ms. Lewinsky could face prosecution on charges of lying under oath about her relationship with the President."

[*New York Times*, February 5, 1998]

FBI director Louis Freeh's leaked memo in December 1997 endorsing the creation of an independent counsel to investigate Democratic fund raising placed him in this picture. As Attorney General Janet Reno testifies before the House Government Reform and Oversight Committee, Freeh, center, huddles with a lawyer to prepare his own testimony which followed. His presentation undermined his boss's appearance before the Republican controlled committee and questioned her decision not to authorize a probe.

In another incident in December 1997, Attorney General Janet Reno announced that the Justice Department and FBI investigation of campaign finance violations in President Clinton's 1996 reelection campaign had turned up too little evidence to warrant the appointment of a special prosecutor. Her announcement was greeted with great derision and Republican calls for her resignation because two days earlier someone at the FBI had leaked Director Louis Freeh's memo to Reno in which he maintained that sufficient evidence *did* exist to justify a probe by a special prosecutor. The leak was viewed among the local political *cognoscenti* in the bureau's effort to disassociate itself from the attorney general's decision and the criticism that would surely follow.

Reporters and Their News Organizations

Both the broadcast and print news outlets rely heavily on the talents of their reporters and correspondents, who work directly with politicians and other sources in uncovering stories and following leads. Sometimes, a close relationship with a source will allow the reporter to scoop a story for his or her news organization or gain an exclusive interview.

The role of reporter is so pivotal to making news that a professional creed has grown up around the job and sets its members apart from others who work in the news business. Reporters make the initial decisions as to the newsworthiness of a story and may play the chief role in defining the context or framework within which the story will be eventually reported. Within their organizations, reporters may act as a story's sponsor; "selling" a story to the editor is a venerable challenge and source of journalistic pride.

The advent of twenty-four-hour news outlets has put new pressure on reporters for television all-news cable networks such as CNN to "feed the monster," as they call it, with a steady stream of reports, interviews, and observations by the pundits. For print reporters, all-news television compounds their struggle to find fresh news. By the time their newspaper is opened in the morning their readers will already have witnessed the same news on television. The reporter's dilemma becomes his or her publisher's dilemma as readers increasingly discover they can dispense with reading the paper altogether.

The Beat. Both the newspapers and broadcast media cover the regular sources of important stories in a systematic fashion by permanently assigning reporters to certain venues, traditionally called **beats.** At the national level, regular news beats include the White House, Congress, the Supreme Court, and the State Department. Moreover, during political campaigns reporters are assigned to cover each of the major candidates. Every campaign organization in turn assigns staff members to serve as the reporters' contacts. At the White House, reporters receive much of their information at the daily briefings conducted by the president's press secretary. In fact, nearly all government agencies and senior officials have press staffs who are responsible for providing the media with information. More often than not, these are the agents who initiate "news" by issuing a statement or talking with a reporter.

The beat system has several important implications for news. Because news organizations rely on a continuous flow of stories, beat reporters routinely file a story every day or so, regardless of its newsworthiness. The president is a favorite subject for daily reporting; rarely will a national news broadcast omit mention of the president, even if only to report a golf score. Recognizing reporters' need for material, the office of the White House press secretary supplies them with favorable copy and ample photo opportunities.

If a particular government agency is not on a beat, it is less likely to generate news. In the late 1980s a major scandal was uncovered at the Department of Housing and Urban Development in which an undersecretary awarded government subsidies and consulting contracts as political favors. Although the scandal involved many clear violations of the law and millions of dollars, the story first broke in an obscure trade journal devoted to housing issues. The national newspapers and networks had failed to assign a correspondent to monitor HUD, but this specialized journal had. Beats allow news organizations to work efficiently and their agents in the field to specialize in a particular sector of the government. But they also steer the news toward sometimes-trivial events while missing more important ones.

Another implication of the beat system is that reporters for rival publications and networks tend to write about the same limited range of events. Moreover, while on the beat they are in daily contact with other correspondents whom they regard more as colleagues than as competitors. The White House press corps are members of an organized club that has been in continuous operation for over a half-century. Given the close proximity in which reporters on the same beat work, news reports emanating from a particular beat tend to be very similar across newspapers and even across the news media. Occasionally, these social dynamics create a conspicuously narrow or skewed representation of an event. On such occasions, critics charge reporters with practicing **pack journalism.**

Selecting the News. To accommodate their various carrying capacities, the news media must exercise discretion in allocating time and space to news stories. The media employ various criteria in deciding which stories to include in their papers and broadcasts. The first criterion is the authority and status of the source. Like no other politicians, presidents command the front pages of the nation's press and the lead stories of the network evening news programs. Far behind are the Senate and its members who edge out members of the House of Representatives.[39] A secondary consideration, according to some media observers, is the number of "talking heads," which might explain why the less populous Senate does better than the House. The rest of Washington is normally relegated to wire service stories (Associated Press, Reuters, UPI) which may or may not make the inside pages of the nation's newspapers.

A second criterion is level of controversy: conflict and controversy are preferred to consensus. In their efforts to sell stories to editors and in their news organizations' competitive efforts, the news media often create controversy where it does not exist. In early 1995 Speaker Newt Gingrich dressed down the press corps for refusing to cast a bipartisan meeting with President Clinton in a favorable light. After announcing that the recently elected Republican Congress looked forward to working constructively with the Democratic president, a reporter asked, "What do you think it [bipartisanship] will break down over?" Gingrich retorted, "You just heard the leaders of the Republican Party say that the Democratic president today had a wonderful meeting on behalf of America; we're

Controversy attracts the press. Above, each day of the impeachment trial dozens of reporters filled the Senate Press gallery, but six weeks later the room was almost vacant for a debate on a bill to give states latitude in spending federal school aid.

trying to work together. Couldn't you try for twenty-four hours to have a positive, optimistic message as though it might work?"[40]

A third criterion, closely related to the second, is negativity—bad news is more desirable than good news. Economic downturns attract greater news attention than rising prosperity. Similarly, the news media find far more to criticize than praise in politicians' performances. Presidents cry foul more than most, but Congress fares a little better.[41] In 1993, when asked pointedly in a press conference why he thought his popularity had dropped fifteen percentage points in only two months, President Clinton quickly shot back, "I bet not five percent of the American people know that we passed a budget . . . and it passed by the most rapid point of any budget in 17 years. I bet not one in 20 American voters knows that because . . . success and the lack of discord are not as noteworthy as failure."[42]

The systematic evidence on this issue suggests that presidents' complaints are not far off the mark. One study, which scored every evening network news statement about Presidents Bush and Clinton during the first three years of each president's administration, showed that both presidents garnered mostly negative coverage (Fig-

ure 14–6). Only for four of the twenty-four quarters did they average as much favorable as unfavorable network news. Even during the first quarter of 1991 when the Gulf War lifted Bush's Gallup poll approval rating to a record-

Figure 14–6 Television News Evaluations of Bush and Clinton

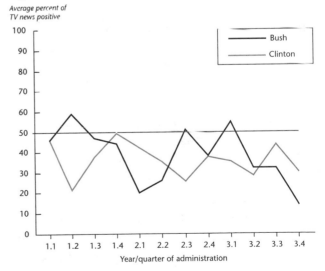

Source: Ratings based on content analysis of sound bites on ABC, NBC, and CBS evening news programs provided by the Center for Media and Public Affairs, Washington, D.C. *Note:* Clinton data are from his first term.

By one count over ten thousand government officials in Washington alone are in some way involved in press and public relations. Senate minority leader Tom Daschle (right) of South Dakota and his press secretary, Marc Kimball, are no exceptions as they confer in the Democrats' "Intensive Communications Unit," where senators conduct news media interviews.

setting 88 percent, the president still barely managed to win mostly favorable coverage. By these standards a president who musters a 40:60 ratio of favorable to unfavorable news is doing pretty well.

The news media are not a neutral conduit through which a source's message flows to an intended audience; they actively filter and interpret those messages. It is not that they have somehow seized power that should legitimately reside elsewhere. Rather, they must contend with the congestion posed by a great number of sources vying for limited news space. The number of messages proposed each day far surpasses the carrying capacity of even the most thorough newspaper. By one count, over ten thousand government officials in Washington alone are in some way involved in press and public relations on a daily

basis. And the number of trade associations and other interest groups also seeking to influence public opinion must easily surpass this number. For many would-be sources of news, the greatest barrier to success is the sheer volume of competing news stories being offered to media outlets on any news day. Moreover, as commercial enterprises, newspapers and televisions ultimately depend on audience satisfaction with the product they offer. This, too, prompts them to select and slant the news in ways that allows them to compete successfully for consumers and advertisers.

Strategic Relations between Politicians and Reporters

In many respects, relations between politicians and reporters have not changed much since the early days of the Republic when a newspaperwoman spotted President John Quincy Adams skinny-dipping in the Potomac and threatened to scream if he came out of the water before giving her an interview on his policy toward the state banks.[43] (President Adams had been hiding in the White House hoping to avoid public statements on the issue.) This amusing scene is a reminder of the tension inherent in the relationship between politicians and reporters. If they could, each side would exploit the other since each possesses (and would prefer not to surrender) something the other need. The politician needs sympathetic access to voters, and the reporter needs information that makes for a good story. Both are, in some sense, costly to obtain. No working journalist wants to appear to be a publicist for some politician. And the conveyed information that best serves the politician's purpose will rarely coincide with that coveted by the reporter. President Adams clearly thought no story at all would best suit his purposes, but the intrepid reporter caught him at an unguarded moment.

With mutual dependence blended with mutual suspicion governing relations between politicians and re-

Shortly after the 1962 California gubernatorial election, the defeated Richard Nixon held what was then termed his "last press conference." There he made bitter reference to his treatment by the press, saying they "would not have Nixon to kick around any more."

porters, these actors find themselves in a classic prisoner's dilemma. As we have seen in earlier chapters, this dilemma, which is fundamental to all political relations, has been resolved by the creation of institutions and processes to enforce commitments and nurture trust. But no such institutional development has been able to fully resolve the tension between politicians and reporters. As a result, reporters and politicians are ever mindful of manipulation by the other side. As unamused spectators to the intramural bickering that frequently surfaces between these actors, the public has demoted both politicians and reporters to the lower ranks of professional prestige. Yet this dilemma to cooperation is precisely what the Framers had in mind when they placed protection for the press immediately after freedom of speech in the First Amendment. Anyone suspicious of the concentration of government authority should applaud the wariness with which these actors engage one another.

The tension inherent to their relations does not condemn all politicians and reporters to a Machiavellian game of mutual exploitation. Some have found ways to minimize risk and thereby maximize the rewards of cooperation. Clearly for any politician, "managing the press" is a valuable skill. For example, John Kennedy, who as a senator numbered more Washington journalists than Senate colleagues among his friends, had the press eating out of his hand throughout his 1960 presidential campaign. By contrast, Richard Nixon, his opponent in 1960, stumbled from one confrontation to the next with the press. He managed to attract the enmity of many journalists on the campaign trail in 1960, and after a second defeat in the 1962 California gubernatorial race, he vented his long pent-up anger at the press as no politician had before.

The Numbers Game

As important as personality and skill are to explaining why some politicians (and reporters) are more successful than others in cultivating relations with the other side, the situations in which these actors must engage one another appear to determine their capacity to discover a cooperative solution to their dilemma. In a very real sense, both politicians and reporters find themselves in a numbers game.

When, for example, one or a few politicians control sought-after information, they will enjoy the upper hand in defining what information is reported and how it is conveyed to the audience. For their part, reporters will chaff under the concessions this unfavorable ratio imposes. Manipulation through control of access is a common complaint among reporters who cover presidential electoral campaigns.[44] Not only are they fed a bland diet of the candidate's self-congratulatory press releases, but they also soon find their individual access to the candidate for interviews and more interesting information governed by how well they treated the candidate in the previous story. The "boys on the bus" who cooperate are rewarded with access and good "copy." But those who portray the candi-

The "boys" on the bus? Women journalists occupy seats on the press bus as well. Here the audience for George W. Bush's June 1999 "campaign" appearance in Iowa creates a classic backdrop for the dozens of reporters who are chasing the candidate for a story.

date and campaign in an unflattering light soon find themselves bearing the stigma "access denied" and may even be replaced on the "beat" as their organizations seek to reestablish a conduit to news stories.

In the opening to this chapter, the press's "villain" was not a presidential candidate but the military, in another illustration of how asymmetry of control over information can define press relations. Forced to bow to military strictures on access to information about the execution of the war against Iraq, some irate reporters took matters into their own hands by heading out into the desert in rented cars. They simply found their professional predicament intolerable.

Such imbalances, however, will sometimes be reversed with too many politicians chasing too few news outlets. These adversely situated politicians will be just as unhappy as the reporters shoved to the back of the campaign

bus or the hapless CBS correspondent tearing across the desert in search of a war story. In the heyday of the newspaper syndicates, before radio news programming, politicians found themselves kowtowing to the imperious lords of the newspaper industry. In their sometimes frenzied competition for readers and advertisers, these national chains lurched from one sensational story to the next, appearing to drag politicians along with them. When Joseph Pulitzer's New York *World* and its competitors became absorbed by events playing out in Cuba in 1898 and leading up to the Spanish-American War, leaders in Washington were compelled to respond. When Congress found itself some twenty-five years later creating a regulatory environment for assigning radio licenses, members, fearful of monopoly control of news, wrote the rules carefully so that newspapers would be hampered in their efforts to extend their control over this emerging news medium.

Politician–Press Relations Then and Now

Veteran newspaper reporters sometimes wax nostalgically about the "good old days" when the print journalists ruled the news and worked closely with politicians on the basis of mutual trust and profit. The "good old days" probably never were as rosy as hindsight allows, but a look back at politician–press relations during the 1930s and 1940s does reveal much more relaxed and mutually satisfactory relations than one finds today. It was an era in which news about national politics was dominated by a small number of Washington correspondents who had organized themselves professionally to reduce cutthroat competition. These Washington fixtures cultivated close, frequently chummy, relations with the comparatively few politicians who actively sought to influence the news.

Then, as now, the president was at the center of the news media's attention. During his years in the White House, Franklin Roosevelt (1933–1945) conducted 998 biweekly press conferences with a regular group of White House correspondents. The president used these "family gatherings," as he called them, as occasions to make significant announcements. Reporters favored press confer- ences because it created a level playing field and limited competition for stories. Once when Roosevelt violated their expectations and granted an interview to a senior editor of the *New York Times,* one of their representatives chastised him at a later news conference. "My head is on the block," quipped the president in half-jest, but he promised never to do it again and for the next eight years he did not.

Reporters came to the Oval Office expecting hard news that would secure them a byline on the front page of the next day's paper. "He never sent reporters away empty-handed," reminisced one veteran, adding that cor- respondents "are all for a man who can give them several laughs and a couple of top-head dispatches in a twenty- minute visit."[45] In return they gave him and his New Deal full and generally sympathetic coverage. Both sides, then, got what they needed from their long-standing relation- ship. Two key elements to their success in finding a solu- tion to the prisoner's dilemma and working cooperatively was the community's stability and small size. The presi- dent served as an authoritative and routinely available source, and he knew them all on a first-name basis. This allowed these well-organized reporters to develop collec- tively an ongoing *quid pro quo* with the president.

Some students of the news media attribute the mod- ern era's strained relations between politicians and the press to specific events: Vietnam and Watergate. Charges of presidential manipulation became daily occurrences during the Vietnam War, which took place largely on Lyn- don Johnson's watch. Before the "credibility gap" had much chance to dissipate, the Watergate scandal broke, and eventually through the persistent efforts of reporters President Nixon was forced to resign in 1974. Both events found presidents concealing information from reporters. In 1977 Jimmy Carter moved into the White House and publicly vowed, "I'll never lie to you," which only appears to have doubled reporters' efforts to catch him in one. While these incidents surely contributed to politicians'

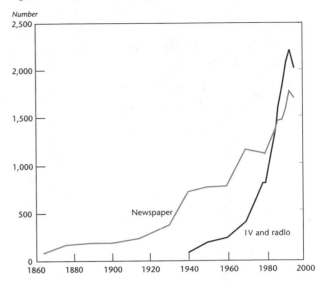

Figure 14–7   Growth of Congressional Press Corps, 1864–1995

Source: Harold W. Stanley and Richard G. Niemi, *Vital Statistics on American Politics, 1997–1998.* (Washington, D.C.: Congressional Quarterly, 1998), Figure 4–1.

Note: Press corps members are those correspondents entitled to admission to the Senate and House press galleries and radio and television galleries. Prior to 1986, the number of press corps members was recorded approximately every ten years.

modern "credibility gap" with reporters, a credibility gap of sorts is embedded in the tension between reporters' and politicians' preferred news story. Under ripe condi- tions, mutual suspicion is bound to flourish.

If the cozy relations of the earlier era reflected its set- ting, so too might the frequently stormy relations that characterize modern relations between these actors in which charges of lying, manipulation, and bias occasion- ally become topics of presidential press conferences. To- day's free-wheeling marketplace of politicians and re- porters is a far cry from the cartel-like setting once permeating politician–press relations. Present-day Wash- ington finds many more politicians engaged in political talk, trying to capture the news media's attention. To- day's Washington also contains a far larger, more diverse population of reporters who compete as much with each other as with politicians to define the news. One could

MEDIATING THE MESSAGE

From 1968 to 1988 national politicians were replaced by network correspondents as the primary ingredients of network news stories. This can be seen in the following transcripts taken from network coverage of two presidential campaigns a month before the election. In 1968 the major party candidates were Democrats Hubert Humphrey and running mate Edmund Muskie and Republicans Richard Nixon and running mate Spiro Agnew. Third party candidate George Wallace and his running mate, Gen. Curtis LeMay, received extensive coverage by the media as well. Twenty years later Democrats Michael Dukakis and running mate Lloyd Bentsen took on Republicans George Bush and Dan Quayle. Note how much longer the candidates' sound bites were in 1968. Moreover, the CBS anchor, Walter Cronkite, moderates the candidate presentations by explaining the context and issues, while in 1988 ABC anchor Peter Jennings and correspondents Sam Donaldson and Barry Serafin devote their time to relating secondhand what the candidates said and conjecturing on the political motivations of their actions.

CBS Evening News, October 8, 1968

Walter Cronkite

Walter Cronkite: Hubert Humphrey said today that the nuclear age calls for new forms of diplomacy, and he suggested regular summit meetings with the Soviet Union. He made the proposal to a meeting of the nation's newspaper editors and publishers in Washington.

Humphrey (speaks for 1 minute, 26 seconds.)

Cronkite (over video of press conference): Humphrey was asked about the battered state of the Democratic party.

Humphrey (speaks for 49 seconds.)

Cronkite: Last Thursday when he became George Wallace's running mate, retired General Curtis LeMay characterized nuclear weapons as, quote, "just another weapon in the arsenal." He made clear he did not advocate their use in Vietnam. But in his words, "I think there are many occasions when it would be most efficient to use nuclear weapons." Today at a news conference in Los Angeles the subject came up again.

LeMay (speaks for 1 minute, 29 seconds, including an exchange with a reporter at his press conference.)

Cronkite: Campaigning in Connecticut today, George Wallace appealed at one stop for, quote, "the support of people of all races and colors." And at another stop he attacked the 1968 open housing law. In Wallace's words, "when both parties joined together to destroy the adage that your home is your castle, they're not fit to run this country."

Cronkite (following commercial break): Sources close to Richard Nixon say he believes that George Wallace reached his peak last week and will decline in strength. Today Nixon stepped up his attacks on the third party candidate. Bill Plante has that story in Michigan.

Plante (over video of Nixon striding through crowd to the podium): In Flint Nixon made the same appeal as he did last week in the South, because the threat is the same: George Wallace. Several local unions here have endorsed Wallace. He divides the state enough so that Nixon and Humphrey are running almost even. Therefore Nixon's tactic is to convince the voters that a vote for him is the only real vote for change.

Nixon (speaks for 32 seconds.)

Plante (over video of Nixon shaking hands with exuberant children): Earlier Nixon brought his motorcade to a sort of scheduled unscheduled stop at the Michigan State School for the Deaf where he told the youngsters of his Aunt Olive, a missionary though afflicted by deafness, and encouraged them. The Dean interpreted his remarks.

Nixon (44 seconds): When a person may not be able to hear, then he develops other qualities. Qualities of the heart. Qualities of understanding that people who may be able to hear do not develop to the same extent. It shows you that in the world in which you will be living that your country needs you, and that what you learn here in this school will give each of you a chance to render wonderful service to this country.

ABC World Tonight, October 4, 1988

Peter Jennings: Ever since the first presidential debate turned out to be pretty much of a draw, Dukakis's campaign staff has been seeking new ways to get at Vice President Bush. Here's ABC's Sam Donaldson.

Sam Donaldson

Donaldson (over video of Dukakis rally): The Dukakis game plan has three parts. First an increasingly strident stump attack on George Bush's record by the candidate himself. Here's today's version.

Dukakis: He was asked to head up a task force on international terrorism. What happened? Mission failed. When he was asked to lead the war on drugs, we all know what happened. The mission has failed.

Donaldson: To be sure, Dukakis still talks about his own solutions to national problems.

Dukakis (talking to workers in a factory): I wanna make sure that every working family in this nation has basic health insurance. You have it here—it's terrific.

Donaldson: But more and more his stump speech is aimed at cutting Bush down.

Dukakis (in factory): They asked Bush about it; he said, "Well we're going to help the unemployed buy into Medicaid." Tell me what that means. You're unemployed, you haven't got any money, George can't buy into anything.

Donaldson (over video from Dukakis TV ad): Part two of the strategy is to run television ads aimed at undercutting Bush's own attacks on Dukakis. Actors play the part of cynical Bush advisers who try to hoodwink the voters.

Cynical Bush adviser: How long do you expect to get away with this furlough thing?

Second adviser: Hey Bernie, how long till the election? (Laughter.)

Announcer (over graphics): They'd like to sell you a package. Wouldn't you rather choose a president?

Donaldson (over video of Bush-Dukakis debate, then Quayle, then Bentsen): Part three of the strategy is to show up better in the televised debates. In this Wednesday's Bentsen versus Quayle, the Dukakis camp is counting on Bentsen to look like the heavyweight.

Campaign Chairman Paul Brountas: He knows the issues and I expect he will do a very good job.

Donaldson: This strategy, they believe, will produce a winner.

Adviser Francis O'Brien: We are making steady progress, and again, it's all the pieces fitting together.

Donaldson: The themes of this campaign have turned out to be more negative than positive. But the Dukakis people believe they can still win that way. If they can't help you like their man more, they believe they can help you like his opponent less. Sam Donaldson, ABC News, Toledo.

[A report on the Bush campaign followed. Here are a few excerpts:]

Barry Serafin: Under criticism even from some Republican party elders for not talking enough about the issues, and seeking to blunt Democratic charges of callousness, Bush unveiled a new proposal called YES, Young Engaged in Service, aimed at enlisting wealthy kids to help poor ones.

Bush: The end result, I hope, is that citizen service will become a real and living part of every young American's life.

Serafin: But by the second stop of the day . . . the vice president was back to the tried and true, the one-liners that in California, for example, have helped him erase a double-digit deficit on crime.

Bush: I support our law enforcement community.

Serafin: On education:

Bush: I will be the education president.

Serafin: And another familiar refrain:

Bush: Read my lips: No new taxes!

Source: Daniel C. Hallin, "Sound Bite News: Television Coverage of Elections, 1968–1988," in *Do the Media Govern? Politicians, Voters, and Reporters in America,* ed. Shanto Iyengar and Richard Reeves (Thousand Oaks, Calif.: Sage, 1997), 57–65.

sense this emerging reconfiguration as early as 1961, when President Kennedy conducted his first press conference on live, prime-time television. Networks news bureaus relished their new-found access to the press conference and quickly turned FDR's "family gathering" into a media event. Veteran news reporters understandably despised the intrusion of network cameras, likening it to "making love in Carnegie Hall."[46] Derision directed at modern television-based journalism remains commonplace. One White House newspaper correspondent recently characterized televised news as "souffle journalism . . . a recipe that calls for one part information mixed with two parts attitude and two parts conjecture. And after twenty-four hours or so, the analysis it contains has fallen flat."[47]

Television proved a formidable competitor for audiences and advertisers. Today, Internet appears poised to have the same impact. "An item can emerge on an Internet Web site," complained a former network correspondent, "worm its way into a late-night comedian's act, appear as a topic on the morning radio show, and catapult onto the pages of the *New York Times*—all within the space of a few hours."[48] This new, still-evolving environment is ill-suited for the cultivation of cozy politician–press relations. Rather, it is conducive to the flourishing of a prisoner's dilemma arising from competition and manipulation.

Politicians whose survival depends on successful adaptation to this altered media environment have become savvier about staging events in ways that attract the attention of television network correspondents with their huge audiences. Network reporters have responded by redoubling their efforts to control the content of the news. Among other techniques, they aggressively edit presidential rhetoric and editorialize about its purposes. They also have cut back on the amount of time allotted to the president and presidential candidates on the evening network news. As late as 1968, these politicians spoke on camera without interruption for an average of about forty seconds. Since then, however, the average presidential sound bite has dwindled to less than nine seconds.[49]

At a conference of former press secretaries and network news officials, the chicken versus the egg question was raised about the shrinking sound bite. This led to the following exchange between NBC Nightly News anchor John Chancellor and President Jimmy Carter's press secretary, Jody Powell.

Chancellor: . . . I think television reporters out in the field—when presented with pre-packaged, pre-digested, plastic coated phrases and with no opportunity to question a president—want to get something that isn't just pre-packaged and pre-digested, and that's why you are getting a more contentious kind of reporting in the twenty seconds at the end of the spot. I had an argument with [CBS correspondent] Tom Pettit during the 1988 election, and I said, "Why is it that all of our correspondents end their pieces with some little snippy, nasty saying? Why don't they just say, 'And tomorrow the president goes to Cleveland.'" And Pettit says, "It wouldn't come out that way. They would say, 'Tomorrow the president goes to Cleveland and no one knows why.'"

. . . So you compress the political propaganda on the one hand, or increase the reactive hostility on the other hand, and that's what a minute-and-a-half television spot is today. I think both sides are probably equally responsible for it, but I think that the politicians started it.

Powell: I will just raise a logical question. Assuming that there are other things to do in a White House and now and then, . . . why would you go to all of the trouble to [package the president's message] if you did not find yourself faced with a situation in which it's the way to deal with it? . . . Are we supposed to believe that one morning ten, fifteen years ago somebody in the Johnson White House or the Nixon White House . . . woke up and said, "We don't need to do this, but just for the hell of it, why don't we create this whole structure here about going out on the road and doing that sort of thing?" Or rather perhaps it was a reaction—maybe intelligent, maybe unwise, maybe in the public interest, maybe not— . . . to a set of circumstances which they saw and said, "We've got to do something."

Bypassing the News Media

This exchange raises the question of why politicians do not break out of this unproductive relationship and

How Cable Ended the Golden Age of Presidential Television

The ability of modern presidents to lead the nation has rested at times on their ability to communicate directly to the American public over national television. In the 1960s, when more households in America had a television than a toilet and all were tied to the networks via their antennas, presidents enjoyed an extraordinary entrée into America's homes. When presidents sought a prime-time slot to broadcast an address to the nation or a press conference, the networks always accommodated them. Moreover, to minimize the risk of losing their audience to another channel, the three networks—acting like a classic oligopoly—always agreed to carry the president's appearance at precisely the same time and even to share cameras so that viewers would not be tempted to change channels during the broadcast. Audience research found that almost all viewers stayed tuned, patiently watching the president and waiting for resumption of their favorite shows. Thus presidents won access to the networks' large, and largely captive audience, and the networks minimized the revenue losses incurred from interrupting their programming.

Then came cable, and this congenial arrangement between presidents and the networks fell apart. From 1970 to 1998 the share of households connected to the cable grew from 6 percent (mostly to strengthen a distant network signal) to 67 percent. During these years the cable offering grew as well, from a half dozen or so channels to over forty-five alternative channels on average. As networks attracted smaller audiences, so too did presidents (see graph).

But the problems for presidents do not end here. Ronald Reagan may have been the first to suffer the indignity of

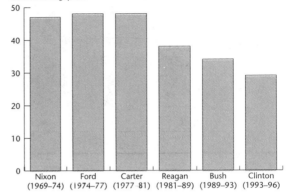

The Declining Prime-Time Audience for Presidential Addresses, 1969–1996

Percent of households with television viewing speech

Source: A.C. Nielsen Media Research and CBS Audience Research.

having a network executive inform him that his proposed address was insufficiently meritorious to deserve prime time, but every president since then has found that such a request, which once triggered automatic compliance, requires serious negotiation. After all, broadcasters opting to carry a presidential message may lose their viewers to cable channels for the rest of the evening. Thus in the absence of captive viewers, networks also now frequently rotate the obligation to air the president, further eroding the president's potential audience.

Source: Matthew A. Baum and Samuel Kernell, "Has Cable Ended the Golden Age of Presidential Television?" *American Political Science Review* 93 (March 1999): 99–114.

Sen. Joseph McCarthy, the master of props, was effective at giving the media what it needed in its earlier days. Fistfuls of papers, pointers, and maps were among the many devices he used in the fifties for his frequent "photo-ops."

communicate directly with their constituencies? As we found in Chapter 7, modern presidents are increasingly inclined to do an end run around the news media in this way. President Clinton addressed the American people every Saturday over a national radio network. And he hit the road. During each of his first three years in office Clinton averaged nearly two months of political travel during which he made over 150 public addresses a year to conferences and conventions. But frequent visits to the constituency packed with appearances and speaking engagements are nothing new. Members of Congress have been practicing direct communication for two centuries. Moreover, they have long enlisted the cutting-edge communications technology of their age. The "franking" privilege gave nineteenth-century members of Congress free access to the postal system, a device they still embrace. The modern congressional staff without a resident Webmaster is rare.

Most politicians, however, find themselves in a bind

where reliance on direct communication is too expensive and they are attracting too little news attention to get their message to voters. So most politicians "buy" as much direct communication as they can afford and chase as much news attention as their skill and position of authority permits. To that end, many of them have perfected techniques of generating favorable coverage. Presidents, for example, have long appreciated that foreign travel and visits to disaster sites generate more favorable news. Television viewers crave visual images, and savvy politicians have learned how to feed them irresistible ones. In the 1950s, anticommunist witch hunter senator Joseph McCarthy always appeared with loose sheets of paper that he could wave at any warm camera and claim they contained his list of 205 or 81 or 57 (the number changed daily) known communists in the State Department.[50] Civil rights leaders in the 1960s realized that by confronting southern segregation through often-violent television images, they could validate their claims of racism to the rest of the nation. Their success with highly telegenic passive resistance continues to inspire the media strategies of those who engage in protest.

As noted, presidents find themselves uniquely positioned among politicians in attracting news coverage. Modern communications technology affords them the possibility of becoming more self-reliant by taking their case directly to the public. At more modest levels, other politicians are following the president's lead in enlisting modern technology to substitute direct communication for mediated news. Congress has its own broadcast studios allowing members to send live television feeds to the local stations in their districts and states. Similarly, bureaucrats send out a steady stream of announcements and newsletters to their clients. Finally, the White House, most members of Congress, and virtually every interest group in Washington maintain Web sites that are being used increasingly by technophile constituents to register their questions, compliments, and complaints. The U.S.

Chamber of Commerce even created a cable channel promoting conservative causes.

Communication: Fundamental to Democracy

Democracy hinges on communication between citizens and their representatives. Through communication, citizens can check on the performance of their elective officeholders; politicians, in turn, use it to have as much influence as possible over what citizens learn about their government. Most of this communication takes the form of news. Anyone living in this era where newsroom ethics prescribe "if it bleeds, it leads" might have trouble appreciating the essential role of the news media in American democracy. Yet the Framers understood this role and thus provided in the First Amendment for a free press unfettered by government policy. In a real sense, the Framers' legacy is today's sprawling, chaotic news media shaped by the opportunities presented by technological developments and the dictates of the marketplace.

The evolution of the news media has followed the democratization of the nation itself. Beginning with the penny press in the 1830s, each new technology and each innovative business response made news cheaper and more widely available to more citizens. This trend continues as evidenced by the recent emergence of the Internet as a source of political news and an influence on all media. With the Internet, the history of technological and market innovation that began with the penny press is being reenacted in full. Emergent media continuously redefine the content of news and alter politicians' and reporters' strategies as they engage one another in its production.

Key Terms

audience / 464   leak / 469
beat / 471   pack journalism / 472
carrying capacity / 464   unit cost / 456

Suggested Readings

Ansolabehere, Stephen, Roy Behr, and Shanto Iyengar, *The Media Game: American Politics in the Television Age.* New York: Macmillan, 1993. A brief overview of news and politics, this book offers especially useful treatments of the news and information in election campaigns and reports the latest experiments in media effects on public opinion.

Bennett, W. Lance. *News: The Politics of Illusion.* 3d ed. New York: Addison-Wesley, 1995. A comprehensive discussion of the implications of present and future communications technology.

Esptein, Edward Jay. *News From Nowhere.* New York: Vintage Books, 1973. One of the first and still an authoritative consideration of how the television medium dictates news production by the networks. This book is well written and rich with observations and insights based on extensive field studies.

Iyengar, Shanto, and Richard Reeves, eds. *Do the Media Govern? Politicians, Voters, and Reporters in America.* Thousand Oaks, Calif.: Sage, 1997. This fine anthology combines social science research with journalistic introspection. Taking together, these essays offer a comprehensive survey of scholarship on politics and the news media.

Schudson, Michael. *Discovering the News: A Social History of American Newspapers.* New York: Basic Books, 1978. Perhaps the best short historical treatment of the transformation of the nineteenth-century newspaper industry. The book is historical, but the author's purpose is to discern how and why new communications technologies are adopted and in turn alter the extent and way news is presented to the public.

Underwood, Doug. *When MBAs Rule the Newsroom.* New York: Columbia University Press, 1993. As the title suggests, this is a lively and critical assessment of the news industry.

Chapter 15

THE DILEMMAS OF INSTITUTIONAL REFORM

☆ *All political institutions are, by design, biased in some way. Are the biases embodied in existing U.S. institutions systematic and cumulative, or do they offset one another?*

☆ *What does the logic of American politics tell us about the wisdom of popular institutional reforms such as legislative term limits?*

☆ *How can individual citizens participate effectively in a political system dominated by large institutions?*

On August 22, 1787, a small group of delegates at the Constitutional Convention strolled down to Philadelphia's Front Street wharf to catch a preview of the industrial revolution. From the wharf, they watched a machine noisily defying the currents of the Delaware River. According to an eyewitness, it "walked the waters like a thing of life."[1] The "thing" was one of the early prototypes of the steamboat. It was built not by the "father of the steamboat," Samuel Fulton, who was in the vicinity and may have witnessed the demonstration, but by one John Fitch. Unlike Fulton, Fitch was never able to attract the sustained financing needed to refine and manufacture his invention.

Fitch's presence in Philadelphia on that hot summer day was not a coincidence. With the encouragement of Virginia's delegates to the convention (George Washing-ton and James Madison, among others), Fitch was staging this demonstration to lure the convention into an adopting an industrial policy—namely, subsidizing his venture.[2] But the implications of the event eluded the delegates, unable, as they were, to envision the future of steam power in transportation and manufacturing. There is no mention of the demonstration in the proceedings of the convention, but, in fairness to the delegates' acumen, the boat only travelled a short distance at an estimated three miles an hour, a speed that even Fitch admitted was too slow to demonstrate its commercial value.

Even had they been able to foresee the coming industrial age, the delegates probably would not have gone down different paths at the convention. They sweated through the sweltering Philadelphia summer not to prepare for a speculative future, but to deal with the immedi-

485

ate crises that engulfed the young nation. They finally settled on an institutional framework for national government that carried some hope of remedying current problems and, equally important, of winning support across the often disunited states.

Remarkably, the core of their work has endured through more than two centuries of social, economic, and technological change far exceeding anything they could have imagined. This achievement serves as eloquent testimony to both the soundness of their political logic and the staying power of well-designed institutions. The Framers' triumph of institutional design was as much a product of good theory as of astute balancing among the competing economic and regional interests of their day. Drawing on such intellectual giants as Locke, Montesquieu, Harrington, Hume, and Newton, they thought deeply about how institutions could be arranged to induce self-interested citizens and ambitious politicians to work together for common purposes, believing, with considerable justification, that popular government would end in violent conflict and dictatorship if they failed.

Their efforts succeeded in part because the Constitution provided a framework within which a multitude of subsidiary political institutions, official and unofficial, public and private, could flourish. If we have succeeded in fulfilling the promise implicit in our title, it should be clear by now that these institutions also embody intelligible political logic. Every institution examined in the preceding chapters has been shaped by strategies for overcoming the familiar obstacles to collective action—internal conflicts, coordination and free-rider problems, excessive transaction costs—as well as for minimizing agency losses from the delegations of authority so often used to cope with these problems.

Each institution also reflects the politics of its origin, embodying the maneuvers of successful coalitions to shape future decisions to their liking. Indeed, by design

political institutions favor some groups, interests, or values over others. For example, delegates to the Constitutional Convention from the small states won the battle to have a Senate apportioned by state and coequal to the House (see Chapter 2), and to this day, the distribution formulas governing numerous federal programs favor the least populous states at the expense of the most populous ones. A century ago, upper-crust Progressive reformers changed the rules governing civil service jobs, voter registration, candidate selection, and balloting in a deliberate and eventually successful attack on the power of party machines run by leaders of "slender social distinction" (see Chapter 12). Liberal House Democrats tightened party control over conservative committee chairs in 1974 by making their selection subject to a secret caucus ballot (see Chapter 6). Arising from competition among interests for political advantage, bias affects all political institutions to some degree; they inevitably favor some segments of society over others.

The question, then, is not whether particular political institutions are biased—they certainly are. Rather, it is to what extent are their biases cumulative, imposing overarching biases on the entire political system. If the system itself *is* biased or otherwise falls short, how should ideas about how to change it be appraised? And if people decide that particular changes are warranted, what can they, as individual citizens, do to bring them about?

The answers to these questions are considered in the rest of this chapter. We begin by identifying two clear systematic biases that flow from the political institutions and practices covered in this book. Then we will look at how best to think about and evaluate proposals for revising political institutions and practices to reduce or alter these biases. Finally, we consider how individual citizens can participate effectively in a political system in which so much of the action takes place within and among large institutions.

The Bias of American Institutions

To what extent are the biases inherent in each particular institution cumulative? Certainly different institutions favor different combinations of interests, and the luxuriant proliferation of elected government bodies, administrative agencies, electoral organizations, and interest groups allows a wide range of demands and preferences to receive their due. But, while the political system remains wide open to competing influences, pluralism does not by itself guarantee that institutional biases will offset one another to achieve a roughly equitable balance. Indeed, they do not.

Collectively, American political institutions display at least two broad, enduring, systematic biases. First, American politics favors those groups that are better able to overcome their own collective action problems and that, once they do, have greater resources for pursuing political objectives. To be sure, (nearly) universal suffrage makes numbers count. Other things being equal, larger groups and more widely shared interests receive more favorable attention because ultimate government authority is held by politicians who need votes to win and keep their jobs. But all things never are equal: political resources and the capacity to act collectively are distributed very unequally. Indeed, the analyses in Chapters 10–13 revealed that groups with more money, organization, knowledge, internal agreement, skilled leadership, and moral commitment find it easier to solve their collective action problems than groups commanding fewer of these assets. And because bargaining is at the heart of politics, success in achieving political objectives depends on the skill and resources participants can bring to the bargaining table.

Success, moreover, tends to be self-reinforcing. Economic sectors able to obtain their "own" cabinet departments, such as agriculture, thereby enlist government officials to help them overcome future collective action problems. Legislation giving private persons standing to sue to enforce laws protecting the environment drastically cut the cost of pursuing certain environmental goals. The Voting Rights Act of 1965 threw the resources of the Department of Justice behind the fight against racial discrimination in voter registration.

Together, differences in bargaining resources and the capacity to act collectively introduce a detectable class bias to U.S. politics. On the whole, the preferences and values of people with greater wealth, education, social status, and links to powerful institutions count more in politics than those of people without these advantages. People in the vast middle class prevail through numbers when they are sufficiently adamant and united, as they are, for example, on the value of the Social Security and Medicare programs. But on many less-salient or consensual issues, numbers matter less, other resources more. People who are poor, uneducated, or socially marginal remain at a clear disadvantage in both resources and, compared with the middle class, numbers. Because they are harder to mobilize, their numbers count for relatively less.

This being said, the interests of the poor or dispossessed are not invariably ignored, nor do the wealthy and well connected win every time. The government spends billions of dollars on a host of services for poor people; legal segregation is no more; a progressive income tax still takes a larger share of larger incomes; and auto manufacturers lost battles against mandatory catalytic converters and air bags. But the political playing field on which these victories were achieved has never been a level one. The Framers, intent on protecting the rights of the propertied against a propertyless majority, did not design it to be level. Despite the eventual achievement of universal suffrage, the institutions they devised, combined with the uneven distribution of political resources other than votes, has kept the field tilted in favor of the people and groups at the upper end of the social and economic scale.

The American system also is fundamentally biased in favor of the status quo. Such a bias is typical of all political institutions, for they are designed, among other things, to stabilize power relationships and to make political deals durable enough for people to bother making them in the first place. But the status quo bias inherent in U.S. institutions is abnormally strong. It is not automatically a conservative bias, as Republicans have learned from two decades of failed attempts to dismantle the Department of Education. Nor does it automatically reinforce the system's upper-class bias. Rather, it is a bias against adopting new institutions and policies and in favor of preserving old ones, regardless of their ideological or class tenor. The "checks" side of the Constitution's proverbial checks and balances remains in full force because policy-making authority continues to be shared by separate institutions, within which authority also is often fragmented. Any innovation requiring legislation faces the hurdles lodged in the lawmaking process described in Chapter 6; bureaucratic agencies and federal courts also can be used to stifle change. Once in place, however, new programs and the agencies that administer them are protected by the very same lawmaking hurdles and bureaucratic obstacles. Institutions create interests, whose advocates can exploit the system's many veto points to preserve what they have won. The politicians who designed the Constitution opted for institutions that keep transaction costs high to keep conformity costs low; the system's powerful status quo bias is an enduring legacy of their handiwork.

Ironically, this unwieldy system regulates the political transactions of the most dynamic society the world has yet seen. If its political institutions favor the status quo, America's capitalist market economy, permeable borders, social fluidity, and zeal for technological change keep it under perpetual attack. A framework designed for an eighteenth-century society only beginning to imagine steamboats was not easily adapted to a twentieth-century world in which the first powered flight and the first landing on the moon could take place within the span of a single lifetime. It will be no easier adapting this framework to the political challenges posed by life in the hyperspeed, information-driven world of the twenty-first century. Because social and economic changes continually generate new problems and recast old ones, demands for institutional innovations designed to cope with them are always on the political agenda. For example, instantaneous global transmission of images, ideas, and capital has left the old regulatory regimes governing pornography, intellectual property (patents and copyrights), and banking in tatters. The question of how, if at all, elected leaders can reassert effective national authority over these domains remains unanswered, although not for want of competing ideas and proposals.

The Tricky Business of Institutional Reform

Institutional shortcomings inevitably become targets for reform; some people in every generation want to "reinvent government." Those who believe that particular rules and practices or the system as a whole slight their interests or thwart necessary changes naturally look for alternative arrangments that would redress these problems. But designing effective institutions—ones that accomplish what their designers intend—is tricky business. The political world is so densely interconnected and human beings are so clever at discovering and exploiting opportunities that the full impact of any significant institutional innovation is impossible to predict; every significant change is likely to have unintended and unwanted consequences. For example, in the early 1970s reformers who wanted to limit the impact of "special interest" money in campaigns enacted a set of rules governing the organization and activities of nonparty political committees, familiarly known as PACs. But by clearing up the cloudy legal status of such organizations, the new rules helped them to flourish, and the same reformers now view PACs as a menace. A similar situation played out after the Interstate Commerce Commission was abolished in 1995 (deregulation had eliminated its primary tasks—setting rates and allocating routes for the rail and trucking industries). People were inadvertently left with nowhere to go when they were swindled by household moving companies, and unscrupulous movers took to demanding thousands of dollars more than the contracted payment before completing delivery—in effect, holding furniture for ransom.[3]

The risk of unintended consequences is no reason to shrink from institutional change, but it does suggest the importance of thinking carefully about how proposed changes would work in practice. The (mostly Democratic) sponsors of the independent counsel law, enacted in 1978 in response to the Watergate scandal, failed signally to do so. Intent on securing independent investigation and prosecution of crimes committed by high executive branch officials, they neglected to impose adequate checks on the counsel's authority. An independent counsel was appointed by a three-judge panel on the attorney general's finding of "reasonable grounds to believe that further investigation [into misconduct by a high government official] is warranted." He or she then enjoyed an unlimited budget, unlimited time, and a potentially limitless jurisdiction, and could be fired only for "good cause."[4] Constraints, if any, were largely self-imposed. After witnessing independent counsel Kenneth Starr's sprawling $40 million, five-year investigation of Bill and Hillary Clinton (and many of their unlucky associates), culminating in exposure of the Lewinsky sex scandal and a report to the House laying out the case for impeaching the president, Democrats joined Republicans in concluding that the law was a mistake. Remarkably, even Kenneth Starr declined to defend the law when it came up for renewal in 1999, testifying that it unconstitutionally tried to "cram a fourth branch of government into our three-branch system."[5]

Some important consequences of institutional innovations *can* be anticipated. Madison certainly would have predicted that unchecked authority would eventually be abused. More broadly, any reform that alters individual incentives changes behavior in predictable ways because in politics most people, most of the time, are engaged in the strategic pursuit of transparent goals. Indeed, proposals for change that do not anticipate at least the obvious strategic responses to them are fundamentally misguided.

In enacting the independent counsel law in 1978, Congress failed to impose adequate constraints on the counsel's authority. Even independent counsel Kenneth Starr, whose $40 million, five-year investigation of Bill and Hillary Clinton led eventually to the president's impeachment in 1999, declined to defend the law when it came up for renewal the same year. The law was not renewed.

For example, proponents argue that congressional term limits would improve representation by replacing "career politicians" with "citizen legislators" closer to the people. But limiting the number of terms a member can serve would alter incentives in a way virtually guaranteed to weaken representation. After all, what quality service should principals expect from agents destined to lose their jobs on a certain date no matter how well or poorly they perform? By artificially truncating careers in office, term limits would reduce the political costs of ignoring voters' wishes and lower the payoffs for developing close ties

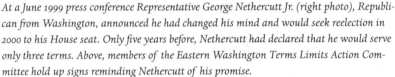

At a June 1999 press conference Representative George Nethercutt Jr. (right photo), Republican from Washington, announced he had changed his mind and would seek reelection in 2000 to his House seat. Only five years before, Nethercutt had declared that he would serve only three terms. Above, members of the Eastern Washington Terms Limits Action Committee hold up signs reminding Nethercutt of his promise.

with constituents. Rational agents would care more about pleasing prospective future principals—in other constituencies, in the executive branch, or in the private sector—than about satisfying their current principals. Term limits are therefore much more likely to degrade rather than improve representation, weakening the influence of the ordinary citizens. Indeed, term limits would not even serve the narrower partisan interests of their Republican backers now that their party has shown itself capable of winning control of Congress without them.

More generally, any institutional reform whose success requires political actors—whether politicians or independent counsels—to routinely ignore their own interests is certain to disappoint. The Framers, well informed by both theory and experience, did not make this mistake, one important reason why their work has lasted. Thus the first task for anyone intent on redesigning institutions to

produce more desirable outcomes (as they define them) is to map out how proposed changes would change incentives and thus the strategic behavior of political actors. Do the revised rules and reformed institutions tempt politicians to renege on collective pursuits when citizens would want them to cooperate, or conversely, does it invite their collusion where the citizenry's interests would best be served by healthy competition? Does the reform encourage agents to shirk or in other ways violate their responsibilities to their principals? Does it produce desirable collective goods without the large economic inefficiencies that political logic sometimes generates? By this test, many popular reforms besides term limits—including constitutionally mandated balanced federal budgets, the line-item presidential veto, and many proposed campaign finance reforms—come up short.

Effective institutional changes also acknowledge the

centrality of politics and the value of allowing political entrepreneurs to do their jobs. As we noted in Chapter 1, politics requires getting people who disagree on values and goals to agree nonetheless on common courses of action so that they can live together peacefully. The difficulty and value of doing politics successfully are easily underestimated, but the bloody civil conflicts that plague the world today serve as a reminder that politics can be a matter of life and death. Reflexive disdain for politicians and their trade is simply foolish; what deserves praise or blame is how skillfully they do their work and to what ends.

In doing politics, experience and talent help (another reason to be skeptical of legislative term limits), but appropriate institutional rules and practices are even more important. Changes that inadvertently make it harder to do politics can easily backfire on their proponents. For example, "sunshine" laws requiring political business to be done in public, a popular reform of the 1970s meant to weaken the influence of lobbyists, inhibit the give and take needed to reach agreement, for no one wants to be the first to "sell out" by suggesting compromise, especially if others cannot be trusted to follow suit (the prisoner's dilemma). Sunshine laws may even increase the influence of lobbyists; after all, they get paid to attend meetings and monitor politicians' decisions, while ordinary citizens have no material incentive to show up (a free-rider problem). We saw in Chapter 6 (Congress) how a 1986 tax reform bill that eliminated a host of special interest tax breaks to achieve a broad reduction in marginal tax rates moved forward only when negotiations were moved behind closed doors. The Constitution itself was written behind closed shutters by delegates who kept their deliberations strictly confidential.

Or consider the reforms of the presidential nominating process discussed in Chapter 12. The system now in place allows outsiders with little Washington experience and few political ties to other elected leaders to end up in the White House, where they then have to undergo an of-

ten rocky period of on-the-job training in how to deal politically with Congress and the rest of the Washington establishment. Even the best-intentioned reforms can have ill effects. Ethics rules adopted in 1995 prohibit members of Congress from accepting free meals from lobbyists. It is not clear that the new rules have reduced the influence of "special interests," but they have reduced the number of informal opportunities for members to socialize across party lines. With fewer cross-party friendships forged in the convivial atmosphere occasioned by free food and drink, partisan conflicts become more intense and intractable.

In different ways, each of these changes unwittingly raised political transaction costs, thereby reducing the prospects for successful collective action. Whether these new costs outweighed other benefits (at least to their proponents) is a question that cannot be answered here, but these examples underline the essential point that, when it comes to designing institutions, tradeoffs are unavoidable. Arrangements that make it easier to achieve some goals make it harder to achieve others. The Internal Revenue Service, for example, can take steps to be more customer-friendly or better at catching tax cheats, but not both. Members of Congress can enjoy greater latitude for participation or speedier collective action, but not both. States can be freer to adapt policies to local conditions or more accountable to national majorities, but not both. There are no institutional panaceas; transaction costs and conformity costs are always at odds, delegation is always risky to principals, some goals can be achieved only at the expense of others. Thus even if institutional changes would work as intended, reformers must always consider whether the tradeoffs they entail are worth it.

None of this is to argue against changing institutional rules and practices; indeed, there is no way to avoid innovation if people want to make any headway against old policy failures and new policy problems or to redress the system's biases. It is, however, an argument for weighing reform proposals carefully for the soundness of their political logic. What are the innovations supposed to achieve? How successful are they likely to be, given how they would alter individual incentives and affect the possibilities for doing politics? What tradeoffs do they require between conformity costs and transaction costs, and are the benefits worth the cost in these terms? It also is an argument for incremental change. Tinkering with the machinery rather than replacing it wholesale is neither glorious nor satisfying to people frustrated by the shortcomings and biases of current institutions, but it does reduce the magnitude of unintended consequences and, partly for this reason, has the advantage of greater political feasibility. Finally, reformers must remember that all institutions are indeed biased and therefore must be alert to the new biases that any change is bound to introduce. People who believe in democratic equality should be particularly skeptical of changes that might reinforce existing class biases and welcome changes that might counteract them. And those worried about policy gridlock should be especially alert to how changes would affect transaction costs.

What Can Individual Citizens Do?

As we have seen throughout this book, politics is the domain of institutions. But where does this leave individual citizens? How can they change institutions or policies they find objectionable or defend those they like against challenge? The inescapable reality is that citizens are collectively mighty but individually almost powerless. With rare exceptions, citizen action is effective only as collective action. As we have seen, however, collective action is often problematic. Because so much of politics is about the provision of collective goods, each individual has an incentive to ride free on the efforts of others. But if everyone follows the same logic (and why shouldn't they?), there are no efforts on which to ride free, and no collective goods are obtained.

The paradox of individual participation is that people can provide themselves with collective goods through politics only if they work for their provision for reasons *other* than enjoying the goods. Voting, contributing to parties or lobbying groups, writing letters to senators and representatives, marching in demonstrations, virtually any form of political action taken by individual citizens has no *instrumental* payoff to any one of them because no single participant's contribution will have a decisive effect on the outcome one way or the other. If everyone responds only to instrumental incentives (that is, just to get the right political outcome), everyone rationally rides free and there is no instrumental payoff. To get the payoff, people must pursue it for some *noninstrumental reason*— say, out of a sense of obligation to contribute one's share, or for the intrinsic satisfaction of participating, or in response to social pressure. This is why moral commitment was included as an asset in the earlier list of the advantages and disadvantages enjoyed by different groups. Ironically, when collective goods are at stake, moral incentives can produce instrumental payoffs where instrumental incentives would not.

Moral or other individual incentives are rarely enough, however. They may discourage free riding, but they cannot fully stop it; many will feel passionately but act rationally. Nor do they solve the coordination problems that inhibit collective action. Although coordination is sometimes spontaneous, as when irate French citizens converged on the Bastille as a hated symbol of the old regime at the onset of the French Revolution, sustained collective action requires the kind of coordination that only leadership and organization can provide—that is, citizens who want to participate in governing themselves have no choice but to hook up with institutions. Opportunities to do so abound. At the forefront are electoral institutions—primary and general elections and the parties active in them. But behind them are thousands of other institutions capable of coordinating action in pursuit of some collective good. It is difficult to think of any political goal to which some organization is not dedicated (see Chapter 13), but if an appropriate or effective organization is lacking, the solution is to create one. Effective collective action requires citizens either to coordinate their participation by accepting the leadership of existing organizations or to become political entrepreneurs themselves.

Why should they bother? Why not be content to ride free on the efforts of others? Because participation in politics is often fun. Because it is an opportunity to express identities and values. Because it is a way of taking part in history. Because institutions often make it easy and cheap to participate. And because when enough individuals convince themselves, against reason, that their personal participation makes a difference, collectively they do indeed make a difference.

REFERENCE MATERIAL

Appendixes

Appendix 1

DECLARATION OF INDEPENDENCE

On June 11, 1776, the responsibility to "prepare a declaration" of independence was assigned by the Continental Congress, meeting in Philadelphia, to five members: John Adams, Benjamin Franklin, Thomas Jefferson, Robert Livingston, and Roger Sherman. Impressed by his talents as a writer, the committee asked Jefferson to compose a draft. After modifying Jefferson's draft the committee turned it over to Congress on June 28. On July 2 Congress voted to declare independence; on the evening of July 4, it approved the Declaration of Independence.

In Congress, July 4, 1776,

The Unanimous Declaration of
the Thirteen United States of America,

When in the Course of human events, it becomes necessary for one people to dissolve the political bands which have connected them with another, and to assume among the Powers of the earth, the separate and equal station to which the Laws of Nature and of Nature's God entitle them, a decent respect to the opinions of mankind requires that they should declare the causes which impel them to the separation.

We hold these truths to be self-evident, that all men are created equal, that they are endowed by their Creator with certain unalienable Rights, that among these are Life, Liberty and the pursuit of Happiness. That to secure these rights, Governments are instituted among Men, deriving their just powers from the consent of the governed. That whenever any form of Government becomes destructive of these ends, it is the Right of the People to alter or to abolish it, and to institute new Government, laying its foundation on such principles and organizing its powers in such form, as to them shall seem most likely to effect their Safety and Happiness. Prudence, indeed, will dictate that Government long established should not be changed for light and transient causes; and accordingly all experience hath shown, that mankind are more disposed to suffer, while evils are sufferable, than to right themselves by abolishing the forms to which they are accustomed. But when a long train of abuses and usurpations, pursuing invariably the same Object evinces a design to reduce them under absolute Despotism, it is their right, it is their duty, to throw off such Government, and to provide new Guards for their future security. Such has been the patient sufferance of these Colonies; and such is now the necessity which constrains them to alter their former Systems of Government. The history of the present King of Great Britain is a history of repeated injuries and usurpations, all having in direct object the establishment of an absolute Tyranny over these States. To prove this, let Facts be submitted to a candid world.

He has refused his Assent to Laws, the most wholesome and necessary for the public good.

He has forbidden his Governors to pass Laws of immediate and pressing importance, unless suspended in their operation till his Assent should be obtained; and when so suspended, he has utterly neglected to attend to them.

He has refused to pass other Laws for the accommodation of large districts of people, unless those people would relinquish the right of Representation in the Legislature, a right inestimable to them and formidable to tyrants only.

He has called together legislative bodies at places unusual, uncomfortable, and distant from the depository of their Public

Records, for the sole purpose of fatiguing them into compliance with his measures.

He has dissolved Representative Houses repeatedly, for opposing with manly firmness his invasions on the rights of the people.

He has refused for a long time, after such dissolutions, to cause others to be elected; whereby the Legislative Powers, incapable of Annihilation, have returned to the People at large for their exercise; the State remaining in the mean time exposed to all the dangers of invasion from without, and convulsions within.

He has endeavored to prevent the population of these States; for that purpose obstructing the Laws of Naturalization of Foreigners; refusing to pass others to encourage their migration hither, and raising the conditions of new Appropriations of Lands.

He has obstructed the Administration of Justice, by refusing his Assent to Laws for establishing Judiciary Powers.

He has made Judges dependent on his Will alone, for the tenure of their offices, and the amount and payment of their salaries.

He has erected a multitude of New Offices, and sent hither swarms of Officers to harass our People, and eat out their substance.

He has kept among us, in times of peace, Standing Armies without the Consent of our legislature.

He has affected to render the Military independent of and superior to the Civil Power.

He has combined with others to subject us to a jurisdiction foreign to our constitution, and unacknowledged by our laws; giving his Assent to their acts of pretended legislation:

For quartering large bodies of armed troops among us:

For protecting them, by a mock Trial, from Punishment for any Murders which they should commit on the Inhabitants of these States:

For cutting off our Trade with all parts of the world:

For imposing taxes on us without our Consent:

For depriving us in many cases, of the benefits of Trial by Jury:

For transporting us beyond Seas to be tried for pretended offences:

For abolishing the free System of English Laws in a neighbouring Province, establishing therein an Arbitrary government, and enlarging its Boundaries so as to render it at once an example and fit instrument for introducing the same absolute rule into these Colonies:

For taking away our Charters, abolishing our most valuable Laws, and altering fundamentally the Forms of our Governments:

For suspending our own Legislature, and declaring themselves invested with Power to legislate for us in all cases whatsoever.

He has abdicated Government here, by declaring us out of his Protection and waging War against us.

He has plundered our seas, ravaged our Coasts, burnt our towns, and destroyed the lives of our people.

He is at this time transporting large armies of foreign mercenaries to compleat the works of death, desolation and tyranny, already begun with circumstances of Cruelty & perfidy scarcely parallel in the most barbarous ages, and totally unworthy the Head of a civilized nation.

He has constrained our fellow Citizens taken Captive on the high Seas to bear Arms against their Country, to become the executioners of their friends and Brethren, or to fall themselves by their Hands.

He has excited domestic insurrections amongst us, and has endeavoured to bring on the inhabitants of our frontiers, the merciless Indian Savages, whose known rule of warfare, is an undistinguished destruction of all ages, sexes and conditions.

In every stage of these Oppressions We have Petitioned for Redress in the most humble terms: Our repeated Petitions have been answered only by repeated injury. A Prince, whose character is thus marked by every act which may define a Tyrant, is unfit to be the ruler of a free People.

Nor have We been wanting in attention to our British brethren. We have warned them from time to time of attempts by their legislature to extend an unwarrantable jurisdiction over us. We have reminded them of the circumstances of our emigration and settlement here. We have appealed to their native justice and magnanimity, and we have conjured them by the ties of our common kindred to disavow these usurpations, which would inevitably interrupt our connections and correspondence. They too have been deaf to the voice of justice and of consanguinity. We must, therefore, acquiesce in the necessity, which denounces our Separation, and hold them, as we hold the rest of mankind, Enemies in War, in Peace Friends.

We, therefore, the Representatives of the United States of America, in General Congress, Assembled, appealing to the Supreme Judge of the world for the rectitude of our intentions, do, in the Name, and by Authority of the good People of these Colonies, solemnly publish and declare, That these United Colonies are, and of Right ought to be Free and Independent

States; that they are Absolved from all Allegiance to the British Crown, and that all political connection between them and the State of Great Britain, is and ought to be totally dissolved; and that as Free and Independent States, they have full Power to levy War, conclude Peace, contract Alliances, establish Commerce, and to do all other Acts and Things which Independent States may of right do. And for the support of this Declaration, with a firm reliance on the Protection of Divine Providence, we mutually pledge to each other our Lives, our Fortunes and our sacred Honor.

John Hancock.

New Hampshire:
Josiah Bartlett,
William Whipple,
Matthew Thornton.

Massachusetts-Bay:
Samuel Adams,
John Adams,
Robert Treat Paine,
Elbridge Gerry.

Rhode Island:
Stephen Hopkins,
William Ellery.

Connecticut:
Roger Sherman,
Samuel Huntington,
William Williams,
Oliver Wolcott.

New York:
William Floyd,
Philip Livingston,
Francis Lewis,
Lewis Morris.

Pennsylvania:
Robert Morris,
Benjamin Harris,
Benjamin Franklin,
John Morton,
George Clymer,
James Smith,
George Taylor,
James Wilson,
George Ross.

Delaware:
Caesar Rodney,
George Read,
Thomas McKean.

Georgia:
Button Gwinnett,
Lyman Hall,
George Walton.

Maryland:
Samuel Chase,
William Paca,
Thomas Stone,
Charles Carroll of Carrollton.

Virginia:
George Wythe,
Richard Henry Lee,
Thomas Jefferson,
Benjamin Harrison,
Thomas Nelson Jr.,
Francis Lightfoot Lee,
Carter Braxton.

North Carolina:
William Hooper,
Joseph Hewes,
John Penn.

South Carolina:
Edward Rutledge,
Thomas Heyward Jr.,
Thomas Lynch Jr.,
Arthur Middleton.

New Jersey:
Richard Stockton,
John Witherspoon,
Francis Hopkinson,
John Hart,
Abraham Clark.

Appendix 2

CONSTITUTION OF THE UNITED STATES

The United States Constitution was written at a convention that Congress called on February 21, 1787, for the purpose of recommending amendments to the Articles of Confederation. Every state but Rhode Island sent delegates to Philadelphia, where the convention met that summer. The delegates decided to write an entirely new constitution, completing their labors on September 17. Nine states (the number the Constitution itself stipulated as sufficient) ratified by June 21, 1788.

The Framers of the Constitution included only six paragraphs on the Supreme Court. Article III, Section 1, created the Supreme Court and the federal system of courts. It provided that "[t]he judicial power of the United States, shall be vested in one supreme Court," and whatever inferior courts Congress "from time to time" saw fit to establish. Article III, Section 2, delineated the types of cases and controversies that should be considered by a federal—rather than a state—court. But beyond this, the Constitution left many of the particulars of the Supreme Court and the federal court system for Congress to decide in later years in judiciary acts.

We the People of the United States, in Order to form a more perfect Union, establish Justice, insure domestic Tranquility, provide for the common defence, promote the general Welfare, and secure the Blessings of Liberty to ourselves and our Posterity, do ordain and establish this Constitution for the United States of America.

ARTICLE I

Section 1. All legislative Powers herein granted shall be vested in a Congress of the United States, which shall consist of a Senate and House of Representatives.

Section 2. The House of Representatives shall be composed of Members chosen every second Year by the People of the several States, and the Electors in each State shall have the Qualifications requisite for Electors of the most numerous Branch of the State Legislature.

No Person shall be a Representative who shall not have attained to the age of twenty five Years, and been seven Years a Citizen of the United States, and who shall not, when elected, be an Inhabitant of that State in which he shall be chosen.

[Representatives and direct Taxes shall be apportioned among the several States which may be included within this Union, according to their respective Numbers, which shall be determined by adding to the whole Number of free Persons, including those bound to Service for a Term of Years, and excluding Indians not taxed, three fifths of all other Persons.][1] The actual Enumeration shall be made within three Years after the first Meeting of the Congress of the United States, and within every subsequent Term of ten Years, in such Manner as they shall by Law direct. The Number of Representatives shall not exceed one for every thirty Thousand, but each State shall have at Least one Representative; and until such enumeration shall be made, the State of New Hampshire shall be entitled to chuse three, Massachusetts eight, Rhode-Island and Providence Plantations one, Connecticut five, New-York six, New Jersey four, Pennsylvania eight, Delaware one, Maryland six, Virginia ten, North Carolina five, South Carolina five, and Georgia three.

When vacancies happen in the Representation from any State, the Executive Authority thereof shall issue Writs of Election to fill such Vacancies.

The House of Representatives shall chuse their Speaker and other Officers; and shall have the sole Power of Impeachment.

Section 3. The Senate of the United States shall be composed of two Senators from each State, [chosen by the Legislature thereof,][2] for six Years; and each Senator shall have one Vote.

Immediately after they shall be assembled in Consequence of the first Election, they shall be divided as equally as may be into three Classes. The Seats of the Senators of the first Class shall be vacated at the Expiration of the second Year, of the second Class at the Expiration of the fourth Year, and of the third Class at the Expiration of the sixth Year, so that one third may be chosen every second Year; [and if Vacancies happen by Resignation, or otherwise, during the Recess of the Legislature of any State, the Executive thereof may make temporary Appointments until the next Meeting of the Legislature, which shall then fill such Vacancies.][3]

No Person shall be a Senator who shall not have attained to the Age of thirty Years, and been nine Years a Citizen of the United States, and who shall not, when elected, be an Inhabitant of that State for which he shall be chosen.

The Vice President of the United States shall be President of the Senate, but shall have no Vote, unless they be equally divided.

The Senate shall chuse their other Officers, and also a President pro tempore, in the Absence of the Vice President, or when he shall exercise the Office of President of the United States.

The Senate shall have the sole Power to try all Impeachments. When sitting for that Purpose, they shall be on Oath or Affirmation. When the President of the United States is tried, the Chief Justice shall preside: And no Person shall be convicted without the Concurrence of two thirds of the Members present.

Judgment in Cases of Impeachment shall not extend further than to removal from Office, and disqualification to hold and enjoy any Office of honor, Trust or Profit under the United States: but the Party convicted shall nevertheless be liable and subject to Indictment, Trial, Judgment and Punishment, according to Law.

Section 4. The Times, Places and Manner of holding Elections for Senators and Representatives, shall be prescribed in each State by the Legislature thereof; but the Congress may at any time by Law make or alter such Regulations, except as to the Places of chusing Senators.

The Congress shall assemble at least once in every Year, and such Meeting shall [be on the first Monday in December],[4] unless they shall by Law appoint a different Day.

Section 5. Each House shall be the Judge of the Elections, Returns and Qualifications of its own Members, and a Majority of each shall constitute a Quorum to do Business; but a smaller Number may adjourn from day to day, and may be authorized to compel the Attendance of absent Members, in such Manner, and under such Penalties as each House may provide.

Each House may determine the Rules of its Proceedings, punish its Members for disorderly Behaviour, and, with the Concurrence of two thirds, expel a Member.

Each House shall keep a Journal of its Proceedings, and from time to time publish the same, excepting such Parts as may in their Judgment require Secrecy; and the Yeas and Nays of the Members of either House on any question shall, at the Desire of one fifth of those Present, be entered on the Journal.

Neither House, during the Session of Congress, shall, without the Consent of the other, adjourn for more than three days, nor to any other Place than that in which the two Houses shall be sitting.

Section 6. The Senators and Representatives shall receive a Compensation for their Services, to be ascertained by Law, and paid out of the Treasury of the United States. They shall in all Cases, except Treason, Felony and Breach of the Peace, be privileged from Arrest during their Attendance at the Session of their respective Houses, and in going to and returning from the same; and for any Speech or Debate in either House, they shall not be questioned in any other Place.

No Senator or Representative shall, during the Time for which he was elected, be appointed to any civil Office under the Authority of the United States, which shall have been created, or the Emoluments whereof shall have been encreased during such time; and no Person holding any Office under the United States, shall be a Member of either House during his Continuance in Office.

Section 7. All Bills for raising Revenue shall originate in the House of Representatives; but the Senate may propose or concur with Amendments as on other Bills.

Every Bill which shall have passed the House of Representatives and the Senate, shall, before it become a Law, be presented to the President of the United States; If he approve he shall sign it, but if not he shall return it, with his Objections to that House in which it shall have originated, who shall enter the Objections at large on their Journal, and proceed to reconsider it. If after such Reconsideration two thirds of that House shall agree to pass the Bill, it shall be sent, together with the Objections, to the other House, by which it shall likewise be reconsidered, and if approved by two thirds of that House, it shall become a Law. But in all such Cases the Votes of both Houses shall be determined by yeas and Nays, and the Names of the Persons voting for and against the Bill shall be entered on the Journal of each House respectively. If any Bill shall not be returned by the President within ten Days (Sundays excepted) after it shall have been presented to him, the Same shall be a Law, in like Manner as if he had signed it, unless the Congress by their Adjournment prevent its Return, in which Case it shall not be a Law.

Every Order, Resolution, or Vote to which the Concurrence of the Senate and House of Representatives may be necessary (except on a question of Adjournment) shall be presented to the President of the United States; and before the Same shall take Effect, shall be approved by him, or being disapproved by him, shall be repassed by two thirds of the Senate and House of Representatives, according to the Rules and Limitations prescribed in the Case of a Bill.

Section 8. The Congress shall have Power To lay and collect Taxes, Duties, Imposts and Excises, to pay the Debts and provide for the common Defence and general Welfare of the United States; but all Duties, Imposts and Excises shall be uniform throughout the United States;

To borrow Money on the credit of the United States;

To regulate Commerce with foreign Nations, and among the several States, and with the Indian Tribes;

To establish an uniform Rule of Naturalization, and uniform Laws on the subject of Bankruptcies throughout the United States;

To coin Money, regulate the Value thereof, and of foreign Coin, and fix the Standard of Weights and Measures;

To provide for the Punishment of counterfeiting the Securities and current Coin of the United States;

To establish Post Offices and post Roads;

To promote the Progress of Science and useful Arts, by securing for limited Times to Authors and Inventors the exclusive Right to their respective Writings and Discoveries;

To constitute Tribunals inferior to the supreme Court;

To define and punish Piracies and Felonies committed on the high Seas, and Offences against the Law of Nations;

To declare War, grant Letters of Marque and Reprisal, and make Rules concerning Captures on Land and Water;

To raise and support Armies, but no Appropriation of Money to that Use shall be for a longer Term than two Years;

To provide and maintain a Navy;

To make Rules for the Government and Regulation of the land and naval Forces;

To provide for calling forth the Militia to execute the Laws of the Union, suppress Insurrections and repel Invasions;

To provide for organizing, arming, and disciplining, the Militia, and for governing such Part of them as may be employed in the Service of the United States, reserving to the States respectively, the Appointment of the Officers, and the Authority of training the Militia according to the discipline prescribed by Congress;

To exercise exclusive Legislation in all Cases whatsoever, over such District (not exceeding ten Miles square) as may, by Cession of particular States, and the Acceptance of Congress, become the Seat of the Government of the United States, and to exercise like Authority over all Places purchased by the Consent of the Legislature of the State in which the Same shall be, for the Erection of Forts, Magazines, Arsenals, dock-Yards, and other needful Buildings;—And

To make all Laws which shall be necessary and proper for carrying into Execution the foregoing Powers, and all other Powers vested by this Constitution in the Government of the United States, or in any Department or Officer thereof.

Section 9. The Migration or Importation of such Persons as any of the States now existing shall think proper to admit, shall not be prohibited by the Congress prior to the Year one thousand eight hundred and eight, but a Tax or duty may be imposed on such Importation, not exceeding ten dollars for each Person.

The Privilege of the Writ of Habeas Corpus shall not be suspended, unless when in Cases of Rebellion or Invasion the public Safety may require it.

No Bill of Attainder or ex post facto Law shall be passed.

No Capitation, or other direct, Tax shall be laid, unless in Proportion to the Census or Enumeration herein before directed to be taken.[5]

No Tax or Duty shall be laid on Articles exported from any State.

No Preference shall be given by any Regulation of Commerce or Revenue to the Ports of one State over those of another; nor shall Vessels bound to, or from, one State, be obliged to enter, clear, or pay Duties in another.

No Money shall be drawn from the Treasury, but in Consequence of Appropriations made by Law; and a regular Statement and Account of the Receipts and Expenditures of all public Money shall be published from time to time.

No Title of Nobility shall be granted by the United States: And no Person holding any Office of Profit or Trust under them, shall, without the Consent of the Congress, accept of any present, Emolument, Office, or Title, of any kind whatever, from any King, Prince, or foreign State.

Section 10. No State shall enter into any Treaty, Alliance, or Confederation; grant Letters of Marque and Reprisal; coin Money; emit Bills of Credit; make any Thing but gold and silver Coin a Tender in Payment of Debts; pass any Bill of Attainder, ex post facto Law, or Law impairing the Obligation of Contracts, or grant any Title of Nobility.

No State shall, without the Consent of the Congress, lay any Imposts or Duties on Imports or Exports, except what may be absolutely necessary for executing it's inspection Laws: and the net Produce of all Duties and Imposts, laid by any State on Imports or Exports, shall be for the Use of the Treasury of the United States; and all such Laws shall be subject to the Revision and Controul of the Congress.

No State shall, without the Consent of Congress, lay any Duty of Tonnage, keep Troops, or Ships of War in time of Peace, enter into any Agreement or Compact with another State, or with a foreign Power, or engage in War, unless actually invaded, or in such imminent Danger as will not admit of delay.

ARTICLE II

Section 1. The executive Power shall be vested in a President of the United States of America. He shall hold his Office during the Term of four Years, and, together with the Vice President, chosen for the same Term, be elected, as follows

Each State shall appoint, in such Manner as the Legislature thereof may direct, a Number of Electors, equal to the whole Number of Senators and Representatives to which the State may be entitled in the Congress: but no Senator or Representative, or Person holding an Office of Trust or Profit under the United States, shall be appointed an Elector.

[The Electors shall meet in their respective States, and vote by Ballot for two Persons, of whom one at least shall not be an Inhabitant of the same State with themselves. And they shall make a List of all the Persons voted for, and of the Number of Votes for each; which List they shall sign and certify, and transmit sealed to the Seat of the Government of the United States, directed to the President of the Senate. The President of the Senate shall, in the Presence of the Senate and House of Representatives, open all the Certificates, and the Votes shall then be counted. The Person having the greatest Number of Votes shall be the President, if such Number be a Majority of the whole Number of Electors appointed; and if there be more than one who have such Majority, and have an equal Number of Votes, then the House of Representatives shall immediately chuse by Ballot one of them for President; and if no Person have a Majority, then from the five highest on the list the said House shall in like Manner chuse the President. But in chusing the President,

the Votes shall be taken by States, the Representation from each State having one Vote; A quorum for this Purpose shall consist of a Member or Members from two thirds of the States, and a Majority of all the States shall be necessary to a Choice. In every Case, after the Choice of the President, the Person having the greatest Number of Votes of the Electors shall be the Vice President. But if there should remain two or more who have equal Votes, the Senate shall chuse from them by Ballot the Vice President.][6]

The Congress may determine the Time of chusing the Electors, and the Day on which they shall give their Votes; which Day shall be the same throughout the United States.

No Person except a natural born Citizen, or a Citizen of the United States, at the time of the Adoption of this Constitution, shall be eligible to the Office of President; neither shall any Person be eligible to that Office who shall not have attained to the Age of thirty five Years, and been fourteen Years a Resident within the United States.

In Case of the Removal of the President from Office, or of his Death, Resignation, or Inability to discharge the Powers and Duties of the said Office,[7] the Same shall devolve on the Vice President, and the Congress may by Law provide for the Case of Removal, Death, Resignation or Inability, both of the President and Vice President, declaring what Officer shall then act as President, and such Officer shall act accordingly, until the Disability be removed, or a President shall be elected.

The President shall, at stated Times, receive for his Services, a Compensation, which shall neither be encreased nor diminished during the Period for which he shall have been elected, and he shall not receive within that Period any other Emolument from the United States, or any of them.

Before he enter on the Execution of his Office, he shall take the following Oath or Affirmation:—"I do solemnly swear (or affirm) that I will faithfully execute the Office of President of the United States, and will to the best of my Ability, preserve, protect and defend the Constitution of the United States."

Section 2. The President shall be Commander in Chief of the Army and Navy of the United States, and of the Militia of the several States, when called into the actual Service of the United States; he may require the Opinion, in writing, of the principal Officer in each of the executive Departments, upon any Subject relating to the Duties of their respective Offices, and he shall have Power to grant Reprieves and Pardons for Offences against the United States, except in Cases of Impeachment.

He shall have Power, by and with the Advice and Consent of the Senate, to make Treaties, provided two thirds of the Senators present concur; and he shall nominate, and by and with the

Advice and Consent of the Senate, shall appoint Ambassadors, other public Ministers and Consuls, Judges of the supreme Court, and all other Officers of the United States, whose Appointments are not herein otherwise provided for, and which shall be established by Law: but the Congress may by Law vest the Appointment of such inferior Officers, as they think proper, in the President alone, in the Courts of Law, or in the Heads of Departments.

The President shall have Power to fill up all Vacancies that may happen during the Recess of the Senate, by granting Commissions which shall expire at the End of their next Session.

Section 3. He shall from time to time give to the Congress Information of the State of the Union, and recommend to their Consideration such Measures as he shall judge necessary and expedient; he may, on extraordinary Occasions, convene both Houses, or either of them, and in Case of Disagreement between them, with Respect to the Time of Adjournment, he may adjourn them to such Time as he shall think proper; he shall receive Ambassadors and other public Ministers; he shall take Care that the Laws be faithfully executed, and shall Commission all the Officers of the United States.

Section 4. The President, Vice President and all civil Officers of the United States, shall be removed from Office on Impeachment for, and Conviction of, Treason, Bribery, or other high Crimes and Misdemeanors.

ARTICLE III

Section 1. The judicial Power of the United States, shall be vested in one supreme Court, and in such inferior Courts as the Congress may from time to time ordain and establish. The Judges, both of the supreme and inferior Courts, shall hold their Offices during good Behaviour, and shall, at stated Times, receive for their Services, a Compensation, which shall not be diminished during their Continuance in Office.

Section 2. The judicial Power shall extend to all Cases, in Law and Equity, arising under this Constitution, the Laws of the United States, and Treaties made, or which shall be made, under their Authority; — to all Cases affecting Ambassadors, other public Ministers and Consuls; —to all Cases of admiralty and maritime Jurisdiction; —to Controversies to which the United States shall be a Party; —to Controversies between two or more States; —between a State and Citizens of another State;[8] —between Citizens of different States; —between Citizens of the same State claiming Lands under Grants of different States, and between a State, or the Citizens thereof, and foreign States, Citizens or Subjects.[8]

In all Cases affecting Ambassadors, other public Ministers and Consuls, and those in which a State shall be Party, the supreme Court shall have original Jurisdiction. In all the other Cases before mentioned, the supreme Court shall have appellate Jurisdiction, both as to Law and Fact, with such Exceptions, and under such Regulations as the Congress shall make.

The Trial of all Crimes, except in Cases of Impeachment, shall be by Jury; and such Trial shall be held in the State where the said Crimes shall have been committed; but when not committed within any State, the Trial shall be at such Place or Places as the Congress may by Law have directed.

Section 3. Treason against the United States, shall consist only in levying War against them, or in adhering to their Enemies, giving them Aid and Comfort. No Person shall be convicted of Treason unless on the Testimony of two Witnesses to the same overt Act, or on Confession in open Court.

The Congress shall have Power to declare the Punishment of Treason, but no Attainder of Treason shall work Corruption of Blood, or Forfeiture except during the Life of the Person attainted.

ARTICLE IV

Section 1. Full Faith and Credit shall be given in each State to the public Acts, Records, and judicial Proceedings of every other State. And the Congress may by general Laws prescribe the Manner in which such Acts, Records and Proceedings shall be proved, and the Effect thereof.

Section 2. The Citizens of each State shall be entitled to all Privileges and Immunities of Citizens in the several States.

A Person charged in any State with Treason, Felony, or other Crime, who shall flee from Justice, and be found in another State, shall on Demand of the executive Authority of the State from which he fled, be delivered up, to be removed to the State having Jurisdiction of the Crime.

[No Person held to Service or Labour in one State, under the Laws thereof, escaping into another, shall, in Consequence of any Law or Regulation therein, be discharged from such Service or Labour, but shall be delivered up on Claim of the Party to whom such Service or Labour may be due.][9]

Section 3. New States may be admitted by the Congress into this Union; but no new State shall be formed or erected within the Jurisdiction of any other State; nor any State be formed by the Junction of two or more States, or Parts of States, without the Consent of the Legislatures of the States concerned as well as of the Congress.

The Congress shall have Power to dispose of and make all

needful Rules and Regulations respecting the Territory or other Property belonging to the United States; and nothing in this Constitution shall be so construed as to Prejudice any Claims of the United States, or of any particular State.

Section 4. The United States shall guarantee to every State in this Union a Republican Form of Government, and shall protect each of them against Invasion; and on Application of the Legislature, or of the Executive (when the Legislature cannot be convened) against domestic Violence.

ARTICLE V

The Congress, whenever two thirds of both Houses shall deem it necessary, shall propose Amendments to this Constitution, or, on the Application of the Legislatures of two thirds of the several States, shall call a Convention for proposing Amendments, which, in either Case, shall be valid to all Intents and Purposes, as Part of this Constitution, when ratified by the Legislatures of three fourths of the several States, or by Conventions in three fourths thereof, as the one or the other Mode of Ratification may be proposed by the Congress; Provided [that no Amendment which may be made prior to the Year One thousand eight hundred and eight shall in any Manner affect the first and fourth Clauses in the Ninth Section of the first Article; and][10] that no State, without its Consent, shall be deprived of its equal Suffrage in the Senate.

ARTICLE VI

All Debts contracted and Engagements entered into, before the Adoption of this Constitution, shall be as valid against the United States under this Constitution, as under the Confederation.

This Constitution, and the Laws of the United States which shall be made in Pursuance thereof; and all Treaties made, or which shall be made, under the Authority of the United States, shall be the supreme Law of the Land; and the Judges in every State shall be bound thereby, any Thing in the Constitution or Laws of any State to the Contrary notwithstanding.

The Senators and Representatives before mentioned, and the Members of the several State Legislatures, and all executive and judicial Officers, both of the United States and of the several States, shall be bound by Oath or Affirmation, to support this Constitution; but no religious Test shall ever be required as a Qualification to any Office or public Trust under the United States.

ARTICLE VII

The Ratification of the Conventions of nine States, shall be sufficient for the Establishment of this Constitution between the States so ratifying the Same.

Done in Convention by the Unanimous Consent of the States present the Seventeenth Day of September in the Year of our Lord one thousand seven hundred and Eighty seven and of the Independence of the United States of America the Twelfth. IN WITNESS whereof We have hereunto subscribed our Names,

George Washington, *President and deputy from Virginia, and thirty-eight other delegates.*

[The language of the original Constitution, not including the Amendments, was adopted by a convention of the states on September 17, 1787, and was subsequently ratified by the states on the following dates: Delaware, December 7, 1787; Pennsylvania, December 12, 1787; New Jersey, December 18, 1787; Georgia, January 2, 1788; Connecticut, January 9, 1788; Massachusetts, February 6, 1788; Maryland, April 28, 1788; South Carolina, May 23, 1788; New Hampshire, June 21, 1788.

Ratification was completed on June 21, 1788.

The Constitution subsequently was ratified by Virginia, June 25, 1788; New York, July 26, 1788; North Carolina, November 21, 1789; Rhode Island, May 29, 1790; and Vermont, January 10, 1791.]

AMENDMENTS

Amendment I

(First ten amendments ratified December 15, 1791.)

Congress shall make no law respecting an establishment of religion, or prohibiting the free exercise thereof; or abridging the freedom of speech, or of the press; or the right of the people peaceably to assemble, and to petition the Government for a redress of grievances.

Amendment II

A well regulated Militia, being necessary to the security of a free State, the right of the people to keep and bear Arms, shall not be infringed.

Amendment III

No Soldier shall, in time of peace be quartered in any house, without the consent of the Owner, nor in time of war, but in a manner to be prescribed by law.

Amendment IV

The right of the people to be secure in their persons, houses, papers, and effects, against unreasonable searches and seizures, shall not be violated, and no Warrants shall issue, but upon probable cause, supported by Oath or affirmation, and particularly describing the place to be searched, and the persons or things to be seized.

Amendment V

No person shall be held to answer for a capital, or otherwise infamous crime, unless on a presentment or indictment of a Grand Jury, except in cases arising in the land or naval forces, or in the Militia, when in actual service in time of War or public danger; nor shall any person be subject for the same offence to be twice put in jeopardy of life or limb; nor shall be compelled in any criminal case to be a witness against himself, nor be deprived of life, liberty, or property, without due process of law; nor shall private property be taken for public use, without just compensation.

Amendment VI

In all criminal prosecutions, the accused shall enjoy the right to a speedy and public trial, by an impartial jury of the State and district wherein the crime shall have been committed, which district shall have been previously ascertained by law, and to be informed of the nature and cause of the accusation; to be confronted with the witnesses against him; to have compulsory process for obtaining witnesses in his favor, and to have the Assistance of Counsel for his defence.

Amendment VII

In Suits at common law, where the value in controversy shall exceed twenty dollars, the right of trial by jury shall be preserved, and no fact tried by a jury, shall be otherwise re-examined in any Court of the United States, than according to the rules of the common law.

Amendment VIII

Excessive bail shall not be required, nor excessive fines imposed, nor cruel and unusual punishments inflicted.

Amendment IX

The enumeration in the Constitution, of certain rights, shall not be construed to deny or disparage others retained by the people.

Amendment X

The powers not delegated to the United States by the Constitution, nor prohibited by it to the States, are reserved to the States respectively, or to the people.

Amendment XI *(Ratified February 7, 1795)*

The Judicial power of the United States shall not be construed to extend to any suit in law or equity, commenced or prosecuted against one of the United States by Citizens of another State, or by Citizens or Subjects of any Foreign State.

Amendment XII *(Ratified June 15, 1804)*

The Electors shall meet in their respective states and vote by ballot for President and Vice-President, one of whom, at least, shall not be an inhabitant of the same state with themselves; they shall name in their ballots the person voted for as President, and in distinct ballots the person voted for as Vice-President, and they shall make distinct lists of all persons voted for as President, and of all persons voted for as Vice-President, and of the number of votes for each, which lists they shall sign and certify, and transmit sealed to the seat of the government of the United States, directed to the President of the Senate; — The President of the Senate shall, in the presence of the Senate and House of Representatives, open all the certificates and the votes shall then be counted; — The person having the greatest number of votes for President, shall be the President, if such number be a majority of the whole number of Electors appointed; and if no person have such majority, then from the persons having the highest numbers not exceeding three on the list of those voted for as President, the House of Representatives shall choose immediately, by ballot, the President. But in choosing the President, the votes shall be taken by states, the representation from each state having one vote; a quorum for this purpose shall consist of a member or members from two-thirds of the states, and a majority of all the states shall be necessary to a choice. [And if the House of Representatives shall not choose a President whenever the right of choice shall devolve upon them, before the fourth day of March next following, then the Vice-President shall act as President, as in the case of the death or other constitutional disability of the President. —][11] The person having the greatest number of votes as Vice-President, shall be the Vice-President, if such number be a majority of the whole number of Electors appointed, and if no person have a majority, then from the two highest numbers on the list, the Senate shall choose the Vice-President; a quorum for the purpose shall consist of two-thirds of the whole number of Senators, and a majority of the whole number shall be necessary to a choice. But no person constitutionally ineligible to the office of President shall be eligible to that of Vice-President of the United States.

Amendment XIII *(Ratified December 6, 1865)*

Section 1. Neither slavery nor involuntary servitude, except as a punishment for crime whereof the party shall have been duly convicted, shall exist within the United States, or any place subject to their jurisdiction.

Section 2. Congress shall have power to enforce this article by appropriate legislation.

Amendment XIV *(Ratified July 9, 1868)*

Section 1. All persons born or naturalized in the United States, and subject to the jurisdiction thereof, are citizens of the United States and of the State wherein they reside. No State shall make or enforce any law which shall abridge the privileges or immunities of citizens of the United States; nor shall any State deprive any person of life, liberty, or property, without due process of law; nor deny to any person within its jurisdiction the equal protection of the laws.

Section 2. Representatives shall be apportioned among the several States according to their respective numbers, counting the whole number of persons in each State, excluding Indians not taxed. But when the right to vote at any election for the choice of electors for President and Vice President of the United States, Representatives in Congress, the Executive and Judicial officers of a State, or the members of the Legislature thereof, is denied to any of the male inhabitants of such State, being twenty-one years of age,[12] and citizens of the United States, or in any way abridged, except for participation in rebellion, or other crime, the basis of representation therein shall be reduced in the proportion which the number of such male citizens shall bear to the whole number of male citizens twenty-one years of age in such State.

Section 3. No person shall be a Senator or Representative in Congress, or elector of President and Vice President, or hold any office, civil or military, under the United States, or under any State, who, having previously taken an oath, as a member of Congress, or as an officer of the United States, or as a member of any State legislature, or as an executive or judicial officer of any State, to support the Constitution of the United States, shall have engaged in insurrection or rebellion against the same, or given aid or comfort to the enemies thereof. But Congress may by a vote of two-thirds of each House, remove such disability.

Section 4. The validity of the public debt of the United States, authorized by law, including debts incurred for payment of pensions and bounties for services in suppressing insurrection or rebellion, shall not be questioned. But neither the United States nor any State shall assume or pay any debt or obligation incurred in aid of insurrection or rebellion against the United States, or any claim for the loss or emancipation of any slave; but all such debts, obligations and claims shall be held illegal and void.

Section 5. The Congress shall have power to enforce, by appropriate legislation, the provisions of this article.

Amendment XV *(Ratified February 3, 1870)*

Section 1. The right of citizens of the United States to vote shall not be denied or abridged by the United States or by any State on account of race, color, or previous condition of servitude.

Section 2. The Congress shall have power to enforce this article by appropriate legislation.

Amendment XVI *(Ratified February 3, 1913)*

The Congress shall have power to lay and collect taxes on incomes, from whatever source derived, without apportionment among the several States, and without regard to any census or enumeration.

Amendment XVII *(Ratified April 8, 1913)*

The Senate of the United States shall be composed of two Senators from each State, elected by the people thereof, for six years; and each Senator shall have one vote. The electors in each State shall have the qualifications requisite for electors of the most numerous branch of the State legislatures.

When vacancies happen in the representation of any State in the Senate, the executive authority of such State shall issue writs of election to fill such vacancies: *Provided,* That the legislature of any State may empower the executive thereof to make temporary appointments until the people fill the vacancies by election as the legislature may direct.

This amendment shall not be so construed as to affect the election or term of any Senator chosen before it becomes valid as part of the Constitution.

Amendment XVIII *(Ratified January 16, 1919)*

Section 1. After one year from the ratification of this article the manufacture, sale, or transportation of intoxicating liquors within, the importation thereof into, or the exportation thereof from the United States and all territory subject to the jurisdiction thereof for beverage purposes is hereby prohibited.

Section 2. The Congress and the several States shall have concurrent power to enforce this article by appropriate legislation.

Section 3. This article shall be inoperative unless it shall have been ratified as an amendment to the Constitution by the legislatures of the several States, as provided in the Constitution, within seven years from the date of the submission hereof to the States by the Congress.][13]

Amendment XIX (Ratified August 18, 1920)

The right of citizens of the United States to vote shall not be denied or abridged by the United States or by any State on account of sex.

Congress shall have power to enforce this article by appropriate legislation.

Amendment XX (Ratified January 23, 1933)

Section 1. The terms of the President and Vice President shall end at noon on the 20th day of January, and the terms of Senators and Representatives at noon on the 3d day of January, of the years in which such terms would have ended if this article had not been ratified; and the terms of their successors shall then begin.

Section 2. The Congress shall assemble at least once in every year, and such meeting shall begin at noon on the 3d day of January, unless they shall by law appoint a different day.

Section 3.[14] If, at the time fixed for the beginning of the term of the President, the President elect shall have died, the Vice President elect shall become President. If a President shall not have been chosen before the time fixed for the beginning of his term, or if the President elect shall have failed to qualify, then the Vice President elect shall act as President until a President shall have qualified; and the Congress may by law provide for the case wherein neither a President elect nor a Vice President elect shall have qualified, declaring who shall then act as President, or the manner in which one who is to act shall be selected, and such person shall act accordingly until a President or Vice President shall have qualified.

Section 4. The Congress may by law provide for the case of the death of any of the persons from whom the House of Representatives may choose a President whenever the right of choice shall have devolved upon them, and for the case of the death of any of the persons from whom the Senate may choose a Vice President whenever the right of choice shall have devolved upon them.

Section 5. Sections 1 and 2 shall take effect on the 15th day of October following the ratification of this article.

Section 6. This article shall be inoperative unless it shall have been ratified as an amendment to the Constitution by the legislatures of three-fourths of the several States within seven years from the date of its submission.

Amendment XXI (Ratified December 5, 1933)

Section 1. The eighteenth article of amendment to the Constitution of the United States is hereby repealed.

Section 2. The transportation or importation into any State, Territory, or possession of the United States for delivery or use therein of intoxicating liquors, in violation of the laws thereof, is hereby prohibited.

Section 3. This article shall be inoperative unless it shall have been ratified as an amendment to the Constitution by conventions in the several States, as provided in the Constitution, within seven years from the date of the submission hereof to the States by the Congress.

Amendment XXII (Ratified February 27, 1951)

Section 1. No person shall be elected to the office of the President more than twice, and no person who has held the office of President, or acted as President, for more than two years of a term to which some other person was elected President shall be elected to the office of the President more than once. But this Article shall not apply to any person holding the office of President when this Article was proposed by the Congress, and shall not prevent any person who may be holding the office of President, or acting as President, during the term within which this Article becomes operative from holding the office of President or acting as President during the remainder of such term.

Section 2. This article shall be inoperative unless it shall have been ratified as an amendment to the Constitution by the legislatures of three-fourths of the several States within seven years from the date of its submission to the States by the Congress.

Amendment XXIII (Ratified March 29, 1961)

Section 1. The District constituting the seat of Government of the United States shall appoint in such manner as the Congress may direct:

A number of electors of President and Vice President equal to the whole number of Senators and Representatives in Congress to which the District would be entitled if it were a State, but in no event more than the least populous State; they shall be in addition to those appointed by the States, but they shall be considered, for the purposes of the election of President and Vice President, to be electors appointed by a State; and they shall meet in the District and perform such duties as provided by the twelfth article of amendment.

Section 2. The Congress shall have power to enforce this article by appropriate legislation.

Amendment XXIV *(Ratified January 23, 1964)*

Section 1. The right of citizens of the United States to vote in any primary or other election for President or Vice President, for electors for President or Vice President, or for Senator or Representative in Congress, shall not be denied or abridged by the United States or any State by reason of failure to pay any poll tax or other tax.

Section 2. The Congress shall have power to enforce this article by appropriate legislation.

Amendment XV *(Ratified February 10, 1967)*

Section 1. In case of the removal of the President from office or of his death or resignation, the Vice President shall become President.

Section 2. Whenever there is a vacancy in the office of the Vice President, the President shall nominate a Vice President who shall take office upon confirmation by a majority vote of both Houses of Congress.

Section 3. Whenever the President transmits to the President pro tempore of the Senate and the Speaker of the House of Representatives his written declaration that he is unable to discharge the powers and duties of his office, and until he transmits to them a written declaration to the contrary, such powers and duties shall be discharged by the Vice President as Acting President.

Section 4. Whenever the Vice President and a majority of either the principal officers of the executive departments or of such other body as Congress may by law provide, transmit to the President pro tempore of the Senate and the Speaker of the House of Representatives their written declaration that the President is unable to discharge the powers and duties of his office, the Vice President shall immediately assume the powers and duties of the office as Acting President.

Thereafter, when the President transmits to the President pro tempore of the Senate and the Speaker of the House of Representatives his written declaration that no inability exists, he shall resume the powers and duties of his office unless the Vice President and a majority of either the principal officers of the executive departments or of such other body as Congress may by law provide, transmit within four days to the President pro tempore of the Senate and the Speaker of the House of Representatives their written declaration that the President is unable to discharge the powers and duties of his office. Thereupon Congress shall decide the issue, assembling within forty-eight hours for that purpose if not in session. If the Congress, within twenty-one days after receipt of the latter written declaration, or, if Congress is not in session, within twenty-one days after Congress is required to assemble, determines by two-thirds vote of both Houses that the President is unable to discharge the powers and duties of his office, the Vice President shall continue to discharge the same as Acting President; otherwise, the President shall resume the powers and duties of his office.

Amendment XXVI *(Ratified July 1, 1971)*

Section 1. The right of citizens of the United States, who are eighteen years of age or older, to vote shall not be denied or abridged by the United States or by any State on account of age.

Section 2. The Congress shall have power to enforce this article by appropriate legislation.

Amendment XXVII *(Ratified May 7, 1992)*

No law varying the compensation for the services of the Senators and Representatives shall take effect, until an election of Representatives shall have intervened.

SOURCE: U.S. Congress, House, Committee on the Judiciary, *The Constitution of the United States of America, as Amended*, 100th Cong., 1st sess., 1987, H Doc 100–94.

NOTES: 1. The part in brackets was changed by section 2 of the Fourteenth Amendment.

2. The part in brackets was changed by the first paragraph of the Seventeenth Amendment.

3. The part in brackets was changed by the second paragraph of the Seventeenth Amendment.

4. The part in brackets was changed by section 2 of the Twentieth Amendment.

5. The Sixteenth Amendment gave Congress the power to tax incomes.

6. The material in brackets was superseded by the Twelfth Amendment.

7. This provision was affected by the Twenty-fifth Amendment.

8. These clauses were affected by the Eleventh Amendment.

9. This paragraph was superseded by the Thirteenth Amendment.

10. Obsolete.

11. The part in brackets was superseded by section 3 of the Twentieth Amendment.

12. See the Nineteenth and Twenty-sixth Amendments.

13. This amendment was repealed by section 1 of the Twenty-first Amendment.

14. See the Twenty-fifth Amendment.

FEDERALIST NO. 10

The Same Subject Continued: The Union as a Safeguard Against Domestic Faction and Insurrection.

From the New York Packet
Friday, November 23, 1787.
Author: James Madison

To the People of the State of New York:

AMONG the numerous advantages promised by a wellconstructed Union, none deserves to be more accurately developed than its tendency to break and control the violence of faction. The friend of popular governments never finds himself so much alarmed for their character and fate, as when he contemplates their propensity to this dangerous vice. He will not fail, therefore, to set a due value on any plan which, without violating the principles to which he is attached, provides a proper cure for it. The instability, injustice, and confusion introduced into the public councils, have, in truth, been the mortal diseases under which popular governments have everywhere perished; as they continue to be the favorite and fruitful topics from which the adversaries to liberty derive their most specious declamations. The valuable improvements made by the American constitutions on the popular models, both ancient and modern, cannot certainly be too much admired; but it would be an unwarrantable partiality, to contend that they have as effectually obviated the danger on this side, as was wished and expected. Complaints are everywhere heard from our most considerate and virtuous citizens, equally the friends of public and private faith, and of public and personal liberty, that our governments are too unstable, that the public good is disregarded in the conflicts of rival parties, and that measures are too often decided, not according to the rules of justice and the rights of the minor party, but by the superior force of an interested and overbearing majority. However anxiously we may wish that these complaints had no foundation, the evidence, of known facts will not permit us to deny that they are in some degree true. It will be found, indeed, on a candid review of our situation, that some of the distresses under which we labor have been erroneously charged on the operation of our governments; but it will be found, at the same time, that other causes will not alone account for many of our heaviest misfortunes; and, particularly, for that prevailing and increasing distrust of public engagements, and alarm for private rights, which are echoed from one end of the continent to the other. These must be chiefly, if not wholly, effects of the unsteadiness and injustice with which a factious spirit has tainted our public administrations.

By a faction, I understand a number of citizens, whether amounting to a majority or a minority of the whole, who are united and actuated by some common impulse of passion, or of interest, adversed to the rights of other citizens, or to the permanent and aggregate interests of the community.

There are two methods of curing the mischiefs of faction: the one, by removing its causes; the other, by controlling its effects.

There are again two methods of removing the causes of faction: the one, by destroying the liberty which is essential to its existence; the other, by giving to every citizen the same opinions, the same passions, and the same interests.

It could never be more truly said than of the first remedy, that it was worse than the disease. Liberty is to faction what air is to fire, an aliment without which it instantly expires. But it could not be less folly to abolish liberty, which is essential to political life, because it nourishes faction, than it would be to wish the annihilation of air, which is essential to animal life, because it imparts to fire its destructive agency.

The second expedient is as impracticable as the first would be unwise. As long as the reason of man continues fallible, and he is at liberty to exercise it, different opinions will be formed. As long as the connection subsists between his reason and his self-love, his opinions and his passions will have a reciprocal influence on each other; and the former will be objects to which the latter will attach themselves. The diversity in the faculties of men, from which the rights of property originate, is not less an insuperable obstacle to a uniformity of interests. The protection of these faculties is the first object of government. From the protection of different and unequal faculties of acquiring property, the possession of different degrees and kinds of property immediately results; and from the influence of these on the sentiments and views of the respective proprietors, ensues a division of the society into different interests and parties.

The latent causes of faction are thus sown in the nature of man; and we see them everywhere brought into different degrees of activity, according to the different circumstances of civil society. A zeal for different opinions concerning religion, concerning government, and many other points, as well of speculation as of practice; an attachment to different leaders ambitiously contending for pre-eminence and power; or to persons of other descriptions whose fortunes have been interesting to the human passions, have, in turn, divided mankind into parties, inflamed them with mutual animosity, and rendered them much more disposed to vex and oppress each other than to co-operate for their common good. So strong is this propensity of mankind to fall into mutual animosities, that where no substantial occasion presents itself, the most frivolous and fanciful distinctions have been sufficient to kindle their unfriendly passions and excite their most violent conflicts. But the most common and durable source of factions has been the various and unequal distribution of property. Those who hold and those who are without property have ever formed distinct interests in society. Those who are creditors, and those who are debtors, fall under a like discrimination. A landed interest, a manufacturing interest, a mercantile interest, a moneyed interest, with many lesser interests, grow up of necessity in civilized nations, and divide them into different classes, actuated by different sentiments and views. The regulation of these various and interfering interests forms the principal task of modern legislation, and involves the spirit of party and faction in the necessary and ordinary operations of the government.

No man is allowed to be a judge in his own cause, because his interest would certainly bias his judgment, and, not improbably, corrupt his integrity. With equal, nay with greater reason, a body of men are unfit to be both judges and parties at the same time; yet what are many of the most important acts of legislation, but so many judicial determinations, not indeed concerning the rights of single persons, but concerning the rights of large bodies of citizens? And what are the different classes of legislators but advocates and parties to the causes which they determine? Is a law proposed concerning private debts? It is a question to which the creditors are parties on one side and the debtors on the other. Justice ought to hold the balance between them. Yet the parties are, and must be, themselves the judges; and the most numerous party, or, in other words, the most powerful faction must be expected to prevail. Shall domestic manufactures be encouraged, and in what degree, by restrictions on foreign manufactures? are questions which would be differently decided by the landed and the manufacturing classes, and probably by neither with a sole regard to justice and the public good. The apportionment of taxes on the various descriptions of property is an act which seems to require the most exact impartiality; yet there is, perhaps, no legislative act in which greater opportunity and temptation are given to a predominant party to trample on the rules of justice. Every shilling with which they overburden the inferior number, is a shilling saved to their own pockets.

It is in vain to say that enlightened statesmen will be able to adjust these clashing interests, and render them all subservient to the public good. Enlightened statesmen will not always be at the helm. Nor, in many cases, can such an adjustment be made at all without taking into view indirect and remote considerations, which will rarely prevail over the immediate interest which one party may find in disregarding the rights of another or the good of the whole.

The inference to which we are brought is, that the CAUSES of faction cannot be removed, and that relief is only to be sought in the means of controlling its EFFECTS.

If a faction consists of less than a majority, relief is supplied by the republican principle, which enables the majority to defeat its sinister views by regular vote. It may clog the administration, it may convulse the society; but it will be unable to execute and mask its violence under the forms of the Constitution. When a majority is included in a faction, the form of popular government, on the other hand, enables it to sacrifice to its ruling passion or interest both the public good and the rights of other citizens. To secure the public good and private rights against the danger of such a faction, and at the same time to preserve the spirit and the form of popular government, is then the great object to which our inquiries are directed. Let me add that it is the great desideratum by which this form of government can be rescued from the opprobrium under which it has so long labored, and be recommended to the esteem and adoption of mankind.

By what means is this object attainable? Evidently by one of two only. Either the existence of the same passion or interest in a majority at the same time must be prevented, or the majority, having such coexistent passion or interest, must be rendered, by their number and local situation, unable to concert and carry into effect schemes of oppression. If the impulse and the opportunity be suffered to coincide, we well know that neither moral nor religious motives can be relied on as an adequate control. They are not found to be such on the injustice and violence of individuals, and lose their efficacy in proportion to the number combined together, that is, in proportion as their efficacy becomes needful.

From this view of the subject it may be concluded that a pure democracy, by which I mean a society consisting of a small number of citizens, who assemble and administer the government in person, can admit of no cure for the mischiefs of faction. A common passion or interest will, in almost every case, be felt by a majority of the whole; a communication and concert result from the form of government itself; and there is nothing to check the inducements to sacrifice the weaker party or an obnoxious individual. Hence it is that such democracies have ever been spectacles of turbulence and contention; have ever been found incompatible with personal security or the rights of property; and have in general been as short in their lives as they have been violent in their deaths. Theoretic politicians, who have patronized this species of government, have erroneously supposed that by reducing mankind to a perfect equality in their political rights, they would, at the same time, be perfectly equalized and assimilated in their possessions, their opinions, and their passions.

A republic, by which I mean a government in which the scheme of representation takes place, opens a different prospect, and promises the cure for which we are seeking. Let us examine the points in which it varies from pure democracy, and we shall comprehend both the nature of the cure and the efficacy which it must derive from the Union.

The two great points of difference between a democracy and a republic are: first, the delegation of the government, in the latter, to a small number of citizens elected by the rest; secondly, the greater number of citizens, and greater sphere of country, over which the latter may be extended. The effect of the first difference is, on the one hand, to refine and enlarge the public views, by passing them through the medium of a chosen body of citizens, whose wisdom may best discern the true interest of their country, and whose patriotism and love of justice will be least likely to sacrifice it to temporary or partial considerations. Under such a regulation, it may well happen that the public voice, pronounced by the representatives of the people, will be more consonant to the public good than if pronounced by the people themselves, convened for the purpose. On the other hand, the effect may be inverted. Men of factious tempers, of local prejudices, or of sinister designs, may, by intrigue, by corruption, or by other means, first obtain the suffrages, and then betray the interests, of the people. The question resulting is, whether small or extensive republics are more favorable to the election of proper guardians of the public weal; and it is clearly decided in favor of the latter by two obvious considerations:

In the first place, it is to be remarked that, however small the republic may be, the representatives must be raised to a certain number, in order to guard against the cabals of a few; and that, however large it may be, they must be limited to a certain number, in order to guard against the confusion of a multitude. Hence, the number of representatives in the two cases not being in proportion to that of the two constituents, and being proportionally greater in the small republic, it follows that, if the proportion of fit characters be not less in the large than in the small republic, the former will present a greater option, and consequently a greater probability of a fit choice.

In the next place, as each representative will be chosen by a greater number of citizens in the large than in the small republic, it will be more difficult for unworthy candidates to practice with success the vicious arts by which elections are too often carried; and the suffrages of the people being more free, will be more likely to centre in men who possess the most attractive merit and the most diffusive and established characters.

It must be confessed that in this, as in most other cases, there is a mean, on both sides of which inconveniences will be found to lie. By enlarging too much the number of electors, you render the representatives too little acquainted with all their local circumstances and lesser interests; as by reducing it too much, you render him unduly attached to these, and too little fit to comprehend and pursue great and national objects. The federal

Constitution forms a happy combination in this respect; the great and aggregate interests being referred to the national, the local and particular to the State legislatures.

The other point of difference is, the greater number of citizens and extent of territory which may be brought within the compass of republican than of democratic government; and it is this circumstance principally which renders factious combinations less to be dreaded in the former than in the latter. The smaller the society, the fewer probably will be the distinct parties and interests composing it; the fewer the distinct parties and interests, the more frequently will a majority be found of the same party; and the smaller the number of individuals composing a majority, and the smaller the compass within which they are placed, the more easily will they concert and execute their plans of oppression. Extend the sphere, and you take in a greater variety of parties and interests; you make it less probable that a majority of the whole will have a common motive to invade the rights of other citizens; or if such a common motive exists, it will be more difficult for all who feel it to discover their own strength, and to act in unison with each other. Besides other impediments, it may be remarked that, where there is a consciousness of unjust or dishonorable purposes, communication is always checked by distrust in proportion to the number whose concurrence is necessary.

Hence, it clearly appears, that the same advantage which a republic has over a democracy, in controlling the effects of faction, is enjoyed by a large over a small republic,—is enjoyed by the Union over the States composing it. Does the advantage consist in the substitution of representatives whose enlightened views and virtuous sentiments render them superior to local prejudices and schemes of injustice? It will not be denied that the representation of the Union will be most likely to possess these requisite endowments. Does it consist in the greater security afforded by a greater variety of parties, against the event of any one party being able to outnumber and oppress the rest? In an equal degree does the increased variety of parties comprised within the Union, increase this security. Does it, in fine, consist in the greater obstacles opposed to the concert and accomplishment of the secret wishes of an unjust and interested majority? Here, again, the extent of the Union gives it the most palpable advantage.

The influence of factious leaders may kindle a flame within their particular States, but will be unable to spread a general conflagration through the other States. A religious sect may degenerate into a political faction in a part of the Confederacy; but the variety of sects dispersed over the entire face of it must secure the national councils against any danger from that source. A rage for paper money, for an abolition of debts, for an equal division of property, or for any other improper or wicked project, will be less apt to pervade the whole body of the Union than a particular member of it; in the same proportion as such a malady is more likely to taint a particular county or district, than an entire State.

In the extent and proper structure of the Union, therefore, we behold a republican remedy for the diseases most incident to republican government. And according to the degree of pleasure and pride we feel in being republicans, ought to be our zeal in cherishing the spirit and supporting the character of Federalists.

PUBLIUS.

Appendix 4

FEDERALIST NO. 51

The Structure of the Government Must Furnish the Proper Checks and Balances Between the Different Departments

From the New York Packet.
Friday, February 8, 1788.
Author: Alexander Hamilton or James Madison

To the People of the State of New York:

TO WHAT expedient, then, shall we finally resort, for maintaining in practice the necessary partition of power among the several departments, as laid down in the Constitution? The only answer that can be given is, that as all these exterior provisions are found to be inadequate, the defect must be supplied, by so contriving the interior structure of the government as that its several constituent parts may, by their mutual relations, be the means of keeping each other in their proper places. Without presuming to undertake a full development of this important idea, I will hazard a few general observations, which may perhaps place it in a clearer light, and enable us to form a more correct judgment of the principles and structure of the government planned by the convention. In order to lay a due foundation for that separate and distinct exercise of the different powers of government, which to a certain extent is admitted on all hands to be essential to the preservation of liberty, it is evident that each department should have a will of its own; and consequently should be so constituted that the members of each should have as little agency as possible in the appointment of the members of the others. Were this principle rigorously adhered to, it would require that all the appointments for the supreme executive, legislative, and judiciary magistracies should be drawn from the same fountain of authority, the people,

through channels having no communication whatever with one another. Perhaps such a plan of constructing the several departments would be less difficult in practice than it may in contemplation appear. Some difficulties, however, and some additional expense would attend the execution of it. Some deviations, therefore, from the principle must be admitted. In the constitution of the judiciary department in particular, it might be inexpedient to insist rigorously on the principle: first, because peculiar qualifications being essential in the members, the primary consideration ought to be to select that mode of choice which best secures these qualifications; secondly, because the permanent tenure by which the appointments are held in that department, must soon destroy all sense of dependence on the authority conferring them. It is equally evident, that the members of each department should be as little dependent as possible on those of the others, for the emoluments annexed to their offices. Were the executive magistrate, or the judges, not independent of the legislature in this particular, their independence in every other would be merely nominal. But the great security against a gradual concentration of the several powers in the same department, consists in giving to those who administer each department the necessary constitutional means and personal motives to resist encroachments of the others. The provision for defense must in this, as in all other cases, be made commensurate to the danger of attack. Ambition must be made to counteract ambition. The interest of the man must be connected with the constitutional rights of the place. It may be a reflection on human nature, that such devices should be necessary to control the abuses of government. But what is government itself, but the greatest of all reflections on human nature? If men were angels, no government would be necessary. If angels were to govern men, neither external nor internal controls on government would be necessary. In framing a government which is to be administered by men over men, the great difficulty lies in this: you must first enable the government to control the governed; and in the next place oblige it to control itself. A dependence on the people is, no doubt, the primary control on the government; but experience has taught mankind the necessity of auxiliary precautions. This policy of supplying, by opposite and rival interests, the defect of better motives, might be traced through the whole system of human affairs, private as well as public. We see it particularly displayed in all the subordinate distributions of power, where the constant aim is to divide and arrange the several offices in such a manner as that each may be a check on the other that the private interest of every individual may be a sentinel over the public rights. These inventions of prudence cannot be less requisite in the distribution of the supreme powers of the State. But it is not possible to give to each department an equal power of self-defense. In republican government, the legislative authority necessarily predominates. The remedy for this inconveniency is to divide the legislature into different branches; and to render them, by different modes of election and different principles of action, as little connected with each other as the nature of their common functions and their common dependence on the society will admit. It may even be necessary to guard against dangerous encroachments by still further precautions. As the weight of the legislative authority requires that it should be thus divided, the weakness of the executive may require, on the other hand, that it should be fortified. An absolute negative on the legislature appears, at first view, to be the natural defense with which the executive magistrate should be armed. But perhaps it would be neither altogether safe nor alone sufficient. On ordinary occasions it might not be exerted with the requisite firmness, and on extraordinary occasions it might be perfidiously abused. May not this defect of an absolute negative be supplied by some qualified connection between this weaker department and the weaker branch of the stronger department, by which the latter may be led to support the constitutional rights of the former, without being too much detached from the rights of its own department? If the principles on which these observations are founded be just, as I persuade myself they are, and they be applied as a criterion to the several State constitutions, and to the federal Constitution it will be found that if the latter does not perfectly correspond with them, the former are infinitely less able to bear such a test. There are, moreover, two considerations particularly applicable to the federal system of America, which place that system in a very interesting point of view. First. In a single republic, all the power surrendered by the people is submitted to the administration of a single government; and the usurpations are guarded against by a division of the government into distinct and separate departments. In the compound republic of America, the power surrendered by the people is first divided between two distinct governments, and then the portion allotted to each subdivided among distinct and separate departments. Hence a double security arises to the rights of the people. The different governments will control each other, at the same time that each will be controlled by itself. Second. It is of great importance in a republic not only to guard the society against the oppression of its rulers, but to guard one part of the society against the injustice of the other part. Different interests necessarily exist in different classes of citizens. If a majority be united by a common interest, the rights of the minority will be insecure. There are but two methods of providing against this evil: the one by creating a will in the community independent of the majority that is, of the society itself; the other, by comprehending in the society so many separate descriptions of citizens as will render an unjust combination of a majority of the whole very improbable, if not impracticable. The first method prevails in all governments possessing an hereditary or self-appointed authority. This, at best, is but a precarious security; because a power independent of the society may as well espouse the unjust views of the major, as the rightful interests of the minor party, and may possibly be turned against both parties. The second method will be exemplified in the federal republic of the United States Whilst all authority in it will be derived from and dependent on the society, the society itself will be broken into so many parts, interests, and classes of citizens, that the rights of individuals, or of the minority, will be in little danger from interested combinations of the majority. In a free government the security for civil rights must be the same as that for religious rights. It consists in the one case in the multiplicity of interests, and in the other in the multiplicity of sects. The degree of security in both cases will depend on the number of interests and sects; and this may be presumed to depend on the extent of country and number of people comprehended under the same government. This view of the subject must particularly recommend a proper federal system to all the sincere and considerate friends of republican government, since it shows that in exact proportion as the territory of the Union may be formed into more circumscribed Confederacies, or States oppressive combinations of a majority will be facilitated: the best security, under the republican forms, for the rights of every class of citizens, will be diminished: and consequently the stability and independence of some member of the government, the only other security, must be proportionately increased. Justice is the end of government. It is the end of civil society. It ever has been and ever will be pursued until it be obtained, or until liberty be lost in the pursuit. In a society under the forms of which the stronger faction can readily unite and oppress the weaker, anarchy may as truly be said to reign as in a state of nature, where the weaker individual is not secured against the violence of the stronger; and as, in the latter state, even the stronger individuals are prompted, by the uncertainty of their condition, to submit to a government which may protect the weak as well as themselves; so, in the former state, will the more powerful factions or parties be gradnally induced, by a like motive, to wish for a government which will protect all parties, the weaker as well as the more powerful. It can be little doubted that if the State of Rhode Island was separated from the Confederacy and left to itself, the insecurity of rights under the popular form of government within such narrow limits would be displayed by such reiterated oppressions of factious

majorities that some power altogether independent of the people would soon be called for by the voice of the very factions whose misrule had proved the necessity of it. In the extended republic of the United States, and among the great variety of interests, parties, and sects which it embraces, a coalition of a majority of the whole society could seldom take place on any other principles than those of justice and the general good; whilst there being thus less danger to a minor from the will of a major party, there must be less pretext, also, to provide for the security of the former, by introducing into the government a will not dependent on the latter, or, in other words, a will independent of the society itself. It is no less certain than it is important, notwithstanding the contrary opinions which have been entertained, that the larger the society, provided it lie within a practical sphere, the more duly capable it will be of self-government. And happily for the REPUBLICAN CAUSE, the practicable sphere may be carried to a very great extent, by a judicious modification and mixture of the FEDERAL PRINCIPLE.

PUBLIUS.

PRESIDENTS, VICE PRESIDENTS, SPEAKERS, AND CHIEF JUSTICES, 1789–1999

President/Vice President	Term	Congress	Speaker of the House	Chief Justice of the United States
George Washington[1] John Adams	(1789–1797)	1st 2nd 3rd 4th	Frederick A.C. Muhlenberg, Pa. Jonathan Trumbull, F-Conn. Muhlenberg Jonathan Dayton, F-N.J.	John Jay (1789–1795) John Rutledge (1795) Oliver Ellsworth (1796–1800)
John Adams, F Thomas Jefferson, D-R	(1797–1801)	5th 6th	Dayton Theodore Sedgwick, F-Mass.	Ellsworth John Marshall (1801–1835)
Thomas Jefferson, D-R Aaron Burr (1801–1805) George Clinton (1805–1809)	(1801–1809)	7th 8th 9th 10th	Nathaniel Macon, D-N.C. Macon Macon Joseph B. Varnum, Mass.	Marshall
James Madison, D-R George Clinton[2] (1809–1812) Elbridge Gerry[2] (1813–1814)	(1809–1817)	11th 12th 13th 14th	Varnum Henry Clay, R-Ky. Clay/Langdon Cheves, D-S.C. Clay	Marshall
James Monroe, D-R Daniel D. Tompkins	(1817–1825)	15th 16th 17th 18th	Clay Clay/John W. Taylor, D-N.Y. Philip P. Barbour, D-Va. Clay	Marshall
John Quincy Adams, D-R John C. Calhoun	(1825–1829)	19th 20th	Taylor Andrew Stevenson, D-Va.	Marshall
Andrew Jackson, D John C. Calhoun[3] (1829–1832) Martin Van Buren (1833–1837)	(1829–1837)	21st 22nd 23rd 24th	Stevenson Stevenson Stevenson/John Bell, W-Tenn. James K. Polk, D-Tenn.	Marshall Roger B. Taney (1836–1864)
Martin Van Buren, D Richard M. Johnson	(1837–1841)	25th 26th	Polk Robert M.T. Hunter, D-Va.	Taney
William Henry Harrison,[2] W John Tyler	(1841)			Taney
John Tyler, W	(1841–1845)	27th 28th	John White, W-Ky. John W. Jones, D-Va.	Taney
James K. Polk, D George M. Dallas	(1845–1849)	29th 30th	John W. Davis, D-Ind. Robert C. Winthrop, W-Mass.	Taney

(continued)

President/Vice President	Term	Congress	Speaker of the House	Chief Justice of the United States
Zachary Taylor,[2] W Millard Fillmore	(1849–1850)	31st	Howell Cobb, D-Ga.	Taney
Millard Fillmore, W	(1850–1853)	31st 32nd	Cobb Linn Boyd, D-Ky.	Taney
Franklin Pierce, D William R. King[2] (1853)	(1853–1857)	33rd 34th	Boyd Nathaniel P. Banks, R-Mass.	Taney
James Buchanan, D John C. Breckinridge	(1857–1861)	35th 36th	James L. Orr, D-S.C. William Pennington, R-N.J.	Taney

Abraham Lincoln,[2] R
  Hannibal Hamlin (1861–1865)
  Andrew Johnson,[4] D (1865)
	(1861–1865)	37th
		38th
			Galusha A. Grow, R-Pa.
			Schuyler Colfax, R-Ind.
				Taney
				Salmon P. Chase (1864–1873)

Andrew Johnson, D	(1865–1869)	39th 40th	Colfax Colfax/Theodore M. Pomeroy, R-N.Y.	Chase

Ulysses S. Grant, R
  Schuyler Colfax (1869–1873)
  Henry Wilson[2] (1873–1875)
	(1869–1877)	41st
		42nd
		43rd
		44th
			James G. Blaine, R-Maine
			Blaine
			Blaine
			Michael C. Kerr, D-Ind./
			  Samuel J. Randall, D-Pa.
				Chase
				Morrison R. Waite (1874–1888)

Rutherford B. Hayes, R William A. Wheeler	(1877–1881)	45th 46th	Randall Randall	Waite
James A. Garfield,[2] R Chester A. Arthur	(1881)			Waite
Chester A. Arthur, R	(1881–1885)	47th 48th	Joseph Warren Keifer, R-Ohio John G. Carlisle, D-Ky.	Waite
Grover Cleveland, D Thomas A. Hendricks[2] (1885)	(1885–1889)	49th 50th	Carlisle Carlisle	Waite Melville W. Fuller (1888–1910)
Benjamin Harrison, R Levi P. Morton	(1889–1893)	51st 52nd	Thomas Brackett Reed, R-Maine Charles F. Crisp, D-Ga.	Fuller
Grover Cleveland, D Adlai E. Stevenson	(1893–1897)	53rd 54th	Crisp Reed	Fuller

William McKinley,[2] R
  Garret A. Hobart[2] (1897–1899)
  Theodore Roosevelt (1901)
	(1897–1901)	55th
		56th
			Reed
			David B. Henderson, R-Iowa
				Fuller

Theodore Roosevelt, R Charles W. Fairbanks (1905–1909)	(1901–1909)	57th 58th 59th 60th	Henderson Joseph G. Cannon, R-Ill. Cannon Cannon	Fuller
William Howard Taft, R James S. Sherman[2] (1909–1912)	(1909–1913)	61st 62nd	Cannon James B. "Champ" Clark, D-Mo.	Fuller Edward D. White (1910–1921)
Woodrow Wilson, D Thomas R. Marshall	(1913–1921)	63rd 64th 65th 66th	Clark Clark Clark Frederick H. Gillett, R-Mass.	White
Warren G. Harding,[2] R Calvin Coolidge	(1921–1923)	67th	Gillett	William Howard Taft (1921–1930)

President/Vice President	Term	Congress	Speaker of the House	Chief Justice of the United States
Calvin Coolidge, R	(1923–1929)	68th	Gillett	Taft
Charles G. Dawes (1925–1929)		69th	Nicholas Longworth, R-Ohio	
		70th	Longworth	
Herbert C. Hoover, R	(1929–1933)	71st	Longworth	Taft
Charles Curtis		72nd	John Nance Garner, D-Texas	Charles Evans Hughes (1930–1941)
Franklin D. Roosevelt,[2] D	(1933–1945)	73rd	Henry T. Rainey, D-Ill.	Hughes
John Nance Garner (1933–1941)		74th	Joseph W. Byrns, D-Tenn./	Harlan F. Stone (1941–1946)
Henry A. Wallace (1941–1945)			William B. Bankhead, D-Ala.	
Harry S. Truman (1945)		75th	Bankhead	
		76th	Bankhead/Sam Rayburn, D-Texas	
		77th	Rayburn	
		78th	Rayburn	
		79th	Rayburn	
Harry S. Truman, D	(1945–1953)	79th	Rayburn	Stone
Alben W. Barkley (1949–1953)		80th	Joseph W. Martin Jr., R-Mass.	Frederick M. Vinson (1946–1953)
		81st	Rayburn	
		82nd	Rayburn	
Dwight D. Eisenhower, R	(1953–1961)	83rd	Martin	Vinson
Richard Nixon		84th	Rayburn	Earl Warren (1953–1969)
		85th	Rayburn	
		86th	Rayburn	
John F. Kennedy,[2] D	(1961–1963)	87th	Rayburn/John W. McCormack,	Warren
Lyndon B. Johnson			D-Mass.	
		88th	McCormack	
Lyndon B. Johnson, D	(1963–1969)	88th	McCormack	Warren
Hubert H. Humphrey (1965–1969)		89th	McCormack	
		90th	McCormack	
Richard Nixon,[3] R	(1969–1973)	91st	McCormack	Warren
Spiro T. Agnew[3] (1969–1973)		92nd	Carl Albert, D-Okla	Warren E. Burger (1969–1986)
Gerald R. Ford[5] (1973–1974)		93rd	Albert	
Gerald R. Ford, R	(1974–1977)	93rd	Albert	Burger
Nelson A. Rockefeller[5]		94th	Albert	
Jimmy Carter, D	(1977–1981)	95th	Thomas P. O'Neill Jr., D-Mass.	Burger
Walter F. Mondale		96th	O'Neill	
Ronald Reagan, R	(1981–1989)	97th	O'Neill	Burger
George Bush		98th	O'Neill	William Rehnquist (1986–)
		99th	O'Neill	
		100th	Jim Wright, D-Texas	
George Bush, R	(1989–1993)	101st	Wright/Thomas S. Foley, D-Wash.	Rehnquist
Dan Quayle		102nd	Foley	
Bill Clinton, D	(1993–)	103rd	Foley	Rehnquist
Al Gore		104th	Newt Gingrich, R-Ga.	
		105th	Gingrich	
		106th	J. Dennis Hastert, R-Ill.	

NOTES: The vice president's term or party is noted when it differs from that of the president. Key to abbreviations: D—Democrat; D-R—Democratic-Republican; F—Federalist; R—Republican; W—Whig.

1. Washington belonged to no formal party.   2. Died in office.

3. Resigned from office.   4. Democrat Johnson and Republican Lincoln ran under the Union Party banner in 1864.

5. Appointed to office.

Minneapolis-
St Paul area
| 4 | 5 |

Milwaukee area
| 4 | 5 |

Chicago area
| 1 – 10 |

Cleveland area
| 10 | 11 |

Detroit area
| 12 | 14 | 15 |

Cincinnati area
| 1 | 2 |

St. Louis area
| 1 – 3 |

Pittsburgh area
| 14 | 18 |

Boston &
coastal areas
| 4 | 6 – 10 |

New York City
area
| 2 – 18 |

Northern New
Jersey area
| 7 – 10 | | 13 |

Philadelphia
area
| 1 – 3 |

Baltimore area
| 3 | 7 |

Northern
Virginia area
| 8 | 11 |

Houston area
| 7 | 8 | 9 | 18 |
| 22 | 25 | 29 |

Tampa St.-
Petersburg area
| 10 | 11 |

Miami area
| 17 – 19 | 21 | 22 |

Fort Worth area
| 6 | 12 | 24 | 26 |

Dallas area
| 3 | 4 | 6 | 24 |
| 26 | 30 |

San Antonio area
| 20 | 21 | 23 | 28 |

SOURCE: Congressional Quarterly, 1999.
NOTE: Map depicts current congressional districts, which are based on population data gathered in the 1990 census. After the 2000 census, the 435 seats in the House of Representatives will be reapportioned and, if necessary, the states will redraw the district lines.

POLITICAL PARTY AFFILIATIONS IN CONGRESS AND THE PRESIDENCY, 1789–1999

Year	Congress	House Majority party	House Principal minority party	Senate Majority party	Senate Principal minority party	President
1789–1791	1st	AD-38	Op-26	AD-17	Op-9	F (Washington)
1791–1793	2nd	F-37	DR-33	F-16	DR-13	F (Washington)
1793–1795	3rd	DR-57	F-48	F-17	DR-13	F (Washington)
1795–1797	4th	F-54	DR-52	F-19	DR-13	F (Washington)
1797–1799	5th	F-58	DR-48	F-20	DR-12	F (John Adams)
1799–1801	6th	F-64	DR-42	F-19	DR-13	F (John Adams)
1801–1803	7th	DR-69	F-36	DR-18	F-13	DR (Jefferson)
1805–1807	9th	DR-116	F-25	DR-27	F-7	DR (Jefferson)
1807–1809	10th	DR-118	F-24	DR-28	F-6	DR (Jefferson)
1809–1811	11th	DR-94	F-48	DR-28	F-6	DR (Madison)
1811–1813	12th	DR-108	F-36	DR-30	F-6	DR (Madison)
1813–1815	13th	DR-112	F-68	DR-27	F-9	DR (Madison)
1815–1817	14th	DR-117	F-65	DR-25	F-11	DR (Madison)
1817–1819	15th	DR-141	F-42	DR-34	F-10	DR (Monroe)
1819–1821	16th	DR-156	F-27	DR-35	F-7	DR (Monroe)
1821–1823	17th	DR-158	F-25	DR-44	F-4	DR (Monroe)
1823–1825	18th	DR-187	F-26	DR-44	F-4	DR (Monroe)
1825–1827	19th	AD-105	J-97	AD-26	J-20	DR (John Q. Adams)
1827–1829	20th	J-119	AD-94	J-28	AD-20	DR (John Q. Adams)
1829–1831	21st	D-139	NR-74	D-26	NR-22	DR (Jackson)
1831–1833	22nd	D-141	NR-58	D-25	NR-21	D (Jackson)
1833–1835	23rd	D-147	AM-53	D-20	NR-20	D (Jackson)
1835–1837	24th	D-145	W-98	D-27	W-25	D (Jackson)
1837–1839	25th	D-108	W-107	D-30	W-18	D (Van Buren)
1839–1841	26th	D-124	W-118	D-28	W-22	D (Van Buren)
1841–1843	27th	W-133	D-102	W-28	D-22	W (W. Harrison) W (Tyler)
1843–1845	28th	D-142	W-79	W-28	D-25	W (Tyler)
1845–1847	29th	D-143	W-77	D-31	W-25	D (Polk)
1847–1849	30th	W-115	D-108	D-36	W-21	D (Polk)
1849–1851	31st	D-112	W-109	D-35	W-25	W (Taylor) W (Fillmore)
1851–1853	32nd	D–140	W–88	D–35	W24	W (Fillmore)
1853–1855	33rd	D-159	W-71	D-38	W-22	D (Pierce)

Year	Congress	House		Senate		President
		Majority party	Principal minority party	Majority party	Principal minority party	
1855–1857	34th	R-108	D-83	D-40	R-15	D (Pierce)
1857–1859	35th	D-118	R-92	D-36	R-20	D (Buchanan)
1859–1861	36th	R-114	D-92	D-36	R-26	D (Buchanan)
1861–1863	37th	R-105	D-43	R-31	D-10	R (Lincoln)
1863–1865	38th	R-102	D-75	R-36	D-9	R (Lincoln)
1865–1867[1]	39th	U-149	D-42	U-42	D-10	U (Lincoln)
						U (A. Johnson)
1867–1869	40th	R-143	D-49	R-42	D-11	R (A. Johnson)
1869–1871	41st	R-149	D-63	R-56	D-11	R (Grant)
1871–1873	42nd	R-134	D-104	R-52	D-17	R (Grant)
1873–1875	43rd	R-194	D-92	R-49	D-19	R (Grant)
1875–1877	44th	D-169	R-109	R-45	D-29	R (Grant)
1877–1879	45th	D-153	R-140	R-39	D-36	R (Hayes)
1879–1881	46th	D-149	R-130	D-42	R-33	R (Hayes)
1881–1883	47th	R-147	D-135	R-37	D-37	R (Garfield)
						R (Arthur)
1883–1885	48th	D-197	R-118	R-38	D-36	R (Arthur)
1885–1887	49th	D-183	R-140	R-43	D-34	D (Cleveland)
1887–1889	50th	D-169	R-152	R-39	D-37	D (Cleveland)
1889–1891	51st	R-166	D-159	R-39	D-37	R (B. Harrison)
1891–1893	52nd	D-235	R-88	R-47	D-39	R (B. Harrison)
1893–1895	53rd	D-218	R-127	D-44	R-38	D (Cleveland)
1895–1897	54th	R-244	D-105	R-43	D-39	D (Cleveland)
1897–1899	55th	R-204	D-113	R-47	D-34	R (McKinley)
1899–1901	56th	R-185	D-163	R-53	D-26	R (McKinley)
1901–1903	57th	R-197	D-151	R-55	D-31	R (McKinley)
						R (T. Roosevelt)
1903–1905	58th	R-208	D-178	R-57	D-33	R (T. Roosevelt)
1905–1907	59th	R-250	D-136	R-57	D-33	R (T. Roosevelt)
1907–1909	60th	R-222	D-164	R-61	D-31	R (T. Roosevelt)
1909–1911	61st	R-219	D-172	R-61	D-32	R (Taft)
1911–1913	62nd	D-228	R-161	R-51	D-41	R (Taft)
1913–1915	63rd	D-291	R-127	D-51	R-44	D (Wilson)
1915–1917	64th	D-230	R-196	D-56	R-40	D (Wilson)
1917–1919	65th	D-216	R-210	D-53	R-42	D (Wilson)
1919–1921	66th	R-240	D-190	R-49	D-47	D (Wilson)
1921–1923	67th	R-301	D-131	R-59	D-37	R (Harding)
1923–1925	68th	R-225	D-205	R-51	D-43	R (Coolidge)
1925–1927	69th	R-247	D-183	R-56	D-39	R (Coolidge)
1927–1929	70th	R-237	D-195	R-49	D-46	R (Coolidge)
1929–1931	71st	R-267	D-167	R-56	D-39	R (Hoover)
1931–1933	72nd	D-220	R-214	R-48	D-47	R (Hoover)
1933–1935	73rd	D-310	R-117	D-60	R-35	D (F. Roosevelt)
1935–1937	74th	D-319	R-103	D-69	R-25	D (F. Roosevelt)
1937–1939	75th	D-331	R-89	D-76	R-16	D (F. Roosevelt)
1939–1941	76th	D-261	R-164	D-69	R-23	D (F. Roosevelt)
1941–1943	77th	D-268	R-162	D-66	R-28	D (F. Roosevelt)
1943–1945	78th	D-218	R-208	D-58	R-37	D (F. Roosevelt)
1945–1947	79th	D-242	R-190	D-56	R-38	D (F. Roosevelt)
						D (Truman)

(continued)

(continued)

Year	Congress	House Majority party	House Principal minority party	Senate Majority party	Senate Principal minority party	President
1947–1949	80th	R-245	D-188	R-51	D-45	D (Truman)
1949–1951	81st	D-263	R-171	D-54	R-42	D (Truman)
1951–1953	82nd	D-234	R-199	D-49	R-47	D (Truman)
1953–1955	83rd	R-221	D-211	R-48	D-47	R (Eisenhower)
1955–1957	84th	D-232	R-203	D-48	R-47	R (Eisenhower)
1957–1959	85th	D-233	R-200	D-49	R-47	R (Eisenhower)
1959–1961	86th	D-283	R-153	D-64	R-34	R (Eisenhower)
1961–1963	87th	D-263	R-174	D-65	R-35	D (Kennedy)
1963–1965	88th	D-258	R-177	D-67	R-33	D (Kennedy) D (L. Johnson)
1965–1967	89th	D-295	R-140	D-68	R-32	D (L. Johnson)
1967–1969	90th	D-247	R-187	D-64	R-36	D (L. Johnson)
1969–1971	91st	D-243	R-192	D-57	R-43	R (Nixon)
1971–1973	92nd	D-254	R-180	D-54	R-44	R (Nixon)
1973–1975	93rd	D-239	R-192	D-56	R-42	R (Nixon) R (Ford)
1975–1977	94th	D-291	R-144	D-60	R-37	R (Ford)
1977–1979	95th	D-292	R-143	D-61	R-38	D (Carter)
1979–1981	96th	D-276	R-157	D-58	R-41	D (Carter)
1981–1983	97th	D-243	R-192	R-53	D-46	R (Reagan)
1983–1985	98th	D-269	R-165	R-54	D-46	R (Reagan)
1985–1987	99th	D-252	R-182	R-53	D-47	R (Reagan)
1987–1989	100th	D-258	R-177	D-55	R-45	R (Reagan)
1989–1991	101st	D-259	R-174	D-55	R-45	R (Bush)
1991–1993	102nd	D-267	R-167	D-56	R-44	R (Bush)
1993–1995	103rd	D-258	R-176	D-57	R-43	D (Clinton)
1995–1997	104th	R-230	D-204	R-53	D-47	D (Clinton)
1997–1999	105th	R-227	D-207	R-55	D-45	D (Clinton)
1999–2001	106th	R-222	D-211	R-55	D-45	D (Clinton)

SOURCES: U.S. Bureau of the Census, *Historical Statistics of the United States, Colonial Times to 1970* (Washington, D.C.: Government Printing Office, 1975); and U.S. Congress, Joint Committee on Printing, *Official Congressional Directory* (Washington, D.C.: Government Printing Office, 1967–); *CQ Weekly*, selected issues.

NOTE: Figures are for the beginning of the first session of each Congress. Key to abbreviations: AD—Administration; AM—Anti-Masonic; D—Democratic; DR—Democratic-Republican; F—Federalist; J—Jacksonian; NR—National Republican; Op—Opposition; R—Republican; U—Unionist; W—Whig

1. The Republican Party ran under the Union Party banner in 1864.

SUMMARY OF PRESIDENTIAL ELECTIONS, 1789–1996

Year	No. of states	Candidates		Electoral vote		Popular vote	
1789[a]	10	*Fed.* George Washington		*Fed.* 69		——[b]	
1792[a]	15	*Fed.* George Washington		*Fed.* 132		——[b]	
1796[a]	16	*Dem.-Rep.* Thomas Jefferson	*Fed.* John Adams	*Dem.-Rep.* 68	*Fed.* 71	——[b]	
1800[a]	16	*Dem.-Rep.* Thomas Jefferson Aaron Burr	*Fed.* John Adams Charles Cotesworth Pinckney	*Dem.-Rep* 73	*Fed.* 65	——[b]	
1804	17	*Dem.-Rep.* Thomas Jefferson George Clinton	*Fed.* Charles Cotesworth Pinckney Rufus King	*Dem.-Rep* 162	*Fed.* 14	——[b]	
1808	17	*Dem.-Rep.* James Madison George Clinton	*Fed.* Charles Cotesworth Pinckney Rufus King	*Dem.-Rep* 122	*Fed.* 47	——[b]	
1812	18	*Dem.-Rep.* James Madison Elbridge Gerry	*Fed.* George Clinton Jared Ingersoll	*Dem.-Rep* 128	*Fed.* 89	——[b]	
1816	19	*Dem.-Rep.* James Monroe Daniel D. Tompkins	*Fed.* Rufus King John Howard	*Dem.-Rep* 183	*Fed.* 34	——[b]	
1820	24	*Dem.-Rep* James Monroe Daniel D. Tompkins	——[c]	*Dem.-Rep* 231	——[c]	——[b]	
1824[d]	24	*Dem.-Rep* Andrew Jackson John C. Calhoun	*Dem.-Rep* John Q. Adams Nathan Sanford	*Dem.-Rep* 99	*Dem.-Rep.* 84	*Dem.-Rep* 151,271 41.3%	*Dem.-Rep* 113,122 30.9%

(continued)

(continued)

Year	No. of states	Candidates		Electoral vote		Popular vote	
1828	24	*Dem.-Rep.* Andrew Jackson John C. Calhoun	*Nat.-Rep.* John Q. Adams Richard Rush	*Dem.-Rep.* 178	*Nat.-Rep.* 83	*Dem.-Rep.* 642,553 56.0%	*Nat.-Rep.* 500,897 43.6%
1832[e]	24	*Dem.* Andrew Jackson Martin Van Buren	*Nat.-Rep.* Henry Clay John Sergeant	*Dem.* 219	*Nat.-Rep.* 49 54.2%	*Dem.* 701,780	*Nat.-Rep.* 484,205 37.4%
1836[f]	26	*Dem.* Martin Van Buren Richard M. Johnson	*Whig* William H. Harrison Francis Granger	*Dem.* 170	*Whig* 73	*Dem.* 764,176 50.8%	*Whig* 550,816 36.6%
1840	26	*Dem.* Martin Van Buren Richard M. Johnson	*Whig* William H. Harrison John Tyler	*Dem.* 60	*Whig* 234	*Dem.* 1,128,854 46.8%	*Whig* 1,275,390 52.9%
1844	26	*Dem.* James Polk George M. Dallas	*Whig* Henry Clay Theodore Frelinghuysen	*Dem.* 170	*Whig* 105	*Dem.* 1,339,494 49.5%	*Whig* 1,300,004 48.1%
1848	30	*Dem.* Lewis Cass William O. Butler	*Whig* Zachary Taylor Millard Fillmore	*Dem.* 127	*Whig* 163	*Dem.* 1,233,460 42.5%	*Whig* 1,361,393 47.3%
1852	31	*Dem.* Franklin Pierce William R. King	*Whig* Winfield Scott William A. Graham	*Dem.* 254	*Whig* 42	*Dem.* 1,607,510 50.8%	*Whig* 1,386,942 43.9%

Year	No. of states	Candidates		Electoral vote		Popular vote	
		Dem.	*Rep.*	*Dem.*	*Rep.*	*Dem.*	*Rep.*
1856[g]	31	James Buchanan John C. Breckinridge	John C. Fremont William L. Dayton	174	114	1,836,072 45.3%	1,342,345 33.1%
1860[h]	33	Stephen A. Douglas Herschel V. Johnson	Abraham Lincoln Hannibal Hamlin	12	180	1,380,202 29.5%	1,865,908 39.8%
1864[i]	36	George B. McClellan George H. Pendleton	Abraham Lincoln Andrew Johnson	21	212	1,812,807 45.0%	2,218,388 55.0%
1868[j]	37	Horatio Seymour Francis P. Blair, Jr.	Ulysses S. Grant Schuyler Colfax	80	214	2,708,744 47.3%	3,013,650 52.7%
1872[k]	37	Horace Greeley Benjamin Gratz Brown	Ulysses S. Grant Henry Wilson		286	2,834,761 43.8%	3,598,235 55.6%
1876	38	Samuel J. Tilden Thomas A. Hendricks	Rutherford B. Hayes William A. Wheeler	184	185	4,288,546 51.0%	4,034,311 47.9%
1880	38	Winfield S. Hancock William H. English	James A. Garfield Chester A. Arthur	155	214	4,444,260 48.2%	4,446,158 48.3%
1884	38	Grover Cleveland Thomas A. Hendricks	James G. Blaine John A. Logan	219	182	4,874,621 48.5%	4,848,936 48.2%

Year	No. of states	Candidates Dem.	Candidates Rep.	Electoral vote Dem.	Electoral vote Rep.	Popular vote Dem.	Popular vote Rep.
1888	38	Grover Cleveland Allen G. Thurman	Benjamin Harrison Levi P. Morton	168	233	5,534,488 48.6%	5,443,892 47.8%
1892[l]	44	Grover Cleveland Adlai E. Stevenson	Benjamin Harrison Whitelaw Reid	277	145	5,551,883 46.1%	5,179,244 43.0%
1896	45	William J. Bryan Arthur Sewall	William McKinley Garret A. Hobart	176	271	6,511,495 46.7%	7,108,480 51.0%
1900	45	William J. Bryan Adlai E. Stevenson	William McKinley Theodore Roosevelt	155	292	6,358,345 45.5%	7,218,039 51.7%
1904	45	Alton B. Parker Henry G. Davis	Theodore Roosevelt Charles W. Fairbanks	140	336	5,028,898 37.6%	7,626,593 56.4%
1908	46	William J. Bryan John W. Kern	William H. Taft James S. Sherman	162	321	6,406,801 43.0%	7,676,258 51.6%
1912[m]	48	Woodrow Wilson Thomas R. Marshall	William H. Taft James S. Sherman	435	8	6,293,152 41.8%	3,486,333 23.2%
1916	48	Woodrow Wilson Thomas R. Marshall	Charles E. Hughes Charles W. Fairbanks	277	254	9,126,300 49.2%	8,546,789 46.1%
1920	48	James M. Cox Franklin D. Roosevelt	Warren G. Harding Calvin Coolidge	127	404	9,140,884 34.2%	16,133,314 60.3%
1924[n]	48	John W. Davis Charles W. Bryant	Calvin Coolidge Charles G. Dawes	136	382	8,386,169 28.8%	15,717,553 54.1%
1928	48	Alfred E. Smith Joseph T. Robinson	Herbert C. Hoover Charles Curtis	87	444	15,000,185 40.8%	21,411,991 58.2%
1932	48	Franklin D. Roosevelt John N. Garner	Herbert C. Hoover Charles Curtis	472	59	22,825,016 57.4%	15,758,397 39.6%
1936	48	Franklin D. Roosevelt John N. Garner	Alfred M. Landon Frank Knox	523	8	27,747,636 60.8%	16,679,543 36.5%
1940	48	Franklin D. Roosevelt Henry A. Wallace	Wendell L. Willkie Charles L. McNary	449	82	27,263,448 54.7%	22,336,260 44.8%
1944	48	Franklin D. Roosevelt Harry S. Truman	Thomas E. Dewey John W. Bricker	432	99	25,611,936 53.4%	22,013,372 45.9%
1948[o]	48	Harry S. Truman Alben W. Barkley	Thomas E. Dewey Earl Warren	303	189	24,105,587 49.5%	21,970,017 45.1%
1952	48	Adlai E. Stevenson II John J. Sparkman	Dwight D. Eisenhower Richard M. Nixon	89	442	27,314,649 44.4%	33,936,137 55.1%
1956[p]	48	Adlai E. Stevenson II Estes Kefauver	Dwight D. Eisenhower Richard M. Nixon	73	457	26,030,172 42.0%	35,585,245 57.4%

(continued)

(continued)

Year	No. of states	Candidates		Electoral vote		Popular vote	
		Dem.	Rep.	Dem.	Rep.	Dem.	Rep.
1960[q]	50	John F. Kennedy Lyndon B. Johnson	Richard M. Nixon Henry Cabot Lodge	303	219	34,221,344 49.7%	34,106,671 49.5%
1964	50*	Lyndon B. Johnson Hubert H. Humphrey	Barry Goldwater William E. Miller	486	52	43,126,584 61.1%	27,177,838 38.5%
1968[r]	50*	Hubert H. Humphrey Edmund S. Muskie	Richard M. Nixon Spiro T. Agnew	191	301	31,274,503 42.7%	31,785,148 43.4%
1972[s]	50*	George McGovern Sargent Shriver	Richard M. Nixon Spiro T. Agnew	17	520	29,171,791 37.5%	47,170,179 60.7%
1976[t]	50*	Jimmy Carter Walter F. Mondale	Gerald R. Ford Robert Dole	297	240	40,830,763 50.1%	39,147,793 48.0%
1980	50*	Jimmy Carter Walter F. Mondale	Ronald Reagan George Bush	49	489	35,483,883 41.0%	43,904,153 50.7%
1984	50*	Walter F. Mondale Geraldine Ferraro	Ronald Reagan George Bush	13	525	37,577,185 40.6%	54,455,075 58.8%
1988[u]	50*	Michael S. Dukakis Lloyd Bentsen	George Bush Dan Quayle	111	426	41,809,083 45.6%	48,886,097 53.4%
1992	50*	William J. Clinton Albert Gore	George Bush Dan Quayle	370	168	43,728,275 43.2%	38,167,416 37.7%
1996	50*	William J. Clinton Albert Gore	Robert J. Dole Jack F. Kemp	379	159	47,401,054 49.2%	39,197,350 40.7%

SOURCES: Harold W. Stanley and Richard G. Niemi, *Vital Statistics on American Politics 1997–1998* (Washington, D.C.: CQ Press, 1998), 23–27; *Guide to U.S. Elections,* 3d ed. (Washington, D.C.: Congressional Quarterly, 1994), 358–410; Federal Election Commission.

NOTE: Dem.-Rep.—Democratic-Republican; Fed.—Federalist; Nat.-Rep.—National-Republican; Dem.—Democratic; Rep.—Republican.

a. Elections from 1789 through 1800 were held under rules that did not allow separate voting for president and vice president.

b. Popular vote returns are not shown before 1824 because consistent, reliable data are not available.

c. 1820: One electoral vote was cast for John Adams and Richard Stockton, who were not candidates.

d. 1824: All four candidates represented Democratic-Republican factions. William H. Crawford received 41 electoral votes and Henry Clay received 37 votes. Because no candidate received a majority, the election was decided (in Adams's favor) by the House of Representatives.

e. 1832: Two electoral votes were not cast.

f. 1836: Other Whig candidates receiving electoral votes were Hugh L. White, who received 26 votes, and Daniel Webster, who received 14 votes.

g. 1856: Millard Fillmore, Whig-American, received 8 electoral votes.

h. 1860: John C. Breckinridge, southern Democrat, received 72 electoral votes. John Bell, Constitutional Union, received 39 electoral votes.

i. 1864: Eighty-one electoral votes were not cast.

j. 1868: Twenty-three electoral votes were not cast.

k. 1872: Horace Greeley, Democrat, died after the election. In the electoral college, Democratic electoral votes went to Thomas Hendricks, 42 votes; Benjamin Gratz Brown, 18 votes; Charles J. Jenkins, 2 votes; and David Davis, 1 vote. Seventeen electoral votes were not cast.

l. 1892: James B. Weaver, People's party, received 22 electoral votes.

m. 1912: Theodore Roosevelt, Progressive party, received 88 electoral votes.

n. 1924: Robert M. La Follette, Progressive party, received 13 electoral votes.

o. 1948: J. Strom Thurmond, States' Rights party, received 39 electoral votes.

p. 1956: Walter B. Jones, Democrat, received 1 electoral vote.

q. 1960: Harry Flood Byrd, Democrat, received 15 electoral votes.

r. 1968: George C. Wallace, American Independent party, received 46 electoral votes.

s. 1972: John Hospers, Libertarian party, received 1 electoral vote.

t. 1976: Ronald Reagan, Republican, received 1 electoral vote.

u. 1988: Lloyd Bentsen, the Democratic vice-presidential nominee, received 1 electoral vote for president.

* Fifty states plus the District of Columbia.

Appendix 9

THE AMERICAN ECONOMY

**The Federal Government Dollar—
Where It Comes From**

**The Federal Government Dollar—
Where It Goes**

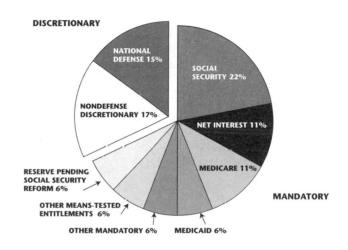

Source: Office of Management and Budget, *Budget of the United States Government, Fiscal Year 2000* (Washington, D.C.: U.S. Government Printing Office, 1999), 7, 10.

Year	GDP (in constant 1992 dollars)	Federal Government Spending (billions) (in constant 1992 dollars)			National Debt (current dollars)	
		National Defense	Non-defense	Total	Debt held by the public (millions)	As a percentage of GDP
1940	$941.2	$20.8	$88.3	$109.2	$42,722	43.7
1941	1,101.8	69.5	80.6	150.2	48,223	41.8
1942	1,308.9	223.7	110.3	334.0	67,753	46.6
1943	1,523.0	525.2	143.9	669.1	127,766	71.1
1944	1,644.7	680.5	144.8	825.5	184,796	89.4
1945	1,626.7	765.4	97.8	862.4	235,182	108.2
1946	1,447.7	432.4	96.4	529.0	241,861	111.0
1947	1,430.7	122.0	154.1	276.2	224,339	98.2
1948	1,491.0	88.3	144.3	232.5	216,270	85.3
1949	1,479.8	123.4	178.6	302.0	214,322	79.5
1950	1,611.3	129.1	190.1	319.3	219,023	80.3
1951	1,734.0	215.8	134.9	350.6	214,326	66.8
1952	1,798.7	383.1	123.6	507.0	214,758	61.5
1953	1,881.4	396.7	131.9	528.5	218,383	58.6
1954	1,868.2	363.9	110.8	474.6	224,499	59.5
1955	2,001.1	311.9	139.1	450.9	226,616	57.3

(continued)

(continued)

Year	GDP (in constant 1992 dollars)	Federal Government Spending (billions) (in constant 1992 dollars)			National Debt (current dollars)	
		National Defense	Non-defense	Total	Debt held by the public (millions)	As a percentage of GDP
1956	$2,040.2	$291.3	$149.9	$440.9	$222,156	52.1
1957	2,078.5	291.0	159.0	449.9	219,320	48.7
1958	2,057.5	286.2	171.9	458.1	226,336	49.3
1959	2,210.2	272.5	208.0	480.4	234,701	47.9
1960	2,262.9	257.2	200.9	458.2	236,840	45.7
1961	2,314.3	258.6	215.4	473.9	238,357	44.9
1962	2,454.8	267.2	244.7	511.8	248,010	43.7
1963	2,559.4	261.9	252.5	514.4	253,978	42.4
1964	2,708.4	265.7	273.5	539.0	256,849	40.1
1965	2,881.1	245.6	285.1	530.9	260,778	38.0
1966	3,069.2	270.8	315.4	586.2	263,714	35.0
1967	3,147.2	320.0	345.0	665.0	266,626	32.8
1968	3,293.9	349.2	372.3	721.5	289,545	33.4
1969	3,393.6	333.5	371.2	704.7	278,108	29.3
1970	3,397.6	310.7	369.9	707.6	283,198	28.1
1971	3,510.0	283.0	432.2	715.1	303,037	28.1
1972	3,702.3	262.3	476.3	738.7	322,377	27.4
1973	3,916.3	239.6	509.6	749.1	340,910	26.1
1974	3,891.2	228.3	531.2	759.4	343,699	23.9
1975	3,873.9	224.1	623.6	847.6	394,700	25.4
1976	4,082.9	216.8	668.7	885.4	477,404	27.6
TQ[1]	n/a	52.1	168.9	221.0	495,509	27.2
1977	4,273.6	216.4	685.1	901.4	549,103	27.9
1978	4,503.0	217.4	727.1	944.5	607,125	27.4
1979	4,630.6	221.8	735.1	957.0	640,308	25.7
1980	4,615.0	229.3	786.2	1,015.5	709,838	26.1
1981	4,720.7	241.8	814.4	1,056.3	785,338	25.8
1982	4,602.3	263.7	822.6	1,086.3	919,785	28.6
1983	4,803.7	284.0	839.5	1,123.5	1,131,596	33.1
1984	5,140.1	287.4	841.6	1,129.1	1,300,498	34.1
1985	5,323.5	306.2	902.7	1,209.0	1,499,908	36.6
1986	5,487.7	324.8	905.7	1,230.4	1,736,709	39.7
1987	5,649.5	330.0	883.8	1,213.8	1,888,680	41.0
1988	5,865.2	333.9	911.7	1,245.6	2,050,799	41.4
1989	6,062.0	338.3	946.4	1,284.7	2,189,882	40.9
1990	6,136.3	324.6	1,029.1	1,353.7	2,410,722	42.4
1991	6,079.4	283.3	1,082.8	1,366.1	2,688,137	45.9
1992	6,244.4	298.4	1,083.3	1,381.7	2,998,834	48.8
1993	6,386.1	286.2	1,088.5	1,374.8	3,247,471	50.2
1994	6,608.4	270.9	1,122.4	1,393.2	3,432,117	50.2
1995	6,742.2	255.5	1,155.2	1,410.6	3,603,373	50.1
1996	6,906.8	242.1	1,177.5	1,419.6	3,732,964	49.9
1997 est.	n/a	237.4	1,208.1	1,445.6	3,875,775	49.3
1998 est.	n/a	224.7	1,231.4	1,456.1	4,021,358	48.9
1999 est.	n/a	220.7	1,258.9	1,479.6	4,159,413	48.3
2000 est.	n/a	219.9	1,264.6	1,484.6	4,268,984	47.2
2001 est.	n/a	215.0	1,255.5	1,470.4	4,327,965	45.6
2002 est.	n/a	213.5	1,247.8	1,461.3	4,333,122	43.5

1. Transitional quarter when fiscal year start was shifted from July 1 to October 1.

SOURCES: Compiled from U.S. Department of Commerce, *Survey of Current Business* (Washington, D.C.: U.S. Government Printing Office, May 1997), 10, 14; Office of Management and Budget, *Budget of the United States Government, Fiscal Year 1998, Historical Tables* (Washington, D.C.: U.S. Government Printing Office, 1997), 95–103.

NOTES

Chapter 1. The Logic of American Politics
pages 2–23

1. William Booth, "California, U.S. Buy Redwoods," *Washington Post,* March 3, 1999, A1.

2. This text concentrates on politics in the American national government, but it also draws freely on examples from other settings because the logic embedded in political processes is by no means confined to matters related to government.

3. In 1832 the Prussian general Carl von Clausewitz proclaimed famously that war is "politics by other means." Clausewitz writes, "War is not merely an act of policy but a true political instrument, a continuation of political intercourse, carried on with other means." Carl von Clausewitz, *On War,* ed. and trans. Michael Howard and Peter Paret (Princeton, N.J.: Princeton University Press, 1976), 87.

4. James Harrington, *The Common-wealth of Oceana and a System of Politics* (1656; reprinted, ed. J. G. Pocock, New York: Cambridge University Press, 1992).

5. Collective action is defined as the efforts of a group, be it a social club, a nation, or even the international community, to reach and implement agreements.

6. Consider how remarkable it is that in 1999 the senators engaged in trying an impeached president found themselves consulting what the Framers had to say about this provision of the Constitution more than two hundred years earlier.

7. C. R. Hallpike, "Functionalist Interpretations of Primitive Warfare," *Man* (September 1973). Cited in Russell Hardin, "Hobbesian Political Order," *Political Theory* (May 1991): 168.

8. Thomas Hobbes, *Leviathan, or The matter, forme, & power of a common-wealth ecclesiasticall and civil* (1651; reprint, Oxford: Clarendon Press, 1958).

9. Moreover, serious "indirect" costs may be associated with delegating enforcement authority to offices—a factor examined later in this chapter (see "Delegation").

10. Alternately, two-thirds of the state legislatures can ask Congress to call a national convention to propose amendments, but this has never been done.

11. Conformity costs are equivalent to Buchanan and Tullock's "external" costs. The label "conformity costs," however, avoids confusion with the concept of "externality" introduced later in the chapter. See James M. Buchanan and Gordon Tullock, *The Calculus of Consent* (Ann Arbor: University of Michigan Press, 1962).

12. *Federalist* No. 51.

13. They were, among others, the French philosopher Baron de Montesquieu (1689–1755) and the English philosopher John Locke (1632–1704).

14. While this discussion focuses on the consumption of economic goods, the argument applies equally well to religious and social "consumption." In the absence of a state religion, each denomination prospers according to consumer attraction to its appeal.

15. Think of externalities as the flip side of conformity costs: rather than society imposing a less-than-ideal public good on each of its members, some members impose undesired "goods" on society.

16. Henry Jones Ford, *The Rise and Growth of American Politics* (New York: Macmillan, 1898).

Chapter 2. The Constitution   pages 24–57

1. Wayne Carp, *To Starve the Army at Pleasure: Continental Army Administration and American Political Culture, 1775–1783* (Chapel Hill: University of North Carolina Press, 1984), 197. During 1780 Washington frequently repeated this warning in correspondence with political leaders.

2. On learning of Franklin's plan King George III declared, "I am the colonies' legislature."

3. At the time, the only British taxes on the colonies were duties on imports from outside the British Empire, designed less to raise revenue than to regulate commerce.

4. Earlier, the Sugar Act of 1764 levied new duties on certain foreign imports and introduced new efforts to interdict Yankee smuggling to circumvent import duties. At the same time Parliament passed another inflammatory law, the Currency Act, which forbade the colonies from printing their own currency, thus requiring merchants to raise scarce hard cash in order to do business.

5. "Nothing else is talked of," wrote Sally Franklin to her father, Benjamin, in London. "The Dutch [Germans] talk of the stompt act the Negroes of the tamp, in short every body has something to say."

Mary Beth Norton et al., *A People and a Nation: A History of the United States* (Boston: Houghton Mifflin, 1990), 117.

6. When some colonies' assemblies were enjoined from meeting, they would adjourn to a local tavern and resume doing business as an unofficial provincial convention.

7. Letter from John Adams to Timothy Pickering, August 22, 1822, in John Adams, *Life and Works*, Vol. II, ed. Charles Francis Adams (Boston, 1850–1856).

8. Joseph R. Conlin, *The Morrow Book of Quotations in American History* (New York: Morrow, 1984). Whether drafting Virginia's first law guaranteeing religious freedom as a member of its House of Burgesses, revising Virginia's constitution, or founding the University of Virginia, Jefferson consistently devoted himself to those activities liberating the inherent capacities of his fellow citizens.

9. Among the items deleted: "He [King George III] has waged cruel war against human nature itself, violating its most sacred rights of life and liberty in the persons of a distant people who never offended him, captivating them and carrying them into slavery in another hemisphere, or to incur miserable death in their transportation thither." In *Thomas Jefferson* (New York: Library of America, 1984), 21–22.

10. Under the Articles, the president served more or less as the chief clerk of Congress.

11. Payments were to be roughly proportionate to a state's wealth, which was assumed to be proportionate to its population.

12. Ten years later these advocates of congressional authority would form the core group of nationalists, led by James Madison and Alexander Hamilton, pressing the nation for a new constitution.

13. This expression comes from Revolutionary War general Nathaniel Greene—see Carp, *To Starve the Army at Pleasure*, 196. Remarkably, while the field commanders showered Congress with contempt, none ever suggested that the military could do a better job of running the government.

14. Hamilton also argued that Congress must delegate administration to "great officers of State—A secretary for foreign affairs—A President of War—A President of Marine—A Financier." In effect, Hamilton was calling for an autonomous national government with a legislature at its center and a separate executive branch.

15. Gordon S. Wood offers this assessment: "The economic and social instability engendered by the Revolution was finding political expression in the state legislatures at the very time they were larger, more representative, and more powerful than ever before in American history." Wood, *The Creation of the American Republic: 1776–1787* (New York: Norton, 1969), 405–410.

16. Letter to Thomas Jefferson, October 17, 1788, in William T. Hutchinson et al., eds., *The Papers of James Madison*, Vol. 9 (Chicago: University of Chicago Press, 1962).

17. This discussion follows David P. Szatmary's treatment in *Shays's Rebellion: The Making of an Agrarian Insurrection* (Amherst: University of Massachusetts Press, 1980), 120–134.

18. John Locke, *Essay Concerning the True Original Extent and End of Civil Government. Second Treatise of Government*, ed. C. B. Macpherson (Indianapolis, Ind.: Hackett, 1980).

19. Unable to fathom the purpose of certain provisions of the ancient constitutions he had examined, Madison was determined not to leave future generations in the dark about the rationale of this new constitution. Thus he carefully recorded the business of the convention. This discussion closely follows Madison's *Notes on the Federal Convention*, discovered after his death in 1837. The government paid his widow $30,000 for them and published them three years later.

20. Early in debate of the Virginia Plan Hamilton introduced a resolution calling for any product of the convention to move beyond a "merely federal" plan or treaty of the states. Instead, "a national government ought to be established consisting of a supreme Legislative, Executive and Judiciary." Everyone was surprised when the resolution passed six states to one, with five abstentions. See Alfred H. Kelly and Winfred A. Harbison, *The American Constitution*, 3d ed. (New York: Norton, 1963), 123–124. Much of the analysis of the politics of the convention draws on William Lee Miller, *The Business of May Next: James Madison and the Founding* (Charlottesville: University Press of Virginia, 1992).

21. Madison's forces did make one significant concession, accepting an amendment that gave the states sole authority to select the members of the upper house. Thus the Senate began to assume its ultimate form. But the delegates from small states pressed for more: equal state representation in both chambers.

22. Chapter 3, Federalism, traces the nationalization of public policy via the necessary and proper clause.

In addition to listing what Congress can do, the Constitution lists what it—and the states—cannot do. Article I, Section 9, restricts Congress from granting titles of nobility, spending unappropriated funds, suspending the writ of *habeas corpus*, passing ex post facto laws, levying income taxes, and taxing state exports. Section 10 imposes restrictions on states, prohibiting them from conducting foreign policy (through entering into treaties or alliances, or conducting war), printing money, passing laws undermining contracts, and imposing tariffs or duties on trade.

23. Miller, *Business of May Next*, 87.

24. In the Judiciary Act of 1789 the First Congress exercised this option and created a lower federal court system.

25. *Marbury v. Madison*, 1 Cr. 137 (1803).

26. And there are others. Article IV provides for the extradition of criminals and assures the states that the records, acts, and proceedings of each state will be given "Full Faith and Credit" in other states and that citizens of individual states will be entitled to all the "Privileges and Immunities" of citizens in other states.

27. Other trade and business-related provisions appear in Article I. One provision prevents the government from passing laws impairing the obligations of private contracts; others mandate that the national government create bankruptcy and patent laws.

28. The three-fifths rule had been devised under the Articles to resolve a sectional dispute over apportioning states' tax contributions according to population. At that time the northerners had had a stake in recognizing the humanity of slaves—if slaves were people their numbers should be fully counted in apportioning tax obligations. Southerners had countered that, since they marketed slaves as property, slaves should be counted no more than any other property. After extended haggling, the groups agreed to add three-fifths of the number of slaves to a state's free population.

29. The committee that drafted this language proposed the ban on regulation end in 1800, but a coalition of New Englanders and southerners added eight years to the ban. Only Madison spoke out against extending the deadline. The delegates from Virginia, all of whom owned slaves at one time or another, voted against extension.

30. As Madison wrote to explain the decision, "An understanding on the two subjects of *navigation* and *slavery,* had taken place between those parts of the Union, which explains the vote on the Motion." Quoted in Miller, *Business of May Next*, 135.

31. Quoted in James MacGregor Burns, *The Vineyard of Liberty* (New York: Vintage Books, 1983), 28.

32. Catherine Drinker Bowen, *Miracle at Philadelphia: The Story of the Constitutional Convention, May to September 1787* (Boston: Atlantic-Little, Brown, 1966), 278.

33. Under pressure from small farmers, many state legislatures had printed cheap paper money (making it easier for the farmers to pay off their debts), overturned court decisions unfavorable to debt-laden farmers, and provided some with direct subsidies and relief. Thus these constituencies were reluctant to see their state legislatures subordinated to some more distant government that would assume control of critical activities such as currency and bankruptcy. The farmers failed to recognize, however, that the ascendancy of the national government would benefit them by shifting public finance away from property taxes and toward import duties. Some northeastern merchants who foresaw this shift lobbied their delegates to oppose ratification.

34. Jefferson had helped to draft a constitution for Virginia in 1776, and Madison had shepherded it through the House of Burgesses.

35. Although they became famous, the *Federalist* essays, according to most historians, had a negligible impact on the outcome of the ratification process. Perhaps too many hard economic interests were in play for abstract arguments about the general welfare to do more than justify and dress up positions grounded firmly in self-interests. The New York convention shifted toward ratification only after New York City threatened to secede from the state if the vote went against ratification.

36. See Locke, *Essay Concerning the True Original Extent and End of Civil Government,* and David Hume, "The Perfect Commonwealth," in *Essays, Moral, Political, and Literary,* ed. Eugene F. Miller (Indianapolis: Liberty Fund, 1987). In 1776 Madison had urged fellow members of the Virginia House of Burgesses to embrace a multitude of religious sects in promoting religious reform, proposing that "all men are equally entitled to enjoy the free exercise of religion, according to the dictates of conscience." Ralph Ketcham, *James Madison: A Biography* (Charlottesville. University Press of Virginia, 1990), 72. In an essay on the "vices" of republican governments, he fleshed out the argument more fully and applied it to political factions. Also see Douglas Adair, "'That Politics May Be Reduced to a Science,' David Hume, James Madison and the Tenth Federalist," *Huntington Library Quarterly* (1957), reprinted in Douglas Adair, *Fame and the Founding Fathers* (New York: Norton, 1974), 93–106.

37. In an earlier version of this passage, delivered at the convention in defense of the Virginia Plan, Madison had added that those who owned slaves and those who did not had distinct and antithetical interests. He may well have omitted this reference to slavery here because it had proven controversial with southern delegates. After all, this is a public argument intended to persuade readers to support adoption of the Constitution.

38. Here space joins population numbers as an issue because it is difficult to organize a majority faction across a great expanse. The Framers also hoped to discourage collusion by calling for members of the electoral college to cast their votes in their state capitals rather than in the nation's capital.

39. At one point in *Federalist No. 47*, Madison panders to his opponents by invoking Montesquieu—whom he calls a "great oracle"—as the inspiration of the Constitution's separation of powers doctrine. Despite the complimentary reference here, Madison rarely cited Montesquieu.

40. See Robert Dahl, *A Preface to Democratic Theory* (Chicago: University of Chicago Press, 1956), and E. E. Schattschneider, *Party Government* (New York: Holt, Rinehart and Winston, 1942), 18–21.

Chapter 3. Federalism   pages 58–87

1. This account of the 1906 earthquake was drawn from daily reports in the *New York Times,* April 19–30, 1906.

2. For an assessment of FEMA's performance, see Saundra K. Schneider, "FEMA, Federalism, Hugo, and 'Frisco,'" *Publius* 20 (summer 1990): 97–113.

3. In this text and elsewhere, the terms *federal* and *national* are used interchangeably. This practice also characterized discussions leading to the formation of the Union. Any difference in usage was largely a matter of stress—that is, the term *federal* reflected the user's cognizance of the state elements in the national government. Hans Sperber and Travis Trittschuh, *American Political Terms* (Detroit: Wayne State University Press, 1962), 148–149.

4. This definition comes directly from Parris N. Glendening and Mavis Mann Reeves, *Pragmatic Federalism,* 2d ed. (Pacific Palisades, Calif.: Pacific Palisades Publishing, 1984), 11.

5. David Firestone, "Gun Lobby Begins Concerned Attacks on Cities' Lawsuits," *New York Times,* February 9, 1991, C5.

6. For a review of contemporary state-local relations, see Russell L. Hanson, *Governing Partners: State-Local Relations in the United States* (Boulder, Colo.: Westview Press, 1998).

7. Farmers 2–7 do not have to worry about one of their neighbors trying to free ride; everyone understands that if any one of them drops out the project will become too costly for the others and it will falter. It is assumed that farmers 1 and 8 have a sincere lack of interest in the project and are not free riding.

8. But if the special district is governed by consensus, then any one of the shaded farmers could effectively veto the road maintenance proposal. Thus one of the most important decisions these farmers will make in the early stages of their collective undertaking will deal not with roads but with the rules governing how they would make such decisions in the future. Indeed, one could even imagine a variety of perverse outcomes that hark back to Madison's fear of majority tyranny. For example, a minimum majority of farmers (nine in this example) could pass a law requiring all farmers to contribute to paving the driveways of the majority.

9. This history is well told by Robert H. Wiebe in *The Search for Order, 1877–1920* (New York: Hill and Wang, 1967).

10. Unlike the federal government, most state governments are forbidden by their constitutions from enacting annual budgets that incur a deficit.

11. The commerce clause permits Congress to "regulate Commerce with foreign Nations, and among the several States." After the *McCulloch* decision in 1819 (described later in this chapter), the commerce clause receded as a source of tension in federal-state relations. Indeed, other than its efforts to prevent unionization of workers and maintain high, protective tariffs, the national government rarely intruded into private commerce. *McCulloch v. Maryland,* 4 Wheat. 316 (1819).

12. Daniel Patrick Moynihan, *Maximum Feasible Misunderstanding: Community Action in the War on Poverty* (New York: Free Press, 1969).

13. The Fishery Conservation Management Act of 1976 established three Regional Fishery Management Councils. They are, along with the secretary of commerce, jointly responsible for fisheries management.

14. The case was *United States v. F. W. Darby Lumber Co.,* 312 U.S. 100 (1941). Passage cited in Lee Epstein and Thomas G. Walker, *Constitutional Law for a Changing America: A Short Course* (Washington, D.C.: CQ Press, 1996), 206.

15. MADD did meet some resistance in the low drinking age states that benefited economically from the commerce in alcohol.

16. *South Dakota v. Dole*, 483 U.S. 203 (1987).

17. Timothy Egan, "Struggle over Gun Control Laws Shifts to States and Tests N.R.A.," *New York Times*, October 13, 1997.

18. *Federalist* No. 46.

19. William H. Riker, "The Senate and American Federalism," *American Political Science Review* 49 (1955): 452–469.

20. For a discussion of the Senate's special role in spawning presidential candidates, see Nelson W. Polsby, *Political Innovation in America* (New Haven: Yale University Press, 1984).

21. See Article I, Section 9.

22. It also is known as the necessary and proper clause.

23. Opponents of national gun control legislation claim that the "right to bear arms" stated in the Second Amendment is a fundamental personal right. The full text, however, clearly refers to the rights of the states to maintain a militia in order to deter encroachments from the national government. In reality, the Second Amendment was drafted to protect federalism.

24. *McCulloch v. Maryland*, 4 Wheat. 316 (1819).

25. *Gibbons v. Ogden*, 22 U.S. 1 (1824).

26. *Garcia v. San Antonio Metropolitan Transit Authority*, 469 U.S. 528 (1985).

27. *United States v. Lopez*, 514 U.S. 549 (1995). The Gun-Free School Zones Act established a zone around public schools in which anyone caught having a gun was charged with a federal felony.

28. Kenneth T. Palmer and Eward B. Laverty, "The Impact of *United States v. Lopez* on Intergovernmental Relations: A Preliminary Assessment," *Publius* 26 (summer 1996): 109–126. This revisionism continued in a 1997 case where the Court invalidated a provision of the 1993 Brady handgun law that required local law enforcement officials to run background checks on purchasers of handguns. Dan Carney, "Brady Decision Reflects Effort To Curb Congress' Authority," *Congressional Quarterly Weekly Report*, June 28, 1997, 1524–1525.

29. John Kincaid, "Constitutional Federalism: Labor's Role in Displacing Places to Benefit Persons," *PS* (June 1993): 172.

30. Carol S. Weissert and Sanford F. Schram, "The State of American Federalism, 1995–1996," *Publius* 26 (summer 1996): 1–9.

31. Surprising allies of categorical grant makers are the administrators of the state agencies these grants support. For them, conversion to block grants would introduce uncertainty over their budgeting. Funds from an alcohol and drug abuse program, for example, might be shifted from outpatient methadone facilities to prison construction and, in the process, from one state agency to another.

32. The one exception was the Hatch Act (1940), which sought to clean up corruption by preventing federal and state employees from engaging in a variety of partisan political activities.

33. L. Nye Stevens, "Unfunded Mandates—Reform Act Has Had Little Effect on Agencies' Rulemaking Actions, Report to the Committee on Governmental Affairs, U.S. Senate," General Accounting Office, Washington, D.C., 1998.

Chapter 4.   Civil Rights   pages 88–123

1. Barry Bearak, "Rights Groups Ducked a Fight, Opponents Say," *New York Times*, November 22, 1997, A1.

2. John M. Broder, "Clinton, Softening Slap at Senate, Names 'Acting' Civil Rights Chief," *New York Times*, December 16, 1997.

3. The Framers, by giving each state two senators regardless of size, weakened the Senate both as a representative institution and as an arena where a variety of political views would be heard.

4. In 1787 Benjamin Franklin convened an abolition society meeting in his home and invited delegates to the Constitutional Convention to attend.

5. As late as 1858, Abraham Lincoln, in his famous Senate race debates in Illinois with Stephen Douglas, was distinguishing between citizenship rights based on equality and fundamental rights. He protected his flank by stating there was "no purpose to introduce political and social equality between the white and black races." But then, in one of the most progressive statements made by any elected officeholder of the time, he asserted: "There is no reason in the world why the negro is not entitled to all the natural rights enumerated in the Declaration of Independence. . . . I hold that he is as much entitled to these as the white man." Donald G. Nieman, *Promises to Keep: African-Americans and the Constitutional Order, 1776 to the Present* (New York: Oxford University Press, 1991), 43.

6. This achievement stemmed in part from the Senate's insistence that the former Confederate states ratify the amendment as a condition of their reentry into the Union.

7. Mary B. Norton et al., *People and a Nation: A History of the United States*, 2 vols., 3d ed. (Boston: Houghton Mifflin, 1987), 1:238.

8. Chaplain W. Morrison, *Democratic Politics and Sectionalism: The Wilmot Proviso Controversy* (Chapel Hill: University of North Carolina Press, 1967).

9. *Dred Scott v. Sandford*, 19 How. 393 (1857).

10. According to David Donald, perhaps Lincoln's foremost biographer, the president's policies corresponded closely to those that would have been produced by "a rather simple computer installed in the White House, fed the elementary statistical information about election returns and programmed to solve the recurrent problems of winning re-election. . . ." David Donald, *The Politics of Reconstruction, 1863–1867* (Baton Rouge: Louisiana State University Press, 1965).

11. Of the eleven referendum votes held from 1865 through 1869 in eight northern states on constitutional changes to provide blacks with the ballot, only those in Iowa and Minnesota in 1868 succeeded. The white voters of Illinois, Indiana, Pennsylvania, and New Jersey never voted on the issue, which may have indicated a higher intensity of racial prejudice in those states than in Connecticut, New York, and Ohio, where equal suffrage was defeated. LaWanda and John H. Cox, "Negro Suffrage and Republican Politics: The Problem of Motivation in Reconstruction Historiography," *Journal of Southern History* 33 (August 1967): 318–319.

12. Even the most ardent abolitionists admitted that freedmen could not be transformed instantly into full citizens. One of these was Republican senator Charles Sumner of Massachusetts, who before the war had earned his abolitionist credentials the hard way by being severely caned after a floor speech. The assailant was a southerner with apparently tender sensibilities. Sumner's reservations on this score were seconded by no less than journalist William Lloyd Garrison, as militant an abolitionist as there ever was. "According to the laws of development and progress," Garrison concluded, the franchise "is not practical." Garrison justified his conservative stance with a prescient appreciation of freedmen's circumstances in the South, where "as soon as the state was organized and left to manage its own affairs, the white population, with their superior intelligence, wealth, and power, would unquestionably alter the franchise in accordance with their prejudices, and exclude those [freedmen] thus summarily brought to the polls. Coercion would

gain nothing." C. Vann Woodward, *The Burden of Southern History* (Baton Rouge: Louisiana State University Press, 1968), 90.

13. He also estimated that thirty-seven of all southern seats would be accounted for by the region's black population. The fact that few African Americans would be allowed to vote did not matter; it had never mattered in the North, where they always had been counted in congressional apportionment but in most states had never voted.

14. Had they remained in force, the black codes would have effectively reinstituted a de facto form of slavery. Among other things, these laws forbade African Americans to own property, carry firearms, appear in court, and marry whites.

15. Quoted in Woodward, *Burden of Southern History*, 95.

16. Johnson's policies were designed to return the South rapidly to the Union and allow the former rebels to take control of their states. Arguably, he was following the same policies favored by Lincoln shortly before his assassination on April 16, 1865. Johnson did manage to render one policy toothless, however. Confederate civilian and military leaders who had not received a presidential pardon were barred from holding office, but Johnson apparently pardoned anyone who requested it.

17. Similarly, in Alabama there were approximately twenty thousand more white men than black men but forty thousand more black voters. Woodward, *Burden of Southern History*, 98–99.

18. Ibid.

19. C. Vann Woodward, *Reunion and Reaction: The Compromise of 1877 and the End of Reconstruction* (Boston: Little, Brown, 1966).

20. Similarly, interpreting the Fifteenth Amendment, the Supreme Court ruled in *United States v. Reese* (1876) that state laws denying voting rights to African Americans were indeed permissible unless they could be shown to be motivated by considerations of race. By applying the poll tax or literacy test to everyone, or even claiming to do so, the southern legislatures could satisfy the Court. *United States v. Reese*, 92 U.S. 214 (1876).

21. *Plessy v. Ferguson*, 163 U.S. 737 (1896).

22. According to Woodward, Republican politicians tended to be conservative at the end of Reconstruction. Acknowledging the rapid industrialization during these years, they aligned themselves with urban, business constituencies for whom black civil rights in the South were a low priority. Woodward, *Reunion and Reaction*, 22–50.

23. While President Roosevelt had been reluctant to back federal antilynching and anti–poll tax legislation, many congressional Democrats introduced and championed hundreds of bills targeted at these and other civil rights issues. (The legislation repeatedly passed in the House of Representatives but, just as in the antebellum era, failed in the Senate where the South held a greater share of the membership.)

24. This is not to say that racial discrimination was on the verge of extinction in the 1940s. Jim Crow still had strong roots in the South. Moreover, in the wake of the December 7, 1941, bombing of Pearl Harbor, thrusting the United States into war with Japan, the federal government created a comprehensive program for the removal of Japanese Americans from the West Coast to internment camps. In 1944 the Supreme Court upheld that removal and confinement. Even though the Court recognized that "all legal restrictions which curtail the civil rights of a single racial group are immediately suspect," it concluded that "pressing public necessity may sometimes justify the existence of such restrictions." As in the case of civil liberties, civil rights were readily sacrificed during wartime.

25. In Detroit, for example, the African American population doubled from 8 percent in 1930 to 16 percent in 1950 and to 44 percent by 1970 (Table 4-1). Although Detroit had the most dramatic growth in black population, a similar trend was evident in every major urban center throughout the nation. Edward G. Carmines and James A. Stimson, *Issue Evolution: Race and the Transformation of American Politics* (Princeton: Princeton University Press, 1989), Table 2.1.

26. James Rowe, a former Roosevelt aide, initiated the famous "Clifford Memorandum" of November 10, 1947, in which this excerpt appeared, and about three-quarters of the final text was his. But, revealing his background, this New Dealer offered no more than a passing reference to the black vote. The addition of this new constituency was the handiwork of Clark Clifford, who represented the next generation of Democratic strategists. Clark Clifford with Richard Holbrooke, *Counsel to the President: A Memoir* (New York: Random House, 1991), 192.

27. Carmines and Stimson, *Issue Evolution*.

28. *Brown v. Board of Education of Topeka*, 347 U.S. 483 (1954).

29. *Smith v. Allwright*, 321 U.S. 649 (1944).

30. *Brown v. Board of Education of Topeka*, 349 U.S. 294 (1955).

31. Some civil rights leaders, suspicious of Lyndon Johnson, accused him of selling out their cause. Later they would retract their criticism. Every civil rights law passed over the next decade also bore LBJ's stamp.

32. Organizations—from civil rights organizations to black churches—recruited and "rewarded" demonstrators with status and personal support. Movement leaders provided the essential coordination, channeling protesters' activities in the most productive direction. Dennis Chong, *Collective Action and the Civil Rights Movement* (Chicago: University of Chicago Press, 1991).

33. David J. Garrow, *Bearing the Cross: Martin Luther King, Jr., and the Southern Christian Leadership Conference* (New York: Morrow, 1986), 91.

34. Paul Burstein, "Public Opinion, Demonstrations, and the Passage of Antidiscrimination Legislation," *Public Opinion Quarterly* 43 (1979): 157–172.

35. Taylor Branch, *Parting the Waters: America in the King Years, 1954–1963* (New York: Simon and Schuster, 1988).

36. Some southern Democrats and Republicans who were unsympathetic to the civil rights goals actually worked to strengthen the House version of the bill in order to make it unattractive to border state senators, who might have been willing to vote to end a southern filibuster on whatever bill came to the Senate floor.

37. Gerald M. Pomper, "From Confusion to Clarity: Issues and American Voters, 1956–1968," *American Political Science Review* (June 1972): 419.

38. Robert M. Axelrod, "Where the Votes Come From: An Analysis of Electoral Coalitions, 1952–1958," *American Political Science Review* (March 1972).

39. From Gary Orfield, *Congressional Power: Congress and Social Change* (New York: Harcourt Brace Jovanovich, 1975), 102.

40. Until the Supreme Court ruled them unconstitutional in 1968, *restrictive covenants* were commonly embedded in property deeds preventing owners from selling the property to Jews and African Americans. *Jones v. Alfred H. Mayer Co.*, 392 U.S. 409 (1968).

41. *Johnson v. Transportation Agency of Santa Clara County*, 480 U.S. 646 (1987).

42. *Adarand Constructors, Inc. v. Pena*, 515 U.S. 200 (1995).

43. *Texas v. Hopwood*, 135 L. Ed. 2d 1095 (1996).

44. The rise of the abortion issue after the Supreme Court legalized abortions in its 1973 *Roe v. Wade* decision stalled ERA. Jane Mansbridge, *Why We Lost the ERA* (Chicago: University of Chicago Press, 1986).

45. Gallup poll cited in ibid., 214.

46. *Romer v. Evans*, 134 L. Ed. 2d 855 (1996).

Chapter 5. Civil Liberties   pages 124–159

1. *Reno v. ACLU*, 138 L. Ed. 2d 874 (1997).

2. From a speech to Congress, June 8, 1789. Quoted in *The Papers of James Madison*, ed. William T. Hutchinson et al. (Chicago: University of Chicago Press, 1962), 197–206.

3. *Employment Division, Department of Human Resources of Oregon v. Smith*, 494 U.S. 872 (1990). This case is described more fully in the section "Free Exercise."

4. *City of Boerne v. Flores*, 136 L. Ed. 2d 709 (1997).

5. Linda Greenhouse, "Laws Urged to Restore Religion Act," *New York Times*, August 15, 1997.

6. Donald S. Lutz, "The State Constitutional Pedigree of the U.S. Bill of Rights," *Publius* 22 (spring 1992): 19–45.

7. Quoted in Alpheus Thomas Mason, *The States' Rights Debate* (New York: Oxford University Press, 1972), 174. Madison informed the House of Representatives: "I will not propose a single alteration which I do not wish to see take place, as proper in itself, or proper because it is wished by a respectable number of my fellow citizens."

8. *Barron v. Baltimore*, 7 Pet. 243 (1833).

9. Andrew W. Young, *Introduction to the Science of Government*, 3d ed. (Rochester, N.Y.: William Alling, 1843).

10. This discussion of incorporation follows the presentation in Lee Epstein and Thomas G. Walker, *Constitutional Law for a Changing America: Rights, Liberties, and Justice*, 3d ed. (Washington, D.C.: CQ Press, 1998), 66–88. Indeed, this text provides a thorough review and treatment of all issues described in this chapter.

11. *The Butchers' Benevolent Association of New Orleans v. The Crescent City Livestock Landing and Slaughterhouse Co.; Esteben v. Louisiana* (The Slaughterhouse Cases), 16 Wall. 36 (1873).

12. *Hutardo v. California*, 110 U.S. 516 (1884).

13. Throughout the nineteenth century litigants were mostly contesting property rights, not personal liberties. As a result, not much case law on the subject accumulated. In 1897, when the Supreme Court first incorporated the Bill of Rights into the Fourteenth Amendment's due process clause, it selected for incorporation the Fifth Amendment's ban on taking private property without compensation.

14. *Palko v. Connecticut*, 302 U.S. 319 (1937). In 1937 the Court in *Palko* designated criminal rights a special class of rights and refused to assume federal jurisdiction over a double jeopardy case. Although the Court ruled that the First Amendment guarantees were rightly applied to both state and federal governments—for "neither liberty nor justice would exist if they were sacrificed"—it found that protection against double jeopardy was not so fundamental. States could elect to disregard it and "justice still be done."

15. John L. Sullivan, James E. Piereson, and George E. Marcus, *Political Tolerance and American Democracy* (Chicago: University of Chicago Press, 1982). The authors caution, however, that the trend toward increased tolerance may not be nearly so great when one takes into account that public opinion toward groups changes over time. Communists, for example, seem less despised now that the cold war is over than in the 1950s. By first asking respondents to identify which group they most despised and then applying the tolerance questions to this target group, these researchers found that respondents registered levels of intolerance comparable to those directed at "communists" in the 1950s.

16. *Prudential Insurance Co. v. Cheek*, 259 U.S. 530 (1922), quoted in Richard C. Cortner, *The Supreme Court and the Second Bill of Rights* (Madison: University of Wisconsin Press, 1981), 57. The Court's refusal to incorporate free expression occurred in the context of a "Red Scare" spurred by fear of the 1917 Bolshevik Revolution in Russia and the creation of the Comintern in 1919, whose avowed purpose was to destroy capitalism. The result was a wave of legislation across the states that forbade the advocacy of violence or other "unlawful" means to change the government.

17. *Schenck v. United States*, 249 U.S. 47 (1919).

18. *Gitlow v. New York*, 268 U.S. 652 (1925).

19. *Dennis v. United States*, 341 U.S. 494 (1951).

20. *Brandenburg v. Ohio*, 395 U.S. 444 (1969).

21. *National Socialist Party of America v. Village of Skokie*, 432 U.S. 43 (1977).

22. *Tinker v. Des Moines*, 393 U.S. 503 (1969).

23. *Texas v. Johnson*, 491 U.S. 397 (1989).

24. *United States v. Eichman*, 496 U.S. 310 (1990).

25. Only 50 percent of respondents, however, believed an amendment on flag burning was "worth the effort." ABC News / *Washington Post* poll, July 9–12, 1998.

26. This led to the celebrated lower court case, *United States v. One Book Entitled Ulysses*, 72 F. 2d 705 (1934), in which the judge proposed a new standard distinguishing intentional from unintentional obscenity.

27. *Roth v. United States*, 354 U.S. 476 (1957).

28. Epstein and Walker, *Constitutional Law*, 371.

29. *Miller v. California*, 413 U.S. 15 (1973).

30. *Jacobellis v. Ohio*, 378 U.S. 184 (1964).

31. Epstein and Walker, *Constitutional Law*, 371.

32. *Reno v. ACLU*, 117 S. Ct. 2329, 138 L. Ed. 2d 874 (1997).

33. *Near v. Minnesota*, 283 U.S. 697 (1931).

34. *New York Times Co. v. United States*, 403 U.S. 713 (1971).

35. *Sheppard v. Maxwell*, 384 U.S. 333 (1966).

36. *Globe Newspaper Co. v. Superior Court*, 457 U.S. 596 (1982).

37. This doctrine was first employed in 1964 in *New York Times Co. v. Sullivan*, 376 U.S. 254 (1964).

38. In private correspondence with Jefferson, Madison offered precisely the same argument in favor of religious diversity that he later would offer for factions. By letting a thousand denominations bloom, he reasoned, none would attract sufficient popular support to dominate the others.

39. One of Madison's favorite observations on this score came from Voltaire: "If one religion only were allowed in England, the government would possibly be arbitrary; if there were but two, the people would cut each other's throats; but, as there are such a multitude, they all live happy and in peace." Ralph Ketcham, *James Madison* (Charlottesville: University Press of Virginia, 1971), 166.

40. Jefferson referred to a "wall of separation" between church and state in an 1802 letter written to the Danbury Baptist Association.

41. *Bradfield v. Roberts*, 175 U.S. 291 (1899).

42. *Everson v. Board of Education*, 330 U.S. 1 (1947).

43. Frank J. Sorauf, *The Wall of Separation* (Princeton: Princeton University Press, 1976), 257. In the Midwest and West these figures were much lower—18 and 11 percent, respectively.

44. *Lemon v. Kurtzman, Earley v. DiCenso*, 403 U.S. 602 (1971).

45. *Lynch v. Donnelly*, 465 U.S. 668 (1984); *County of Allegheny v. ACLU, Greater Pittsburgh Chapter*, 492 U.S. 573 (1989).

46. Leonard W. Levy, *The Establishment Clause* (New York: Macmillan, 1986), 128.

47. *Board of Education of Kiryas Joel Village School District v. Grumet*, 512 U.S. 687 (1994).

48. *Engel v. Vitale*, 370 U.S. 421 (1962).

49. *School District of Arlington Township v. Schempp*, 374 U.S. 203 (1963).

50. *Wallace v. Jaffree*, 472 U.S. 38 (1985).

51. *Lee v. Weisman*, 505 U.S. 577 (1992).

52. Robert Birkby, "The Supreme Court in the Bible Belt: Tennessee Reaction to the *Schempp* Decision," *American Journal of Political Science* 10 (1966): 304.

53. Kevin Sack, "In South, Prayer Is a Form of Protest: A Ruling Is Opposed in Classrooms, Courtroom and Statehouse," *New York Times*, November 8, 1997, A7.

54. *Cantwell v. Connecticut*, 310 U.S. 296 (1940). The Court concluded that, "in spite of the probability of excesses and abuses, [religious] liberties are, in the long view, essential to enlightened opinion and right conduct on the part of citizens of a democracy." See Cortner, *The Supreme Court and the Second Bill of Rights*, 99–108, for a thoughtful review of this case.

55. Epstein and Walker, *Constitutional Law*, 54.

56. *Employment Division, Department of Human Resources of Oregon v. Smith*.

57. *Church of the Lukumi Babalu Aye, Inc., et al. v. City of Hialeah*, 508 U.S. 502 (1993).

58. Cited in Kenneth Janda, Jeffrey M. Berry, and Jerry Goldman, *The Challenge of Democracy*, 4th ed. (Boston: Houghton Mifflin, 1995), 537.

59. *Brown v. Mississippi*, 297 U.S. 278 (1936).

60. Harold W. Stanley and Richard G. Niemi, *Vital Statistics on American Politics, 1997–1998* (Washington, D.C.: CQ Press, 1998), 155.

61. *Mapp v. Ohio*, 367 U.S. 643 (1961).

62. *United States v. Leon*, 468 U.S. 897 (1984); *Massachusetts v. Sheppard*, 468 U.S. 981 (1984).

63. *Nix v. Williams*, 467 U.S. 431 (1984).

64. *Minnesota v. Carter*, 97–1147 (1998) dealt with guests in homes.

65. *Mallory v. Hogan*, 378 U.S. 1 (1964).

66. *Miranda v. Arizona*, 384 U.S. 436 (1966).

67. William Glaberson, "Miranda Ruling Faces Its Most Serious Challenge," *New York Times*, February 25, 1999, A1.

68. *Benton v. Maryland*, 395 U.S. 784 (1969).

69. *Gideon v. Wainwright*, 372 U.S. 335 (1963).

70. *Argersinger v. Hamlin*, 407 U.S. 25 (1972).

71. *Furman v. Georgia*, 408 U.S. 238 (1972). This description of the case is taken from Lee Epstein and Thomas G. Walker, *Constitutional Law for a Changing America: A Short Course* (Washington, D.C.: CQ Press, 1996), 623–624.

72. *Gregg v. Georgia*, 428 U.S. 153 (1976).

73. Death Penalty Information Center, <http://www.essential.org/dpic/> (January 21, 1999).

74. *Griswold v. Connecticut*, 381 U.S. 479 (1965).

75. *Griswold v. Connecticut*.

76. *Eisenstadt v. Baird*, 410 U.S. 113 (1972), extended access to contraceptives to unmarried women.

77. But as Justice Byron White wrote in his dissent from the *Roe* decision, "the upshot is that the people and the legislatures of the fifty states are constitutionally disentitled to weigh the relative importance of the continued existence and development of the fetus, on the one hand, against a spectrum of possible impacts on the mother, on the other hand." *Roe v. Wade*, 410 U.S. 113 (1973).

78. *Planned Parenthood of Southeastern Pennsylvania v. Casey*, 505 U.S. 833 (1992).

79. *Bowers v. Hardwick*, 478 U.S. 186 (1986). The Georgia law imposed up to a twenty-year sentence for convictions, although in this case the defendant, Michael Hardwick, had never actually been charged with the crime. In *Romer v. Evans* (described in Chapter 4) the Court ruled that homosexuals could not be excluded from explicit civil rights protections. *Romer v. Evans*, 134 L. Ed. 2d 855 (1996).

80. *Cruzan v. Director, Missouri Department of Health*, 497 U.S. 261 (1990).

81. *Vacco v. Quill*, 138 L. Ed. 2d 834 (1997); *Washington v. Glucksberg*, 138 L. Ed. 2d 772 (1997).

Chapter 6. Congress   pages 160–207

1. Jon Healy, "Jubilant GOP Strives to Keep Legislative Feet on the Ground," *Congressional Quarterly Weekly Report*, November 12, 1994, 3214.

2. Ibid., 3211.

3. In the past some states elected some or all of their U.S. representatives in statewide "at-large" districts. This practice was ended by a Supreme Court decision requiring that districts have equal populations (see note 4). One state, Georgia, requires an absolute majority of votes to win general elections to Congress. If no candidate wins such a majority, a runoff election is held between the top two finishers.

4. *Wesberry v. Sanders*, 376 U.S. 1 (1964).

5. *Thornburg v. Gingles*, 478 U.S. 30 (1986).

6. *Davis v. Bandemer*, 478 U.S. 109 (1986).

7. *Thornburg v. Gingles*.

8. *Shaw v. Reno*, 590 U.S. 630 (1993).

9. *Miller v. Johnson*, 115 S. Ct. 2475 (1995).

10. Alan I. Abramowitz and Jeffrey A. Segal, *Senate Elections* (Ann Arbor: University of Michigan Press, 1992), 18.

11. The Progressive Era and its effects on U.S. politics are described more fully in Chapter 12, Political Parties.

12. Richard F. Fenno Jr., *Home Style: House Members in Their Districts* (Boston: Little, Brown, 1978), chaps. 1–5.

13. Data collected and analyzed by the authors.

14. Jerrold G. Rusk, "The Effects of the Australian Ballot Reform on Split Ticket Voting, 1876–1908," in *Controversies in Voting Behavior*, ed. Richard G. Niemi and Herbert F. Weisberg (San Francisco: W. H. Freeman, 1976), 485–486.

15. Gary C. Jacobson, *The Politics of Congressional Elections*, 4th ed. (New York: Longman, 1997), 19–34.

16. Norman J. Ornstein, Thomas E. Mann, and Michael J. Malbin, *Vital Statistics on Congress, 1997–1998* (Washington, D.C.: Congressional Quarterly, 1998), 151–153.

17. David R. Mayhew, *Congress: The Electoral Connection* (New Haven: Yale University Press, 1974), 37.

18. Gary C. Jacobson and Samuel Kernell, *Strategy and Choice in Congressional Elections*, 2d ed. (New Haven: Yale University Press, 1983), chaps. 2–3.

19. Gary C. Jacobson and Michael A. Dimock, "Checking Out: The Effects of Bank Overdrafts on the 1992 House Elections," *American Journal of Political Science* 38 (August 1994): 601–624.

20. John Kingdon, *Congressmen's Voting Decisions*, 2d ed. (New York: Harper and Row, 1981), 47–50.

21. John R. Johannes, *To Serve the People: Congress and Constituency Service* (Lincoln: University of Nebraska Press, 1984), 19.

22. Exceptions are the seven states that have one representative—see Figure 6–1.

23. Jacobson, *Politics of Congressional Elections*, 130–134.

24. Clinton's 66 percent job approval rating in 1998 was the highest for any president at a midterm election since the Gallup Poll began asking the question more than fifty years ago. In part as a consequence, the 1998 midterm election was only the second since the Civil War in which the president's party gained House seats (the other was 1934). See Gary C. Jacobson, "The 1998 Congressional Elections," *Political Science Quarterly* 114 (spring 1999): 31–51.

25. Gary C. Jacobson, "The 105th Congress: Unprecedented and Unsurprising," in *The Elections of 1996*, ed. Michael Nelson (Washington, D.C.: CQ Press, 1997), 143–166.

26. Roger H. Davidson and Walter J. Oleszek, *Congress and Its Members*, 6th ed. (Washington, D.C.: CQ Press, 1998), 123.

27. Mayhew, *Congress*, 87–97.

28. Gary W. Cox and Mathew McCubbins, *Legislative Leviathan: Party Government in the House* (Berkeley: University of California Press, 1993), part 2.

29. David Rohde, *Parties and Leaders in the Postreform House* (Chicago: University of Chicago Press, 1991), chap. 3.

30. President pro tempore is now, by tradition, the majority member with the greatest Senate seniority; in the 106th Congress (1999–2000), ninety-six-year-old Strom Thurmond, a South Carolina Republican first elected to the Senate in 1956, filled the office.

31. George B. Galloway, *The History of the House of Representatives* (New York: Crowell, 1961), 12.

32. Barbara Hinckley, *Stability and Change in Congress*, 4th ed. (New York: Harper and Row, 1988), 155.

33. Garry Young and Joseph Cooper, "Multiple Referral and the Transformation of House Decision Making," in *Congress Reconsidered*, 5th ed., ed. Lawrence C. Dodd and Bruce I. Oppenheimer (Washington, D.C.: CQ Press, 1993), 212.

34. John W. Ellwood and James A. Thurber, "The New Congressional Budget Process: The Hows and Whys of House-Senate Differences," in *Congress Reconsidered*, ed. Lawrence C. Dodd and Bruce I. Oppenheimer (New York: Praeger, 1977), 168.

35. Joseph White and Aaron Wildavsky, *The Deficit and the Public Interest: The Search for Responsible Budgeting in the 1980s* (Berkeley: University of California Press, 1989), chaps. 16–17.

36. Barbara Sinclair, *Unorthodox Lawmaking: New Legislative Processes in the U.S. Congress* (Washington, D.C.: CQ Press, 1997), chaps. 2–3.

37. Mathew D. McCubbins and Thomas Schwartz, "Congressional Oversight Overlooked: Police Patrols vs. Fire Alarms," *American Journal of Political Science* 28 (February 1984): 165–179.

38. Barbara Sinclair, "Regular Order? New Legislative Processes in the Contemporary Congress" (paper presented at the annual meeting of the American Political Science Association, New York, September 1–4, 1994), table 3. Also see Sarah A. Binder and Steven S. Smith, *Politics or Principle? Filibustering in the United States Senate* (Washington, D.C.: Brookings, 1997).

39. "Six Bills Vetoed," *Congressional Quarterly Weekly Report*, December 14, 1996, 3386.

40. Kingdon, *Congressmen's Voting Decisions*, 47–54.

41. George Hager and David S. Cloud, "Democrats Tie Their Fate to Clinton's Budget Bill," *Congressional Quarterly Weekly Report*, August 7, 1993, 2212–2219.

42. Harold W. Stanley and Richard G. Niemi, *Vital Statistics on American Politics*, 6th ed. (Washington, D.C.: Congressional Quarterly, 1998), 252.

43. John R. Hibbing and Elizabeth Theiss-Morse, *Congress as Public Enemy: Public Attitudes toward American Political Institutions* (New York: Cambridge University Press, 1995), 46–61.

Chapter 7. The Presidency   pages 208–245

1. David E. Rosenbaum, "In Appeal for Support for Budget, President Calls Plan Best for Now," *New York Times*, October 3, 1993, A1.

2. Michael Oreskes, "Advantage: Democrats," *New York Times*, October 29, 1990, A14; Maureen Dowd, "From President to Politician: Bush Attacks the Democrats," *New York Times*, October 30, 1990, A13.

3. Bob Woodward, *The Agenda: Inside the Clinton White House* (New York: Simon and Schuster, 1994).

4. Robert Brownstein, "Washington Outlook, Clinton's Political Recovery Will Be Fleeting Unless He Sticks to Course," *Los Angeles Times*, December 4, 1995.

5. Ibid.

6. Dennis Farney, "Clinton Seems to Have Emerged in Good Shape from the Blame Game over the Budget Impasse," *Wall Street Journal*, November 21, 1995.

7. Christopher Georges, "Balanced-Budget Talks between GOP, White House Stall after Three Days," *Wall Street Journal*, December 1, 1995. Clinton had similarly advised Democratic lawmakers: "We have to exercise a high degree of humility. We're going to make some very complicated demands, and the American people are going to judge us on how we handle this debate." David E. Rosenbaum, "With Crisis Over, Clinton Now Seeks the High Ground," *New York Times*, November 21, 1995.

8. Richard E. Neustadt, *Presidential Power and the Modern Presidents: The Politics of Power from Roosevelt to Reagan* (New York: Free Press, 1990).

9. Theodore Roosevelt, *The Works of Theodore Roosevelt* (New York: Charles Scribner, 1926), 347.

10. Marcus Cunliffe, *The Presidency* (Boston: Houghton Mifflin, 1968).

11. David Herbert Donald, "Lincoln, The Politician," in *Lincoln Reconsidered: Essays on the Civil War Era* (New York: Random House, 1956).

12. As a result, Congress sometimes finds itself presented with a presidential *fait accompli*. In 1907, for example, a startled Congress learned that President Theodore Roosevelt had sent the entire U.S. fleet on a two-year world cruise intended to impress other nations, especially Japan, with the U.S. resolve to play an active role in world affairs.

13. Neustadt, *Presidential Power*, 34.

14. There were, however, a few "litmus test" issues such as the tariff, and during moments of national crisis the president's policy preferences would suddenly matter a great deal—such as Lincoln's position on slavery in the territories in 1860.

15. Louis Fisher, *Constitutional Conflicts between Congress and the Presi-*

dent, 3d ed. (Lawrence: University of Kansas Press, 1991), 103.

16. Ibid., 93; Glendon A. Schubert Jr., "Judicial Review of the Sub-delegation of Presidential Power," *Journal of Politics* 12 (1950): 668.

17. Since those days, budgeting has become far more complex. One of the most important changes occurred in the 1970s, when the law governing the budgetary process was changed to require budgets to cover both revenue (taxes) and spending. Congress created new committees to reconcile the two sides of the ledger and new agencies to help it forecast economic changes that would affect the budget. Allen Schick, *The Federal Budget: Politics, Policy, Process* (Washington, D.C.: Brookings, 1994).

18. Sterling Denhard Spero, *Government as Employer* (Carbondale: Southern Illinois University Press, 1972), 117–143.

19. Richard E. Neustadt, "The Presidency and Legislation: The Growth of Central Clearance," *American Political Science Review* 48 (September 1954): 461–671.

20. Yet Congress may curb even this administrative prerogative. For example, in 1982, during a Republican administration, House Democrats pushed a law through Congress that prevented the Office of Management and Budget from revising or delaying submissions of certain mandated reports to Congress. Morton Rosenberg, "Congress's Prerogative over Agencies and Agency Decisionmakers: The Rise and Demise of the Reagan Administration's Theory of the Unitary Executive," *George Washington Law Review* 57 (January 1989).

21. Theodore J. Lowi and Benjamin Ginsberg, *American Government: Freedom and Power,* 4th ed. (New York: Norton, 1996), 625.

22. Noble E. Cunningham Jr., *In Pursuit of Reason: The Life of Thomas Jefferson* (Baton Rouge: Louisiana State University Press, 1987).

23. John Hart, *The Presidential Branch: From Washington to Clinton,* 2d ed. (Chatham, N.J.: Chatham House, 1995), 31.

24. Quoted in Samuel Kernell, "New and Old Lessons on White House Management," in *Executive Leadership in Anglo-American Systems,* ed. Colin Campbell and Margaret Jane Wyszomirski (Pittsburgh: University of Pittsburgh Press, 1991), 350.

25. Terence Smith, "Carter Liaison Aide with Jews to Quit White House," *New York Times,* March 9, 1978.

26. Donald T. Regan, *For the Record: From Wall Street to Washington* (New York: Harcourt Brace Jovanovich, 1988), 245.

27. William Cavala, "Changing the Rules Changes the Game: Party Reform and the 1972 California Delegation to the Democratic National Convention," *American Political Science Review* 68 (March 1974): 27–42.

28. Democratic Party leaders had employed the unit rule to take full control of a state's bloc of votes. This rule allowed a majority of a state's delegation to cast all of the delegation's votes as a "unit" for a particular candidate.

29. Nelson W. Polsby and Aaron B. Wildavsky, *Presidential Elections,* 9th ed. (Chatham, N.J.: Chatham House, 1996).

30. Jimmy Carter, *Keeping the Faith: Memoirs of a President* (New York: Bantam Books, 1982). For a more detailed treatment of the rise of outsiders, see Samuel Kernell, "Campaigning, Governing, and the Contemporary Presidency," in *The New Direction in American Politics,* ed. John E. Chubb and Paul E. Peterson (Washington, D.C.: Brookings, 1985), 117–141.

31. The same consideration had prompted Colorado senator Gary Hart to forgo a promising reelection race in 1986 in order to seek the Democratic Party's presidential nomination in 1988.

32. Theodore Lowi calls these outsider politicians "personal presidents." Theodore J. Lowi, *The Personal President: Power Invested, Promise*

Unfulfilled (Ithaca: Cornell University Press, 1985).

33. Alison Mitchell, "Clinton Seems to Keep Running Though the Race Is Run and Won," *New York Times,* February 12, 1997, A1, A12.

34. Douglass Cater, "How a President Helps Form Public Opinion," *New York Times Magazine,* February 26, 1961, 12. In a similar vein in 1978 Carter aide Gerald Rafshoon sent the president a memorandum that established the president's media strategy for the rest of his tenure. Rafshoon cautioned, "The power of presidential communication is great, but not unlimited. You may be able to talk to the people all day . . . but the people can only handle so much. *Investment of that power in too wide a range of issues will dissipate it. This has happened over the last eighteen months*" (emphasis added). After elaborating on this theme, Rafshoon concluded, "Your involvement should always be weighed with an eye towards preventing the devaluation of presidential currency." From a memorandum to President Carter, June 30, 1978, personal papers of Gerald Rafshoon.

35. In late 1987 and early 1988 the big three television networks refused to broadcast addresses by President Reagan on two separate occasions, an unprecedented rebuke for the "Great Communicator." In June 1992 President Bush was denied network time for an evening press conference, and six of President Clinton's appearances (through January 1998) failed to attract full network coverage. Matthew A. Baum and Samuel Kernell, "Has Cable Ended the Golden Age of Presidential Television?" *American Political Science Review* 93 (March 1999): 99–114.

36. J. F. TerHorst and Ralph Albertazzie provide a lively chronology of presidential air travel in *The Flying White House: The Story of Air Force One* (New York: Coward, McCann, and Geoghegan, 1979)

37. Alexis de Tocqueville, *Democracy in America,* ed. J. P. Mayer (Garden City, N.Y.: Doubleday Books: 1969), 122.

Chapter 8. The Bureaucracy   pages 246–283

1. *Newsweek,* October 6, 1997, 30.

2. Michael Nelson, "A Short, Ironic History of Bureaucracy," *Journal of Politics* 44 (1982): 750.

3. Leonard D. White, *The Jeffersonians: A Study in Administrative History, 1801–1829* (New York: Macmillan, 1961), 139–140.

4. James Q. Wilson, "The Rise of the Bureaucratic State," in *The American Commonwealth, 1976,* ed. Nathan Glazer and Irving Kristol (New York: Basic Books, 1976), 78.

5. Nelson, "A Short, Ironic History of Bureaucracy," 756.

6. Leonard D. White, *The Federalists: A Study in Administrative History* (New York: Macmillan, 1961), 427–431.

7. White, *Jeffersonians,* 357.

8. Quoted in Leonard D. White, *The Jacksonians: A Study in Administrative History, 1829–1861* (New York: Macmillan, 1963), 318.

9. Ibid., 320.

10. Matthew A. Crenson, *The Federal Machine: Beginnings of Bureaucracy in Jacksonian America* (Baltimore: Johns Hopkins University Press, 1975), 4.

11. House Ways and Means Committee, Report 641, 24th Cong., 1st sess., 1836, 2, quoted in ibid., 137–138.

12. Paul P. Van Riper, *History of the United States Civil Service* (Evanston, Ill.: Row, Peterson, 1958), 74–75.

13. Nelson, "Short, Ironic History of Bureaucracy," 767.

14. Donald R. Whitnah, ed., *Government Agencies* (Westport, Conn.: Greenwood Press, 1983).

15. Ibid., 152–172.

16. Terry M. Moe, "The Politics of Bureaucratic Structure," in *Can the Government Govern?* ed. John E. Chubb and Paul E. Peterson (Washington, D.C.: Brookings, 1989), 276.

17. Harold Seidman and Robert Gilmour, *Politics, Position, and Power: From the Positive to the Regulatory State* (New York: Oxford University Press, 1986), 316–319.

18. Theodore J. Lowi, *The End of Liberalism: The Second Republic of the United States,* 2d ed. (New York: Norton, 1979).

19. James Q. Wilson, *Bureaucracy: What Government Agencies Do and Why They Do It* (New York: Basic Books, 1989), 82–83.

20. Ibid., 130.

21. Ibid., 235.

22. B. Dan Wood and Richard W. Waterman, "The Dynamics of Political Control of the Bureaucracy," *American Political Science Review* 85 (September 1991): 801–828.

23. Hugh Heclo, *Government of Strangers: Executive Politics in Washington* (Washington, D.C.: Brookings, 1977), 195–198.

24. Richard W. Waterman, *Presidential Influence and the Administrative State* (Knoxville: University of Tennessee Press, 1989), chap. 7.

25. Martin Shapiro, *Who Guards the Guardians? Judicial Control of Administration* (Athens, Georgia: University of Georgia Press, 1988), 57.

26. Wilson, *Bureaucracy,* 91.

27. Jack L. Walker, *Mobilizing Interest Groups in America: Patrons, Professions, and Social Movements* (Ann Arbor: University of Michigan Press, 1991), 30–33.

28. Kenneth R. Mayer, *The Political Economy of Defense Contracting* (New Haven: Yale University Press, 1991), 158–174.

29. R. Douglas Arnold, *Congress and the Bureaucracy: A Theory of Influence* (New Haven: Yale University Press, 1979), 136–137.

30. Douglas Cater, *Power in Washington* (New York: Vintage Books, 1964).

31. Hugh Heclo, "Issue Networks and the Executive Establishment," in *The New American Political System,* ed. Anthony King (Washington, D.C.: American Enterprise Institute, 1978), 87–124.

32. Joel D. Aberbach, "The Federal Executive Under Clinton," in *The Clinton Presidency: First Appraisals,* ed. Colin Campbell and Bert A. Rockman (Chatham, N.J.: Chatham House, 1996), 179.

33. Wilson, *Bureaucracy,* 127.

34. Ibid.

35. Seidman and Gilmour, *Politics, Position, and Power,* 15.

Chapter 9. The Federal Judiciary   pages 284–315

1. Donald O. Dewey, *Marshall versus Jefferson: The Political Background of* Marbury v. Madison (New York: Knopf, 1970). On pages 42–43, Dewey cites various evidence that Marshall seriously entertained his elevation. He reportedly promoted it as "legal" among colleagues, and one biographer spotted Marshall's pen in anonymous newspaper endorsements of this option. On hearing of this plot, Virginia's Democratic-Republican governor and future president, James Monroe, warned vaguely that force would be enlisted to remove Marshall, Virginian or not.

2. In the end, though, Burr proved to be Jefferson's ideal running mate; he scared many Federalists even more than the radical from Monticello. Burr later took up dueling and assumed imperial aspirations—raising "soldier of fortune" armies to seize western territories from the French and create his own country.

3. If anyone doubted the partisan purpose of this last-minute reform, they had only to consult the provision that reduced the size of the Supreme Court from six members to five. It was slated to take effect after President Adams had filled the current chief justice vacancy and after one of the members had left. In effect, then, the law deprived Democratic-Republicans of the right to appoint a member of the Court and of the chance to breach this hastily constructed Federalist barricade to republicanism.

4. In his message to the new Congress, President Jefferson understated his plans: "The judiciary system of the United States, and especially that portion of it recently erected, will of course present itself to the contemplation of Congress."

5. Letter from Jefferson to John Dickinson, December 19, 1801, cited in Dewey, *Marshall versus Jefferson,* 63.

6. To avoid an immediate collision with the Court, Congress then suspended the Court's schedule for the next thirteen months. This move not only would ease the dismantling of the eliminated courts but also would prevent the Court from continuing the partisan battle while Congress was out of session.

7. *Stuart v. Laird,* 1 Cr. 299 (1803).

8. Marshall's decision is sometimes presented as a trick pulled on an unsuspecting administration. Robert Lowry Clinton argues persuasively that those who presented the case were aware of this possibility and argued that the Court did indeed enjoy the jurisdiction given by Congress. See Robert Lowry Clinton, Marbury v. Madison *and Judicial Review* (Lawrence: University Press of Kansas, 1989), 8–30.

9. The act, Marshall found, contradicted the description of original Court jurisdiction set forth in Article III, Section 2, of the Constitution.

10. *Marbury v. Madison,* 1 Cr. (5 U.S.) 137 at 177–180 (1803), emphasis added.

11. Although the Supreme Court left *Marbury* alone for much of the nineteenth century, there is evidence that early on it came to be accepted as legal dogma. *Marbury* was cited numerous times by lower courts and in lawyers' arguments. Whenever Jefferson encountered these citations, he objected. As late as 1823 he griped to one of his Supreme Court appointees, "This case of Marbury and Madison is continually cited by bench & bar, as if it were settled law, without any animadversion on its being *merely* an obiter dissertation by the Chief Justice." Letter from Jefferson to Justice William Johnson, June 12, 1823, cited in Dewey, *Marshall versus Jefferson,* 145 (emphasis added).

12. *McCulloch v. Maryland,* 4 Wheat. 316 (1819).

13. *Scott v. Sandford,* 19 How. (60 U.S.) 393 (1857).

14. The opinion in *Scott v. Sandford* was only the second time the Court had overruled an act of Congress. Considering that in the first instance, *Marbury,* the Court merely asserted its authority, the Dred Scott decision may represent the real, if inauspicious, beginning of judicial review of federal law.

15. Quoted by Paul Brest and Sanford Levinson in *Processes of Constitutional Decisionmaking,* 3d ed. (Boston: Little, Brown, 1992), 75.

16. *Fletcher v. Peck,* 6 Cr. 87 (1810).

17. *Munn v. Illinois,* 94 U.S. 113 (1877); *Mugler v. Kansas,* 123 U.S. 623 (1887).

18. *Lochner v. New York,* 198 U.S. 45 (1905).

19. *Muller v. Oregon,* 208 U.S. 412 (1908).

20. *Bunting v. Oregon,* 243 U.S. 426 (1917).

21. Robert McCloskey and Sanford Levinson, eds., *The American Supreme Court,* 2d ed. (Chicago: University of Chicago Press, 1994); and Lawrence Baum, *The Supreme Court,* 6th ed. (Washington, D.C.: CQ Press, 1998), 208.

22. *West Coast Hotel v. Parrish,* 300 U.S. 379 (1937).

23. The nonconstitutional courts are classified as legislative courts. They are created by Congress under Article I and are designed to fulfill some special purpose; their judges are appointed by the president for fixed terms. Examples are the U.S. Court of Military Appeals, the U.S. Tax Court, and bankruptcy courts.

24. *Jaffree v. Board of School Commissioners,* 554 F. Supp. 1104, 1128 (S.D. Ala. 1983).

25. When a lower court appears to have disregarded such a directive, the Court may hear the case a second time, rebuke the lower-court judge, issue a writ of mandamus ordering the lower-court judge to take a specified action, or assign the case to a different court.

26. *Brown v. Board of Education,* 347 U.S. 483 (1954).

27. Under certain circumstances, resistance to Supreme Court decisions might lead to a judge's advancement by an administration that disagrees with current Court policy.

28. J. Woodford Howard Jr., *Courts of Appeals in the Federal Judicial System* (Princeton, N.J.: Princeton University Press, 1981), 76.

29. Peter Linzer, "The Meaning of Certiorari Denials," *Columbia Law Review* 79 (1979): 1227–1305.

30. David O'Brien, *Storm Center: The Supreme Court in American Politics,* 4th ed. (New York: Norton, 1996).

31. David A. Savage, "Jurists Improve Turnover Rate: California-Based Ninth Circuit Has 13 of 17 Rulings Reversed by Supreme Court. In Previous Year, Justices Overruled 28 of 29," *Los Angeles Times,* July 2, 1998.

32. Gregory A. Caldeira and John R. Wright, "Organized Interest and Agenda Setting in the U.S. Supreme Court," *American Political Science Review* 82 (1988): 1109–1127.

33. Lori Hausegger and Lawrence Baum, "Inviting Congressional Action: A Study of Supreme Court Motivations in Statutory Interpretation," *American Journal of Political Science* 43 (January 1999): 162–185.

34. Mathew McCubbins, Roger G. Knoll, and Barry R. Weingast, "Political Control of the Judiciary: A Positive Theory of Judicial Doctrine and the Rule of Law," *University of Southern California Law Review* (September 1995): 1631–1683.

35. In order of their appointment, the Four Horsemen were Willis Van Devanter (1911), James McReynolds (1914), George Sutherland (1922), and Pierce Butler (1922).

36. William N. Eskridge Jr., "Overriding Supreme Court Statutory Interpretation Decisions," *Yale Law Journal* 101 (1991): 331–455. Another study found that Congress passed new laws to reverse 41 of 569 Supreme Court decisions declaring state or federal law unconstitutional from 1954 through 1990. See James Meernik and Joseph Ignagni, "Judicial Review and Coordinate Construction of the Constitution," *American Journal of Political Science* 41 (April 1997): 446–467.

37. *Mobile v. Bolden,* 446 U.S. 55 (1980).

38. David Stout, "Judges May Review Deportation Orders, Appeals Court Rules," *New York Times,* May 19, 1998.

39. *Nixon v. United States,* 418 U.S. 683 (1974).

40. *Immigration and Naturalization Service v. Chadha,* 462 U.S. 919 (1983).

41. Louis Fisher, "The Legislative Veto: Invalidated, It Survives," *Law and Contemporary Problems* 56 (1993): 288.

42. In January 1998 the Clinton administration changed its policy. It moved in federal court to shut down the marijuana clubs. Sabin Russell, "California Pot Clubs Targeted," *San Francisco Chronicle,* January 10, 1998.

43. *Guide to the U.S. Supreme Court,* 3d ed., ed. Joan Biskupic and Elder Witt (Washington, D.C.: Congressional Quarterly, 1997), 832.

44. Lincoln Caplan, "The Tenth Justice," pt. 1, *New Yorker,* August 10, 1987, 40.

45. Nevertheless, a group of Republican senators led by Phil Gramm of Texas, dissatisfied with their influence over the appointment of these appeals judges, proposed in 1997 that the Senate Judiciary Committee clear all nominees with those Republican senators whose states are covered by the nominee's circuit jurisdiction. Neil A. Lewis, "Republicans Seek Greater Influence in Naming Judges," *New York Times,* April 27, 1997.

46. Robert A. Carp and Ronald Stidham, *The Federal Courts,* 2d ed. (Washington, D.C.: CQ Press, 1991), 102.

47. Baum, *Supreme Court,* 45. Eisenhower might not have used those exact words, but the story probably is an accurate reflection of his attitude toward these two justices.

48. John H. Cushman Jr., "Senate Imperiling Judicial System, Rehnquist Says," *New York Times,* January 1, 1998.

49. Mark Helm and Stewart Powell, "Clinton, GOP Strike a Deal on Judges," [New Orleans] *Times-Picayune,* May 6, 1998. More recently, Neil A. Lewis, "Environment and Politics Enter Debate on Judgeship," *New York Times,* May 9, 1999.

50. Lee Epstein et al., *The Supreme Court Compendium: Data, Decisions, and Developments,* 2d ed. (Washington, D.C.: Congressional Quarterly, 1996).

Chapter 10. *Public Opinion*   *pages* 316–347

1. CBS News/*New York Times* poll, March 8–10, 1994.

2. ABC News/*Washington Post* poll, February 24–27, 1994.

3. NBC News/*Wall Street Journal* poll, July 23–26, 1994.

4. *Public Perspective,* September/October 1994, 24.

5. V. O. Key Jr., *Public Opinion and American Democracy* (New York: Knopf, 1967), 14.

6. Quoted in Susan Herbst, *Numbered Voices: How Opinion Polling Has Shaped American Politics* (Chicago: University of Chicago Press, 1993), 108.

7. George C. Edwards III, "Frustration and Folly: Bill Clinton and the Public Presidency," in *The Clinton Presidency: First Appraisals,* ed. Colin Campbell and Bert A. Rockman (Chatham, N.J.: Chatham House, 1996), 234.

8. Alison Mitchell, "Clinton Seems to Keep Running Though the Race Is Run and Won," *New York Times,* February 2, 1997, A1.

9. Samuel Kernell, *Going Public: New Strategies of Presidential Leadership,* 3d ed. (Washington, D.C.: CQ Press, 1997), 23.

10. "Survey Bolsters Global Warning Fight," *Los Angeles Times,* November 21, 1997, A4.

11. William W. Lambert and Wallace E. Lambert, *Social Psychology* (Englewood Cliffs, N.J.: Prentice Hall, 1964), 50.

12. Warren E. Miller and Santa Traugott, *American National Election Studies Sourcebook, 1952–1986* (Cambridge, Mass.: Harvard University Press, 1989), 94.

13. Robert S. Erikson and Kent L. Tedin, *American Public Opinion,* 5th ed. (Boston: Allyn and Bacon, 1995), 65–78.

14. Stanley Feldman and John Zaller, "The Political Culture of Am-

bivalence: Ideological Responses to the Welfare State," *American Journal of Political Science* 36 (1992): 268–307.

15. George F. Bishop, Robert W. Oldendick, and Alfred J. Tuchfarber, "Pseudo-Opinion on Public Affairs," *Public Opinion Quarterly* (1980): 189–209.

16. John Zaller and Stanley Feldman, "A Simple Theory of Survey Response: Answering Questions versus Revealing Preferences," *American Journal of Political Science* 36 (1992): 581.

17. John E. Mueller, *War, Presidents, and Public Opinion* (New York: Wiley, 1973), 100.

18. Michael W. Traugott and Paul J. Lavrakas, *The Voter's Guide to Election Polls* (Chatham, N.J.: Chatham House, 1996), 108–109.

19. Philip E. Converse, "The Nature of Belief Systems in Mass Publics," in *Ideology and Discontent*, ed. David Apter (New York: Free Press, 1964); Christopher Achen, "Mass Political Attitudes and Survey Response," *American Political Science Review* 69 (1995): 1218–31.

20. Zaller and Feldman, "Theory of Survey Response," 585–586.

21. Shanto Iyengar and Donald R. Kinder, *News That Matters* (Chicago: University of Chicago Press, 1987), 63–72.

22. Benjamin I. Page and Robert Y. Shapiro, *The Rational Public* (Chicago: University of Chicago Press, 1992), 63.

23. Ibid., 130.

24. James A. Stimson, *Public Opinion in America: Moods, Cycles, and Swings* (Boulder, Colo.: Westview Press, 1991), 29–31.

25. Michael B. MacKuen, Robert S. Erikson, and James A. Stimson, "Macropartisanship," *American Political Science Review* 83 (1989): 1125–1142.

26. Stimson, *Public Opinion,* 125.

27. Arthur Lupia and Mathew D. McCubbins, *The Democratic Dilemma: Can Citizens Learn What They Really Need to Know?* (New York: Cambridge University Press, 1998).

28. Herbert McClosky and John Zaller, *The American Ethos* (Cambridge, Mass.: Harvard University Press, 1984), 38.

29. Herbert McClosky and Ada Brill, *Dimensions of Tolerance* (New York: Basic Books, 1983).

30. McClosky and Zaller, *American Ethos,* 83.

31. Ibid., 84.

32. Page and Shapiro, *Rational Public,* 74.

33. *American National Election Study, 1998,* variable 980505.

34. Barbara Hinkson Craig and David M. O'Brien, *Abortion and American Politics* (Chatham, N.J.: Chatham House, 1993), 266–270.

35. Page and Shapiro, *Rational Public,* 112.

36. Richard A. Brody, *Assessing the President* (Stanford: Stanford University Press, 1991).

37. Mueller, *War, Presidents, and Public Opinion,* 58–63.

38. Mark Peffley and Jon Hurwitz, "International Events and Foreign Policy Beliefs: Public Responses to Changing U.S.-Soviet Relations," *American Journal of Political Science* 36 (May 1992): 431–461.

39. Erikson and Tedin, *American Public Opinion,* 189–190.

40. Ibid., 210.

41. "Portrait of the Electorate," *New York Times,* November 10, 1996.

42. "The New Electorate: Where Do You Fit?" *Los Angeles Times,* September 21, 1994, A16.

Chapter 11. Voting, Campaigns, and Elections
pages 348–381

1. Chilton Williamson, *American Suffrage: From Property to Democracy 1760–1860* (Princeton, N.J.: Princeton University Press, 1960), 49.

2. Alexis de Tocqueville, *Democracy in America* (New York: Vintage Books, 1990), 57.

3. Quoted by David Morgan in *Suffragists and Democrats: The Politics of Women's Suffrage in America* (East Lansing: Michigan State University Press, 1972), 84.

4. Ibid., 124.

5. Steven J. Rosenstone and John Mark Hansen, *Mobilization, Participation, and Democracy in America* (New York: Macmillan, 1993).

6. Ibid., 150.

7. Ibid., 241.

8. Ibid., 214–218.

9. Ruy A. Teixeira, *The Disappearing American Voter* (Washington, D.C.: Brookings, 1992), 86–101; Michael M. Gant and William Lyons, "Democratic Theory: Nonvoting and Public Policy: The 1972–1988 Presidential Elections," *American Politics Quarterly* 21 (April 1993): 194–195.

10. Martin P. Wattenberg, *The Decline of American Political Parties, 1952–1992* (Cambridge, Mass.: Harvard University Press, 1994), 155–157, 171–180.

11. Angus Campbell et al., *The American Voter* (New York: Wiley, 1960), chaps. 6 and 7.

12. Morris P. Fiorina, *Retrospective Voting in American National Elections* (New Haven, Conn.: Yale University Press, 1981), chap. 5.

13. "Outlook: Kansas," *Congressional Quarterly Weekly Report,* October 11, 1989, 2432.

14. Samuel L. Popkin, *The Reasoning Voter: Communication and Persuasion in Presidential Campaigns,* 2d ed. (Chicago: University of Chicago Press, 1994), 1.

15. Paul R. Abramson, John H. Aldrich, and David W. Rohde, *Continuity and Change in the 1992 Elections* (Washington, D.C.: CQ Press, 1994), 56–57.

16. Stephen J. Wayne, *The Road to the White House 1996: The Politics of Presidential Elections* (New York: St. Martin's Press, 1997), 260–261.

17. Paul S. Herrnson and Clyde Wilcox, "The 1996 Presidential Election: A Tale of a Campaign That Didn't Seem to Matter," in *Toward the Millennium: The Elections of 1996,* ed. Larry J. Sabato (Boston: Allyn and Bacon, 1997), 136.

18. Alan Ehrenhalt, "Technology, Strategy Bring New Campaign Era," *Congressional Quarterly Weekly Report,* December 7, 1985, 2559.

19. Stephen Ansolabehere et al., "Does Attack Advertising Demobilize the Electorate?" *American Political Science Review* 88 (December 1994): 829–838.

20. Nelson W. Polsby and Aaron Wildavsky, *Presidential Elections,* 9th ed. (Chatham, N.J.: Chatham House, 1996), 215–216.

21. Paul Taylor, "Accentuating the Negative," *Washington Post* (national weekly ed.), October 20, 1986, 6.

22. Joel Bradshaw, "Strategy, Theme, and Message" (paper presented at the Conference on Campaign Management, American University, Washington, D.C., December 10–11, 1992), 114.

23. *Buckley v. Valeo,* 424 U.S. 1 (1976).

24. *Colorado Republican Federal Campaign Committee v. Federal Election Commission,* 518 U.S. 604 (1996).

25. In congressional elections, individuals may give no more than

$1,000 per candidate per campaign, with primary, runoff, and general election campaigns treated as separate campaigns. Non-party committees (PACs) are limited to $5,000 per candidate per campaign. Parties may give no more than $5,000 to a House candidate and $17,500 to a Senate candidate. The $1,000 individual contribution limit also applies to presidential primary candidates; presidential candidates who accept public funds for the general elections may not accept any other direct contribution to their campaigns. Contributions from foreign sources are illegal in all federal elections.

26. The same differences in spending among types of candidates hold for Senate elections, but variations in state populations and states holding elections (only two-thirds of the states hold Senate elections in any given election year, with the same set repeating only at six-year intervals) make year-to-year comparisons of the kind presented in Figure 11–3, page 374, less informative.

27. Gary C. Jacobson, *The Politics of Congressional Elections* (New York: Longman, 1997), 96–105.

28. In Maine and Nebraska the electoral vote can be divided if one congressional district votes for a candidate who loses statewide.

29. Wayne, *Road to the White House*, 225–226, 264.

Chapter 12. Political Parties   pages 382–419

1. Larry Sabato, *The Party's Just Begun: Shaping Political Parties for America's Future* (Glenview, Ill.: Scott, Foresman, 1988), 133.

2. American National Election Study, 1980.

3. American National Election Study, 1998.

4. E. E. Schattschneider, *Party Government* (New York: Holt, Rinehart, Winston, 1942), 1.

5. John F. Hoadley, *The Origins of the American Party System* (Lexington: University of Kentucky Press, 1986), 51.

6. See Alexander Hamilton's discussion of the electoral college in *Federalist No. 68*. This device is described in Chapter 7, The Presidency.

7. Noble E. Cunningham Jr., "The Development of Parties," in *After the Constitution: Party Conflict in the New Republic*, ed. Lance Banning (Belmont, Calif.: Wadsworth, 1989), 104.

8. Paul Goodman, *The Democratic Republicans of Massachusetts: Politics in a Young Republic* (Cambridge, Mass.: Harvard University Press, 1964), 204.

9. Quoted in Richard H. Brown, "The Missouri Crisis, Slavery, and the Politics of Jacksonianism," in Banning, *After the Constitution*, 446.

10. Michael F. Holt, *Political Parties and American Political Development from the Age of Jackson to the Age of Lincoln* (Baton Rouge: Louisiana State University Press, 1992), 41.

11. James S. Chase, *Emergence of the Presidential Nominating Convention, 1798–1832* (Urbana: University of Illinois Press, 1973), 85.

12. Richard P. McCormick, "Political Development and the Second Party System," in *The American Party Systems: Stages of Political Development*, 2d ed., ed. William Nesbit Chambers and Walter Dean Burnham (New York: Oxford University Press, 1975), 108.

13. William N. Chambers, "Election of 1840," in *History of American Presidential Elections*, vol. 1, ed. Arthur M. Schlesinger Jr. and Fred L. Israel (New York: Chelsea House, 1971), 687.

14. Alexander B. Callow, "The Rise of the Boss," in *The City Boss in America: An Interpretive Reader*, ed. Alexander B. Callow (New York: Oxford University Press, 1976), 7.

15. Ibid., 8.

16. Nelson W. Polsby, *Consequences of Party Reform* (New York: Oxford University Press, 1983), chaps. 2 and 3.

17. Stephen J. Wayne, *The Road to the White House 1996: The Politics of Presidential Elections* (New York: St. Martin's Press, 1997), 107.

18. Martin P. Wattenberg, *The Decline of American Political Parties, 1952–1992* (Cambridge: Harvard University Press, 1994), 174.

19. Gary C. Jacobson, *The Electoral Origins of Divided Government: Competition in U.S. House Elections, 1946–1988* (Boulder, Colo.: Westview Press, 1990), 15–19.

20. Morris P. Fiorina, *Divided Government*, 2d ed. (Boston: Allyn and Bacon, 1996),72–81.

21. Jacobson, *Electoral Origins of Divided Government*, 105–120.

22. American National Election Study, 1998.

23. Fiorina, *Divided Government*, 24–25.

24. Bruce E. Keith et al., *The Myth of the Independent Voter* (Berkeley: University of California Press, 1992), chap. 4.

25. Warren E. Miller and J. Merrill Shanks, *The New American Voter* (Cambridge, Mass.: Harvard University Press, 1996), 141–145.

26. Paul S. Herrnson, *Party Campaigning in the 1980s* (Cambridge, Mass.: Harvard University Press, 1988).

27. John H. Aldrich, *Why Parties? The Origin and Transformation of Party Politics in America* (Chicago: University of Chicago Press, 1995), 273.

Chapter 13. Interest Groups   pages 420–451

1. Darrell M. West and Burdett A. Loomis, *The Sound of Money: How Political Interests Get What They Want* (New York: Norton, 1998), 160–161.

2. This account is taken from ibid., chap. 6; and Dan Carney, "Congress Fires Its First Shot in Information Revolution," *Congressional Quarterly Weekly Report*, February 3, 1996, 289–294.

3. Robert Scheer, "Special Interests Push Out Public Interest," *Los Angeles Times*, June 1, 1999, B5.

4. Alison Gilbert Olson, *Making the Empire Work: London and American Interest Groups, 1690–1790* (Cambridge, Mass.: Harvard University Press, 1992), 56.

5. Ibid., 119.

6. Ibid., 146.

7. Karl Schriftgiesser, *The Lobbyists: The Art and Business of Influencing Lawmakers* (Boston: Little, Brown, 1951), 4.

8. Ibid., 3.

9. Alexis de Tocqueville, *Democracy in America,* ed. Andrew Hacker (New York: Washington Square Press, 1964), 71.

10. Ibid., 182.

11. Mary Rulkotter Dearing, *Veterans in Politics: The Story of the G.A.R.* (Baton Rouge: Louisiana State University Press, 1952), 1.

12. David B. Truman, *The Governmental Process* (New York: Knopf, 1951).

13. E. E. Schattschneider, *The Semi-Sovereign People: A Realist's View of Democracy in America* (Hinsdale, Ill.: Dryden Press, 1960), 34–35.

14. Mancur Olson, *The Logic of Collective Action: Public Goods and the Theory of Groups* (Cambridge, Mass.: Harvard University Press, 1965).

15. Jack L. Walker Jr., *Mobilizing Interest Groups in America: Patrons, Professions, and Social Movements* (Ann Arbor: University of Michigan Press, 1991), 1.

16. David Vogel, *Fluctuating Fortunes: The Political Power of Business in America* (New York: Basic Books, 1988), 220–227.

17. Walker, *Mobilizing Interest Groups,* 29.

18. Ibid., 31.

19. Daniel Kahneman and Amos Tversky, "Prospect Theory: An Analysis of Decision under Risk," *Econometrica* 47 (1979): 263–291.

20. William P. Browne, "Issue Niches and the Limits of Interest Group Influence," in *Interest Group Politics,* 3d ed., ed. Allan J. Cigler and Burdett A. Loomis (Washington, D.C.: CQ Press, 1991), 348.

21. James Q. Wilson, *Political Organizations* (New York: Basic Books, 1973), chap. 13.

22. Ibid., 356.

23. Kay Lehman Schlozman and John T. Tierney, *Organized Interests and American Democracy* (New York: Harper and Row, 1986), 150.

24. Unidentified lobbyist quoted in Jeffrey M. Berry, *The Interest Group Society* (Boston: Little, Brown, 1984), 117; emphasis in the original.

25. Schlozman and Tierney, *Organized Interests,* 333.

26. "UFO Supporters Urge Disclosure," *Los Angeles Times,* July 6, 1993.

27. Andrew J. Polsky, "Giving Business the Business," *Dissent* (winter 1996): 33–36.

28. Jonathan D. Salant, "GOP Bumps Up against Court Precedent in Trying to Block AFL-CIO," *Congressional Quarterly Weekly Report,* April 13, 1996, 997.

29. See, for example, Philip Stern, *The Best Congress Money Can Buy* (New York: Pantheon Books, 1988); Brooks Jackson, *Honest Graft: Big Money and the American Political Process* (New York: Knopf, 1988); Elizabeth Drew, *Politics and Money: The New Road to Corruption* (New York: Macmillan, 1983).

30. John R. Wright, *Interest Groups and Congress* (Boston: Allyn and Bacon, 1996), 136–145; Frank J. Sorauf, *Inside Campaign Finance: Myths and Realities* (New Haven, Conn.: Yale University Press, 1992), 163–174.

31. Richard L. Hall and Frank W. Wayman, "Buying Time: Monied Interests and the Mobilization of Bias in Congressional Committees," *American Political Science Review* 84 (1990): 797–820.

32. Robert S. Salisbury, *Institutions and Interests: Substance and Structure in American Politics* (Pittsburgh: University of Pittsburgh Press, 1992), 348.

33. William P. Browne, *Private Interests, Public Policy, and American Agriculture* (Lawrence: University of Kansas Press, 1988), 248–252.

34. Schlozman and Tierney, *Organized Interests,* 399–403.

35. Lester C. Thurow, *The Zero-Sum Society* (New York: Basic Books, 1980); Mancur Olson, *The Rise and Decline of Nations* (New Haven, Conn.: Yale University Press, 1982).

Chapter 14. The News Media   pages 452–483

1. After CNN lost its satellite link with Baghdad, CNN anchor Bernard Shaw and reporters Peter Arnett and John Holliman used their telephone link to CNN headquarters in Atlanta to render a blow-by-blow, eyewitness account of the attack.

2. This description of media coverage of the Gulf War is based largely on Everette E. Dennis et al., *The Media at War* (New York: Freedom Forum, 1991), 1.

3. Ibid., 18.

4. Letter to Edward Carrington, January 16, 1787, and found in *The Papers of Thomas Jefferson,* Vol. 2, ed. Julian P. Boyd (Princeton, N.J.: Princeton University Press, 1955), 49.

5. This concept is unavoidably flaccid, accommodating as it does the enormous range of activities that "make" and transmit news to the public. The Washington bureau chief of the *New York Times* and the program news manager of the local television station both assign reporters to cover stories and decide which ones will be used. Yet vastly different considerations guide their assignments, their perceptions of who is their audience, and, ultimately, what they regard to be "news." As we will discuss later in this section, newspapers, magazines, radio, television, and Internet news providers necessarily approach the news differently and provide consumers with a different product.

6. Timothy Cook, *Governing with the News: The News Media as a Political Institution* (Chicago: University of Chicago Press, 1998), 22.

7. Charles E. Clark, *The Public Prints: The Newspaper in Anglo-American Culture, 1665–1740* (New York: Oxford University Press, 1994), 195–196.

8. Edwin Emery, *The Press and America,* 2d ed. (Englewood Cliffs, N.J.: Prentice-Hall, 1962), 107–124.

9. This tradition continued after Independence in the debates over the Constitution's ratification. *The Federalist Papers,* as well as the Anti-Federalist essays, were published first in various newspapers and then collected and distributed in pamphlet form.

10. Richard Hofstadter, *The Idea of the Party System* (Berkeley: University of California Press, 1969), 8.

11. Thomas C. Leonard, *The Power of the Press: The Birth of American Political Reporting* (New York: Oxford University Press, 1986), 57.

12. The union of press and party politics was fully consummated during the administration of Andrew Jackson (1829–1837). Three of the five members of Jackson's inner "kitchen cabinet" were seasoned journalists, including Postmaster General Amos Kendall who was dubbed "Jackson's lying machine" by the opposition press. Jackson also developed a very close relationship to Francis Blair, editor of the *Washington Globe,* which involved an exchange of favorable news and government printing contracts. In fact, altogether Jackson appointed fifty-seven editors to patronage positions, primarily as postmasters or customs agents. This ostentatious use of the spoils of victory led even some of Jackson's supporters to worry that freedom of the press would be compromised by placing so many editors on the public payroll.

13. By the time he had finished his unhappy tenure as president, the badly bruised Thomas Jefferson held the press in absolute contempt. They had fallen to a "putrid state" of "malignity, vulgarity and mendacious public spirit," and Jefferson quit reading newspapers. It is this legacy of partisanship, rather than the lofty status of independent agent of the people, that marks the history of journalism in America and against which the professionalization of journalism in the twentieth century represents a reaction.

14. Note that several contemporaneous social changes also aided the rise of the penny press. Kobre identifies these factors as including the growth of cities, modernization of transportation, the rise of a larger working class, onset of mass production of consumer items, and increases in literacy, among others. Sidney Kobre, *The Development of American Journalism* (Dubuque, Iowa: William C. Brown, 1969), 208.

15. In the first edition of the *Herald,* its publisher, John Gordon Bennett, a longtime Democratic Party functionary who had clashed with others in the party, denounced allegiances to all political parties and political principles. He claimed that the *Herald* would support no party or faction. Instead, he said, it would concentrate on reporting the news "stripped of verbiage and coloring." Frederic Hudson, *Journalism in the*

United States (New York: Harper and Brothers, 1972) 433; and Michael Schudson, *Discovering the News: A Social History of American Newspapers* (New York: Basic Books, 1978), 22.

16. Willard Grosvenor Bleyer, *Main Currents of the History of American Journalism* (Boston: Houghton Mifflin, 1927), 377.

17. Alfred M. Lee, *The Daily Newspaper in America* (New York: Macmillan, 1937), 214–217.

18. Some rising stars in the news industry, in fact, tried to exploit their influence with public opinion by running for elective office. The most famous instance arose in 1872, when New York publisher Horace Greeley won the Democratic Party's nomination for president. The power of the media was not lost on incumbent Republican Ulysses S. Grant, who welcomed another newspaper publisher, Henry Wilson, to be his running mate. The fact that Greeley lost the election badly does not detract from the feat of this political novice in winning the nomination for his party's highest office without ever having previously served in an elected office.

19. *New York Journal,* May 8, 1898, 1.

20. Ithiel de Sola Pool, *Technologies of Freedom* (Cambridge, Mass.: Harvard University Press, 1983), 47.

21. *Historical Statistics of the United States: Colonial Times to 1970,* Vols. 1 and 2 (Washington, D.C.: Government Printing Office, 1975), series R104–5.

22. Emery, *Press and America,* 663.

23. Erik Barnouw, *The Golden Web,* Vol. 2 (New York: Oxford University Press, 1968), 18–22.

24. Although one cannot be sure that responses to the survey questions actually reflect respondents' consumption habits, the strong trend confirms that Americans are increasingly relying on television for their news.

25. Stephen Ansolabehere, Roy Behr, and Shanto Iyengar, *The Media Game: American Politics in the Television Age* (New York: Macmillan, 1993), 42–46.

26. Sola Pool, *Technologies of Freedom,* 110. Under the Radio Act of 1912, the Department of Commerce had tried to allocate radio stations across the spectrum, but a 1926 federal court ruling left the industry unregulated and set the stage for the 1927 law.

27. This legislation was preceded by a narrower law, the Radio Act of 1927, which distributed stations across the spectrum. New technological developments in directional transmission, which sharply increased the number of possible stations, and a confusing mix of bureaucratic responsibilities led to the 1934 revision.

28. The decision to lodge these regulatory responsibilities in an independent agency rather than the established bureaucracy—say, the Department of Commerce—was inspired more immediately by politics than by abstract considerations for designing institutions to shield civil liberties. With newspaper barons still rumbling across the political landscape, members of Congress fully appreciated the political power inherent in control of mass communication. And they feared that some future administration might use its licensing authority to favor friends and punish enemies and thereby extract a partisan advantage.

29. The FCC sought a similar balance in the presentation of controversial ideas and individuals. In 1969 the courts awarded antismoking advocates time to refute cigarette commercials, and the next year opponents of the Vietnam War won rebuttal time to a speech on the war by President Richard Nixon. Also in the 1960s the opposition party was given time to respond to the president's nationally televised messages—a practice that remains in place today. When groups tried to push the "fairness doctrine" beyond certain limits, the FCC and the courts generally sided with the networks and stations which claimed that different points of view were adequately reported in their news broadcasts.

30. In 1987 Congress tried to forestall the FCC's change in policy by passing legislation that would have made the doctrine a law. President Reagan vetoed the legislation. Subsequent efforts to override the veto and pass new bills have thus far failed.

31. Paul Lazarsfeld concluded an early study of radio listeners with the optimistic forecast that radio news would actually increase newspaper consumption. See his *Radio and the Printed Page* (New York: Duell, Sloan and Pierce, 1940).

32. Figures calculated from Table 4–4 of Doris A. Graber, *Mass Media and American Politics,* 5th ed. (Washington, D.C.: CQ Press, 1997), 110–111.

33. See Ansolabehere et al., *Media Game,* 45. These results were confirmed in a recent *Wall Street Journal*/NBC News poll, in which Americans expressed greater confidence in every broadcast news outlet over every other media outlet (with the exception of CNBC/MSNBC—the lowest-rated broadcaster listed—which tied with the top-rated print outlet, *Time* magazine). Albert R. Hunt, "Washington Events Fuel Disdain for Media, Politics," *Wall Street Journal,* September 17, 1998.

34. News stories that do not have culprits tend to be ignored. The savings and loan crisis in the 1980s was arguably the most expensive domestic policy fiasco in American history, costing American taxpayers nearly $150 billion. But it never achieved sustained network coverage. Meanwhile, discovery of routine congressional overdrafts in 1992, which involved no illegal activity and did not cost taxpayers a dime, became the news media's scandal of the year.

35. W. Russell Neuman, Marion R. Just, and Ann N. Crigler, *Common Knowledge* (Chicago: University of Chicago Press, 1992), 87–95.

36. Leon V. Sigal, *Reporters and Officials: The Organization and Politics of News Reporting* (Lexington, Mass.: D. C. Heath, 1973), 122.

37. Howard Kurtz of the *Washington Post,* appearing on ABC News *Nightline,* January 30, 1998.

38. John Donovan, ABC News. Howard Kurtz said, "The White House decided the way that it could inoculate itself was to do the leaking itself, to do what they called document dumps, to get this stuff out, take their hits early and then, Fred Thompson and other investigating senators came along, the White House could say well this is old news. This has all be in the papers. We already know all this stuff." ABC News *Nightline,* March 11, 1998.

39. Stephen Hess, *Live from Capitol Hill* (Washington, D.C.: Brookings, 1991).

40. Joseph N. Cappella and Kathleen Hall Jamieson, *Spiral of Cynicism: The Press and the Public Good* (New York: Oxford University Press, 1997), 3–5.

41. Coverage of Congress is mostly neutral, but when it is not, it tends to be negative. See Charles M. Tidmarch and John J. Pitney Jr., "Covering Congress," *Polity* 17 (1985): 463–483.

42. Transcript, presidential press conference, May 7, 1993, Washington, D.C.

43. Paul F. Boller Jr., *Presidential Anecdotes* (New York: Penguin Books, 1982), 63–64.

44. Timothy Crouse, *Boys on the Bus: Riding with the Campaign Press Corps* (New York: Ballantine, 1996).

45. James E. Pollard, *The Presidents and the Press* (New York: Macmillan, 1947), 775.

46. Cited in Worth Bingham and Ward S. Just, "The President and the Press," *Reporter* 26 (April 12, 1962): 20.

47. Tom Rosentiel, *The Beat Goes On: President Clinton's First Year with the Media* (New York: Twentieth Century Fund, 1994), 31.

48. Marvin Kalb, "The Rise of the 'New' News" A Case Study of Two Root Causes of Modern Scandal Coverage" (discussion paper D-34, John F. Kennedy School of Government, Harvard University, October 1998).

49. Daniel C. Hallin, "Sound Bite News: Television Coverage of Elections, 1968–1988," in *Do the Media Govern? Politicians, Voters, and Reporters in America,* ed. Shanto Iyengar and Richard Reeves (Thousand Oaks, Calif.: Sage, 1997), 57–65.

50. Richard H. Rovere, *Senator Joe McCarthy* (Cleveland: Meridian Books, 1966), 124.

Chapter 15. The Dilemmas of Institutional Reform
pages 484–493

1. This account is drawn from John S. Morgan, *Robert Fulton* (New York: Mason/Charter, 1977); and John Fitch's memoirs, published as *The Autobiography of John Fitch,* ed. Frank D. Prager (Philadelphia: American Philosophical Society, 1976).

2. Some delegates were sufficiently impressed to propose to the Continental Congress a gift of western lands to Fitch upon completion of a successful prototype.

3. "New Rules Urged to Rein in Rogue Interstate Movers," *Los Angeles Times,* May 10, 1999, A1.

4. Dan Carney, "Senators Say Independent Counsel Law Should Lapse if Not Radically Changed," *Congressional Quarterly Weekly Report,* February 27, 1999, 474.

5. Dan Carney, "Independent Counsel Holds No Brief for the Law that Empowered Him," *Congressional Quarterly Weekly Report,* April 17, 1999, 885.

GLOSSARY

access The ability of privileged outsiders, such as interest group officials, to obtain a hearing from elected officials or bureaucrats. *(Page 378.)*

ad hoc committee A congressional committee appointed for a limited time to design and report a specific piece of legislation. *(Page 190.)*

affirmative action Policies or programs designed to expand opportunities for minorities and women and usually requiring that an organization take measures to increase the number or proportion of minorities and women in its membership or employment. *(Page 89.)*

agency loss The discrepancy between what citizens ideally would like their agents to do and how the agents actually behave. *(Page 16.)*

agent Someone who makes and implements decisions on behalf of someone else. *(Page 15.)*

aggregate partisanship The distribution, or percentage, of the electorate that identifies with each of the political parties. *(Page 332.)*

ambivalence A state of mind produced when particular issues evoke attitudes and beliefs that pull one in opposite directions. *(Page 329.)*

amicus curiae "Friend of the court." A brief filed in a lawsuit by an individual or group that is not party to the lawsuit but that has an interest in the outcome. *(Page 298.)*

Articles of Confederation The compact among the thirteen original states that formed the basis of the first government of the United States. The Articles were the formal basis of the national government from 1777 to 1789, when they were supplanted by the Constitution. *(Page 27.)*

attitude An organized and consistent manner of thinking and feeling about people, groups, social issues, or, more generally, any event in one's environment. *(Page 323.)*

audience The segment of the public who listens to or reads a particular media communication. *(Page 464.)*

Australian ballot A ballot prepared and distributed by government officials that places the names of all candidates on a single list and is filled out by voters in private. First adopted in the United States in 1888, the Australian ballot replaced oral voting and party-supplied ballots. *(Page 402.)*

authority The right to make a decision and to implement that decision. *(Page 15.)*

beats Regularly assigned venues that news reporters cover on an ongoing basis. *(Page 471.)*

bicameral legislature A legislature composed of two houses or chambers. The U.S. Congress (House and Senate) and every U.S. state legislature (with the exception of Nebraska's, which is unicameral) are bicameral legislatures. *(Page 32.)*

block grants Broad grants of money given by the federal government to state governments. The grants specify the general area (such as education or health services) in which the funds may be spent but leave it to the state to determine the specific allocations. *(Page 81.)*

bureaucracy A complex structure of offices, tasks, and rules in which employees have specific responsibilities and work within a hierarchy of authority. Government bureaucracies are charged with implementing policies. *(Page 248.)*

bureaucratic culture The norms and regular patterns of behavior found within a bureaucratic organization. Different agencies often develop their own norms which shape the behavior of those who work in the agency. *(Page 273.)*

cabinet The formal group of presidential advisers who head the major departments and agencies of the federal government. Cabinet members are chosen by the president and approved by the Senate. *(Page 17.)*

candidate   A person who is running for elected office. *(Page 364.)*

carrying capacity   The amount of information a communication technology can deliver to its audience. Newspapers have much higher carrying capacities than television news programs. *(Page 464.)*

casework   The activity undertaken by members of Congress and their staffs to solve constituents' problems with government agencies. *(Page 172.)*

categorical grant   A federal grant of money to states or localities for a specific purpose. These grants usually require states to provide matching funds and to adhere to federal guidelines in spending the funds. *(Page 81.)*

caucus   A closed meeting of a political or legislative group to choose candidates for office or to decide issues of policy. *(Page 419.)*

central clearance   A presidential directive requiring that all executive agency proposals, reports, and recommendations to Congress—mostly in the form of annual reports and testimony at authorization and appropriations hearings—be certified by the Office of Management and Budget as consistent with the president's policy. *(Page 229.)*

checks and balances   A constitutional mechanism giving each branch some oversight and control of the other branches. Examples are the presidential veto, Senate approval of presidential appointments, and judicial review of presidential and congressional actions. *(Page 42.)*

civil liberties   Constitutional and legal protections from government interference into personal rights and freedoms such as freedom of assembly, speech, and religion. *(Page 91.)*

civil rights   The powers or privileges conferred on citizens by the Constitution and the courts entitling them to make claims upon the government. Civil rights protect individuals from arbitrary or discriminatory treatment at the hands of the government. *(Page 90.)*

clear and present danger test   A rule used by the Supreme Court to distinguish between speech protected and not protected by the First Amendment. Under this rule, speech aimed at inciting an illegal action is not protected by the First Amendment. *(Page 135.)*

clientele   The category of people, or groups, served by a bureaucratic agency. *(Page 257.)*

closed rule   An order from the House Rules Committee limiting floor debate on a particular bill and disallowing or limiting amendment. *(Page 193.)*

cloture   A parliamentary procedure used to close debate. Cloture is used in the Senate to cut off filibusters. Under the current Senate rules, three-fifths of senators must vote for cloture to halt a filibuster. *(Page 200.)*

coalition   An alliance of unlike-minded individuals or groups to achieve some common purpose such as lobbying, legislating, or campaigning for the election of public officials. *(Page 17.)*

cognitive shortcut   A mental device allowing citizens to make complex decisions based on a small amount of information. For example, a candidate's party label serves as a shortcut by telling voters much about his or her position on issues. *(Page 333.)*

collective action   An action made by a group of like-minded individuals to achieve a common goal. *(Page 7.)*

collective goods   Goods that are collectively produced and freely available for anyone's consumption. *(Page 21.)*

commander in chief   The title given to the president by the Constitution that denotes the president's authority as the head of the national military. *(Page 221.)*

commerce clause   The clause in Article I, Section 8, of the Constitution that gives Congress the authority to regulate commerce with other nations and among the states. *(Page 71.)*

concurring opinion   A written opinion by a Supreme Court justice who agrees with the decision of the Court but disagrees with the rationale for reaching that decision. *(Page 303.)*

confederation   A political system in which states or regional governments retain ultimate authority except for those powers they expressly delegate to a central government. *(Page 33.)*

conference committee   A temporary joint committee of the House and Senate appointed to reconcile the differences between the two chambers on a particular piece of legislation. *(Page 190.)*

conformity costs   The difference between what a person ideally would prefer and what the group with which that person makes collective decisions actually does. Individuals pay conformity costs whenever collective decisions produce policy outcomes that do not *best* serve their interests. *(Page 12.)*

coordinated spending   Spending by the Democratic and Republican Party committees in behalf of individual congressional candidates. *(Page 373.)*

conservative   In the United States, a proponent of a political ideology that favors small or limited government, an unfettered free market, self-reliance, and traditional social norms. *(Page 324.)*

constitution A document outlining the formal rules and institutions of government and the limits placed on its powers. *(Page 6.)*

constitutional courts Category of federal courts vested with the general judicial authority outlined in Article III of the Constitution. The most important are the Supreme Court, the ninety-four district courts, and the courts of appeals. Their authority derives from that of the Supreme Court, and they are supposed to conform to its decisions. *(Page 294.)*

core values Moral beliefs held by citizens that underlie their attitudes toward political and other objects. As integral parts of an individual's identify, these beliefs are stable and resistant to change. *(Page 324.)*

court of appeals The second tier of courts in the federal judicial system (between the Supreme Court and the district courts). One court of appeals serves each of eleven regions, or circuits, plus one for the District of Columbia. *(Page 294.)*

Court packing plan An attempt by President Franklin D. Roosevelt, in 1937, to remodel the federal judiciary. Its purpose ostensibly was to alleviate the overcrowding of federal court dockets by allowing the president to appoint an additional Supreme Court justice for every sitting justice over the age of seventy. The legislation passed the House of Representatives but failed in the Senate by a single vote. If it had passed, Roosevelt could have added six new justices to the high bench, thereby installing a new Court majority sympathetic to his New Deal programs. *(Page 291.)*

Declaration of Independence The document drafted by Thomas Jefferson and adopted by the Second Continental Congress on July 4, 1776, declaring the independence of the thirteen colonies from Great Britain. *(Page 32.)*

de facto segregation Segregation that results from practice rather than from law. *(Page 117.)*

de jure segregation Segregation enacted into law and imposed by the government. *(Page 117.)*

delegation The act of one person or body authorizing another person or body to perform an action on its behalf. For example, Congress often delegates authority to the president or administrative agencies to decide the details of policy. *(Page 14.)*

direct democracy A system of government in which citizens make policy decisions by voting on legislation themselves rather than delegating that authority to their representatives. *(Page 16.)*

dissenting opinion The written opinion of one or more Supreme Court justices who disagree with the ruling of the Court's majority. The opinion outlines the rationale for their disagreement. *(Page 302.)*

district courts The trial courts of original jurisdiction in the federal judicial system. The ninety-four district courts are the third tier of the federal judicial system, below the courts of appeals and the Supreme Court. *(Page 294.)*

divided government A term used to describe government when one political party controls the executive branch and the other political party controls one or both houses of the legislature. *(Page 412.)*

dual federalism A system of government in which the federal government and state governments each have mutually exclusive spheres of action. *(Page 64.)*

due process clause A clause found in both the Fifth and Fourteenth Amendments to the Constitution protecting citizens from arbitrary action by the national and state governments. *(Page 131.)*

elastic clause Another name given to the "necessary and proper clause" of the Constitution (see "necessary and proper clause"). *(Page 78.)*

electoral college A body of electors in each state, chosen by voters, who formally elect the president and vice president of the United States. Each state's number of electoral votes equals its representation in Congress; the District of Columbia has three votes. An absolute majority of the total electoral vote is required to elect a president and vice president. *(Page 44.)*

enrolled bill A bill that has been passed by both the Senate and the House and has been sent to the president for approval. *(Page 231.)*

entitlement A benefit that every eligible person has a legal right to receive and that cannot be taken away without a change in legislation or due process in court. *(Page 192.)*

enumerated powers The explicit powers given to Congress by the Constitution in Article I, Section 8. These include the powers of taxation, coinage of money, regulation of commerce, and provision for the national defense. *(Page 77.)*

equal protection clause A Fourteenth Amendment clause guaranteeing all citizens equal protection of the laws. The courts have interpreted the clause to bar discrimination against minorities and women. *(Page 131.)*

establishment clause The first clause of the First Amendment. The establishment clause prohibits the national government from establishing a national religion. *(Page 142.)*

exclusionary rule A judicial rule prohibiting the police from using evidence at a trial that was obtained through illegal search and seizure. *(Page 148.)*

executive agreement An agreement between the president and one or more other countries. An executive agreement is similar to a treaty, but, unlike a treaty, it does not require the approval of the Senate. *(Page 220.)*

executive order A presidential directive to an executive agency establishing new policies or indicating how an existing policy is to be carried out. *(Page 215.)*

externalities Public goods or bads that are generated as a byproduct of private activity. For example, air pollution is an externality (public bad) because it is, in part, the byproduct of the private activity of driving a car. *(Page 19.)*

faction A group of people sharing common interests who are opposed to other groups with competing interests. James Madison defined a faction as any group with objectives contrary to the general interests of society. *(Page 52.)*

federalism A system of government in which power is divided between a central government and several regional governments. In the United States the division is between the national government and the states. *(Page 63.)*

Federal Register A government publication listing all proposed federal regulations. *(Page 263.)*

filibuster A tactic used in the Senate to halt action on a bill. It involves making long speeches until the majority retreats. Senators, once holding the floor, have unlimited time to speak unless a cloture vote is passed by three-fifths of the members. *(Page 200.)*

focus group A method of gauging public opinion by observing a small number of people brought together to discuss specific issues, usually under the guidance of a moderator. *(Page 364.)*

framing Providing a context that affects the criteria citizens use to evaluate candidates, campaigns, and political issues. *(Page 329.)*

free exercise clause The second clause of the First Amendment. The free exercise clause forbids the national government to interfere with the exercise of religion. *(Page 142.)*

free-rider problem A situation in which individuals can receive the benefits from a collective activity whether or not they helped to pay for it, leaving them with no incentive to contribute. *(Page 9.)*

gag rule An executive order prohibiting all federal employees from communicating directly with Congress. *(Page 229.)*

gerrymandering Drawing legislative districts in such a way as to give one political party a disproportionately large share of seats for the share of votes its candidates win. *(Page 167.)*

government The institutions and procedures through which people are ruled. *(Page 6.)*

grandfather clause A statute stating that only those people whose grandfather had voted before Reconstruction could vote, unless they passed a literacy or wealth test. After the Civil War this mechanism was used to disenfranchise African Americans. *(Page 101.)*

grant-in-aid Funds given by Congress to state or local governments for a specific purpose. *(Page 81.)*

grassroots lobbying Lobbying conducted by rank-and-file members of an interest group. *(Page 443.)*

home rule Power given by a state to a locality to enact legislation and manage its own affairs locally. Home rule also applies to Britain's administration of the American colonies. *(Page 28.)*

ideology A comprehensive, integrated set of views about government and politics. *(Page 324.)*

independent spending Campaign spending by a person or organization for or against a political candidate that is not controlled by or coordinated with any candidate's campaign. *(Page 373.)*

insider lobbying Interest group activity that includes normal lobbying on Capitol Hill, working closely with members of Congress, and contributing money to incumbents' campaigns. Contrasts with *outsider lobbying*. *(Page 425.)*

interest group An organized group of citizens seeking to influence public policy. *(Page 423.)*

intervenor A third party introduced in the rulemaking process in Congress to guarantee a desired balance of interests in regulatory policy making. *(Page 267.)*

iron triangle A stable, mutually beneficial political relationship among a congressional committee (or subcommittee), administrative agency, and organized interests concerned with a particular policy domain. *(Page 276.)*

issue network A loose, informal, and highly variable web of relationships among representatives of various interests who are involved in a particular area of public policy. *(Page 280.)*

issue publics Groups of citizens who are more attentive to particular areas of public policy than are average citizens because they have some special stake in the issues. *(Page 334.)*

issue voting Voting for candidates based on their positions on specific issues, as opposed to their party or personal characteristics. *(Page 362.)*

Jim Crow laws A series of laws enacted in the late nineteenth century by Southern states to institute segregation. These laws created "whites only" public accommodations such as schools, hotels, and restaurants. *(Page 100.)*

joint committee Permanent congressional committees made up of members of both the House and the Senate. Joint committees do not have any legislative authority; they monitor specific activities and compile reports. *(Page 190.)*

judicial doctrine The practice of prescribing in a decision a set of rules that are to guide future decisions on similar cases. Used by the Supreme Court to guide the lower courts in making decisions. *(Page 299.)*

judicial review The authority of a court to declare legislative and executive acts unconstitutional and therefore invalid. *(Pages 45 and 289.)*

leak Strategically consequential information given to reporters on the condition that its source not be identified by name. *(Page 469.)*

legislative veto A procedure that allows one or both houses of Congress to reject an action taken by the president or executive agency. In 1983 the Supreme Court declared legislative vetoes unconstitutional, but Congress continues to enact legislation incorporating the veto. *(Pages 265 and 305.)*

libel A published falsehood or statement resulting in the defamation of someone's character. Libelous statements are not protected by the First Amendment. *(Page 141.)*

liberal In the United States, a proponent of a political ideology that favors extensive government action to redress social and economic inequalities and tolerates social behaviors that conservatives view as deviant. Present-day liberals advocate policies benefiting the poor, minority groups, labor unions, women, and the environment and oppose government imposition of traditional social norms. *(Page 324.)*

literacy test A legal barrier used to exclude African Americans from voting. Local white registrars would require prospective black voters to read and interpret arcane passages of the state's constitution. Since few satisfied these registrars' rigorous demands, by 1910 fewer than 10 percent of black males were voting in the South. *(Page 101.)*

lobbying Activities though which individuals, interest groups, and other institutions seek to influence public policy by persuading government officials leaders to support their groups' position. *(Page 423.)*

lobbyists Professionals who work to influence public policy in favor of their clients' interests. *(Page 422.)*

logrolling Legislative vote trading. For example, legislators representing urban districts may vote for an agricultural bill provided that legislators from rural districts vote for a mass transit bill. *(Page 175.)*

majority leader The formal leader of the party controlling a majority of the seats in the House or the Senate. In the Senate the majority leader is the head of the majority party. In the House the majority leader ranks second in the party hierarchy behind the Speaker. *(Page 185.)*

majority rule The principle that decisions should reflect the preferences of more than half of those voting. Decision making by majority rule is one of the fundamental procedures of democracy. *(Page 14.)*

measurement error Uncertainties in public opinion as revealed by responses to polls that arise from the imperfect connection between the wording of survey questions and the terms in which people understand and think about political objects. *(Page 332.)*

message The central thematic statement in a political campaign of why voters ought to prefer one candidate over others. *(Page 364.)*

minority leader The formal leader of the party controlling a minority of the seats in the House or the Senate. *(Page 185.)*

multiple referral The act of sending a proposed piece of legislation to more than one committee in the same chamber. *(Page 194.)*

national party convention A gathering of delegates to select a party's presidential and vice-presidential ticket and to adopt its national platform. *(Page 395.)*

necessary and proper clause The last clause of Article I, Section 8, of the Constitution. This clause grants Congress the authority to make all laws that are "necessary and proper" and to execute those laws. *(Page 41.)*

negative campaigning The act of attacking an opposing candidate's platform, past political performance, or personal characteristics. *(Page 367.)*

New Deal Coalition An electoral alliance that was the basis of Democratic dominance from the 1930s to the early 1970s. The alliance consisted of Catholics, Jews, racial minorities, urban residents, organized labor, and white southerners. *(Page 406.)*

nullification A doctrine developed by states' rights advocate John Calhoun in the 1830s declaring that the states can, in effect, declare acts of Congress unconstitutional. *(Page 78.)*

obscenity Defined as publicly offensive acts or language, usually of a sexual nature, with no redeeming social value. The Supreme Court has offered varying definitions in its rulings over the years. *(Page 138.)*

open rule   A provision governing debate of a pending bill that permits any germane amendment to be offered on the floor of the House. *(Page 199.)*

open seats   Seats in states or districts being contested by candidates of whom none currently holds the office. Congressional seats become "open" when the incumbent dies or does not run for reelection. *(Page 373.)*

opinion leader   A citizen who is highly attentive to and involved in politics or some subarea of it and to whom other citizens turn for political information and cues. *(Page 332.)*

outsider lobbying   Interest group activities designed to influence elected officials by threatening to impose political costs on them if they do not respond. Tactics include marches, demonstrations, campaign contributions to opponents, and electoral mobilization. *(Page 444.)*

pack journalism   A method of news gathering in which news reporters all follow the same story in the same way because they read each other's copy for validation of their own. *(Page 472.)*

parliamentary government   A form of government in which the chief executive is chosen by the majority party or by a coalition of parties in the legislature. *(Page 17.)*

party identification   An individual's enduring affective or instrumental attachment to one of the political parties; the most accurate single predictor of the vote. *(Page 362.)*

party label   A label carrying the party's "brand name," incorporating the policy positions and past performance voters attribute to it. *(Page 362.)*

party machines   State or local party organizations based on patronage. They work to elect candidates to public offices that control government jobs and contracts which, in turn, are used by party leaders (often denigrated as "bosses") to reward the subleaders and activists who mobilize voters for the party on election day. *(Page 399.)*

patronage   The practice of awarding jobs, grants, licenses, or other special favors in exchange for political support. *(Page 391.)*

penumbras   Judicially created rights based on various guarantees of the Bill of Rights. The right to privacy is not explicitly stated in the Constitution, but the Supreme Court has argued that such a right is implicit in various clauses found throughout the Bill of Rights. *(Page 154.)*

performance voting   Basing votes for a candidate or party on how successfully the candidate or party performed while in office. *(Page 362.)*

pluralism   A theory describing a political system in which all significant social interests freely compete with one another for influence over the government's policy decisions. *(Page 54.)*

plurality   A vote in which the winning candidate receives the greatest number of votes (but not necessarily a majority—50 percent). *(Page 15.)*

pocket veto   A method by which the president vetoes a bill passed by both houses of Congress by failing to act on it within ten days of Congress's adjournment. *(Page 204.)*

political action committee (PAC)   A federally registered fund-raising group that pools money from individuals to give to political candidates and parties. *(Page 169.)*

political socialization   The process by which citizens acquire their political beliefs and values. *(Page 325.)*

politics   The process by which individuals and groups reach agreement on a common course of action even as they continue to disagree on the goals that action is intended to achieve. *(Page 4.)*

poll tax   A tax imposed on people when they register to vote. In the decades after the Civil War this tax was used primarily to disenfranchise African American voters. With passage of the Twenty-Fourth Amendment, in 1964, it became unconstitutional. *(Page 100.)*

pork barrel legislation   Legislation that provides members of Congress with federal projects and programs for their individual districts. *(Page 175.)*

preemption legislation   Laws passed by Congress that override or preempt state or local policies. The power of preemption derives from the supremacy clause (Article VI) of the Constitution. *(Page 80.)*

president pro tempore   In the absence of the vice president, the formal presiding officer of the Senate. The honor is usually conferred on the senior member of the majority party, but the post is sometimes rotated among senators of the majority party. *(Page 186.)*

primary elections   An election held before the general election in which voters decide which of a party's candidates will be the party's nominee for the general election. *(Page 402.)*

principal   An individual with the authority to make some decision. This authority may be delegated to an agent who is supposed to act in the principal's behalf. *(Page 15.)*

prior restraint   A government agency's act to prohibit the publication of material or speech before the fact. Prior restraint is forbidden by the courts except under extraordinary conditions. *(Page 140.)*

prisoner's dilemma A situation in which two (or more) actors cannot agree to cooperate for fear that the other will find its interest best served by reneging on an agreement. *(Page 9.)*

private goods Benefits and services over which the owner has full control of their use. *(Page 19.)*

Progressive Era A period of American history extending roughly from 1880 to 1920 associated with the reform of government and electoral institutions in attempt to reduce corruption and weaken parties. *(Page 427.)*

proportional representation An electoral system in which legislative seats are awarded to candidates or parties in proportion to the percentage of votes received. *(Pages 165 and 390.)*

public goods Goods that are collectively produced and freely available for anyone's consumption. *(Page 19.)*

public interest lobby A group that promotes some conception of the public interest rather than the narrowly defined economic or other special interests of its members. *(Page 425.)*

quotas Specific shares of college admissions, government contracts, and jobs set aside for population groups that have suffered from past discrimination. The Supreme Court has rejected the use of quotas wherever it has encountered them. *(Page 118.)*

red tape Excessive paperwork leading to bureaucratic delay. The term originated in the seventeenth century when English legal and governmental documents were bound with red-colored tape. *(Page 280.)*

republic A form of democracy in which power is vested in elected representatives. *(Page 17.)*

representative government A political system in which citizens select government officials who, acting as their agents, deliberate and commit the citizenry to a course of collective action. *(Page 16.)*

restricted rule A provision governing consideration of a bill that specifies and limits the kinds of amendments that may be made on the floor of the House of Representatives. *(Page 199.)*

revenue sharing Nonspecific grants of money by the federal government to the states based on size and population. *(Page 81.)*

reverse discrimination A term applied to the discrimination exerted against majority groups such as whites or males in an effort to counter, or rectify, discrimination against minority groups. *(Page 89.)*

rider An amendment to a bill that is not germane to the legislation. *(Page 200.)*

rotation in office The practice of citizens serving in public office for a limited term and then returning to private life. *(Page 251.)*

rule A provision that governs consideration of a bill by the House of Representatives by specifying how the bill is to be debated and amended. *(Page 199.)*

segregation The political and social practice of separating whites and blacks into dual and highly unequal schools, hospitals, prisons, public parks, housing, and public conveyances. *(Page 100.)*

select committee A temporary legislative committee created for a specific purpose and dissolved after its tasks are completed. *(Page 190.)*

selective incorporation The judicial doctrine stating that most, but not all, of the protections found in the Bill of Rights also apply to the states (via the Fourteenth Amendment). *(Page 131.)*

senatorial courtesy An informal practice in which senators are given veto power over federal judicial appointments in their home states. *(Page 308.)*

seniority rule The congressional practice of appointing the members of the majority with the most years of committee service as committee or subcommittee chairs. *(Page 180.)*

separate but equal doctrine The Supreme Court–initiated doctrine that separate but equivalent facilities for African Americans and whites are constitutional under the equal protection clause of the Fourteenth Amendment. *(Page 101.)*

separation of powers The distribution of government powers among several political institutions. In the United States, at the national level power is divided between the three branches: Congress, the president, and the Supreme Court. *(Page 17.)*

shared federalism A system in which the national and state governments share in providing citizens with a set of goods. *(Page 65.)*

single-issue voters People who base their votes on candidates' or parties' positions on one particular issue of public policy, regardless of the candidates' or parties' positions on other issues. *(Page 360.)*

soft money Money used by political parties for voter registration, public education, and voter mobilization. The government imposes no limits on contributions or expenditures for such purposes. *(Page 370.)*

solicitor general The official responsible for representing the U.S. government before the Supreme Court. The solicitor general is a ranking member of the U.S. Department of Justice. *(Page 299.)*

Speaker of the House   The presiding officer of the House of Representatives. The Speaker is elected at the beginning of each congressional session on a party-line vote. As head of the majority party the Speaker has substantial control over the legislative agenda of the House. *(Page 185.)*

special committee   A temporary legislative committee, usually lacking legislative authority. *(Page 190.)*

split ticket voting   The act of voting for candidates from different political parties for different offices—for example, voting for a Republican for president and a Democrat for senator. *(Page 402.)*

spoils system   A system in which newly elected officeholders award government jobs to political supporters and members of the same political party. The term originated in the saying "to the victor go the spoils." *(Page 251.)*

standing   The right to bring legal action. *(Page 267.)*

standing committee   A permanent legislative committee specializing in a particular legislative area. Standing committees have stable memberships and stable jurisdictions. *(Page 188.)*

stare decisis   "Let the decision stand." In court rulings, a reliance on precedents or previous rulings in formulating decisions in new cases. *(Page 299.)*

suffragettes   Women who campaigned in the early twentieth century for the right of women to vote. *(Page 120.)*

superdelegate   A delegate to the Democratic National Convention who is eligible to attend because he or she is an elected party official. The Democrats reserve a specific set of delegate slots for party officials. *(Page 409.)*

supremacy clause   A clause in Article VI of the Constitution declaring that national laws are the "supreme" law of the land and therefore take precedence over any laws adopted by states or localities. *(Page 45.)*

"take care" clause   The provision in Article II, Section 3, of the Constitution instructing the president to "take care that the Laws be faithfully executed." *(Page 215.)*

ticket splitting   (See *split ticket voting.*) *(Page 170.)*

transaction costs   The costs of doing political business reflected in the time and effort required to compare preferences and negotiate compromises in making collective decisions. *(Page 12.)*

two-party system   A political system in which only two major parties compete for all of the elective offices. Third party candidates usually have few, if any, chances of winning elective office. *(Page 389.)*

unanimous consent agreement   A unanimous resolution in the Senate restricting debate and limiting amendments to bills on the floor. *(Page 187.)*

unit costs   The costs of transmitting a news product to a consumer. *(Page 456.)*

unitary government   A system of government in which a single government unit holds the power to govern the nation (in contrast to a federal system in which power is shared among many governing units). *(Page 63.)*

veto   The formal power of the president to reject bills passed by both houses of Congress. A veto can be overridden by a two-thirds vote in each house. *(Page 44.)*

whip   A member of a legislative party who acts as the communicator between the party leadership and the rank and file. The whip polls members on their voting intentions, prepares bill summaries, and assists the leadership in various other tasks. *(Page 185.)*

white primary   A practice that permitted political parties to exclude African Americans from voting in primary elections. Because historically in the South winning the Democratic primary was tantamount to winning the general election, this law in effect disenfranchised black voters in southern states. *(Page 100.)*

writ of certiorari   An order given by a superior court to an appellate court, directing the lower court to send up a case the superior court has chosen to review. This is the central means by which the Supreme Court determines what cases it will hear. *(Page 297.)*

writ of mandamus   "We command." A court-issued writ, commanding a public official to carry out a specific act or duty. *(Page 288.)*

INDEX

Murray, Alan S., 174
Mussolini, Benito, 13
Mutual influence, federalism and, 64

N
Nader, Ralph, 433
Nation, The, 426
National Aeronautics and Space Administration (NASA), 260, 276
National Albanian American Council, *342*
National Association for the Advancement of Colored People (NAACP), 105–107, 151
National Association of Business Political Action Committees (NABPAC), 437
National Audubon Society, 434
National Automobile Altered Number file, 277
National Endowment for the Arts (NEA), 203
National Environmental Policy Act of 1969, 267, 444
National health insurance, 205
National Institutes of Health, 270
National Labor Relations Board, 263
National Organization for Women (NOW), 121, 435
National Park Service, 22, 259
National Partnership for Reinventing Government, 279
National party conventions, 395–397
   delegate selection rules of, 408–409
   delegates to, 410, 411
   Jackson and, 236
   nineteenth century, 225–226
   outsiders and, 237–238
   reforms in, 236–237
National Performance Review (NPR), 279, 280, 281
National policy, Congress and, 162
National Railroad Passenger Corporation, 264
National Republicans, 395–396, 398
National Rifle Association, 127, 202, 361, 434, 443
National Science Foundation (NSF), 266
National security
   freedom of press and, 140–141
   freedom of speech and, 134–135
   Shays's Rebellion and, 219

National Security Committee, House, 189
National Security Council (NSC), 230, 231
National Socialist Party, 137
National Trades Union, 426
National Transportation Safety Board, 263
National Voter Registration Act of 1993, 359
Nationalization, 66–75
   historic transfers in, 70–72
   logic of, 66–69
   paths to, 69–75
   political logic of, 74–75
Native Americans, 178, 344
Nativity scenes, 143
Natural Death Act of 1976 (Calif.), 156
Natural resources, free-rider problem and, 73
Navy, U.S. Department of the, 254
Near, Jay, 140
Necessary and proper clause, U.S. Constitution, 41–42, 45, 165
Negative campaigning, 367–368
Negative news, 473
Negotiations, rules/procedures for, 4
Nelson, Michael, 241, 245, 538n25, 539n2, 539n5, 539n13
Nethercutt, George, Jr., 490
Neuman, W. Russell, 545n35
Neustadt, Richard E., 213, 245, 538n8, 538n13, 539n19
Neutrality doctrine, establishment of religion and, 143–144
New Christian Right, 407
New Deal coalition, FDR's, 70–71, 102–103, 406–407
   Court packing plan and, 291–292, 304
   political socialization and, 326–327
   public opinion on, 338
New Guinea, tribal prisoner's dilemma in, 10–11
New Hampshire
   presidential primary in, 373
   U.S. Constitution ratification and, 51
New Jersey Plan for U.S. Constitution, 41
New Orleans, La., Reconstruction era riot, 99
New York, U.S. Constitution ratification by, 51
New York Daily Advertiser, 52
New York Herald, 457
New York Journal, 459, 460

New York Sun, 457
New York Times v. United States (1971), 140–141
New York Times/CBS News poll, 239, 410
New York World, 457, 459, 476
Newberry v. United States (1921), 405
News media, 453–483
   broadcasting, 460–463
   bypassing, 480, 482–483
   campaign messages and, 368, 375–376
   on campaign spending, 378
   on Clinton's scandal, 334, 335
   colonial newspaper economics, 455–456
   content of, 464–466
   development of, 455–466
   "earned" media, 376
   FECA, soft money and, 371
   format of, 466
   J. E. Hoover's use of, 277
   information control and, 475–476
   interest group pressure using, 442
   leaks to, 232, 469, 470, 471
   legislative votes and, 202
   mediating the message by, 478–479
   news as consumer product, 463–466
   nineteenth-century presidential coverage by, 225
   partisan press and, 319
   penny press, 456–458
   political parties and, 412
   politician–press relations, 476–477, 480
   politics of, 466–474
   public officials and, 468–469
   regulation of, 463
   reporters for, 471–472
   State of the Union address and, 217, 219
   story selection process of, 472–474
   See also Hearst, William Randolph; Pulitzer, Joseph
Newspapers
   versus broadcast news, 460–463
   carrying capacity of, 464–465
   penny press, 456–460
Newton, Isaac, 38, 486
Nicaraguan contras, public opinion on, 342
Nieman, Donald G., 534n5
Niemi, Richard G., 23, 145, 255, 263, 331, 332, 341, 394, 457, 477, 528, 537n14, 537n60, 538n42

Nineteenth Amendment, 46, 119–120, 354
Ninth Amendment, 133, 154
Ninth Circuit Court of Appeals, San Francisco, Calif., 298, 308, 312
Nixon, Richard, 231, 232, 242, 409, 478–479
   appointments of, 270, 308
   block grants and, 82
   coalitions of, 407
   election campaigns of, 371
   impoundment by, 193
   judicial appointments of, 133, 139
   Pentagon Papers and, 140–141
   press relations of, 475, 477
   revenue sharing and, 81
   vetoes War Powers Act of 1973, 222
   Watergate tapes and, 305
Nixon v. Herndon (1927), 405
Nonparticipation, logic of, 8
Nonthreatening speech/expression, 137–138
North American Treaty Organization (NATO), 222
North Carolina, gerrymandering in, 168–169
Norton, Mary Beth, 57, 94, 531–532n5, 534n7
Nuclear Regulatory Commission, 263
Nullification doctrine, 56, 78

O
Oates, Stephen B., 123
O'Brien, David M., 541n30, 542n34
O'Brien, Francis, 479
Obscenity, 138–140, 300
Occupational Safety and Health Administration, 226, 261
O'Connor, Sandra Day, 302, 309
Office of Administration, 230
Office of Management and Budget (OMB), 195, 229, 230, 231, 271, 274
Office of Technology Assessment (OTA), 195
Office of the Vice President, 230
Ogilvie, Lloyd, 144
Old Age Assistance, 71
Oldendick, Robert W., 542n15
Older Americans Act of 1965, 436
Oleszek, Walter J., 199, 538n26
Olson, Alison Gilbert, 543n4–6
Olson, Mancur, 430, 451, 543n14, 544n35
O'Neill, Thomas P. "Tip," 186, 240
Open rule, 199

PHOTO CREDITS

Samuel Kernell (Ph.D., University of California, Berkeley) is Professor of Political Science at the University of California, San Diego, where he has taught since 1977. Previously, he taught at the University of Mississippi and the University of Minnesota. Kernell's research interests focus on the presidency. His previous books include *Going Public: New Strategies of Presidential Leadership* (Third Edition, 1997, CQ Press) and, with Gary C. Jacobson, *Strategy and Choice in Congressional Elections* (Second Edition, 1983, Yale University Press). He is currently working on a biography of James H. Rowe.

Gary C. Jacobson (Ph.D., Yale University) is Professor of Political Science at the University of California, San Diego, where he has taught since 1979. He previously taught at Trinity College, the University of California at Riverside, Yale University, and Stanford University. Jacobson specializes in the study of U.S. elections, parties, interest groups, and Congress. He is the author of *Money in Congressional Elections, The Politics of Congressional Elections* (Fourth Edition, 1997, Longman), and *The Electoral Origins of Divided Government* (1990), and is coauthor with Samuel Kernell of *Strategy and Choice in Congressional Elections* (Second Edition, 1983, Yale University Press). Jacobson is a Fellow of the American Academy of Arts and Sciences.